Series in Health and Social Justice

Series Editors

Avi Chomsky
Margaret Connors
Shelly Errington
Paul Farmer
Kenneth Fox
Jennifer Furin
Jim Yong Kim
Joe Rhatigan
Haun Saussy

Women, Poverty, and AIDS

Sex, Drugs, and Structural Violence

Edited by

Paul Farmer
Margaret Connors
Janie Simmons

Common Courage Press *Monroe, Maine*

Library of Congress Cataloging-in-Publication Data
Women, poverty, and AIDS: sex, drugs, and stuctural violence/
[edited by] Paul Farmer, Margaret Connors, Janie Simmons.
p. cm.
Includes bibliographical references and index.
ISBN 1-56751-075-2 (cloth: alk. paper).
ISBN 1-56751-074-4 (pbk.: alk. paper)
1. AIDS (Disease)--Social aspects. 2. AIDS (Disease)--Sex factors.
3. Poor women--Diseases. I. Farmer, Paul (Paul Edward), 1959-   .
II. Connors, Margaret. III. Simmons, Janie.
RA644.A25W657 1996   96-27349
362.1'969792--dc20   CIP

Common Courage Press
P.O. Box 702
Monroe, ME 04951
207-525-0900
fax: 207-525-3068

The Institute for Health and Social Justice
Partners In Health
113 River Street
Cambridge, MA 02139
617-441-6288
fax: 617-661-2669

First Printing

Contents

Acknowledgments

Writing and editing *Women, Poverty, and AIDS* has been a communitarian experience. We called ourselves the "WPA team," and although the team itself seemed, at most times, frighteningly small, we had a good deal of assistance. The book is a project of the fledgling Institute for Health and Social Justice. Like most fledglings, the IHSJ has received its share of nurturing pushes. We'd like to thank Howard Hiatt, the patron saint of the IHSJ, and also the Aaron Diamond and Merck Foundations; their support made the year's many activities possible.

These activities are structured around a "fellowship experience" in the true sense of those now debased words, and we're grateful to the 1994-1995 IHSJ fellows, Sally Zierler and Janie Simmons. Joyce Millen, our 1995-1996 fellow, has of course pitched right in on *Women, Poverty, and AIDS*, bringing her significant experience and abundant good will to bear on a project that was to have been finished prior to her arrival. Thanks, Joyce—we'll repay the favor before the year is over.

We're also grateful for the constitutive and editorial assistance of Bill Rodriguez and Kristin Nelson.

A number of students, most of them from Harvard University, contributed to this effort, notably Keith Joseph, Ana Blohm, Cassis Henry, Orestes O'Brien, Alec Irwin, and Benny Gavi (others, who shared authorship or editing responsibilities, are credited in the following pages). The Department of Social Medicine of Harvard Medical School provides a home for the IHSJ seminar and also an academic appointment for our fellows. More importantly, Arthur Kleinman, Kris Heggenhougen, Leon Eisenberg, and other colleagues at the department afford their unstinting moral support for these efforts, located as they are in that liminal space between theory and practice. Marshall Wolf of the Brigham and Women's Hospital facilitated this project in a similarly reliable manner, as did our colleague Gail Levine. Jonathan Mann, Daniel Tarantola, and their colleagues at the François-Xavier Bagnoud Center for Health and Human Rights at the Harvard School of Public Health offered not only assistance and data, but also the sterling example of their own work. *AIDS in the World*, oft-cited in these pages, remains a key tool for those seeking to understand the many dynamics of global HIV transmission.

The perspectives advanced here, though often hashed out in seminar rooms, are most decidedly those of the front lines. We thank our partners there, including the many people who responded to our inquiries about community-based and service organizations attempting to make common cause with poor women. For case material and encouragement, we're indebted to Anitra Pivnick, Sarthak Das, and Margaret Cerullo. Mindy and Bob Fullilove provided their unique *mélange* of wisdom and solidarity. We thank, too, the clinicians and service providers who have contributed to this book or to our own development, sometimes merely by talking about the struggles and courage of people living with AIDS. Susan Larrabee ("Redistribute!") comes immediately to mind, as do other members of the HIV team at the Brigham and Women's Hospital. Special thanks to Matt Clark, also of the Brigham, for assistance with graphs.

Several people helped us, at the last minute of course, in editing a team work in order to lend consistency of tone and also to enhance the scholarly buttressing of our arguments. Haun Saussy, of UCLA and Stanford, is a grizzled veteran of Partners in Health efforts. If many years ago Haun thought that he could escape to the library, he was long ago disabused of this notion (we suspect, however, that he actually chooses to help us). Shelly Errington and Vinh Kim Nguyen, more recent conscripts from the University of California at Santa Cruz and McGill, respectively, may live to regret their offers of assistance, as may Ken Fox.

Maggie Steber took the arresting and affecting photograph on the book's cover. We will look at it whenever we wish to be reminded of the power of pragmatic solidarity.

Our publishers, Greg Bates and Flic Shooter, are also our friends and fellow travelers. Greg has endured the angst of working with people who put clinical and community work above writing and deadlines, but we hope the vitality of practice sparkles through in some of these pages.

If the vitality of practice sparkles at all, it is thanks to our patients (P.F.) and to our partners in Perú, Chiapas, and, most importantly, in Haiti. With funds from the World AIDS Foundation, our sister organization, Zanmi Lasante, has made a name for itself by working with and for poor women to prevent HIV transmission in rural Haiti. This book could not have been written without their steering and example. We add special thanks to Maxi Raymonville and the members of Proje Sante Fanm.

Finally, we thank our partners here in the Boston area. We will not acknowledge the writers and annotators, as their names appear in the text, but would like to thank the many participants in the first IHSJ seminar, as they sharpened our understanding of these materials and of the debates that surround them; the insights of Nina Kammerer and Pat Symonds were especially appreciated. Those "here in the house" might appropriately enough note that it's not customary to thank close kin, but we claim editors' prerogative in order to express our deep gratitude to Jim Kim, Kristin Nelson, Loune Viaud, Tom White (the patron saint of Partners In Health), Mercedes Becerra, María Contreras, Anne Hyson, Matthew Olins, Arnie Chien, and Ophelia Dahl.

This book is dedicated to our teachers—women now living with both poverty and HIV. Because these women are so accustomed to having their eloquent—and damning—critiques silenced, we do not ask for their blessings on a book, no matter how well-intentioned. But we do hope that we have somehow captured in its pages both their courage in the face of adversity and the radicality of their resistance.

Paul Farmer,
Margaret Connors,
and Janie Simmons
Cambridge, Massachusetts

Introduction

"Most heterosexuals will continue to have more to fear from bathtub drowning than from AIDS."

Michael Fumento,
The Myth of Heterosexual AIDS, 1990

"From 1993 to 1994, the death rate for HIV infection for white men aged 25-44 years did not change, and rates for women and black men increased; in 1994, the rate for black women aged 25-44 years surpassed that for white men in that age group."

Centers for Disease Control, 1996

1.

Women, Poverty, and AIDS is the inaugural volume in a new series, "Health and Social Justice," which will be published by Common Courage Press and the Institute for Health and Social Justice (IHSJ).

We intend to bring forth at least one volume each year. Although the topics will vary, the general approach and intent will not. These books are meant to address what we see as a failure. Put simply, we live in an age of unprecedented advance in science and in communications technology. In a flash of electronic mail, collaborators on this book can confer with colleagues across the globe. New technologies permit the production of documents that a mere decade ago would have involved the most laborious manuscript preparation.

We can disseminate materials widely—at least in a geographical sense.

As regards AIDS, a staggering number of new studies and a profusion of scientific and clinical journals are the result, in part, of these advances in communication; in part they are the result of important basic science and clinical research. The rapid growth of a computerized AIDS database—available now to many students, clinicians, researchers, and to certain patients, in a matter of seconds—is a reflection of both the advances in technology and a rapidly expanding knowledge base about a new disease.

And yet, science fails us. Not everyone has access to what we know. Nor do the data thus made available adequately reflect all that is most important about AIDS. A look at the AIDS database is instructive in this regard. If one conducts a search using the term "AIDS," over 100,000 references are instantaneously available. In restricting the search by adding the terms "women" to "AIDS," one finds, at this writing, well over 2000 references.

If you seek to further restrict your search by adding "poverty" to "women" and "AIDS," however, the computer will inform you that "there are no references meeting these specifications." As recently as October 22, 1994, two researchers writing in *The Lancet* could report that they were "not aware of other investigators who have considered the influence of socioeconomic status on mortality in HIV-infected individuals."[1]

That is the knowledge gap, and the communication gap, these books are meant to fill. Many would now agree—if not in print, then in informal discussion—that poverty and other forms of social inequality, including gender-based discrimination, are the leading co-factors in the grim advance of the world pandemic of AIDS. In 15 large U.S. cities, complications of HIV infection became the leading cause of death for all women 25 to 44 years old by 1991.[2] Among African-American women in this age group, regardless of place of residence it is the leading cause of death: the death rate is nine times as high for black women as for white women.[3] In cities throughout the world, and in certain rural areas as well, complications of HIV disease have become the leading cause of death of young women.[4]

Poverty and gender inequality are two reasons why the fastest-growing epidemics are among women, who in some regions of the world already constitute the majority of those infected. Large-scale social forces—economic, political, and cultural factors—are now placing millions of women at increased risk for HIV infection. At the same time, these same forces render many of the aforementioned scientific advances altogether irrelevant for most women at increased risk. As women living in poverty, they were already denied access to such goods and services before HIV came along to further complicate their lives. Thus does a new disease reveal old problems.

An appreciation of this sad state of affairs led Partners in Health, a community-based organization with long experience in the provision of health care and other services to poor communities, to found both the Institute for Health and Social Justice and to initiate this book series with a critical reexamination of how AIDS has, in a single generation, eclipsed other causes of death among many of the world's women.

2.

It is hardly an insight to note that the fruits of science, and of scholarship in general, are not evenly shared. Those who do not regard this uneven distribution as a failure might find little of interest in this book and its successor volumes. But those who do find much to deplore in the status quo are hereby invited to join us in a rethinking of the processes by which such disparities are created, maintained and, indeed, entrenched as the scientific revolution advances.

This book series is but one part of that process of *rethinking*. Most of these volumes will contain an introduction and a series of critical essays, written by us or by experts in the field, which attempt to reexamine a particular issue—in this case, AIDS—through the eyes of persons living in poverty. A difficult exercise, certainly, but one too rarely attempted. Whenever possible, we will draw on the experiences and critical viewpoints of the poor with and for whom Partners in Health works.

Most volumes will further offer a *rereading* of selected literature on the topic at hand. The latter half of this book is, in a sense, an annotated bibliography—a term that suggests a tedious enumeration of arcane studies of interest only to a tiny community of scholars. But we believe you will find our rereading stimulating and perhaps even the most interesting part of the series. In it, important studies and influential publications will be replayed in a new hermeneutic key. The purpose of our reexamination is simply to ask: how are these texts relevant to the struggles of poor and otherwise oppressed people?

Other, related questions guide this rereading. How is the production of these texts related to the social context in which risks and burdens are so unevenly distributed? In the current volume, the axes of socioeconomic class and gender frame our reanalysis. Specifically, how have various bodies of literature obscured—or brought into focus—the interrelations between gender, class and, often enough, "race," in the present-day global economic order? How has the highlighting of one category (gender, say, or sexual preference) contributed to the disappearance or devaluation of other categories and conditions (e.g., social class and poverty)? Are each of these factors equally susceptible to erasure? How have academics and health-care providers contributed, or failed to contribute, to community-based efforts to slow the advance of HIV? To improve care and services for those already infected? Given these shortcomings—for, manifestly, medical science has failed to stop the spread of HIV—how might social-justice concepts serve as correctives in future efforts? How might these concepts serve to reinvigorate efforts currently underway?

Accordingly, *Women, Poverty, and AIDS* is divided into three main parts. The first, "Rethinking AIDS," attempts to reflect on the AIDS pandemic from the perspectives of poor women, whether living in rich countries or in poor countries. Part II, "Rereading AIDS," reexamines, using this same analytic key, portions of the social science, public health, and clinical literature on AIDS. As you will see, we have found that mainstream scientific publications have often obscured the real nature of women's risk—with the expected results in preventive efforts. Many of us who worked on Part II regard our critical rereading as an exercise in self-critique.

Finally, many of the IHSJ volumes will contain a resource guide under the rubric "Pragmatic Solidarity." In Part III of *Women, Poverty, and AIDS*, we have attempted to describe the AIDS-related work of organizations whose efforts are of relevance to poor women. How often can these organizations or collectives point to their efforts and declare victories? Seldom, if ever, but what they can say is that they have made common cause with poor women infected with HIV. For this reason alone, we extend a "hermeneutic of generosity" to community-based efforts.

Combining as they do critiques of specialist literature with the testimony of the poor and their advocates, these books will pose by their very structure a thorny question: Just who is their intended audience? Many of us have published through the standard academic venues, and know all too well how the arcane terminologies of our subfields serve as barriers to interdisciplinary collaboration—to say nothing of our work's impenetrability to those denied access to higher education. Rather than dupe ourselves about our likely readership, we hope this series will be of interest to scholars who would sharpen their thinking as regards the poor; our books will speak to the health-care professional, the social activist and the scholar of intercultural relations by casting a critical light on the concerns of all three.

We hope also to appeal to those working in community-based organizations, who might find this book useful in preparing grant proposals and reports, and to providers who devote themselves to the care of women (and others) with HIV disease. We hope, too, for a broad audience interested in social-justice issues, and are confident that students of disciplines ranging from public health to anthropology might find the IHSJ series a useful adjunct to more conventional topical overviews.

In summary, then, it is our hope that these books, and also the critical essays that the IHSJ will publish periodically, will have several purposes. One purpose is to supplement existing scholarly work. Many of us are already involved in academic research, but feel constricted by the canons of our fields; the IHSJ series will publish books with attitude. Although openly partisan, we have attempted to maintain a rigorous approach to our rereadings even as we acknowledge our stance of advocacy for those living in poverty. Another goal is corrective: we are convinced that the errors of omission and misinterpretation we have found in the academic literature on AIDS are symptomatic of serious flaws in the conduct and interpretation of research.

A third purpose is constitutive. We seek to create a forum for new voices in debates about AIDS. Through these and related efforts, we hope to forge a community of scholars and health care providers committed to social justice. In fact, we have already discovered, in little over a year of operation, a wide network of students and established scholars who agree that it is time for a social-justice approach to many contemporary health problems.

We acknowledge, then, that our publications emerge from and will doubtless bear the marks of an inegalitarian social, medical and educational world. Speaking "for" the poor is not a mission to be claimed lightly. But we will attempt to remain true to the radicality of our patients' and co-workers critique: stopping AIDS will call for fundamental changes in our increasingly inegalitarian society.

3.

Although there are clearly many ways to marginalize groups of people, and many consequent forms of suffering, the IHSJ has made a commitment to those living in poverty. What is meant here by the terms "poverty" and "poor people"? There is, of course, a large literature on this subject. It is not to be dismissed, and we have made some effort, in this book and elsewhere, to engage this varied body of work.

At the same time, we have eschewed a relativism that we feel obscures the nature of suffering in an increasingly interconnected world. Those who repeat the received wisdom that "poverty is relative" are usually not those who have experienced the grinding deprivation of the people to whom we feel most indebted. Those who insist that "all suffering is relative" are not, as a rule, subject to the same daily threats faced by those we attempt to serve, whether in Haiti or Perú or in the crumbling cities of the United States. Perhaps it would be truer to say that "suffering is relative from the vantage point of those who are not presently suffering."

We have also eschewed nationalism or geographic parochialism. The women who have acted as subjects in—and provided inspiration for—this book are from various cities and countries, but their shared status as women who live in poverty links them, and not only in the eye of the beholder. They are also linked, increasingly, by their subordination within a *global* economic network that has limited many women's choices. The boundaries between the global and the local are increasingly blurred by important ties. It is thus not enough to "think globally and act locally."

Explorations of these linkages, so often obscured, will be one of the central tasks of the IHSJ. To bring home this point, we open *Women, Poverty, and AIDS* with a series of portraits of poor women with HIV disease. These women live in very different settings; their paths toward infection with HIV were in some ways different. They do not share access to the same level of medical care; they are not subject to identical types of discrimination. They do not share language and culture. These women are not of the same "race" or ethnic background. In fact, what these women have in common is almost exclusively their poverty and their gender, as anthropologist Martha Ward has pointed out:

> The collection of statistics by ethnicity rather than by socio-economic status obscures the fact that the majority of women with AIDS in the United States are poor. Women are at risk for HIV not because they are African-American or speak Spanish; women are at risk because poverty is the primary and determining condition of their lives.[5]

The health problems of poor people, especially those of this hemisphere, will continue to be the IHSJ's focus in coming years. The second volume of the series, *Life Studies/Death Studies*, is subtitled "An Anthropology of Structural Violence," as it draws on material from Haiti to suggest that "endpoints" ranging from tuberculosis to death in police custody are manifestly related to the same large-scale socioeconomic and political forces examined in *Women, Poverty, and AIDS*.

The IHSJ's central theme for 1995-96 is "The New World Order and the Health of the Poor." Throughout the year, we again ask how seemingly impersonal "macro" forces come to have their effects on individuals, families, and communities. The book series continues with *The New World Order and the Health of the Poor*. This time, however, the forces under consideration are not racism and gender inequality, but rather a broad range of international trade policies from GATT to NAFTA and the transnational businesses whose interests are represented by such treaties. We ask how these "free-trade" agreements, and also the structural adjustment programs of the World Bank and the International Monetary Fund, come to have their impacts on poor communities. A fourth volume will be based on a dialogue on this subject between Gustavo Gutiérrez and Noam Chomsky.[6]

The two central themes—AIDS among poor women and the effects of the "new world order" on the health of the poor—are more closely related than is initially apparent, as the work of anthropologist Brooke Schoepf has suggested:

> Globally, AIDS is best regarded as a 'disease of development' and 'under-development.' It has struck with particular severity in communities struggling under the burdens of economic crises caused by stagnation in the global economy, distorted internal production structures inherited from colonialism, unfavorable terms of trade, and widening disparities of wealth fueled by the channeling of public funds into private pockets.[7]

Similar analyses have been advanced by several other social scientists, but the biomedical and epidemiological literatures were, until this year, altogether silent on this matter. In the summer of 1995, writing in the journal *AIDS*, Peter Lurie and co-workers advanced a similar thesis, suggesting a link between structural adjustment programs, migration, and high rates of HIV transmission. Although they did not offer a close examination of any particular setting, they drew on data from throughout sub-Saharan Africa, and also from parts of Asia and Latin America. Their conclusions were politely put: alternative development strategies are necessary, but, in the interim, the World Bank should call for "AIDS Impact Reports." These would "require the parties to any loan agreement to explicitly stipulate the potential impact of the proposed loan on HIV transmission."[8]

Interestingly, representatives of the World Bank responded with some vehemence, accusing Lurie and co-workers of having a quarrel with "the whole process of development." Lurie *et al.* do not carry their arguments to their logical conclusion, wrote the Bank's representatives, "since that would mean a return to the Stone Age: that would doubtless slow the spread of HIV."[9]

So acrid an exchange between the World Bank and those calling for alternative development strategies is emblematic of many health-related debates before us today, from AIDS to a national health plan. In each instance, the voices of the poor are muted, or not heard at all. When even timid calls for widening the scope of debate are heard, those charged with protecting orthodoxy intervene to protect their interests and shout down the poor.

Women, Poverty, and AIDS and subsequent volumes in the series will attempt to broaden the scope of debate around key health issues. We do this in the hope that the scholarly enterprise can better serve the interests of those who have lost out in world orders old and new.

Paul Farmer and Jim Yong Kim
Partners in Health

PART I

Rethinking AIDS:
Locating Poor Women

CHAPTER ONE

Women, Poverty, and AIDS

Paul Farmer

"These days, whenever someone says the word 'women' to me, my mind goes blank. What 'women'? What is this 'women' thing you're talking about? Does that mean me? Does that mean my mother, my roommates, the white woman next door, the checkout clerk at the supermarket, my aunts in Korea, half the world's population?"

JeeYeun Lee,
"Beyond Bean Counting"

"Macroeconomic conditions operating in a context of pervasive gender inequality have different effects upon the lives of women in different regional, class, and family circumstances. Different circumstances also produce different negotiating strengths among women as well as different HIV risks."

Brooke Schoepf,
"Gender, Development, and AIDS"

1.

AIDS was first recognized as a distinct clinical syndrome in the summer of 1981, when physicians in California and New York noted clusterings of unusual infections and cancers in their patients. Almost all of these patients were young, gay men, a group not previously known to have such "opportunistic" infections. In August, a mere two months after the

3

first cases were reported in men, the same syndrome was identified in a woman.[1] Within a year, AIDS cases were registered among men and women who injected drugs, among hemophiliacs and some of their sexual partners, and among women and men from poor countries, including Haiti, who seemed to share none of the risk factors seen in the other patients.

Since that time, both AIDS and commentary on it have swept the globe. Never before has a single sickness been the subject of such intense and sustained scrutiny. Given the intensity of public awareness and fear of AIDS, it is unsurprising that so many myths and misunderstandings about AIDS have thrived and even proliferated. Though surely there is a compelling interest in getting the facts right and developing appropriate responses on the basis of accurate research, fantasies and junk science have often dominated public discussions of AIDS.

The initial misunderstanding—that AIDS was a disease of men—can be attributed, perhaps, to historical accident: the new disease was first characterized in the technologically advanced United States, where it did, initially at least, primarily afflict men.[2] But, from the outset of the world pandemic, it was apparent that women were also vulnerable to AIDS, and, within in a year or two, there were data to suggest that women were at least as likely to become infected as men.

Evidently, AIDS cases involving women did not count for much. In 1985, a cover story in *Discover*, a popular science magazine, dismissed the idea of a major epidemic in women. Because the "rugged vagina," in contrast to the "vulnerable anus," was designed for the wear and tear of intercourse and birthing, it was unlikely that women would ever be infected in large numbers through heterosexual intercourse. AIDS, we were informed, "is now—and is likely to remain—largely the fatal price one can pay for anal intercourse."[3]

Such mistaken verdicts were slowly called into question. By late 1986, it was becoming clear that AIDS incidence was declining among gay men even as it was climbing among those classed as the "heterosexual exposure group."[4] "Suddenly," proclaimed the cover of *U.S. News and World Report* in January, 1987, "the disease of them is the disease of us." The accompanying illustration depicted the "us" in question (honestly enough) as a white, yuppie couple.[5] In her study of the gradual evolution of U.S. AIDS discourse, Paula Treichler discerns a "diversification" of commentary about women and AIDS in the spring of 1987. Nonetheless, one still heard voices maintaining that women would never constitute a significant proportion of AIDS victims. *The Myth of Heterosexual AIDS*, released in 1990 by a major commercial publisher, typifies that sort of thinking: "Among the great wide percentage of the nation the media calls 'the general population,' that section the media and the public health authorities has [sic] tried desperately to terrify, there is no epidemic. AIDS will pick off a person here and there in this group, but the original infected partner will be one of the two groups in which the disease is epidemic. Most heterosexuals will continue to have more to fear from bathtub drowning than from AIDS."[6]

The irony here is not one of false predictions. Even as such projections were being written, millions of women—whose partners were neither bisexual men nor intravenous drug users—had already been "picked off" by HIV. Even in the United States, where the epidemic among women had initially been closely linked to injection drug use, the proportion of women reported exposed by a partner whose risk was not specified—in other words, not an injecting drug user—quintupled from 1983-84 to 1989-90. In the five years preceding the publication of *The Myth of Heterosexual AIDS*, the percentage increase in annual AIDS incidence was higher among the "heterosexually-acquired" exposure group than in any other.[7] By 1991, AIDS was the leading killer of young women in most large U.S. cities.[8]

The mismatch between reality and representation led Paula Treichler to pose, in 1988, the following question: "Given the intense concern with the human body that any conceptualization of AIDS entails, how can we account for the striking silence, until very recently, on the topic of women in AIDS discourse (including biomedical journals, mainstream news publications, public health literature, women's magazines, and the gay and feminist press)?"[9] In other words, why did many continue to think of AIDS as a disease of men?

More poignantly, perhaps: why were the voices of women with AIDS absent from scientific and popular commentary a full decade into the pandemic?[10]

One explanation for this partiality is that the majority of women with AIDS had been robbed of their voices long before HIV appeared to further complicate their lives. In settings of entrenched elitism, they have been poor. In settings of entrenched racism, they have been women of color. In settings of entrenched sexism, they have been, of course, women.

If it is finally recognized that AIDS poses enormous threats to poor women, this wisdom comes too late. Throughout the world, millions of women are already sick with complications of HIV infection. In the United States and in Latin America, the epidemics among women are increasing at a rate much higher than that registered among other groups: AIDS is already the leading cause of death among young African-American women living in the United States.[11] In Mexico, the male:female ratio of HIV infection went from 25:1 in 1984 to 4:1 in 1990. In Sao Paulo, Brazil, seroprevalence among pregnant women has increased sixfold in only three years.[12]

Similarly disturbing trends are registered elsewhere in the world, particularly in developing countries, where 90% of all adults and 98% of all children infected with HIV live.[13] In many sub-Saharan African nations, there are already more new infections among women than among men. In 1992, the United Nations Development Program estimated that, "Each day a further three thousand women become infected, and five hundred infected women die. Most are between 15 and 35 years old."[14] The World Health Organization has predicted that, during the course of the 365 days of the year 2000, between six and eight million women will become infected with HIV.[15]

Once we have begun to see the extent of these problems, further questions emerge. By what mechanisms do most seropositive women come to be infected with HIV? If not all women are at high risk, which groups of women are most likely to be exposed to the virus? How is women's risk similar in vastly different settings? How is it different? Has scholarly research—whether clinical investigation, epidemiology, or social science—kept pace with the advancing AIDS pandemic? Finally, what effects have persistent misunderstandings about women and AIDS had on the allocation of resources designed to prevent, detect, or treat the complications of HIV infection?

Throughout this book, we will continue to return to these questions. But we begin by examining the experience of three women living with HIV. These women are from very different backgrounds: "Darlene" is an African-American woman from Harlem; "Guylène" is the daughter of poor peasants from rural Haiti; "Lata" was living in a rural Indian village when, at the age of 15, she was sold into prostitution in Bombay. Their stories, similar in some ways and different in others, speak to many of the questions raised above.

2. DARLENE

Darlene Johnson was born in Central Harlem in 1955, one of three children born to a mother who was chronically homeless, leaving her husband and children for long periods of time.[16] Darlene remembers her parents having terrible fights in which her father hit her mother and her mother "cried for days." When Darlene was five, her mother sent her to Alabama to live with her maternal grandmother.

Darlene was shuttled back to New York City when she was eleven, and left to the care of her brother, ten years older than she. Darlene's brother, angry that this new burden narrowed his own life's chances, beat her frequently. With no other means of support, Darlene lived with her abusive brother until after eleventh grade, when she married a "hardworking man." The couple soon had two children. "No welfare," she says. "We never did it, not even when things were hard."

Things were often hard. The couple had many problems. Chief among them was their mutual passion, not for each other, but for heroin: "I didn't love him," she recalls. "He beat me, sometimes in front of the kids. It was drugs." After six years of abuse, Darlene found a way to leave. She and her children went to live with her estranged father.

A short while after moving in with her father, Darlene met her second husband. This marriage was for love. Her husband, also a heroin user, worked. They had two sons. Her two older children also loved this man, and things were looking up. Darlene insists that, although she used heroin, it didn't interfere with taking care of her children. "It just made things smooth," she said.

In 1987, her stepbrother, also a heroin user, was diagnosed with AIDS. "He just died," said Darlene; no mess, no fuss. Everyone in the family was stunned. Shortly thereafter, Darlene's stepfather had a fatal heart attack. Upon autopsy, he, too, was found to be HIV-infected.

Darlene grieved but was determined to keep her family together. Then her husband began to have high fevers and night sweats. He refused to go to the doctor, but Darlene knew it must be AIDS. By this time, she was tortured by the memory of all the times that she, her husband, and her stepbrother had shared needles. Darlene was tested and learned that she was indeed HIV-positive.

Her husband died two months later. Alone with four children, Darlene was heartbroken: she had lost her husband, her stepbrother, and her stepfather in a single year. Two women who were her baby's godparents and who had also shared needles became ill and they, too, had died.

Darlene was not only heartbroken. She was also broke, obliged to add the constant struggle to make ends meet to the struggle to overcome her grief. Her children kept her going. She suspected that her youngest son, sick from birth with one thing or another, was also infected. His first serious bout with pneumonia made everything clear: "I didn't know he had it till they took my baby to the hospital." At this time, Darlene was, by her own account, in a state of shock. "Too many close people" had died.

Darlene decided to set up her home to care for her son. She didn't want to abandon him in the hospital and so learned to do everything she could for him. When her older children began to act up, cutting school and hanging out in the streets, Darlene tried to get them help, to no avail. There was nothing for them. The counselors in their schools couldn't be trusted not to give out information about AIDS.

Soon the children were completely out of hand. By this time, the baby stared at Darlene as if he didn't know who she was. Crack, she explains, came to be the only way she could find to ease her pain. But, as always, there was a price to pay. She began to lose patience with her children. She yelled often, she didn't cook regular meals for them. She was relieved when they were away. Darlene felt she had nothing but pain:

> This social worker was telling everybody I had the virus . . . The police came looking for me when my little son ran away, he ran away with my big son; my big son brought him home. When I came downstairs, the cops jumped all the way down the stairs. 'Oh, you supposed to be in the hospital cause you got AIDS.' Everybody on the street was looking at me . . . [The social worker] told my kids' friends, their parents. A little boy was up in the fire escape, he said, 'Oh, look—there's David's mother; she got AIDS.'

Darlene concluded that her children were suffering and neglected. She felt there was no family. Everyone had died. So she turned to the Department of Social Services and asked that her three oldest children be placed in foster care while she tried to care for the youngest, now dying of AIDS. "I just didn't want to live any more and I didn't want the kids to be running in the street, to be hungry."

The children were placed in separate homes. The oldest was sent to a home in the Bronx, but he ran away to live with a friend of Darlene's who wanted him and who supports him. Darlene also wanted the child to be with her friend, but knew city authorities would never have given her custody of him, so she said nothing. Darlene's daughter was placed with a woman Darlene knew to be a drug user: "They put my daughter in a house where they sell drugs, crack. My daughter watches this lady's kids." Darlene is powerless to change the placement.

One of Darlene's sons was placed in New Jersey with a family that Darlene likes. He is well cared for and she expects the family to adopt him when she dies. She is grateful for them and wants the adoption to happen. She attends family therapy sessions with this family. This son, she feels, will be all right.

Having given her children to foster care, and left alone with her youngest, Darlene found it painful to care for him. The little boy suffered terribly, she recalls. His stomach became more and more distended and he stopped responding to her. Finally, one night, as he lay in bed with her, he stopped breathing. This death "took me out completely," Darlene said. "He was three years old. It took him six months to die." Now six people in her life had died in a single year.

Darlene gave in to crack completely and hit rock bottom. She lived on the streets for three months, but was desperate "not to die that way." The children counted on seeing her. She went into the hospital to detoxify from crack, and was enrolled in a methadone program. Once in the program, she saw a doctor. All during the year of deaths, she had never gone to a doctor for herself. She thinks she must have been very depressed.

Darlene, too, has been diagnosed with AIDS, but mostly she worries about her two oldest children. She could have used some help with them when all the deaths began. Darlene sees the two children who live near her every day. She visits the son who lives in New Jersey every week. She says she'll see them this way until she dies. She only hopes she doesn't linger.

3. GUYLÈNE

Guylène Adrien was born in Savanette, a dusty village in the middle of Haiti's infertile central plateau.[17] Like other families in the region, the Adriens fed their children by working a small plot of land and selling produce in regional markets. Like other families, the Adriens were poor, but Guylène recalls that they "had enough to get by." She was the third of four children, a small family by Haitian standards. It was to become smaller still: Guylène's younger sister died in adolescence of cerebral malaria. Guylène's oldest sister is said to be somewhere in the Dominican Republic, where she has been living, if she is living, for over a dozen years. Guylène's other surviving sister lives with her mother and two children, working the family plot of land for ever-diminishing returns.

Guylène recounts her own conjugal history in the sad voice reserved for retrospection. When she was a teenager—"perhaps 14 or 15"— a family acquaintance, Occident Dorzin, took to dropping by to visit. A fairly successful peasant farmer, Dorzin had two or three small plots of land in the area. In the course of these visits, he made it clear to Guylène that he was attracted to her. "But he was already married, and I was a child. When he placed his hand on my arm, I slapped him and swore at him and hid in the garden."

Dorzin was not so easily dissuaded, however, and eventually approached Guylène's father to ask for her hand, not in marriage, but in *plasaj*, a potentially stable form of union widespread in rural Haiti. Before she was 16, Guylène moved with Dorzin, a man 20 years her senior, to a village about an hour away from her parents. She was soon pregnant. Occident's wife, who was significantly older than Guylène, was not at all pleased, and friction between the two women eventually led to dissolution of the newer union. In the interim, however, Guylène gave birth to two children, a girl and then a boy.

After the break with Dorzin, Guylène and her nursing son returned to her father's house. She remained in Savanette for five months, passing through the village of Do Kay on her way to the market in Domond or to visit her daughter, who remained in Occident's care. It was during these travels that she met a young man named Osner, who worked intermittently in Port-au-Prince, the capital city, as a laborer or a mechanic. One day he simply struck up a conversation with Guylène as she visited a friend in Do Kay. "Less than a month later," she recalled, "Osner sent his father to speak to my father. My father agreed." Leaving her toddler son in her parents' household, Guylène set off to try conjugal life a second time, this time in Do Kay.

The subsequent months were difficult. Guylène's father died later that year, and her son, cared for largely by her sister, was often ill. Guylène was already pregnant with her third child, and she and Osner lacked almost everything that might have made their new life together easier. Osner did not have steady work in Port-au-Prince, but, as a mechanic, he was occasionally able to find part-time jobs.

After the baby was born, in 1985, they decided to move to the city: Osner would find work in a garage, and Guylène would become involved in the marketplace. Failing that, she could always work as a maid. In the interim, Osner's mother would care for the baby, as Do Kay was safer for an infant than was Port-au-Prince.

Osner and Guylène spent almost three years in the city. These were hard times. Political violence was resurgent, especially in their neighborhood of Cité Soleil, a vast and notorious slum on the northern fringes of the city. The couple was often short of work: he worked only irregularly as a mechanic; she split her time between jobs as a maid and selling fried food on the wharf in Cité Soleil. Guylène much preferred the latter:

> Whenever I had a little money, I worked for myself selling, trying to make [her capital] last as long as I could. When we were broke I worked in ladies' houses . . . If the work is good, and they pay you well, or the person is not too bad, treats you well, you might stay there as long as six or seven months. But if the person treats you poorly, you won't even stay a month. Perhaps you only go for a single day and then you quit . . . Rich women often hate poor women, so I always had trouble working for them.

When asked what she meant by decent pay, Guylène stated that the equivalent of $20 a month was passable, as long as you were able to eat something at work.

In 1987 (Darlene Johnson's year of losses), three "unhappy occurrences" came to pass in quick succession. A neighbor was shot and killed during one of the military's regular nighttime incursions into the slum; bullets pierced the thin walls of Guylène's and Osner's own house. A few weeks later, Guylène received word that her son had died abruptly. The cause of death was never clear. And, finally, Osner became gravely ill. It started, Guylène recalled, with weight loss and a persistent cough.

Osner returned to the clinic in Do Kay a number of times in the course of his illness, which began with pulmonary tuberculosis. In the case of a young man returning from Port-au-Prince with tuberculosis, it was routine practice to consider HIV infection in the differential diagnosis, and it was suggested as a possibility at that time. In the clinic, Osner reported a lifetime total of seven sexual partners, including Guylène. With one exception, each of these unions had been monogamous, if short-lived.

When Osner did not respond, except transiently, to biomedical interventions, many in the village began to raise the possibility of AIDS. At his death in September, 1988, it was widely believed that he had died from the new disease. His doctors concurred.

Guylène subsequently returned to Savanette, to a cousin's house. She tried selling produce in local markets, but could not even support herself, much less the child she had left in the care of Osner's mother. She was humiliated, she said, by having to ask her mother-in-law for financial assistance, even though she informed her that she was pregnant with Osner's child. Finally, a full year after Osner's death, the fetus "frozen in her womb" (as she put it) began to develop. It was, she insisted, Osner's baby (others identified a man from her hometown of Savanette as the child's father). She had the baby, a girl, in November of 1989. Osner's mother always referred to the child as her granddaughter.

A month after her confinement, Guylène returned to Savanette with the baby. She was unemployed; her mother and sister were barely making ends meet. Guylène and others in the household often went hungry. Feeling as if she were a burden, Guylène finally went to the coastal town of Saint-Marc, where she had cousins. She worked as a servant in their house until the baby became ill; Guylène, too, felt exhausted. Since medical care was readily available only in Do Kay, she returned again to the home of Osner's mother. Guylène's and Osner's first child had already started school there, and Osner's mother allowed she could always find food for two more.

By early June, 1992, Guylène was ill: she had lost weight and become amenorrheic. Later that month, a doctor at the clinic heard her story with some alarm. Yes, Guylène said, she had heard of AIDS; some had even said that Osner had died from it, but she knew that was not true. After reviewing Osner's chart, the physician suggested that she be tested for HIV. She was leaving for Port-au-Prince, Guylène informed him, but would return for the results. The child's physical exam was unremarkable except for pallor and a slightly enlarged liver. The baby was treated, empirically, for worms and also for anemia, and sent home.

The next day, Guylène returned to Port-au-Prince. She worked a few days as a maid, but found the conditions intolerable. She tried selling cigarettes and candy, but remained hungry and fatigued; the city was in the throes of its worst economic depression in recent decades. "I was ready to try anything," she said. Shortly thereafter, Guylène's fourth baby died quite suddenly of cardiac failure, presumed secondary to HIV cardiomyopathy: although the child had never been tested for antibodies to the virus, Guylène's test had come back positive a few days prior to the tragedy.

Guylène was informed of her positive serology on the day following her return; she listened impassively as a physician went through the possible significance of the test and made plans to repeat it. Careful physical examination and history suggested that Guylène had not yet had a serious opportunistic infection. Her only manifestations of HIV infection at that time were severe anemia, amenorrhea, weight loss, occasional fevers, and some swelling of her lymph nodes.

Guylène began visiting the clinic regularly following confirmation of her positive HIV serology. Her doctors spoke with her regularly—"too often," she once remarked—about HIV infection and its implications. She was placed on prophylactic isoniazid, iron supplement and multivitamins, and also a protein supplement. Guylène did not return to Port-au-Prince, but rented a house with the financial aid she received through an AIDS-treatment program based in the village.

Although Guylène experienced significant improvement in less than a month, she remained depressed and withdrawn. A young man named René had been visiting her, but Guylène discouraged him and he disappeared—"he went to Santo Domingo, I think, because I never heard from him again." In mid-November, however, Guylène responded to the advances of a soldier stationed in Péligre. A native of a large town near the Dominican border, with a wife and two children there, the soldier had only been in the region about a month. Although residents of Péligre said that he had a regular partner in that village as well, Guylène insists that she was his only partner in the region:

He saw me here, at home. He saw me only a couple of times, spoke to me only a couple of times, before announcing that he cared for me. After that, he came to visit me often. I didn't think much of it until he started staying over. I got pregnant at about the time they announced that he was being transferred back to [his home town]. He said he'd be back, but I never saw or heard from him again.

Because Guylène's physicians had gone to some trouble to advise her against unprotected sexual intercourse, they were anxious to know how conversations about this subject may have figured in her decision to conceive another child, if indeed the pregnancy was the result of a decision. That Guylène understood what it meant to be an asymptomatic carrier of HIV seemed clear from a metaphor she used to describe herself: "You can be walking around big and pretty, and you've got a problem inside. When you see a house that's well built, inside it's still got ugly rocks, mud, sand—all the ugly, hidden things. What's nice on the outside might not be nice on the inside."

Guylène understands, too, that her child might well be infected with HIV. But she is impatient with questions, tired of talking about sadness and death: "Will the baby be sick? Sure he could be sick. People are never not sick. I'm sick . . . he might be sick too. It's in God's hands."

Now Guylène draws to the close of her fifth pregnancy, which may well culminate in another death. Two of her children are dead; two others have long looked to a father or grandmother for the bulk of their parenting. Guylène's own sisters are dead, missing, or beaten into submission by the hardness of Haiti. Few of her nephews and nieces have survived into adulthood. Guylène assures her physicians that she is without symptoms, but seems inhabited by a persistent lassitude.

4. LATA

When Lata first entered the world somewhere in rural Maharastra, in a small thatched hut lit only by lanterns, her mother began weeping—tears not of joy, but of shame that she had brought yet another daughter into the world.[18] "God must not have been very happy with me that day," she said. Lata does not know what month she was born

into her untouchable *Harijan* family with two sisters and three broth-
ers, but the year was 1967. Her father farmed a very small plot in
Solapur, a small agricultural village, yet as she remembers it, her
mother did nearly all of the remaining work:

> So much of my childhood is a blur to me. I remember when my father
> would return home he would beat my mother for her cooking or because
> one of us was crying. And if he had drunk too much he would beat my sis-
> ter and me, the whole time my mother running around to prepare better
> food or make us quiet so father could eat. It seems every day passed like
> this, the only difference being that father got meaner as he grew older.

Never permitted to attend school, Lata by the age of six was
tilling and weeding with her father. "Years passed like this," she
remarked, examining her hands as if for traces of blisters. Her two
elder sisters were married at the ages of 15 and 16, respectively, and
both weddings came at a heavy price to Lata's family. One sister's
dowry totaled 10,000 rupees—almost twice her father's earnings for
that year. Predictably, both marriages forced the family to turn to the
local moneylender, a man who maintained interest rates as high as
25%—compounded quarterly. Lata's father, already faced with selling off more of his tiny plot in order to service his debt, lived in fear
of another wedding.

Lack of rainfall during the 1982 monsoon season brought a
poor harvest, leaving the family in the worst financial state it had
ever experienced. "My father was drinking more every day," recalled
Lata. "Sometimes I recall him not even going out to the fields, yet
forcing us to go, and beating us more than he ever had. I know he was
worried about my getting married and when he was drunk he would
curse my mother, blaming her for bringing him yet another daughter."

In this context, the arrival of a man who would take Lata from
the despair of her village life was regarded as a godsend. Like so
many other *dalals* ("middlemen," many of whom are women) who
come from Bombay, Prasant had for some years been making a
"decent" living in the flesh trade. Working the same route from the
villages of Southern Maharastra to the bordellos of Bombay, his

scheme was identical in almost every settlement. Upon arrival in a village, Prasant would seek out a local moneylender and, often with the help of a small bribe, extract information about area families with young daughters and heavy debt. Prasant, like other *dalals*, then approached the male heads of families, claiming to have work for their daughters as servants or seamstresses in Bombay. In Lata's case, her father was told that she would be given work as a dishwasher: "After [Prasant] arrived, my father took my mother aside and told her that jobs were available in Bombay, and this man would give him 11,000 rupees as a payment for me washing dishes and housecleaning. He said I would be able to mail money home every month and allowed to visit Solapur after six months of work. Not for one moment did anyone suspect or question what he told us."

Desperate, hungry, facing the most acute poverty his family had ever experienced, Lata's father saw opportunity and relief in his daughter's departure. A few hours after he and Prasant had spoken, Lata was told to pack her two cotton saris, her bangles and sandals. She would leave for Bombay in the morning.

A frail and frightened 15 year old, Lata had difficulty holding back tears as she waved goodbye, her father's gaze stoic, while tears streamed down her mother's face. It was the last time she would ever see her parents.

She remembered nothing of her trip to Bombay, although it was her first train ride. Her inability to recollect, she suspects, was the result of a drug she had been given. The next memory she had was of a taxi in Bombay. Lata was entering the city's red light district. Barely awake, she was brought to Number 27, Falkland Road, where Prasant sold her to a pimp for 15,000 rupees—about $500. His tidy profit of 4,000 rupees was more than enough to carry him through the month.

Lata had arrived in the Kamathipura district of Bombay, and she was about to become one of its 30,000 sex workers. Lata recalled that she came to complete consciousness in a "cage"— a cramped room full of girls putting on makeup, oiling their hair, and tightening their petticoats and blouses. Lata had no comprehension of where she was:

I saw all of these girls wearing nothing but colored blouses, makeup, and skirts, and asked the madam, 'What is this?' She told me it was a place for working girls. I still didn't understand, frightened by the very clothes these women wore . . . Sapna, the madam, told me I would be staying with her and ordered me to put on clothes that lay on the floor for me and then stand outside. I began crying and told her I couldn't stay. She slapped me hard and I remember I couldn't stop crying. I told her to let me go and she looked me straight in the eye and said, 'You want to leave, fine. Give me 15,000 rupees and you're free. Until then, get dressed and start paying back your *kurja*.'

Lata's *kurja* was her debt, the mechanism by which she was indeed trammeled as if in a cage. She did not join the other girls on the street that day, nor the day after. She slept and lay in the corner of the room, pretending to be ill, eating the food she was given, and listening to the other girls call out to customers on the Falkland Road and watching the parade of men and girls in and out of the adjacent room, furnished only with a bed. On the third day in Bombay, Sapna's patience had been exhausted: she ordered one of her managers to "break Lata in."

No matter how many years pass, Lata says she always has trouble recounting this part of her story. Arun, a manager whose main responsibility was to bring in new customers, also had the duty of making sure the girls were bringing in enough money and "working" hard. As one madam put it, "There are times when they won't listen to us, so the managers and pimps keep the girls in line." Lata recalls:

I had been sitting in the same corner for days, pretending I was not feeling well, frightened, and wishing Sapna would let me go. Finally Arun came to me and pulled me by my ear, telling me to put on the clothes and stand outside. I was a fifteen-year-old village girl and didn't even know what sex was, let alone prostitution. How could I understand what was going on? He took me to the room with the bed and closed the door and forced me to have sex with him. Afterwards, he said, 'Now do you understand?' and laughed and told me to get to work. I remember being silent while the other girls stared at me when I came out. I'm sure they knew what he did. And for the first time I began to accept that there was no way out—I was here to stay.

That day, Lata, clad in a purple blouse and pink petticoat, nervously joined the thousands of prostitutes of Bombay's red light districts. It was her first night on the streets and the beginning of a long and painful career.

Unlike most other girls, who stand in front of the cages, beckoning to passing men, Lata stood quietly, receiving no business during her first three days out. The days were long: bathing at around 10 in the morning, out on Falkland Road by 11, lunch at 4 p.m., and back on the street until 2 or 3 a.m., with dinner if she was lucky. On an average day, a Bombay prostitute may see four to five customers a day. Times may vary, but generally late evening is when they are busiest. Early in the afternoon of her fourth day, Lata was finally approached:

> An Arab man came and after seeing me spoke with the madam for some time and wanted to take me to the Taj Hotel for three days. I saw him give her many hundred rupee notes, and then he took me into his taxi and to the hotel. I was terrified of being alone with him, you have to remember that he was my first customer and I had no idea what to do. The first night we slept in separate beds and the next day he took me to sari and jewelry shops, buying me clothes and gold. When he would go out in the day, he would lock me in the room. But the more he bought, the more scared I became of what he would expect. On the second night, he told me to dress in all of the clothes he bought for me. Frightened as I was, I knew that I had no choice. At that moment, I remember saying to myself, 'This is now my life,' truly accepting it for the first time . . . No longer willing to fight him or my own self, I had sex with him.

Upon her return to Falkland Road, Lata settled into the routine of a Bombay prostitute. Slowly, she came to know the stories of the girls in her brothel, and others nearby. Although they hailed from many villages and even from Nepal, most had similar experiences. Like the others, she gave half of her daily earnings to the madam as repayment for her *kurja*. Yet Lata knew that she, and all girls sold into prostitution, had little hope of ever buying their freedom; her initial debt of 15,000 rupees was accruing an interest of 20 to 25% a month. If a pimp brought a customer to her, she owed him 25%. And in most areas, police regularly extort money from sex workers with the threat of jail. With an average of four or five customers per day, each paying about 20 to 30 rupees, she could be left with as little as 20 rupees to cover food, clothing, and other basic needs.

At this writing, Lata has been in Bombay for 13 years. She is a well-known figure at Number 27 Falkland Road, a small brothel sandwiched between a tea stall and a large pink building brimming with Nepali girls. Proudly wearing her gold bangles, her hair always neatly oiled and braided, Lata is now a respected "veteran" of the red-light community. At 28 years of age, she continues to see an average of four or five customers a day.

Rumor of AIDS did not reach the red light district of Bombay until 1989 or so—surely well after the virus itself had arrived. "Back then I and other people on Falkland Road started to know about AIDS, but we did not take it seriously. Then the Indian Health Organization people came and gave us free condoms."

In 1991, Lata became one of the first sex workers to volunteer as a peer AIDS educator, and she pushes her fellow prostitutes to demand that their clients use condoms: "I tell the girls, it's your life. If he refuses to wear one, send him away. And even if he offers you one million for sex without a condom, you don't do it. But I know this is hard. There are too many hungry girls. Too many scared girls. And the madams are always watching, putting on pressure."

Preventive messages came too late for Lata, who now knows that she is infected with HIV. She continues to work as both an AIDS outreach worker and a prostitute.

5. SEX, DRUGS, AND STRUCTURAL VIOLENCE

The stories of Darlene, Guylène, and Lata—recounted in detail in order to bring into relief the forces constraining their options—reveal both differences and commonalities. But how locally representative is each of these experiences? Darlene Johnson's experiences, though tragic, are all too commonplace among African-American women. As a heroin user, a habit clearly tied to a poverty structured by racism, her chances of avoiding HIV were slim, even if she had wanted to quit prior to her diagnosis. In 1987, the year that Darlene's world was burst asunder by AIDS, there were 338,365 treatment slots available to the nation's estimated four million addicts, and most of these programs predominantly served men. As a pregnant woman, Darlene would have found it next to impossible to find treatment for her addiction.[19] Writing of women who are addicted, of color, and living in poverty, Janet Mitchell and co-workers have recently noted that "Access to care and services has traditionally been marginal for women with any one of these three criteria. Any two of these . . . essentially put a women in the extremely limited access category. Women with all three of these characteristics fall into the no access category."[20]

In the United States, HIV has moved, almost unimpeded, through poor communities of color. By 1991, African Americans, who comprise approximately 12% of the U.S. population, accounted for 30% of all reported AIDS cases. During the eighties, the cumulative incidence of AIDS was more than 11 times higher for black women than for white women. Although many early cases were among those who injected drugs, the epidemic is fast expanding among women with no such history. As noted above, AIDS is the leading cause of death among African-American women from 25 to 44; for Latinas in this age group, it is now the third leading cause of death.[21] When the first multi-center study of AIDS among U.S. women was funded, almost 78% of over 1300 patients recruited were women of color.[22]

Understanding the strikingly patterned U.S. epidemic is less a matter of knowing one's geography, and more a matter of understanding a limited number of events and processes—the "synergism of plagues" discussed by Rodrick Wallace—that range from unemployment to the destruction of housing by fires.[23] "Urban poverty in the United States has created the perfect machinery for the continued propagation of HIV," notes Robert Fullilove. "Inner city poor neighborhoods often shelter a vigorous drug trade, numerous opportunities for strangers to engage in drug-mediated, unprotected sex, and numerous locations where these and other risk behaviors go virtually unchallenged."[24] Darlene's lamentable experience is, alas, all too typical.

In Haiti, similarly, little about Guylène's story is unique. There is a deadly monotony in the stories told by rural Haitian women with AIDS. In a study conducted in the clinic where Guylène receives her care, the majority of new AIDS diagnoses are registered among women, most of them with a trajectory similar to Guylène's. As young women—or teenaged girls—they had been driven to Port-au-Prince by the lure of an escape from the harshest poverty. Once in the city, each worked as a domestic, but none managed to find the financial security so elusive in the countryside. The women interviewed were straightforward about the non-voluntary aspect of their sexual activity: in their opinions, they had been driven into unfavorable unions by poverty.[25] Indeed, such testimony calls into question facile notions of "consensual sex."

Lata's painful experience also exemplifies that of hundreds of thousands of poor girls in India, Nepal, and elsewhere. It has been estimated that up to 50% of Bombay's prostitutes were recruited through trickery or abduction.[26] Although no real population-based surveys have yet been conducted, it is highly likely that most of India's prostitutes have high rates of HIV infection. In the late 1980s, some 700 sex workers were arrested and forcibly taken to the city of Madras, where 70% of them were found to have antibodies to HIV. Many of these women were jailed or subjected to other forms of harassment, including that of having their names publicly listed.[27]

In short, the experiences of Darlene, Guylène, and Lata are all too typical. One clear lesson is that both the immediate and systemic causes of increased risk need to be elucidated. For example, heroin use—and needle sharing—put Darlene at increased risk of HIV infection. Sex work—or, rather, unprotected sex work—put Lata at risk of HIV infection. But in Harlem and Bombay, it seems fair to assert that the decisions made by the women profiled were linked to their impoverishment and their subordinate status as women. Furthermore, it is important to remember that Darlene and Guylène and Lata were born into poverty. Their attempts to escape poverty were long bets that failed—and AIDS was the form their failure took.

The stories recounted here force a difficult question: How many girls are, from birth, at inordinate risk of AIDS or some other dreadful destiny? "For some women," notes the founder of an AIDS support group for women, "HIV is the first major disaster in their lives. For many more, AIDS is just one more problem on top of many others."[28] In fact, those in the former category—women for whom HIV is an altogether unprecedented misfortune—are in the minority. Attentiveness to the life stories of women with AIDS usually reveals it to be the latest in a string of tragedies. "For poor women," notes anthropologist Martha Ward, "AIDS is just another problem they are blamed for and have to take responsibility for. They ask, 'How am I going to take care of my family?' 'I have to put food on the table now.' 'You think AIDS is a problem! Let me tell you—I got real problems.'"[29]

Millions of women living in similar circumstances—but with very different psychological profiles and cultural backgrounds—can thus expect to meet similar fates. Their sickness may be thought of as a result of "structural violence," because it is neither nature nor pure individual will that is at fault, but rather historically given (and often economically driven) processes and forces that conspire to constrain individual agency.[30] Structural violence is visited upon on all those whose social status denies them access to the fruits of scientific and social advances.

If meaningful responses to AIDS are to be presented, the differential political economy of risk must be revealed. Structural violence means that some women are, from the outset, at high risk of HIV infection, while other women are shielded from risk. Reflecting on the experiences detailed above and adopting this point of view—that a political economy of risk can be described, and that this exercise helps to explain where the AIDS pandemic is moving and how quickly—we begin to see why similar stories are legion in sub-Saharan Africa and India. They are fast becoming commonplace in Thailand and other parts of Asia. The experiences recounted here may be considered textbook cases of vulnerability, but their moral is deciphered only if it is made clear that these women have been rendered vulnerable to AIDS through *social* processes. By social processes, we mean the economic, political, and cultural forces that can be shown to shape the dynamics of HIV transmission. The anthropologist Brooke Schoepf, writing from Zaïre, explains how AIDS has "transformed many women's survival strategies into death strategies":

> Women, who often lack access to cash, credit, land or jobs, engage in 'off-the-books' activities in the informal sector. Some exchange sex for the means of subsistence. Others enter sex work at the behest of their families, to obtain cash to purchase land or building materials, to pay a brother's school fees, or to settle a debt. Still others supplement meager incomes with occasional resort to sex with multiple partners. Married or not, the deepening economic crisis propels many to seek 'spare tires' or 'shock absorbers' to make ends meet.[31]

Taken together, the dynamics of HIV infection among women and responses to its advance reveal much about the complex relationship between power/powerlessness and sexuality. All sexually active women share to some extent biological risk, but it is clear that the AIDS pandemic among women is strikingly patterned along social, not biological, lines. And many questions remain unanswered. For example, by what mechanisms, precisely, do social forces (such as poverty, sexism and other forms of discrimination) become embodied as personal risk? What role does inequality per se play in promoting HIV transmission?

Although many would agree that forces such as poverty and gender inequality are the strongest enhancers of risk for exposure to HIV, this subject has been neglected in both the biomedical and social science literature on HIV infection. The extent of this neglect will be explored in Part II of this book, but let us take, as an example, a recent investigation of heterosexually transmitted HIV infection in "rural" Florida. The study, published in the *New England Journal of Medicine*, was conducted by Ellerbrock and co-workers, who revealed that fully 5.1% of 1,082 asymptomatic women attending a public prenatal clinic in rural Florida had antibodies to HIV. What "risk factors" might account for such high rates of infection? The researchers reported a statistically significant association between HIV infection and having used crack cocaine, having had more than five sexual partners in a lifetime, or more than two sexual partners per year of sexual activity. Also associated with seropositivity to HIV were histories of exchanging sex for money or for drugs or of having had sexual intercourse with a "high-risk partner."

These associations are unsurprising. How are they interpreted? The study concludes that "in communities with a high seroprevalence of HIV, like this Florida community, a sizable proportion of all women of reproductive age are at risk for infection through heterosexual transmission."[32] Is this, in fact, the most significant (or the most pragmatically valuable) conclusion to be drawn from such a study? In settings with an even higher seroprevalence of HIV, such as New York City, it is clear that not all women of reproductive age are at increased risk of HIV infection: poor women, who in this country are usually women of color, are at high risk.

Such a conclusion is possible only if the "community" under study is placed under a Bell jar, so that both the glittering towers of West Palm Beach and the vast fields of sugarcane, and their owners, are outside the field of analysis. But if these parts of the "community" are invisible, so too is the political economy of AIDS, for many of these women, like their partners, have worked in these wealthy communities or in the nearby fields. Thus, arbitrarily constricting the social field generates the illusion of equally shared risk. It obscures inequalities central to the advance of HIV. The equivalent exercise would be to recount Darlene's story as if Central Harlem were an island nation, rather than a rich city's ghetto. Guylène's narrative would make no reference to the wealthy households in which she was obliged to work. Lata's social field would be bordered by the margins of the Kamathipura district, into which no wealthy clients entered.

A closer look at the language in which Ellerbrock's and coworkers' conclusions were couched suggests that a meaningful discussion of risk cannot be limited to medical issues narrowly construed. Nowhere in their article does the word "poverty" appear, even though the authors mention that over 90% of the women who knew their incomes belonged to households earning less than $10,000 per year.[33] Nowhere in the article do we see the words "racism," even though in Florida, as elsewhere, the African-American and Latino communities are those most affected by the epidemic. The terms "sexism," "despair," and "powerlessness" are also absent from the discussion, even though many of the women studied were pulled into the region by the possibilities of jobs as servants or farmworkers. One might as easily conclude by arguing that, in Palm Beach County, it is the women who are "at risk" of attending a public prenatal clinic who are at higher risk of acquiring HIV—unemployed women of color, that is, who are more likely to have unstable sexual unions or to exchange sex for drugs or money.[34]

Like all societies characterized by extreme inequality or structural violence, the linked societies of Darlene, Guylène, and Lata require other kinds of violence in order to maintain the status quo, which is so unbearable for the majority. In the United States, the enormous number of African Americans in prisons also reflects this violence, as do death squads in Haiti. Other forms of structural violence are more strikingly gendered. Police brutality in Bombay is to be understood in the context of a political economy favoring the import of poor Nepali girls, say, to India's economic powerhouse.

HIV and direct violence against women are intimately linked. Among sex workers, risk of assault and risk of HIV are both highest among the poorest prostitutes.[35] Many of the estimated 4,000,000 U.S. women who are assaulted by their male partners are precisely those at heightened risk for HIV. As Sally Zierler notes, "This figure, awful as it is, obscures the fact that some women are more at risk than others. For like HIV's distribution, partner violence against women follows social divisions marked by class position, and race/ethnicity, creating strata of extreme vulnerability to violence victimization."[36]

Finally, in an era of widespread and instantaneous communication, *symbolic* violence is also used to accomplish these ends: structural violence requires its apologists, witting or unwitting, and we now turn to the role played by researchers and other opinion shapers in buttressing the myths and mystifications related to the topic of women and AIDS.

6. WOMEN AND AIDS:
MYTHS AND MYSTIFICATIONS

Throughout the world, the majority of women with HIV infection are poor. They are denied access not merely to resources and services but also to symbolic capital. In her thoughtful examination of the gendering of American AIDS discourse, Paula Treichler asks, "Why were women so unprepared? And why do they continue to take it so quietly?"[37] She responds to her question with a candor that is all too rare:

> As evidence of AIDS in women mounted, speculations linked the disease to prostitutes, intravenous drug users, and women in the Third World (primarily Haiti and countries in central Africa). It was not that these three groups were synonymous but, rather, that their differentness of race, class, or national origin made speculation about transmission possible—unlike middle-class American feminists, for example. American feminists also by this point had considerable access to public forums from which to protest ways in which they were represented, while these other groups of women were, for all practical purposes, silenced categorically so far as public or biomedical discourse was concerned.[38]

This silencing refers to the silence of poor women in public forums ranging from conferences to published material—for they have not, in fact, been silent. They have been, rather, unheard. In rural Haiti, for example, a group of poor women committed to preventing AIDS worked together in 1991 to generate a list of common myths about women and AIDS.[39] The document prepared by the group made reference to the following myths:

AIDS is a Disease of Men

The data are overwhelming: AIDS was never a disease of men. Given transmission dynamics, AIDS may in fact become a disease afflicting predominantly women.

"Heterosexual AIDS" Won't Happen

Heterosexual AIDS has already happened. Indeed, in many parts of the world, AIDS is the leading cause of death among young women.

Women's Promiscuity Causes AIDS

Most women with AIDS do not have multiple sexual partners; they have never used i.v. drugs; they have not received tainted blood transfusions. Their major risk factor is being poor. For others, the risk is being married and unable to control not only their husbands but also what jobs their husbands have to perform to make a living.

Women are AIDS Vectors

Women are too often perceived as agents of transmission who infect men and "innocent babies." Prostitutes have been particularly hard hit by such propaganda, but prostitutes are far more vulnerable to infection than to infecting: AIDS is an "occupational risk" of commercial sex work, especially in settings in which sex workers cannot safely demand that clients use condoms.[40]

Condom as Panacea

Gender inequality calls into question the utility of condoms in settings in which women's ability to insist on "safe sex" is undermined by a host of less easily confronted forces. Furthermore, many HIV-positive women choose to conceive children, which means that barrier methods that prevent conception are not the answer for many. Woman-controlled viricidal preventive strategies are necessary, if women's wishes are to be respected.

While these were the myths deemed salient in rural Haiti, other, related mystifications are to be found in every setting in which poor women must now add HIV to a long list of quotidian threats. In the United States, anthropologist Martha Ward complains of "urban folklore" about mothers with AIDS: "'Those women' have food stamps. They buy alcohol or luxury items. They have infected their innocent babies. They should use birth control, get abortions, get a job, finish school, use condoms, and say 'no' to drugs."[41]

What many of the dominant myths and mystifications have in common is an exaggeration of personal agency, often through highlighting certain psychological or cultural attributes, even though it is not at all clear that these attributes are in any way related to women's risk for HIV infection. Condoms are a classic case in point. As noted, several studies have revealed that most U.S. women at high risk of

HIV infection are already aware that condoms can prevent transmission, but many of these women are unable to insist that they be used. Although most acknowledge the link between poverty and low rates of condom use, few studies have carefully explored the association. A recent study among African-American women in Los Angeles showed that condoms were less likely to be used by couples in which the woman was dependent upon her male partner for rent money.[42]

There is nothing wrong with underlining personal agency, but there is something unfair about using personal agency as a basis for assigning blame while simultaneously denying those blamed the opportunity to exert agency in their lives. "A patronage that simultaneously grants 'victims' powerlessness and then assigns them blame for that powerlessness is nothing new," notes Jan Grover. "It is therefore important to make connections between the construction of AIDS victimhood and similar constructions of the poor, who also suffer the triple curse of objectification, institutionalized powerlessness, and blame for their condition."[43]

The objectification of "the poor" is, of course, a risk run by any who use the term at all, but striving to understand a person's material constraints is hardly tantamount to a refusal to recognize the salience of personal experience. Recognizing a commonality of constraint—in addition to, say, a commonality of psychology or of culture—is an important part of unraveling the nature of risk. Indeed, as Margaret Connors argues in Chapter 3, failure to embed personal experience in the larger social and economic matrices in which it takes on meaning is often synonymous with intense focus on personal psychology or "deviant subcultures."

Among the myriad mystifications important in obscuring the nature of women's risk, three are recurrent: one, as noted, is the focus on local factors and local actors to the exclusion of broader analyses that would implicate powerful forces and powerful actors outside of the field of view. A second is the conflation of structural violence and cultural difference. A third, centrally related to the others, is absence of serious considerations of social class.[44] These are not infrequently the mechanisms by which personal agency is exaggerated in both scholarly and popular commentary. To cite Brooke Schoepf again, "the structure of the wider political economy establishes the situations and restricts the options that people can choose as a means of survival. A focus on 'sub-cultures,' as on individual behaviors, tends to obscure the underlying causes of social interaction."[45]

These expedient erasures and exaggerations are buttressed, rather than challenged or exposed, by research published in a host of key journals. For example, a review of the ever-enlarging epidemiological literature reveals that although racism, sexism, and powerlessness go unmentioned, there usually is mention of culture.[46] Take a study conducted by Nyamathi and co-workers in the Los Angeles area among 1173 women aged 18 to 75 years of age. Half were African-Americans; half were called "Latina," and described as either "high-acculturated" or "low-acculturated." Recruited through homeless shelters or drug-treatment programs, all of these women had histories of drug use or of being the sexual partner of an injecting drug user or of being homeless or of having a history of a sexually transmitted disease. Some had histories of sex work; some had multiple sexual partners. A survey administered to these women revealed that "African-American and Latina women were equally knowledgeable about AIDS symptomatology; the etiologic agent of AIDS; and behaviors known to reduce risk of HIV infection, such as using condoms and cleaning works used by intravenous drug users."[47] Greater differences existed as regards knowledge of modes of transmission, but the women surveyed tended to overestimate transmissibility, not to underestimate it.

In a sense, then, what the researchers found was that ignorance about HIV was not really the issue for these women. What put them at risk for HIV was something other than cognitive deficits. But the interpretation of their findings, published in the influential *American Journal of Public Health*, was not in keeping with the data: "These findings suggest the need for culturally sensitive education programs that cover common problems relating to drug use and unprotected sex and, in addition, offer sessions for women of different ethnic groups to address problematic areas of concern."[48] Was this truly a key implication of the research? By the researchers' own standards, these women were by and large fully aware of transmission of HIV through injection drug use and unprotected sex. Moreover, the more women had used drugs or had multiple sexual partners, the more likely they were to perceive themselves, correctly, as being at increased risk of HIV infection.

By insisting that "culturally sensitive education programs" have a large role to play in protecting poor women from AIDS, the authors are suggesting, all evidence to the contrary, that ignorance of the facts is centrally related to high HIV risk, and thus that the means of altering risk is through increasing knowledge. Through this cognitivist legerdemain, we have expediently moved the locus of the problem—and thus the interventions—away from certain features of an inegalitarian society and towards the women deemed "at risk." The problem is inherent in the women, thus the interventions should change the women.

The cost of all this desocialization might well be significant, for cognitivist, behaviorist, or culturist assumptions often privilege effects over cause. Immodest claims of causality, and even undue focus on the psychological or cultural peculiarities of those with AIDS, are not only incorrect emphases, they also serve to expediently deflect attention away from the real engines of the AIDS pandemic. Thus when the *éminences grises* of STD control examine possibilities for effective AIDS control in developing countries, their list of interventions ranges from public lectures to "long-term psychotherapy for HIV-positive individuals" and "group therapy for commercial sex workers."[49]

Similar themes are widely echoed in a society known for its obsession with individualism. It is not surprising, then, to hear the same exaggerations of agency even from those most committed to preventing AIDS. Often, we hear about a certain community's "denial" of risk, or about the epidemic of "low self-esteem" among those living with HIV infection. These cultural and psychological factors are then granted etiologic power: rather than the effects, they are construed as the source of increased risk. Sadly, if predictably, the same calculus of causality is to been found in the comments of those afflicted by AIDS. The founder of one group for women living with HIV infection put it this way: "Low self-esteem is a significant 'co-factor' that led many women to be at risk of acquiring HIV."[50] Surely there are co-factors for "low self-esteem"— and poverty, otherwise known in post-welfare America as hunger and homelessness, is the obvious leader among them. Other variations on this theme of inequality, including racism and sexism, are also high on the list.

Such immodest claims of causality, as noted, serve to deflect attention away from structural violence. No wonder U.S. Republicans and their friends among the Democrats have had so little difficulty promoting the same hypotheses. In the recently promulgated "Personal Responsibility Act," A.F.D.C. recipients are called to work a minimum of 35 hours per week in a designated "work slot." Since these women have, unlike the Act's authors, more than a passing knowledge of math, they will see that with a median disbursement of $366 per month and an hourly wage in such "slots" of well under $3.00, participants will be unable to assemble the funds necessary to provide daycare, let alone health care and safe housing, for their children. Even in cities with modest costs of living, a single mother of two children would need an hourly wage of $10.00 in order to cross the poverty line.[51] We are left to surmise that these women's infants and toddlers will prepare their own formula and meals. As Valerie Polakow, who recently interviewed scores of single American mothers, bitterly notes, this experience should give these babies an early lesson in the importance of personal responsibility. "As their rhetoric against won't-work mothers and promiscuous teens escalates," concludes Polakow, "it advances the pernicious idea that poverty is a private affair, that destitution and homelessness are simply products of bad personal choices."[52]

From typhoid to tuberculosis and AIDS, blaming the victim is a recurrent theme in the history of epidemic disease.[53] In case after case, analysis of the problem may lead researchers to focus on the patients' shortcomings (e.g., failure to drink pure water, failure to use condoms, ignorance about public health and hygiene) or else on the conditions that structure people's risk (lack of access to potable water, lack of economic opportunities for women, unfair distribution of the world resources). The results are not indifferent. One of the chief benefits of choosing to see illness in global-systemic terms is that it encourages physicians (and others concerned to protect or promote health) to make common cause with people who are both poor and sick. Another benefit of analyses that resolutely embed person experience in the larger social fields in which such experience takes on its meaning is that such analyses have far more explanatory power in examining epidemics of infectious disease—particularly those which, like AIDS, move along the fault lines of our interlinked societies.

In conclusion, the most frequently encountered and easily circulated theories about women and AIDS are far more likely to include punitive images of women as purveyors of infection—prostitutes, for example, or mothers who "contaminate" their innocent offspring—than to include images of homelessness, barriers to medical care, a social-service network that doesn't work, and an absence of jobs and housing. Dominant readings are likely to foster images of women with AIDS that suggest they have had large numbers of sexual partners, but less likely to show how girls like Lata are abducted into the flesh trade, and even less likely to reveal how political and structural violence—for example, the increasing landlessness among the rural poor and the gearing of economies to favor export—come to be important in the AIDS pandemic today.

For women most at risk of HIV infection, life choices are limited by racism, sexism, political violence and grinding poverty. It is a wonder, then, that discussions of AIDS so rarely focus on these issues. Complex indeed are the mechanisms by which such structural violence can be effaced and the apparent significance of personal choice (or cultural difference) inflated. But when dominant myths about women and AIDS are contrasted with the experiences of Darlene and Guylène and Lata, we are forced to call into question many of these understandings.

7. WHAT NOW?

In rural Haiti in 1991, a group of poor women, some of them living with HIV, met to consider AIDS and its effects on their communities. They agreed that, although many were infected with HIV through means well beyond their own control, not enough had been done to educate the people in the region. How could they join forces to make up for this deficiency? It was out of the question to use written materials in a setting of nearly universal illiteracy, and the military government had just taken control of many of the area's radio stations. In the end, these women—who had never had electricity in their homes and had never owned televisions—decided to produce a videotape that told a story very similar to Guylène's. They then worked with Partners In Health to acquire a portable generator, a video projector, and a screen. Condom demonstrations and community discussion accompanied each showing of the video.[54]

Proud of their success, the women subsequently spoke of their experience at a number of meetings and conferences held in rural Haiti. In one of these conferences, a Haitian physician (herself not unsympathetic to the trials of the women who had made the video) listened to a presentation by one of the women and saw the video. During the discussion, the doctor faced the project participant, who had proudly introduced herself as a *malerez*, a "poor woman," and asked, "So what? In other words, if we are manifestly failing to prevent HIV transmission in this region, what is the significance of your project?"

The *malerez* did not hesitate in answering: "Doctor, when all around you, liars are the only cocks crowing, telling the truth is a victory."

Telling the truth about the nature of women's risk would be no mean feat in the current climate, and much of this book attempts to do just that. A sound analytic purchase on the dynamics of HIV transmission among poor women is one of the key desiderata of the group collaborating on this volume. Throughout it, we will question standard interpretations of existing data and also call, in certain cases, for new research.

A second, and related, set of tasks concerns prevention. Making condoms readily available is an altogether insufficient response. Getting the right message across remains a priority and always will, as HIV is unlikely to be eradicated soon. This means that adolescents everywhere in the world simply must learn about STDs prior to become sexually active. Universal HIV education needs to become part of growing up, and might also help to attenuate AIDS-related stigma. Clearly, such efforts will need to be different in different settings, but the universal finality (and obstinacy) of AIDS have changed the way we think about sexuality and sexism, and teens throughout the world need to learn about the relationship between HIV transmission and social forces such as poverty and gender inequality.

A third set of activities might be targeted towards specific groups of those at risk for HIV infection. In northern Tanzania, for example, improving the quality and accessibility of treatment for STDs reduced the incidence of HIV by 42%.[55] Injecting drug users need ready access to drug-treatment programs, but we know that needle-exchange efforts can decrease the incidence of new infections even in the absence of adequate clinical treatment.[56] Stopping prostitution will require addressing poverty, gender inequality, and racism, but in the absence of serious societal programs aimed at doing that, public health authorities can make a priority of protecting, rather than punishing, sex workers.[57] Commercial sex workers have benefited from high-quality medical care, especially when provided with prostitutes' well-being—rather than that of their clients—in mind: "It is important," notes one advocate, "that a full range of health care services, including health care for their children and not just STD services, be made more accessible—and more acceptable—to prostitutes."[58] Again, attacking AIDS-related stigma will require attacking the stigmatization of sex workers, gays, and other scapegoat groups.

For women already living with HIV disease, improved clinical services are critical. This means, among other things, educating health-care professionals about women and AIDS.[59] HIV infection is underrecognized in women, with many cases diagnosed during pregnancy—or at autopsy. When AIDS case definitions were changed to include, among other conditions, invasive cervical cancer, the number of AIDS diagnoses in U.S. women doubled in a single year.[60] Improving services further implies the removal of barriers that currently prevent poor women, regardless of their HIV status, from obtaining much-needed resources. These resources range from access to certain medications to safe housing. Although data are lacking, research currently underway in the urban United States suggests that, in one large cohort of women, the majority with advanced HIV disease were not receiving *Pneumocystis* prophylaxis, to say nothing of antiretroviral therapy. In the same cohort, most women did not have housing security; almost 20% stated that they had "no safe place to live."[61] Given that HIV-positive Americans face AIDS-related discrimination ranging from insults to loss of jobs and housing, the tasks before us are indeed challenging, if less so than the tasks facing those who would change the frightful conditions endured by poor women living in poor countries. Scrupulous attention to these matters could, in principle, prolong the lives of millions of women already infected.[62]

Finally, it is important to recall that women are also affected by AIDS in indirect ways, for it is women who bear the brunt of caring for the sick, regardless of age or gender.[63] For this reason, improving the quality of care for all people living with AIDS will improve the lives of the women who care for them.

Through these three sets of tasks alone—that is, setting the record straight, rethinking prevention activities, and improving the array of services available to women and to all persons with AIDS— much can be done to strengthen the hand of women living in poverty. With perseverance and commitment, such measures might eventually result in the slowing of the rate of HIV transmission to poor women. We will discuss these and other efforts in Chapters 3 and 4, and throughout Part III, "Pragmatic Solidarity."

As important as these AIDS-focused activities are, they largely attack the symptoms of a deeper malaise. Endeavors focused on AIDS, though crucial, must be linked to efforts to empower poor women. The much-abused term "empower" is not here meant vaguely; it is not a matter of self-esteem or even parliamentary representation. Those choosing to make common cause with poor women must seek to give them control over their own lives. Control of lives is related to the control of land, systems of production, and the formal political and legal structures in which lives are enmeshed. In each of these arenas, poor people are already laboring at a vast disadvantage; poor women's voices are almost unheard.

The occurrence of HIV in the wealthy countries, where even those living in poverty control more resources than women like Guylène and Lata, reminds us that HIV tracks along steep gradients of power. In many settings, HIV risks are enhanced not so much by poverty in and of itself, but by inequality. Increasingly, what people with AIDS share are not personal or psychological attributes. They do not share culture or language or a certain racial identity. They do not share sexual preference or an absolute income bracket. What they share, rather, is a social position—the bottom rung of the ladder in inegalitarian societies. Writing from Bombay, Sarthak Das underlines similarities in the experience of the untouchable castes of India and poor people of color in U.S. cities: "We need only replace the categories of 'Black' and 'Hispanic' with the low caste, untouchable titles of *Harijan* and *Sudra* in order to observe a parallel epidemiological pattern on the subcontinent."[64]

This is why efforts to promote pragmatic solidarity must not only engage local inequalities, but also global ones. The trials of women like Guylène and Lata pose challenges to women—and, of course, to all people of good will—in the rich countries. Can we somehow lessen the huge and growing disparities that characterize our world? Within rich countries, the struggles of women like Darlene Johnson are even more of a rebuke, challenging facile notions of sisterhood and solidarity. Unlike Guylène and Lata, Darlene lives within a mile of a world-class medical center. At key points in her experience, however, that center might as well have been half a world away. With no insurance, Darlene did not have ready access to it.

The rapidly growing literature on women and AIDS is well-stocked with pieties about solidarity, but the progress of the disease among women seems to take particular advantage of the lack of solidarity among the members of an AIDS-affected society. Very often, when solidarity fails, the reasons are less about color and more about class. A working-class lesbian writes that "HIV makes a mockery of pretend unity and sisterhood." Those most affected, she notes, are women of color and poor white women, many of whom are "struggling with long histories of shooting drugs or fucking men for the money to get those drugs. These are not the women usually identified as the women the feminist movement or the lesbian movement most value and try to organize to create a progressive political agenda."[65] Guylène reserved some of her harshest commentary for the women for whom she worked as a servant: "Rich women often hate poor women, so I always had trouble working for them." In Bombay, not only are the madams, of course, women, but so are many of the *dalals* who abduct teenage girls from their home villages.

One of the contributors to *Listen Up*, a recently published collection of feminist essays, observes that, "Many feminists seem to find the issues of class the most difficult to address; we are always faced with the fundamental inequalities inherent in late-twentieth-century multinational capitalism and our unavoidable implication in its structures."[66] A view of those structures and the ways lives are entangled in them is precisely the perspective of our book. Whose interests are served by writing of one group of women with AIDS while ignoring millions of others because of nationality? Clearly, HIV cares little for national boundaries.

Collaborators in this book aim to link deep concern with pragmatic interventions—projects designed to prevent or better treat complications of HIV infection—with more utopian aspirations. For if the hypothesis that inequality is an important co-factor in this pandemic is correct, then stopping AIDS will require a more ambitious agenda, one that calls for the fundamental transformation of our world. What is at stake in these tasks is well expressed by anthropologist and activist Brooke Schoepf: "Unless the underlying struggles of millions to survive in the midst of poverty, powerlessness, and hopelessness are addressed, and the meanings of AIDS understood in the context of gender relations, HIV will continue to spread."[67]

In embracing a pessimism of the intellect, we nonetheless permit ourselves a certain optimism of the spirit. To paraphrase Patricia Hill Collins: as surely as HIV may be linked to oppression, so too are the conditions of oppression inherently unstable.[68]

CHAPTER TWO

A Global Perspective

Janie Simmons, Paul Farmer,
and Brooke G. Schoepf

I n the eyes of many in the United States, the typical person with AIDS is a gay white man. This is no surprise in a country in which the syndrome has been labelled everything from GRID—Gay-Related Immune Deficiency—to "The Lavender Peril." The stigma associated with this stereotype is well known.[1] Like so many AIDS-related stereotypes, the image has the added disadvantage of being inaccurate. While it is still true that in some parts of the United States most of the burden of advanced HIV disease is borne by gay men, in the developing world women are afflicted as often as men. The epidemiological pattern of women's increasing risk is emerging in the despoiled cities of the United States. Furthermore, because AIDS is the late manifestation of an infection that has occurred, often, more than a decade earlier, the dynamics of the pandemic are better assessed by serosurveys of asymptomatic populations or by examination of the incidence of HIV transmission. While data on the distribution of HIV are even thinner than data on the distribution of AIDS, what evidence exists suggests that, in many settings throughout the world, the highest rates of new infections are registered among women.

Increasingly, then, the face of AIDS is a woman's face. However, not all women are at increased risk of infection with HIV. Among women, as among men, the incidence of new infections has a striking pattern. It is poor women, by and large, who must wrestle with this grave danger. The cumulative effects of lives of poverty and sexual exploitation force many women into circumstances where sex becomes a survival strategy. In many settings, stable sexual unions are torn asunder by war and social dislocation. In others, women living in poverty turn to drugs or to male sexual partners who inject drugs—men who have themselves been brutalized, often enough, by similar social forces like racism, labor exploitation, and occupational apartheid.

In all of these situations, high rates of HIV transmission to women have been the rule since early in the pandemic. To best explain these patterns, a thorough understanding of the local and gendered dynamics of HIV transmission must be fully alive to processes and events which are, increasingly, global or at least transnational in nature. This chapter will provide a brief overview of the status of women in the global AIDS pandemic. As we shall see, HIV has afflicted women from the outset, and in no setting can HIV risk be shown to be decreasing among women. This is especially true in sub-Saharan Africa, but it is also the case in U.S. cities and throughout Southeast Asia, India, the Caribbean, and in parts of Latin America. We review data on risk and infection in these areas of the world to cast in bold relief the complex and changing dynamics of HIV infection among women.

1. REEXAMINING THE GLOBAL PANDEMIC

The Global AIDS Policy Coalition estimates that, as of January, 1996, 30.6 million people worldwide have been infected with HIV since the beginning of the pandemic.[2] The cumulative number of HIV infections among adults has tripled since 1990, from nearly 10 million then to over 30 million in 1996. Figure 2.1 depicts the estimated geographic distribution of HIV infection as of January 1, 1996. Strikingly, 93 percent of these infections have occurred in the developing world, with 63 percent of all infections occurring in sub-Saharan Africa. Another 23 percent have occurred in Southeast Asia, and approximately 10 percent in Latin America and the Caribbean. Less than four percent of cumulative infections have been registered in the industrialized world.

While Figure 2.1 offers a static representation of the worldwide distribution of the virus, the true picture of the pandemic is complex and evolving. HIV is not one disease but many, for the global pan-

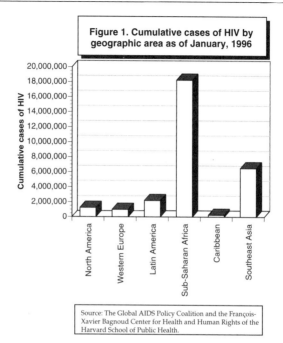

Figure 1. Cumulative cases of HIV by geographic area as of January, 1996

Source: The Global AIDS Policy Coalition and the François-Xavier Bagnoud Center for Health and Human Rights of the Harvard School of Public Health.

demic is composed of thousands of interrelated subepidemics, many with unique local dynamics.[3] Our understanding of these subepidemics has evolved, but not as rapidly as the pandemic itself. This incomprehension has surely contributed to our failures to prevent AIDS. On both a global and a national scale, experts note, efforts to slow the transmission of HIV have been ineffective: "The course of the pandemic with and through global society is not being affected—in any serious manner—by the actions taken at the national or international level."[4] In 1995 alone, approximately 4.7 million more people became infected with HIV, an average of 13,000 infections each day.

In the face of this tragedy, it is clear that the resources committed to intervention efforts have proven grossly inadequate, in part because of the skewed distribution of the disease. Of the 4.7 million infections thought to have occurred in 1995, 1.9 million of them occurred in sub-Saharan Africa—not coincidentally, the poorest region of the world. Fully 2.5 million are estimated to have occurred in Southeast Asia—the region where the numerical majority of the world's poor live. This region is already home to more than three times the total number of infected people in the entire industrialized world, where some 170,000 persons were infected during the course of 1995. Thus, the industrialized countries of the northern hemisphere, which alone boast an infrastructure adequate to the task of caring for the sick, accounted for less than four percent of new infections worldwide.

How have women been affected in the pandemic? Of the 4.7 million new infections which are estimated to have occurred among adults in 1995, 1.7 million, or 39 percent, occurred among women. Given steep increases in incidence among women in both the industrialized and the developing world, and given, too, the greater facility of male-to-female transmission, women are now considered to be the population most at risk for HIV infection. The percentage of women with HIV is expected to increase dramatically in 1996 and beyond, particularly in Southeast Asia and India, where infection rates are currently soaring.

Even where it has been reported that rates of total new infections have reached a plateau, as in Western Europe, or declined, as in North America, incidence among the poor and among women—two overlapping social groupings—is still sharply rising. The U.S. epidemic has been most pronounced among men, yet the male:female ratio fell from 15:1 in 1982 to 9:1 in 1990.[5] Surveillance data for 1992 report a male:female ratio of 5:1 in the United States as a whole,[6] but these static ratios obscure the fact that shifts have been dramatic. Between 1991 and 1992, the Centers for Disease Control (CDC) documented a 17 percent increase in AIDS cases attributable to heterosexual transmission. This occurred in the setting of a one percent decrease in cases attributed to homosexual or bisexual transmission.[7] Furthermore, national data obscure trends within particular subepidemics. In much of the industrialized world, with the notable exception of a handful of cities with high-quality needle-exchange programs, rates of new infections have risen steadily among injection drug users, men and women alike.[8] The majority of injection drug users are poor men, but women who inject drugs or whose sexual partners do so are increasingly found to be infected through heterosexual contact.[9] As is the case internationally, the incidence of HIV infection is, like the incidence of addiction, heavily skewed by class. In certain U.S. populations tested, such as Job Corps candidates and armed services recruits, both programs which target poor youth, seroprevalence has not only been high, but equal to, or even greater than, rates found among women.[10]

Among women, African-Americans and Latinas have been the chief victims of HIV infection in the inner cities of the United States, leading one activist to comment: "Whenever you hear about women and AIDS, think women of color. That should be your first image, because that gets lost."[11] Whether or not this image gets lost or is systematically ignored, the fact remains that since the beginning of the U.S. epidemic, HIV has disproportionately affected women of color. As early as 1987, AIDS was the leading cause of death among 15- to 45-year-old Black and Latina women living in New York City.[12] These trends have since become even more pronounced. African-American and Latina women comprise the majority of women living with HIV. In 1993, 77 percent of all women infected with HIV in the United States were African-American or Latina.[13] That same year, in nine U.S. cities, AIDS became the leading cause of death among women of childbearing age.[14]

How might we explain the staggering differentials in risk for HIV? As we shall see in Chapter Three, these trends have more to do with poverty and inequality than with supposed predispositions attributable to "race," ethnicity, or culture. The injustices born of racism, sexism and poverty also victimize women in other parts of the world where years of exploitation and neglect are even more dramatically linked to the rapidly expanding subepidemics of AIDS. In Thailand, where the sex industry is marketed in the industrialized world as a tourist attraction, male STD patients and brothel-based prostitutes had seroprevalence rates as high as 63 percent based on 1991 data from Chiang Rai, one of Thailand's northernmost provinces. Five years earlier, seroprevalence among Thai sex workers and injection drug users was almost zero.[15] In Zaïre and Uganda, where more than half of newly infected adults are women, AIDS is now the leading cause of death among young adults.[16] In Côte d'Ivoire, where the first AIDS case was reported in 1985, as many as 40 percent of all patients in a public hospital serving the urban poor were found to be seropositive in 1991.[17] In Rwanda, where murder has recently become the leading cause of death, complications of HIV infection are not far behind. Even before the mass rapes and genocide, national surveillance data from 1986 found 30 percent of pregnant women in urban areas to be infected.[18]

Wherever women are affected, so too are children. Some have argued that, ultimately, it was concern for children, including the unborn children of "women of reproductive age," which brought women's risk into the limelight.[19] As early as 1988, AIDS had already become the leading cause of death among Latino children in New York and New Jersey, and the number two cause of death among African-American children.[20] Maternal-fetal transmission rates in New York City range between 20 and 30 percent.[21] In much of the developing world, perinatal transmission rates are even higher—as many as 43 percent of infants born to infected mothers will also succumb to the disease.[22] In addition, the health of HIV-negative children of women with AIDS is also adversely affected.[23]

For an altogether different set of reasons, adolescents are also highly vulnerable. Given the years that elapse between infection and diagnosis of HIV disease, many men and women diagnosed with AIDS as adults actually became infected as teenagers. But, again, this risk is gendered, with teenage girls at higher risk than boys. Worldwide, the proportion of women reported with AIDS exceeds the number of men reported with AIDS in the youngest age distribution categories, again reflecting infection during adolescence.[24] Compared with both more mature women and with adolescent boys, teenaged girls are also more at risk of acquiring AIDS during their first sexual encounter.[25] For these and other reasons, the CDC has added "young adults and adolescents with multiple sex partners, and those with sexually transmitted diseases" to their list of women at highest risk of heterosexually acquired infection.[26]

In a perverse twist, fear of HIV infection has led to further exploitation of children in many parts of the world. Men seek low-risk sexual partners and so press "virginal" adolescent girls for sexual relations. This logic has actually increased the numbers of sex tourists with deep pockets who participate in a highly lucrative transnational flesh trade in some poor countries. In Thailand, for example, children as young as 8 or 10 years old are sold into sexual slavery or are coerced into commercial sex. Estimates of the number of child prostitutes in Thailand range from an optimistic 100,000 to over 800,000. To heap injury upon injury, 50 to 80 percent of these children may have already been infected with HIV.[27] Poor children have also been victimized in this way in the Philippines, Sri Lanka, India, Kenya, Brazil, and in parts of the Caribbean and Eastern Europe.[28]

In the areas hardest hit by AIDS, staggering numbers of children have also been orphaned. UNICEF estimates that 9 million children will be orphaned in Africa by the year 2000.[29] In Uganda, one of every 10 children is already parentless.[30] In the United States, the increasing number of boarder babies and orphans is but another marker of the rising incidence of infection among women, especially poor women of color. Suffering and death are highly concentrated in the cities most afflicted by what one observer aptly called "a synergy of plagues."[31]

The above-cited estimates and projections hint at an incalculable amount of suffering as people already assailed by harsh living conditions and inadequate medical services become infected, sicken and die. Women, young and old, many of whom are sick themselves, are the principal caregivers for ill spouses, relatives, and children orphaned by AIDS and other calamities, including war, forced migration, and infectious diseases.[32] As bereaved and burdened women struggle to care for the sick and dying, the numbers of new infections continue to rise.

2. EXPLAINING THE DYNAMICS
OF SPREAD TO POOR WOMEN

One of the most pressing questions the pandemic raises is seldom asked and never answered: What are the precise mechanisms by which AIDS has become, in the space of a generation, a leading cause of death among poor women throughout the world? As noted in Chapter One, 92 percent of all adults, 97 percent of all women, and 98 percent of all children infected with HIV live in the developing world.[33] However, geography is inadequate to explain this observation. Sub-Saharan Africa, where most infections have occurred from the beginning of the pandemic, is one of the least densely populated regions of the world.[34] High rates of infection are now found in both cities and rural areas. Those areas of the world with the highest rates of infection are in both "developed" and underdeveloped nations. Distinctions between the processes which place U.S. women like Darlene Johnson at risk and those which place women like Guylène and Lata at risk in Haiti and India are easy to recognize. However, many of the conditions which shaped these three women's lives and deaths are, on closer inspection tragically similar. Their lives, like the lives of many women, are shaped by forces generated far beyond the geographic borders of the places where they live and die.

Lack of information regarding how the virus is transmitted, "promiscuity," lack of condoms, and "denial" may all contribute to an individual's level of risk. Indeed, these three factors receive heavy rotation in academic writings on AIDS risk. However, the forces which render women more vulnerable to infection than men, poor women more vulnerable than their wealthier counterparts, and adolescent girls more vulnerable than adult women, have much more to do with the relationships between poverty, gender inequality, and biological vulnerability.

Biological vulnerability is important, as a growing body of research has demonstrated that the virus is more efficiently transmitted from men to women than vice versa.[35] Nevertheless, the social status of women further places them at risk. In many areas of the world, women are forced to choose between what Zimbabwean researchers Bassett and Mhloyi have called "biological death" or "social death."[36] Pressed to maintain stable relationships with husbands or lovers, or short-term liaisons with clients, poor women are often forced to assent to unprotected sex even when they know their lives are in danger.[37] Young women are extremely vulnerable because, often, they are in no position to refuse risky sex. In many settings characterized by high rates of HIV infection, women's lives are also endangered by rape and other forms of sexual violence.[38]

The unavailability and excessive costs of female-controlled prevention technologies, as well as the negative social meanings associated with condom use, also heighten women's risk.[39] Furthermore, surveys of women living with HIV have shown that many wish to bear children. In diverse settings worldwide, childbearing is tightly linked to respect and economic stability. Where the barriers to power, joy, and opportunity are so great, condom-promotion campaigns are bound to fail.[40] As Carovano notes, "To provide women exclusively with HIV prevention methods that contradict most societies' fertility norms is to provide many women with no options at all."[41]

We will consider these complexly interrelated forces by more closely examining women's increased biological vulnerability, gender inequality and poverty, below.

Biological Factors

As noted in Chapter One, dissemination of the view that AIDS poses little threat to women is all the more remarkable given the fact that HIV is, as McBarnett has noted, a "biologically sexist" organism.[42] Certain studies suggest that per-exposure transmission from man to woman during genital-genital intercourse is two to five times more efficient than from woman to man.[43] Other investigations have prompted researchers to argue that HIV is up to 20 times more efficiently transmitted from men to women than vice versa.[44] HIV is more highly concentrated in seminal fluids than in vaginal secretions and may more easily enter the bloodstream through the extensive convoluted lining of the vagina and cervix. Vulnerable penile surface area is much smaller—in circumcised men without genital ulcerations, only the urethral meatus is involved; in uncircumcised men, this area as well as the skin under the foreskin are potentially vulnerable.[45] One recent study suggests that certain strains of HIV may grow better in a type of cell lining the vaginal wall. [46]

Young women are especially vulnerable to infection. While genital trauma is also a factor in more mature women's risk (especially if culturally-sanctioned practices such as using herbs or foregoing foreplay in order to keep the vagina "dry and tight" are followed), young women are even more likely to experience genital trauma. Before menstruation begins, the lower reproductive tract is anatomically and physiologically immature. The multiple cell layers and secretions that provide adult women with some protection develop gradually so that a girl's vaginal mucosa is not as well lined with protective cells as that of a more mature woman. Trauma and bleeding are thus more likely to occur, especially during first coitus.[47] This biological vulnerability is aggravated wherever adolescent girls are sought by older men. Furthermore, older men are more likely to be infected than are younger men as a result of having had more sexual partners. As illustrated in Figure 2.2, girls and women aged 10 to 29 years are infected at much higher rates than are boys and men of the same age.

This vulnerability is not only experienced in the developing world. Figure 2.3, based on U.S. data, suggests that the high risk experienced by certain groups of girls is faced across national and cultural boundaries. Why are 91 percent of U.S. adolescents who

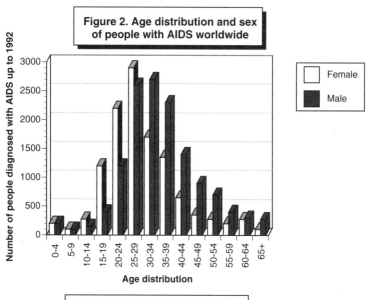

Figure 2. Age distribution and sex of people with AIDS worldwide

Source: de Bruyn, Jackson, Wijermars, *et al.*, *Facing the Challenges of HIV/AIDS/STDS: A Gender-based Response.*

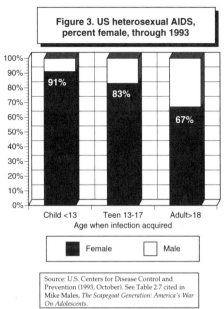

Figure 3. US heterosexual AIDS, percent female, through 1993

Source: U.S. Centers for Disease Control and Prevention (1993, October). See Table 2.7 cited in Mike Males, *The Scapegoat Generation: America's War On Adolescents.*

acquire HIV before their thirteenth birthday female? Poverty-accentuated gender inequality fuels transmission rates in the United States, as well.

Co-infection with other sexually transmitted diseases further increases HIV risks for women and girls. Early studies suggested that chancroid, syphilis, and genital herpes, all of which cause genital ulcers, have been associated with increased risks of acquiring HIV from an infected partner.[48] More recently, non-ulcerative sexually transmitted diseases, including gonorrhea and chlamydia, have also been associated with increased risks.[49] The presence of a concurrent STD has been shown to increase the risk of infection at least three- to five-fold.[50] HIV is also known to lead to altered manifestations of other, concurrent STDs and promote their spread.[51] Here again, women are more susceptible to infection. A man infected with gonorrhea, for example, will transmit it to a female sexual partner approximately two-thirds of the time, whereas a woman will transmit it to a male sexual partner only one-third of the time.[52] Infection rates for "classic" STDs are higher in women than in men, and, as with HIV, women tend to acquire these STDs at a younger age than do men. In the United States, for example, rates for gonorrhea and syphilis among adolescents are three times that of the non-adolescent, sexually active population.[53]

In addition to being disproportionately affected, women are also especially vulnerable to complications of undiagnosed or untreated STDs. Gonorrhea and primary syphilis may be asymptomatic in 50 to 80 percent of women, but only 10 percent of men.[54] Furthermore, many men do not inform their partners when they are infected. Even when women have symptoms, these may be too subtle—or too low on a long list of concerns—to cause them to seek medical attention. When women do suspect infection, they may be too ashamed to seek treatment, since STDs are often popularly associated with prostitution and STD clinics have historically been frequented mainly by men and by female sex workers.[55] Even when treatment is available and women try to avail themselves of it, it may be inadequate, prohibitively expensive, or proffered in an offensive or otherwise undignified manner. As a result of these factors, women are less likely to seek or receive treatment.[56]

Poor women in the developing world are also made more vulnerable to HIV infection through tainted blood transfusions used to treat endemic diseases such as iron-deficiency anemia, often caused by worms or malaria and worsened by menstrual losses and malnutrition. Complicated pregnancies and lack of access to safe and legal abortions further magnify poor women's risks for transfusion-associated AIDS. While blood tends to be screened in the developing world's capital cities, equipment is often lacking or non-functional in smaller cities and rural areas.[57] In settings throughout the world, transfusion-associated HIV transmission continues apace, and women are disproportionately affected.

Gender Inequality

As noted, biological risk alone does not explain soaring infection rates among women. Women's precarious social status, a direct result of gender inequality and amplified poverty, magnifies each of these biological predispositions. In addition to the gendered power differentials characterizing most sexual unions, women are denied equal access to economic resources, housing, health care, legal protection, land, schooling, inheritance, and employment in the formal sector of most societies. Wage-earning women may be obliged to supply sex to supervisors as a condition of employment. Domestic workers are particularly vulnerable to this kind of abuse. Women who work in the low-wage informal sector may also be forced to supplement meager earnings with sex work. Still others can find no employment in the informal sector except sex work. Male violence, whether threatened or actualized, is also all too commonly used to control women throughout their lives and increases their vulnerability to infection. In many cases, such violence is legally as well as socially sanctioned.[58]

Extensive evidence suggests that gender inequality has a direct impact not only on HIV transmission, but also on the course of HIV disease. Research conducted in the United States and reviewed in Chapter Seven, lends credence to the claim that once infected, women die sooner than men. Although survival studies have predominantly been conducted in the industrialized countries, reports suggest that similar trends have been registered in the southern hemisphere, as well. In the early years of the Brazilian epidemic, for example, it was estimated that "the mean survival time was 16.9 months for men and only 5.8 months for women."[59] This difference is clearly related to access to care, which seems to have been monopolized by men even in settings where there has always been gender parity in rates of sickness. As Danziger has pointed out: "In Africa, where roughly equal numbers of men and women are sick as a consequence of AIDS, most hospital beds for people with AIDS are filled by men."[60]

Few studies have examined the mechanisms by which gender inequality comes to influence disease distribution, however. Those that do exist tend to underline the significance of "gendered poverty." As Krieger and Margo observe

> ...the priorities and policies that put women last—and the factors that increase their risk of HIV infection—are the concrete and deadly expression of social, political, economic, and cultural conflicts that contribute to women's oppression and are deeply embedded in the diverse societies in which AIDS has taken root.[61]

Other studies, when re-examined with the question of the relationship between social forces and disease distribution in mind, shed some light on this subject. For example, Zierler suggests the importance of gender inequality in a critical re-reading of a study of discordant Italian couples (couples with one seropositive member and one seronegative member).[62] The epidemiologists who designed the study made no comment on the gender issue, despite compelling quantitative evidence of gender inequality. Of 730 discordant heterosexual couples, 524 of them included an uninfected woman. Of these 524 couples, 71 percent of the HIV-infected men stated that they never used condoms. But when the HIV infected member of the couple was a woman, as was the case in 206 of the couples, only 35 percent of the men never used condoms. Therefore, HIV-infected men were twice as likely to engage in sex without a condom than seronegative men where transmission was a possible outcome. This suggests that the uninfected women in this study were at least twice as likely to be exposed to HIV as the uninfected men, a risk further amplified by the fact that HIV is transmitted more efficiently from men to women than vice versa. No data was collected on the relative economic dependence or independence of men and women in this study, but, as Zierler rightly concludes, "As an index for the relative power differential between women and men, the condom use data offer a strategy for quantifying the effect of sexual politics on women's risk of infection."[63]

As has often been commented, sexual politics are also visible in the unavailability of a preventive technology controlled by women. We can do no better than echo Carovano, who observes that "Supporting efforts to develop women-controlled reproductive technology that provides women with real choices is also critical, given the reality of many women's lives."[64]

Poverty

Ninety percent of new cases of STDs occur in the developing world. Classic STDs, like HIV disease, "tend to be diseases of poverty, enhanced by conditions of economic deprivation, social disenfranchisement, and gender inequality."[65] Poverty, we have tried to argue, cannot be considered as just another co-factor to be considered along with biological considerations, gender inequality, and cultural considerations. All of the biological factors predisposing girls and women to increased risk of infection—from chronic anemias to genital mutilation and early first coitus—are aggravated by poverty. A recent United Nations document notes that

> A lack of control over the circumstances in which the intercourse occurs may increase the frequency of intercourse and lower the age at which sexual activity begins. A lack of access to acceptable health services may leave infections and lesions untreated. Malnutrition not only inhibits the production of mucus but also slows the healing process and depresses the immune system.[66]

In addition, poverty and gender inequality are inextricably intertwined. Poverty plays a large role in structuring dependent relationships with a male partner, whether that relationship be marriage or another type of union. Increasingly, women are the sole heads of households, but the absence of men in a household does not translate into increased independence for the poor women who head such households. Instead, when full responsibility for children and other dependents is shouldered by women, the family is likely to plunge deeper into poverty. This is now the case in half of the households in rural Africa, and in the poorest settlements of urban Latin America.[67]

Poverty is the most pernicious and least studied risk factor for AIDS. Through myriad mechanisms, it creates an environment of risk. As we have suggested in Chapters One and Six, epidemiological studies have often obscured this dynamic, in part because of outmoded or inadequate concepts. As Zwi and Cabral, and increasingly many others, have argued, "the terms 'risk groups' and, more recently, 'risk behaviors'... have limitations: 'risk groups' may be stigmatizing and non-specific; 'risk behaviors' may fail to identify the determinants of behavior."[68] These terms, unless carefully contextualized, also exaggerate individual agency, and leave unacknowledged and unexplained the ways in which large-scale social and economic factors structure risk for individuals and groups, particularly those who are systematically marginalized from power and from access to the goods, services, and opportunities which power ensures.

The sexual politics described in the previous section are linked to women's need to secure economic resources, a need heightened by changing demographics, migration, war, and unjust or failed economic policies. Women are disproportionately represented among the poor, despite—or perhaps because of—decades of economic and "development" strategies. In many instances, these strategies have impoverished and further destabilized the most vulnerable populations around the world.[69] A recent report from the United Nations estimates that over one billion people currently live in poverty; some 600 million of these people are "extremely poor," meaning that most of their energy and resources are consecrated solely to the provision of food for their families.[70] This report also notes that 70 percent of the world's poor are women, even though women and girls shoulder most of the workload in poor households.[71]

The following paragraph reads as if it had been written to describe AIDS in women, but the "disease" in question is poverty:

> Two out of three women in the world presently suffer from the most debilitating disease known to humanity. Common symptoms of this fast-spreading ailment include chronic anemia, malnutrition, and severe fatigue. Sufferers exhibit an increased susceptibility to infections of the respiratory and reproductive tracts. And premature death is a frequent outcome. In the absence of direct intervention, the disease is often communicated from mother to child, with markedly higher transmission rates among females than males. Yet, while studies confirm the efficacy of numerous prevention and treatment strategies, to date few have been vigorously pursued. The disease is poverty.[72]

A persistent lack of goods and services, as well as the pervasive sense of hopelessness that this abominable condition creates, has consistently translated into poor health outcomes for women and children, even before AIDS arrived to further complicate their lives. Poverty produces what is rather crassly termed "excess" death and disability among poor women and children, most often due to illnesses which are both preventable and treatable. In places like Bangladesh, Brazil, Nigeria and Uganda, 50 percent of deaths among women of childbearing years are the result of complications due to pregnancy, child-birth or other "reproductive causes."[73] This statistic is even more alarming when we consider that women are far more likely to receive health care associated with their reproductive functions than other types of medical services, such as primary or preventive care.[74]

As with other scourges, the populations least able to bear the brunt of the AIDS pandemic are precisely those which are most heavily affected. According to 1988 WHO data, the cities of New York and Kinshasa, Zaïre were faced with epidemics of roughly similar proportions: the annual incidence among New York adults was then estimated to be 110 per 100,000 men and 12 per 100,000 women; the annual incidence among men and women in Kinshasa was estimated at 55-100 per 100,000 population. The similarities stop there, however: the per capita income of Zaïre is approximately one percent of that of the United States. Kinshasa is home to the sole large teaching hospital in all of Zaïre, a nation of almost 32 million inhabitants; the New York metropolitan area alone can boast dozens of far superior facilities. Further, an epidemic that cripples Kinshasa cripples the nation, as the city is the nexus of Zaïre's political and economic activity. In spite of federal sluggishness in responding to the epidemic, it should be noted that New York received a substantial amount of the one billion federal dollars allocated, in 1989, for research on and treatment of HIV infection: this sum is greater than three times the size of Zaïre's total annual foreign assistance in 1987.

As striking a contrast as this is, the situation is even grimmer in other countries: "Zambia, Rwanda, Haiti and Uganda are already finding AIDS from 20-100 times more of an economic burden than in the United States."[75] In Haiti, for example, where seropositivity rates have been high among poor urban dwellers since the beginning of the pandemic and now are increasing in rural areas, total governmental per capita expenditures on health were only $27 in 1990. Only a handful of Haitian families can afford to buy health care on their own, since annual per capita incomes for most Haitians ranges from about $315 in urban areas, to around $100 in rural areas, based on figures from 1983.[76] In comparison, the U.S. government spent $2,765 per person on health that same year.[77] Given the lack of basic medical care in much of the world, there can be little doubt that many HIV-positive persons die not from late opportunistic infections, but from untreated tuberculosis and even malnutrition, both quite preventable problems. Of course, even vast national resources mean little in terms of health when these resources are distributed inequitably throughout the population. As Darlene Johnson's experience and Chapter Four suggest, not all people benefit equitably from federal health outlays even when they are relatively high.

Another problem with defining poverty in national terms stems from the fundamentally transnational nature of poverty. The relationship between global economic forces and disease rates among particular populations are rarely examined in scholarly publications or the mainstream media. However, research from Africa, Haiti, India, and Southeast Asia reveals that high rates of AIDS are intimately linked to histories of underdevelopment and worsening inequality. Many of these investigations, which will be reviewed below, rejected readily-accepted speculations about "hidden homosexuality," "exotic sexual practices" or "promiscuity" as the determinants of high rates of infection in the populations studied. Instead, they examined the ways in which national economies, shaped by a century or more of colonial rule, had given rise to an increasingly marginalized peasant labor force, the social disintegration of rural society, massive migrations to cities in search of work, and the unprecedented growth of urban poverty—with attendant unemployment and prostitution. These conditions, coupled with poor women's precarious social status and their increased biological susceptibility to HIV, led to soaring seropositivity levels among poor women throughout much of the developing world.

Given these conditions, viewing the AIDS pandemic as a set or even a series of smaller, bounded epidemics occurring within nation-states may obfuscate or distort our understanding of the nature of HIV transmission among the poor. Questions regarding the increased HIV risks borne by poor women must be posed in light of the much larger, and to some extent, less easily recognizable, historical, political, economic and social forces which are, at the very least, transnational, if not always global. HIV infection among women has not only affected women throughout the world; it is itself a result of global, as well as local, processes. We turn now to overviews of studies that seek to reveal these complex realities.

3. ILLUSTRATIONS AND PARTICULARS

While we have argued that national and geographical analyses often obscure important and shifting transmission dynamics, these reports often contain the only data available for large parts of the world. Existing surveillance systems rely heavily on the categories of "nation" and "nation-state", as do large-scale epidemiological studies. We will, therefore, refer to these nationwide figures, with the caveats mentioned above and also with an eye to revealing hidden dynamics—dynamics which are far more likely to be linked to power differentials, large-scale and local, than to national cultures and histories. We complement these data with our own research and observations in order to critically reexamine studies that might reveal what is at stake, in the pandemic, for women living in poverty.

Because we have worked extensively in three of the world's most AIDS-affected countries—the United States, Haiti, and Zaïre—we draw heavily on data from these regions. Although there are distinct limitations in such an approach, we believe that the social (economic, cultural, and political) forces which place poor women at risk are manifest in both the poorest countries and in the wealthy ones. Clearly, the dynamics of these multiple subepidemics differ, as do local cultural considerations; but striking commonalities exist as well. These differences and similarities will be made explicit in the following discussion.

North America and Europe

Approximately four percent of the world's AIDS cases are registered in North America and Europe. HIV initially and disproportionately afflicted gay men and hemophiliacs in the industrialized world, but injection drug users and their "female sexual partners" have always borne a level of risk disproportionate to their numbers in the population. Attack rates continue to climb. Infections among women have been increasing at a faster rate than any other population group.

Transmission among women increasingly occurs as a result of heterosexual contacts, although infection as a result of drug use continues
to be an important mode of transmission among women. In turn,
perinatal transmission has driven the dramatic rise in HIV infection
among children. Thus, infection in the industrialized world, as elsewhere, is no random accident of history. To illustrate, we will turn to
a discussion of HIV/AIDS among women in the United States. Later
we embark on a discussion of the dynamics of HIV/AIDS among
poor women in other parts of the world.

　　Poor women were dying of AIDS in the United States long
before their contributions to death statistics were officially recognized.[78] In New York City and Washington, D.C., higher unexplained
rates of deaths among young women were reported as early as 1981,[79]
the same year that AIDS was first described among gay men in San
Francisco.[80] Between 1981 and 1986, total deaths among women
increased dramatically in areas of the United States later shown to
have high reported rates of AIDS. Among women aged 15-44, deaths
from all causes (excluding traffic deaths) rose by 21 percent in New
York City, 18 percent in New Jersey, 30 percent in Connecticut, 8
percent in Maryland, and 17 percent in Washington, D.C. The numbers of women dying from respiratory and other infectious diseases
subsequently felt to be AIDS-related also increased dramatically in
those areas of the United States reporting the most AIDS cases. For
example, pneumonia and influenza deaths increased from 50 cases to
127 cases (an increase of 157 percent) among women ages 15-44 in
New York City during this period. Deaths from these infections
increased during this period by 267 percent in Maryland, by 133 percent in Connecticut, and by 38 percent in New Jersey. Elevated
death rates such as these were not recorded in places, like Idaho, with
no known AIDS cases at the time.[81]

　　Although retrospective analyses now suggest that excess mortality among these urban women was most likely AIDS-related, this
was not appreciated during the first years of the epidemic. Poverty
and gender inequality were likewise rarely invoked in discussions of
the U.S. epidemic's trends. From the outset, deaths from infections
were also registered among women in public health facilities and

prisons, but public health officials failed to recognize these infections as AIDS-related. The first report of AIDS in women was published by the CDC in 1983. In this document, the women were described as the "female sexual partners" of males with AIDS: a "37 year old Black female who had been a steady sexual partner of an IV drug user," and a "27 year old Hispanic whose only sexual partner was bi-sexual."[82] These women thus became the first women qua women to be "officially" recognized as having AIDS between 1981 and 1987, even though one woman had been reported among "heterosexual intravenous drug users" in one of the initial, 1981 reports[83] and a third of all heterosexual patients being followed clinically for Kaposi's sarcoma and PCP between June 1, 1981 and May 28, 1982 were women.[84] How many women remained undiagnosed, even as they exhibited symptoms of AIDS, is not known, but one source estimates this figure to be as high as 63 percent of reported cases.[85]

In 1986, the CDC "re-classified" a significant number of AIDS cases involving transmission to or from women. These cases had until that time been classified as "unexplained" or "other."[86] Despite activism on the part of infected women and their allies,[87] the enormous threat posed by AIDS to U.S. women was not recognized fully in published reports until Guinan and Hardy reported that "heterosexual contact is the only transmission category where women with AIDS outnumber men with AIDS. The proportion of women in this category increased annually between 1982 and 1986."[88] These researchers identified two factors to explain this trend: (1) "A greater proportion of men are infected, and therefore a woman is more likely than a man to encounter an infected partner; and (2) the efficiency of transmission of HIV from man to woman may be greater than from woman to man."[89] More conclusive evidence on the efficiency of transmission did not surface until 1991, when an article reported that "the odds of male-to-female transmission were significantly greater than female-to-male transmission" and that "low rates (among women) may be attributed to what is as yet a relatively early phase of the epidemic among heterosexuals, especially women, and may explain why we observe fewer symptomatic female index cases."[90]

Even after the CDC recognized that women were at risk, the identification of infected women was compounded by the fact that the CDC's initial case definitions of AIDS were based on disease manifestations registered in men. The first case definition did not include gynecological infections or cervical cancer, often early manifestations of HIV disease in women. In addition, male-biased case definitions for AIDS were used by insurers and other agencies to allocate life-sustaining resources to people with AIDS. Thus, the absence of infections unique to women in the case definition led not only to misdiagnosis and underreporting but also to women's decreased access to treatment, insurance and disability benefits, participation in drug trials, and specialized housing.[91]

The CDC first changed the case definition in 1985 and then again in 1987; the latter revision included conditions more common to women and drug users, enabling physicians to use the case definition to more accurately make clinical diagnoses. Still, none of the 12 indicator diseases were women-specific. Finally, after intense activism in 1991, the CDC revised the case definition again—this time to include some common reproductive tract infections as indicator diseases for AIDS. When this new case definition went into effect in 1992, case rates among women tripled as a result, as Figure 4 suggests.[92]

Despite a leveling off of infections among some groups in the United States, incidence among women as a group continues to rise. Between 1991 and 1992, as noted, the rates of increase among AIDS cases attributable to heterosexual transmission were more than an order of magnitude higher than increases in any other category; accordingly, the rates of increases among women and children topped the list, with African-American women again affected more than any other group.[93] The trend has continued. In 1994, the CDC recorded 14,081 AIDS cases among women in the U.S., and the proportion of reported AIDS cases increased annually between 1988 to 1994 from 10 percent to 18 percent.[94] Of the 1994 cases, 41 percent were believed to have occurred through injection drug use, 38 percent were attributed to heterosexual contact, and 2 percent from contaminated blood or blood products. For the remaining 19 percent, no

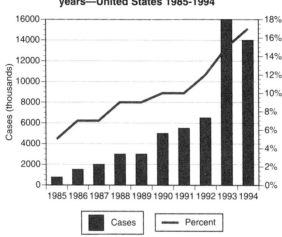

Figure 4. Number and percentage of AIDS cases among women aged 13 years—United States 1985-1994

Cases (thousands)

Cases   Percent

Note: The AIDS surveillance case definition was expanded in 1993 by the CDC.

Source: U.S. Department of Health and Human Services, Public Health Service. Cited in Centers for Disease Control, *Mortality and Morbidity Weekly Report,* 1995

mechanism of exposure could be identified.[95] And AIDS is only the tip of the iceberg, as serosurveys of asymptomatic women reveal far greater numbers of infections.

In spite of the increasing difficulty of masking the dimensions of the epidemic among U.S. women, other factors still have prevented HIV-infected women, the majority of whom were already impoverished, from receiving the care they need and deserve. Growing appreciation of the feminization of the U.S. epidemic did not alter this, a fact noted by the authors of *Searching for Women: A Literature Review on Women, HIV and AIDS in the United States:*

> The new surveillance definition may be a step towards a more complete picture of who and how many people living in the United States are sick with serious HIV disease, but it is unrealistic to assume that such a new case definition of AIDS can directly make a major impact on the lives of women at risk of HIV or AIDS ... The socioeconomic status of many women, the eligibility rules for health insurance and the lack of availabil-

ity of physicians sensitive to the needs of this population are not con-ducive to meeting the needs of the women most at risk of HIV disease.[96]

As in the developing world, the majority of U.S. women with HIV and AIDS are poor. In the United States that means that most infected women are women of color. African-American and Latina women accounted for more than three-quarters of the 14,081 cases reported among women in 1994, despite the fact that they represent only 21 percent of all U.S. women. Rates of AIDS among U.S. women were 16 times higher among Black women and 7 times higher among Latinas than among white women in 1994.[97]

Many of these women have children. Approximately 7,000 HIV-infected women give birth each year in the United States, and approximately one-quarter of these infants are born HIV-infected.[98] Early in the epidemic, AIDS had already become a substantial killer of minority children. It ranked number one as a cause of death among Latino children in New York and New Jersey, and was the second leading cause of death among African-American children.[99] AIDS is now a major cause of death among children aged one to four, ranking seventh overall in the United States in 1992.[100] Five years ago, more than half of all children estimated to be orphaned by AIDS in the United States and its territories lived in New York City. Other blighted cities are catching up. At this writing, it is estimated that one in three motherless American children live in New York City. As Carol Levine of the New York Orphans Project points out, this pro-portion is falling not because deaths from AIDS are diminishing in New York, but because the rates of AIDS deaths among women have been rising sharply in other cities.[101] In the United States, it is has been estimated that between 72,000 and 125,000 children and ado-lescents will be motherless as a result of AIDS by the year 2000.[102] Sixty percent of these orphans will live in New York, Newark, Miami, Los Angeles, Washington, D.C. and San Juan, but the remainder will be scattered in small cities, and in suburban and rural areas.[103]

In part because of these alarming trends among poor women of color and their children, research has focused inordinately on "race" and ethnicity rather than on socio-economic status. The causal fac-tors relating risk differences across socio-economic statuses are rarely if ever examined. Epidemiologists have used "race" not simply as a marker, but as an explanatory variable.[104] As Connors explains in Chapter Three, many researchers writing about AIDS in the United States have observed, quite correctly, that HIV-infected women have been predominantly African American and Latina, but they have then turned to narrowly construed "culturalist" explanatory frameworks to define risk or to target interventions. Yet Black and Latina urban residents of inner cities in San Francisco, New York, Newark, Boston, Hartford, Miami and San Juan do not share a single culture or a single set of origins. They are Puerto Rican, Dominican, Jamaican, Haitian, Mexican, Salvadoran, and U.S.-born. What they do share is a low social position within a context rife with economic and gender inequality. They share the disadvantages of unemployment and underemployment at less than a living wage. They share lives of overt discrimination as well as the more subtle, pervasive forms of disempowerment that institutional racism and sexism create.

Because many researchers think and write as if "race" and ethnicity can stand alone as explanatory paradigms, many studies neglected important underlying factors and dynamics at work during the first decade of the pandemic. Epidemiologists stressed risk from "casual sex," or risk from sex with "high-risk" partners and were oblivious to the threats facing many women, including married women, who did not consider their relationships to be casual or their partners to be high-risk.[105] Few studies mentioned women's relative powerlessness to negotiate condom use—especially poor women whose livelihoods, and those of their children, hinged on their relationships with men who might or might not want to use condoms. The significance of these constraints is brought into new light by examining the AIDS pandemic in the countries held in underdevelopment.

Sub-Saharan Africa

At this writing, most women with HIV infection live on a single continent: Africa. AIDS was first recognized in Africans in 1983.[106]

Today Africa's sub-Saharan regions now contain the largest numbers of infected women. Thus far, the region has borne the brunt of cumulative AIDS cases, new infections, and AIDS deaths among men, women, and children. Already, the burdens of morbidity and mortality have been staggering. Of an estimated global total of 8.5 million AIDS cases worldwide, 7 million people, or 82 percent, live in Africa. Eighty-six percent of the world's 7.5 million AIDS deaths occurred among Africans. In 1994 alone, 1.2 million people from sub-Saharan Africa are believed to have died of AIDS-related causes. This number represents 80 percent of all AIDS-related deaths worldwide for that year. More than half of these deaths, 478,000 out of an adult total of 913,000, were among women. Another 282,000 were children.

AIDS cases and AIDS deaths are but the tip of an African iceberg. HIV transmission, particularly among women, has continued to advance relentlessly in this area of the world. With an estimated 1993 population of 560 million, Africa may have as many as 17.3 million HIV-positive inhabitants. This represents 67 percent of the global cumulative number of HIV infections as of January, 1995—at least half among women and girls. The male:female sex ratio in sub-Saharan Africa has been 1:1.2 since the beginning of the pandemic. This means that for every 10 males who acquire HIV in sub-Saharan Africa, as many as 12 females become infected.[107] Females predominate the younger age groups. Prevalence among women aged 15 to 19 is several times higher than men of the same age, as indicated in Figure 2.3.[108]

Why is there so much sickness and death in this area of the world, and why have women, particularly young women, been infected at such high rates since the beginning of the pandemic? These questions have produced a curious assortment of explanations, many of them groundless. Neither latitude—the epidemics of San Francisco and New York show that AIDS is not a tropical malady— nor overcrowding is a believable causal factor. Sub-Saharan Africa has one of the world's lower population densities, with fewer than 20 persons per square kilometer, and rural (less-populated) areas are increasingly affected as the pandemic progresses.[109] We shall examine some of the more commonly heard explanations and attempt to understand their appeal, an exercise continued in Part II of this volume. Much of the confusion about the answers has stemmed from the fact that research and intervention efforts were focused primarily in and on industrialized countries during the early years of the pandemic.[110] Reports of African physicians and researchers rarely made it into print in influential, indexed scientific journals.[111]

Because researchers latched onto the paradigm of a "gay plague," the discovery of heterosexual transmission in Africa was initially constructed as fundamentally distinct from AIDS in the United States and Europe. When the worldwide distribution of AIDS became evident, epidemiologists characterized the pandemic as comprising three distinct transmission patterns with entire continents grouped in a "typical" pattern. In Pattern I areas, AIDS initially appeared chiefly among homosexual and bisexual men and injection drug users, as in North America and Europe during the mid to late 1970s. Pattern II areas were defined primarily by the predominance of heterosexual transmission during this same time period. Sub-Saharan Africa, Latin America and the Caribbean were considered Pattern II areas. Pattern III areas was described for low-prevalence areas having "contact" with Pattern I and II areas or with imported blood or blood products. Eastern Europe, the Middle East, North Africa, Asia and the Pacific were considered Pattern III areas. With greater understanding of the changing and dynamic nature of HIV transmission, this nomenclature was modified—the category of Pattern I/II was developed in 1989—and eventually discarded. By 1990, as Mann and co-workers explain, the WHO classificatory scheme had become outdated and had led to "static thinking and global complacency."[112]

A central flaw of the WHO categories lay in their stasis. The categories constructed obscured the dynamics of a moving target. However, the model did more than neglect changing transmission patterns. The classificatory scheme was not systemic. It obliterated intracontinental and intranational variability. No country can claim that a national AIDS epidemic has been controlled within its borders; and no border, whether geographical, social, political or economic, has proven impermeable.[113] For this reason, static models using the nation-state as the prime unit of analysis could not adequately represent the scope of the pandemic or the connections between sub-epidemics which constitute the present crisis.

Essentialist notions of African and Haitian "otherness" reinforced a hazardous tendency to conflate the outcomes of structural violence and cultural differences. These misconceptions led researchers and policy makers to ignore the lessons which might have been learned most effectively from the African case—namely, that AIDS explodes in contexts characterized by social inequalities and dislocations.

Other misconceptions led to other intellectual misadventures. The sufferers were also alienated by the stereotypes conjured up at their expense.[114] Although there were no early studies of the effects of war, urbanization or economic crisis on rates of HIV transmission, there was great fascination regarding "hidden homosexuality," genetic difference, and the "exotic" sexual or ritual practices of Africans.[115] Some of these studies and commentaries have been derisively termed "armchair anthropology." For example, in 1986 British authors bent on showing how simian viruses were at the root of the AIDS pandemic asserted the following: "Monkeys are often hunted for food in Africa. Once caught, monkeys are often kept in huts for some time before they are eaten. Dead monkeys are often used as toys by African children."[116] A number of equally farfetched theories also made their way into print, while more sober reflections and empirically-grounded research often went ignored.[117] In much of this material, women continued to be absent from epidemiological discourse apart from their presumed status as "vectors of transmission." Poverty was addressed mainly in relation to the economic damage done by AIDS to national economies, even though the immediate costs of AIDS in poor communities were almost always borne by poor families.[118]

As the dust has settled, what have been the chief features of the African pandemic? Some authors state that "the stage on which this epidemic is unfolding has been set by the social realities in Africa: the migrant labor system, rapid urbanization, constant war with high levels of military mobilization, landlessness, and poverty."[119]   Most cases of HIV and AIDS in sub-Saharan Africa have occurred in the more densely populated urban areas. However, rural areas, linked to these urban centers via commercial trading routes, have also been hard hit.[120] One example is in the Rakai district in Uganda, an area located in the South-Western part of the country where the first AIDS cases in Uganda were recognized.[121] In the mid- to late-eighties, the areas with the highest infection rates in Africa included cities in the Central African Republic, the Republic of the Congo, Zaïre, Burundi, Rwanda, Uganda, Zambia, Ivory Coast, Kenya, Tanzania, Malawi and Cameroon.[122] Since then, HIV has spread across the continent. Not surprisingly, young urban women living in poverty are at highest risk.

Sex workers have been particularly affected by this new occupational hazard. Between 40 and 90 percent of poor prostitutes—women whose major source of subsistence comes from the sale of sex to multiple partners—are reported to be HIV infected in numerous African cities. In Kinshasa, the rate among sex workers rose from 27 percent of those tested in 1985 to 35 percent in 1988.[123] Far higher rates are routinely reported. In Nairobi, prostitutes showed an increase in seroprevalence from eight percent in 1980 (determined by retrospective serology on stored blood) to 59 percent of samples drawn in 1985.[124] Infection was related to the presence of other STDs and to length of time in the trade, with over 72 percent of women becoming infected after four to five years. Interviews with and testing of male partners who sought STD treatment revealed that 10 percent of the women's clients were seropositive. Simple mathematics suggest just how high rates of exposure are for these women. Serving as many as five partners daily, "these women had intense exposure to HIV, on the order of three to four HIV antibody positive, and presumably infectious, contacts per week.[125]

Researchers, early on, labeled prostitutes as "reservoirs of disease" ignoring their increased risk and focusing instead on the risks to their male clients.[126] By the end of 1991, researchers began to acknowledge that working-class male migrants, along with truck drivers and soldiers, were also implicated in the spread of HIV to both sex workers and rural women. One small survey of Kenyan truck drivers and their assistants found 35.2 percent to be HIV-infected.[127] Another study revealed that these men had travel histories involving as many as seven different eastern and central African countries.[128] The early propagative role of elite men (Africans and expatriates, businessmen, officials and technicians) largely escaped notice.[129]

Although female-to-male transmission was clearly occurring, it has been difficult to document, which makes the labelling of sex workers as vectors less tenable to argue. Referring to data from the United States, Carovano notes that "despite the portrayal of prostitute-as-vector, as of January 1989 . . . there [had] been no documented cases of men becoming infected through contact with a specific prostitute."[130] In Africa, Simonsen and colleagues were among the first biomedical researchers to examine social factors in relation to HIV transmission, calling for the "reduction of the social circumstances which create the necessity for women to resort to prostitution,"[131] but they did not actually focus on poverty and inequality as causal factors in the pandemic itself. This group was, however, one of the first to begin effective condom education for sex workers.[132]

Commercial sex workers in Africa, as in other areas of the world, were not the only women at risk. Blood samples of women delivering in Kinshasa hospitals in 1986 revealed that six to eight percent of the women were HIV-infected. Between 25 percent and 40 percent of the infants born to seropositive mothers also were infected; the majority of these babies died before the age of two years. Most of the mothers in this sample were married, and those aged 20 to 30 years were more likely to be seropositive than their older peers.[133] In addition, seroprevalence among young women who earned below-subsistence wages in formal sector jobs, such as hospital workers or textile factory workers, was high. One Kinshasa survey showed that, among hospital workers tested, 16.7 percent were seropositive in 1986. Among factory workers, 11.1 percent were seropositive that same year. Most of these women were single.

When socioeconomic data are available, they show that HIV prevalence rates are skewed by class. At Kenyatta Hospital, which serves Nairobi's middle class, two to three percent of parturient women were seropositive between 1986 and 1988.[134] HIV prevalence among 4,883 women tested at a health center serving a poor Nairobi neighborhood increased from 6.5 percent in 1989 to 13 percent in 1991.[135] Most of these women reported no "risky behaviors" and the already low number reporting multiple partners declined over the three years of the study. In Malawi, seroprevalence in urban parturient women rose rapidly, reaching 17.6 percent of 461 women tested in 1989.[136] The latter two studies found HIV strongly associated with untreated syphilis, itself linked to poverty. The most rapid rise in infection was seen in teens and women less than 25 years of age.

In Rwanda, as noted, national surveillance data from 1986 had already recorded levels of HIV infection as high as one-fifth of urban women and one-seventh of urban men.[137] In Kigali, the capital, HIV rates were highest among women 26 to 40 years old: 30 percent of mothers were seropositive at delivery in 1986.[138] Most reported having only one sexual partner.[139] The major risk factor identified for these women was not multiple partners, but a wage-earning husband who drank alcohol.[140] A more recent 1989-1993 longitudinal study in Butare Préfecture found that teenage women were at highest risk.[141]

Infections have continued to spread as a result of military and paramilitary men using rape as an instrument of genocide and intimidation.[142] Similar patterns have been noted elsewhere in Africa:

> women living in areas plagued by civil unrest or war may be in a situation of higher risk. In many countries, relatively high percentages of male military and police personnel are infected and their unprotected (voluntary or forced) sexual encounters with local women provide an avenue for transmission. Patterns of female infection have been correlated with the movements of members of the military in parts of Central and Eastern Africa.[143]

These studies confirm what many African women have known all along: not only sex workers are at high risk. Monogamous, married women of childbearing age are also at high risk, as are young girls, many of whom are infected at first coitus. Studies also confirm another reality: women do not control resources that allow them to live independently of men, and so are in no position to refuse unsafe sex. Still, even as researchers demonstrated that even monogamous women were at risk, and that HIV had already spread beyond the "core groups" of prostitutes and truck drivers, officials continued to promote the core-group model. This focus was counter-productive when applied to prevention approaches, since many men avoided the term "prostitutes" and defined their casual partners as "friends." And, because AIDS and condoms are associated with the stigma of prostitution, women with multiple partners were reported to refuse condoms in order to protect their virtue, even when condom use was a possible option.

Prevention is also made more difficult by most African women's lack of access to effective treatment for STDs. STDs increase the risk of acquiring HIV from an infected partner. While urban women with disposable income can consult private practitioners and pay for a full course of antibiotic treatment, this is extremely difficult, if not impossible, for women living in poverty. Poor women's access to treatment is further limited when user-fees are charged, a policy mandated as part of structural adjustment programs imposed by the World Bank. Visits by Nairobi women to an STD specialty clinic dropped to 65 percent of the already low level attained before user charges had been levied.[144] This is particularly disturbing since transmission rates have continued to escalate among African women, and research has shown that improved access to both free STD treatment and condoms increases their use.[145]

To better understand the roots of these escalating transmission rates among women, it is necessary to analyze linkages between political economy, gender, culture and AIDS. Most of sub-Saharan Africa, like much of the developing world, is in the throes of an ever-deepening economic crisis. In these times poor women bear the brunt of increased workloads, declining incomes and increased sickness.[146] Schoef and her colleagues have analyzed these linkages in Zaïre, an example, perhaps, of a worst case scenario, but one which is not without relevance in other areas of sub-Saharan Africa. The underlying causes of this scenario are broadly similar to what is occuring throughout much of the continent. In many African nations, poor terms of trade, the contradictions of distorted post-colonial economies, which generate class disparities and burdensome debt service, have created what now appears to be an entrenched crisis.[147]

In a number of African countries this crisis began in 1974 with the rise in oil prices, and declining prices for many major export commodities. Over the next decade, economic stagnation was fueled in some countries by widespread drought; in others stagnation was the consequence of corruption. Foreign debt grew. Per capita incomes are ranked among the world's lowest, ranging between an estimated $90 (U.S. dollars) per year in 1993 for Mozambique and Tanzania, to $960 (U.S. dollars) per year in Gabon.[148] Incomes have since continued to decline. In a recent study of the dynamics of AIDS transmission, Quinn underlines the importance of this decline: "Twenty-four countries in sub-Saharan Africa with a total population of over 400 million were worse off in terms of average income per capita at the end of the 1980s that at the beginning of the decade."[149]

Moreover, average per capita figures mask huge disparities in wealth, and steep gradients of this sort seem to promote HIV transmission in and of themselves.[150] As "Economic Recovery" and Structural Adjustment Policies shifted national burdens to the poor, many families' incomes were outpaced by hyper-inflation in the costs of basic necessities. Those just scraping by in the 1980s have since fallen into extreme poverty. In cities where people had been accustomed to eating two and three meals per day, they now eat a single meal, or skip food for days; malnutrition is widespread. Ever more desperate economic conditions have reduced the poor, and many formerly middle-class families, to "zones of non-existence." School attendance has declined, especially among girls. Banditry and gendered violence have increased.

Throughout the continent, in fact, poor women and children have experienced most severely the effects of structural adjustment policies and the deepening crisis. Economic crisis and gendered structures of employment shape present sociocultural configurations.

In most countries, lack of schooling and discrimination keep the numbers of women in formal sector employment to between four to 10 percent of the work force. Moreover, stagnant or declining economies with low levels of industrialization find 40 to 60 percent of the male workforce un- or underemployed. These men and the vast majority of women without special qualifications resort to the "informal sector" of petty commodity production and trade. Here, too, occupations are gender-segregated, with women concentrated in the lowest-paid, and often unlicensed, activities. These include petty trade, food preparation, market gardening, sewing, hairdressing, domestic work, smuggling and prostitution.

Most of these occupations yield very low and often erratic incomes, and at the same time, render their practitioners vulnerable to extortion and violence from police, petty officials and the military. Even the more lucrative activities, such as money-changing, sale of imported cloth and appliances, or diamond and gold smuggling are subject to political protection, which can be withdrawn. Produce trade and smuggling take place over long distances, across borders and continents. Consequently, whether coerced or for pleasure, sexual relations with several partners are not uncommon.

Another consequence of macrolevel crisis is to render the already crowded microlevel informal sector increasingly less profitable for small operators- especially those who must use part of their capital to meet urgent expenses. With the crisis, women, who formerly relied upon steady contributions from male sex partners and from their extended families, report that these sources are dwindling; others, too, are hard-pressed to make ends meet. Sexual patron-client relations and multiple partner strategies that supplement poor women's incomes have become increasingly important to survival.

Some of these macrolevel forces are illustrated in the AIDS pandemic in South Africa. Although reported cases of AIDS in this country are low, measures of HIV infection show an increasing infiltration of HIV into this country. For example, in the Transvaal area, the seroprevalence rate increased among pregnant women from 0.036 percent in 1987 to 0.217 percent in 1988.[151] A study reported by Jochelson, Mothibeli, and Leger examines the impact of the colonial system, which has disrupted family structures, on the pattern of HIV infection and AIDS in South Africa. The study, based on interviews with 20 male migrant workers and 24 female commercial sex workers, discusses how many migrant workers, who must leave home to earn money, are separated from their families for long periods of time. During this separation, they often become involved in relationships with other women. The relationships between men and city women may reduce the finances available to the wives of the migrant workers because the men will often send less money home. The authors state: "Migrancy also subjects marriages to great strain, and divorce or abandonment deprives women of economic support. With access to few opportunities on the labor market, some women may choose prostitution as the only means of economic survival."[152] The researchers also found that women who worked as prostitutes and served the male migrant workers "come from socially and economically marginalized groups in rural and urban areas".[153] Many had been abandoned by their husbands and lovers or had left their husbands after years of physical abuse. They worked as commercial sex workers in order to support themselves and their children. Almost half of these women had migrated illegally to South Africa from Lesotho. Their marriages ended, and they were thus required to earn their livings as prostitutes. The authors state: "The collapse of their marriages and their entry into prostitution were related to the way the migrant labor system interacts with women's subordinant and dependent social and economic position in rural Sotho society."[154]

Poverty, inequality, and the socially constructed meanings of gender are crucial to understanding heterosexual HIV transmission. Both Western and African researchers have focused on women female sex workers as "vectors" or "reservoirs of infection." The most influential epidemiological voices argue that the pandemic can be controlled by reducing sexual transmission among "core transmitters" of the virus. Married women, who contract infection from their husbands and may infect their children, have been neglected by the gaze of most. Needless to say, this orientation was already the basis of earlier, failed STD control campaigns.

But while public health campaigns target sex workers, many African women take a different view of AIDS epidemiology and prevention. In their view, the epidemiology of HIV and Africa's economic crises suggest that HIV spreads not because of the "exotic sexual practices" of Africans but because of the conditions of daily life within which women struggle to survive. Most women at risk are not engaged in sex work, and those sex workers who are in harm's way, are placed there by people who make choices about what human lives are valuable and what lives are disposable. Most risky situations are not under women's control. While on some levels, gender relations are subject to negotiation, African women's struggles to improve their condition do not take place in circumstances of their own making. Moreover, despite those struggles, women often lose.

African women who live in poverty lose these struggles because the forces arrayed against them are intricate and entrenched. "Low-intensity" warfare has killed millions and decimated industrial, commercial and social infrastructures in much of Africa. Terror has created countless refugee populations across the continent, shredding social safety nets, and deflowering promises of post-colonial Africa.

The full effects of violence and grinding poverty upon their greatest victims, the poorest who have abandoned hope, are underdocumented. The distribution of HIV makes it difficult to mask the effects of structural violence. Despite early fascination with exotic sexual and ritual practices, recent commentaries have been less likely to claim these as causal theories. In 1995, Quinn examined three new hypotheses to explain the rapid spread of HIV in East Africa: the "truck town" hypothesis, the "migrant labor" hypothesis, and ethnically patterned troop movements. Quinn concluded that "probably all three hypotheses together help explain the spread of HIV within Uganda."[155] Further south, he notes, the high rates of STDs seen among "South African" miners—many in fact from impoverished neighboring states—are not to be understood without reference to economic pressures that drive migration. Indeed, the explosiveness of the African AIDS pandemic is not to be understood without reference to the large-scale forces discussed throughout this book:

In sub-Saharan Africa, between 1960 and 1980, urban centers with more than 500,000 inhabitants increased from 3 to 28, and more than 75 military coups occurred in 30 countries. The result was a massive migration of rural inhabitants to urban centers concomitant with the spread of HIV-1 to large population centers. With the associated demographic, economic, and social changes, an epidemic of sexually transmitted diseases and HIV-1 was ignited.[156]

Add to this list pervasive gender inequality, and the recipe for vast human disaster on the African continent is complete.

Latin America and the Caribbean

The Global AIDS Policy Coalition estimates that as of January 1995, eight percent of the world's cumulative AIDS cases were registered in Latin America and the Caribbean. While we will focus most of our attention on Haiti in this review, it is instructive to reflect on the distribution of HIV and AIDS in the nations which make up the Caribbean basin. Latin America and the Caribbean, including Puerto Rico, were originally classified by the WHO as a Pattern II area, reflecting the fact that "heterosexual intercourse has been the dominant mode of HIV transmission from the start. Blood transfusion, the reuse of contaminated needles, and intravenous drug use contribute to a variable degree, but homosexuality generally plays a minor role in this pattern."[157] However, careful review of the region's AIDS pandemic reveals that it is comprised of multiple subepidemics initially derived from the larger pandemic to the north. Because of their origins, the region's earliest cases did not, in fact, reflect Pattern II epidemiology. Instead, risk factors were initially very similar to those seen in the United States. As we have noted elsewhere, socioepidemiological research has convincingly demonstrated that the virus came to Haiti, the Dominican Republic, Jamaica, Trinidad and Tobago and the Bahamas from the United States, probably through tourism and transnationals returning home from abroad. Thus despite growing similarities to patterns of transmission in Africa, the pandemic in this region is undeniably of American descent.

Caribbean tourism serves, in fact, as an index of dependence on North America. In a country as poor as Haiti—the poorest country in the hemisphere—AIDS might be thought of as an occupational hazard for workers in the tourist industry. Indeed, the relation between the degree of dependence on trade with North America and prevalence of HIV was suggested by an exercise comparing AIDS attack rates to U.S.-Caribbean trade indices which reflect the influence of U.S.-based markets. By 1986, the five countries with the largest number of AIDS cases were as follows: the Dominican Republic, the Bahamas, Trinidad/Tobago, Mexico, and Haiti. In both 1983 and 1977, these same five countries were the countries most dependent on the United States for the sale of exports. Haiti, the country with the most AIDS cases, was also the most economically dependent on the United States. By an order of magnitude, Cuba has the fewest AIDS cases in the region; it is also the least dependent on U.S. trade and tourism, given the 36-year-old embargo imposed on Cuba by the United States. Cuba, while still a poor country, is also the least marked in terms of economic inequality of all the nations mentioned, including the United States. Recent efforts to open Cuba to tourism and the rise of prostitution may lead to substantial increases in seropositivity in this island nation.[158]

How have women been affected by AIDS in the Caribbean? Gravely. In 1991, a total of 2,091 cases of AIDS in women were reported to the Pan American Health Organization from Latin America and 347 from the Caribbean subregion. This reflects incidence rates of 9.4 per million women in Latin America and 79.0 for the Caribbean. Incidence rates among women for 1991 range from a high of 673.0 per million in the Bahamas and 136.1 per million in Bermuda to a low of 0.0 for countries such as Bolivia, the Cayman Islands, and Montserrat. Rates among "women at high risk" may be as elevated as 69 percent.[159]

Haiti may be taken as a case in point. In the early eighties, the Haitian epidemic seemed to have an epicenter in the city of Carrefour, a center of prostitution bordering the south side of Port-au-Prince. In the beginning, Haitian researchers documented high prevalence, among the first Haitians with AIDS, of "accepted risk factors," i.e. the risk factors for AIDS identified by the CDC, including histories of homosexual contact.[160] Over time, however, HIV infection has become a predominantly heterosexually transmitted disease. By 1986, heterosexual transmission—or, in the language of the day, transmission among those with "no risk factor"—was demonstrated or strongly suspected in approximately 70 percent of Haitian AIDS cases. Additional evidence for heterosexual transmission of HIV was to be found in high rates—over 50 percent—of infection among female sex workers in the Port-au-Prince area, the ever-decreasing male:female ratio among Haitians with AIDS, and the growing number of pediatric AIDS cases.[161]

How far has HIV spread in Haiti? During 1986 and 1987, sera from several cohorts of ostensibly healthy urban adults were analyzed for antibodies to HIV, revealing high rates of seropositivity. In a group of individuals working in hotels catering to tourists, HIV seroprevalence was a sobering 12 percent. In a group of 502 mothers of children hospitalized with diarrhea and among 190 urban adults with a comparably low socioeconomic background, the seroprevalence rates were 12 percent and 13 percent, respectively. Among urban factory workers, 5 percent were found to have antibodies to HIV. In all series, rates were comparable for men and women, which suggested to many observers that the high attack rate in Haitian men would slowly give way to a pattern like that seen in parts of Africa. As in Africa, poor teenaged girls were particularly hard-hit:

> the high seropositivity rate (8 percent) found in pregnant women 14 to 19 years of age suggests that women [in an urban slum] appear to acquire HIV infection soon after becoming sexually active. Moreover, this age group is the only one in which a higher seropositivity rate is not associated with a greater number of sexual partners. Women with only one sexual partner in the year prior to pregnancy actually have a slightly higher prevalence rate (although not significantly so) than the others. This suggests that they were infected by their first and only partner.[162]

In summary, then, large numbers of urban Haitians have been exposed to HIV. Clearly, HIV infection is most often a heterosexually transmitted disease in urban Haitian settings. But what of rural regions? Scant ethnographic and epidemiologic research has been conducted in rural Haiti. However, one study reported that almost 70 percent of all patients with symptomatic HIV disease were young women.[163] A small case-control study of 40 women revealed that none had a history of prostitution or used illicit drugs; and none had a history of transfusion. None of the women reported more than six sexual partners. In fact, several of the afflicted women had had only one sexual partner. Although women in the study group had (on average) more sexual partners than controls, the difference was not striking—and the average for each group was less than three lifetime partners per woman. The chief risk factors in this small cohort involved not the number of partners, but rather the occupations of these partners. Most of the women with HIV disease had histories of sexual contact with soldiers or truckdrivers. Of the women diagnosed with HIV disease, none had a history of sexual contact exclusively with peasants. Among the seronegative controls, none reported contact with soldiers, and most had sexual relations only with peasants from the region. Histories of extended residence in Port-au-Prince and work as a domestic were also strongly associated with a diagnosis of HIV disease. This and complementary studies led us to conclude that conjugal unions with non-peasants, salaried soldiers and truckdrivers who are highly mobile—socially and geographically—and who are paid on a daily basis, reflect these women's quest for economic security. In this manner, truckdrivers and soldiers have served as "bridges" to the rural population, just as North American tourists seem to have served as bridges to the urban Haitian population. But just as North Americans are no longer important in the transmission of HIV in Haiti, truckdrivers and soldiers will soon no longer be necessary components of the rural epidemic.

Careful review of studies from urban and rural Haiti, and also extensive ethnographic research on AIDS, permitted the identification of a number of differentially weighted, synergistic factors promoting HIV transmission in Haiti. In spite of a large number of hypotheses invoking everything from voodoo practices to ritualized homosexuality, many of the factors actually found to be associated with HIV infection are similar to those described for Africa. As land becomes more exhausted, more and more peasants abandon agriculture for the lure of wage-labor in cities and towns. Indeed, one of the most striking recent demographic changes has been the rapid growth of Port-au-Prince: in 1950, the urban population was 12.2 percent of the total population of this highly agrarian nation; it had increased to over 20 percent in 1971 and reached almost 30 percent by 1980. Demographers estimate that, by the year 2000, urban dwellers will constitute close to 40 percent of the total population.[164]

As is the case with many developing countries, internal migration has played the most significant role in the growth of the capital. One observer estimates that "between 1950 and 1971 rural-urban migration accounted for 59 percent of Haitian urban growth, while natural population increase accounted for only 8 percent."[165] As Neptune-Anglade has noted, the growth of Port-au-Prince is substantially the result of a "feminine rural exodus." In fact, approximately 60 percent of the population of Port-au-Prince is female. The most common form of employment among younger women of rural origin is that of servant: "In the cities, the [economically] active 10-14 year-old girls are essentially all domestics . . . These 'restaveks' find themselves at the very bottom of the social hierarchy."[166] It is this social position that will later determine to a large extent, their increased risk for HIV infection.

Population shifts, when coupled with the unremitting immiseration of Haiti, have had a palpable effect on longstanding patterns of sexual union. Stable unions have been undermined by the economic pressures to which women with dependents are particularly vulnerable. In the wake of these pressures, new patterns have emerged: "serial monogamy" might describe the monogamous but weak unions that lead to one child but do not last much longer than a year or so. After such unions have dissolved, women find themselves with new dependents and even more in need of reliable partners. Equally risk-inducing has been the quest for unions with financially secure partners. In rural Haiti, men of this description once included a substantial fraction of all peasant landholders. In recent decades, however, financial security has become elusive for all but a handful of truckdrivers, representatives of the state (*viz.*, soldiers and petty officials), and landholders. As noted, truckdrivers and soldiers are clearly groups with above-average rates of HIV infection—and above-average access to women.

The Haitian economy counts a higher proportion of economically active women—most of them traders—than any other developing society, with the exception of Lesotho.[167] But sexism is clearly a force in political, economic, and domestic life, and it would be difficult to argue with Neptune-Anglade when she states that, in all regards, rural women "endure a discrimination and a pauperization that is worse than that affecting [rural] men."[168] As elsewhere, gender inequality weakens Haitian women's ability to negotiate safe sexual encounters.

It is unfortunate indeed that HIV arrived in Haiti shortly before a period of massive and prolonged social upheaval. Political unrest has clearly undermined preventive efforts and may have helped, through other mechanisms, to spread HIV. For example, although AIDS prevention has been identified as one of the top priorities of the Haitian ministry of health, the office charged with coordinating preventive efforts has been hamstrung by six *coups d'état*, which have led, inevitably, to personnel changes—and worse. By this writing, there have been no comprehensive efforts to prevent HIV transmission in rural Haiti.

Political upheaval did not just hobble the chance of a coordinated response to the epidemic. It has had far more direct effects. One of the most epidemiologically significant events of recent years may prove to be the violent *coup d'état* of September, 1991 in which the democratically elected president, Jean-Bertrand Aristide, was driven from the country by a military junta. As noted, a number of surveys of asymptomatic adults living in urban slums revealed seroprevalence rates of approximately 10 percent. Following the coup, these areas were targeted by the army for brutal repression. A number of journalists and health-care professionals estimated that fully half of the adult residents of this slum fled to rural areas following the army's lethal incursions. It takes little imagination to see that such flux substantially changes the equations describing HIV transmission dynamics in low-prevalence rural areas sheltering the refugees.

Finally, in seeking to understand the Haitian AIDS epidemic, it is necessary to underline the contribution of an inert public health system. Medical care in Haiti is something of an obstacle course, one in which innumerable barriers are placed before poor people seeking care. As in Africa, failure to have an STD treated means persistence of important co-factors. Thus vaginal and cervical diseases, even those as ostensibly minor as trichomoniasis, may increase the risk of HIV transmission through "microwounds." Inflammation associated with these diseases may also increase the risk of transmission since lymphoctyes are, after all, the target cells of HIV. Although important data about STDs are now being collected in Port-au-Prince,[169] there are as yet no careful studies being conducted in rural areas. There are no data to suggest that villagers are more sexually active than their urban counterparts; there is even less reason to believe that rural Haitians are more sexually active than age-matched controls from North America. What is clear is that a majority of STDs go untreated, which certainly suggests that sores, other lesions, and inflammation will persist far longer in rural Haiti than in many areas of the world that have adequate health care systems.

Failure to treat pulmonary tuberculosis, Haiti's most common "opportunistic infection," means rapid progression of HIV disease and death, to say nothing of its impact on HIV-negative individuals. Contaminated blood transfusions may be the only alternative to no transfusions at all. Condoms are often not available even to those who want them. The cost of pharmaceuticals, always prohibitive, has skyrocketed in recent years. Antivirals are effectively unavailable: in February, 1990, "local radio stations announced . . . that for the first time, the drug AZT is available in Haiti. It might as well have been on Mars. A bottle of 100 capsules costs $343—more than most Haitians make in a year."[170]

Another country in Latin America that looms large in the AIDS pandemic is Brazil. Brazil has the third highest absolute numbers of people with AIDS in the world. More recently, HIV has been reported to be increasing among Brazilian women. The proportion of women with AIDS in São Paulo, where 60 percent of AIDS cases are located, has risen dramatically since 1985. At that time, the ratio of male to female AIDS cases was 38 to one. By 1991 that ratio had dropped to seven to one. Goldstein suggests that that by the year 2000, the number of AIDS cases in women will equal that in men.[171]

Brazil is a country riven by economic inequality: it is estimated that 10 percent of the population earn 47 percent of the income there.[172] It is interesting to note that Brazil also has one of the largest total foreign debts of all countries in the developing world.[173] In fact, Lurie, Hintzen, and Lowe state that Brazil's debt "illustrates the role of commercial sex work as a link bewteen poverty and HIV."[174] They assert that a decrease in state spending on education has forced 8 million Brazilian children to leave school and go to work. Many children have been abandoned by their parents because their parents could no longer afford to care for them. Alone and with no support, many of these children have turned to commercial sex work in order to survive and the use of drugs in order to ease the pain of that survival. HIV seroprevalance among these "street children" may be quite high.[175]

An Asian Enigma?

HIV and AIDS were not known in Asia until relatively late in the pandemic. A late start did not preclude, however, a seemingly relentless surge in transmission. At this writing, HIV infection rates are soaring in Southeast Asia, particularly in Thailand, but also in Myanmar, Vietnam, Laos, Cambodia, China and the Philippines. The Global AIDS Coaliton has estimated that the number of people currently infected with HIV in South East Asia alone outnumbers the total number of people infected in the entire developed world and is expected to exceed the number of infected in sub-Saharan Africa by the turn of the century.[176] The World Health Organization (WHO) estimates that, by the year 2000, approximately 3 million to 6 million people will be infected with HIV in Thailand; another 10 million will be infected in India. If these projections are correct, these countries alone may be home to half of the world's infected by the year 2000.[177]

Many of the mechanisms of this rapid spread are revealed by data from Thailand. "The first few cases of HIV infection were not documented until 1985," notes Quinn, "and it was not until 1988-1990 that the transmission of HIV escalated to epidemic proportions."[178] One 1985 survey of 600 "high-risk" individuals (sex workers, STD patients, and injection drug users) revealed HIV seroprevalence of less that 0.5 percent. Three years later, injection drug users in the same region could be shown to have a prevalence of 40 percent, with seroconversion rates as high as three to five percent per month.[179] The next wave of the Thai epidemic seemed to strike sex workers, with one nationwide survey showing that rates of infection among prostitutes increased steadily from 3.7 percent in 1989 to 15 percent in 1991.[180] Sex workers were held to have an amplificatory role, infecting non-drug-using clients, who in turn infected their "low-risk" non-prostitute wives and girlfriends.[181] Regardless of the pathways of transmission, the rates of spread are impressive. "If this rate of HIV transmission continues," notes one analyst, "there will be 2-4 million cumulative HIV infections by the year 2000."[182]

How are these explosions usually explained? Although insights from other settings—urban North America, Africa, and Haiti—are clearly relevant to the Thai epidemic, the same tendency to invoke "mysterious forces" was registered in much commentary on these trends. One 1991 study of AIDS in Thailand reports that "the reason and dynamics behind the timing and rapidity of the 1988 epidemic in IDUs (injection drug users) are unknown."[183] The authors speculate that needle-sharing between Thai injection drug users and expatriates in prison, together with the annual pardon of prisoners, may have triggered the spread among the nation's injection drug users. Terming the exceptionally high rates of HIV among "brothel-based, lower-class prostitutes" in Chiang Mai (where seroprevalence was as high as 63 percent) an "enigma," the authors suggest that the explanation for the rapid spread among Thai women "is likely to come from research on sexual behavior and related diseases given a lack of evidence of genetic factors in the human host nor virulence of the etiologic agent to explain it."[184] The authors do mention that male patronage of prostitutes is part of the pattern of spread in Thailand, as well as in adjacent regions such as Burma, Laos, China and India. No mention is made, however, of the economic conditions in which prostitution, sex tourism, or increased drug use are a last option among few options for the poorest in the nation.

As in other parts of the developing world, prostitutes have been blamed for the rapid rise in infection rates rather than the economic and social conditions which foster prostitution. The sex industry is estimated to employ four percent of Thai women. Increasingly, teenagers and even younger children are pulled in as well, sometimes abducted or sold into sex slavery to offset the economic crises facing their families amongst the poorest sectors of Thailand's hilltribes. According to one observer, "Underlying the spread of HIV among (Thai) highlanders is the complex interrelationship between old and new cash crops, the eradication of poppy cultivation, poverty—both inadequate subsistence and a felt lack of desired consumer goods—and tourism, including sex tourism." [185] Most brothel-based sex workers are paid by the brothel, not by their clients, and have little negotiating power with their clients or brothel-owners. The commercial sex workers most at risk for having little negotiating power are the "younger and younger women sought by brokers in distant highland villages to meet the demand for 'AIDS-free' prostitutes."[186]

Despite the concern triggered by these projections, official reports have described successive waves of spread in this area of the world with little mention of the transnational nature of Asia's sex tourism and its drug trade. Sex tourism, characterized by large numbers of foreign visitors who come for the services of commercial sex workers, has been an important component of Thailand's economic resurgence. This explains to some extent the high-level of complacency and denial which first characterized the Thai response; the importance of sex tourism also helps to explain the deliberate manipulation of statistics. In 1987, Thailand's "Year of Tourism," the Thai Ministry of Health claimed that only seven prostitutes among thousands tested for antibodies were seropositive to HIV. The good news was short-lived: in 1988, when the Year of Tourism was over, the Ministry of Health released "new" findings confirming that 40 percent of prostitutes tested in Bangkok and Chiang Mai were infected.[187]

What of Asia's second most populous country? A decade ago, there were almost no cases of HIV infection reported in India, but an explosive pandemic is now spreading across the subcontinent. One recent review opens with the assertion that, by the beginning of the next century, "India will have more new cases of HIV infection per year than any single country and probably the largest number of HIV-infected people as well."[188] As if the above-cited estimates were not sufficiently dire, others are even worse: "Projections are that in India 3 million people may be infected in 1996 and 20 million by the year 2000."[189]

The people most affected by the disease thus far, according to published reviews, are injection drug users, with reported seroprevalence rates as high as 64 percent, and female commercial sex workers, with reported seroprevalence rates as high as 30 percent.[190] In one large survey in northeast India, none of the 2,322 injecting drug users tested between 1986 and 1989 were seropositive for HIV. In the same region, more than half tested in June, 1990, were found to be infected.[191] HIV seropositivity rates among Bombay sex workers rose from two percent in 1988-1989 to nearly 40 percent in 1991.[192] In the city of Vellore, seroprevalence among prostitutes increased from 0.5 percent in 1986 to 34.5 percent in 1990.[193] The pandemic has spread far beyond those involved in sex work, however, with over 1 million people infected in the past six years; "if unchecked this number could increase dramatically, exceeding even the number of HIV infections in Africa."[194]

As is so often the case, many of these surveys assert that women working as commercial sex workers are the people primarily responsible for the spread of the disease into the "general population." As an explanation, this logic hides more than it reveals. Commercial sex work is an occupation of poor women and of uneducated women. Of Calcutta prostitutes interviewed in one study, 49.1 percent became commercial sex workers to escape extreme poverty; 84.4 percent of the women in the study were illiterate; 21.6 percent reported "family disturbances" which led them to becoming prostitutes.[195] More importantly, other studies have shown that HIV infection is not confined to women working in the commercial sex industry. In a study of pregnant women attending an antenatal clinic in Vellore, 20 were found to be HIV positive. Only two of these women were commercial sex workers. Among the 20 women who were HIV infected, the "risk factor" the majority shared was poverty. In fact, 85 percent of the HIV positive women in this study were of lower socio-economic status.This data reminds us that linking HIV infection solely to female commercial sex work is misguided.[196]

In explanations for the lamentable states of affairs in India, immodest claims of causality again abound.[197] One report cites "denial, ignorance, fear and stigmatization" and "tradition" rather than the violent coercion, lack of choices, inequality, or disruptions of traditional work and life which also describe the setting. For example, "HIV Thrives in Ancient Traditions"—as if these factors stand alone outside of the forces of history as adequate explanations for the dynamics of HIV transmission in India.[198] One of the traditions in question involved the selection and preparation of a *harijan*, or low-caste, girl who happens to catch the fancy of "village landlords." At puberty, after receiving training in meeting the sexual needs of her patrons, she is publicly auctioned. Men outbid one another to become her first sexual partner. Is this not a story at least as much about unequal relations of power, gender, inequality, and poverty as it is about ancient traditions?

Although other nations in Asia are not as severely affected as Thailand and India in terms of sheer numbers, similar types of epidemics, in which poverty and inequality place certain segments of the population at risk, can still be seen. China is a huge country which still reports a small epidemic. In all, there are 36 cases of AIDS reported. Of 2.8 million HIV antibody tests performed, only 1,243 people tested positive.[199] Most of these cases came from Yunnan province which is located in the "golden triangle," a major crossroads in the international drug trade. This area has traditionally had a relatively high prevalence of injection drug use, particularly among men, though opiates were more commonly smoked rather than injected until recent years. An estimated 50 percent of the injection drug users in this province are believed to be infected with HIV. Farmers and manual laborers who inject often share needles. Ten percent of the wives of these HIV-positive men are HIV-positive as well.[200] Many of the infected Yunnan women are actually Burmese immigrants. Though the province of Yunnan is located in an area of high levels of drug trafficking, poverty and inequality again play major roles in the AIDS pandemic there. Yunnan is considered to be home of China's "national minorities." In fact, one minority group, the Dai, accounted for two thirds of the HIV-infected individuals living in Yunnan in 1990.[201] Much of the data about the Chinese AIDS pandemic is centered around injecting drug users in the province of Yunnan, yet one study asserts that "...heterosexual transmission will probably become the dominant mode of transmission elsewhere in the country."[202] In fact, while injection drug users accounted for 83 percent of the cases of HIV infection in 1990, they only accounted for 72 percent of cases of HIV infection tabulated two years later.[203]

The Philippines also reports relatively low numbers of HIV infection. As of December, 1993 only 467 HIV infections had been reported to the AIDS Registry in the Department of Health in Manilla.[204] Some authors point out that there may be severe under-reporting of HIV in the Philippines: "The Registry has been vulnerable to the vagaries of...a passive system of case reporting."[205] A "passive" system of reporting is no surprise in a country that spends only 1.9 percent of its budget on health care while up to two thirds of all Filipino deaths occur in the absence of medical attention of any sort. What is sadly surprising is that despite this state of affairs, the Philippines is the greatest exporter of health professionals in the world.[206] Although the highest rates of HIV infection are seen among men who have sex with men, injection drug users, military personnel, and female sex workers also have high rates of HIV infection. In fact, one out of every six HIV-positive women are sex workers.[207] These women are exploited by the vast "sex tourism" industry in the Phillipines. Prostitution here, as in many other places in the world, is "caused mainly by severe economic privation."[208] Women earning a living as sex workers in this setting are often severely exploited and in no position to negotiate risk.[209] In addition to the subordination of women in the commercial sex industry, other factors such as economic recession, political instability and structural adjustment programs have contributed to severe deficiencies in the provision of healthcare.[210]

What about the richest country in Asia? Japan's epidemic is small, but it follows the trends registered in other countries: inequality serves as a virulent co-factor. Data collected by the AIDS Surveillance System, established by the Ministry of Health in order to monitor the spread of HIV, suggest that accelerated spread of HIV infection in Japan began in 1991. Much of this change is due to an increase in heterosexual transmission of the disease. As of April, 1993, a total of 62 AIDS cases in Japan were reported with heterosexual contact as the risk factor. Of these 62 cases, 51 were men and 11 were women. But a very different picture is seen when less advanced HIV disease is examined. Of the 498 people in Japan with HIV infection attributed to heterosexual contact, 176 are men and 322 are women. The number of HIV and AIDS cases reported in women with heterosexual contact as a risk factor rose from 26 in 1987 to 253 in 1992. Similar trends were not reported among men in Japan. By 1992, women accounted for 65 percent of the people in Japan with HIV and AIDS who became infected with the disease through heterosexual contact.[211]

Although the AIDS pandemic seemed slow to start, HIV infection is firmly established in various countries throughout Asia.[212] Some researchers have stated that: "The speed with which the epidemic moved into this region has not left time for adequate information sharing."[213] More work needs to be done to adequately describe the dynamic of HIV transmission in the different countries in Asia.[214] However, what data exist suggest that the pandemic in Asia is in fact no enigma. The same factors which are linked with HIV infection everywhere in the world—including poverty and gender inequality—are also seen to go hand and hand with the pandemic in Asia.

4. CONCLUSIONS

It has been our intention to offer an honest portrayal of the conditions in which AIDS has become, in the course of a decade, a leading cause of death among poor women. By critically reexamining research on the distribution and spread of HIV among women, we have sought to cast in bold relief the mechanisms through which the impoverishment and sexual exploitation of women have become the norms of HIV transmission throughout the world. We call for a renewed commitment to understanding the true nature of the AIDS pandemic and we hope that this understanding will help transform the structures that generate the trends already registered. The following ideas will be reexamined in the chapters that follow:

1. Poor women have been afflicted by HIV since the beginning of the pandemic, even in those parts of the industrialized world where the majority of early cases were among gay men.

2. The AIDS pandemic has not been significantly contained anywhere in the world, and it is advancing most rapidly among women living in poverty. Preventing the spread of HIV will require preventing transmission to women.

3. Gender inequality is an important co-factor in the AIDS pandemic. Therefore, preventing AIDS will also require recognition and redress of the global and local forces which drive inequality.

4. Old models for understanding the spread of HIV are inadequate. The majority of infected women reside in the world's poorest countries and communities because poverty and gender inequality act to increase women's HIV risks. This dynamic has not been the focus of scientific or public debate. Further, conventional modes of inquiry have obscured existing trends. Currently, poverty is more likely to be identified as an outcome of AIDS rather than as a force that generates risk. Proxies for class, such as "race" and ethnicity, are discussed in relation to exposure categories, but not in relation to socioeconomic status as a determinant of risk. As a result, theoretical frameworks

for discussing risk in relation to poverty are either ignored or buried. Researchers and policy makers seem to be unable to imagine change beyond the level of individual change. Unfortunately, individual change is terribly constrained by the structural violence which defines the lives of women and other subordinated groups.

5. New models are needed. Prevention of HIV transmission to women will require serious consideration of the means by which poverty and gender inequality enhance transmission and, ultimately, thwart conventional attempts to prevent AIDS. More powerful explanatory frameworks must be dynamic, systemic, and critical: they must explain the pandemic's rapid change and predict its future course; they must reveal the transnational linkages elided in many accounts based on national reporting; they must reveal the ways in which inequalities inevitably play a role in local subepidemics and in the larger pandemic.

Around the world, women have made enormous contributions to the physical, emotional, spiritual, and material well-being of their families and communities by supporting the sick and dying, the orphaned, and the exploited. Rather than crassly accept this norm as women's lot, or the lot of the poor, we must demand that the life conditions of all women be improved through compassionate and effective medical, social, economic, political and legal strategies for change.

CHAPTER THREE

Sex, Drugs, and Structural Violence

Unraveling the Epidemic Among Poor Women in the United States

Margaret Connors

"I was in the bathroom, and I remember I was sitting on the toilet and there was one of those heaters on the wall. I don't know why, but I said, 'I'm going to open that.' I pulled it out and I found the needle, a cooker and the thing they tie themselves with, the rubber hose. When I saw that my heart went to my feet."[1]

1. INTRODUCTION

These words come from the story of Mildred, a 29-year-old minister's daughter and mother of three who "was going to die for having loved a heroin addict." Mildred ignored rumors that her husband was injecting drugs until she found evidence that he was in fact using heavily. From that time on her life changed forever. Mildred's story was chronicled by a *Boston Globe* journalist over the course of a year and a half as she battled the virus, placed her children with relatives, and attempted to save a love relationship strained by the demands of the care she required.

It took Mildred almost four years to reveal her HIV infection publicly, using one excuse after another to explain days spent depressed, sick in bed, and struggling to get to her job. But after four years of living with HIV, she developed headaches and extreme exhaustion that proved to be due to meningitis. Believing that death was near, she videotaped a farewell message for her family to see after she died. During the two days of taping, Mildred had forty seizures. She recovered with only enough time to prepare for the next onslaught. She then battled illness after illness. At one time, her weight sank to as little as 62 pounds. Yet Mildred was still alive a year and a half after this journalist began her story. She attributes her survival to the benefits of early intervention with experimental drugs. Having been given a "death sentence" in 1984, she now says that her life has become a "curious kind of waiting."

While Mildred is no different from most women who become infected, the circumstances of her infection fail to conform to any of the exaggerated stereotypes of "women who get AIDS." She is neither a sex worker, nor a drug user, nor a woman who "sleeps around." In fact she was infected at about age 23 by the young man she fell in love with at 12 and he 13—"puppy love," she calls it.

This story is about one individual's life. Yet tales like Mildred's—stories about women, about poverty, about drug use, about children deprived of their parents, and much more—are multiplying daily, because women constitute the fastest-growing group of AIDS sufferers. We could tell these stories as hundreds and hundreds of individual accounts of suffering, each with its own unique configuration of personalities and circumstances.

There are, in fact, many versions of the AIDS story. Versions told with statistics often lose the immediacy and concreteness of the tales told about an individual life, but can provide insights about the spread of the disease. We know from demographic data that women are the fastest–growing group of AIDS sufferers. We know that it is not just any woman who is likely to contract AIDS, because it is not merely the individual decisions of women that "cause" them to become infected. Structural factors—social class and economic status—far more than individual decisions and aspirations, explain why HIV increasingly affects women in the United States and elsewhere.

We could go so far as to say that the root cause of the HIV

infection is, simply, poverty. Poverty is a condition which puts women at greater and greater risk of contracting the HIV virus. Of course, we might say that there are other factors besides poverty that put women at risk for contracting AIDS—factors such as drug use and prostitution. But, as this chapter will illustrate, drug use and transactional sex often occur as the consequence of poverty.

One way to imagine these "factors" (poverty, gender inequality, racism, drug use) is as vectors that converge in the bodies and lives of individuals; in some lives, more factors converge, placing those people at higher risk of contracting disease. But these vectors do not intersect each other mechanically or add up quantitatively. Ethnographic research suggests a more complex picture, in which each factor tends to implicate the other, forming complex constellations of conditions from which it is difficult for "at-risk" individuals to escape. And poverty, increasing in the United States and worldwide, is at the base of them all.

Many individual women who become HIV-infected do not conform to the often-heard profile of the AIDS victim. Mildred, for instance, was neither a sex worker nor a drug user, and was, at least statistically, less at risk than such persons. But the overriding risk factor for Mildred was her poverty. As a poor woman in the United States, she is more likely to be sexually involved with an injection drug user. Mildred, like thousands of other women, embodies and lives out statistical risk and structural disadvantage, even as she struggles against them. While many women are at risk for HIV infection because they are partners of injection drug users, at least currently more women are at risk because they are drug users themselves. This chapter depicts the lives of drug-using women in Massachusetts, at risk of being infected or already infected with HIV.[2] Women often find themselves in situations where they must weigh the risk of becoming infected against other risks including homelessness, assault, and loss of essential income. The social forces that make HIV infection more likely become embodied as personal risk. Examining these women's lives helps make sense of the circumstances in which many poor women are forced to choose between the risk of HIV and other dangers.

These are the basic facts. But the story of why poor women are at greater risk of contracting the virus does not end there. Systematic disregard by government and state agencies has compounded the devastating effect of poverty in women's lives. Since the beginning of the epidemic, women have been denied federal assistance once gravely ill, denied admission to drug treatment if pregnant or caring for their children, and most recently denied income for basic sustenance through drastic welfare cuts. After detailing the overlap of poverty and AIDS risk for women, this chapter will analyze the ways in which the U.S. government has obscured the disproportionate risk that women bear in the AIDS epidemic.

Nor does the story end there. Social science studies could illuminate the structural reasons for the spread and perpetuation of this disease in certain populations. But, in fact, social scientists have also tended to sidestep the effect of poverty in their analysis of HIV transmission. Entering the public health arena as cultural experts, they have created a discourse that stresses the idea that cultural sensitivity can have a meaningful impact on HIV risk reduction. Unfortunately, culture has been made the focus at the expense of exploring issues of political economy—that is, how economic instability places women and ethnic minorities at risk for HIV infection. The third section of the chapter analyzes some of this literature, arguing that, in contrast to economic factors, few if any cultural or personality traits directly place people at an increased risk for HIV.

2. STRUCTURAL AND GENDER INEQUALITIES OF RISK AMONG INJECTION DRUG-USING WOMEN

Who is most likely to contract AIDS?

AIDS became the leading cause of death among Massachusetts residents aged 25-44 in 1993 and among all U.S. citizens in this age category in 1995.[3] Twenty percent of new cases diagnosed in the state are women, up 8 percent from just two years ago. David Mulligan, the Massachusetts Commissioner of Public Health recently said that "AIDS is becoming more heterosexual."[4] What this really means is that AIDS is becoming more gendered; seventy percent of these "heterosexual" cases are now among women.[5]

AIDS is simultaneously becoming less white. Black women die of AIDS nine times more often than white women, Latina women six times more often and nearly two-thirds of all children with AIDS are black.[6] Black and Hispanic men die three times more often than white men, often leaving women alone to provide for children. In fact, the number of African Americans who became newly infected with HIV/AIDS exceeded that of whites last year, although African Americans represent only 12 percent of the nation's population.[7]

New cases also continue to climb among injection drug users (IDUs), as they plateau among gay men. Thirty percent of all people with AIDS are injection drug users and 70 percent of injection drug users with AIDS are minorities.[8] In New York City and the state of Massachusetts, the most common means of infection is now through syringe injection.[9] Nearly fifty percent of women are infected through the use of a dirty needle and 80 percent are IDUs or the sex partner of an IDU. In the Massachusetts prison population, females inmates have about twice the HIV infection rate of men in prison and all those testing HIV-positive have a history of injection drug use.[10]

Not unlike plagues that have come before, the worst of the epidemic will ravage the most disadvantaged in our communities. In the United States, as in much of the world, women—particularly drug-addicted women—will bear much of the burden of this disease. It is necessary to explain how the constellation of large-scale forces affect personal risk for HIV among injection drug users, for there are particular sets of circumstances that make infection likely for women in the United States.

Why are female injection-drug users more at risk than males?

To me it's like a hopeless situation. I sit here, and I watch the disease of addiction. The rates of recovery are so terrible, like one in a hundred. And everybody I know, let's say out of a hundred people, only five have not tested positive—I'm just saying in the clique that I was running with. And you're seeing a lot of reinfection there too, because they're taking the attitude that we're all gonna go, so why bother. And I don't see any cut down in, say, prostitution. There are just as many guys who want it now as before.

As Anne, a 15-year veteran of the drug war who had survived its abuses until AIDS came along, describes typical life on the streets, it is clear that she is aware of the multiple risks for drug-addicted women. Nearly half (45%) of all U.S. women currently diagnosed with AIDS became infected through injection drug use.[11] Women become infected through this method of transmission because, as injection drug users, they must assume greater risk than men in virtually every circumstance. Why are these women so much at risk? Drug-using women typically engage in sex for money or drugs with little power to enforce condom use. These women suffer from deep despair because they are, in fact, often powerless to do anything about their situation. They experience intense isolation, and they have less access than their male counterparts to facilities with which to arrest their addiction.

How are sex, money, and drugs tied together for poor women, and why are their risks thereby increased?

Drug users typically have "running partners"—people who shoot up together, scam, and generally spend time together. Drug-using women prefer male running partners for the protection they afford. But men prefer not to run with women and would rather have sexual relationships with "good" (non-drug using) women. Therefore, women tend to go to great lengths to secure a male running partner which often entails increased needle sharing, sex for protection, and for access to drugs.

Needle sharing is more likely to occur among female IDUs as a means of securing protection and due to their unequal access to clean syringes. Unchanged from early on in the epidemic is the fact that women IDUs are more likely to borrow needles to avoid arrest for possession and more likely to lend needles as a form of life insurance in order to secure help in the event of overdose.[12] Consequently, female IDUs are more often found to be sexually involved with another IDU, than male IDUs—doubling their risk of infection through two possible modes of transmission: injection drug use and sex with an infected man.[13] Needle exchange programs have been introduced in several major cities in order to address the rising rates of HIV infection among injection drug users. These needle-exchange programs, which seem to quickly replace the black market as a primary source of syringes in San Francisco, New York City, and Boston,[14] appear to be successful at reducing HIV transmission. But studies are indicating the possibility that these programs are less effective among women than among men.[15] Recent ethnographic research in New York City found that women drug users were more likely to share the same syringe with a companion, to inject with other users present, and to have drug users as sexual partners. Moreover, as compared to their male counterparts, these women used a more limited personal network of family, friends, and sexual partners for access to new syringes.[16] In sum, even with needle exchange programs reducing the rate of HIV transmission, women continue to be more at risk than men.

The statistics lay bare the disproportionate risk of infection for women. In Brooklyn, New York, new female injectors are becoming infected at twice the rate of male injectors the same age.[17] Unequal access to clean needles has been found to negatively impact women from the start. Female initiates to injection drug use are particularly likely to put themselves at risk for HIV as a consequence of differential access to clean needles. A recent Baltimore study of drug initiation among young women (18-22 years old) found that despite knowledge of HIV when first introduced to injection drugs, more than three quarters of the women used a "hitter" (someone to inject the drugs for them) and half injected with a used cooker (a component of drug injection paraphernalia, usually a bottle cap, used to heat the drug and from which the drug is extracted into the syringe).[18] First use of injection drugs often requires assistance and is thus a particularly likely time for infection to occur. Initiates are taught how to tie off, find a vein, "flag" it (determine that the needle is actually in the vein by pulling blood into the syringe), and then inject. All this is often demonstrated with a borrowed syringe. Here we see how social policies, such as paraphernalia laws, together with gender inequalities, affect the day-to-day survival of drug-addicted women. What naturally follows is the fact that nearly one hundred percent of HIV-infected women in Massachusetts state prisons have injection drug use as their primary risk factor.[19]

Sex and drugs tend to be linked in drug-using women's lives. It is not uncommon for women to provide sexual favors to drug dealers out of desperation for drugs, a circumstance to which women crack users appear to be particularly susceptible.[20] In New York City, research suggests that 75 percent of crack-addicted sex workers engage in fellatio exclusively for drug money, an activity that clearly puts women at greater risk than men. The virus gains easy entrance into the bloodstream through mouth lacerations from crack smoking as well as due to the higher rates of genital ulcerations among female crack users.[21]

Ironic as it may seem, women resort to prostitution for drug money (as they do with needle sharing and the development of sexual relationships with fellow IDUs) partly because they tend to be more risk-aversive than their male counterparts.[22] They do not choose to sell sex for money or drugs because prostitution is safe—women are often raped and beaten while working the streets. They sell sex because the legal repercussions of arrest are minimal compared to alternative forms of crime: e.g, drug dealing, robbery, or fencing stolen goods. Arrest for prostitution usually entails a night in jail and payment of a $50-100 fine. Most women working on the streets have children to care for and cannot risk more severe sentences.

The irony is that the very measures women take to protect themselves—to reduce the risk of arrest and violence, and the need to resort to dangerous and demeaning acts— make them more vulnerable to HIV infection. The decision of addicted women to be "safe" on some fronts almost forces them to put themselves at risk for AIDS.[23]

Female sex-workers face particular challenges in trying to protect themselves from infection. In a desperate attempt to communicate the need for condom use to "johns," female sex-workers spray-painted a message on an abandoned city billboard in Worcester, Massachusetts, with the warning "WE CHARGE FOR _SEX_, _AIDS_ IS

FREE!" Women were driven to devise shopping lists of strategies to protect themselves and their clients from infection when men resisted condom use. An HIV-positive, 15-year veteran of those very streets details the difficulties of negotiating condom use, which to the john often means less gratification and "dirty" sex:

Interviewer: "Do you think these guys realize the risk and they just don't care?"

Ann: "I just think that they're ignorant slobs, basically. Some of these guys are business men driving around in Mercedes and BMWs and they'll look at me and they'll go, "I'm clean, are you?" What are you gonna say, "No, I'm a festering pool of pus, but give me all your money?" I mean, from the guy who doesn't even own a car to a Cadillac [owner], that's it—I know I'm clean, are you. A lot of them will say to you, "Do you use drugs?" If I say no, that clears their conscience. Now what girl out there is about to say, "Yeah I do?"

Interviewer: When he says, "I'm clean, are you?" Do you say...

Ann: Yeah, I lie.

Interviewer: And then do you use a condom?

Ann: Well, first you start off dickering on money. I have had guys who don't want to wear rubbers and want vaginal sex. And what I say is " I've had the test, and it came back negative, and I don't know who you've been with—probably every other hooker in the city!" Usually I throw a little guilt on them. I'll say, "Do you really want to take it home to your wife or girlfriend?" With vaginal sex, I would say most men do [use a condom].

What is the link between isolation, powerlessness, and the spread of HIV?

The common denominator for poor, drug-using women appears to be their limited power to control the course of their lives. Women fare worse than men not because of their gender, but because of sexism: unequal power relations between the sexes. More often than not, assertion of power (no matter what the context) is not even an option for poor women. One drug-using woman's explanation of why she injects sheds some light on how drug abuse and powerlessness go hand in hand:

I was really confused about where my place was in society: that I didn't even deserve to hold a job. Sometimes I felt like I didn't deserve to eat 'cause I didn't feel worth anything.

Knowing how someone with HIV became infected is to know only where the misery of their lives has led, not when it began and for how long it has been endured. [24] It is often assumed that a woman becomes HIV-infected because she has failed to protect herself sufficiently. Yet, we find that the social forces limiting women's control over whether they can support their children through work, find prenatal care when needed, and find an affordable place to live are the very same forces that affect their control over HIV risks. It should therefore not be surprising to find particularly high rates of sexual and physical abuse among poor women, especially among drug-using women. A recent study of women receiving HIV care at Boston City Hospital found that 74-80 percent had undergone injury and/or nonconsensual sex and had identified domestic violence as a significant health concern.[25] A New York City study of female IDUs found that over 60 percent had been physically abused as adults. The study concludes that long histories of drug and physical abuse "leave many women believing that they cannot control their lives or bodies—especially in transactions with men involving drugs and sex."[26] National studies show that 78 percent of sex workers interviewed underwent forced sexual intercourse before the age of fourteen.[27] Virtually all of the 100 crack users interviewed in a South Bronx drug treatment center were found to have experienced violent trauma in their lives.[28] The circumstances in which women are forced to have sex against their will are very often the same circumstances in which women become infected with HIV. A recent study at the Massachusetts Correctional Facility for Women found that inmates who report sexual abuse as children were three times more likely to be infected with HIV.[29] In many ways, women drug users are the most obvious victims of structural violence.

Drug-using women experience loneliness, isolation, and depression, if not more often, then certainly more profoundly than others do.[30] And no wonder. They are often stigmatized and marginalized, assumed to be disease-carriers, even by other drug-users. One male IDU, asked by an interviewer about how he would react if a female sex partner asked him to use a condom, illustrates how women are likely to be distrusted:

Remi: I don't know, I haven't crossed that bridge.

Interviewer: Do you think you'd say ...?

Remi: I don't know, it probably depends on what condition I was in at the time. Whether I was sober or drunk. Probably would. Basically, I probably look at them like they was crazy. I guess my second thought would be, "What, you got something?" Then my antennas would come up. "What's happening?"

Interviewer: Cause it seldom happens to you?

Remi: It never happens.

Interviewer: You'd immediately think...

Remi: Yeah, something's wrong with her.

A series of interviews with the predominantly female sexual partners of male injection drug users (many of whom also had substance abuse problems) show that 82 percent experienced depression and anxiety about aspects of their lives over which they felt they had no control, such as finding a place to live, obtaining a better life for their children, and finding a job. A woman from Boston spoke with particular clarity about the sources of her pain:

> One, I don't have no money. I was homeless and had anxiety. I got tired of looking for a job, runnin' to this place and that place. To handle my depression the only way is to sell drugs. The money was there. It kind of lifted me up.

Mary, who sought recovery from addiction when her ten year old said to her, "Momma, we don't want to live with you anymore," talks about the burdens of being a single mother and a drug addict:

> When I started to see the things I didn't care to see, the loneliness, unhappiness and emptiness, I did drugs to ease the pain... I tried to carry the world by myself. When the weight of the world became too heavy, I escaped, time after time, by doing drugs.

It is easy to see how poverty can induce social isolation and depression, but one might ask how isolation affects one's risk for HIV infection. Consider one Worcester woman's explanation of why an addict would share a needle for reasons other than a lack of access:

> Addicts tend to isolate themselves. You're out there on the streets and
> you're all by yourself. And most people out there are very lonely. It's
> almost a way of communicating or making a bond between people. I've
> seen many people get together and say, 'Okay, what do you have?' And
> they'll put it together. The next question is, 'Who's got the works?' It's a
> way of bonding 'em together, you know? [31]

One possible way out of the drug-addicted lifestyle and consequent risk of contracting HIV is to seek recovery from addiction.
However, we find that women with drug problems are marginalized to
an even greater extreme than others, which may impede their recov-
eries. Just six years ago drug treatment programs in this country did
not admit pregnant women.[32] Such programs simply announced that
they were not equipped to handle pregnant women. A recent study of
the accessibility of drug treatment for women in five major U.S. cities
found that while most programs will now accept a pregnant woman,
her options for treatment are severely restricted if she is seeking childcare or is a Medicaid recipient.[33] One grave consequence of women's
exclusion from drug treatment is the rising number of children born
to HIV infected mothers. In New York City between 1991 and 1993
the number of foster children born to infected mothers increased 26
percent.[34] Based on a collection of studies, the GAO (General
Accounting Office) reports that 78 percent of foster children in New
York City, Pennsylvania, and Los Angeles are at high risk for HIV
based on a single risk factor: injection drug use by their mothers.[35] My
own research among drug-using women suggests that women most
want to recover when they are pregnant.

Although there are many factors that deter women from seeking help for drug dependency, the institutional barriers are the most
significant. With jail often the only place where women experience
life without drugs, it is hardly surprising that many find it difficult to
break out of the cycle of addiction. Until a successful class action suit
in 1992, the only recourse for pregnant women wanting treatment
was imprisonment; no treatment program would have them. Many
then thought of jail time as detox time. As Tammy exclaimed when
interviewed while in treatment for the first time, "This is the first
time that I've been clean this long without having to be locked up."

But as we have seen all along, "One step forward, two steps back." As the "war on drugs" continues to escalate, the most recent effort to "crack down" on the drug user denies pregnant women the option to utilize the treatment programs they have recently won the right to enter. Twenty-four states have already prosecuted women for ingesting drugs when pregnant and for murder if their children died. The number of these prosecutions tripled between 1990 and 1992.[36] It should come as no surprise that the majority of these women were poor and African-American—women who are especially vulnerable to this type of structural violence.

3. THE GOVERNMENT'S ROLE IN HIV INFECTION AMONG WOMEN

How have women been ignored?

The history of the AIDS epidemic in the United States has been a history of a struggle against disinformation. This fact has been especially true for women. There has been no lack of information on women's risk of AIDS, but it has been mostly misinformation. Women were told that they were much less at risk for HIV than men, and that they did not have AIDS, even as they *were* dying from it. Thousands of women have died from AIDS without receiving any financial assistance and without gaining access to experimental drugs, to clinical trials, or even to proven therapies that could have prolonged their lives. Despite testing HIV-positive and exhibiting symptoms of depressed immune function, women were excluded from clinical trials because their symptoms simply did not match the criteria for an AIDS diagnosis.[37]

Throughout the epidemic, women's risk for HIV and the reasons for their disproportionate risk have been obscured. Overwhelming evidence of this fact became apparent during 1993 when the Centers for Disease Control revised its case definition to include opportunistic infections in women, effectively tripling AIDS case rates.

The U.S. government has not recognized women's economic needs as the primary caretakers of children. It has not recognized women as prisoners of domestic abuse, and in its decision to make enormous cuts in Medicaid, the principal health care program for poor women, it is certainly ignoring the obvious link between poverty and risk of HIV infection. Such efforts to balance the budget on the backs of poor women are destined to diminish further the opportunities for poor women to benefit from early detection of HIV infection and treatment.[38] The biggest obstacle to reducing the spread of HIV is neither a lack of resources nor a lack of knowledge, but a lack of political resolve to use existing resources and information in order to reduce the number of lives HIV will take.[39]

In addition to deceiving the public about women's risk for HIV, the government has, in many ways, also worsened the conditions that put women at greater risk. For the last decade two sets of policy changes have further impoverished women: changes in policy that are related directly to HIV, as well as changes in anti-poverty policies that have immediate effects on women's health.

Gaining access to health care is increasingly difficult for women in the United States. They are more likely to be uninsured or underinsured and are less represented in a variety of clinical trials (two-thirds of federal funding for STDs goes to treating men).[40] Moreover, women bear the burden of pathology (e.g., sterility, pelvic inflammatory disease, and salpingitis).[41] Despite their greater health care needs during the child-bearing years, the proportion of women receiving early prenatal care actually declined between 1980 and 1989: by nearly two percent for all women and three percent for black women, after a steady increase during the 1970s.[42]

Despite evidence from European cities as early as 1986 that needle exchange programs have a profound effect on curbing the epidemic among drug users and their sexual partners, a two-year pilot program was not instituted in Boston until 1993. The sluggish response of the state has, in effect, permitted infection rates among Boston's IDUs to rise an average of four percent each year since 1990—from 17 percent to a current rate of over 40 percent.[43] With nearly half of all women becoming infected through injection drug use, this failure to act promptly has harmed women particularly.

States bear much of the burden of providing substance abuse treatment because the federal government has reallocated substance abuse prevention to state and private industry over the past 15 years, and because most drug users lack medical insurance. In the face of the expanding AIDS epidemic, the Commonwealth of Massachusetts has cut spending on the treatment of substance abuse by 20 percent during the last five years.[44] For those who choose recovery to avoid the risk of HIV infection or transmission, it takes longer to get into treatment than it did three years ago.

In short, Massachusetts has not just displayed a lack of commitment to the problem of addiction; the state has actually reduced services in the inner city amidst an epidemic. This is exactly what some African Americans feared in their opposition to needle exchange, which they regarded as "a threat to the efforts to prevent drug abuse."[45] With decreasing access to treatment, the original goal of needle exchange as an interim step to reduce harm becomes compromised. Boston's new needle exchange project, for example, gives drug users the choice to inject with a clean needle, but less choice about whether they will die from addiction itself.[46]

Annual increases in the number of female-headed households, the continuing tradition of women working for 60 percent of men's wages, and the exportation of wage-labor jobs to the third world are obvious threats to women's economic survival. Data from the Center for Budget and Policy Priorities in 1991 show that two-thirds of U.S. citizens living in poor families with children were living with a tax-paying worker.[47] The GAO, an independent watchdog agency for government programs, found that to be eligible for Aid to Families with Dependent Children (AFDC) benefits—a program for single parent families—recipients must have monthly incomes that are well below the poverty line. In fact, women were forced to make less money in 1988 than in 1980 before being eligible for government services.[48] Increases in the number of those living in poverty were particularly felt among single-parent families with children, pushing over one million more families below the poverty line.[49] As of January 1994, the poverty threshold for a family of three was $1,027 per month, and many states have income eligibility cutoffs that are less than half that amount.[50]

Work is simply not enough to lift many families out of poverty.[51] In fact, the two types of families examined by the GAO

(AFDC and the working poor) were frequently the same families observed at different points in time. While almost 64 percent of welfare recipients are back in the workforce within two years, between two-thirds and three-quarters who leave welfare return within five years.[52]

How does the "war on drugs" affect poor women, in particular?

One factor that accounts for this cycling in and out of dire poverty is that women increasingly find themselves on their own raising children.[53] And one reason for this increase in single parenting is that so many men are in prison. In fact, the fastest growing public housing in this country is the prison system, where 60 percent of men in prison serve time for drug-related charges.[54] With one out of every three young black men involved with the criminal justice system (in prison, awaiting trial, or on probation), the problem of fatherless children cries for deeper analysis.

Unjust criminal sentences for small-time drug dealers and the "three strikes and you're out" crime bill (mandating that state judges impose life sentences on third-time "violent" offenders) exemplify the reactionary stance of government policy makers who see poverty and substance abuse as personal problems with individualistic solutions.[55] Mandatory minimum sentences almost exclusively target those in poor urban communities (where often the only thriving business is the drug trade). Possession of five grams of crack cocaine, for example, translates into a mandatory five-year prison sentence. Possession of the same amount of powdered cocaine results in a minimum 10 months of probation. Increasingly hard to ignore is the fact that crack is the poor man's high.[56] One effect of the large black prison population is that there are fewer young black men for women to marry and fewer stable families.[57]

We have seen that there are numerous trends contributing to the institutionalized poverty of women: AFDC cuts, minimum wage employment, and the incarceration of black men. These are not simple problems, other than in the sense of what is right and wrong.

What is inexplicably wrong with this social scenario is that when young men are sent to jail, women are also penalized. In an era when even middle class families need two incomes to make ends meet, women are consequently forced to take minimum-wage jobs on which they cannot support a family, forced to become welfare recipients, and forced to experience the pain and misery of poverty in a country with more billionaires than any other country in the world. The war on drugs is increasingly a war on the drug user and on entire communities where poverty makes drug use one of the few viable economies.

What remains when we take the
"personal" out of poverty?

In her accounts of the lives of welfare mothers, Valerie Polakow stresses that proponents of social policies that export working class jobs, raise the taxes of the poor, and demonize those who suffer the consequences have succeeded in "advancing the pernicious idea that poverty is a private affair, that destitution and homelessness are simply products of bad personal choices."[58] In fact, poverty and the stigma of HIV infection share a common legacy of being popularly linked to personal responsibility.

The strictly medical "cause" of AIDS is a virus that lodges and multiplies in human bodies in a fashion that systematically destroys the immune response to fight infection. But humans exist not just in their bodies but in a social world, and therefore the etiology of AIDS is often seen as not just a virus. AIDS is commonly perceived as a sign of moral weakness, of promiscuity and illegal behavior. Beyond the beliefs about how AIDS is contracted, a more fundamental (and certainly more empirically accurate) cause of the perpetuation of AIDS is poverty. Poverty as a dynamic force requires individuals to reprioritize their lives based on survival, often at the expense of well-being. Poverty destabilizes lives, crushes self-esteem, and creates an apartheid between those who have economic power and those who do not. I offer the following narrative from Keith, a now recovered drug user, as a source of insight into the social forces at issue:

The ghetto to me was like living in a maze. There was no way out. What I did was to just keep filtering in and out, in and out of the maze trying to find a way out. By the time I understood that there was an open door, that I could actually get out, I was comfortable enough that I didn't even want to. I felt like I had wasted so much time and done so much bad, that I wouldn't even be accepted into the new world.

Just at that time, a program that trains you for a good job came into my life and made me feel that maybe I could change the way my life was going. I got a job at the Department of Employment Security. I felt like I was on top of the world. But really, I was uncomfortable. I was in a place that I thought I shouldn't be. It was a whole new world. I'd sit in the lunchroom and I'd hear people talking about advancement and I didn't think that I had the qualifications to bring myself up. My actions were so totally different from other people's. I had like a "ghetto mentality" even though I could act "as if" very, very well. They taught me that in technical language from the start. But I wasn't feeling what I was doing. I wasn't feeling good about where I was. I didn't know anything about accomplishments. If I had known all of that I think I could have made it, but I didn't know the steps. I was told in my neighborhood that I was a "token nigger" 'cause I worked downtown. That hurt me so I had to get high on the job to feel comfortable. There weren't many blacks working in my office and the guys in the neighborhood helped me doubt myself. It worked well because that was my whole life anyway, downing myself. I got promoted, I had my own office, my own desk, name plate and telephone, and that scared the hell out of me and I resigned.

Keith poignantly shows us that poverty is about the mechanisms that keep people in their "proper" place. It marginalizes, stigmatizes, and erodes human agency and leads to dependence and powerlessness. Poverty effectively prevents individuals and entire communities from reconceptualizing problems, imagining different alternatives, and creating new solutions.[59] This is how the personalization of poverty is internalized.

Poverty is not a single condition: its causes and effects on poor people change historically. In the aftermath of the colonial era, which had ravaged entire cultures through slavery, slaughter, and redistribution of land to the wealthy, the resultant poverty needed to be managed. "Development" programs were instituted throughout the world. While the structures of misery are perpetuated through the same sources of oppression domestically, development rhetoric such as "lifting peasants from the chains of poverty" did not extend to our own urban poor. In the United States, low-income persons are, by the "nature" of their social realities, criminally suspect.[60] To be poor in a rich society implies the additional burden of social exclusion. This is particularly true for women and minorities.[61]

The most severely poor have been labeled as "the underclass." These "undeserving" poor are commonly perceived as poor not because of economic realities such as lost employment, low wages, or other factors they could not control, but because they will not work and exist at the margins of society. The underclass could "bring down the great cities, sap resources from the entire society and, lacking the usual means to survive, prey upon those who possess them."[62] Only in the United States, says sociologist Wacquant, is "public assistance presumed to cause rather than alleviate urban ills." [63]

While perceptions of the poor have changed little, this is not the case for the cause of poverty. In *The New American Poverty*, Michael Harrington emphasized that we must speak of *poverties*, because the poverty in America today is different from the poverty of the 1930s or the 1960s. There are new structures of misery in the 1980s and 1990s.[64] Contemporary poverty can no longer be understood primarily as a lack of material resources and economic power. In a new world order that generates inequalities by design, we must consider new social policies and institutions in order to understand poverty.[65] In the 1970s, writes Harrington, the American poor began to suffer in unprecedented ways as a result of a reshaping of the occupational structure of the U.S. economy. This reshaping has in effect created a poverty more difficult to defeat than any before it. These new structures of misery for the U.S. poor are characterized by the disappearance of manufacturing jobs, unions that no longer represent a vital social and political force, and an absence of domestic policies to keep U.S. multinational corporations loyal to workers in this country.

During the recessions of the 1980s, changes in tax policy and sharp cuts in social security and welfare under the Reagan administration reinforced the general downward trend for the nation's poor. Taxes for the poorest fifth in the nation jumped from 9 percent to 12 percent of their income. Tax rates for the richest fifth actually declined by 0.5 percent. In the Reagan era, Americans turned against the poor. Fearing for their own economic security, Americans "who had welcomed the War on Poverty now supported the war on the poor."[66] This posturing continues as the seven-year budget plans are implemented with political support from both Republicans and Democrats, making cuts in welfare spending six and one-half times deeper than Reagan's.[67]

To blame the poor for their plight, when social policies reinforce the difficulties of escaping poverty, represents a kind of structural violence. Structural violence puts people at risk for poor health and social outcomes like drug use, incarceration, family dysfunction, and HIV. Poor women's HIV risk has been created not by neglect, but rather by a social planning which redistributes wealth as if the poor do not matter.[68]

4. THE USE OF CULTURE AND THE CONSTRUCTION OF DENIAL TO EXPLAIN THE GROWING AIDS EPIDEMIC AMONG WOMEN

How have social scientists overlooked the driving force of poverty in their research on AIDS?

Modern poverty is the product of political decisions. Governments choose to deny the poor basic social goods. Many social scientists ignore this social reality in their analysis of HIV transmission. AIDS researchers, in effect, obscure the relationship between poverty and HIV infection among women by using explanatory models focused on the "beliefs" and "attitudes" of infected individuals. Some of these models have inadequate theories of "culture" or focus on "culture" as the main cause of the spread of the virus; some use psychological labels such as "denial" to explain HIV infection among women. The absence of a critical analysis of the role of poverty as a driving force in accelerating rates of HIV among women limits the development of programs to address the fundamental determinants of risk. Social scientists have surrendered either to following in ignorance the public health principles of disease prevention or to ethnicizing the issue. This is done at the expense of seeing some of the most glaring, historical economic disparities.[69] The time has come to abandon the false belief that individual behaviors and cultural norms, once they are "corrected," will prevent further spread of HIV.

While no single approach dominates ethnographic studies of HIV prevention and understanding of AIDS, social scientists have positioned themselves as the "cultural experts." The scholarly tradition of social science developed as a discipline to explore the richness of cultural differences and the means by which culture shapes human action. As HIV prevention strategies emerged, many called for "culturally sensitive and appropriate" education. We produced thick descriptions of the nuances and intricacies of sex and drug-taking practices. We linked these behaviors with "cultural beliefs" and connected AIDS meanings with "social context," so as to inform prevention education.

Ostensibly, our orientation to the problem of AIDS prevention offered a new perspective on the *causes* of AIDS because we addressed topics like culture. So far much of our published research has informed colleagues about sectors of society previously unexplored through the ethnographic lens. Our work has introduced a certain reading public to the underworld of the street addict ("the drug culture") and to the sex lives of gay bathhouse patrons, teens, and others.

Social scientists' mode of inquiry and investigation has demonstrated to government funding institutes that our methods of data collection often generate very interesting results. What other kind of academic would "hang out" in a shooting gallery in order to understand the nuances of needle sharing and the negotiations of needle cleaning among drug users? Similarly, ethnographic work has led many to discover the category of men who have sex with men but do not consider themselves gay or bisexual, and, more recently, a population ignored by HIV prevention educators—the transgendered population.[70] In the decade of social science research on AIDS, such methodologies have put social scientists on the map and back into the network of government funding agencies such as the National

Institute on Drug Abuse and the National Institutes of Mental Health. Rare indeed are the major research projects that do not now call for an ethnographer on the team.

An aspect of our work that has generated particular appeal is our insistence that HIV prevention programs be developed in a manner that is culturally sensitive, culturally appropriate, and culturally innovative (a creative reshaping of existing values to accomplish the objectives of behavior change-oriented prevention programs).[71] This chapter addresses the issue of cultural sensitivity and its use in social science research on AIDS not because social scientists take this approach as "the answer" to successful HIV prevention, but because it is both a common approach and one that is gaining popularity in other disciplines. Increasingly, researchers perceive this approach as *the* contribution of social scientists and as the direction in which they should proceed.

Yet there lurks a dark side to this newly popularized approach. How we use culture to talk about AIDS may generate more harm than good. In particular, promoting a culturally sensitive approach at the expense of addressing structural issues— poverty, economic vulnerability, and legislation that negates poor women's needs— obscures the fundamental forces continuing to drive up the incidence of infection. Essentially, this prevailing orientation to culture in HIV research and prevention planning has done little good for poor women and threatens to do them much harm.

The following three articles are emblematic of this trend of using "culture" to explain rising HIV infection rates. In their article, "Barriers to Condom Use and Needle Cleaning Among Impoverished Minority Female Injection Drug Users and Partners of Injection Drug Users," Nyamathi and colleagues argue that AIDS education programs must be culturally sensitive in order to "motivate effectively women and their partners to reduce risky behavior and reinforce new health-promoting behavior."[72] In "HIV Seroprevalence in Female Intravenous Drug Users: The Puzzle of Black Women's Risk," Lewis and Watters propose that a culturally appropriate approach to prevention might help to alleviate the denial of HIV risk among black drug-using women. And Bayer (working in the field of public health) embraces the social science emphasis on culture in his article, "AIDS Prevention and Cultural Sensitivity: Are They Compatible?" He cautions, though, that the role of culture can be overemphasized, but not because such overemphasis marginalizes the role of other social forces. Instead, he argues that cultural issues can become inextricably tied up with political and moral issues, a development to be avoided at all costs. He offers as an example the early opposition to needle exchange by members of the African American community. The first two sets of authors acknowledge the effect of poverty on HIV transmission, but keep it at arm's length, while Bayer seems to want to skirt these issues altogether. As we shall see in Chapter 5, these articles are examples of a much larger body of literature which ignores, marginalizes, or depoliticizes the profound impact of poverty on the rising rates of HIV infection among U.S. women.

This critique of these articles should be understood not as a critique of the authors, but as an example of how social scientists with the best of intentions can come to make immodest claims of causality. Many of us are guilty of emphasizing cultural and subcultural "explanations" of HIV transmission at the expense of issues of poverty and powerlessness. After all, we are called on *because* we are supposed to be the cultural experts. In each case, the critiques that follow are not meant to extend to authors' work as a whole.

Nyamathi and colleagues' (1995) study was undertaken to describe sexual behaviors, drug use, and other factors that inhibit condom use and needle cleaning among "impoverished women" who are injection drug users or sexual partners of IDUs. This study also investigated whether risky sexual behavior or barriers to risk reduction differ with ethnicity and level of acculturation.[73] Their research is based on the findings of a series of questionnaires administered to 378 "impoverished minority women" (256 African American and 122 Latinas between 18 and 69 years of age), primarily recruited from Los Angeles homeless shelters, drug treatment programs, and— in a few cases— directly from the street. All these women were either injection drug users and/or the sexual partners of IDUs. Over 80 percent injected drugs or used crack cocaine. The research sought to determine the frequency of unprotected sex and barriers to condom use and needle cleaning among these women. The article briefly describes factors related to drug abuse and obstacles to AIDS prevention which primarily focus on individual behavior and culture (particularly the gender roles in "Latino culture").

The study found that the most common barriers to condom use were women believing that their partners did not have AIDS, limited skills in the use of condoms, lack of access to condoms, and a lack of skills negotiating condom use with their partner. The most pervasive barriers to needle cleaning were not having access to needles, not having a hiding place for needles, no interest in cleaning when high, and not having disinfectant to clean with. Sexually-active women who reported having an injection drug-using partner were more likely to engage in unprotected sex than women who were only IDUs. Women with multiple partners were more likely to report unprotected sex. On the other hand, of all the women in the study over 80 percent had unprotected sex and close to 60 percent reported needle sharing with 40 percent not making any attempt to disinfect.

As is the case with many articles on the topic of women and AIDS, Nyamathi and colleagues minimize the distress of poverty. They refer to "impoverished women" throughout the article and yet fail to operationalize the term, essentially glossing over it as if it were simply a given for this population. Even when they find that there are no significant differences in risk behaviors between these women based on ethnicity or acculturation, they continue to focus on these two factors and the non-statistically-significant *differences* between them rather than on what these poor women might have in common. In fact, like Lewis and Watters, they psychologize the problems of poverty and focus on culturally competent delivery of AIDS education.

Examples of this bias come through when Nyamathi and co-workers write of: "the strong belief among impoverished women that their partners do not have AIDS"[74] Is this any different than middle-class and rich women who are also likely to believe strongly that their partners do not have AIDS? Similarily, they assert that "Culturally competent strategies are necessary to motivate women and their partners to reduce risky behaviors and reinforce new health-promoting behavior."[75] How culturally competent strategies can help convince "unmotivated" women to take precautions is never explained. If motivation is really the problem, would it not be more productive to assist women around the issue of being poor and drug-addicted in the hope that seeing a way out of their poverty might make a difference in their level of motivation?

The authors also promote a naive assumption that these women's sexual encounters are with sexual *partners*. Given the high rate of injection drug use in the sample (62 percent) and the fact that the non-injectable drug of choice was crack (even among non-IDUs), how women defined their sexual encounters was left unexplored. Nyamathi and co-workers either assumed that sexual partners include those with whom the women had sex purely for money or drugs, or that the issue of transactional sex was unimportant to the study. It was suggested that empowering women with assertiveness skills to use and negotiate the use of condoms is needed. More than likely, many of the women's assumed sexual partners are actually sexual encounters for obtaining money or drugs and are therefore unlikely occasions for *insisting* on condoms (even though condoms are more likely to be used in these encounters than in intimate relationships).

The authors do mention that financial, transportation, and childcare issues are barriers to attending health clinics and risk reduction education, but this is noted as an aside and not explored. Recommendations for culturally competent prevention still takes precedence. Despite the fact that more than 80 percent of the women took no precautions when having sex and more than 50 percent made no attempt to disinfect when sharing needles, the authors engage in the minutiae of comparing the two ethnic groups and even look at acculturation as a potential factor for increased risk-taking. What goes unmentioned is the fact that all or most of the women in the study are drug-addicted women and that poverty more than acculturation and ethnic/cultural differences continues to leave these women with little choice but to engage in risk.

In an article written on HIV seroprevalence among female IDUs, Lewis and Watters indicate that cultural sensitivity can bring understanding to the plight of HIV infection among black female drug users.[76] They allude to black women's generally poorer health status and higher rates of STDs, but then explain that the answer to "the mystery of black women's risk" is to be solved, ultimately, through generating "more culturally appropriate ways to elicit sensitive information." [77] The authors cite a study which found through intensive reinterviewing of blood donors that "87 percent of HIV-positives had initially denied high risk behavior." [78] They postulate that probing second interviews could uncover "denial" as the case for black women as well—a term becoming more and more popular among social and behavioral scientists as the epidemic worsens.

Lewis' and Watters' research failed to get to the bottom of why black women are the targets of HIV infection more often than white women. Like Nyamathi and colleagues, who call for a culturally sensitive approach, they essentialize this aspect of minority women's risk of HIV. Focusing on cultural sensitivity as the means of reducing HIV transmission resembles family planners' shortsighted focus on family size as the solution to poverty. [79]

In the paper's conclusion, Lewis and Watters make a disturbing link between risk behaviors and culture when they discuss "established" risk behaviors among women of color. "Our research suggests that established risk behaviors may be expressed in a more complex and less well understood manner among drug users and other populations at risk for the virus." [80] This formulation depoliticizes the phenomenon of HIV risk-taking and misapprehends the determinants of transmission. Within the communities Lewis and Watters discuss, what is "established" are the conditions of poverty which require women to bear risks they would otherwise not have to take. For poor women, sex can become a strategy for economic and psychological survival both in cases where sex is engaged in purely for money and drugs, and in relationships where women must depend on their sexual partners for food and rent money.

Lewis and Watters also postulate that women's "denial" plays a large role in their risk of infection and that culturally-relevant educational material can help break through the self-deception. This, they imply, is one of the positive results of culturally-appropriate research and prevention. Social and behavioral scientists and medical researchers increasingly use this label of "women in denial" in talk about risk for HIV in order to explain why women do not put knowledge of risk to use.[81]

While the term denial is rarely defined in this literature, researchers use it in ways which imply a reluctance to accept the shared reality of AIDS and a refusal to admit "the truth" about one's HIV risk-taking behaviors. Denial in this sense serves, however inadvertently, as a mechanism of blaming the victim. Faced with obvious failures to slow the rate of HIV transmission, HIV prevention theorists and educators seldom ask, "What are *we* doing wrong?" Too often they ask instead, "What are *they* doing wrong?"[82]

We cannot dismiss denial or culture altogether as factors affecting the response to AIDS among the poor. But most poor women clearly know about AIDS. They do not deny its existence, though often their responses are based on fear. They are afraid that they may become infected and that they will be labeled as "diseased" if they suggest to their partners that they use protection for mutual safety. The meaning of AIDS is constructed on the basis of one's personal, class, gender, and cultural experiences. For poor women touched by AIDS, the experiences of sexism, racism, and poverty dominate life and determine, above and beyond how AIDS is defined, what AIDS *means*. In light of this fact, commonly-heard statements mean more than merely a denial of or even resistance to the AIDS message:

> How can I avoid needle sharing or turn down a 'trick' who refuses a condom?

> Maybe I deserve to get this.

> They're trying to wipe us off the earth.

> They tell us to do the bleach and the water and the bleach and the water, but I don't trust that... [83]

When researchers speak only of how the women most at risk engage in self-deception and distortion of their vulnerability, these researchers ignore the essential context in which meanings are made. Some women are reluctant to believe that AIDS exists and appear to deny its gravity, but when we understand AIDS meanings within the context of extreme economic and psychological vulnerability, then "denial" begins to lose its explanatory power.

We should strike denial from our vocabulary, if we do not redefine its meaning to include the mechanisms by which the poor are at far greater risk for HIV. "Denial" scapegoats, dehumanizes, and especially depoliticizes women's struggle against structural violence. The "myth" of denial erases the context of fear, economic need, and relationships of power that shape poor women's decisions about HIV prevention. In fact, we should not use the term until we are ready to discuss the policy makers' denial of structural violence against poor women and the policy makers' ready recognition of cultural differences among different classes of women.[84] Responsible use of denial should include an explanation of how the poor are often powerless to avoid risk.

Whereas Lewis and Watters see a culturally-sensitive approach as a way to uncover denial, Bayer promotes limited use of cultural sensitivity in HIV education. But Bayer's work critiques cultural sensitivity not because it obfuscates the overriding factors of structural violence but because he sees that cultural sensitivity can illuminate political and moral issues which he claims have no place in public health discourse and practice.

Bayer expresses some appreciation for social scientists' use of cultural sensitivity in his article "Compatibility of AIDS Prevention and Cultural Sensitivity." [85] He stresses that AIDS prevention efforts that are not culturally sensitive are doomed to fail because they do not reach their intended audience as understandable or as acceptable messages. But he cautions readers against taking cultural sensitivity to the extreme and explains how the concept can degenerate into a dangerous radical form. He defines three kinds of cultural sensitivity (two beneficial, one detrimental): 1) semantic (sensitivity to cultural vernacular and language meaning); 2) instrumental (sensitivity defined as empowering women to be agents of change and resist prevailing sexist norms and practices—for example, empowering sex workers to demand their clients use condoms); 3) principled cultural sensitivity (the detrimental kind), in which respect for cultural integrity gives way to a relativism that ultimately defeats the objectives of public health. Bayer notes the "fierce opposition of the African American community to needle exchange" as an example of this principled cultural sensitivity. According to Bayer, this type of cultural sensitivity goes too far. He claims that the two "weakest" forms of cultural sensitivity "raise few problems" for public health, but "the strongest use of the term is incompatible with the goals of AIDS prevention" because it "compels us to think carefully about [the] political and moral warrant for public health intervention."[86]

Bayer's attack on "principled cultural sensitivity" inadvertently exalts structural violence. He advocates helping women in the sex industry "demand" safe sex (the sex worker version of Nancy Reagan's "just say no to drugs" campaign, because women are placed as the central focus of change), but chastises African Americans' insistence on addressing the structural conditions that have led to the rapid spread of HIV among minority IDUs. Political and moral issues do not belong in public health's efforts to prevent AIDS, he chides. In reply, we need only ask the organizers of ACT UP how many more thousands of gay men, drug users, and women would have died if ACT UP did not challenge the political and moral warrant of a public health response to this epidemic.

Bayer's call to remove political and moral issues from public health parallels the message of an earlier article "AIDS, Privacy, and Responsibilities" (1989), where he stresses that America needs a "cultural transformation" towards greater moral responsibility to limit the spread of AIDS. Here he clarifies that responsibility and morality have their place in limiting the AIDS epidemic, they just do not belong in public health policy and practice.

Bayer argues that America must assume the task of remaking American culture so as to "affect the private choices which determine the future of AIDS in America." He points to three behaviors as examples of impediments: needle sharing ("uninfected addicts will have to give up the ritual of needle sharing"), individual choice ("profound transformations" are required "in the way men, women, and adolescents choose to behave in the face risk... we are ultimately dependent on the emergence of a culture of restraint and responsibility to shape such choices"), and our capacity for denial ("Only a cultural transformation can affect the private choices that will determine the future of AIDS in America... impeding that transformation will be the psychological capacity for denial").[87] Bayer's prescription for HIV prevention calls for the "cultural transformation" of gay men, poor women, and injection drug users—but not for the structural transformation of a society that distributes risks so unevenly.

Why have researchers tended to minimize the effects of structural violence in poor women's lives?

In the social science literature in general, a focus on the personal lives of those most at risk has introduced a dialogue that encourages the use of psychological labels such as "HIV risk denial" to explain individual and community responses to this epidemic.[88] It is imperative that we re-read AIDS prevention literature to understand how both public health professionals and social scientists have used and coopted culture to explain (if only in part) the greater incidence of AIDS among minority populations. Phrases such as "cultural resistance" (Bayer's comment on the African American community's opposition to needle exchange), "cultural barriers to behavior change," and Lewis' and Watters' allusion to black women's "denial" of established risk behaviors are troubling examples of how researchers have collapsed culture into AIDS. Social scientists have rewritten social theory in order to distance themselves from the notion of a culture of poverty only to be found constructing a "culture of AIDS."[89]

Poor women will hear and understand standard HIV prevention messages, but they will not be able to heed them if their more immediate needs are not addressed. When a woman has little hope that her efforts to negotiate safer sex with clients or to enter drug treatment will be successful, there is little reason for her to face these problems. The constraints imposed by poverty and the blame levied by the powerbrokers and policy-makers who serve their own interests predate the epidemic. These factors constitute the conditions of social oppression that have brought HIV disproportionately to poor women. Why then have so many researchers tended to exaggerate the agency of women with HIV infection?

While important for any comprehensive prevention program, culturally sensitive approaches to HIV prevention fall short of explaining why current HIV prevention has not been effective at curtailing this epidemic. These approaches are limited, but not because they could become "too radical," as Bayer fears. They fall short because they often neglect to address class, poverty, and gender and the ways in which these factors shape and define culture. When we bring inequality and poverty to the foreground we develop a more fundamental set of questions, and we can move beyond vexations about how to convince individuals to change risky behavior. Our focus should be on the synergistic effects of these social afflictions and their impact on HIV transmission.[90]

The rates of HIV infection continue to rise among women of color. This problem creates an imperative: the problem of AIDS' disproportionate effect on "minority" communities should be understood *not* as a problem that rests with culture, "established risks," or "black resistance." To control the AIDS epidemic among women and ethnic minorities requires that we understand what they have in common, not simply what makes them culturally distinct. It is not the traditions of culture that place women, drug users, and ethnic minorities at risk for AIDS, but rather the traditions of poverty: that is, how mechanisms of control over resources are passed down from one generation to another and continually require a reinforcement of survival strategies, as those who have little are being forced to make do with less. Too great an emphasis on cultural beliefs and behaviors as barriers to HIV prevention obscures the truths of women's and ethnic minorities' lives.[91] The story of poverty and how it constrains the lives of women is one that should be told more often in social science research on AIDS.

5. CONCLUSION

We now know that substance abuse will be most prevalent among the oppressed, especially when their oppression involves direct assaults on personal dignity and cultural heritage. High rates of alcoholism among Native Americans and drug abuse among aborigines of Australia and African Americans in the United States are not to be understood without recourse to history. Theories that would "naturalize" the existing social order and disparate patterns of risks and burdens are ultimately both superficial and unambitious, as they seek to explain only the end results of long and painful processes.

A similarly rhetorical "War on Drugs" targets its victims. Small-time drug dealers go to prison, while boulevards are named after financiers who profit from this multibillion dollar trade. In the absence of effective treatment programs, the war on drugs has been a war on drug users.

This war on drugs takes many prisoners and leads to many unintended casualties, among them poor women. At this writing, a wave of enthusiasm for "welfare reform" is registered among the powerful, themselves the beneficiaries of corporate welfare. As corporate tax breaks rise, support for AFDC, public housing, Head Start, and other child-care programs dwindles. The total annual income from a minimum-wage job is $8,800, which would leave a family of three about $3,000 below the poverty line. For America's poor women, prospects for survival become even grimmer, especially for those with dependent children. HIV transmission is entangled in this struggle for survival. As one African American woman with AIDS deftly sums up the situation: "Gonna be a lot of $5, $10 AIDS going 'round. Gonna be people getting AIDS for a box of Pampers."[92]

Popular political discourses like the recent "Personal Responsibility Act" fit neatly into a time-honored tradition of hiding the agents of structural violence. Or perhaps it is we, the researchers, who slip too comfortably into the war against the poor? By relentlessly exploring the role of personal responsibility, and theorizing essential cultural and psychological links between the epidemics of drug addiction and AIDS, researchers may help to obscure the relationships between these scourges and their ultimate causes.

Despite ten years of research and prevention directed towards drug users, no social movement has emerged that is responsive to those who face unremitting violence in their lives. With respect to HIV prevention, we need to ask how poverty and marginality (in all their forms: racism, sexism, and classism) serve to undermine and crush the "positive behavior changes" we tout as the standards of HIV-prevention education.

A first step towards understanding women's unequal risk for AIDS is to characterize prevailing relationships of power. In order to speak of poverty, we must speak of power. If we fail to do so, we run the risk of poverty becoming (or rather, remaining) an empty word, a word that speaks of inevitability. "Poverty is a part of life." "There will always be poor people."

What can social scientists do beside cataloging the intricacies of the irrational calculations and behaviors through which individuals come into contact with this deadly virus? How can researchers avoid depoliticizing, psychologicalizing, and medicalizing social suffering in our writing on AIDS? How can we forcefully critique our work in ways that address the structures which put women at great and unequal risk? Wrestling with these questions is a key to unraveling the epidemic among poor women. Ultimately, the social sciences' contribution to the study of AIDS will be to show how systems generate inequality and how inequality structures AIDS risks and burdens.

CHAPTER FOUR

Women and HIV Infection

A Different Disease?

Johanna Daily, Paul Farmer, Joe Rhatigan,
Joel Katz and Jennifer Furin

1. INTRODUCTION

Although prevention is the most important strategy for curbing the AIDS pandemic, clinicians are called upon when prevention fails. Since we discuss prevention efforts in other chapters, we limit our discussion here to the care of women already infected with HIV. Through the experience of three women with HIV disease, we review a number of issues—gender-based differences in survival, under-recognition of HIV infection in women, and the effects of poverty and gender inequality on the course of HIV disease. We seek to ground our discussion in practical considerations, as our guiding question is a pragmatic one: what steps might be taken to deliver effective, high-quality care to *all* women with HIV infection?

Although this is a chapter for clinicians, it must be acknowledged at the outset that the clinics and hospitals in which we work mirror the inequalities of our world. Clinical issues—quality of care, the natural history of disease, algorithms for HIV management, pharmacological questions—cannot be divorced from the social and political realities which constrain medical care. Indeed, the gap between standard of care and the services now delivered are reflections of the structural violence discussed throughout this book. Although our discussion will focus on the clinical details of the three cases we present, we recognize that many clinical problems arise from and are complicated by systemic failures to provide adequate medical care to women living in poverty.

2. MONICA VINCENT

Monica Vincent was one of three children who had, by her own account, a difficult childhood involving multiple foster-care placements. As a teenager growing up in urban Connecticut, she briefly experimented with drugs, often sharing needles. At the age of 17, Monica gave birth to a daughter, but relinquished her to adoption, in large part because she was using drugs at the time. Not long after her pregnancy, she stopped taking drugs, never to use them again. She met Paul, a truck driver, when she was 21, and they were married three years later. Monica described their relationship as warm, strong, and healthy.

In 1991, Monica gave birth to Sandra, her second child and the couple's first. During this pregnancy, she discovered that she was infected with HIV. Her husband was found to be seronegative, as was their daughter.

Following her pregnancy, plagued by thrush, Monica sought further evaluation. Her physicians found that she had a CD4 count of less than $100/mm^3$. Zidovudine and trimethoprim/sulfamethoxazole were prescribed, but she stopped using them because of side effects. Alternative prophylaxis for *Pneumocystis carinii* pneumonia (PCP) was not prescribed.

Monica felt it was necessary to keep her HIV infection a secret from her family, except for her spouse, and from her friends. Her lack of attention to her own health worried her husband, but he felt unable to force the issue, according to later discussions with a social worker.

Monica and her husband had not planned her third pregnancy, which began in 1994. She received routine prenatal care, though her obstetrician was unaware of her HIV infection. She smoked cigarettes until about the twentieth week of gestation, when she abruptly stopped because she began to experience shortness of breath upon minimal exertion. As her dyspnea progressed, Monica was prescribed an oral antibiotic and bronchodilators.

In early May 1995, Monica presented to a community hospital emergency department with complaints of shortness of breath at rest. She was afebrile and tachypneic and required supplemental oxygen. A chest radiograph was felt to be consistent with an atypical pneumonia. The next morning, increasingly short of breath, she was transferred to a large teaching hospital for further management.

Physicians there started her on trimethoprim/sulfamethoxazole and prednisone for presumed PCP, a diagnosis subsequently confirmed by special stains of induced sputum. They also began therapy with zidovudine in order to minimize the risk of perinatal HIV transmission.

As Monica's oxygen requirements increased over the first day, she was transferred to the intensive care unit (ICU). In the ICU, Monica did well until early in the second week of her stay, when an episode of coughing led to severe hypoxia, requiring endotracheal intubation. The heart rate of her fetus began to slow approximately 15 minutes after intubation, and she underwent an emergency Cesarean-section delivery of a 3.3-pound baby girl. The infant was admitted to the neonatal ICU for mild respiratory distress, anemia, and prematurity, but did well during her stay there and was subsequently found to be HIV-negative.

When Monica became febrile the next day, the ICU team broadened her antibiotic coverage. Although she was still on a ventilator, she was able to see her baby for the first time that day. Two days after delivery, Monica's condition deteriorated. Although her antibiotic regimen had been tailored to cover potential aspiration, fungal, and cytomegaloviral pneumonias, she continued to do poorly. A week after delivery, she developed a left-sided pneumothorax, requiring placement of a chest tube.

After two weeks of intubation, hypoxic and febrile, Monica was only intermittently responsive. At the end of May, she developed septic shock and multisystem organ failure. Her family, including her husband, mother, and sister, agreed that her physicians should make no attempts at resuscitation. Monica Vincent died early on the morning of June 7, 1995. At autopsy, organizing pneumonia was found throughout both of her lungs with evidence of PCP and diffuse infection with cytomegalovirus.

3. FLOR BECERRA

Flor Alvarez was born in a small town in the Dominican Republic, where she lived until the age of 18, when she moved to the capital city. There she met Luis Becerra, a trader who traveled frequently to San Juan, Puerto Rico. They soon married, and Flor shortly thereafter had her first child, a boy. Two more children were born during their first four years of marriage.

Luis emigrated to Puerto Rico in 1979 and then to Florida a few months later. Flor and their youngest child followed him in 1980; the oldest two children remained in the care of Luis' mother. In the United States, Flor worked as a housekeeper and never sought medical care in the decade after her arrival because she was, in her estimation, "perfectly healthy." She gave birth to a fourth child in a public hospital in south Florida.

In July 1992, Flor presented to the emergency room of a large teaching hospital complaining of chest-wall pain. Her past medical history was significant only for cervical dysplasia and four uncomplicated vaginal deliveries. She took no medications. A physical exam revealed vesicular chest-wall lesions consistent with herpes zoster.

With no regular physician, Flor was referred to a county health facility for follow-up care with a public health nurse. A skin test for tuberculosis was markedly positive. Flor reported that she had a negative PPD test when she entered the United States in 1980, although she had received BCG vaccine in infancy. She was unaware of any recent exposure to people with active tuberculosis. It is unknown whether anyone ever offered her isoniazid or whether she did not accept treatment. In any case, she received no prophylaxis for tuberculosis.

Flor gave informed consent for serologic tests for HIV infection, and she received pretest counseling in Spanish. Her serologies were positive. Flor did not return for her test results, however, and no one was able to contact her by telephone.

In the emergency room of the same teaching hospital, physicians saw Flor again in January, 1993, when she presented with symptoms later attributed to *Candida* vaginitis. She was also found to be pregnant. During Flor's pregnancy, her husband was hospitalized with severe pneumococcal pneumonia and was himself diagnosed with HIV infection.

In July 1993, Flor gave birth to a low-birth-weight baby girl, subsequently found to be HIV-positive. Flor's CD4 count was 506/mm³ after a repeat HIV serology was positive.

For a period of eight months after delivery, Flor was said to have "disappeared." She received no follow-up care until March, 1994, when she returned to the same emergency room. Her chief complaints at that time were fevers and malaise, and she had lost over 20 pounds since her daughter's birth. Physical exam was significant for a temperature of 102 degrees and an enlarged spleen. She was anemic, with a hematocrit of 26 percent. A chest radiograph was felt to be unremarkable. Bacterial and mycobacterial sputum cultures were negative. Special stains of the same specimen for PCP were also negative. A "relatively high" CD4 count was cited as reassurance that her symptoms were unlikely to be due to an opportunistic pathogen, and further invasive workup was not pursued. Flor was sent home with a diagnosis of "viral syndrome."

Flor returned to the emergency room one week later with fevers up to 105 degrees, chills, and an increased cough. Unable to eat, she had lost another four pounds. A chest radiograph again revealed no infiltrates. Repeat sputum studies were negative for PCP, and Flor was admitted to the hospital with a diagnosis of "fever of unknown origin."

Persistent fevers, chills, and worsening dyspnea marked Flor's hospital course. A repeat CD4 count was 484/mm³. On her third hospital day, bilateral infiltrates developed, and she was started on trimethoprim/sulfamethoxazole as well as supplemental oxygen. She had a negative PPD test, although she was noted to be anergic. Stains from a bronchoscopy were non-diagnostic.

On hospital day four she was transferred to the ICU for worsening hypoxemia and increasing lung infiltrates. On hospital day nine, attending physicians added empiric antituberculous therapy after a miliary pattern was noted on chest radiograph. Flor required mechanical ventilation shortly thereafter. Stains from a repeat bronchoscopy were again non-diagnostic.

Flor died four days later. Specimens from both of her bronchoscopies grew *Mycobacterium tuberculosis* susceptible to all first-line antituberculous agents. At this writing, Luis Becerra has advanced to AIDS. Their four children in the United States, including the newborn, are in the care of an aunt.

4. MARIE ANGE VIAUD

Marie Ange Viaud, a 24-year-old native of rural central Haiti, presented in April, 1989 to a small clinic with complaints of cough and night sweats for three weeks. She had lost weight, and had been amenorrheic for more than two months. But it was an episode of hemoptysis—about "a cupful" of bright red blood—that precipitated her first visit to the clinic. She was then afebrile, with a normal blood pressure, and weighed 96 pounds. Physical exam was significant only for rhonchi in her right upper lung fields. A chest radiograph revealed two large cavitary lesions in the right apex as well as a right paratracheal infiltrate and old, healed granulomata in the left hilum and apex. Sputum was floridly positive for acid-fast bacilli, and Marie Ange was started, that day, on antituberculous therapy. Within two weeks, her cough and night sweats had resolved. She gained seven pounds in her first month of treatment and tolerated the medications well.

Marie Ange was seen on a monthly basis over the next year. She continued to gain weight, and experienced no recrudescence of symptoms, although a community health worker associated with her care suggested that she was not fully compliant with her medications. In October, 1989, Marie Ange's husband, also a native of the region, presented with tuberculosis. His chest radiograph, like Marie's, suggested reactivation disease, rather than primary tuberculosis. Not much was made of this coincidence, however, until February 1990, when Marie Ange returned with recurrent night sweats, fevers, and cough. She had lost six pounds over the three preceding months and also complained of intermittent diarrhea. Her sputum was again laden with acid-fast bacilli. Stools were negative for ova and parasites. Other studies revealed a mild anemia. It was not possible, at that time, to obtain a chest radiograph.

Marie Ange claimed she was taking her antituberculous medications, but both her husband and the community health worker, who was making home visits at that time, contested her claim. Two additional drugs were added to her regimen, and she also received an empiric course of mebendazole to treat a possible parasitic infection as the cause of her diarrhea.

Marie Ange began receiving daily visits from her community health worker, and physicians from the clinic, who as part of a retreatment protocol saw her weekly, also visited her at home. Two weeks after she was diagnosed with recurrent tuberculosis, an HIV test was performed; it was positive, as was her husband's.

Marie Ange again responded to antituberculous medications, and her symptoms resolved fairly promptly. In May 1990, however, she presented to the clinic with low-grade fevers, a sore throat, and persistent diarrhea. Her weight was stable. Examination of her oropharynx suggested thrush. Her lungs remained clear. Laboratory studies at that time showed *Isospora belli* cysts in stool and yeast in her sputum. She had a more significant anemia, and her CD4 count was estimated to be $280/mm^3$. A pregnancy test was positive.

When Marie Ange learned that she was pregnant, she stated that her chief concern was prevention of transmission of HIV to the fetus, and she asked if there were medications that might prevent this. Her physicians offered her zidovudine. By May, 1990, she thus had more than 20 pills to take each day, some every five hours. This proved to be a difficult regimen for Marie Ange, who felt burdened by the sheer number of pills. She also experienced nausea, sometimes accompanied by vomiting which necessitated (on more than one occasion) rehydration. However, her diarrhea and thrush resolved.

In late December, 1990, Marie Ange gave birth to a normal-birth-weight infant who subsequently proved to be HIV-negative. The child did not suffer from any problems attributable to his mother's medications. In the months following delivery, Marie Ange began to experience severe muscle pains in both legs, suggesting an adverse reaction to zidovudine; these symptoms resolved when the medication was discontinued. In May, 1991, Marie Ange experienced recurrent diarrhea, again found to be due to *Isospora*. Her diarrhea responded to high-dose trimethoprim/sulfamethoxazole, and Marie-Ange was maintained on suppression doses of this drug in spite of decreasing blood counts.

Marie Ange felt well throughout the summer of 1991, and she was able to resume work as a produce seller in regional markets. In October, 1991, however, she fell from a truck, injuring her spine. Left with complete lower-extremity paralysis, she developed a deep decubitus ulcer in May, 1992. The ulcer eventually healed, but Marie Ange continued to lose weight throughout the summer of 1992, and she remained anemic until her death in September of that year. No discrete terminal infection or event was documented.

5. DISCUSSION:
POVERTY, GENDER, AND HIV DISEASE

The illness trajectories of Monica Vincent, Flor Becerra, and Marie Ange Viaud are, of course, unique in many senses. But they are typical in others. These stories illustrate some of the commonly registered clinical features of HIV disease among poor women. These stories also speak volumes about shortcomings in the care given to poor women living with HIV disease. These shortcomings, and the forces that shape them, often result, we believe, in differential survival: gender inequality and poverty lead to worse outcomes among those infected with HIV.

Poor outcomes are not inevitable, however. These stories offer us a starting point for a discussion of how to improve delivery of effective and high-quality care to a disadvantaged population. Such a discussion is necessarily prefaced by a more general examination of the means by which poverty and gender inequality impact upon clinical outcomes.

As noted throughout this volume, poverty and its attendant social circumstances are clear risk factors for HIV acquisition.[1] In addition, cross-sectional studies document that women with HIV infection are more likely than their male counterparts to be living in poverty.[2] But what is the evidence that gender or income, individually or in combination, affect survival or the course of HIV? How might the poverty of these three women have impacted their care, and why?

Many studies suggest that both poverty and social marginalization are risk factors for premature mortality in the United States and the United Kingdom: differences in survival between socioeconomic groups have widened since 1930.[3] The importance of poverty as a risk factor for adverse outcomes has been well described for many diseases; there is little reason to believe that AIDS might be exempt from this pernicious synergy.[4] Only a few studies have directly addressed the question of how economic status affects HIV disease progression and mortality, but all seem to point to adverse outcomes among the poor.[5]

A number of mechanisms may contribute to shortened survival among the poor. For example, in a review of 12,068 inpatient admissions for various illnesses, Weissman and co-workers found that participants who were African-American, poor, and uninsured were much more likely to report a delay in health care. After controlling for diagnosis and severity of illness, they found that these patients required hospital stays nine percent longer, on average, than those of other patients. In this population, gender was not in and of itself a risk for receiving fewer services, but poverty was a major risk factor for delays in diagnosis and entry into the health care system.[6]

The under-funded urban clinics which serve uninsured patients are characterized by long waits, uncoordinated care, and a lack of follow-up. In addition to delays in receiving health care, income-related differential use of tests and procedures may contribute to adverse health outcomes for poor people. For example, in a study of HIV-positive patients who presented with pulmonary symptoms,

Horner *et al.* found that Medicaid patients were less likely to undergo bronchoscopy, were less likely to have a diagnosis of PCP confirmed, and were more likely to die in the hospital than were privately insured patients.[7] Loue and co-workers found similar results in their analysis of the relationship between insurance status and health services utilization. Using logistic regression, they found that patients with PCP who had publicly funded insurance were only about half as likely as were privately insured patients to undergo bronchoscopy with bronchoalveolar lavage at the time of their first PCP episode.[8] Uninsured patients were also less likely to participate in therapeutic trials, and this was associated with a higher risk of death.[9]

What about gender-related adverse outcomes? The feminization of poverty often makes this difficult to study. It is also difficult to ascribe differential outcomes to biological differences between men and women. If HIV-infected women are at greater risk for poor outcomes than are HIV-infected men—if AIDS among women is "a different disease"—are these differences predominantly biological or social? The literature examining survival differences between women and men is reviewed in detail in Chapter 7. Most evidence suggests that survival is not significantly different in women and men when studies control for disease stage, utilization of services and medications, and socioeconomic factors. Earlier, uncontrolled studies were misleading in suggesting shorter survival in women.[10] In a sense, the early studies obscured how closely poverty and gender are associated in this epidemic, for the vast majority of women with HIV are poor.

Although biological sex in and of itself appears not to be a risk factor for rapid disease progression or death, gender inequality *is* a risk factor in that it poses numerous barriers to utilization. Studies among woman with a variety of conditions, particularly women of color, reveal significant gaps in care delivery.[11] These gaps may be related to barriers to utilization affecting women; they include failure to screen women for HIV, failure to diagnose HIV-associated manifestations in women, and failure to deliver effective and coordinated care to women with HIV. Social stigma, discrimination, and fear also keep women from obtaining appropriate screening and care, as do women's disproportionate burdens of caring for others.

Anecdotally, it is not uncommon to ask women why they do not utilize the health care system to its full potential and to have them answer that the demands of their dependents or work for income supersede their own health care. Women, who are often caretakers of children, spouses, and parents, frequently lack both time and money for treatment.[12]

Lack of screening

HIV screening and testing are essential preventive and therapeutic interventions, yet health care workers consistently fail to utilize them appropriately, as a number of U.S. studies reveal. Makadon *et al.* have shown that, even in the 1990s, the vast majority of physicians do not routinely discuss the issue of HIV with patients.[13] Schoenbaum and co-workers have shown that health care providers do not diagnose women with HIV in a timely manner, even though women see health care providers more often than do men. In an investigation of HIV screening patterns, Wortley *et al.* reviewed 2,441 cases of AIDS diagnosed at various state health departments between 1990 and 1992. They found that women and non-whites were more likely to be diagnosed at a late stage of illness than were men and whites. It is notable that the authors focused their discussion on differential treatment along race and gender lines, but did not discuss the significance of socioeconomic status.[14]

Lack of HIV screening and appropriate testing is not only a problem in the United States. In countries throughout the world, HIV testing may not be an option for many people because it does not exist. When discussing HIV testing in Africa, Allen *et al* state: "Voluntary HIV testing is not widely available, and the efficacy of confidential or anonymous testing and counseling in promoting risk reduction has not been studied."[15] Thus, while lack of HIV screening and testing may constitute a significant problem for many women in the United States, it appears to be an even greater difficulty for most women living in the developing world.

"Targeted" screening will remain a problem as long as the nature of HIV risk among women is poorly understood. Although in many settings, women constitute the fastest growing group of HIV-infected individuals, their risk factors are often unrecognized by themselves and by their health care providers. In a study of anonymous HIV testing of women attending an urban prenatal clinic, Barbacci and co-workers demonstrated that 43% of HIV-positive women reported no "traditional" risk behavior on a risk assessment questionnaire.[16] Ward *et al.* have shown that nearly half of the women found to be HIV-positive at blood donation could not identify a risk factor for their infection.[17] For women such as Flor and Marie Ange, the only risk factor may be the risk behavior of their one and only partner, of whose behavior they may not be fully apprised. Improved screening strategies and the redefining of "risk factors" must be the subject of further research.

Under-recognition

The stories of Monica Vincent, Flor Becerra and Marie Ange Viaud illustrate the under-recognition of typical manifestations of HIV disease in women. All three women were diagnosed with AIDS late in the course of their infection. All three suffered from potentially preventable HIV-related complications.

Flor Becerra presented with cervical dysplasia, recurrent *Candida* vaginitis, and herpes zoster infection, conditions seen in normal hosts, but also strongly associated with HIV infection. Marie Ange Viaud presented with tuberculosis—again, a common comorbid infection and in many settings the harbinger of HIV infection. Of course, tuberculosis is a significant cause of morbidity and mortality even among individuals without HIV infection.[18] This is certainly true in Haiti, where tuberculosis was the leading cause of death in Marie Ange's age group long before the advent of HIV. However, tuberculosis is also the leading "opportunistic infection" among Haitians with HIV disease. Because tuberculosis often occurs with HIV infection, many feel that all patients with active tuberculosis should be counseled regarding HIV testing. Marie Ange's diagnosis was delayed when physicians in a busy clinic did not elicit a history of chronic diarrhea that might also have led to more timely HIV testing.[19]

Under-utilization of medical therapy

For a variety of reasons, which may have been related to her gender and social circumstances, Monica Vincent was receiving neither PCP prophylaxis nor zidovudine—two therapies with proven benefit for people in her circumstances. The under-use of both prophylactic medications and antiretroviral therapy has been repeatedly documented in U.S. women.[20] Results from the HER Study showed that less than 23% of women with CD4 counts of less than 200/mm3 were receiving PCP prophylaxis.[21] These differences involved "race": whites were more likely to be offered or to receive zidovudine than were people of color;[22] whites were more likely to receive PCP prophylaxis than were blacks.[23]

Trimethoprim/sulfamethoxazole is the most effective PCP prophylaxis, and it would follow that the under-use of this in any population would lead to an increase in poor outcomes among people with HIV. Vanishingly small percentages of poor, African women living with advanced HIV infection are receiving any prophylaxis at all.

Access

Another reason for differential survival between men and women, besides under-use of medicines and diagnostic tests, includes late entry into the health care system. Although definitive research on this topic is lacking, it appears that women in the United States are more likely to present for treatment of HIV infection later in the course of their illness than are men, as is evidenced by their presenting disease manifestations. As noted, this may reflect either under-utilization of health care or lack of HIV screening.[24] Women are also more likely to present with symptomatic AIDS than are men, who, in the United States and Europe at least, are often diagnosed with asymptomatic HIV infection. Women are more likely than men to be first diagnosed with AIDS at the time of their death.[25]

Poor women's difficulties with access persist even after they are receiving care. One study found that after entering the health care system, women with AIDS received fewer services than did men with AIDS.[26] A multivariate analysis of Medicaid payments found that

HIV-infected women in Michigan received fewer HIV-related medical services than did male recipients even when utilization was controlled for disease stage.[27]

HIV status is often revealed during pregnancy and, here again, many women are found to have advanced disease. In two of our cases, the diagnosis of HIV was discovered or rediscovered during pregnancy. In a study conducted in Miami, the average length of survival of a newly diagnosed HIV-positive woman after delivery was only 201 days.[28]

Other factors

In the United States, HIV positive women are often assumed to be injection drug users, which is one reason many hide their HIV disease from friends and family. But throughout the world, public knowledge of HIV infection exposes women to prejudice, discrimination, and violence.[29] Among 238 HIV seropositive women in Kinshasa, Zaire, 97 percent stated they were unwilling to inform their sexual partners of their serostatus because of fear of divorce, physical harm, and public scorn.[30] Similar fears motivate women in the United States as well.[31]

Relatives, friends, and the general public are not the only groups of people who stigmatize women with HIV. Surveys of physicians show that they too have been guilty of making harsh judgments and stigmatizing AIDS patients.[32] Many poor women with HIV often feel AIDS-related stigma might erode the social supports upon which they depend for survival. Thus they may avoid obtaining critically important care, as was tragically seen in the case of Monica Vincent.

As the HIV pandemic preferentially afflicts poor communities and as economic disparities increase, one would suspect that poverty-related adverse HIV outcomes will become increasingly common. By merely living in poverty, the women whose stories are recounted above were at increased risk for poor outcomes from a number of conditions, including HIV disease. Gender inequality complicates this dynamic with its own insidious mechanisms, very few of which are exclusively biological.

6. CONCLUSIONS

Several issues were identified at the outset of this chapter, including gender-based survival differences, the under-recognition of HIV disease in women, and economic forces which affect the health care poor people receive. These issues are of particular concern to poor women, a group of people disproportionately affected by HIV disease. In the following paragraphs, we will examine the specific ways in which these issues operate in the lives of poor women.

Just as Monica Vincent's and Flor Becerra's stories illustrate some of the problems in the care of women with HIV infection living in the United States, Marie Ange Viaud's experience reveals some of the problems affecting HIV-infected women in poor countries. Throughout the world, women do not have access to even the most rudimentary medical services, such as chest radiographs.

Marie Ange's access to first-line diagnostic and therapeutic measures was compromised by the limited infrastructure and impoverishment of her country. In the face of severe pulmonary symptoms, she was unable to obtain a chest radiograph. Following her spinal-cord injury, no imaging was available in all of Haiti, which was, at the time, wracked by political violence. The only laboratory able to determine CD4 subsets was in faroff Port-au-Prince, and this test alone cost more than her annual income, which in rural Haiti is less than $250 per capita. The issue of access to therapy comes to the fore when we reflect on the costs of the 10 medications prescribed for Marie Ange: retail costs of these agents are well in excess of $10,000 per year, a heavy burden in even a wealthy country.

Yet Marie Ange's story also shows some of the ways that, despite limited resources, good care can be delivered to women with HIV disease. At the time of her AIDS diagnosis, Marie Ange Viaud was a 26-year-old pregnant woman with relapsed (versus re-infection) pulmonary tuberculosis, oral candidiasis, and diarrhea due to *Isospora*. Once diagnosed with HIV infection, however, Marie received quality care. She had ready access to knowledgeable clinicians, antiretroviral therapy, and treatment and prophylactic regimens for opportunistic infections. Unfortunately, these options are virtually non-existent in most of Haiti, throughout sub-Saharan Africa, and in parts of Southeast Asia.

In each of the cases presented, early diagnosis might have improved outcomes. But timely diagnoses were compromised by inadequate community-based care and even, perhaps, by inappropriate case definitions of AIDS. For example, cervical dysplasia and tuberculosis are two diseases that often herald HIV infection in women. In addition to this fact, poor women are much more susceptible to infection with human papilloma virus and *Mycobacterium tuberculosis* than are women not living in poverty.[33] Because tuberculosis and HPV were not "AIDS-defining" illnesses according to CDC criteria, women presenting with these problems were overlooked.

Finally, there are numerous issues surrounding the widespread use of serologic tests to diagnose HIV infection in asymptomatic women. Many clinicians agree that early diagnosis can extend survival in HIV infection. For this reason, early diagnosis and treatment are of extreme importance in promoting the health of women with HIV. The problem with HIV testing, however, is that people found to be HIV-positive may well face discrimination. They may lose their jobs, their homes, and their health-care coverage, in the event they are fortunate enough to have it. As long as AIDS-related discrimination can lead to loss of housing, insurance, and employment, it is difficult for us to fully endorse HIV testing of women on a large scale.

Since the beginning of the AIDS pandemic, men have been more likely than women to enjoy the benefits of life-prolonging therapeutic interventions. The consequences of women not receiving standard care for advanced HIV infection are illustrated by two of the stories presented at the beginning of the chapter. Monica was not receiving PCP prophylaxis, and died, in essence, from complications of that preventable disease. Flor was not started on isoniazid and later died from reactivation tuberculosis. This occurred even though it is widely recognized that tuberculosis due to drug-susceptible strains is highly responsive to therapy in persons co-infected with HIV.

Many authors who document the decreased use of proven therapies among women call for greater availability and access to those therapies, a call we strongly endorse. However, what is striking to us is the lack of utilization of those resources by the women who could most benefit from them, even though they appear to be geographically close and available. What barriers are these women facing? Investigations of this question need to move beyond useless critiques of personal behaviors and values and into a more honest and clear-sighted look at the subtle—and sometimes not-so-subtle—ways our present delivery of medical care rebukes rather than welcomes these women.

The women whose stories are told in this chapter also suffered from a lack of communication between their health care providers. When primary prevention fails, only surveillance and ready access to coordinated primary care are likely to retard the advance of HIV infection in poor women. In each of the cases examined, improved access to coordinated care might well have increased survival. By "coordinated," we mean community-based and involving teams of providers, including social workers, nurses, and outreach workers. By "coordinated," we also mean care characterized by effective communication between patients and providers. In the case of Flor Becerra, this coordination was hampered by both linguistic and bureaucratic communication barriers. Such barriers are particularly important in the United States, where HIV disproportionately affects Hispanic Americans but where many facilities providing HIV-related care have a dearth of services available in Spanish.

By "coordinated care," we also signal the importance of clear communication between providers. In two of the cases, a disheartening lack of such communication may have led to substandard care. In the case of Monica Vincent, the miscommunication occurred between an internist and an obstetrician; in the case of Flor Becerra, between the county health clinic and the teaching hospital.

The care provided to poor women with HIV must also be coordinated with the rhythms of these women's lives. It must take into account that many women are caretakers of homes and families. Marie Ange, Flor, and Monica all had children and households to tend. Unless the idea of medical care is broadened to include services (such as child and respite care), women will continue to neglect their own health, and remain deprived of resources that often are within minutes of their homes.

The experiences of Monica Vincent, Flor Becerra, and Marie Ange Viaud suggest that more research would serve the interests of women with HIV infection. It is discouraging, but perhaps not surprising, that too little is known of HIV disease in women. As Hankins and Handley noted in 1992,

> Seemingly little attention has been paid to the unique features of HIV infection in women. Much of what is currently known about the natural history of HIV disease has been learned through the prospective study of large cohorts of gay men. In contrast, the bulk of literature describing HIV disease in women consists of case reports, cross-sectional studies, and retrospective evaluations published primarily in conference proceedings.[34]

As one can see in perusing the major clinical trials which are annotated in Part II of this book, men have formed the vast majority of subjects in the studies which serve as the foundation for our current treatment of HIV infection with antiretroviral therapy as well as our best knowledge about prophylaxis and treatment of opportunistic infections.[35] Although this is starting to change, Cotton and coworkers reviewed data regarding accrual of patients to multicenter trials and found that only 6.7 percent of participants were women.[36] They found that women were less likely to be told by their doctors about trials. In addition to this lack of information, there are other contributing factors, such as a lack of day care and transportation support, which effectively prevent women from participating in such trials.

Women's health has suffered from a lack of research on the unique biological manifestations of HIV disease in women. An attendant lack of research on therapies for these manifestations has been inevitable. Thus, new research is important, and we join others in calling for a rapid expansion of the AIDS knowledge base. The need for investigations regarding subjects ranging from case definitions to drug safety profiles arise from consideration of the cases presented in this chapter. But one central issue deserves emphasis here: *existing* therapies and technologies could dramatically improve outcomes among women with HIV disease were these made universally available.

Thus, HIV disease in women is a "different disease" for many reasons, and most of them are social. What is of critical importance is that women with HIV often lack the resources to access HIV-related health care. These issues are strikingly important in the lives of poor women with HIV. In each of the domains discussed above, structural violence and its attendant inequities are manifest along gender and class lines. Inferior care is the inevitable result. For example, access to quality care is not guaranteed to all in the United States, and, as we have seen, this lack of health-care security is manifest in lack of access to health information, effective prophylaxis, and clinical trials. But calls for universal access and increased availability of services are not enough. We must clearly examine the myriad economic, social, and cultural forces that routinely deny poor women access to care, despite its availability and their legal access to it. No honest appraisal of these forces can fail to take into account women's inferior position to men in terms of economic resources, control over sexual and reproductive decisions, and political power. Genuine attempts to remedy the deficiencies in care discussed here must call for the economic, social, and political empowerment of women—especially poor women of color—both in the United States and throughout the world.

Our case-based exploration of the experience of three women with fatal complications of HIV infection leads us to offer a series of suggestions for clinicians working with women everywhere. To improve care offered to women potentially at-risk for HIV, clinicians could:

- learn to assess the nature of HIV risk and present these risk factors to women in non-judgmental ways.

- assess how economic status may thwart attempts at risk-behavior reduction. Work on strategies to overcome personal *and* socioeconomic barriers to implementing risk-reduction efforts as a part of standard treatment plans.

- assess, prior to HIV testing, a woman's environment and how knowledge of HIV serostatus may affect her physical and emotional safety.

To improve services for women already living with HIV, clinicians could:

- identify barriers to health-care utilization by women and devise systems to overcome them. These barriers may include financial difficulties, time priorities (e.g. care-taking obligations), lack of control over environment (jobs, housing, phones, physicians), and linguistic and cultural divides. Many poor patients, particularly women, report an inherent distrust of and unfamiliarity with the large institutions that are so often the sole providers of AIDS-related services. Making these institutions more democratic would also demand heightened efforts to increase the number of women providers.

- ensure equal access to care, including universal medical insurance and social security, for women with HIV.

- underwrite HIV therapies with proven efficacy, including antiretrovirals and prophylactic antibiotics.

- coordinate care on both a community and hospital level.

- address women's lack of economic, social and political power by voicing solidarity with movements, both domestic and abroad, that seek to empower poor women.

Calls for more research and improved clinical services can only go so far. Our own experience as clinicians leads us to recognize the limitations of good will and of good science. As the International Federation of Gynecology and Obstetrics noted in 1992, "an improvement in women's social, economic, and political status will alleviate many of the AIDS-related problems they face."[37] Physicians and other health care providers also have a role to play in the struggle for social justice for women living in poverty—not simply for citizens of the United States, but for women everywhere. Although such aspirations may sound utopian, we make these statements with people like Marie Ange in mind. National boundaries need not serve as curbs on compassion. Certainly, the virus itself has had no difficulties vaulting across whatever boundaries nations and national health regimes have put in its way.

PART II

Rereading AIDS:
Examining Claims of Causality

CHAPTER FIVE

Rereading Social Science

Paul Farmer, Margaret Connors, Kenneth Fox, and Jennifer Furin, editors

with David Devine, Steven Lamola, Joyce Millen and Janie Simmons

"Very little of the current research that is being done on sexual risk behaviour acknowledges the import of systemic poverty on sexual risk behaviour. Moreover, research paradigms that continue to place a premium on the study of behavioural frequencies and dubious notions of motive are unsuited to the task of identifying ways in which to foster 'actionable' changes in high-risk sexual behaviour. Certainly this fact reflects a failure of political will, but it should also call into question the kinds of priorities that have been established in the AIDS prevention research industry."

> Michael Clatts, "Disembodied Acts: On
> the Perverse Use of Sexual Categories
> in the Study of High Risk Behaviors"

"There seem to be, in the eyes of critics, only two types of social scientists: those who are frequently wrong but never in doubt, and those who say, 'Well, it's all very complex' and then hang up the phone."

> Richard Shweder and Donald Fiske,
> "Uneasy Social Science"

The body of social science literature on AIDS and AIDS prevention is enormous and rapidly growing. However, the topic of women and AIDS, the subject of a few notable books and "special issues" of scholarly journals, accounts for only a fraction of that outpouring. Even within that small group of publications, scrutiny of *poor* women and AIDS has been neglected.

This chapter draws widely on social science writing relevant to the topic of poor women and AIDS. Influential publications in this small, underattended domain have ranged from essays (or even compelling polemics) to careful empirical research. Moreover, writing in the social sciences—anthropology, psychology, sociology, "behavioral"—is underpinned by highly disparate theories and methods. No disease has undergone more intensive social-science study than has AIDS. We have selected a number of interesting, influential or otherwise exemplary papers and offer a close reading of them. This bid for an analytic purchase on women and AIDS is structured by a four-step process. First, we examine writings on the subject of women, poverty, and AIDS. The major strengths and shortcomings of these texts are revealed by a close and critical rereading. Second, we explore the influence of behaviorism and cognitivism on the AIDS literature and critique its lines of inquiry and claims of causality. Third, we offer notes on a series of publications by anthropologists, sociologists, psychologists, and others writing in the humanist tradition. Finally, we attempt to review the major problems that disable scholarly work on this subject. As we shall see, despite the heterogeneity of social science writing on women and AIDS, the field is marked by a few recurrent themes.

Our goal in this exercise is to be critical. However, the criticism for which we aim is a constructive one. The research and writing of our colleagues has helped shed light on certain aspects of the AIDS epidemic, and for this and other reasons, it is valuable. But much more needs to be done. As this chapter will show, the social sciences are far from understanding AIDS and its multiple dynamics. This is due, in large part, to a dearth of scholarly research and writing on poverty, gender inequality, and AIDS. Thus, when we assert that these issues have often been overlooked, it is not to assign blame but rather to suggest new avenues of research. The ultimate goal of our rereading is to bring to the forefront neglected issues and problems in an effort to better understand AIDS and to slow its rapid movement among women.

First, a few definitions are in order. Of our three key words—women, poverty, and AIDS—only poverty is a widely contested concept. By poverty, we refer to a lack of material resources, but also to the contexts and consequences of vast, unmet human needs. *The Dictionary of Development* defines poverty as a "morally unacceptable condition of upwards of one-third of all people, characterized by frequent death of children, lack of education, health care, access to other basic necessities, and exploitation by a variety of forces including local politicians, major landowners, criminals, government, transnational banks, and transnational corporations."[1]

Poverty may thus be construed as a broad human-rights issue generated by and experienced within the context of global political, economic and social forces. And poverty is not an accident of nature: "The poor are simply seen as those who have nothing," note Boff and Boff. "There is a failure to see that the poor are oppressed and made poor *by others*."[2]

1. MAKING IT EXPLICIT:
WOMEN, POVERTY, AND AIDS

Despite robust traditions of feminist and class-based critique, the social sciences have thus far failed to direct adequate attention to explorations of the relationship of poverty, gender inequality, and AIDS. Further, most of the small handful of works examining the relationship between gender and AIDS have truncated discussion of the role of economic factors. One exception to this rule is the recently published *Women Resisting AIDS*, edited by sociologists Schneider and Stoller. The introduction, by the editors, is excellent and hard-hitting. "There is no question," they write, "that the social, sexual, political, and economic subordination of women structures their vulnerability in the epidemic. Globally, women are poor, with few material resources."[3]

This auspicious theme, though echoed in several of the book's 19 chapters, is conspicuously absent from some sections. The collection's diversity quickly gives way to unevenness. Some chapters are well documented; others are not. Some contributors make their assumptions explicit; others are strikingly unselfconscious about the epistemological questions that underpin their commentary. There is no index.

The book is divided into four parts, the first of which—
"Women Confront the Problem of AIDS"—is composed of essays
taking a broad view of the pandemic. One piece, Esu-Williams's 1992
keynote address to the plenary session of the VIIIth International
Conferences on AIDS, reveals an awareness of structural violence:
"To enable women to protect themselves, there are three issues at
stake: improving the social and economic status of women, providing a method over which they have sufficient control, and getting
more men to adopt safer sex."[4] Esu-Williams notes with alarm the
disproportionate AIDS burdens borne by poor countries and calls for
the industrialized countries to "support poorer nations to address the
pandemic."[5] With the exception of a passing reference to structural
adjustment, however, there is scant attention paid to relationships
between health, wealth, and power in some countries and illness,
poverty, and immiseration in others.

Other chapters engage legal issues of significance chiefly to
U.S. women. The first of these, by Hunter, offers a helpful overview
of legal problems regarding access to health care, decisions related to
pregnancy and parenting, and mandatory HIV testing of women and
newborns. Although Hunter underlines the importance of the
"intersection of gender, race, and class," it is not always reflected in
her assertions:

> One of the major achievements in the gay male community during the
> 1980s was the creation of innovative educational programs encouraging
> behavior changes to reduce the risk of HIV transmission. *As a result*, the
> incidence of new HIV infections among gay men fell sharply. Women face
> a challenge at least as formidable in the 1990s—to develop prevention
> programs that tackle the issue of negotiating safer sex between women
> and their partners that are sensitive to the diverse ethnic and cultural
> backgrounds of women affected by HIV. The primary role of law on this
> question should be to ensure that the government is not permitted to
> choke off the most effective programs because of concerns about the con-
> troversial nature of their content.[6]

Several assumptions underpin Hunter's statement: the gay
male "community" is homogeneous; educational programs—rather
than other events, processes, and conditions—led to a sharp decrease

in HIV transmission within these communities; men and women engage in sexual relationships for similar reasons; the chief challenge for women is to develop more "innovative" programs; these programs will decrease HIV transmission among women as they seem to have among gay men; and finally, the most important laws will be those that aim to protect freedom of expression, since "overly explicit communication" has been the source of most of the legal problems related to AIDS.

Each of these assumptions is open to criticism. First, gay male communities are hardly homogeneous.[7] Decreases in incidence of new HIV infections has been registered among older, *middle-class* gay men, who are disproportionately white.[8] Within this socially heterogeneous category, gay men, there are many communities. French sociologist Michael Pollak shows that class and the degree of engagement in urban, cosmopolitan gay culture are determinants of access to AIDS education.[9] It is doubtful that AIDS education, no matter how explicit, will have equal effects on groups stratified by class and "race" within capitalist and racist contexts. Innovative educational campaigns might have little or no effect in communities in which risk is determined not by lack of knowledge concerning HIV, but by one's subordinate position in an inegalitarian society. Second, there are many reasons for engaging in sexual relations. For many poor women, and for some poor men, particularly drug users and gay adolescents, sex is a survival strategy.[10] In this way, sexual behavior is less "malleable" than behavior among social equals. Third, HIV prevention might be low on the list of priorities for women living in poverty. For them, access to basic services, rather than innovation in programming, would seem to be a more important priority in AIDS prevention.[11]

In Part II of the book, "Women and the Problems of HIV Prevention," five very different prevention arenas are examined from different perspectives. Greenblat's examination of women in families with hemophilia offers pragmatic assistance to certain groups, advancing role-playing as an important AIDS teaching tool. The chapter focuses on what are termed key "communication issues." These are distilled into a "balanced set of 20 items," and this set includes eroticizing safer sex, issues regarding college applications, and HIV and marriage proposals. Rereading the chapter from the point of view of women living in poverty, the set would seem to be balanced for certain people, but not for others. Among poor women, notes anthropologist Martha Ward, "The idea of post-AIDS spirituality or eroticizing safe sex draws a blank response. The idea of eating right and living well has little meaning for a group of women subject to chronic ill health and for whom the economic barriers to adequate nutrition are frequently insurmountable."[12] In short, although the interventions described by Greenblat make reference to a "larger social world," there is, at times, a failure of social imagination: poor women are apparently not part of this social world. In many settings in which AIDS is endemic, for example, any blood dyscrasia—even sickle-cell anemia—is a death sentence, given the disparity of access to advanced technology or even basic primary health care.

Such failure of imagination, easily linked to provincialism, is by no means unique to Greenblat's paper; it is pervasive in North American and European writings on AIDS.[13] One obvious way of countering this problem would be to juxtapose North American reflections on improving AIDS education with those from very different social realities. Unfortunately, the paper from South Africa, Mtshali's "Transferability of American AIDS Prevention Models to South African Youth," is marred by sweeping generalizations. "Traditional healers are highly trusted," we read; "the supernatural aspect of the relationship produces confidence."[14] But South Africa is a highly heterogeneous nation, and recourse to "traditional healers" is by no means universal there. More troubling, perhaps, are other statements: "If [youth] are given the tools to prevent and avoid contact with the virus, then there is hope that one day a cure or vaccine will be found, and that HIV/AIDS can be counted with the likes of tuberculosis, leprosy, and smallpox."[15] *Tuberculosis?* AIDS can already be counted with the likes of tuberculosis, in that together they are now two of the leading causes of death among young South Africans. In fact, such comments reveal a spectacular achievement of international propaganda: in reality, tuberculosis, while long in decline in the developing countries and among the wealthy, has remained the world's leading cause of infectious deaths.[16] The problem is that a disease that disproportionately affects the poor is, by definition, not a problem, as Mtshali's comment suggests. The central questions have not yet been posed: Will AIDS be allowed to follow the path of misery traced by tuberculosis? Will AIDS become another disease that disproportionately strikes the poor without occasioning much scholarly comment or investigation? The author notes that "South Africans are still in a world of their own concerning AIDS."[17] In fact, as noted in Chapter 2 of *Women, Poverty and AIDS*, the transmission of HIV in South Africa is tightly tied to the disruption of stable sexual unions by large scale, *transnational* forces ranging from labor migration to land seizure. South Africans know all too well the hazards of living in this world—"living in a world of their own" is by comparison less of a problem.

Part III, "Women Organize AIDS Care and Foster Social Change," consists of seven chapters detailing the experiences of women on the "front lines" in the AIDS pandemic. This section is the most experience-near and ethnographically rich, in large part because women, note the editors, have been "crucial to slowing the spread and managing the consequences of the epidemic."[18] But the vast disparity in resources available and the thinly veiled social divisions between groups of women emerge clearly. AIDS, note Schneider and Stoller, has "sharpened important differences between women in poorer, less industrialized countries, by showing the different stakes of middle-class, working-class, and peasant women."[19] Important differences in the experiences of U.S. women are also brought into view. Hollibaugh, Director of the Lesbian AIDS Project of Gay Men's Health Crisis, writes of "Lesbian Denial and Lesbian Leadership in the AIDS Epidemic." As we have noted in Chapter 3 of this volume, facile use of the word "denial" is common, and there is ample reason to avoid it in social science writing. But Hollibaugh's essay, which draws on the author's many years of organizing gender politics, is cast in the confessional and insider mode.[20] Although few data are offered to support her claim, Hollibaugh reasonably posits that HIV is present among lesbians and should thus be a focus of aggressive preventive efforts.[21] Among the

reasons that it is not a focus, according to Hollibaugh, are the prejudices of movement élites who control resources and symbolic capital.
She sees hope in the more "independent" pockets of lesbian communities: "It is there, in working-class lesbian political and social organizations, that I see the most innovative and least judgmental struggle to integrate HIV knowledge into daily lesbian life."[22]

The account of "The Role of Nurses in the HIV Epidemic," by
Fraser and Jones, is unpretentious and powerful. Both authors were
members of the first inpatient AIDS unit in the United States, formed
at the San Francisco General Hospital in 1983. Their reflections regarding what recent epidemiological trends in the U.S. epidemic have
meant for nurses make for fascinating reading. In the epidemic's first
years, most of their patients were middle-class gay men. More recently,
they have cared for "those individuals who are the most alienated and
compromised by the system's inefficiencies and inequities."[23] The
hard-won experience of Fraser and Jones seems to have left them with
a no-nonsense understanding of what empowerment is really about:

> When a patient is homeless, no amount of tender loving care on the part
> of a committed and dedicated nurse will be able to change that fact.
> Instead, the nurse is seen as an accomplice to an unjust system that allows
> people with terminal diseases to be discharged to homeless shelters and
> addicts to go untreated for their addictions.[24]

The experience of Fraser and Jones was in many ways unique,
since they were present from the outset of the epidemic and were
working within a world-class medical infrastructure. In their
account, "the AIDS epidemic" means, of course, the U.S. subepi-
demic. What, one wonders, was the experience of nurses struggling
with the new epidemic in Haiti, say, or Zaïre? Still, many of Fraser
and Jones' insights apply across a broad range of contexts, as do their
deeply affecting conclusions. One such conclusion is that quality
health care should be "the right of every individual in society."
Another conclusion, found in the closing lines of the chapter,
deserves quotation in full:

> So what is our message? It is simply that we value our work, our patients,
> and our contribution. The spiritual aspects of our job, the social activism,

the connections with human souls in need, and the opportunity to practice exquisite caring are all part of the payback we receive. It is an honor to share this struggle with the thousands of people with HIV/AIDS we have known.[25]

The fourth and final section of the book, "Problems and Policies for Women in the Future," consists of three excellent essays by leaders in the field. In "Challenges and Possibilities: Women, HIV, and the Health Care System in the 1990s," Rodriguez-Trias and Marte review the structural features of the U.S. health care system that render it "not made for women." Their experience with wasteful, costly, and fragmented care in many ways parallels that described in Chapter 4 of *Women, Poverty, and AIDS*. The fiscal aspect of the current health care crisis, they optimistically argue, "opens the door for dialogue on the most substantive issues: reintegrating health care for women and their families; redirecting reproductive rights policies; establishing prevention as a health care priority; replacing punitive with supportive policies for the social problems of the poor."[26]

Pies reviews "AIDS, Ethics, Reproductive Rights," concluding that "there are no easy answers." Although focused on U.S. women, the review is more broadly applicable because the fundamentally economic nature of these issues is recognized: "The women who are represented in the U.S. HIV/AIDS statistics are basically the same population of women who are frequently overrepresented in every adverse outcome of pregnancy."[27] Her conclusion is worth citing in full:

As long as a significant percentage of women live in poverty; as long as unemployment continues to rise and extension of unemployment benefits is denied; as long as women are denied an opportunity to education, job training, and equal pay for equal work; as long as these same women are denied welfare benefits for having children or are having those benefits reduced due to state budget cutbacks; as long as poor women are denied access to abortion (while they can barely afford to support the children they do have); as long as our society expects everyone to make a "reasonable" choice—and what is reasonable is determined by those in power—any efforts to find resolution to the many compelling ethical issues discussed above must involve a broader social, political, and economic view of the problem of HIV infection and pregnancy.[28]

Indeed, a broader social, political, and economic view of AIDS makes terms such as "our society" problematic, as the superb essay by Bianco suggests. In "How AIDS Changes Development Priorities," Bianco reminds us of the effects of HIV among the poor living in poor countries. The World Health Organization estimates that, during the course of the year 2000 alone, between six and eight million women will become infected with HIV. Bianco takes much of the mystery out of this harrowing fact by noting that "AIDS is already a disease of the poor" and that structured inequality is very much a transnational affair. Thus reversing these unwelcome trends will call for a truly new world order: "Whatever this new international order turns out to be, it would imply a growing and continuous flow of resources from rich countries to poor countries."[29] The virus, on the other hand, will no doubt flow in the opposite direction. Not only do social inequalities account in large part for the unequal distribution of HIV disease, they also account for its course after infection:

> Other social inequities between rich and poor all over the world which become more evident with AIDS are differences in purchasing power and in access to education, health, recreation, and other benefits. Perhaps the only positive contribution of AIDS to the evolution of mankind is the possibility of bringing these conflicts to a boiling point and exposing them for what they are.[30]

A number of contributions to *Women Resisting AIDS* bear closer scrutiny. The essay by the founder of WORLD—"Women Organized to Resist Life-threatening Diseases"—is in the confessional mode: "To explain how and why I started WORLD," writes Denison, "you need to understand what it was like before."[31] Upon learning of her HIV infection, feeling alone and adrift, Denison "realized that I needed a women's HIV support group."[32] The group subsequently formed sponsored a series of retreats in which participants "talked, painted, went for walks by the beach, gathered sage from the hill to do a healing ritual. It was an artificially created community of women," she allows, "but a community all the same."[33] Although much of the essay seems peculiarly American and rooted in middle-class strivings—the longing for New-Age spirituality and for a women's HIV support group was not, in any case, a prime concern of Haitian women living with AIDS—there is much of value here. For example, Denison candidly tells the story of how WORLD's plans to start a local newsletter for HIV-positive women met resistance *within* the AIDS-service community. "Please don't," responded one activist, upon hearing of the proposal. "My organization's applying for a grant to do one, and if they see you're doing it for free, the funders won't give us the money."[34]

There are, in Denison's testimony, important acknowledgements that it is not merely gender, but also "race" and class, that structure U.S. women's experience with AIDS and with other life-threatening disease. "For some women," she notes, "HIV is the first major disaster in their lives. For many more, AIDS is just one more problem on top of many others."[35] WORLD's retreats were held in order to constitute "a place where women most readily transcend the barriers erected by centuries of racism and classism, to share their grief and support for one another. In spite of all the 'isms' that divide, a mother's love for her children is universal."[36] If Denison's essay, like much of *Women Resisting AIDS*, is flawed by a nation-state focus, it is fully alive to the struggles of the poor within our borders.

The women who organized WORLD were not, by and large, élite professionals. The organization was "grassroots" in the sense that it was brought into existence by women living with HIV and familiar with quotidian struggles for access to basic resources. But there is nonetheless a significant gap between women whose lives might be meaningfully improved by newsletters and retreats and those who, like Darlene and Guylène and Lata, struggle for survival. The experience of women living in extreme poverty—women sharing, often, extremely high risks for HIV—invades our consciousness as we read comments such as the following: "Before we could apply for grants, we had to learn how to make grant applications, how to develop programs, how to use the computer, how to incorporate and apply for nonprofit status, how to function as a board of directors, how to recruit and use volunteers. All of this takes time."[37] It takes more than time, sadly. It takes access to basic resources—literacy and electricity, say—that elude the majority of women with HIV infection.

Women Resisting AIDS contains two chapters by women who identify with the prostitutes' rights movement. One of their lessons is that, even among U.S. sex workers, community organizing is riven by class differences. In "Sex Workers Fight Against AIDS," Alexander, for 17 years a community activist and researcher, offers a careful and well-documented overview of recent efforts to organize sex workers. She contrasts two distinct types of societal responses to STDs among prostitutes: reglementary STD-control responses, which have a long and undistinguished history, and community-based responses, which are new and owe much, she notes, to AIDS. The chapter reviews the underpinnings of these responses, and then proceeds to a report on the status of community-based organizing on five continents. As might be expected, the rights of prostitutes in certain wealthy European countries and in Australia and New Zealand are better protected than are those working in the United States or in poor countries, but there are heartening reports from Africa and countries such as Thailand. Alexander also reports that, in 1991, a "Network of Sex Work-related HIV/AIDS Projects" was formed "in order to facilitate the sharing of information, strategies, and other ideas between projects around the world, especially in developing countries."[38]

The shortcomings of this fine review are to be found in a number of comments that reveal conventional wisdom about the nature of causality as regards both prostitution and the AIDS pandemic. For example, Alexander claims that "the nature of the discourse on prostitution has a profound effect on both the form and the outcome of AIDS prevention interventions, and thus on the course of AIDS."[39] The two claims in this declaration—that discourse on prostitution directly affects AIDS interventions and that AIDS interventions directly affect the course of the pandemic—are hypotheses, and not yet supported by empirical research. Indeed, in some settings, both distribution and outcome of HIV infection (like other STDs before it) vary quite independently of both ideologies about the disorder and of interventions to prevent their spread. In some passages, Alexander seems to acknowledge this: "The reality," she notes, "is that, regardless of laws, commercial sex occurs in every country and culture, its extent determined largely by economic forces."[40]

In her overview of interventions, Alexander reports with enthusiasm the efforts of sex workers from across the globe to protect themselves by promoting condom use through various forms of "social marketing" (stickers, posters, wallet-sized cards, buttons, and "camera-ready logos" are cited as examples). Again, the efficacy of such strategies, which are touted by many large development agencies, varies enormously in different settings. The triumph of social marketing in a country like Switzerland, a success cited by Alexander, does not necessarily predict success in the red-light district of Bombay, to say nothing of other settings in which mere survival is the key goal of sexual liaisons, as Guylène's story suggests. In many such unions, conception of a child is a desired result of intercourse (since the child's birth can result in improved life chances for the mother and, often, her other dependents). Condoms are thus not part of the scenario. As Carovano has noted: "To provide women exclusively with HIV prevention methods that contradict most societies' fertility norms is to provide many women with no options at all."[41]

Alexander's work is pioneering, and these weaknesses suggest not the need to broaden her geographical scope, which is admirably broad, but rather to doggedly insist that questions regarding, say, the adoption of certain practices (e.g., condom use) be rooted in broader social analyses. Another weakness is Alexander's plea for the specificity of local knowledge and her affirmation of prostitutes' discernment: "As workers on the front lines, prostitutes know best the obstacles to behavioral change, whether it is the frequency with which police confiscate or damage condoms; sex workers' belief that ingesting semen keeps one young, healthy, and attractive; managers' fear of lost business; or clients' belief that health certificates guarantee noninfection."[42] Is this really a list of the most striking "obstacles to behavior change" now facing the majority of the world's sex workers? It may be a start, but sex workers driven through desperation to standing on the street, selling sex for pennies, face a different set of obstacles. Africanist historian Iliffe writes of "subsistence prostitution by women driven by poverty." Kinshasa's call girls (vedettes) are far outnumbered by the city's despised chambres d'hôtel, one of whom told an anthropologist, "I am a woman and I have no learning: what work is there for me except prostitution?"[43] In the Amhara region of Ethiopia, of women questioned for a 1987 study about their "chief reason" for becoming prostitutes, 40% cited lack of employment, 30% cited divorce, and 13% needed to augment meager incomes: "During the day we wear our old clothes and go begging," according to one. "At night we go out with men."[44] Most of these women are now dead from AIDS, and many of their children are dead, as well.

There are enormous regional variations in the push-pull forces that lead, ultimately, to sex work: "Many organizations that originally were formed to fight 'trafficking in women' quickly recognized that the problems faced were not simply those of women victimized by 'traffickers.' Often women migrate with the conscious intent to work as prostitutes in the host country, as a way to improve their own economic status or to help their families at home."[45] Here, Alexander over-simplifies the question of agency, for migration with "conscious intent to work as a prostitute" does not perforce mean that women are not victimized. Many would argue that steep grades of inequality almost always characterize situations in which women move from one country to another in order to engage in sex work. The analysis of prostitution must also be transnational, not merely centered on individuals' "conscious intent." How else will we explain German tourists in Thai brothels? Nepali girls in Bombay streets? Korean women shipped to Japan and classified as "military supplies"?

Similarly dissonant notes might be sounded in response to the sex workers' movement's push for the professionalization of prostitutes, for the process tends, in many instances, to widen the gap—and lessen the chance for solidarity—between professionals and the more vulnerable "subsistence" prostitutes.[46] The review glosses over rifts within the prostitutes' rights movements, which figures prominently in a chapter based on a 1993 interview with Gloria Lockett, who became involved in political organizing when she was arrested for prostitution and conspiracy in 1982—a charge she found to be "stupid, racist, sexist, and biased." The essay is subtitled "The Struggle to Survive," and describes the experience of CAL-PEP, the

California Prostitutes Education Project. Lockett writes about some of the other prostitutes' rights organizations:

> One of the problems I have with other organizations, like COYOTE, is that they're just too white for me. Most of those people don't go to jail, mainly because they're white and they're call girls. I mean, it's not their fault. The police want to bust people who are easier for them to bust, and that's the women who are on the streets. It's that simple. People of color, especially blacks and Latinas, are the ones who are in jail most, and that's not because they commit more crimes. They're just easier to get, and people can believe that they committed a crime easier than they can believe that blondes commit crimes.[47]

The experiences of women in CAL-PEP—which actually received funding for safer-sex workshops from the CDC—are quite distinct from experiences of poor sex workers in poor countries, where, often enough, there is no discernible "community" of prostitutes.[48]

Another interesting and textured chapter, by sociologist Reback, is "Constructing the Outreach Movement: Street Interventions to Women at Risk." This chapter is helpful because it makes its theoretical underpinnings explicit and offers "thick description" in the form of dialogue with several of the outreach workers who staff the Los Angeles branch of Women and AIDS Risk Network (WARN), a multisite project AIDS-prevention program funded by NIDA. To judge from the description offered by Reback, these women have made remarkable contributions to the struggle against AIDS. Most of them have personal histories of addiction or abuse; almost all have been the victims of structural violence. The author asserts: "The paraprofessional outreach workers come from the communities they now work in, so they are culturally sensitive and have personal knowledge of high-risk sex and drug behavior."[49] For Reback, then, a life of tribulations educates and strengthens one to do culturally sensitive outreach work. "When an outreach worker enters the field," notes Reback, "she has been trained to be confident that each woman she will meet has her own inner strength."[50] "Inner strength" and "empowerment" are two of the chapter's catchphrases. "Empowerment is the hub of WARN," she notes. It is realized through: "(1) listening to the women; (2) entering the field with a value-free attitude; (3) working with a woman according to her own agenda; and (4) giving her the tools to achieve her goals."[51]

Among the "tools" in question are gifts. In this project, cosmetics companies donate a series of luxury gifts which the outreach workers distribute to women; these "excite the woman's interest and hold a specific meaning for her. Because they are luxury items," goes the logic, "the giver is coded as a friend, not a patron."[52] As anthropologists, we have no objection to the distribution of gifts, regardless of provenance, but do wonder about just-so stories about such prestations and the process of empowerment:

> The outreach moment is turned around, and the woman decides whether or not to accept the gift, be it a cosmetic, condoms, bleach, or an AIDS pamphlet. The woman does not feel trapped; she is not forced into a situation in which she must explain or defend her behavior. She is given a choice, an option. The moment is hers, the empowerment begins.[53]

This empowerment appears to occur through a process that is more mystical than political: "mutuality of the interaction—listening, suggesting options, and looking at a woman's inner strengths—leads to empowerment."[54]

Reback's chapter is imbued with a complicated admixture of identity politics—"outreach workers must identify on some level with the target population"[55]—and suffused with unexamined but feel-good terms like "community" and "culture." There are also occasional platitudes: "Give a woman a fish, and feed her for a day; teach a woman to fish, and feed her for life." The author is also caught in a paradigm in which efficacy narrowly construed must justify the existence of projects. For some, the provision of employment opportunities is ample justification for a project ("Give a woman a decent job," one might add, "and feed her for life"), given that the much abused term "at-risk" is so often a gloss for unemployed or underemployed and, therefore, poor. A more modest description of the work of AIDS prevention is offered by one of the outreach workers: "For me it's like chopping down a mountain with a toothpick."[56]

Women Resisting AIDS, which is subtitled "Feminist Strategies of Empowerment," is at its weakest whenever immodest claims of causality are advanced. When we read that "Low self-esteem is a significant 'co-factor' that leads many women to be at risk of acquiring HIV,"[57] we would like to ask for the data that support such a claim. To appreciate the ways in which the un-examined language of self-empowerment creeps into the book, one might read Sosnowitz's "AIDS Prevention, Minority Women and Gender Assertiveness," which relates the experience of working with a small group of "minority" teens and young adults on a college campus in the northeastern United States. Clearly, there are major dangers in extrapolating from the experience of a small group of students who met for only 14 weeks.[58] But more serious, in our opinion, are the leaps of faith necessary to follow the author's logic in interpreting the experience. The intervention she describes consisted of "AIDS Discovery Class" for 40 "minority" students, many of whom, she notes, did not understand terms such as "vaginal," "anal," and "oral." "It was obvious," writes Sosnowitz, "that a more personal, understandable method was needed to discuss these terms, so that safe sex could be practiced."[59] Through talk, safe sex becomes an option in the world Sosnowitz describes. Exercises in promoting dexterity with condoms—making jewelry out of condoms and games in which cucumbers must be adroitly sheathed with condoms—are imbued with future transforming power. The author argues that as a result of such games, "The norms of public conversation were being changed. Without self consciousness, the students were discussing condoms openly."[60]

The three major problems arising from this chapter are common to many such overviews, which are often dampened by cliché and rife with generalizations not underpinned by research. For example, we read of "the youthful appetite for sex"; we read of whole cultures characterized by a "lack of openness" or that suffer "cultural paranoia."[61] Sosnowitz discusses "Black responses" and "Latino responses" to AIDS as if vast intergroup diversity did not exist. In discussing Latino responses, for example, the author notes that, "By suggesting that women should be assertive in protecting themselves against disease and pregnancy by discussing sexual histories with their partners, prevention initiatives are asking for gender behavior that is discouraged in Latino cultures."[62] Similarly,

> Sexual responsibility falls to the female in both the black and Latino groups, responsibility particularly difficult for some given these groups lack of openness surrounding the subject. Furthermore, females who feel guilty about having sex are less likely to take precautions against pregnancy or disease. There is also evidence that young women of racial/ethnic groups, like young white women, frequently are unable to insist on methods that could protect them from sexually transmitted diseases . . . The combination of denial and the inability to discuss sex increases the likelihood of minority young women contacting a sexually transmitted disease, including AIDS.[63]

In another sweeping generalization, the author asserts that many of the groups under discussion, beleaguered by social problems, "live in the present." Cultures which are "present-oriented" may have difficulty appreciating the concept of latent infection.[64]

In short, bold claims that culturally constructed "denial" or "inability to discuss sex" directly increase risk for HIV infection are made throughout, as they are made elsewhere in the AIDS literature. In fact, such causal relationships have never been clearly demonstrated. These claims underpin an even more influential leitmotiv: the reason for increased risk and for program failure are located in the minds of "minority" youth. In such a view, it is by changing their cognitive structures—rather than, say, their living conditions—that risk may be altered. Similarly, dependence on essentialist conceptions of "race," ethnicity, and culture set authors up to overemphasize the agency of those who suffer disproportionately.

Ultimately, Sosnowitz makes a number of assertions that conflate cause and effect. Writes Sosnowitz: "Small groups can be used to empower women by providing a setting in which they can express their inner fears and gain acceptance and encouragement from others."[65] This unproven assertion, as we have seen, is commonplace in AIDS-prevention work. We suspect that real empowerment of poor "minority women" will not be achieved through small-group discussion among them, no matter how affirming of their self esteem these talks might be.

One of the few scholarly journals taking AIDS, gender inequality, and poverty as its central problematic was a special issue of *Culture, Medicine and Psychiatry* devoted to "Women, Poverty, and AIDS."[66] The five studies presented are primarily focused on "inner cities" of the United States. In a sense, then, each of them examines what it means to be a poor woman in a rich country. A brief introductory essay added data from Haiti, a setting of far greater material privation. In both rich and poor countries, it was argued that both large-scale and local forces conspire to put women at risk for exposure to HIV early in their adult lives.

In each setting examined, the large-scale forces are similar, but these studies also explore the "local knowledge" usually studied by anthropologists. An exception is the first paper, in which Gupta and Weiss offer an overview of the effects of HIV on women throughout the world. The paper presents findings from the Women and AIDS Program, a research effort undertaken by the International Center for Research on Women. The findings Gupta and Weiss present come from 17 research projects in 13 different countries located in Africa, Asia, Latin America, and the Caribbean. Research associated with these programs provides "insights into the realities of women's lives—their sexual behavior and experiences and the ways in which sociocultural and economic factors affect their vulnerability to HIV."[67]

Specifically, the Women and AIDS Program looks at barriers which affect the adoption of AIDS risk reduction behaviors by women. The barriers examined exist on several levels, including individual lack of knowledge and skills; social norms and beliefs that interfere with or disable women's practice of AIDS risk reduction; and "socioeconomic determinants of women's risk of HIV at the individual and household level that in turn result from broader macro-level economic and social conditions."[68] The socioeconomic barriers cited by Gupta and Weiss include widespread economic recession and poverty, political and economic instability, unequal power among men and women, the persistence of legal discrimination against women,

women's low economic status, women's low educational status, domestic violence against women, women being forced into nonconsensual sexual relationships, the fact that women's status is often tied to their roles as wives and mothers, and the fact that, due to migration and abandonment and divorce, women are left alone to run households.[69]

Gupta and Weiss make several policy and program-oriented suggestions designed to overcome these barriers. Many of these—educating women about AIDS and other STDs, increasing women's ability to use condoms, and providing women with counseling in order to help them practice safer behaviors—are aimed at the level of individual actors. What is important about Gupta and Weiss' suggestions for change, however, is that they also underline the importance of change in the socioeconomic systems that structure HIV risks for women. They advocate, for example, the creation of policies and programs which improve women's social status as well as their economic status. The authors call for more economic opportunites for women by providing access to credit, educational opportunities, job-skills training, and jobs. Gupta and Weiss also signal the importance of programs that rally community support for changing power relations between men and women.[70]

If the Gupta and Weiss paper makes explicit the important roles that poverty and gender inequality play in the AIDS pandemic, Ward's U.S.-focused essay gets to the heart of the matter by arguing that HIV infection in poor women is a "qualitatively different disease" than AIDS as defined in the early 1980s. Drawing on over a decade of experience studying the provision of prenatal and family-planning services to poor women in Louisiana and elsewhere in the United States, Ward examines the impact of HIV among women living in communities already hard-hit by addiction, unemployment, high infant mortality, and the malignant neglect of recent federal administrations. She shows that "the very females at highest risk for HIV are also ones already identified with illness and death. They are the very people who are unlikely to hear the educational messages or to seek medical help from a system already faltering and failing them."[71] Questions of agency are directly addressed, leaving Ward skeptical of preventive messages that trumpet the importance of condom use: "The implication is that women have both political and cortical control over their own sexual practices."[72] She counters naïve social marketing by underlining the social forces that constrain human agency. The most powerful of these, as noted, are gender and class: "It is less risk or risk-taking than an inescapable status that defines the danger to women."[73]

Pivnick, working in the Bronx, details the meanings associated with condoms among a group of poor, urban women on methadone, most of whom were African-American or Latina, and some of whom were HIV-positive. Pivnick found, as have many others working else-where in the urban United States, that although there was wide-spread knowledge about AIDS in general and about the efficacy of condoms in particular, few of these women reported that their part-ners used condoms. Yet these women, including Darlene in Chapter 1, have already been touched by AIDS. In such a setting, Pivnick explores the meanings behind non-use of condoms, which local health officials have pushed as "the only hope" for preventing AIDS. She shows that "condoms do not signify birth control, venereal dis-ease prevention, or, as many had hoped, prevention of HIV trans-mission. Rather, condoms signify the presence of AIDS and therefore death."[74] Not using a condom, in contrast, is invested with an alto-gether different set of meanings: "For the informants in this study, intimacy and fidelity are confirmed by having sex with a partner without a condom."[75]

Working in public maternal-and-child health clinics, Sobo studied a small sample of poor African-American women living in Cleveland. As in the Bronx, condoms were rarely used. In discussing why not, the women interviewed recounted stories, "monogamy nar-ratives," in which their own troubled unions were nonetheless described as "monogamous, caring, satisfying," and "leav[ing] neither partner desirous of sex or love from outside sources."[76] These ideals did not square with condom use, which carried a considerable and nega-tive symbolic load: "Refusing to acknowledge the possibility that one's mate has sex with other women (or men) supports the monogamy narrative. Unsafe sex supports it too: unsafe sex deflects attention from adultery and deceit and focuses it instead on the trust and hon-esty."[77] Ultimately, Sobo reaches a conclusion similar to those reached in Haiti, Louisiana, and the Bronx: condom use was "avoided because of women's structural inability to mandate it. Women refigure the decision to remain condomless as elected rather than imposed in order to avoid having to confront the fact that they are often coerced by and socially and economically dependent upon men."[78]

Glick Schiller combines a more quantitative field survey, conducted in urban New Jersey, with interpretive and critical anthropology to yield a striking reinterpretation of the use of women's labor during the AIDS epidemic. She states that, "In health services research about the utilization by and financing of health services for people with AIDS, women kin as caregivers virtually disappear and the sacrifices made by women kin become socially invisible."[79] Glick Schiller discerns several reasons for this blindness to women's provision of services, including the fact that people with AIDS are often culturally constructed as the "dangerous other." "To be human is to be familiar, that is to have family. By imagining persons with AIDS as people without families, they become unknown entities removed from our empathy."[80] Another reason women's work in the AIDS pandemic has been ignored, according to Glick Schiller, is because the "legitimate" agencies of public health have chosen not to recognize women's contributions.

In addition to being disproportionately affected by AIDS, women are called upon to bear the brunt of caretaking activities. The paper brings into relief the cynicism behind certain calls for more "community-based services." Often, these services are the unpaid labor of women kin:

> For women, the epidemic is not only increasingly a killer in its own right. The manner in which AIDS health services are being represented intensifies the oppressive conditions within which many women live their lives, even as it removes the work of women kin of people with AIDS from public purview. To reveal the unspeakable burdens being shouldered by the women kin who care for family members with AIDS is to challenge the manner in which health services are conceptualized by U.S. health researchers and public officials.[81]

The journal's tenor is gloomy, although the editors note that the "purpose of this collection of papers was not to compile defeatist insights concerning AIDS and women."[82] The message that seems to echo through each of these studies, including that conducted in Haiti, is that the forces helping to place poor women at risk of HIV infection will not be effectively addressed by making AIDS-prevention programs more "culturally appropriate." Poverty, note the editors, "weakens women's ability to negotiate 'safe' sexual encounters, just as it weakens their ability to avoid other dangerous situations. Sexism further erodes this autonomy, as do addiction, violence, concurrent disease, and a host of other problems."[83] Martha Ward summarizes the doubts of all of the authors. Referring to linkages between socioeconomic status and health, she states:

> These linkages suggest that prevention strategies should concentrate on new forms of primary health care for women before behavior-modification campaigns; these linkages also suggest that the primary health care systems for American women were already inadequate without the addition of yet another sexually transmitted disease, already epidemic in poor women and, furthermore, that the health care delivery system is unlikely to improve.[84]

A strength of this collection is its sharp focus on poor women; the papers explicitly explore the relationships between class, culture, and illness causation. But there are shortcomings, as well: there are too few papers, and each is marked by the standard problems seen with ethnographic work: small study sizes and limited generalizability. Here, too, the gaze is not rigorously transnational—most of the papers are based on U.S. materials.[85] Finally, *Culture, Medicine, and Psychiatry*'s circulation is limited, largely, to a small circle of medical anthropologists, who, as noted, have often given short shrift to issues of class.

Both *Women Resisting AIDS* and the special "Women, Poverty, and AIDS" issue of *Culture, Medicine, and Psychiatry* illustrate several problems that need to be addressed in the social-science literature on AIDS. We will explore them, and others, throughout the remainder of the chapter. It is worth noting here, however, that immodest claims of causality regarding both local subepidemics and the pandemic are made throughout even the best literature on women, poverty, and AIDS. In some writings, the quirks of "minority cultures" are held to explain high rates of infection; in others, gender inequality alone explains the disparities in infection rates; in still others, low self-esteem is invoked as the culprit in the maldistribution that is registered.

Further, the "activist" literature is written by leaders and, as such, may not always accountable to the poor, who are themselves rarely in leadership positions. Much of the literature glosses over issues of class that divide feminist approaches. Noting that "HIV makes a mockery of pretend unity and sisterhood," Hollibaugh forthrightly asks, "Who is the 'we' in our sisterhood?"[86] Similarly, immodest claims of program success are often explicitly linked by most of the authors to "empowerment," a catch-all phrase that implies everything from enhanced sense of personal efficacy to successful negotiation of safe sex. Only occasionally do contributors mean by "empowerment" the transfer of resources and power away from some groups and to women living in poverty. And only rarely is it actually acknowledged that it is poor women, not all women, who need to be empowered. Almost never is it acknowledged that many powerful women, like powerful men, often achieve their positions at the expense of poor women.

With rare exceptions, then, analysis is not transnational, although the AIDS pandemic is. Even the international studies are insufficiently systemic. Too often, these investigations refer to certain "communities"—again, a problematic term—as if they existed in isolation from larger, often global, systems that distribute not only resources but also HIV.[87] Class relations within the United States are grounded in, and powerfully forged by, an increasingly global socioeconomic system. Surely the AIDS pandemic, itself shaped by the same emerging system, is best analyzed within a framework that can help explain how the large-scale comes to be manifest in the local. By restricting the scope of the analytic gaze to local actors and local factors, it is possible to miss many of these large-scale forces altogether. As we shall see, one of the means by which such restriction occurs is through behaviorist and cognitivist approaches to AIDS and AIDS prevention.

2. BEHAVIORISM AND OTHER
IMMODEST CLAIMS OF CAUSALITY

Psychological theories about human behavior have had a huge, and largely unexamined, influence on the ways in which AIDS-prevention efforts have proceeded. These theories have appeared in many permutations, some of which have engendered trends and schools within the behavioral sciences. But psychological theories cannot by themselves explain the differential distribution of HIV infection vis-à-vis gender. To do so would require recourse to largely discredited attempts to constitute a generic psychology of women. For similar reasons, disproportionately high rates of infection in many sub-Saharan African regions do not lend themselves to a purely psychological explanation—there is no pan-African psychology.[88]

These issues could be skirted in 1984, when the occurrence of AIDS in women and in poor countries was almost wholly invisible to the scholarly gaze. Gender was not examined so much as sexual preference, a focus that reflected, in a sense, an epidemiological accident: the country with the largest number of behavioral scientists was also that with a large AIDS epidemic afflicting, primarily, gay men. Declaring AIDS a "psychological emergency," some psychologists got busy; they began important inquiries into the effects of the epidemic on gay men, both those infected with the virus and those who witnessed and feared its devastating effects. Counseling strategies were devised, often bringing real comfort to those in need.

However, immodest attempts to build "theories" and "models" were not long in following. There were, for example, a number of attempts to constitute a "psychology of AIDS." In a paper entitled "Psychological Research Is Essential to Understanding and Treating AIDS," Coates and co-workers attempted to relate personality factors to disease progression and survival with AIDS:

> Psychosocial factors; including personality variables and transient states, partially influence susceptibility to environmental stressors. Genetic and environmental factors would also influence susceptibility to stress. Thus, we propose that the interaction of genetic, environmental, and psychosocial factors that may, at various times, protect the organism, predispose the organism to disease onset, or influence the course of disease once contact.[89]

The problem with such models lies as much in what is not discussed—here, the larger social contexts in which the "organism" in question makes decisions, many of them constrained by cultural and, especially, politico-economic factors.[90] Even in 1984, differential survival between, say, a poor Haitian with AIDS and an insured San Franciscan with AIDS was significant. These differences were not explained by personality factors.

Many of the AIDS-related claims of behavioral scientists echoed a common refrain: "Without effective treatments or cures," noted Batchelor in a special issue of *American Psychologist*, "the only hope for stopping the spread of AIDS is through prevention—and the behavioral and social sciences offer the best perspective in changing individual and group behaviors." Batchelor argued further that "The fundamental relationships between psychological/behavioral factors and health/disease status are not generally recognized by health policy officials."[91] A more recent declaration by CDC director, David Satcher, reveals just how influential the behaviorist program has become:

> We cannot overstate the role of behavioral science in our effort to 'get ahead of the curve' with emerging infections. Having the science or laboratory technology to control infectious disease is not enough, unless we can influence people to behave in ways that minimize the transmission of infections and maximize the efforts of medical interventions. For example, even though HIV/AIDS does not have a vaccine or cure, it is almost entirely preventable. For many people, however, reducing the risk for HIV infection and AIDS requires important changes in lifestyle and behavior. We must use our knowledge of human behavior to help people make lifestyle changes and prevent disease.[92]

The assumptions underpinning this statement work on at least three levels. One, echoing many psychologists' claims, is that the means of reducing risk of HIV is through *changing lifestyle and behavior*. Setting aside for a moment the validity of this assertion, the expression itself—"lifestyle and behavior"—merits careful examination.

In the nineties, when the highest incidence of new HIV infections is registered among poor women, most of whom live in the southern hemisphere, attention to the concept "lifestyle" forces a number of questions: Whose lifestyles and whose behaviors does the CDC's Satcher have in mind? In 1995, when the statement was published, it would be addressed to people like Darlene, Guylène, and Lata—women living in poverty—and also to their partners. But is gender inequality part of a particular lifestyle? Can poverty be termed a lifestyle? Addiction to narcotics? Prostitution?

The call to change "lifestyle and behavior" is directed toward precisely those persons whose agency is most harshly constrained. Clearly, *assumptions about the nature of human agency*—the second level of supposition apparent in Satcher's comment—are embedded in the paragraph cited. The term "lifestyle" suggests that people may choose, freely and equally, to avoid or to engage in risk. In certain middle-class strata, individuals do alter risk by lifestyle change. To diminish risk for coronary artery disease, say, one stops smoking, joins a health club, reads nutrition labels and buys low-fat foods. But ignoring or overlooking sociological variables inevitably leads to a spurious understanding of the dynamics of HIV spread. Such misunderstandings are the inevitable result of exclusive focus on individuals, as a recent Institute of Medicine report, *Assessing the Social and Behavioral Science Base for HIV/AIDS Prevention and Intervention*, has noted: "Until now, most behaviorally based AIDS prevention research has focused on the individual...it must also be recognized that all individual behavior is embedded in and influenced by its social and physical environment...But broader social forces such as economics, politics, and international affairs also shape individual decisions."[93] Similar suppositions are firmly rooted in modern epidemiology, as we shall see in Chapter 6.[94]

A third problem, again with theoretical underpinnings and closely related to the previously cited issues, concerns the *scope of analyses*. How is the field of social inquiry on AIDS and AIDS prevention circumscribed? Behavioral scientists' calls to change individual behaviors and lifestyles do not give voice to the strain of structural conditions that restrict human agency in systemic and unequal ways.[95] In the current intellectual division of labor, these structural conditions are more often studied by sociologists, political economists, historians, and some anthropologists.[96] Thus a welcome plea for cross-disciplinary cooperation can serve, ultimately, to frame research and prevention questions in ways that favor certain forms of inquiry over others. More to the point, the individualistic, lifestyle-and-behavior approach to AIDS and AIDS prevention which predominates tends to obscure the crux of the problem now posed by the increasing incidence of AIDS among poor women.[97]

This division of labor is reflected in much AIDS and STD research. Among the many undefined factors and traits discussed in psychological research on AIDS are "neuroticism," "psychoticism," "prudishness," "guilt," and "extraversion." Also explored are relationships between STDs and attributes ranging from "parental indifference" to "mood states" and "emotional insecurity." Thus there are studies which purport to show, for example, "significant and positive correlations between neuroticism and syphilis and gonorrhea."[98] On the other hand, there is relatively little discussion of the possible significance of social structural variables, such as income or educational inequality level, access to medical services, or racism and discrimination.

Many defend restricted fields of inquiry by noting the authors' explicit intentions to examine psychological variables. However, the problem is not so much in the topics chosen for inquiry, but rather in the tendency to elevate these chosen variables to the status of determinants of sexual practices and HIV risk while, at the same time, ignoring other extrapersonal variables which demonstrably affect sexual practices and HIV risk.[99] Indeed, one authority goes beyond arguing that STDs are "behavioral diseases," and insists that "all sociological variables implicated in venereal disease are primarily related to the personality of the individual."[100] In transforming STDs from social disease to behavioral disease, sociological variables are swept under the rug of individual personality traits. The effects of such desocialization are often striking in this constricted field of inquiry.

An illustration of how these assumptions work in AIDS research is a key 1988 review article by Becker and Joseph entitled "AIDS and Behavioral Change to Reduce Risk: A Review." These two influential psychologists were invited by the *American Journal of Public Health* to review the subject of AIDS risk reduction and to comment upon prospects for the future. The review begins with the commonly heard mantra of AIDS prevention: "The prospect for either a vaccine or a definitive treatment for those already infected remains remote, and attention must therefore focus on the only available measure: alteration of those human behaviors essential to transmission of HIV."[101] On one level, these opening lines, are basic and non-controversial. On a deeper level, however, they act to sharply limit the domain of intervention to individual behavior. Vast arenas of action—for example, improving housing for women living in poverty, changing land inheritance laws, or even altering the economic inequalities that seem so linked to AIDS—are neglected in this vision. Becker and Joseph continue:

> Prevention of HIV transmission requires either abstinence from or modi-fication of relevant behaviors. In particular, celibacy and the avoidance of IV drug use would be sufficient to virtually halt the spread of HIV—but widespread compliance with such extreme measures seems unlikely, necessitating control strategies which involve modification rather than elimination of risk-related behaviors.[102]

Where is the locus of control in such a formulation? What models of agency underpin this way of construing risk? How is the social field shaped in this perspective? The answers to these questions are not long in coming: "Despite the specific behavioral imperatives posed by AIDS and the more general public health enthusiasm for individual behavioral risk reduction," continue Becker and Joseph, "idiosyncratic features of HIV infection and AIDS require more care-ful consideration. These features arise from the unique biological characteristics of the retroviruses, from the epidemiological aspects of the epidemic, and from the enveloping social context."[103] Lest we think that the social field will be widened to include, perhaps, the effects of certain social policies on the urban poor, Becker and Joseph restrict even further the frame of analysis. They highlight three of these "features": 1) *Biological* features, to which category they assign "wasting or obvious lesions, disability, dependence, and dementia," 2) *Psychological* features, including the "extreme uncertainty charac-terize[ing] the entire process," which results in "marked psychologi-cal distress," and 3) *Social* features, by which they narrowly mean "disrupted personal or familial relationships," and decidedly not the structural conditions which are so intimately linked to the AIDS pandemic.[104] The individual's social field, in this view, is limited to persons with whom he or she comes into contact on a regular basis. Cultural systems, historical social structures, and power relations have little place in this analytic view.

Becker and Joseph, echoing the researchers they review, find other ways to restrict the analytical field. They note that existing research has been conducted "in the male homosexual/bisexual community." The term "community" is not defined.[105] Becker and Joseph focus on geographical locations—large urban centers in the United States and Europe. As argued in Chapter 1, any geography that is not located in social space obscures the chief forces that drive forward the pandemic.[106]

Becker and Joseph's review does not find fault in studies that fail to contextualize the data they gather. But the theoretical and methodological shortcomings of many of the "KABP" (Knowledge, Attitudes, Beliefs, and Practices) studies they reviewed are significant. From an anthropological perspective, many of the shortcomings of survey data arise from the fact that data are ripped from their social context.[107] Although conducted in large part by social scientists, these investigations rarely explore socioeconomic and cultural variables, even though "race" is occasionally mentioned.

The studies reviewed are largely investigations of gay men, but one must ask what kinds of descriptors characterize their lives outside of gay bars and bathhouses? Were these men college-educated, white? Real explorations require more complex and detailed questions. For example, in one study Becker and Joseph review, the subjects are described as a "well-educated convenience sample of 745 self-identified gay men aged 20-65." Here, three variables are dealt with: education, sexual preference, and age. But is educational level a proxy for other factors which relate more directly to economic privilege? Are variables such as housing and insurance status of HIV-positive persons related to outcomes? Substance abuse is discussed without reference to the poverty and racism which discipline its social distribution in much of the world.

The studies Becker and Joseph review do not, by and large, address key questions of power or stigma. Even when the problem of power differentials flare up in the review, they are quickly extinguished. For example, the discussion of the differences between gay men and injection drug user starts off clearly enough: "Unlike the gay community, which is relatively organized and generally characterized by educational and socioeconomic advantage, more IVDUs are members of minority communities and their average level of education is lower."[108] Quickly deployed, however, is a confusing use of the words "culture" and "subculture." A spurious equality is then advanced: "Language and literacy problems are well recognized, and communication in this subculture is generally oral rather than written. Furthermore, both the majority culture and the IVDU subculture tend to hold negative stereotypes of one another. There is a general impression that IVDUs are incapable of (or disinterested in) changing their behavior, while IVDUs view public health authorities with suspicion and distrust."[109] These kinds of comments must be subjected to careful scrutiny. In absence of such a lack of social detail, these studies lead quickly toward cognitivist and psychological reductionism, and devolve to speculations about "personality predispositions" and "difficulties in sexual impulse control."[110] Left unexamined is a range of social forces that may be much more tightly bound to risk.

KABP studies are pervasive in the social science literature on women and AIDS. Typical of this genre of writing is Nyamathi and co-workers' 1993 study "AIDS Related Knowledge and Behaviors among Impoverished Minority Women," which is reviewed in Chapter 1 of *Women, Poverty, and AIDS*. As noted, their research showed that, among poor women of color in Los Angeles, knowledge of HIV was adequate to prevent transmission, if indeed such cognitive questions were relevant to the prevention of AIDS among these women. But knowledge did not predict practice.[111] The same research team later definitively shows that more education is not related to safer behavior. In fact, in the 1993 study, they find that "greater knowledge of HIV was found to be positively associated with injection drug use in African American women."[112] Despite these findings, the authors still emphasize the need for more education: "clearly, impoverished African-American women are very much in need of culturally sensitive counseling about the risks of non-intravenous drug use and sex with multiple partners."[113]

The researchers show that what women already know has failed to protect them from HIV infection, yet the analysis remains locked in a paradigm in which the only possible remedy is better education. The theme is widely echoed in the literature.[114] Mak and Plum pose the question "Do Prostitutes Need More Health Education Regarding Sexually Transmitted Diseases and the HIV Infection?" From 1988 to 1989, 154 female prostitutes who worked in clubs and behind windows in and around Ghent, Belgium, were recruited at their workplaces. Of these women, 72.1 percent were Belgian, 16.2 percent other European, 8.4 percent North African, and 3.2 percent West and Central African. The participants were asked about their sources of AIDS information (television, social network, newspapers, etc.), their knowledge of safe sex techniques (Which practices are safe? Unsafe? Doubtful?), and sex acts performed with clients as well as clients' reaction to prostitutes' proposals to use condoms. According to the authors, less than half the women gave more than seven correct answers on 11 questions about the safety of various sex techniques. Many of the women, we read, considered intercourse with a condom safer than deep kissing, masturbation, and even massage. But do available data allow us to assert with authority that these rankings are clearly incorrect? What was striking was that 99.4 percent of these women rated sex without a condom as unsafe, and yet in 10 to 20 percent of professional sex contacts, no condoms were used. Proposals for condom use almost always came from the women instead of the clients. The study concludes with a misleading note of equality: "health education efforts to prostitutes and their clients [are] not sufficient and that they should be intensified."[115]

But what is insufficient is sex workers' authority to use the knowledge they already have. When the women asked clients to wear a condom, almost one third of them reported that clients had asked to pay less for sex, and 70.5 percent of the women reported that the clients said they would go elsewhere for sex. The study thus reveals a social mechanism that helps in understanding the greater risk of male-to-female transmission, and it is a mechanism that will not be removed by education alone. Men's unwillingness to use condoms and the economic power of male clients in such encounters suggest that even if women had more knowledge about HIV, this might not efficiently alter their risks. Indeed, one must ask whether women "choose" to have unsafe sex at all.[116]

Questions of agency are scanted in most KABP-type studies, even in those conducted in settings of great poverty. In central Zaïre, Brown and co-workers examined the preference of both men and women for a "dry, tight" vagina. These tactile qualities are held to increase sexual pleasure: both men and women reported receiving greater sexual pleasure from "dry, tight" vaginas, which in this study were popularly associated with female virginity and fidelity. Focus-group participants—poorly educated men and women from minority ethnic groups, petty traders, prostitutes, and mine workers—described the techniques and substances used to produce these desired "drying" and "tightening" effects. Pelvic examinations by a physician evaluated the physical consequences of the use of these substances.

Over one-third of the women had actually used tightening or drying substances at some time. Examinations suggested that these materials disrupt the integrity of the vagina and uterine cervix, increasing the likelihood of trauma-induced lesions for both partners, but particularly for women, during intercourse. Again, the study attributes risk of infection to the sexual preferences of women: "Women...may be placing themselves and their partners at high risk for STDs, including AIDS."[117] Again, the potential role of women's dependence on men in a setting of poverty and gender inequality never enters the frame of inquiry.

Even when questions of agency are central to the inquiry, problems of interpretation abound. Aruffo and co-workers examine "health locus of control" (HLOC) and its relation to knowledge about HIV transmission. Specifically, their goal is to determine the extent to which perceptions of control over health predict knowledge of AIDS transmission and prevention. Five hundred and eighty seven patients from community health centers in Harris County, Texas, were chosen at random and interviewed over a three-month period from October to December, 1987. This largely urban sample consisted of white, black, and Hispanic men and women, in majority poor. The interview attempted to explore knowledge of AIDS risk factors and modes of transmission, contraception use, general sexual practices, sources of AIDS information, and to administer the HLOC Scale, which purports to measure the extent to which people perceive themselves as in control of their health. Lower HLOC scores mean "greater internal LOC orientations," which signify feelings of greater control over health outcomes.

The study found a strong relationship between knowledge of AIDS and the HLOC Scale in the sample, and the authors conclude that HLOC is a strong predictor of AIDS knowledge. The authors demonstrate significant racial-ethnic differences: whites had the greatest knowledge of AIDS, followed by blacks, and then Hispanics. Whites had significantly lower HLOC scores than did blacks or Hispanics. How are these findings interpreted? Aruffo and co-workers assert that lower HLOC scores among whites signal their greater capacity for assuming personal responsibility for health: because whites have lower scores, they are more likely to alter their high-risk behavior in response to AIDS prevention programs. But high HLOC scores among African Americans and Hispanics may simply reflect their ability to accurately assess very real constraints on their agency, rather than beliefs or attitudes or cognitive barriers. The study neglects the social and economic factors which constrain people's ability to respond even where knowledge exists.

Much of the research discussed thus far has incorporated "race" as a variable of study. Wyatt discusses the inadequacies of using the concept in AIDS research, stating "the criteria used to identify racial groups are sometimes inappropriate when ethnic and cultural group patterns are to be examined."[118] Wyatt then goes on to discuss how the different cultural patterns and beliefs of different "ethnic" groups might affect their risk of becoming infected with HIV. Wyatt specifically focuses on what are termed "high context" and "low context" cultures:

> It is also important to understand and integrate the differences in behavior patterns of people referred to as high or low context into AIDS research...Individuals from high context cultures are more group oriented, depend more on family and friends as their support network, and are more likely to consider their involvement in relationships a dimension of their identity.[119]

In order to better incorporate the concept of "ethnicity" into research, Wyatt developed a standardized instrument called the "Wyatt Sex History Questionnaire." The WSHQ was pilot tested in a stratified survey of 248 African-American and White women, recruited by random-digit dialing of telephone prefixes in Los Angeles County. Demographics of sample were as follows: ages, 18 to 36; education from less than ten years to professional degrees; annual incomes, less than $5,000 to greater than $50,000. Women differed in marital status and presence of children. Quotas were used to make samples of African Americans and Whites "comparable on demographic variables," so that comparisons could be made between the two "ethnic groups."[120]

Wyatt correctly concludes that it is important to look beyond the concept of "race" when discussing HIV risk. However, the article's definitions of "ethnic" and "cultural" are also narrow, and bring with them their own limitations. As noted, it is misleading to discuss large, heterogeneous groups of people as if their members all shared the same beliefs and values. This happens when Wyatt characterizes all African-Americans as "high context." Finally, and most significantly, the privileging of "ethnicity" over "race" does not serve to bring into relief the power differentials so important in AIDS: it is often misleading to discuss "race," but it is rarely an error to discuss racism. Similarly, consideration of gender inequality is almost absent from the discussion. For example, when asking women why they did not use contraceptives, one possible answer in the WSHQ is "I or my partner do not like contraceptives," suggesting a gender equality that simply does not exist.[121] The assumption that such a power-laden and private issue as contraceptive choice might be revealed by a questionnaire is one that anthropologists have attacked for years.

Even in AIDS research more grounded in social context, the effects of behaviorism are readily discerned even in solid contributions. For example, Mays and Cochran promise to explore "the influence of ethnic minority culture on the behavior of individual women."[122] Controversies over the very notion of bounded, discrete ethnic minorities are never acknowledged; claims that these groups constitute distinct "cultures" are never challenged. Mays and Cochran engage a model of agency that resembles that registered in many of the papers reviewed by Becker and Joseph. We read that AIDS is a "behaviorally transmitted disease," and that "risk reduction relies on altering the intimate behaviors of individuals during sexual activity." It thus follows, for Mays and Cochran, that "further reductions in the incidence of pediatric AIDS are dependent upon the choices and behavior of infected women, many of whom are unaware of their infection status."[123] In a sense, this is, of course, true. But to say without further qualification that reductions in pediatric AIDS depends upon the "choices and behavior of infected women" exaggerates agency and lays a burden of heavy responsibility upon these women, who in speaking of their plight often attempt to trace responsibility in far different ways. They are likely, for example, to speak of men's behavior and of the life experiences that have so restricted their choices. Unsurprisingly, perhaps, many of these women refuse to exaggerate their own agency—recognizing in enhanced claims of independence and freedom augmented opportunities for blaming the victim.

The first pages of Mays and Cochran's paper make other, similar, claims. They are also marred by problematic formulations that are, in our opinion, reflections of the cognitivist and behaviorist trends noted above. We read of "ethnic women" who are "less behaviorally directed by Euro-American culture," and learn that these women may not know key facts. For example, we read that "Many Hispanics are unaware that spermicides containing nonoxynol-9 may be effective in inactivating HIV and thus possibly reducing risk of infection."[124] So be it. But many physicians are similarly uninformed. Furthermore, the relationship of such knowledge to risk reduction has not been demonstrated in the populations studied by Mays and Cochran.

In spite of these problems, Mays and Cochran can be relied upon to draw solid inferences, even when stated in less than ideal ways: "We must not underestimate the variety of ethnic, racial, cultural, and religious factors that influence sexual behavior patterns."[125] To this enumeration we would add "socioeconomic factors" and "power differentials" of all sorts. And although these tend to be left out of lists of relevant factors, it is clear that Mays and Cochran have a deep understanding of these power differentials, which they discuss more thoroughly under the somewhat inapposite heading, "Perceiving AIDS Risk." "Most women, particularly when their life reality is that of being poor, Black, Latina, or outside the law through drug abuse of street prostitution," they note, "have always lived with risk of some kind. AIDS is simply one more risk with which to be concerned. These women have long histories of facing omnipresent dangers not often experienced by the middle class and mustering what scarce resources exist to cope with these dangers.[126]

Some psychological studies on AIDS do put poverty and gender issues on the front burner. For example, a 1994 article by Brown, Melchior, Reback, *et al.* takes on the issue of mandatory partner notification of HIV-positive women. Their study focuses on the psychosocial issues women might face if mandatory partner notification programs were in effect. The authors recruited 887 women from a 1,200-person NIDA study evaluating two intervention models for maintaining drug-free lifestyles and limiting the spread of HIV. Interviews included structured surveys and unstructured questions. The women were asked about HIV-risk behaviors, financial resources, histories of abuse, social norms, and social support networks. Current levels of depression were assessed using a formal instrument, the CES-D scale. All respondents resided in low-income, inner-city neighborhoods of Los Angeles County, many of which were ravaged in the 1992 urban riots.[127] Most of these women were classed as financially dependent. Twenty seven percent were unemployed and looking for work, 13.4 percent were unemployed and not looking, 8.6 percent were working part-time, 21.2 percent were full-time homemakers, 5.6 percent were disabled and unable to work, and 4.1 percent stated only that they had "another work situation." Fifty-eight percent reported monthly incomes of less than $500; 94.5 percent, less than $1000. Over 41 percent had been arrested at least once. Almost 78 percent of the women were African-American; 20.3 percent were Latina, and 2.2 percent were "Caucasian" or "other." Almost 74 percent lived with children for whom they held primary responsibility.

The results of the study suggested that many of these women are likely to experience some combination of sexual, physical, or psychological abuse in the event of mandatory partner notification. Many already suffered from serious feelings of hopelessness, loneliness, psychological distress: fully 70.6 percent were felt to have clinically significant levels of depression. Many of these women lacked reliable social-support networks and related systems of resources that might minimize the likelihood of abuse: 24.5 percent reported they had no "best friend," and many rated their sex partners as less reliable sources of support than several other kinds of individuals and institutions. The majority of these women lived with children, and the authors stated that "such women may be especially vulnerable to abuse from a sex partner because they fear that their children may be abused."[128] Most of the women were having sex with men who were not wearing condoms.

In summary, review of behavioral science literature on AIDS underlines the need for more than questionnaires ("I or my partner do not like condoms"). Individual behavior and cognition almost invariably constitute the chief focus of psychological and behavioral research on AIDS. Yet the disciplinary gaze artificially delimits the nature of the problem at hand; the problems posed by AIDS and AIDS prevention burst the seams of this mode of inquiry. Increasingly, the best writing in psychology makes it clear that the larger forces that generate risk cannot be neglected if women's risk is to be understood and diminished. Amaro, writing in a recent issue of the *American Psychologist*, "examines how researchers using behavioral approaches to HIV prevention have largely ignored how gender and women's social and familial status affect sexual risk behaviors and their ability to reduce risk of infection." According to Amaro, a lack of attention to gender has hampered "existing models of behavioral risk reduction used in understanding sexual risk behaviors...HIV risk reduction has failed to consider a host of contextual social factors that shape the reality of sexual behaviors and potential for sexual risk reduction among women."[129] These contextual social factors, while of little interest to those working from strictly "behavioral" perspectives, are what thwart efforts to prevent HIV transmission, as even bona fide psychologists are coming to agree:

> Educational approaches that seek to change behavior without seeking to change the causal social conditions are, in the end, disempowering to people...the current strategy of increasing condom use without an understanding of the social conditions that facilitate HIV infection (such as addiction, poverty, racism, and inequality among women and men) is seen as having a reformist purpose...rather than a transforming function with the aim of changing society to meet people's needs.[130]

3. TAKING NOTE OF POVERTY AND GENDER INEQUALITY

Many social science researchers agree that the forces that generate women's economic and social marginality also drive their risk of HIV infection.[131] The inclination to attend to these forces varies widely across disciplines and between individual researchers. Although we have focused, thus far, on failures to account for these forces, many researchers do attend to the roles of poverty and gender inequality in the unfolding AIDS pandemic. The review which follows includes several social science articles that confront these powerful forces.

In a 1994 paper, Wallace, Fullilove, Fullilove, *et al.* link HIV incidence, prevalence, and the possibility of increased strain virulence to urban poverty in the United States. The authors state three aims: 1) to examine the relationships between structured urban poverty and HIV transmission; 2) to challenge the idea that privileged classes are insulated from infection; and 3) to call for radical reforms in order to control HIV and other infectious disease agents in the United States.

Wallace and co-workers explore the mechanisms by which the withdrawal of public services and the physical and social disintegrations which follow might be seen as "causes" of HIV infection. The forces that serve to foster economic and racial segregation and to concentrate poverty in particular settings are manifest in public policies which fail to contain urban physical and social disintegration. For example, the strategic closing of municipal fire stations has fueled the "burnout" and subsequent "desertification" of poor neighborhoods in the South Bronx, thus disrupting previously circumscribed networks of needle-sharing drug users.[132] Public policies that exacerbate poverty fuel the motor that drives the spread of HIV into new spaces, geographical and social. The authors suggest that blighted urban centers are the sites of generation for more virulent evolving forms of HIV. These themes have been explored in a number of studies by Wallace and co-workers.[133]

In this work, there is little speculation about individual agency or lifestyles when causes for this "synergy of plagues" are sought. Instead, deficits of political will and ill-conceived local and national policies are held accountable for the physical and social decay of America's inner cities and, consequently, the spread of HIV. The authors conclude that urban poverty will increase the incidence, prevalence, and, possibly, even the strain virulence of HIV. This will happen within present urban and suburban minority epicenters, but the authors also speculate that HIV infection will increase within predominantly heterosexual, middle class communities as well: "As the United States has begun to mirror Africa in the effects of social disintegration on HIV infection, so too may it begin to resemble certain African nations' patterns of disease transmission within affluent subpopulations."[134]

The authors draw on their own substantial research conducted in New York and California, though they discuss data from other HIV epicenters as well. Their review of the epidemiological literature on diffusion of HIV is exemplary, although they neglect some conditions which may also be important in the spread of HIV—the gendered social and economic subjugation of the poor, or women's elevated biological susceptibility. The article does not emphasize the gendered aspects of the spread of infection. Instead, it focuses on the more generic categories of "heterosexual spread," as well as spread from epicenters characterized by high rates of HIV infection among gay men (e.g. the Castro district in San Francisco) to heterosexual populations—typically constituted by poor, socially stigmatized people of color. A final criticism might be that the analysis is "experience-distant." Attention to the personal, experiential level is under-attended in this approach.

In a 1993 paper entitled "AIDS as a Sociohistorical Phenomenon," Friedman also critiques "individualist" models of HIV prevention. He argues that the U.S. epidemic has been influenced by a series of social and historical factors that have been neglected in behavioral models of HIV disease. These behavioral models tend to focus on individual behaviors and motivations: "Disease and seropositivity seem much more to be functions of social and historical factors than of health beliefs or self efficacy."[135] To make his case, Friedman reviews his own work as well as a significant body of epidemiological and sociological literature. He poses several questions based on this review: Why has there been so much focus on the individual? How can community action be promoted? What are the social barriers for HIV risk reduction? Where do these barriers come from and how can they be removed?

Friedman acknowledges the importance of microsocial and social-psychological factors in the AIDS epidemic but argues that approaches based on these concepts have often been over-utilized at the expense of broader, middle-range approaches which take social and historical factors into account. Some social and historical factors which Friedman notes to be crucial to the spread of HIV are geographic location, local social structures, racism (in that "race" was an indirect indicator of social status), and short-sighted public policy and legislation. To illustrate this point, the article points out that many successful AIDS-intervention strategies (e.g., within certain gay communities) have involved the activity of community organizing. In contrast, other social groups severely affected by HIV, such as

IDUs, have had a more difficult time organizing to protect them-selves, in large part, he argues, because of legal strictures, including police brutality, and other social forces that prohibit self-protection. Poverty is addressed throughout the article by underlining its poten-tiation of the epidemic, but its negative contribution to efforts among IDUs to organize collective action against AIDS, as some European IDUs have managed to do, is perhaps insufficiently addressed.

Friedman concludes that autonomous individuals cannot be responsible for generating or stopping the epidemic. The role of social and historical factors in shaping the AIDS epidemic must be recognized and incorporated into HIV research, prevention, and pro-grammatic activity. These issues are also taken up by Friedman, Stepherson, Woods, and co-workers in "Society, Drug Injectors, and AIDS."[136] The researchers again explore how social, economic and political structures have contributed to the spread of HIV among IDUs and affected efforts to control it.

In short, Friedman and co-workers make solid contributions to the responsible sociography of AIDS among urban IDUs, and also to efforts to call into question the dominant models of scholarly expla-nation and action.[137] These articles are exemplary in their analysis of why many U.S. drugs users find it difficult to avoid HIV infection. The authors point out that behavior change on the part of the drug user cannot occur without simultaneous changes in the structure of a society which oppresses and alienates those most vulnerable to HIV infection. Friedman and his colleagues argue that in order for AIDS-prevention programs to work and reduce drug use among the poor, racism and punitive socioeconomic structures must be attenuated or eliminated.

These papers, focused largely on "race," underemphasize the gendered aspects of the pandemic. The authors do note that "sexism probably affects the spread of HIV because women are deprived of social and economic power" and because society condones the phys-ical and emotional abuse of women by men.[138] Lack of a detailed analysis of how local and large-scale power differentials come to have their effects is a shortcoming of the texts of Friedman and co-workers. Structural forces relevant to the urban epidemic are embedded in a "modern business-oriented society,"[139] but there is too little exploration of the precise mechanisms by which the urban poor are subordinated. Also unexamined is the *transnational* nature of the drug trade.

Other work on HIV among the U.S. urban poor also suggests the dire need for new theoretical frameworks. In a 1994 paper, Singer critiques the current conceptual paradigm of AIDS research. He, too, argues that the dominant modes of inquiry in HIV-related research are inclined to de-emphasize the political-economic and social contexts in which the disease occurs. Singer notes the unhealthy intersection of urban poverty and socially devalued ethnicity in U.S. inner cities, and redefines the AIDS epidemic in the urban United States as a "syndemic"—a set of synergistic, intertwined health and social problems that engulf many of the urban poor. That is, AIDS is tightly linked to sets of conditions such as low birth weight, poor nutritional status, tuberculosis, and substance abuse. These conditions are themselves linked to broader set of political-economic and social factors, like unemployment, poverty, poor housing, and homelessness.[140]

Singer prescribes a "critical medical anthropological" framework to remedy the gaps that exist in research on AIDS. This framework focuses on how AIDS is socially constructed, socially transmitted, and socially located. Each of these complex processes is shaped by myriad political-economic and social forces. According to Singer, class, gender, and racial inequalities contribute directly to the spread of AIDS in U.S. urban centers. Singer asserts that AIDS itself is an "opportunistic infection," a disease of impoverished health and social conditions. He sharply challenges anthropologists and epidemiologists to attend to these issues in their research. He has the sociological scope of the researchers previously cited, but links this broad view to more "experience-near" information. In Singer's work, it is possible to discern the voices of those confronting AIDS on a daily basis. There is, however, little exploration of how women might be particularly vulnerable to syndemic disease. Finally, Singer's essay could be improved, as could our own work, with clearer term definitions. Although the terms "poverty" and "class" are used throughout the article, they are never explicitly defined.

Broad conceptual frameworks which take poverty and gender inequality into account can help to address specific AIDS-related questions. For example, Worth contributes to the social science literature on AIDS by exploring "Why Condom Promotion among Vulnerable Women is Likely to Fail." "Vulnerable" or "high risk" women are defined as women who are IDUs or who are sexual partners of IDUs. The study discusses women's self-reports of their life circumstances that make condom use difficult and is based on data collected in support group discussions in two health centers in New York City. One center housed an educational support program for "high risk" women. These women were predominantly sexually active, white, and working poor; the mean age was 30; many were heads of households with children. The second center housed a methadone-maintenance program. The discussion-group participants here were poly-drug abusers, sexually active, and middle aged; 84 percent were heads of welfare-dependent households with children; one half were Puerto Rican and one fourth African-American. At the second center, an attitudinal questionnaire regarding condoms, contraception, STDs, and AIDS was administered.

Findings from both settings suggested that women often do not use condoms for a variety of social, cultural, and economic reasons, which include lack of power and control in sexual relationships, fear of violence, economic dependence on a sexual relationship, and a need to articulate intimacy by not insisting on partner's condom use. AIDS risk-reduction behaviors, including condom use, were embedded in a set of larger forces which dominated these women's lives. The author implies that economic and cultural forces—including poverty, homelessness, and lack of social support—push women into circumstances of powerlessness. These circumstances, she argues, are largely to blame for the lack of condom use among these women.[141]

Worth recommends that "realistic AIDS education" be implemented. This kind of education which would take into account many forces at work. She writes:

> By not insisting on the use of condoms, women avoid paying the present cost of their use: disruption in a relationship through violence, or through loss of economic support, a 'father figure,' or a place to live, at the expense of protecting themselves from a possible future cost, such as HIV infection or illness.[142]

Realistic AIDS education would target entire communities rather than vulnerable women. Worth recommends broadening women's options for risk reduction while simultaneously insisting that responsibility for risk reduction be more equally shared. Worth does an excellent job portraying the social and cultural contexts in which condom use occurs and does not occur in the lives of poor women in New York. The study includes women from quite disparate backgrounds. One potential problem with this study is that the women who participated were all "service utilizers." Thus their experiences may not be representative of all vulnerable women, in particular those who do not seek or use such services.

Another specific set of behaviors which can be better addressed within a framework which takes "race," class, and gender into account are behaviors related to the use of injection drugs. Des Jarlais, Friedman, and Ward review the public health policy of "harm reduction" in helping IDUs avoid HIV risk-related behaviors.[143] "Harm reduction" attempts to diminish harmful health outcomes among IDUs without necessarily reducing drug use. It draws on many complementary strategies, including needle exchange, provision of bleach disinfectants and condoms, counseling, facilitating social organization among IDUs, and drug treatment. The idea is to offer people several approaches simultaneously, on the assumption that different people who use injection drugs may find some strategies more useful than others. Harm reduction also tries to address IDUs' social marginalization by encouraging the development of politicized social networks. The authors begin by stating that although IDUs are subject to numerous health problems which are related to their drug use, HIV represents a unique health crisis which threatens their lives as well as in the lives of their children and sex partners. The authors go on to discuss the epidemiology of HIV among IDUs, noting that the true extent of the disease often goes unrecognized because many

HIV-positive people who use injection drugs get sick and die from non-AIDS defining illnesses, such as recurrent bacterial pneumonia.[144]

Des Jarlais and co-workers review the results of 18 different evaluations of harm-reduction programs in the United States, Western Europe, and Thailand. The programs ranged from counseling to needle exchange; some were more comprehensive. Most studies reported a number of positive results, including decreases in needle sharing, decreases in the number of sexual partners, and increases in condom use. The review also points out some problems associated with harm reduction. These include a tendency for gains to be temporary (ongoing education and outreach are difficult to sustain), and the tendency to recidivism (attempts to establish safer sex practices among IDUs sometimes fail). The authors recommend that more research be conducted to evaluate the efficacy of harm-reduction programs. They also recommend that new and innovative drug-treatment programs be developed, implemented, and evaluated in order to contain the spread of HIV.[145] The review does not adequately account for the economic, political, and social conditions in which drug use is embedded, nor does it address how harm reduction itself might be hampered by these same conditions. Program participants may be willing to engage in multi-pronged strategies to decrease their risk, but the conditions that shaped their initial chances of addiction persist unaltered.

A social science framework which takes poverty and gender inequality into account is not only important in understanding HIV-related risk behaviors: it is also key in understanding how the disease is conceptualized and discussed. This issue is addressed by Seidel, who, drawing on Foucault, "deconstructs" contested "discourses of HIV/AIDS" in sub-Saharan Africa. Medical, moral/religious/ethical, developmental, legal, patients' rights, and political groups all compete for authority in speaking about AIDS. These ways people "talk about HIV/AIDS," notes Seidel, are derived from "dominant institutional frameworks and categories."[146] In examining discourses on HIV, Seidel discusses "situations of risk" arising from war, destabilization, natural disasters, and "displaced and refugee populations."

Seidel also mentions "the historical roots of poverty and related morbidity patterns" that must be addressed when interpreting patterns of HIV risk and infection. Seidel proceeds to talk about the marginalization of women, noting that Sub-Saharan Africa is a place "where few jobs are available for women; and where women have limited access to the cash economy," a place characterized by "the feminization of poverty."[147] Seidel's analysis is at times admirably hardhitting:

> Women as the least empowered are the most at risk. They need to be involved in the planning process and implementations as autonomous individuals at risk. They need information, appropriate services, including free and confidential STD treatment, and support using a peer model. Women need specific targeting, not just a trickle down effect, and should not be seen primarily as vectors or carriers. They need to be empowered to make informed decisions about their sexual and reproductive lives and reproductive choices.[148]

Seidel's analysis, which also includes discussion of the work of others in the area of poverty and HIV, reminds us once again that the language of behaviorists dominates scholarly talk about the AIDS pandemic. However, the emphasis on language leads Seidel to call for language-oriented interventions, such as "culturally sensitive education" to "empower" women with knowledge of their human rights. Seidel sees African women as subordinates in patriarchal discourses, and many of his suggestions are cast in equally linguistic terms: "People with HIV or AIDS need to be legally empowered *through enabling discourses* of the International Bill of Rights and other documents concerned with human rights," the author concludes.[149] Seidel's emphasis on language leaves underattended issues of political economy, such as the forces that generate poverty and lack of medical care for so many African women—regardless of the currency of "enabling discourses" in their home countries.

The studies reviewed thus far all indicate that women are often ignored in HIV research.[150] Smeltzer's 1992 literature review seeks to understand why this has happened, particularly in biomedical research. She concludes that the evolution of the U.S. epidemic, the male-centered CDC case definition for AIDS (that excluded conditions specific to HIV-infected women), the low-priority status of women's health issues in practice and research in general, and the sexual "division of labor" all conspired to keep the issue of women's HIV risk off the official agenda. The essay also discusses potential consequences of this legacy and suggests remedial action for nurses. This action would include women's advocacy and new nursing research agendas. Although the political economy of women's risk is underemphasized, Smeltzer does note that socially, educationally, and economically disadvantaged minority women bear a disproportionate weight of HIV disease. To compound this situation, these same women also have limited access to health care:

> Disenfranchised women are usually unable to exert the power and decision making necessary to minimize their risks and to obtain required services for themselves and their families. Traditional sex roles and the economic hardship of women make it difficult to control the events in their lives and the practices that put them at risk for HIV.[151]

Smeltzer concludes that to address the epidemic among women one must counsel for risk reduction, eliminate testing and treatment delays, include more women in clinical trials, and bolster social services.

Most of the studies reviewed in this chapter come from the United States. The disproportionate focus on women's HIV risk in wealthy countries is probably an epiphenomenon of the relative scarcity of research dollars in poor countries. However, some research focused on countries in the developing world has looked at gender inequality and poverty in these settings. For example, Ankrah, Mhloyi, Manguyu, *et al.*, in "Women, Children and AIDS," discuss the "sociocultural factors" that condition the "behavioral responses" of African women and children to AIDS. Their essay proposes that "the traditional [African] kinship system, which includes the clan...offers a viable mechanism for protecting women and children" against HIV infection.[152] This "traditional" framework is chosen to avoid concepts of "AIDS orphan" and "person with AIDS," which "tend to focus attention on the individual rather than on the African family and community, which are at the center of much of African social life."[153] The authors discuss how patriarchal cultures which

value women primarily for their childbearing and childrearing functions can influence these women's HIV risk. The authors examine
women's intragroup diversity of risk: young women, women who are
wives and mothers, women with multiple partners, and women as
AIDS survivors.

The authors emphasize culture and developmental status as
shapers of risk for HIV and AIDS: "The predicament of young
African women is explained by two sets of factors...sociocultural
pressures, largely beyond their control, which create high-risk situations" and "developmental [factors] that underlie the behavior of the
young."[154] For example, polygyny and competition among co-wives
lead to high risk situations. The authors further propose that African
adolescents seek "self-actualization, adventure, exploration, and the
formation of relationships," and note that "Denial that they can
become HIV-infected characterizes the response of many young
women."[155] Some of these girls and women fall prey to "sugar dad-
dies"—men who provide money and goods in exchange for sex.

In this essay, economic deprivation is often regarded more as a
consequence of the AIDS epidemic than as cause or co-factor for
infection: "Many African wives and mothers lack formal education
and independent means to free themselves from the quagmire of
problems that AIDS creates."[156] The role of poverty in shaping sexual union is, however, acknowledged: "With increasing socioeconomic disruptions in Africa, premarital and extramarital sexual
arrangements with men could become more common as an economic
survival strategy for young women."[157] The authors also note that, in
certain instances of economic hardship, young girls have to give up
schooling in order to take care of sick family members. Similarly,
family illness or other hardships may force them into early marriage,
or prostitution, in order to support their families.[158]

Ankrah and co-workers' chapter shows that large-scale social
and economic forces put certain sub-Saharan women at risk; it
emphasizes "cultural factors" in risk shaping. A major problem with
such an approach is that it requires recourse to notions of overarching African cultural homogeneity. For example, Ankrah and her co-
workers assert that "African clan structures" can be used to imple-

ment AIDS-prevention measures. But are kinship patterns and meanings really so similar across this vast continent? Just how pervasive is the African clan? Is it a force as great in the cities as the countryside? Even the authors wonder about their own "assumption" and call for research to bolster their hope that "the clan structure can address a modern medical and social crisis."[159]

De Bruyn works from a broader international perspective. She confronts gender inequality as a force that generates HIV risk around the world. She also proposes strategies for increasing women's options for self-protection. Though de Bruyn recognizes biological factors in the distribution of disease, she emphasizes social and economic forces at work in the spread of HIV.[160] De Bruyn does not explicitly use the words "poor" or "poverty" in her article, but instead makes reference to low "female education and literacy levels" and "situations of economic need" in "developing countries" in Africa, Asia, and Latin America.[161] She also refers to "environmental factors," which include social contexts that reproduce women's "economic dependence on men."[162]

De Bruyn challenges the notion of personal and individual power to protect oneself from HIV infection: "The precautions to be taken are influenced by societal norms and customs, social interaction and environmental circumstances which can either facilitate or hinder individual action...In essence, prevailing power dynamics make self-protection by women problematic at best and very difficult or impossible at worst."[163] Effectively refuting the idea that individual behavior alone is responsible for HIV transmission, de Bruyn advocates a series of "strategies to increase self-protection possibilities." These include: 1) Broadening women's educational training and employment opportunities in order to lessen their economic reliance on men or on sex work; 2) Enforcement of laws to prevent gender discrimination; 3) Abstinence from extramarital sex; 4) Education of men towards greater responsibility for safer sex and socialization away from a tendency to sexual coerciveness; 5) Education for women (e.g. role-play) on how to manipulate men into using condoms; and 6) Financing of more research on effective methods of female-controlled protection (e.g.the female condom).

4. RECURRING THEMES:
AIDS AND THE FAILURE OF SOCIAL ANALYSIS

"Social science generalizations are not very general," note Shweder and Fiske in a review of the subject. "Indeed, over the past twenty years, the restrictions that bound social science generalizations seem to have increased, as the results of laboratory experiments did not generalize well outside the lab."[164] If social-science generalizations are so fraught with hazard, what possible utility is there in a critical rereading of social-science literature on women and AIDS? The answer to this question, we believe, is that these shortcomings are neither random in occurrence nor innocuous in impact. Inadequate analyses have tended to blame victims for their misfortunes, even as they exculpate those with greater health, wealth, and power. To add insult to injury, these analyses may actually obscure the true nature of women's risk, mislead our understandings about the pandemic's dynamics, and hamper preventive efforts.

To identify the mechanisms by which such misunderstandings are achieved is the aim of our review. Very often, such research is undertaken with pure motives, as Clatts has recently noted: "It is probably true that the present emphasis in AIDS prevention research on identifying behavioural change models began with the best of intentions, notably the development of community-based, culturally sensitive prevention messages." But these models, he argues, have become "tools of abuse and neglect," leading "down conceptual paths that have little or no relevance to the way people actually live, and hence inevitably to strategies and policies that have no relevance to prevention."[165]

Our rereading leads us to identify a number of recurrent themes. As noted throughout this book, many studies steer clear of consideration of the issue of how income, resources, and power are related to women's HIV risk. In some papers reviewed, however, there *is* general consensus that socioeconomic factors are important enough to include in the results or discussion sections. In many texts, it is implicit or explicit that "economic factors" are fundamental to the transmission *and* prevention of HIV. Some authors refer to "poverty," others to "economic factors," "social and economic issues," "socioeconomic disruption," or "low education and literacy," but rare indeed is any sustained consideration of either the meaning of these terms or their impact on the rising rates of HIV among women. In this analytic vacuum, other factors with less well documented relevance to the dynamics of transmission inevitably creep into the discussion:

> Even those studies that acknowledge the systemic economic inequities that persist in these communities utilize this information for little more than descriptive purposes. Typically these conditions are held as constants, and dubious academic constructions, such as 'self-efficacy' and 'locus of control,' are used to explain variance in behaviour. These same dubious entities then become the target for intervention, again with little or no attention to the structural conditions which give rise to perceptions of self, or to those that recreate these systems of power.[166]

This inattention represents a failure of social analysis. That is, in studies in which psychological or cultural variables are discussed in depth while the larger (extrapersonal) factors inflecting local epidemics are ignored, we discern a failure to embed ethnographically visible data into the larger social nexus from which it takes meaning.[167] This reflects, as noted, the *desocialization* of a very social pandemic.

Desocialization of AIDS has been bemoaned as inevitable in the biomedical enterprise and its ancillary professions. "Service professionals find it easier to work with a sick, even dying, baby," notes Ward in writing of AIDS, "than with the social constellation in which the child is embedded."[168] But this particular form of desocialization is by no means uniquely pronounced in the AIDS pandemic; it is an epiphenomenon of the clinical gaze. "In anthropological perspective," notes Kleinman, "this scientific and clinical world view constructs a particularly narrow definition of disease that separates it from social sources and consequences and studies it as a discrete abnormality in biological structure and functioning."[169]

Our rereading shows us that many social scientists are, ironically, as vulnerable to this visual-field defect as are their biomedical colleagues. Replace, in Kleinman's comment, the words "clinical" and "biological" with "psychological," for example, and a similarly restricted, and misleading, analysis ensues; the discourse of certain behaviorists, adds Kleinman, can be "more starkly inhuman and as narrowly technical as the biomedical discourse on disease."[170]

Very evident, these days, is the lack of what Mills once called the sociological imagination, which "enables its possessor to understand the larger historical scene in terms of its meaning for the inner life and the external career of a variety of individuals."[171] The "larger historical scene" has shaped the world pandemic of HIV disease in important ways. This scene is transnational (and, increasingly, global), though this social fact is something the texts we review too often neglect.

Our conclusion is not that researchers and academic writers refuse to see poverty as a dimension of women's lives that warrants careful attention and analysis. Rather we wonder why and by what mechanisms are these factors so systematically elided in the social science literature on AIDS? A number of key mechanisms have emerged in our rereading, and also in the first half of this volume:

1. The Triumph of Behaviorism

Trends towards cognitivist or behaviorist reductionisms, including the idea that individual psychology may have adequate explanatory power, are firmly entrenched across the human sciences and in epidemiology. These trends reflect broad epistemic shifts felt far beyond the academy. They are, in fact, profound transformations with repercussions in the popular cultures of most industrial societies in Europe and North America. In scholarship and in everyday life, these trends toward individualization/atomization desocialize the social world. Much commented upon in philosophy and social theory, even a cursory review of the effects of these changes in contemporary industrial societies is beyond the scope of this essay.[172] But the influence of behaviorial and psychological determinism can be discerned in works granting enormous explanatory power to women's motivations and "cognitive structures" (including "knowledge, attitudes, beliefs and practices"). The danger in this approach lies not in allowing explorations of these components of the AIDS pandemic, but rather its power to decontextualize such data: "Very little of the current research that is being done on sexual risk behaviour acknowledges the import of systemic poverty on sexual risk behaviour," observes Clatts in a recent and dour review of social-science research on AIDS. "Moreover, research paradigms that continue to place a premium on the study of behavioural frequencies and dubious notions of motive are unsuited to the task of identifying ways in which to foster 'actionable' changes in high-risk sexual behaviour."[173]

Clatts refers to the "AIDS-prevention research industry"—perhaps an overstatement, but countless are the studies in which some brand of behaviorism seeks to "explain" the AIDS pandemic, or, more often, some local variant of it. These explanatory excesses are by no means native to psychology: "The Health Belief Model," notes one anthropologist, "has been used in one form or another by many of us, with extremely disappointing results."[174] The influence of behaviorism is readily discerned even in anthropology, one of the more radically contextualizing social sciences: "Our approaches have tended to be individualistic, a search for individual 'deficiencies' to explain seemingly irrational behaviour," observes Bolton in a hard-bitten assessment of anthropological research on AIDS. "Instead of focusing on cultural and social conditions which provide the context for behaviour, we have reduced the problem to one of the individual actor. For anthropologists to be doing this is odd indeed."[175]

Psychological reductionisms are attractive for many reasons. They are difficult to falsify, as Gergen notes: "I can think of no psychological theory that has yet been abandoned for reasons of clear observational challenge."[176] Futhermore, focusing as they do on *individual's* attributes or shortcomings, psychological explanations rarely rock the boat. An intense focus on local actors and local factors often leaves unexamined the larger systems within which the local takes on meaning. This is particularly problematic, as we have seen, when the analytic gaze is brought to bear on the afflicted themselves.

2. Other Immodest Claims of Causality

Social science writings about AIDS are marred by other immodest claims of causality. The nature of those claims, as noted, is largely determined by the training of the claimmakers. Each of the sociomedical sciences—medical anthropology, sociology, economics, etc.—has tended to stake out "turf" to be regarded as the exclusive domain of that particular subspecialty. Each field then tends to profess its importance in explaining the phenomenon under strutiny—regardless of what that phenomenon happens to be. For certain psychologists, as noted, it is an understanding of individual psychology that will unlock the secrets of personal risk and thus of the pandemic writ large. In anthropology, the trend is to insist that understanding *culture* will unlock the secrets of AIDS. "New Studies Urged on Cultural Factors in Spread of AIDS" ran the headline of an article in *The Chronicle of Higher Education.* Among the cultural factors cited were "scarification rites" in Brazil and "misunderstandings" prevalent among Kenyan youth (Many young people, noted one Kenyan social scientist, "believe that it is 'African to be promiscuous'").[177] Clearly, definitions matter, although this is not the place to review definitions of the term culture. There is enormous variation in usage, but "culture" surfaces, these days, in most social-science research on AIDS. Anthropologists find the usages too narrow or too broad, but the term is no more restricted to anthropology than are notions of behaviorism restricted to psychology. "Culture has come out," notes Frankenberg. "It is too late to drive it back into the closet."[178]

Such claims for culture were little more compelling than the cognitive projects of behaviorists, and yet we anthropologists continue to make them. "What has anthropology to offer those who work in the area of AIDS/STDs? Stated simply: The study of culture."[178] This is the opening gambit of a new book that in fact offers much more than the facile study of culture. The anthropological approach "consists of calling for 'cultural sensitivity,'" notes Bolton, exasperated, in the same volume. "Have we nothing else to offer?"[180] Our answer is that we do have something more to offer. For example, we can do the important work of showing how structural violence and cultural difference are conflated. Too often, poverty and violence against the poor become collapsed into an all-accommodating concept of culture. We can show how "culturally sensitive" explorations have served to undermine explorations of other forces that shape the lives of our subjects.[181] We can help others to use the concept of culture in clear and illuminating ways: "Anthropologists need to educate themselves and others about the use of so power-laden a concept."[182]

3. Exaggeration of Poor Women's Agency

Often laudable efforts to incorporate the sufferers' points of view may obscure powerful constraints on agency experienced by most, but not all, people with, or held to be at risk for, AIDS. A failure to appreciate such constraints has had a pernicious effect on many interventions:

> To continue to pretend that a two-hour session with an AIDS educator, for example, can measurably increase 'self-esteem' in a person who has lived an entire lifetime in a context of violence, discrimination, and abject poverty, or that the problem of 'empowerment' lies solely in convincing the subject that he or she has power, regardless of whether this is the case, is to completely miss the mark about why people engage in risk behaviour.[183]

More pointedly, to make such claims of transformative power on the individual level is to engage in fraud. Sadly, many of those most committed to making common cause with poor women with AIDS also buy into this erroneous analysis. In clinics and social-service centers throughout the world, women are exhorted to "get with the program," to "assume their responsibilities" (this, often in reference to children), to "exercise restraint" or sexual self control.[184] Exaggerations of poor women's agency are consonant with many core U.S. values. In a classless meritocracy of self-sufficient individuals naturally dominated by self-made multimillionaires who profess family values, it's easy to blame poor women for their personal misfortunes.[185]

What seems clear is that poverty and gender inequality erode personal agency. "The relative lack of control by women in relation to men, particularly in the context of sexual relations, places them at increasing risk for AIDS," observes Carovano. "Those women with the least control, generally poor women of color, are those who face the greatest risk."[186] And yet poor women do make choices, clearly, and these choices have ramifications for their futures and the future of the pandemic: choices about sex and procreation, choices about bearing risks to avoid risks, choices about how to live with HIV infection. Their lives, often enough, are rich with improvisation and resistance, and these are not to be dismissed. The work of a new and responsible social science of AIDS is to understand the complex interplay between structure and agency—an endeavor that once generated much interest in social theory, but which is glaringly absent from most existing work in this field.

4. Romanticisms About Resistance, Solidarity, Community

A strong vein of commentary in social-science writing on AIDS has celebrated resistance to the various forces held to promote transmission of HIV. Boff and Boff note that it is necessary to include in any conceptualization of poverty the "resources" which are available to poor people and which are often overlooked in classical definitions of poverty: "strength to resist, capacity to understand their rights, to organize themselves and transform a subhuman situation."[187] We do not wish, in our review, to dismiss these invaluable resources; we simply do not wish to underestimate the power of the forces arrayed against the poor. It is possible to celebrate resistance while registering HIV's rapid advance. It is possible to encourage solidarity while reporting significant rifts among participants in "the" struggle against AIDS (or in "the" women's movement).[188] But it is equally possible to deplore the appropriation of poor women's suffering by those who would exploit identity politics for their own gain.

In Part III of this book, we have tried to eschew romanticism. As we underscore the potential power of real community-centered services, we must also speak truth to the interests of the privileged which aim to extent privatized exclusivity and homogeneity, and remain ever-ready to turn back to the times of legally separate and unequal services.

5. Persistence of Disciplinary Insularity

It appears, in reviewing this literature, that poverty and gender inequality are too often viewed as outside the realm of proper analysis. Psychologists have addressed human behavior torn from its context. Anthropologists have examined beliefs and behaviors in a somewhat broader context, but remain trammeled by a framework which reifies discrete cultures and even "subcultures." Physicians have too often focused narrowly on pathophysiology and ignored the social world altogether, which may be one reason many doctors find it difficult to talk about HIV transmission.[189] Imprisoned by their disciplinary paradigms, researchers, writers and program planners fail to see that we face a single, global pandemic, inflected by countless local variations. Disciplinary insularities are readily palpable in any large AIDS conference. Psychologists, sociologists, anthropologists, physicians, political scientists, and literary critics all talking about AIDS seem to discuss problems that bear only a faint family resemblance to one another.

Finally, this insularity has meant that the divide between individual experience and "structural" analysis has too rarely been bridged in social-science investigations of AIDS. Even the best research reviewed here has an "experience-distant" quality. In their efforts to capture the large-scale forces that sculpt the AIDS pandemic, researchers fail to capture the quiddities of individual experience. The voices of the sufferers are too rarely heard. And yet we "only stand to lose by ignoring how the oppressed analyze their own condition," as Rosaldo notes. "Indeed, the dominated usually understand the dominant better than the reverse. In coping with their daily lives, they simply must."[190]

6. Lack of Accountability

Finally, what role have questions of accountability played in shaping the literature reviewed here? Would the same gaps be present if social scientists were accountable to poor women rather than to governments and powerful funding agencies? Many commonly heard claims—i.e., that "culturally appropriate" prevention will stop

AIDS, or that "education is the only vaccine"—are intended to impress federal bureaucracies and in this way move resources into the hands of researchers. Bureaucracies have a natural aversion to massive, structural changes, which may be one reason that there is little official interest in bringing into relief the large-scale forces that structure HIV risks. And so social science has restricted its gaze accordingly. "We have become public opinion pollsters," notes an anthropologist prominent in AIDS research; "we have become the servants of others with more power over funds."[191] Greater commitment and accountability to poor women living with AIDS is in order if we wish to avoid becoming what Chomsky has called "stenographers of power."

Chapter Six

Rereading Public Health

Joe Rhatigan, Margaret Connors,
and William Rodriguez, editors

with Paul Farmer, Jennifer Furin, Steven Lamola,
David Devine, Janie Simmons, Mercedes Becerra Valdivia,
Sonya Shin, and Sally Zierler

"The minimal research that simultaneously studies the health effects of racism, sexism, and social class ultimately stands as a sharp indictment of the narrow vision limiting much of the epidemiological research conducted within the United States."

> Nancy Krieger, Diane Rowley, Allen Herman, *et al*. "Racism, Sexism, and Social Class: Implications for Studies of Health, Disease, and Well-being"

"Epidemiology today, in developed countries, thus assigns a primary importance to studying interindividual variations in risk. By concentrating on these specific and presumed free-range individual behaviors, we thereby pay less attention to the underlying social-historical influences on behavioral choices, patterns, and population health."

> Anthony McMichael, "The Health of Persons, Populations and Planets: Epidemiology Comes Full Circle"

A comprehensive rereading of the public health literature would be a colossal task, one we do not aspire to undertake in this chapter. Instead we have attempted to look at certain key studies—"key" either because they have been widely quoted or because they reflect the reigning paradigms guiding public-health research on HIV and AIDS. On reviewing these studies, we center our gaze on what measure is taken of poor women's experience. Because this body of literature is so large and varied,[1] we have tried to offer a close rereading of a few representative articles in order to explore some of the mechanisms by which the plight of poor women has been obscured. One fact emerges from even a preliminary review: the majority of the articles we review fails to systematically examine how gender inequality and poverty have contributed to the AIDS epidemic, not only in the United States, but throughout the world.

From its outset, AIDS has been conceptualized as a disease that is spread by certain "risk groups"—including gay men, injection drug users, and prostitutes—and by individual "risk behaviors"— anal and vaginal sex without the use of condoms and sharing of contaminated needles among injection drug users.[2] Implicit in this conception are the notions that these behaviors, some of which are "anti-social," are the products of individual choice, and that persons engaging in them can and should voluntarily curb these behaviors. The questions we hope to raise through the rereading we present here are: does a construction of the epidemiology of HIV disease that focuses on *individual* action adequately address the forces driving HIV transmission? Do the dominant models of public health and epidemiology adequately describe the means by which poverty and gender inequality conspire to increase risk on HIV infection.

1. TRANSMISSION STUDIES

A broad range of transmission studies have attempted to answer several questions about women and HIV. Early work focused on what appears to be a straightforward question: do women contract HIV disease? Once this fact was established, later studies focused on which women become infected with HIV and how they became infected. As we will see, in addressing these questions, epidemiologists often make unexamined assumptions about women. Many of these assumptions are centered around women's ability to make sexual, personal, and "lifestyle" choices independent of social forces ranging from racism and gender inequality to poverty.

Harris *et al.* (1983) conducted one of the first studies to suggest that AIDS may be transmitted sexually between heterosexual men and women. In this early study, written before the discovery of HIV, the authors documented that non-drug-using women were susceptible to AIDS. They offered evidence that women acquired the disease from men through heterosexual contact. The authors studied seven monogamous female sexual partners of heterosexual male patients with the newly identified immune disorder. All of the men were intravenous drug users; their female sexual partners were young, had exclusively heterosexual sexual histories, and had not used injection drugs. The authors found that one woman developed AIDS during the study, another had an AIDS-related syndrome, and four women had clinical or laboratory abnormalities associated with AIDS.

In 1994, 11 years after the initial Harris report of seven "risk-free" women infected with HIV through heterosexual contact, Tortu *et al.* conducted a study which assessed the risk of HIV infection in a cohort of over 5,000 U.S. women with injection drug-using sex partners. Heterosexual women reporting one or more injection drug-using sex partners and no such drug use themselves in the six months prior to their initial interview were recruited for the study. Women in the study were largely women of color—over 50 percent were of African-American descent and 30 percent were Latina. Eighty-five percent were unemployed, and nearly 12 percent were homeless. The women who participated in the study were divided into three groups: (1) women with a single sexual partner; (2) women with multiple partners; and (3) women who exchanged sex for drugs, money, or both.

The authors found that women who exchanged sex for drugs, money, or both were at a far higher risk for acquiring HIV infection than women in the other two groups. The difference persisted even when controlling for selected demographic variables including age, ethnicity, geographic region, level of education, and homelessness. Rates of condom use were higher among women exchanging sex for money, drugs; however, the frequency of unprotected sex remained significantly higher than in the other groups, and more of these women became pregnant.[3]

In explaining these findings, the authors stressed the social conditions of these women: poor education, unemployment, and homelessness. The authors correlated the high rates of sexually transmitted diseases (STDs) with urban poverty, and propose that AIDS is but one concern for women who reside in economically and socially devastated areas of the inner city: "The daily need to survive may take precedence over other motivations, including prevention of AIDS. AIDS is but one of many concerns faced by these women...[and] the goal of HIV prevention may not be realized without addressing the broader social issues affecting these women's lives."[4]   This study is one example of the use of a broader conceptual framework in public health research; this framework examines the impact of larger social forces as well as individual behaviors on HIV risk among women.

Although early observations like those of Harris and co-workers and more recent analyses like Tortu *et al.* implicated social forces in the distribution of HIV, many epidemiologists have not broadened the scope of their analysis to take into account these social forces. This narrow scope is evident in a recent series of studies on the efficacy of HIV transmission between men and women. Padian, Shiboski, and Jewell (1991) identified heterosexual index cases and counseled them to refer their heterosexual partners for testing; if the index case's sexual partner was also HIV-positive, the direction of transmission and the efficacy per sexual contact was explored through detailed history taking. Overall, they recruited 379 couples: 72 male partners of infected women, and 307 female partners of infected men. Controlling for the number of exposures, the authors calculated an odds ratio of 18.7 favoring male-to-female transmission. That is, it was 18.7 times more likely for male-to-female transmission to occur than for female-to-male transmission to occur.

This research brings into focus the complicated interconnections between social forces and biology. However, it does not explore several issues: the authors provide no context in which to place their subjects' lives; there is no mention, for example, of whether the index partner who transmitted the virus knew he or she was infected and whether this person told his or her partner. The study participants reported infrequent condom use, but this crucial issue is left largely unexplored. While fundamentally biological considerations help to explain the differential transmission rates between men and women,[5] biology is not the only factor which enhances the efficacy of male-to-female transmission. These authors do not investigate other potential contributing factors, including differences between men and women in their power to control the timing and mode of sexual contact within relationships and to ensure that condoms are used during intercourse.[6]

In a similar vein, De Vincenzi (1994) reported the results of a large prospective study of HIV transmission between heterosexual partners. The study sought to determine the rate of condom use after HIV counseling, the effectiveness of condoms in preventing HIV transmission, and the rate of infection and risk factors for transmission among couples who failed to use condoms consistently for vaginal and anal intercourse. The sample consisted of 378 couples from ten centers in eight European countries. Data from the couples were included in the analysis if the couples had continued sexual contact during the study and if follow-up was complete. Of the 378 couples, 256 (67.7%) continued to have sexual relations. Among these couples, only 124 (48.4%) used condoms consistently during intercourse. Among the couples who used condoms consistently, none of the seronegative partners became infected with HIV.

De Vincenzi reported that consistent condom use was positively correlated with three factors: an AIDS-defining diagnosis in the index partner before study enrollment; the mode of infection in the index partner (40.1% for IDU-transmitted, 70% for transfusion, 73.2% for sexual contact); and the median duration of the relationship before enrollment. Consistent condom use was not associated with the gender of the index partner nor with age. Among the 121 couples who did not use condoms regularly, the rate of seroconversion was 4.8 per 100 person-years. The risk of transmission increased with advanced stages of HIV infection in the index partner and with concurrent genital infection in the seronegative partner (non-ulcerative infection: relative risk equal to 1.6; ulcerative infection: relative risk equal to 5.2). There were no observed differences between the rates of female-to-male and male-to-female transmission. Among the couples with a male index case that did not use condoms, withdrawal to prevent ejaculation in the vagina had a protective effect, whereas unprotected anal sex resulted in increased transmission rates.

This prospective cohort study demonstrates the effectiveness of condoms in preventing HIV transmission and analyzes the factors associated with consistent condom use.[7] The study does not explore the finding that consistent condom use was reported by almost 82% of persons of European descent but by only 43% of persons of African descent. There is no mention of socioeconomic data, although the possibility exists that the differences in condom use might be correlated with socioeconomic status.[8] The links between individual behavior and larger social forces are not examined. Thus, condom use and early withdrawal are ultimately posed as effective methods of HIV prevention (although women's lack of agency in the second method is noted).

Very different findings were reported by Nicolosi and co-workers from the Italian Study Group on HIV Heterosexual Transmission, from a cross-sectional study of 524 female partners of HIV-infected men and 206 male partners of HIV-infected women. None of the partners had a reported risk factor other than sexual exposure to the HIV-infected partner. Seventy-eight percent of the male index cases used injection drugs as did 69 percent of the female index cases. In an analysis of male-to-female transmission, condoms and oral contraceptives had a protective effect (odds ratios 0.2 and 0.5, although no mention is made of how many couples using oral contraception also used condoms), while vaginitis, an STD, or a partner with overt AIDS significantly increased a woman's chance of contracting HIV from her partner (odds ratio 4.5, 2.9, and 2.6, respectively). In analyzing female-to-male transmission, Nicolosi and co-workers found that condom use decreased transmission (odds ratio 0.3) while having a partner with AIDS or having unprotected intercourse two or more times per week increased the likelihood of transmission (odds ratio 7.8 and 5.2 respectively). Using a multivariate logistic regression analysis to control for these independent risk factors, the authors calculate that among 543 couples who rarely used condoms, male-to-female transmission was 2.3 times more efficient than female-to-male transmission.

The authors postulate that the reason for the increased likelihood of male-to-female transmission is biological, arguing that acidic vaginal secretions are likely to carry a lower viral load than is semen. They further add that the surface area across which transmission takes place is larger in women. If accurate, this biologic explanation has important implications for the need for female-based prevention tools, such as vaginal microbicides, in addition to the male condom. But the study largely neglects the social conditions of women's lives—gender inequality, relative impotence in decision-making around sexual practices, conditions of financial dependence and domestic violence—and their potential role in the increased rate of HIV transmission to women.[9] As Zierler remarked in discussing the Italian study, "The gender disparity of susceptibility to HIV infection extends beyond the anatomical and physiological differences between men and women. The sociocultural and economic context of heterosexual sex throughout the world has had a powerful influence on women's susceptibility to infection."[10]

Mention should also be made here of the lack of information regarding HIV transmission among lesbian and bisexual women.[11] Young et al. (1992) reviewed several of the small number of studies which have provided data on the HIV risks of lesbian and bisexual injection drug users (IDUs).[12] They cite a number of studies that emphasize the discordance between self-reported sexual identity and self-reported sexual practices. In other words, many self-identified lesbians reported having unprotected sex with a male partner. For example, data from the Association for Women's AIDS Research and Education (AWARE), which are reported in the article, show that "women who had at least one female sexual partner in the three years prior to entry [into the study] were much more likely to have engaged in anal intercourse with a male partner than women who had no female partners were (33 percent versus 19 percent)."[13] Young and co-workers also note an increased incidence of injection drug use among homosexual women with HIV. Although much of the data they cite are unpublished, precluding a detailed analysis, the authors bring into focus the "institutional denial"[14] of researchers, policy makers, and medical caregivers that lesbians are at risk for HIV infection. This denial has aggravated the failure to provide HIV-prevention education targeted to lesbian and bisexual IDUs. The authors note that the CDC has made little attempt to study lesbian and bisexual women, and that its study protocols obscure much of the relevant information about HIV risk among lesbian and bisexual IDUs. The authors speculate that, as a result, lesbian IDUs—especially self-identified lesbian IDUs—are at increased risk of HIV infection because they feel safe from HIV by virtue of their lesbian identity.

While agreeing with the need for greater awareness of the risks of HIV among lesbian women, we again note that this article contains no explicit analysis of the role that socioeconomic status plays in HIV risk for lesbian and bisexual IDUs. The authors make passing reference to the fact that the "resources of the groups to which individuals belong"[15] in part determine an individual's risk for infection with HIV. The authors assert all lesbian and bisexual IDUs are "triply marginalized" as women, as IDUs, and as lesbians and bisexuals (or perhaps "quadruply marginalized" if they are lesbians and bisexuals of color). Many of these women are also further marginalized by poverty.

Soto-Ramirez and co-workers recently reported a possible biological mechanism to help explain geographical differences in heterosexual HIV transmission rates. They begin their article with a discussion of the different "subtypes" of HIV-1. This subtype classification is based on the gene sequences of viral envelope and core proteins, and HIV subtypes A through I have been identified. These subtypes are unevenly distributed throughout the world, with type B existing primarily in the United States and Western Europe, types A, C, and D in Africa, and type E found primarily in Thailand. The study examined potential differences between HIV-1 subtypes in terms of the cells in which the viral particles are able to replicate. Specifically, the authors examined viral growth in Langerhans' cells (LCs). Langerhans' cells are found on the surface of oral and genital mucosa. They are present in large numbers on the cervix, but absent from rectal mucosa. Langerhans' cells express CD4 receptors on their surface, which makes them a potential site of HIV-1 entry into the body.[16] Soto-Ramirez and co-workers compared the propensity of HIV-1 subtype B and HIV-1 subtype E to replicate in Langerhans' cells in culture. They obtained viral isolates from 14 homosexual men in the Boston area, from 11 heterosexuals at the Chiang-Mai University Hospital, which is located in Northern Thailand, and from seven heterosexuals in Bangkok. These isolates were then subtyped and inoculated into tissue cultures containing various types of human cells, including Langerhans' cells. Replication was quantified using viral p24 levels at seven, 14, and 21 days.

The authors found that the Thai viral isolates had a higher rate of replication in Langerhans' cells, with p24 levels of 16.06 nanograms per milliliter at 21 days compared with 2.32 nanograms per milliliter for the viral isolates from the United States. In fact, higher p24 levels were seen among the Thai isolates growing in Langerhans' cells at seven and 14 days as well. From this data, the authors conclude: "All of the viruses from the Thai heterosexuals, which were subtype E, grew more efficiently in the LCs than any of the viruses from the U.S. homosexuals, which are subtype B. These results suggest that LC tropism is associated with the efficiency of heterosexual transmission of HIV."[17]

Soto-Ramirez and co-workers link their findings to geographic variations in modes of HIV transmission: "The differences we observed in LC tissue tropism between different virus subtypes could help to explain differences in the frequency of heterosexual transmission of different subtypes of HIV-1."[18] Indeed, their work suggests an important biological mechanism that may help shed light on the differential patterns of HIV infection seen throughout the world. However, there are limitations in taking a study which examined the test-tube behavior of viral isolates from 32 individuals and using the results to explain patterns of the global AIDS pandemic. The authors themselves make note of this difficulty, qualifying their conclusion with the caveat that "differences in rates of heterosexual transmission may also be attributable to sexual behavior practices and perhaps even to host genetic susceptibility."[19] We would add to this list a number of social factors, including poverty and gender inequality. It appears that Soto-Ramirez and co-workers may also be unsatisfied with their desocializing conclusions: "However, in Asia or Africa none of the factors studied have fully explained the heterosexual epidemics there."[20]

2. SEROPREVALENCE STUDIES

Alongside transmission studies investigating *how* women become infected with HIV, seroprevalence studies determining *which* women are already infected have been a mainstay of public-health research on women and HIV. Seroprevalence surveys have been considered essential for the planning and implementation of HIV prevention strategies.[21] These types of studies have been carried out in a variety of populations, ranging from so-called "high-risk groups" to groups that could be considered more representative of the "general population"; HIV seroprevalence studies have been conducted among commercial sex workers,[22] STD clinic patients,[23] injection drug users,[24] prisoners,[25] homeless persons in shelters,[26] runaways,[27] native North Americans and Alaskans,[28] United States military personnel,[29] women of child-bearing age,[30] women attending family-planning clinics,[31] women attending prenatal clinics,[32] women who have just given birth,[33] newborns,[34] tuberculosis clinic patients,[35] an insured population in the United States,[36] persons obtaining a marriage license,[37] blood donors,[38] people living in one particular African-American community,[39] and others.[40] Some hospitals conduct routine surveys of their patients.[41] Serosurveillance of particular groups in New York State has served as a means of documenting trends in infection.[42]

A suggestion of the inherent lack of explanatory significance of these seroprevalence studies came in 1987, when Guinan and Hardy wrote one of the first reports focused exclusively on the epidemiology of AIDS in women in the United States. As of 1986, 27,140 cases of AIDS had been reported to the CDC in adults, of whom 1819 (6.7%) were women. Over half of these women were African-American. The major "transmission categories" for women with AIDS were intravenous drug use (52% of cases) and heterosexual contact (21% of cases). Of all adults who had acquired AIDS heterosexually, 84 percent were women.

Although this was one of the first descriptive reports about the epidemic in U.S. women, it failed to suggest the magnitude of the problem. In the first paragraph, the authors explain the importance of studying AIDS in women lies in its intimate relationship to infection in children and heterosexuals in general: "the occurrence of AIDS in women is of special interest...[because] trends in AIDS in women may help determine future trends for pediatric cases and may be a good surrogate for monitoring heterosexual transmission of infection."[43]   The authors conclude the article with an unrealistic proposal to reduce transmission by encouraging the risk-reducing sexual behaviors of celibacy or lifetime monogamy.

This tendency to overlook the impact of HIV infection on women permeates the approach to and conclusions drawn from many seroprevalence studies. For example, in 1986, Kreiss *et al.* studied the seroprevalence of HIV among 90 female prostitutes in Nairobi, Kenya. Between February and April 1985, the authors tested two groups of prostitutes from different social strata and compared them to both a group of males attending an STD clinic and a control group of medical personnel. The first group consisted of 64 prostitutes from an economically depressed area. On average, these women were 29 years old, had engaged in prostitution for five years, and reported an average of 963 sexual encounters per year at the average price of U.S. $0.50 per encounter. Nearly all encounters involved vaginal intercourse without condoms. Fifty-five percent of these women had laboratory evidence of syphilis; 45 percent tested positive for gonorrhea. The second group comprised 26 women who worked in a bar at a tourist hotel. On average, they were 24 years old and had been working for three years. They catered primarily to travelers and averaged 124 sexual encounters per year, mainly vaginal intercourse without condoms, at the rate of U.S. $5-15 per encounter. Thirty-one percent of these women had evidence of syphilis and 19 percent of gonorrhea.

Study participants, including 40 men attending an STD clinic and 42 medical personnel, were also tested for HIV. Overall, 66 percent of the first group of urban prostitutes (42 of 64) were HIV-positive and 31 percent (8 of 26) of the prostitutes working at the tourist bar were HIV-positive. Eight percent of the men in the STD clinic (3 of 40) were HIV-positive, and two percent (1 of 42) of the medical personnel were HIV-positive. The authors assert that there were no associations between HIV seropositivity and duration of prostitution, number of sexual contacts per year, nor history of injections or transfusions. The only significant associations commented on were a history of having sex with men from Rwanda and current infection with gonorrhea. The authors conclude that, given the then-low prevalence of AIDS in Nairobi, their data suggest the recent spread of HIV infection into the city from central Africa (Rwanda) by male travelers who frequent prostitutes. To limit its spread, they note "there is an urgent need to initiate public health education programs directed at modifying sexual behavior and limiting contacts with persons in high-risk populations."[44] By high-risk populations they presumably mean female prostitutes, a group often labeled as a "vector" in the spread of HIV.

There seems to be a clear difference in seroprevalence between the "low socioeconomic status" prostitutes (i.e the urban prostitutes) and the "higher socioeconomic prostitutes" (i.e. the tourist bar prostitutes).[45] The poorer prostitutes, with eight times as many sexual encounters per year, were more than twice as likely to be HIV infected.

Nowhere do Kreiss and co-workers discuss the social and economic reasons that forced these women to engage in prostitution.[46] The problems inherent in this conceptualization are commented upon by Tortu, and co-workers who state: "Much that has been written about sex workers and AIDS has focused on the role of the former as 'vectors of transmission' into the heterosexual community. The dangers of this type of life for the women themselves have often not been addressed."[47]

In an article which appeared early in the AIDS epidemic, Quinn et al. reviewed the epidemiological and clinical features of

AIDS in Africa and discussed possible strategies to curb its spread. They recounted the recognition of AIDS in Africa in 1983, and discussed the available data regarding its prevalence at this time. They reviewed studies showing that the major mode of transmission in Africa was by sex between males and females, although parenteral exposure via unsterilized needles and blood transfusions, as well as vertical transmission from mothers to newborns, were also hypothesized to play a role. In contrast to North America and Europe, homosexual sex and intravenous drug use were not primary modes of disease transmission. Quinn and co-workers also discuss the clinical spectrum of AIDS in Africa, where weight loss (99% of cases), fever (81% of cases), diarrhea (68% of cases) and oral candidiasis (47% of cases) were the major manifestations. Unlike in North America and Europe, where 67 percent of HIV-infected persons developed PCP, only 14 percent of HIV-positive Africans were diagnosed with PCP.

The authors note that the poverty of many African countries prevents their health ministries from taking steps toward curbing the epidemic. For instance they observe that "one cannot hope to prevent the reuse of disposable injection equipment when many hospital budgets are insufficient for the purchase of antibiotics."[48] They also note that the amount of money the United States must spend to screen its blood banks for HIV is many times more than the entire national health budgets of most African countries. Given these economic realities, the authors conclude that the only way to truly curb the AIDS pandemic in Africa is through an international commitment to providing financial help, as well as scientific assistance, to these countries.

In spite of their awareness of the effects economics have responses to the HIV epidemic, the authors propose that educational programs—both for lay people and health professionals—and surveillance systems will stop the spread of HIV in Africa: "These strategies are expected to lead rapidly to the development of programs to halt the spread of the AIDS virus. For example, creative educational approaches are needed to prevent virus transmission through reductions in the number of sexual partners or through use of condoms...The screening of women of child-bearing age and counseling regarding contraception for HIV-seropositive women are necessary in order to interrupt perinatal HIV transmission."[49] The authors do note the need for an "international commitment" in dealing with the AIDS pandemic, "not only in terms of providing financial help but also in providing scientific, educational, and technical assistance." Their focus, however, appears to be on the level of state health bureaucracies rather than on the individuals who are affected by HIV. While improving conditions with regard to HIV on a national level is important, it is also crucial that issues of gender and class inequality that occur within nations not be overlooked.[50] Furthermore, the theories and methods underpinning much of the research on HIV in the developing world also deserve further examination. As Treichler states:

> To hear the story "AIDS in the Third World," we must confront familiar problems in the human sciences: How do we know what we know? What cultural work will we ask that knowledge to perform? What are our own stakes in the success or failure of that performance? How do we document history as it unfolds? In concrete terms, we certainly need to forsake, at least part of the time, the coherent AIDS narrative of the Western professional and technical agencies and listen instead to multiple sources about and within the Third World.[51]

Numerous seroprevalence studies have been done in the United States. A recent article by Ellerbrock *et al.* presents a descriptive analysis of CDC AIDS surveillance data for U.S. women through December 31, 1990, and a comparison of the epidemiologic trends of AIDS in women with those of heterosexual men in the United States. As of December 31, 1990, a total of 15,493 (10%) of the 158,279 cases of AIDS reported to the CDC were in women. Between 1985 and 1990, the percentage of new AIDS cases among women increased from 6.6 percent to 11.5 percent. The proportion of cases attributed to heterosexual contact doubled, contributing 29 percent of all AIDS cases in women. While IDUs represented 51 percent of all cases through 1990, the proportion of female IDUs with AIDS fell from 1986 to 1990. Most women with AIDS were between the ages of 15 and 44 years (85%), black or Hispanic (72%), and from large metropolitan areas (73%), although the proportion of cases from smaller cities and rural areas had steadily increased since 1986. The authors note that the heterosexual male population with AIDS shared many of these characteristics. The study attributes the rising incidence of heterosexual transmission among women to two factors: first, women in the United States are at greater risk than heterosexual men of encountering an HIV-infected heterosexual partner (because most IDUs and hemophiliacs are men, and because some men infected through homosexual exposure to HIV are bisexual[52]); and second, HIV is more efficiently transmitted from men to women. Otherwise, as they summarize, IDUs and women with high-risk sex partners are simply engaging in "high risk behaviors."[53] The authors note that CDC data are quite likely biased due to underdiagnosis or underreporting of AIDS cases in those demographic, ethnic, and risk groups that are traditionally underserved medically, including poor women of color with little access to health care, many of whom go undiagnosed until late in their disease.

The sociodemographic characteristic left out of the conceptual framework of this study is the broader socioeconomic dimension of the AIDS epidemic. Risk is considered largely in behavioral terms. The review concludes by affirming the need for access to education, counseling, HIV testing, and "appropriate medical follow-up,"[54] but fails to note that these welcome interventions might do little to alter risk among many heterosexual women living in poverty.

In 1990, the CDC published statistics that showed that AIDS cases in women were occurring primarily in minority women. Although black and Hispanic women constituted 19 percent of all U.S. women at that time, they represented 72 percent of all U.S. women diagnosed with AIDS. In 1988, the death rate from HIV infection was nine times higher for black women than for white women. The report also stressed that "many women in the United States are unaware that they are at risk for HIV infection, and HIV infected women often remain undiagnosed until the onset of AIDS or until a perinatally infected child becomes ill."[55] In 1991, the CDC reported that almost half of the HIV tests done by publicly-funded counseling and testing sites were of women, and that black and

Hispanic women were overrepresented at these test sites. It is unfortunate that data on the socioeconomic status of these women is not collected, reported, nor analyzed to see how they are correlated with HIV risk. Although these dynamics are unexamined, economic considerations do arise, as these women are depicted as draining the public coffers. "Many women with HIV infection are of lower socioeconomic status; therefore, prevention efforts, health care, and social services—including those for drug treatment—rely on public resources."[56]

In 1995, the CDC reported an update about AIDS in U.S. women through 1994. They found that the percentage of all new AIDS cases that were women had steadily increased since 1985 to make up 18% of new cases in 1994. Seventy-seven percent of 1994 cases in women occurred in black and Hispanic women. Thirty-eight percent of new cases among women were attributed to heterosexual contact. The editors note that "the disproportionate impact of HIV/AIDS among women in racial/ethnic minority groups reflects social and economic factors."[57] However, because systematic data on social and economic factors were not gathered, an in-depth analysis of these forces and the ways in which they put women at risk for HIV infection is left unaddressed.[58]

In 1994, Hu *et al.* explored the regional trends in AIDS incidence in the United States.[59] National surveillance data for persons diagnosed with AIDS from 1988 to 1991 were analyzed to determine the number of AIDS cases reported from each defined region of the United States (Northeast, Midwest, South, West, and U.S. Territories), and, within each region, the characteristics of reported cases by gender, age group, "race"/ethnicity, and "HIV exposure category." This data shows that, although AIDS rates have declined nationally, rates for specific regions and populations increased during the period 1988-1991. The largest percentage increase in AIDS rates were among women, blacks, Hispanics, and persons exposed to HIV through heterosexual contact. The regions that experienced the greatest increases were the Midwest, the South, and the U.S. Territories, probably due to the late spread of HIV into these regions relative to the Northeast and West. In general the rate of AIDS increase was greater for women than men, and for blacks and Hispanics than for other ethnic groups. Although the authors stress the expanding "regional diversity" of AIDS in the United States, much of what they describe reflects epidemic HIV spread to women through heterosexual contact. The report also notes that, even through the late eighties, the epidemic continued to increase among IDUs. The authors conclude that preventive services need to be expanded geographically; however, diversity, particularly in terms of gender inequality and poverty, *within* the different regions is not discussed nor is the impact of this "diversity" on prevention and therapeutic programs is not discussed.

3. MATERNAL AND INFANT STUDIES

Vertical transmission from mother to child has been a topic of much study in public health research.[60]   In addition to work in this area, studies have also looked at the general health of children born to women with HIV. For example, Halsey, Boulos, Holt *et al.* (1990) studied the impact of maternal HIV-1 infections on infant survival, birth weight, gestational age, and malnutrition in a population of women not using injection drugs or cocaine (the effects of drugs on birth weight and infant mortality have confounded similar studies of high-risk populations in which drug use is common). The authors chose to study mothers and infants from the "high-risk Haitian population"[61] of Cité Soleil, a sprawling slum of Port-au-Prince.[62]   The region was served by a community-based, primary health care program providing prenatal care to more than 80 percent of local pregnant women. Between August 1986 and August 1988, 4,588 pregnant women were enrolled in the study and were interviewed at six to seven months gestation. Birth weights were determined for infants born at three hospitals, where gestational age was estimated. The status of infants born outside the hospital was determined in outpatient clinics, where blood was collected, and mothers were interviewed about their own and their children's health status.

Almost 10% of these ostensibly healthy women were found to be HIV-positive. Infants born to HIV-positive mothers had significantly lower birth weights, were more likely to be premature, and were more likely to become malnourished than were infants born to HIV-negative women. At the age of 12 months, 23.4 percent of infants born to HIV-positive women had died compared to 10.8 percent of the infants born to HIV-negative mothers. The study estimates the mother-to-infant HIV transmission rate to be 23.9 percent, close to rates reported for populations in the United States and Europe.

According to this study, the factors associated with maternal HIV infection were age, marital status, prior syphilis infection, number of sexual partners, and smoking.[63] To different degrees these factors show a bias toward a behavioral explanation that evades in-depth socioeconomic analysis. Low per capita income, unemployment, low literacy, and "economic and political stability" are cited as factors contributing to the increase in infant mortality rates in the community in recent years, but the mechanisms by which these factors might alter rates of HIV transmission were not explored. The article thus notes the economic hardship faced by the Haitian population studied, but never in a way that linked socioeconomic status to HIV infection, even though Cité Soleil is notorious as one of the worst slums of the hemisphere.

In 1990, Chin presented global estimates, calculated by the WHO Global Programme on AIDS, of the growing magnitude of the HIV/AIDS pandemic for women and children. He derived annual incidence of HIV infection in women by combining current regional or national estimates of the prevalence of HIV infection with the estimated time that HIV began to spread to women. The number of HIV-infected infants was derived by factoring in age-specific fertility rates and HIV-transmission rates of infected women from a given region or population. The progression rate of HIV to AIDS (significantly more rapid for children than adults) was used to determine the estimated number of AIDS cases for women and children worldwide. The Global Programme on AIDS estimated that by 1990 more than three million females had been infected with HIV, that these women were predominantly of childbearing age, and that 80 percent were from sub-Saharan Africa. In addition, by the end of 1992 about one million infants were estimated to be

HIV-infected. The author noted in passing that during the late 1980s in many central African cities there were more women aged 15-24 infected with HIV than men of the same age. As in the United States, the majority of adolescents with HIV are females.[64] This differential vulnerability, and its relation to gender inequality and poverty, are not examined in Chin's review.

Though Chin notes that "HIV infections are not randomly distributed in any population,"[65] the paper makes no note of the economic factors that underlie this strikingly patterned distribution. The author refers to the scant attention paid to the economic *impact* of the HIV/AIDS pandemic on women and children, but neglects to mention the role of economic factors in sculpting the contours of the pandemic.

4. AIDS AND SOCIOECONOMIC STATUS

As with most reportable diseases in the United States, AIDS data is not reported with information about socioeconomic status.[66] To investigate the association between socioeconomic status and HIV infection, researchers have needed to devise strategies to compensate for the lack of government-collected data. We will look at a few studies that attempt to work around these shortcomings in U.S. data.

Simon *et al.* (1994) examined the relationship between income and AIDS rates in Los Angeles County by "race" and ethnicity. They used 1990 U.S. census data to classify zip codes by median household incomes into low, middle, and high income brackets. They then calculated AIDS rates for each geographically defined sub-population based on the 15,805 AIDS cases reported from 1987 through 1992. They found that AIDS rates were highest (252.8 per 100,000) in low-income areas and lowest (82.0 per 100,000) in high-income areas. AIDS rates also varied by "race," with blacks having the highest incidence (297.1 per 100,000), followed by whites, Hispanics, and Asians (respectively, 244.1, 113.1, and 30.0 per 100,000). All groups had an inverse relationship between income and AIDS rates, and this was most pronounced among whites. Because blacks and Hispanics were more likely to live in low-income areas, a greater proportion of AIDS cases among blacks and Hispanics occurred in people in low-income areas (77.6% of all cases in blacks were in low income areas, while 67.4% of all cases in Hispanics and 46.9% of all cases in whites lived in low-income areas). The authors acknowledge that, within zip codes, there may be a substantial range of individual incomes which may have introduced significant bias into their results. They also discuss the fact that their results may show an effect of downward economic mobility of AIDS patients rather than increased incidence among poorer people.

One important shortcoming of their study is that they provided no breakdown of their cohort by gender and thus did not analyze how trends in AIDS rates by income and "race" were influenced by gender. Nevertheless, their results show an increased prevalence of AIDS in low-income areas and argue strongly for an increased incidence of AIDS among residents in low-income areas.

In a 1992 paper titled "AIDS Incidence and Income," Fife and Mode examined the relationship between incidence of AIDS, income, "race", and mode of infection through a study of Philadelphia AIDS surveillance data. They classified people with AIDS by the per capita income of their census tracts of residence and looked at all cases of AIDS reported to the Philadelphia Department of Health from 1984 to May 1991. They found that there was a steady rise in AIDS incidence among the lowest income tercile, while the incidence among the highest income tercile leveled off after 1987. Non-whites across all income brackets also showed an increasing incidence, while the incidence for whites began to level off after 1987. When study participants with AIDS were grouped according to race, both whites and non-whites in the lowest income group showed an increasing incidence of AIDS. Survival after diagnosis with AIDS was longer for whites versus non-whites and longer for high-income and middle-income groups as compared with low-income groups.

This study documents the rising tide of AIDS cases among lower-income populations. The survival data also support numerous other studies documenting decreased survival among blacks and Hispanics (largely mediated in the 1980s by decreased use of PCP prophylaxis).[67] Fife and Mode's paper does not look at the impact of gender inequality on AIDS incidence, an unfortunate omission as their database likely contained information on gender. Since this was a large population-based study which used residence as a marker for income, the possibility of confounding by downward mobility and wide variations in income across census tracts was again raised. However, it is clear from their data that poor communities showed rising incidences of AIDS cases through 1991 and that this trend was registered across all "races."

Rumley and Esinhart (1993) examined the evolving AIDS epidemic in rural North Carolina, exploring how larger social forces can affect the shaping of HIV "subepidemics." The authors reviewed and analyzed information from relevant literature, from public-health data (e.g. surveillance reports on AIDS, gonorrhea, syphilis, and tuberculosis) and from an ongoing study of HIV/AIDS patients at the University Medical Center of Eastern Carolina at Pitt County (UMCEC-PC). Data from 737 of 873 UMCEC-PC AIDS patients were analyzed and compared with statistics derived from surveillance reports of AIDS cases, and from the incidence of AIDS, syphilis, and tuberculosis. Rates of HIV were determined for each county. Using a simple linear-regression model, the authors correlate the AIDS incidence rate in each county with other disease-incidence rates, as well as with demographic data on "race," poverty, involvement in migrant and seasonal farm work, and school drop-out rate.

This detailed socioeconomic analysis of the AIDS epidemic in North Carolina reveal it to be an epidemic of poor people, and increasingly of poor women: counties with higher percentages of people living in poverty and a higher proportion of school drop-outs tend to have a higher incidence of AIDS. The UMCEC-PC AIDS patients (all of whom live in rural counties) are more likely to be non-white, non-metropolitan, heterosexual, and female when compared with statewide surveillance data. Rumley and Esinhart's sociodemographic analysis is also revealing. Fifty-two percent of the HIV or AIDS patients migrated into the more rural UMCEC-PC catchment area. Though this percentage decreased over time, it describes a continuing trend in the rural AIDS epidemic: adolescents and young adults migrate from rural farm communities to urban centers to seek economic opportunity: they return using injection drugs (or having used them during their time in the city), HIV-positive, or both.[68] These "urban run-offs" also return home (or to no home) without jobs, training, or medical insurance, and in many cases are unaware of or not acknowledging their HIV status. Most of the cases reported in the Rumley and Esinhart paper were from indigent, non-white communities; they were predominantly injection drug users, and most were male. Unprotected sex or needle sharing with these individuals resulted in an increasing number of "home-grown" HIV cases, rendering poor, non-white women most vulnerable to infection. The authors underlined the role that prostitution and "survival sex" played in extending HIV infection in these rural communities.[69] Because of a lack of medical resources and social and economic services in rural areas, the authors posit that many of these infected persons migrated back to nearby cities when they developed symptomatic AIDS. A migration cycle may have ensued, facilitating the transmission of HIV: The authors suggest that this in turn strained medical resources in these cities, consequently forcing less symptomatic HIV-infected persons in these cities to move to more rural areas, where more persons became infected. Within these rural areas, lack of transportation, income, insurance, social and medical services impeded medical care for HIV-infected persons.

In 1994, Diaz et al. reported the results of a multistate-surveillance project that looked at differences in socioeconomic status among people with AIDS. Between June 1, 1990 and January 31, 1993, 2,898 people with AIDS were interviewed in 11 states. Among men, the investigators found that almost half of those exposed through IDU or heterosexual sex had not completed high school, while only 15 percent of the men exposed through homosexual sex had not completed high school (of U.S. men in general, 22% did not finish high school). Seventy-two percent of men exposed through homosexual sex were unemployed, while 88 percent of men exposed through injection drug use were unemployed. Forty-nine percent of men exposed through homosexual sex had annual incomes of less than $10,000, while 73 percent of men exposed through injection drug use were in this income bracket. Blacks were more likely than whites to be unemployed, have low incomes and to have not finished high school.

Among women, all measures reflected an overall lower socioeconomic status than that of the men in the study. Fully half of all women had not completed high school, 90 percent were unemployed, and 77 percent had an annual income of less than $10,000. Black women were more likely than white women to have not completed high school, to be unemployed, and to have annual incomes of less than $10,000. Although downward mobility due to AIDS may account for some of the results the authors describe, it cannot account for the large differences in education seen between blacks and whites and between men and women, differences that most likely reflect premorbid inequities in socioeconomic status.[70] If downward mobility had the effect of impoverishing people with AIDS, that effect was more pronounced for blacks as compared to whites and for women as compared to men.

5. BEHAVIORAL RISK FACTOR ANALYSIS

Analyzing specific behaviors is one of the most common strategies that modern epidemiological studies use to investigate the risk of contracting HIV infection. Numerous studies have been conducted that identify so-called behavioral risk factors in different sub-populations, such as samples of injection drug users,[71] commercial sex workers,[72] gay or bisexual men,[73] adolescents,[74] juvenile delinquents,[75] runaways,[76] homeless individuals,[77] poor women,[78] poor men,[79] and heterosexual adults.[80]

However, as pointed out by some in the field of epidemiology, "to focus on differences in biomedically defined risk between sets of individuals (who, after routine adjustment for confounders are regarded as being 'otherwise equal') is to overlook larger-scale structural differences in patterns of health between populations."[81] As we have argued elsewhere in this book, an analysis of individual behaviors without a comprehensive assessment of the constraints on individual agency is at best inadequate and at worst misleading. Here, we will look at some studies that examine risk behaviors believed to be associated with HIV infection and assess whether or not they take account of the multiple ways in which the agency of poor women is constrained.

In a 1990 paper called "Intravenous Drug Users' Sexual Partners: Gender and Drug Injection Practices," Kleyn *et al.* explore the bias against the female sexual partners of injection drug users in HIV prevention efforts.[82] They ask the question: do female sexual partners need their own prevention programs? The authors claim that public health officials assume that the male sexual partners of most female IDUs are also IDUs, while the female sexual partners of male IDUs are, on the whole, not injecting drugs. At the time this study was done, according to the authors, there were no programs for the sexual partners of female IDUs—in part because it is assumed that these partners are also drug injectors.

The authors conducted this Seattle-based study to document the number of male and female IDUs who have sexual partners who do not inject drugs. They found little difference between men and women as to whether they had a sex partner who was also an IDU. In fact, most IDUs, regardless of gender, had fellow IDUs as sex partners. When sampling an out-of-treatment population, women had almost as many non-injecting sex partners as did men. The authors conclude that public health officials should not assume that the sexual partners of IDUs are women who do not use injection drugs nor should they assume that only men have sexual partners who are not injecting drugs. If programs exclusively target females in the education of sex partners they will be ineffective, Kleyn and co-workers claim.

Clearly, male sexual partners also need to be targeted for the prevention message to be heeded.[83] Yet, can female and male sexual partners of IDUs be targeted with the same message and in the same manner just because they both happen to share the same position as sexual partners of IDUs? The authors conclude with the statement that "the lesson for public health officials charged with AIDS prevention is that it is important to consider suitable information about the nature of specific target populations rather than relying on data readily available but possibly inappropriate for the task at hand."[84] Ironically, they themselves fail to consider relevant information in their article by relying overmuch on Waldorf's outdated book *Careers in Dope*.[85] For example, when seeking an explanation for female IDUs' failure to enter treatment as often as men, for example, Waldorf asserts that women IDUs have more clients and revenue than do male prostitutes;[86] Kleyn and colleagues accept this as plausible. They further assert that women may have fewer financial, legal and social pressures to "clean up their act."[87]

More recent data from numerous studies suggest that these assertions are far from correct. Most often, women IDUs are single mothers who are forced to prostitute, sell drugs, or run shooting galleries to support their habits. They suffer severe discrimination both inside and outside the drug subculture.[88] What they need is not merely education, but a way out of circumstances in which they necessarily subject themselves to HIV risks. Thus, rather than wondering if we are targeting the right individuals, we might ask if we are targeting the right conditions, namely those which force women to take such risks.[89]

Kaplan *et al.* (1994) undertook a study of New Haven's Needle Exchange Program to determine the effect of needle exchange on probability of HIV infection among injection drug users in that city. The authors ask whether participation in a needle exchange program explains the reduction in circulating HIV-infected syringes. They measured HIV prevalence in needles given to white and non-white clients, average needle circulation time, and frequency of visits to the needle exchange. There was no discussion of demographics other than "race" (white and non-white). Mean circulation time of needles significantly predicted recovery of HIV from the needles leading Kaplan and co-workers to conclude: "needle exchange is responsible for the decline in HIV prevalence in needles returned to the New Haven Needle Exchange Program."[90] Thus, with a needle exchange program in operation, there is less opportunity for drug users to become infected.[91]

Although these are important findings, it is unfortunate that there is no mention of women in the article, either in recruitment of participants or the ratio of those who participated in the program. This is a major oversight, given that 41 percent of all HIV infections in U.S. women are due to injection-drug use.[92] This study, as well as other studies on needle exchange, failed to ascertain whether men and women benefit equally from needle exchange programs, and if not, the reasons why they do not.

In 1988, Brown and Primm examined the propensity of IDUs to have sexual relations with other IDUs versus with persons who do not engage in parenteral drug use. Participants were randomly selected through methadone-maintenance clinics in New York City. Their sample of IDUs was 54 percent black, 35 percent Hispanic, and 11 percent white; 41 percent of the group were women. They found that younger, needle-sharing men were more likely to have a non-IDU sex partner. Among black female IDUs, needle sharing was significantly associated with IDU sexual contacts. The authors also note that an "important corollary was the dual route of HIV infection experienced by female IDUs: sexual contact with male IDUs and their own parenteral drug use. This may, in part, explain the higher HIV-infection rate experienced by female IDUs in many seroprevalence studies."[93] This speculation is then taken one step further: the authors propose that the dual exposure of female IDUs, "coupled with their propensity for prostitution, may also serve as a bridge of HIV infection from IDUs to the general community," thus raising the importance of IDU prostitution as a key target in preventing transmission "to the general population."[94]

Brown and Primm advocate for preventive measures aimed at reducing "promiscuity," as opposed to protecting these doubly-at-risk women from exposure in the first place. The authors do note that "drug treatment may reduce HIV-exposing behaviors in IDUs" by providing "relative stability,"[95] thus acknowledging the external difficulties in reducing HIV-risk, but they do not explain the nature of this stability. While the authors investigate the sexual practices of IDUs to postulate sexual transmission from IDUs as a major mode of HIV spread, they fail to evaluate what determines those relationships in the first place: why some IDUs, particularly women, engage in prostitution and have multiple partners. Are prostitution and addiction to drugs distributed according to behavioral, psychological, or cultural traits? As noted, these conditions afflict primarily poor and disempowered persons regardless of "propensities" or "promiscuity." Thus, the authors look at injection-drug-using practices in order to determine a direct link to "the general community," while ignoring the structural violence that shapes many of those practices and which constitutes the real link between subordinate and dominant groups.

In 1991, Shayne and Kaplan attempted a comprehensive review of issues relevant to HIV transmission in women—especially poor women—in the United States by implicitly linking the rising transmission rates among women to problems related to addiction and poverty. This review is effective at pointing out why it is necessary "to be sensitive to different conceptions of risk."[96] For example, the authors note that "safe sex is an economic compromise for many poor women who rely on sex as a source of employment, as a means to establish ownership or proprietary rights in relationships, or as a means of getting tangible supports, generally short in supply."[97] However, their assessment of the literature in general leads them to stress the "formidable challenges" inherent in *educating* poor women and changing *their* behaviors, rather than addressing the even more formidable structural impediments to risk reduction which poor women face.[98] Shayne and Kaplan also participate in the discourse of risk to the "general population" by framing the article in terms of conflicting arguments concerning the actual risk of transmission to women and by concluding that "the virus is spreading, and the dangers it poses affect us all."[99]

In a 1992 article titled, "Sexual Behavior, Smoking, and HIV-1 Infection in Haitian Women," Halsey and co-workers report the results of a follow-up study which examined the association between HIV infection and smoking among Haitian women. Study participants were women from an urban community-health program who had participated in a previous study of risk factors for HIV infection in Cité Soleil. All the women were six to seven months pregnant when first interviewed. Eighty-nine women who reported that they had smoked in the previous study (a mean of six cigarettes per day was reported), and who had been interviewed in the previous 12 months, were enrolled in the current study. From a randomized list of women who reported that they had never smoked, 329 women were chosen as a control group.

Participants were interviewed twice, and, on both occasions, asked about a number of potential factors associated with HIV infection: their lifetime sexual practices, medical history, health "beliefs and practices," smoking, drug and alcohol use, and whether they were tattooed. They were asked about marital status, religion, age, employment, how long they had lived in the area of the study, whether they owned a home, and whether their home had a dirt or cement floor. The last factor was used as a marker of socioeconomic status, with presence of a dirt floor reflecting lower socioeconomic status.

The study found that smokers had significantly more lifetime sex partners, were less likely to be married, had their first sexual contact at a younger age, and had less stable sexual relationships. They also were more likely to both visit folk healers and be Catholic. According to the authors, adjusting for all these factors associated with both smoking and HIV infection did not eliminate the strong association between smoking and HIV infection. The study concludes that this causal link may be the result of an immune suppressive effect associated with smoking. The study also reports a strong correlation between smoking and having a dirt floor.

Given the possibility that the smoking behavior reported— about six cigarettes per day—might have a biological effect increasing the likelihood of HIV infection among women who are engaged in high risk sexual behavior, it is curious that this association received such attention in the final discussion. The final regression analysis of the study showed that *the odds ratio of having HIV infection and having a dirt floor is more than double the odds ratio of having HIV infection and smoking.* The significance of the association between lower socioeconomic status and HIV infection receives little comment.

Plourde *et al.* (1992) examined risk factors for HIV-1 infection in Kenyan women with STDs. The women recruited for this study were treated for STDs between February 1988 and September 1989 at the Nairobi City Commission Special Treatment Clinic. Of the 600 women studied, 13.8 percent were diagnosed as having HIV infection. Forty-eight of the women who participated in the study identified themselves as prostitutes; 25 of the 48 were HIV-positive. The study found that 12.6 percent of women with STDs who had never directly sold sex were found to be HIV-positive, compared with 44 percent of the women studied who were actively engaged in the sale of sex; only three percent of pregnant women with no STDs were seropositive. A narrowly construed definition of prostitution—by both the researchers and study participants—may have led to an underestimate of women's risk if women who exchanged sex to enhance economic security were not considered "prostitutes." In general the HIV-infected women were more likely to be single, widowed, divorced, or separated, and to have had sex for the first time at a younger age compared with the HIV-negative women. They were also much less likely to be pregnant. Interestingly, HIV-infected women also reported greater lifetime duration of oral-contraception use. Indeed the highest risk associated with HIV-infection was found to be the combination of prolonged (more than 12 months) oral-contraception use and the presence of genital ulcers, with the presence of genital ulcers constituting a significant independent risk.

The authors postulate that oral contraceptives make women more susceptible to HIV infection. They propose three mechanisms by which this increased risk might occur: First, because oral contraceptives cause cervical ectopy, women using them may be more susceptible to HIV infection. Second, oral contraceptives may have an indirect effect on HIV transmission by increasing the risks of C. trachomatis cervicitis or genital ulcers. Finally, oral contraceptives are postulated to have a direct immunosuppressive effect that puts women at greater risk for acquiring HIV infection. While these "biological" mechanisms of increased risk may prove to be important in the spread of HIV among women, they also illustrate the tendency in much of the public health literature to rely on biological factors as the factors of primary importance in understanding the spread of HIV. Plourde and co-workers neither investigate the role of social staus in determining risk for either HIV or C trachomatis, nor do they seek to link the sale of sex to the large-scale social forces that so clearly shape urban prostitution in Kenya.[101]

6. PREVENTION AND RISK REDUCTION

Numerous interventions have tried to reduce HIV-related risk behavior in particular populations, such as injection drug users,[100] and in adolescents.[102] AIDS-education programs have been a mainstay of prevention efforts.[103] Two questions remain not only unanswered but often unasked in this literature: Do AIDS education programs really reduce risks for acquiring HIV? If so, for whom are these risks reduced? Recently, attempts by health educators and researchers to more fundamentally address the factors that affect risk perception and risk-taking has resulted in more attention to cultural issues.[104] In fact, incorporating cultural issues into HIV education is often proposed as *the* answer to increasing knowledge, improving attitudes and changing behavior. Yet, this perspective is also limited because many researchers and educators are still operating under the assumption that the individual is the sole agent of change. Individual cognition thus becomes the focus of interventions. Many public health investigators and educators have not considered the structural barriers to AIDS prevention. If a review of the literature tells us anything, it is that we must move beyond the static analysis of individual cognition and toward an understanding of the social dynamics of HIV transmission.[105] As Susser and Susser state: "The present era of epidemiology is coming to a close. The focus on risk factors at the individual level—the hallmark of this era—will no longer serve. We need to be concerned equally with causal pathways at the society level..."[107]

When AIDS researchers fail to see economic and social vulnerability as factors which mediate HIV infection, groups at risk become evident only after large numbers of individuals become infected. For example, female crack users, have not, until recently, been recognized as a group particularly vulnerable to HIV infection. Perhaps because crack is most often smoked, a practice that most likely does not, in and of itself, *directly* heighten HIV risk, the degree to which AIDS has afflicted this group was unanticipated. The mechanisms by which crack users' risk is increased are largely social. Fullilove *et al.* (1992) explore the trauma-related experiences of female crack users. Due to evidence that suggests that crack use is associated with the dramatic increase in the incidence of STDs among black women nationwide,[107] they sought to understand the relationship between trauma, crack use, and crack-related sexual behavior. Women were described in terms of their socio-psychological profile (i.e., chaotic homelife, history of abuse), and reference to their impoverishment emerged in descriptions of the women's lives (e.g. "An unstable period began when she moved between homeless shelters, the streets, and homes of relatives.")[108]

Three types of trauma are found in interviews with crack-using women: (1) trauma that predated the onset of crack use; (2) trauma that is the direct result of crack use (e.g. removal of children from home); and (3) stigma trauma (a result of the reputation that a female crack user will do anything for a high, including degrading sexual favors). The authors suggest that these traumas and consequent post-traumatic stress must be addressed in the treatment of the female drug user. By highlighting the significance of trauma in the lives of drug-addicted women, Fullilove and co-workers have contributed to an understanding of how drug abuse can be exacerbated by trauma, how trauma and crack use are associated, and how different types of trauma must be considered. Their research provides a starting point for further exploration of the complicated confluence of trauma and addiction, trauma and poverty, and trauma and HIV infection.[109]

Elias and Heise explore the challenges inherent in the development of "female-controlled prevention options" such as vaginal microbicides.[110] They review the literature on the need for this technology given the limitations in current prevention strategies, especially limitations due to gender inequality experienced by women: "Underlying gender power inequalities severely limit the ability of many women to protect themselves from HIV infection, especially in the absence of prevention technology they can use, when necessary, without their partner's consent."[111] The authors view the development of female-controlled prevention technology as an essential goal for women worldwide, recognizing that input from diverse groups of women is necessary in order to ensure compatibility with a wide array of sexual norms and experiences. They also call for the need for a microbicide which would be selective, so as not to interfere with the desire of any particular woman to conceive, as well as one which could be used postcoitally to protect women subjected to non-consensual sex or for other "unplanned" sex (among adolescents, for example, who may feel that "planning" to have sex is unacceptable). Elias and Heise review biological, practical, programmatic, and political-economic issues related to research and development of these products. Because Elias and Heise also explore the "economic, political, and violent realities"[112] of many women's lives (in the United States as well as in sub-Saharan Africa), their research makes explicit many issues related to poverty and gender inequality and their impact upon the development, distribution, and potential use of medical technologies.[113]

To determine the relationship between risks for HIV infection, perceiving oneself at risk, and initiating risk reduction for sexually active young women, Eversley and co-workers conducted a study among adult women attending a California-family planning clinic. They determined that these women were at risk for HIV infection if they reported any of the following "behavioral" risk factors: an IDU partner; a history of STDs; multiple partners in the previous year; five or more partners in the previous five years; concerns that their primary partner may have other partners; inquiring about the number of partners that a sexual partner has had; having had sex outside of primary relationship in past year; or not using condoms with partners other than their primary partner.

A survey instrument was used to collect data regarding ethnicity (participants were classified as white, African-American, or "other"—with the latter category including Asians and Latinas), income, education, and employment status. Survey results were analyzed with respect to ethnic subgroups. Education level was significantly lower in the African-American pool and significantly higher among whites. African-American men were more likely to be unemployed. Monthly income of those employed was lower among African-Americans, with whites having highest monthly income. Finally, women in the "other" group and African-American women more often perceived themselves to be, and indeed were, at greater risk for HIV infection. Thus, while the category of "ethnicity" was the variable of interest to the investigators, the "behavioral" risk factors examined might well have varied as significantly by educational status, income, employment status, or gender. Further analysis comparing African-American women—who were also poorer, less educated, and less likely to be employed—to other "ethnicities" showed them to be at higher risk for HIV infection, especially if they had a history of STDs and believed that their primary partner had multiple partners. The study also showed that these women had adopted fewer risk-reduction behaviors, although the differences were not statistically significant.

The behavioral risk factors analyzed in the study did not include personal injection drug use, only the use of injection drugs by sex partners. Further, risk-reduction strategies were focused on the women's concerns about their partners' behavior rather than their own risk behaviors. The risk-reduction behavior of condom use is dependent on male assent, and changing partners or reducing the number of partners is never addressed.

The authors found that there was no significant relationship between perceiving oneself at risk and adopting risk-reduction strategies. The authors conclude:

> these data suggest that the women in this population may be overly optimistic about their invulnerability to HIV. While those women who perceived themselves to be at risk for becoming sexually infected with HIV were more likely to report high-risk behaviors, perception of risk did not motivate these women to adopt low-risk behavior. These data suggest that simple HIV education and acknowledgment may have little effect on reducing exposure to HIV among the women in this population. Alternative strategies for reducing risk must be explored.[114]

The authors state that HIV education may have little effect on prevention because these women demonstrate that they are already aware of the nature of AIDS risks and their own risk factors. In fact, the authors note in their discussion that perception of risk and risk reduction are correlated among homosexual men and among college students, yet not among other sexually-active adults or among injection drug users.

Holtgrave and co-workers present a recent overview of the effectiveness and efficiency of HIV-prevention programs in the United States. The purpose of their article is to review and summarize the characteristics of successful HIV prevention programs, the general characteristics of the programs that had a favorable or unfavorable impact on behavioral outcomes, the financial costs of these programs, and their cost-effectiveness. A successful program is defined as one that averts or reduces HIV-related risk behaviors or modifies their determinants at minimal cost, is community-based and culturally competent, possesses clear objectives and goals for the intervention, is based on social or behavioral science theory and research, and has a quality-assurance and an evaluation component.

Almost none of the programs were evaluated for the adequacy of attention to women's issues, to say nothing of attention given to the needs of poor women.[115] The major findings of the review are that persons at "no or low risk" for infection benefit from "attitude change," "general education," and reinforcement of low-risk behaviors. The authors identify as at "no or low risk" those in the "general population," youth, and high school students.[116] Persons in high-risk groups were said to benefit from counseling, testing, partner notification, or referral, and, when appropriate, from outreach, drug treatment and needle exchange. Holtgrave and co-workers argued that these programs were cost-effective when compared to the cost of care for an HIV-infected person.

The review's major flaw is its narrow scope. It defines a successful program not as one that saves lives but one that reduces "risk behaviors at a minimal cost."[117] The reduction of risk behaviors, which are self-reported, and, at best, surrogate markers for the multifactorial risk faced by poor women, cannot be an adequate measure of a program's success. Although modification of risk behaviors has no doubt contributed to the leveling off of HIV incidence among certain homosexual men and some IDU populations, poor women's risks of contracting HIV are less under their control when compared to men or to non-poor women. Given the increasing incidence of new HIV infections among poor women, a new paradigm is needed: a paradigm that reveals how inequalities related to gender, "race," and class become embodied as increased AIDS risks.[118]

7. CONCLUSION

In epidemiology, as in the behavioral sciences, it is possible to discern a marked trend towards examination of individual risk.[119] In early public health and epidemiological writings on AIDS, considerations of "risk groups"—itself a flawed term—gave way quickly to "risk behavior," a shift which has, ironically, only enforced this trend. There is thus an enormous body of research examining "high-risk behaviors" and AIDS. AIDS interventions, accordingly, have been designed to educate or persuade individuals to choose to avoid these demonstrably dangerous behaviors.

Such an approach, as we have seen, permits individual risk behaviors to be divorced from the larger social world in which such behaviors are embedded. It also tends to exaggerate the agency of the poor and poor women in particular. In epidemiology and in public health, these individualizing trends have a common tendency to *desocialize the social*. How, precisely, do such paradigmatic shifts come to have their effects in writings about women and AIDS? Take, as an example, the previously discussed paper by Halsey, Coberly, Holt, *et al*. The paper, which appeared in the *Journal of the American Medical Association*, was titled "Sexual Behavior, Smoking, and HIV-1 Infection in Haitian Women." The authors of the study speculate that cigarette smoking may alter the cervical epithelium in ways that directly increase HIV risks: "Although the association between smoking and HIV-1 infection could have been due to unrecognized confounding, a biological association between smoking and HIV-1 infection cannot be ruled out." The authors further add: "While the exact biological significance of these findings is unclear, cigarette smoking induces local changes in the vagina and cervix that could alter the risk of HIV-1 acquisition after sexual exposure."[120]

Although cigarette smoking was singled out as the salient finding of a large-scale survey of women living in a Haitian slum, other "factors" were also correlated with HIV infection in this cohort. One of the factors was the presence of a dirt floor, which, although unexplored in the study, was clearly an indirect marker of socioeconomic status. In an urban shantytown, a dirt floor suggested greater poverty. Why might cigarette smoking, which has not been subsequently shown to increase HIV risks, be the subject of intense scrutiny while substandard housing conditions escape the analytic gaze?[121] The elevation of an individual risk behavior and the erasure of social conditions fits neatly into the now-dominant epidemiological paradigm. "By concentrating on these specific and presumed free-range individual behaviors," notes McMichael, "we thereby pay less attention to the underlying social-historical influences on behavioral choices, patterns, and population health."[122]

Similarly truncated was the discussion of Nairobi sex workers' risk for HIV infection. In the study by Kreiss and co-workers, a host of potentially risk-altering factors were mentioned in passing. Which ones are selected for discussion? Those which focus on biological forces, removed from the social world in which they operate. For example, "It may be that epithelial integrity is an important barrier to viral transmission and that diseases such as gonorrhea, chancroid, or syphilis, which cause mucosal or squamous epithelial discontinuity or bleeding are risk factors for AIDS virus infection."[123] Demoted to textual insignificance are factors which point to more social causes of HIV infection in the women who were studied. Prostitutes from the lower socioeconomic group were more than twice as likely as their counterparts in the higher socioeconomic group to be infected with HIV; this fact is not discussed in the results. Once again, socioeconomic factors which may be driving the spread of HIV are effectively ignored.

In vitro models are sometimes held to explain variations in world epidemiology—as was the case in the paper by Soto-Ramirez and co-workers. When this is done without even the briefest discussion of social factors, the desocialization of the AIDS pandemic is complete.

This narrow scope in the fields of public health and epidemiology has been commented upon by those within these disciplines as well.[124] As Pearce notes: "There are still major socioeconomic differences in health, and the relative differences are continuing to increase. Nevertheless, modern epidemiologists rarely consider socioeconomic factors and the population perspective, except perhaps to occasionally adjust for social class in analyses of the health effects of tobacco smoke, diet, and other lifestyle factors in individuals."[125] Pearce further adds "Epidemiology has become a set of generic methods for measurement of disease occurrence, and there has been a concomitant lack of distinctive theory to permit an understanding of the population patterns of disease occurrence."[126] Furthermore, "Most modern epidemiologists still do studies in populations, but they do so in order to study decontextualized individual risk factors rather than to study population factors in their social and historical context."[127]

Trends towards behaviorist or biological reductionisms, including assertions that either individual risk behaviors or viral strain variations serve to explain the global distribution of HIV, are firmly entrenched in modern epidemiology and public health. These trends reflect broad epistemic shifts registered far beyond the academy. But only by linking *distal* causes and characteristics to the much more complex social conditions that structure women's HIV risks will compelling explanatory models emerge. Standard epidemiology, narrowly focused on individual risk, will not reveal these multiple and complex interconnections. "Modern epidemiology," notes one of its leading contributors, is "oriented to explaining and quantifying the bobbing of corks on the surface waters, while largely disregarding the stronger undercurrents that determine where, on average, the cluster of corks ends up along the shoreline of risk."[128]

CHAPTER SEVEN

Rereading the Clinical Literature

Joe Rhatigan and Johanna Daily, editors

with David Devine, Paul Farmer,
Jennifer Furin, and Joel Katz

"All that matters is that women—even when they are sick—are asked
to take care of their families. I believe the time has come to ask: who
will take care of *them?*"

Antonia Novello
"HIV Infection in Women"

I n rereading the clinical literature on women and AIDS, we have
chosen to focus on a few specific areas: the natural history of HIV
infection in women, survival, and antiretroviral therapy and prophylaxis for opportunistic infections. We have also examined a
number of other articles in the clinical literature because they bring
into relief important issues regarding the current conceptualization of
AIDS within the medical community, particularly the medical community of the United States. We have not attempted to give a comprehensive review of the clinical literature in any of these areas, but
instead have selected key articles published in the influential journals
that form the basis for much of our current clinical practice.

As stated in the introduction to Part II, our hermeneutic key in
rereading these articles is to examine them with an eye towards the

experience of women living with both poverty and HIV infection. This task has been particularly difficult: "AIDS data," as Krieger and Fee note, "are still reported only in terms of race, sex, and mode of transmission; there are no data on social class."[1] The clinical literature on AIDS gives short shrift to gender-specific concerns, and many researchers have failed to examine specifically the combined impact of gender and poverty on health outcomes. Such studies are, by and large, non-existent. Instead, researchers treat gender, class, and "race"—which is rarely defined in the clinical literature—as "confounding variables." This is done in spite of the fact that between 1992 and 1993 48% of AIDS cases in men were in non-whites and fully 75% of women with AIDS were African-American or Hispanic.

One does not need to delve deeply into the medical literature to see that little account is taken of poor women's experiences. We can thus signal many of the literature's attendant shortcomings at the outset. Data about manifestations of HIV infection that are unique to women have been scant and slow in coming; they have certainly not even kept pace with the epidemic in the United States. Clinical researchers have been oblivious, it would seem, to the ten-year-old epidemic in Africa.

Similarly, almost all the clinical trials of antiretroviral therapy have enrolled an overwhelming majority of men. By 1994, the Centers for Disease Control reported that 16% of new AIDS cases occur in women, yet, as we shall see, very recent studies have continued to enroll almost exclusively white, and as far as can be discerned, middle class men. All of these studies have taken place in rich, industrialized countries. The same is true of almost every major trial addressing prophylaxis of opportunistic infections.

The immediate goal of this bibliography and reanalysis is to improve the care that physicians can offer to women with HIV disease. We know it is tiresome to repeatedly point out recurring deficits in study design and interpretation, and we apologize to our readers in advance if we have done so. There is ample reason to believe that application of existing clinical knowledge and currently available therapies will lead to substantial improvements in health outcomes for women infectd with HIV.

1. HIV INFECTIONS IN WOMEN

Before examining the few studies to investigate the unique aspects of HIV infection in women, we will first focus our attention on selected review articles that the reader can turn to for more complete clinical information. In the past few years, there have been several reviews of HIV infection in women, but two reviews are exemplary. In 1991, Minkoff and DeHovitz reviewed current knowledge about HIV infection in women and derived standards of care from available data. This article surveyed literature on cervical disease, gynecologic infections, contraception, prevention of opportunistic infections, antiretroviral therapy, obstetrical care, and social issues in HIV-infected women. Minkoff and DeHovitz formulated a set of clinical guidelines for care of HIV-infected women that stressed the need for heightened surveillance for cervical cancer and for STDs, as well as the need to address women's concerns about reliable contraception. The article underscored the lack of clinical literature addressing HIV infection in women and the absence of consensus guidelines on their care. It is a concise review of the literature that argues that HIV infection affects women differently than men. Most importantly, it notes that this effect is due not merely to differences in physiology, but is also due to differences between HIV-infected men and women in income, risk behavior, "race", and access to medical care.[2]

In 1992, Hankins and Handley also reviewed the current literature about AIDS in women and identified topics that require further study. Their paper reviewed epidemiology, AIDS related illnesses, natural history of HIV infection, and the survival of women with AIDS. Hankins and Handley observed that many of the studies of women with AIDS focused on pregnant and childbearing women. In subtle ways, these studies portrayed the women more as vectors of the disease than as victims of it.[3] Although further research has clarified some of the points raised in this article, the authors' critiques of the papers reviewed are applicable to a great deal of the current literature as well.

In 1992, the year of Hankins' and Handley's review, the American College of Obstetricians and Gynecologists compiled a technical bulletin summarizing certain issues related to women and AIDS including: the pathophysiology of HIV disease, gynecologic care of HIV-infected women, issues around HIV and pregnancy, and counseling issues for women felt to be at risk. Although this publication provided a fair amount of medical information, it failed nonetheless to capture the gravity of the epidemic and the urgent need to increase counseling and preventive strategies for women at risk for HIV infection. Further, in no way did it acknowledge that the U.S. women most at risk were, and are, poor women of color.

In 1994 Spence offered a brief overview of the current literature regarding the epidemiology, diagnosis, and management of HIV disease in women, with a more detailed exploration of the evolving standards of care in the management of gynecologic problems in HIV-infected women. Spence's overview also provided concise clinical guidelines.[4] Similarly, Korn and Landers offered an up-to-date summary of what is known about the interrelation of HIV infection and gynecologic disease.[5] In this article, the authors review recent studies evaluating cervical neoplasia, dysmenorrhea, STDs, and vaginitis, and they discuss contraception and HIV infection. As is often the case with review articles concerning women and HIV disease, these authors skirted critical discussion of the ways in which gender inequality and poverty together compromise both women's access to these services and clinicians' ability to provide first-rate care to those who need it most.

The articles by Minkoff and DeHovitz, Hankins and Handley, Spence, and Korn and Landers provide critical information about women and HIV infection. However, there are many more questions about HIV disease in women which need to be answered. This section will examine a few studies to highlight the research questions they have raised about HIV infection in women. Unfortunately, the medical literature discussing issues such as cervical neoplasia, pregnancy outcomes and menstrual function is difficult to interpret because of small study sizes and referral biases. These small sample sizes may be due to the fact that women have often been overlooked in terms of HIV-related research.

An example of small sample size and the problems it can create can be see in the work done by Maiman, *et al.* These researchers were among the first to study the relationship between HIV infection and cervical neoplasia. Their study compared HIV-infected and uninfected women from a cohort of 37 women with confirmed invasive carcinoma of the cervix presenting to Kings County Hospital, a public hospital in Brooklyn, New York, between 1986 and 1989. All the women were under the age of 50. Seventy-seven women were referred for evaluation of an abnormal Pap smear during the same time period. Nineteen percent of patients with invasive cervical carcinoma (7 of 37) were HIV-positive. All treated HIV-positive patients had recurrent carcinoma, while only 58% of treated HIV-negative women had recurrence. Of the 77 women with cervical dysplasia, HIV-positive women had more multifocal lesions, higher-grade cytological abnormalities, and more dysplastic biopsies.[6] This is a small study with obvious referral bias and it does not clearly describe the details of its case-control design. It is important, however in that it was one of the first studies to suggest an increased incidence and possibly more severe course of cervical carcinoma in HIV-positive women.

Wright *et al.* later tried to define the prevalence of cervical intraepithelial neoplasia (CIN), the validity of Pap smears, and the associations between CIN and risk factors for cervical disease in HIV-infected women. A well-designed study, it addressed questions regarding effective screening strategies for cervical cancer in HIV-positive women. The study enrolled women who had recently tested HIV-negative and women known to be HIV-positive. Twenty percent of the 398 HIV-positive women had confirmed CIN compared with only 4% of the 357 HIV-negative women. Pap smears were 81% sensitive and 87% specific in detecting CIN in the HIV-positive women. CIN was independently associated with HIV infection and with CD4 counts of less than 200. The study noted that over 68% of both HIV-positive and HIV-negative women had incomes of less than $10,000 a year, a statistic which highlights the poverty in which the majority of these women live.[7]

There is a significant debate in the clinical literature regarding pregnancy and HIV infection. In one early review from 1985, Brabin reported modest decreases in maternal CD4 counts during pregnancy.[8] There are, perhaps, theoretically compelling reasons to believe that pregnancy might accelerate the progression of HIV disease. However, in 1990 Berrebi *et al.* failed to demonstrate a significant progression of HIV disease during pregnancy. Their careful review of the literature from the first ten years of AIDS revealed no real consensus regarding the effects of pregnancy on the natural history of HIV infection.[9]

Alger and co-workers assessed the effects of HIV infection on pregnancy outcome and the effects of pregnancy on the progression of HIV disease through a case-control study. The study involved a population of women enrolling for prenatal care who, though asymptomatic, reported a risk factor for HIV infection. All the women underwent testing, and the study matched each HIV-positive woman with a control who was HIV-negative. The outcomes studied were perinatal complications in the infant or the mother and the progression of HIV disease in the mother. Patients were followed up to eight weeks post partum. Among the 101 HIV-positive women enrolled in the study, the authors found no significant effects of HIV infection on the course or outcome of pregnancy. In addition, pregnancy did not appear to influence the course of HIV disease as measured by CD4 count.[10]

The community-based study by Alger's group avoided many of the selection biases and serious confounders (such as drug use and advanced HIV disease) which marred many studies looking at this question previously. Although the study size was small, its results argue for minimal or no effect of asymptomatic HIV infection on pregnancy outcome. There was no clear progression of HIV disease during pregnancy, though the post partum follow-up was very short. Although no specific data is available on these women's incomes, the high proportion of Medicaid patients in this study suggests that this is a representative sample of the women most at risk in the United States.

The effect of HIV on the menstrual cycle has been controversial. Previous studies that found menstrual irregularities in HIV-positive women had not excluded women who were active substance users or who were taking methadone. In order to address the effect of HIV infection on menstruation, Shah and co-workers evaluated both a group of 55 HIV-positive women whom they recruited from a gynecology clinic and a seronegative control group whom they matched with the HIV-positive women for age, parity, and tobacco use. They excluded women who were currently substance abusers or who were taking methadone. The authors found that HIV infection and CD4 count had no effect on menstrual cycles or menstrual symptoms in these otherwise healthy women. This study's subject cohort is small, but it suggests that HIV infection has minimal impact on menstrual function in non-substance abusing women.

2. NATURAL HISTORY

The World Health Organization and the U.S. Centers for Disease Control have adopted classification systems for HIV disease staging in order to predict mortality, manage patients more effectively, and standardize research results. We have selected four articles that deal with HIV disease staging in order to examine the research from the perspective of poor women. The first two articles are from a group working in pre-civil war Rwanda which looked at pragmatic strategies for staging HIV infection. The remaining articles evaluate laboratory methods which have become, or will become, the basis of the HIV classification system in the United States.

It is critical that physicians caring for an HIV-infected patient have a standardized method for determining the patient's stage of disease so that they can reliably assess possible interventions. Although most natural-history studies have been done in industrialized countries, two-thirds of HIV-infected people and 80% of all HIV-infected women live in Africa. This fact underscores the need to better understand the natural history of HIV disease on this continent.

Lindan *et al.* studied the natural history of HIV infection in Rwandan women of childbearing age. They looked at 460 HIV-positive women and 948 HIV-negative women whom they randomly chose from a large, previously enrolled, cohort in a free urban medical clinic in Rwanda. These women were poor. Of the infected women, 46% had an income less than $125 per month; 69% had no personal income and were dependent on their partners; 16% had no formal education. Half of HIV-infected women (53%) had only one lifetime sexual partner. All medicines given to the women were free, and there was 90% compliance with follow up visits in both groups. Twenty-four months into the study, the mortality was 7% among HIV-positive women, but 0.3% among the HIV-negative women. AIDS accounted for 90% of deaths in the combined cohort. Strong predictors of mortality among HIV-infected women were body mass index less than 21 kg/m², chronic diarrhea, low income, and an erythrocyte sedimentation rate greater than 60 mm/hr. The WHO clinical case definition was neither specific nor sensitive in predicting mortality among HIV-infected women.[11]

This important, carefully done study addresses the natural history of HIV in an area of the world with a high prevalence of HIV disease. It used low-cost measures easily obtainable in Rwanda. The authors did explain that low income (less than $125/month) is a risk factor for mortality among HIV-infected women, but they failed to put this observation into perspective with the other risk factors they elucidated. In particular, low body mass index was nearly as prevalent in this population as in the HIV-negative group (46% v. 48%), and both carried nearly identical relative risks (2.6 v. 2.3). Independent of income, these patients had equivalent access to care and medicines. This is significant in that it indicates that low income as a risk factor for mortality cannot simply be explained in terms of lack of access to care. The authors did not explore more fully hypotheses for why low income is a risk factor for death, although they did note that lack of access to food may explain high mortality and that this lack of food could be remediable. This paper clearly calls for a trial of food or monetary supplements for these HIV-infected women as a means of reducing mortality.[12]

Using the same cohort as Lindan, et al., Lifson and coworkers evaluated the WHO staging system to predict mortality in HIV-infected women in sub-Saharan Africa. Of 3,702 Rwandan women who were recruited from pediatric and perinatal clinics from 1986-1987, 412 were randomly selected to participate in the study. The researchers found that the WHO staging system did not reliably predict mortality among the study participants. Based on the data they collected, the authors proposed modifications to the WHO criteria to include oral candidiasis, chronic oral or genital ulcers, and pulmonary tuberculosis as indicative of severe (stage 4) disease and to substitute body mass index for weight loss in the definition of the wasting syndrome. These modifications resulted in a classification system which more reliably predicted mortality.

In the earlier study of the same cohort they noted that low income was a risk factor for mortality from HIV. However, they did not further investigate this nor evaluate it as a variable in their modified staging system. (As an aside, the authors mention that at least half of the women in the study are missing and presumed dead since the Rwandan civil war, a reminder that these women, despite being afflicted with AIDS, were at even higher risk for dying from violence.)

Fahey and co-workers evaluated the ability of three cellular and five serologic markers to predict progression from asymptomatic HIV infection to AIDS. This study drew a random sample of 400 people out of 813 HIV-positive gay men enrolled at the Los Angeles center in the Multicenter AIDS Cohort study. These men were followed every six months for four years or until they were diagnosed with AIDS. The best predictors of progression to AIDS were, in order: CD4 count, serum level of neopterin, and serum level of beta 2-microglobulin.[13] This study was technically well done and clinically valuable in caring for patients with HIV. However, it is not clear that the results from this population of 400 gay men in Los Angeles are generalizable to women, who make up approximately 40% of infected persons worldwide, and to persons living in impoverished nations, who make up approximately 92% of infected persons worldwide.

More sensitive markers for determining disease progression other than the CD4 count have been sought to help guide management of antiretroviral therapy. Saksela *et al.* demonstrated that changes in serum levels of HIV RNA were an independent predictor of disease progression, potentially more sensitive than CD4 count. In 1984, a cohort of gay men in New York City were enrolled in a prospective AIDS study and were followed for as long as eight years in order to monitor disease progression. Stored serum specimens were randomly chosen from patients who had not developed AIDS by the time the specimens were taken. Polymerase chain reaction (PCR) assays for multiply-spliced HIV (messanger RNA) from peripheral-blood mononuclear cells was quantified, and HIV mRNA expression was found to be a strong independent marker for progression to AIDS.[14] This study furthers the understanding of the basic biology of HIV and may help clinicians in determining when to start and or adjust antiretroviral regiments. Branched chain measurements of free HIV RNA are commercially available and are under further study to see if they are as predictive. However, the branched-chain assay is quite expenseive (approximately $200 per test), and, simply based on its cost, it is unlikely that the vast majority of HIV-infected people will ever benefit from this technological advance.

3. SURVIVAL

In 1987, Rothenberg *et al.* published one of the earliest studies to demonstrate differential survival with AIDS among different genders and "races." They reviewed 5,833 AIDS cases reported in New York City from mid-1981 through December 1985 based on the then-current CDC case definition. Their cohort reflected the epidemiology of the disease in the city at that time: 90% of cases were men and 9.5% of cases were women; 47.2% of the cohort were white, 30.3% were African-American, and 22% were Hispanic; 58.3% were gay men and 28.5% were intravenous drug users. More women than men died at the time of diagnosis (16.3% v. 10.9 %, p<.001), and more black and Hispanic patients died at the time of diagnosis than did white patients (14.0% and 14.1% v. 8.5%, both p<.001). Women were likely to die earlier than men once diagnosed with AIDS.[15] Although this study did not control for CD4 counts and used a very early CDC case definition, it raised important questions about survival differences between men and women, between blacks and whites, and between Hispanics and whites. These differences have yet to be fully explored. One of the reasons that the study raised more questions than it answered was that a lack of socioeconomic data greatly weakened the analysis.

In another study looking at a New York City population during the same time period, Friedland and co-workers evaluated 526 patients hospitalized with AIDS at Montifiore Medical Center and North Central Bronx Hospital from 1981 through September 1987. Twenty five percent of patients were female. Disease stage was not controlled for by CD4 count. Survival was significantly predicted by the presenting opportunistic infection or neoplasm. Median survival for patients presenting with Kaposi's sarcoma was 12.8 months. For patients presenting with PCP it was 10.9 months. For patients presenting with other infections and neoplasms it was 4.8 months. Across the series, men survived longer than women. Differences in survival by "race," ethnic background, or risk behavior were not statistically significant.[16] This study confirmed other observations that male patients survived significantly longer than females, though the authors do not discuss potential explanations for these patterns. Preventive therapy during this time period was not standardized and not consistent, which is reflected in the fact that there was no survival difference noted by year of diagnosis. Again, although this study population was noted to be economically disadvantaged, income itself was not evaluated as a variable for survival.

In a prospective study, Lemp et al. compared trends in length of survival for women and men after diagnosis with AIDS. Their group looked at patients diagnosed with AIDS in San Francisco between January 1981 and December 31, 1990. Disease stage was not controlled for by CD4 count. One hundred and thirty nine women and 7,045 men were followed prospectively through May 15, 1991. The median survival for women (11.1 months) was significantly shorter than the survival for men (14.6 months). Antiretroviral therapy was associated with increased survival for both men and women, and this positive effect on survival did not differ by gender. Women, however, were less likely than men to have been treated with zidovudine or didanosine (60.3% v. 71.9%, p<.05).[17] The researchers clearly found shorter survival for women, and suggested it was secondary to decreased antiretroviral use in women. As with other discussions in the clinical literature, such rudimentary understandings of the nature of sociobiological causality, when coupled with an absence of attention to class, can lead to confusion regarding the relationship between gender inequality and poverty. Lemp and co-workers note that "the shorter survival of women may be the result of factors other than gender, possibly including less use of antiretroviral therapy."[18] In more straightforward language, we would argue that gender inequality and poor access to medical care conspire to decrease survival among poor women with advanced HIV disease.

Turner *et al.* attempted to define predictors of survival for women and men after diagnosis of AIDS. Their group looked at 2,948 patients with AIDS enrolled in New York Medicaid from 1988-1990 and found survival after diagnosis of AIDS was the same for non-drug-using women and men. Among drug users, women had a slightly lower risk of death. Women had more outpatient visits than men across groups, though they were less likely to have a primary provider. Men were two times more likely than women to receive either PCP prophylaxis or zidovudine, although this conferred no survival benefit. Men and women were equally likely to have seen an AIDS specialist.[19] This paper argues that women and men with AIDS have the same survival rate. It ascribed the gender differences in use of zidovudine and PCP prophylaxis to the possibility that men had more advanced HIV disease than the women . This explantation seems inadequate in the face of a central question: if the women had less advanced HIV disease, why did they not survive longer than the men?

In a retrospective study that examined gender differences in mortality from the first bout with PCP among HIV-infected men and women, Bastian and co-workers looked at 2,526 men and 544 women who were admitted in 1987 to any of the acute-care hospitals in New York City. Women were more likely than men to (1) be black or Hispanic, (2) lack private health insurance, (3) be admitted through an emergency room, (4) receive care at a hospital with less PCP experience, and (5) die in the hospital. In addition, women were less likely to undergo bronchoscopy, but more likely to require intubation. Patients with private insurance had the lowest mortality rates.[20] The authors used a logistic-regression model to control for hospital-level differences as well as sociodemographic differences and concluded that female sex was not independently associated with hospital death. They point out that there was no biological basis for the difference in survival between men and women, because this real difference in survival became statistically insignificant when differences in type of hospital, admission through the emergency room, and private insurance were controlled for, factors which suggest the overiding importence of socioeconomic status. Nevertheless women were more likely to die than men. Perhaps the most important implication of this study is that gender inequality, however mediated, clearly can decrease access to life-prolonging interventions.

A number of studies have examined the relation between antiretroviral use and survival with HIV infection. Easterbrook *et al* evaluated whether racial-ethnic differences existed in survival, disease progression, or development of myelosuppression in zidovudine-treated patients with advanced HIV disease. They looked at 1,044 patients from 12 metropolitan areas enrolled in a long term study from April 1987 to April 1988. Only 40 of 1,044 subjects were women. They found that Hispanic and African-American patients had more advanced HIV disease when started on zidovudine than did whites. Blacks were less likely to receive PCP prophylaxis and were more likely to develop PCP than whites (66% vs. 46%, p=.0001). Although Black and Hispanic patients presented with significantly more advanced disease, there was no significant difference in survival between groups after adjustment was made for stage of HIV disease.[21] The investigators explain the decreased use of PCP prophylaxis among African Americans by observing that "this disparity was mainly attributable to different levels of use across study centers."[22] In other words, those centers with the lowest use of PCP prophylaxis also tended to be those with the largest number of black participants. They note that if they corrected for these "different levels of use," the statistical excess in incidence of PCP among blacks disappears. But there is no way to "correct" for underutilization of an effective medical therapy. By attempting to do so, the authors engage in a statistical sophistry that minces harsh words about racism and the mechanisms by which it comes to have its material effects.

Moore *et al.* described survival trends among patients with AIDS in Maryland and evaluated how survival was modified by demographic and clinical characteristics, particularly therapy with zidovudine. Their study looked at 596 men and 118 women who were diagnosed with AIDS between April 1987 and June 1989. Median survival for women was substantially shorter than that for men (290 days v. 490 days, p<.03). Non-Hispanic whites survived longer than minorities (600 days v. 400 days, p<.001). Fifty-three percent of the men received zidovudine compared with only 33% of women (p<.001). Sixty-three percent of non-Hispanic whites received the drug, but only 43% of minorities did (p<.001). Median survival was 770 days among persons who received zidovudine as compared with 190 days for persons who never received the drug (p<.001). Of course, many other factors may have played a role in these striking differentials: the authors did not control for disease stage by CD4 count, and they did not discuss the use of PCP prophylaxis. Although the authors highlighted the increased survival among patients receiving zidovudine, the more striking and unexplained findings are how few minorities and women received zidovudine and how both groups had substantially shorter survival once diagnosed with AIDS. The authors concluded that, "the challenge now appears to be to increase the use of that therapy (i.e., zidovudine) in all segments of the population infected with HIV."[23] Another challenge lies in investigating why minorities and women are not treated with standard therapy in the first place.

In a careful study that compared disease progression and mortality between HIV-infected women and men who received similar care, Melnick and co-workers examined 3,779 men and 768 women who had enrolled in any trial of the Terry Beirn Community Programs for Clinical Research on AIDS. The median CD4 count at enrollment was 137 for men and 240 for women. Controlling for this difference, the relative risk of mortality was 33% greater for women (RR women:men = 1.33, CI 1.06-1.69). Overall, more women had bacterial pneumonia, progressive multifocal leukoencephalopathy, and thrush than did men. Men had more Kaposi's sarcoma, PCP, herpes, and oral hairy leukoplakia. The increased relative risk of mortality between men and women was even more pronounced among injecting drug users. Also, for patients with a history of disease progression at enrollment, women were twice as likely as men to have death as the first reported event (27.5% v. 12.2%).[24]

This study controls for CD4 counts at baseline, and its finding that women are at increased risk for mortality from HIV as compared with men contrasts with earlier studies that found no significant difference between the two groups. Although the investigators raise the question of why this finding exists and mention that socioeconomic variables may be a factor, they do not report any data. In a study that required extensive blood sampling at enrollment, it would seem very non-invasive to have collected simple data about income, unemployment, homelessness, childbearing responsibilities, and access to routine medical care. Information on these topics could shed light on the differential mortality between men and women that was observed in this study.

Given the failure to demonstrate a purely biological basis for survival difference between men and women, one may conclude that the difference in survival between men and women is mediated by social and economic factors which may secondarily impact upon medical treatment. The question of whether socioeconomic factors influence mortality with HIV infection has been scantily addressed by the research community. In fact, according to an editorial in *The Lancet*, the first study to specifically address the impact of socioeconomic factors on HIV disease was in October, 1994. An outstanding investigation by Hogg and co-workers prospectively studied the association between socioeconomic status and survival in 364 HIV-infected gay men who were recruited during 1982-84 in Vancouver. Gross annual income from all sources at the time of enrollment in the study was the measure of socioeconomic status. The study divided the men into either high or low income groups, with Can$10,000 as the dividing line between the two groups (this figure was the Canadian government-defined poverty level for single men living alone in metropolitan areas). After adjustment for age, lower-income men experienced a mortality risk about 60% greater than that of higher-income men. This finding persisted despite adjustment for CD4 count, use of antiretroviral therapies, PCP prophylaxis, and year of infection. Income data was taken at time of enrollment in the study, which was either in the course of HIV infection for some men or at the time of diagnosis for others. The proportion of low-income men was similar in the two groups, and low- and high-income groups were comparable with respect to CD4 counts at baseline.[25] Thus, it is unlikely that more rapid HIV progression could have any causal effect on income differences at this early stage.

Although the study evaluated survival only among men, it established a strong link between lower incomes and shorter survival following HIV infection. It convincingly weakened the explanatory power of two alternative explanations of this finding: 1) more rapid HIV progression, or 2) differential access to health care. In Canada's health-care system, both high- and low- income groups received similar treatments, including free antiretroviral therapy, and had equal access to HIV specialists. Race and geographic region can also be excluded as possible factors which might explain differential mortality rates because 98% of men were Caucasian; all lived in the same urban region. The researchers call for further investigation of the precise mechanisms by which socioeconomic status affects HIV treatment and survival.

A study done in the United States clarifying previous research was recently published by Chaisson, Keruly and Moore. It examined the relationship between demographic variables and survival among people with HIV infection receiving medical care from a single center. This study retrospectively examined a cohort of 1,372 patients who presented for care at the Johns Hopkins HIV Clinic between July 1989 and April 1994. Thirty percent of patients were women, 77% were black, and 21% were white. Median annual income was $5,000. Blacks were less likely than whites to have received appropriate PCP prophylaxis or appropriate antiretroviral treatment before enrollment, but these differences were eliminated after enrollment. When corrected for disease stage, there was no significant difference in survival between men and women, intravenous drug users and non-intravenous drug users, whites and people of color, or patients with annual incomes of less than or greater than $5,000.

Factors associated with decreased survival included having CD4 counts of less than 200/mm³ and having AIDS at enrollment. The authors do not tell us if there were any differences in stage of disease or CD4 counts between the above groups at presentation.[26] Although they found no survival difference by income, the majority of their patients were impoverished. There may not have been enough of a range in income to see an effect.

The authors concluded that their results "provide strong evidence that earlier reports of differences in survival were a result of inadequate medical care rather than biologic differences in the natural history of HIV infection."[27] This study is the most convincing evidence so far that previously observed differences in survival are more sociological than biological. However, this was a unique population that had access to one of the best HIV centers in the world. Unfortunately, the previously observed differences in survival between men and women, whites and blacks are real and will persist elsewhere until all patients receive appropriate HIV treatment. The barriers to equal access may be multifactorial, but they are nonetheless deadly.

4. PROPHYLAXIS AND
ANTIRETROVIRAL THERAPY

The research that forms the basis for prophylaxis of opportunistic infections in HIV-infected persons was done predominately on white, largely middle class, men. In the United States, the epidemic was initially recognized in gay men, although by 1982, 6.9% of reported cases of AIDS were in women. This percentage has risen each year. In many instances, it may be reasonable to assume that results derived from studies of HIV disease in men are generalizable to women, but proof for this is lacking. In other instances, such as the use of potentially teratogenic drugs, clinicians have had a difficult time using data from studies that have underrepresented women to guide their clinical practice. Here we will look at several studies that underlie our clinical practice for prevention of opportunistic infec-

tions in HIV infection as well as studies concerning tuberculosis prophylaxis, as tuberculosis is a major complication of HIV infection in
poor nations and among the poor in the wealthy nations.

Schneider *et al.* compared PCP prophylactic efficacy and toxicity of aerosolized pentamidine with the efficacy and toxicity of
trimethoprim/sulfamethoxazole (TMP/SMX) in HIV-infected
patients with CD4 counts below 200/mm3. Their study looked at
215 HIV-infected patients with no history of PCP and with CD4
counts less than 200/mm3 and showed that TMP/SMX was more
effective as primary prophylaxis against PCP than was pentamidine, although adverse drug reactions were more common with
TMP/SMX.[28] This important study forms the basis for current prophylaxis regimens for PCP, but, as in other clinical trials, there is
underrepresentation of women, who make up only 5% of the study
population. This underrepresentation of women is significant for a
number of reasons, including the fact that among TMP/SMX's
adverse effects are megaloblastic and suppressive effects on bone
marrow; women, particularly when pregnant, are more vulnerable
to these sequelae than are men. This fact may explain the lack,
until very recently, of clear guidelines regarding PCP prophylaxis
during pregnancy. In 1992, over a decade after the epidemic was
recognized, Sperling and Stratton could comment that, "Perhaps in
an effort to avoid harm to the fetus, Public Health Service guidelines have avoided recommendations for therapies in pregnancy
and in fact have specifically recommended deferring prophylaxis
against *P. carinii* pneumonia until after pregnancy."[29] In many
instances, concerns over theoretical risk to fetal and newborn
health seem to outweigh very real risks to women with advanced
HIV disease for human teratogeniity has never been demonstrated:
"The fetal and newborn safety of trimethoprim-sulfamethoxazole
in human pregnancy is of concern as both drugs readily cross the
placenta. In some animal models, these agents have been reported
to cause various congenital malformations. Sulfamethoxazole
alone, in corresponding doses, was not embryotoxic. To date,
human teratogenicity with either drug, singularly or in combination, has not been reported."[30]

Nightingale and co-workers analyzed the efficacy of rifabutin as an effective prophylaxis against disseminated *Mycobacterium avium* complex (MAC) in AIDS patients with CD4 counts less than 200/mm^3, through two identical randomized, double-blinded, placebo-controlled studies. In the first study, 31 centers enrolled 590 patients (96% males, 85% white) and assigned half to placebo. MAC bacteremia developed in 8% of rifabutin patients and 17% of placebo patients. In the second study of 556 patients (97% male, 91% white), 9% of rifabutin patients developed MAC bacteremia as compared with 18% of placebo patients.[31] Again, it is interesting to note the paucity of women and people of color enrolled in this important clinical trial, the results of which were published in 1993.

Because tuberculosis is a major cause of disease in HIV-infected people who are poor, studies which address prevention and treatment of active tuberculosis are of great importance. In a retrospective study of 374 HIV-positive, anergic patients in urban Spain, Moreno and co-workers assessed risk for development of active tuberculosis. The risks for developing active tuberculosis in patients not receiving isoniazid were similar for PPD-positive patients (10.4 cases per 100 person years) and anergic patients (12.4 cases per 100 person years). The risks for both of these groups was significantly higher than in PPD-negative non-anergic patients who received isoniazid (5.4 cases per 100 person-years). In patients with positive PPD tests, isoniazid prophylaxis significantly reduced the subsequent development of tuberculosis.

Although this is a retrospective study with a fairly large amount of excluded patients, it convincingly argues for treating anergic, HIV-positive patients living in areas of high tuberculosis prevalence with isoniazid prophylaxis. Women are well represented in this study (approximately 40% of participants). This demonstrates that a significant number of women can be included in large HIV studies and also suggests that, in this case, conclusions can reliably be generalized across gender. Although no specific economic data was presented, we know from previous studies that poverty is also a significant risk factor for tuberculosis. The authors' informed strategy for curbing the deadly toll of tuberculosis should be lauded.

Another study which examined prevention of active tuberculosis was a randomized clinical trial by Pape *et al.* These researchers studied 118 asymptomatic HIV-positive patients in urban Haiti. They gave one group of patients isoniazid plus vitamin B6 and another group vitamin B6 alone. They found that isoniazid reduced the risk of tuberculosis for the entire population and for PPD-positive individuals by 71% and 83% respectively. Isoniazid also significantly reduced the mean time to development of active tuberculosis in PPD-positive individuals. The reduction in incidence of tuberculosis—from 10.0 to 1.7 per 100 person-years—compared favorably with the 60-90% efficacy rates observed in non-HIV-infected PPD-positive patients. [32]

For clinicians wishing a detailed review of prophylaxis for opportunistic infections in persons infected with HIV, Gallant *et al.* wrote an excellent article which effectively distills the current literature into specific clinical recommendations. It reviews the efficacy of prophylaxis for *Pneumocystis carinii* pneumonia, toxoplasma infection, cryptococcosis, *Mycobacterium avium* complex, tuberculosis and other viral and bacterial infections.[33] The reviewers failed to point out that the majority of subjects in the trials were men and that very little data exists about prophylaxis in women. Polypharmacy and drug-drug interactions aside, the sheer cost of the prophylaxis that Gallant *et al.* recommend would be prohibitive. The retail costs for these drugs may reach as much as $40,000 per annum per patient. [34]

If one looks in detail at the landmark antiretroviral trials which have guided clinical practice, one finds a clear underrepresentation of women. In addition, in most of the world, the high cost of antiretrovirals renders most of our knowledge about their efficacy irrelevant for all but the wealthiest, who can afford them. Inexpensive interventions that could be available in poor countries, such as food supplements, have not been evaluated as alternatives to decrease HIV related morbidity and mortality.

In 1987, Fischl *et al.* published one of the first trials to determine if AZT (zidovudine) affected survival or disease progression in patients with advanced HIV disease. The study was a double-blinded, placebo-controlled trial which followed 282 patients (13 were women) with AIDS or ARC randomized to placebo or 1500 mg/day of zidovudine. The study was terminated after the majority of subjects had completed only 16 weeks, because significant decreases in mortality were found in the zidovudine treated group. The zidovudine group also experienced increased Karnofsky scores and CD4 counts. Although this was a very important study, the follow-up period was very short, and over half the deaths were due to PCP in a study that excluded patients on PCP prophylaxis.[35] As in most of the studies cited below, women made up a small percentage, 4.5% , of study participants, not reflective of the 6.9% of people with AIDS who were women at that time.

In 1990, Volberding and co-workers reported a study that evaluated whether zidovudine treatment is safe and effective in preventing disease progression among asymptomatic HIV-infected patients. This was a double-blinded study of patients with CD4<500/mm^3 randomized to placebo or zidovudine (500mg/day or 1,500 mg/day). Endpoints were progression to AIDS, change in CD4 counts and evaluation of side effects. Ninety one percent of subjects were white men and 87% were gay or bisexual. After a mean follow up of 55 weeks, the study was stopped, because the results showed that either dose of zidovudine significantly reduced progression to AIDS in both groups with CD4 <200/mm^3 and CD4 of 200-499/mm^3. The higher dose of zidovudine had significantly more hematologic toxicity.[36] This study was very important in determining when antiretroviral therapy should be recommended, though again it highlights how few women or blacks were enrolled in critical therapeutic trials.

Lenderking et al. were one of the first groups to evaluate whether improved survival in asymptomatic HIV-infected patients treated with zidovudine was associated with improved quality of life. They evaluated patients enrolled in a previously reported protocol of the AIDS Clinical Trials Group where asymptomatic HIV- infected people, with either CD4 <200/mm^3 or 200-499/mm^3, were treated with placebo, zidovudine 500mg/day, or zidovudine 1,500 mg/day. The average time without progression of disease or an adverse event was 15.7 months for placebo and 15.6 months for the zidovudine 500 mg/day group. Overall the authors conclude that "a reduction in the quality of life due to severe side effects of therapy approximately equals the increase in quality of life associated with a delay in the progression of HIV disease."[37] This study was the first to analyze the negative quality of life effect of these interventions.

In 1995, Volberding and co-workers reported a study for the AIDS Clinical Trials Group which compared immediate zidovudine therapy to deferred zidovudine therapy in asymptomatic HIV-infected persons with CD4 counts of greater than 500/mm³. Their study randomized asymptomatic patients to either immediate treatment with zidovudine or deferred therapy once CD4 counts fell to below 500/mm³. We are told that 90% of participants were white men, and it is unclear if any women were enrolled. Patients had an average of five years of follow up and 50% of patients completed the study in each arm. The authors found that there was no difference in AIDS-free survival nor in overall survival between the two groups.[38]

Kinolch de Loes et al. recently evaluated the immediate and long term clinical benefits of treatment with zidovudine in patients with primary HIV infection. They reported the results of 77 patients with an acute retroviral syndrome and known exposure to HIV, who were randomized, in a double-blinded study, to zidovudine or placebo. The patients, of whom 81% completed six months of treatment, were followed for 24 months. There was no difference in the mean duration of the acute retroviral syndrome between the groups, but disease progression was significantly less frequent in the zidovudine group than in the placebo group (p=.009). Treatment with zidovudine resulted in an increase in CD4 counts during treatment as compared with placebo. RNA levels did not differ significantly. No increase in AZT resistance was seen in the treatment group.[39] Although the results of this study offer hope for future strategies to treat HIV infection, it is sobering to note that the vast majority of new cases of HIV infection in the world are among persons with little or no access to zidovudine.

In 1992, Hamilton et al. reported a Veterans Administration Cooperative Study which studied the best time to begin zidovudine treatment in patients with symptomatic HIV infection. The placebo-controlled, double-blinded trial evaluated 1,500 mg/day of zidovudine given either as early (immediate) or late therapy (after

CD4 fell below 200/mm3) in symptomatic HIV-infected patients with CD4 counts between 200 and 500/mm3. Of 338 patients, only three were women. In the early therapy group, 28 patients progressed to AIDS as compared with 48 in the late therapy group (p=.02) during follow up of two years. Early therapy increased the time until CD4 counts fell below 200/mm3, but was associated with more side effects. There was no survival benefit to early therapy over late therapy. As in most studies involving anti-retroviral therapy, this study underrepresents women, yet the authors claim that "we believe this conclusion to be generalizable."[40]

To address the lack of scientific data concerning efficacy of antiretroviral therapy in women and people of color, Lagakos *et al.* did a sub-group analysis to see if the beneficial effects of zidovudine also apply to "minorities and other subpopulations," (i.e. blacks, Hispanics, women, and intravenous drug users). The re-analysis evaluated a subset of an original cohort of 2,048 people with asymptomatic HIV infection enrolled in 2 placebo-controlled randomized clinical trials. This sub-group analysis included 155 black people, 190 Hispanic people, 144 women, and 221 intravenous drug users. Zidovudine had no statistically significant effect in women or IDUs, but did delay progression to AIDS in blacks and Hispanics. Yet the overall risk of progression was the same in men and women.[41] The lack of effect seen in women is most likely due to this small sample size.

To address the underrepresentation of women in clinical trials, Cotton and co-workers analyzed the factors influencing the enrollment of women to a large multicenter HIV clinical trials program. Their study analyzed all trials conducted by the AIDS Clinical Trials Group between 1987 and 1990 and found that women comprised only 6.7% of 11,909 ACTG participants. Women entering these trials were significantly more likely to be white (48.5%) and less likely to have ever used IV drugs (22.6%) than U.S. women reported to have AIDS, (26.5% white, 51.0 % having ever used IV drugs, p<.001). Specific attributes of individual trials did not influence enrollment of women except for trials of asymptomatic persons, which had greater numbers of women. There was wide variation among centers in the number of women recruited. Centers with female principal investigators had more than twice the percentage of female enrollment as did units headed by men. [42] Although the authors are not able to answer why women, and specifically women of color, were underrepresented in these trials, their findings raise important and troubling questions about structural and systemic biases in U.S. clinical AIDS research.

The class, gender, and racial biases noted in clinical intervention trials extend to physicians' clinical practice. Stein and co-workers did an important study which revealed that physicians were less likely to offer zidovudine to women as compared with men, to non-whites as compared to whites, and to people without insurance as to people with insurance. They looked at people with AIDS who were enrolled in the AIDS Health Services Program for at least one month and who consented to an interview. Of 880 people, 113 had never been offered zidovudine. Men were three times more likely to be offered zidovudine than women, and whites were almost twice as likely to be offered zidovudine than non-whites. Injection drug users were less than half as likely to be offered zidovudine as non-injection drug users, and insured people were two times more likely to be offered zidovudine as were people without insurance.[43] Unfortunately the investigators make no assessment of patients' economic status, although they claim to study "socioeconomic factors." This would be an interesting and important piece of data in understanding if the racism and sexism they discovered is mediated by differences in socioeconomic status.

Moore *et al.* attempted to determine whether sociodemographic characteristics of patients influenced the use of drug therapy, i.e., antiretrovirals and PCP prophylaxis. They looked at all patients presenting for the first time to the Johns Hopkins HIV Clinic from March 1990 to December 1992. Of 838 patients enrolled, 79% were black and 20% were non-Hispanic whites (31% of patients were women). No "racial" differences were found in the stage of HIV disease at presentation. Sixty three percent of eligible whites and only 48% of eligible blacks received antiretroviral therapy (p=.003). PCP prophylaxis was received by 82% of eligible whites but only by 58% of eligible blacks. There were no differences observed between men and women . In a logistic regression analysis, "race" was the feature most strongly associated with the receipt of drug therapy. This striking race-associated difference was only found among those with incomes of less than $20,000. Thus it would seem that higher socioeconomic status effaced, to some extent, the disadvantages attributable to racism. These findings warranted significant discussion, as they spoke eloquently to the complex relationship between health outcomes and class, race, and gender, but this discussion does not find its way into these pages. To their credit, however, members of the same team set out to test the obvious hypothesis that mortality differentials are the biological reflections of social inequalities. The way to test this was to remove all social—viz ., born of discrimination against the poor, people of color, and women—barriers to state-of-the-art care. The results of this exemplary study, recently published in the *New England Journal of Medicine*, suggest that ensuring equal access to high-quality care can erase mortality differentials across lines of gender and race.[44]

5. PREVENTION

It is estimated that more than 40,000 cases of HIV infection are diagnosed each year in the United States. Appropriately, there exists a large body of literature about prevention of HIV transmission, but the gender-specific complexities of AIDS prevention continue to defy analysis. For example, although condoms are the most effective means of preventing sexual transmission and are widely available, the pandemic continues to progress. Potential causes for the failure of this inexpensive intervention may be related to women's powerlessness to demand their use, because of social, political, and economic inequalities. Such possibilities need further investigation if we aspire to a sound understanding of HIV transmission dynamics. Here we will examine four articles: a large landmark study, a placebo-controlled trial, and two studies looking at women's beliefs and attitudes about risk factors for HIV transmission.

Connor and co-workers reported the results of a large trial to determine the efficacy and safety of zidovudine in reducing maternal-fetal HIV transmission. They evaluated the effect of zidovudine in a double-blind, randomized, placebo-controlled study in pregnant HIV-positive women of 14-34 weeks gestation. These women had CD4 counts of greater than or equal to 200 and no indications for antiretroviral therapy. Four hundred and seventy seven women were enrolled and 409 gave birth to 415 live born infants. The proportion of infants infected at 18 months estimated by the Kaplan-Meier method were 8.3% in the zidovudine group and 25.5% in the placebo group, corresponding to a 67.5% (95% CI 40.7-82.1%) relative reduction in the risk of maternal-fetal transmission of HIV. There were no significant adverse maternal effects, and no infant deaths attributed to treatment. There was minimal neonatal hematologic toxicity. This well-designed study was terminated at an interim analysis due to the large protective benefit of zidovudine in decreasing vertical transmission.[45]

The prevention of spread of HIV to women was examined in a prospective randomized, placebo-controlled trial by Kreiss *et al*. The study evaluated the efficacy of the nonoxynol-9 contraceptive sponge in preventing the sexual acquisition of HIV among 138 HIV-negative commercial sex workers in Nairobi. All women were urged to continue condom use. The study was stopped due to lack of effect and possible adverse outcomes with the sponge. There was no difference in seroconversion rates but there was an increased frequency of genital ulcers (RR 3.3), as well as an increase in vulvitis with the sponge. (There was, however, a 60% decrease in gonococcal cervicitis with sponge use.)[46] Although this study failed to show a protective effect for sponge use, it clearly acknowledged these women's powerlessness to ensure that their partners wore condoms as well as the dire need to protect this population from HIV. The most disturbing finding was that despite intensive counseling on the use condoms and free condoms available to all women, about half of uninfected women in both groups had seroconverted by the end of the 24 months. This finding suggests that the efforts to protect these women from HIV should be aimed at providing them other options besides prostitution to support themselves and their families.

Numerous studies have examined the efficacy of counseling and education to prevent transmission of HIV. Ickovics and co-workers studied the results of HIV counseling and testing in seroneg-ative women on sexual behavior and psychological outcomes. Their study enrolled seronegative women volunteers seeking HIV testing and counseling and compared them with controls from the same clinic population. At baseline, sexual risk, as defined by the authors, was lower for tested versus non-tested women. For tested women, there was a decrease in the estimated chance of acquiring HIV after a negative test result. For both tested and non-tested groups, there was no significant change in sexual risk during the study.[47] There is some discussion of the implications of a true negative result, but scant discussion of the ways in which individual agency may be con-strained. For example, it is true that most "sexual conduct is a prod-uct of interpersonal interaction."[48] However, the factors impinging upon sexual conduct, and indeed, upon most behavior, vary dramat-ically not simply according to knowledge and cognition—in this case, awareness of serostatus—but also according to socioeconomic factors, gender, culture, age, and in racist societies such as our own, "race." Thus the protective effect of testing and counseling might be dramatic among some groups but, negligible among others.

Flaskerud and Thompson looked at the health-related beliefs of white women with incomes of less than $10,000 per year in commu-nity nutrition programs to describe low income women's beliefs about AIDS and its treatment. Forty-two women were interviewed and most were knowledgeable about HIV transmission risks. There were some misconceptions about casual transmission (e.g., the belief that donating blood was risky), and many associated AIDS with exposure to "impurities," (e.g., anal intercourse, with the vector being feces). Many also thought that exposure to the virus was not sufficient for infection and that the host must also be "susceptible." Although most of the women understood medical and public health models of HIV, they still held significant non-scientific misconcep-tions about the disease and its transmission.[49] The authors use this point to argue that education must be targeted at these beliefs, a use-ful point. Many studies, however, have failed to demonstrate any relationship between beliefs and practice, particularly in the realm of sexuality. As we have seen in other chapters in this book, many—at this point, perhaps most—women know that condoms could offer effective protection from HIV. At the same time, they are unable to insist that condoms be used, and the degree to which they are powerless to insist varies directly with socioeconomic status. Flaskerud and Thompson's conclusion—that women living in poverty need more educational interventions—is a commonly heard refrain, but it avoids discussion of the fact that poverty and gender inequality can often render educational messages meaningless.

6. PHYSICIANS' ATTITUDES

To provide good care to HIV patients, early identification is necessary. Physicians' screening practices are critical to the care and counsel they provide to their potentially infected patients. We examine below a few selected studies that examine screening practices and biases of physicians.

In 1991, Ferguson, Stapleton, and Helms asked all resident and staff physicians at a large, midwestern teaching hospital about both their screening practices for HIV risk factors and their attitudes toward caring for HIV infected patients. Only 11% percent of respondents said they routinely screen for high risk behaviors, and only 44% felt comfortable caring for patients with HIV infection. It is noteworthy that 92% of respondents had cared for at least one patient with HIV infection within the prior three years.[50] Although these physicians' attitudes and practices were probably influenced by the low prevalence of HIV infection in their communities, this study underlines the need to educate many parts of the U.S. health care community about AIDS prevention, screening, and treatment.

Underrecognition of HIV infection in women has been evaluated by a number of investigators. Schoenbaum and Webber reviewed visits of patients attending a Bronx, New York, emergency room and found that only 13% of patients were assessed for HIV risk factors. They demonstrated that HIV infection was three times more likely to be recognized in men than in women. When persons with AIDS-defining illnesses were excluded from analysis, HIV infection in men was still more than twice as likely to be recognized. Even in high-risk groups, such as IDUs, the diagnosis was not considered as likely in women.[51] This marked underrecognition of HIV infection in women represents the initial deficit in care of women with HIV, particularly poor women of color, who often receive their primary care through the emergency room.

Makadon and Silin recently reviewed the literature on physician practices for prevention of HIV among their patients. They found that actual practice incorporated few clinical prevention strategies. One survey found that HIV transmission counseling was given in fewer than 1% of patient visits. In another study, only 15% of patients surveyed had discussed AIDS with their physicians during the previous five years, and almost three-fourths of these conversations were initiated by the patients themselves. They found that important barriers to physician effectiveness in HIV prevention included physician discomfort, prejudicial attitudes about patients with HIV, lack of time for adequate discussions, and confusion about what advice should be conveyed to the patient concerning risk factors for transmission. Their review is a stunning report on the widespread lack of physician involvement in preventing HIV infection.

7. CONCLUSION

One purpose of this chapter has been to critically reexamine the clinical literature on women and HIV disease. For the purposes of organization, the topics discussed were divided into several general categories: the natural history of HIV in women; survival; the use of antiretrovirals and prophylaxis against opportunistic infection; prevention among women; and attitudes of physicians towards women and HIV disease. It bears pointing out, however, that deficiencies in these discrete areas do not act by themselves to affect the health of women with HIV. They are intimately intertwined. For example, an understanding of physicians' attitudes towards HIV disease in women helps to explain patterns of antiretroviral use in women, as do the social and economic factors examined throughout this book.

What is lacking, then, is a general understanding of how multiple factors operating at various levels may act synergistically to influence the health of women as it relates to HIV disease. The newly published volume edited by Minkoff, DeHovitz, and Duerr, *HIV Infection in Women*.[52] is a much-needed review that addresses a wide variety of topics ranging from the psychosocial needs of women living with HIV to the medical management of HIV infection and of other sexually transmitted diseases associated with HIV (e.g. human papillomavirus).

HIV Infection in Women begins with a general overview of the epidemiology of HIV infection in women. Chu and Wortley point out that HIV transmission to women is rapidly changing the face of the pandemic. Noting that AIDS has disproportionately affected minorities (*viz* blacks and hispanics), the authors observe that: "Many socioeconomic factors influence the risk of HIV infection among women, including...changing social structures, poverty, and gender."[53]

The collection explores numerous clinical issues, and is meant to serve "as a user's manual for clinicians who will provide care to HIV-infected women...[the editors] hope this text will be found dog-eared in clinics, turned to by providers as they establish sites to treat women and as they face the unique clinical and interpersonal problems that confront HIV-infected women."[54] Nine chapters are included in the section of the book called "Clinical Considerations." Specifically, the book examines medical management of HIV in women; contraception; pregnancy and HIV infection; human papilloma virus; HIV and other sexually transmitted disease interactions in women; HIV infection in female drug users; HIV counseling and testing for women; starting a clinic for women with HIV; and ethical issues concerning women's rights and newborn screening for HIV. *HIV Infection in Women* highlights the unique issues women face when dealing with HIV, including many issues often overlooked in clinical studies. These include the opportunistic infections not seen in men such as invasive cervical cancer and vulvovaginal candidiasis. In considering opportunistic infections that afflict both men and women with HIV, it is clear that women may have worse outcomes.[55]

Although the distribution, manifestations, and severity of HIV infection in women may differ in men, it is clear that these biological phenomena are not unrelated to social factors considered in other chapters. Many experienced clinicians believe that the most striking differences are social ones, most of them related to women's differential access to fair wages, education, housing, and health care. Still others note that women's obligations to children and others means they receive short shrift when their own problems are at stake. In the introduction to *Women and HIV Infection*, Antonia Novello notes: "Women who are living with HIV have told me that clinics are not open during hours when women can go. They are not found in places women can reach...Women are requested to make too many visits with no consideration for transportation costs and child care. Food is not available in the clinics. Who will feed their children? Too much medication is prescribed without explanation or understanding of what 28 pills a day can do to a woman's life, to a woman's time, to a woman's body."[56]

In addition to exploring how women are differentially affected by issues faced by many people dealing with HIV disease, the volume insightfully addresses issues which are women's alone to bear. They examine issues of pregnancy and birth control, correctly pointing out that women are often not in positions that allow them to make decisions which are optimal for their health where these topics are concerned.

Pragmatic information regarding the provision of care to women with HIV is addressed in a chapter by Kelly, "Starting a Clinic for Women with HIV Disease." This chapter gives guidelines regarding provision of optimal care to women with HIV infection, including obstetric and gynecological services; involving more women in clinical trials; and barriers which may keep women from seeking appropriate attention for their health needs, such as lack of available child care services and provider biases towards women with HIV infection. The goal of such a clinic is "providing culturally sensitive, women-centered health care that encompasses medical and psychological services, prevention, and education."[57]

The volume edited by Minkoff, DeHovitz, and Duerr is in some areas exemplary. Its chapters show how multiple perspectives and challenges facing both women with HIV and those providing care for them can be integrated and confronted. However *HIV Infection in Women* also illustrates some of the overarching flaws seen in the clinical literature on HIV disease and women. Perhaps because gender is the primary focus of the volume, there is a lack of systematic data concerning the effects of poverty and inequality on the transmission and progression of HIV disease in women. Although socioeconomic factors, racism, and gender inequality are noted to complicate HIV disease, little attempt is made to explore their effects in the provision of services or on the course of HIV disease.

In *HIV Infection in Women*, Sherr states that "HIV infection has been prevalent in women from the onset of the epidemic. Yet attention has focused on women only in the second decade of the epidemic...Such delays have hindered the assessment of viral expression and transmission in women, disease course, opportunistic infection ramifications, and prognosis and treatment issues."[58] Unfortunately, similar statements can be made about poverty and HIV infection as well. The disease has disproportionately affected the poor since the start of the epidemic. It is time that the striking effects of poverty on women's health and HIV be recognized. Poverty cannot simply be mentioned away. It is not merely a confounding factor. Rather, it is a key issue that must be researched, understood, and addressed if appropriate care is to be provided to women who live with, fear, and struggle against HIV.

PART III

Reconceptualizing Care:
Pragmatic Solidarity

CHAPTER EIGHT

Confronting Obstacles

Greg Rubin

"AIDS programs for poor women continue to offer little but palliative solutions. Service providers have a continuing orientation to middle class values, and it is hard for them to see that behaviors such as drug dealing and substance abuse might be adaptive. The programs for women do not have the vitality or originality of those for gays; they are only tiny grafts on an already taxed health care system."

Martha Ward,
"Poor and Positive: Two Contrasting
Views from Inside the Epidemic"[1]

1. SOCIAL SERVICE PROVIDERS
IN THE UNITED STATES

The preceding chapters have illustrated the glaring absence of a class analysis within current medical and social discourses about women and HIV/AIDS. As we have noted, these literatures have often failed to address issues of economic injustice, obscuring the deep-rooted structures which have facilitated the explosive growth of AIDS among women in the poorest of communities. The analytic shortcomings described in Parts I and II are not only to be found in the research and writing about women and AIDS; they are also apparent in settings where services are provided to women living with HIV.

As Martha Ward suggests, many service providers have instituted AIDS programs for women which are structurally biased against meeting the needs of those most vulnerable to infection. Women with AIDS are also parents, partners, and caretakers for others with HIV; they are responsible for lives beyond their own. Programs for HIV-positive women which are modeled on those that existed early in the epidemic have too often seen the person with AIDS as an individual in isolation, rather than someone upon whom others are dependent for their basic needs. Occasionally, these programs end up placing additional burdens upon those they intend to help most.

Such biases are far from intentional, yet their presence demonstrates how these services are often painfully inadequate for women facing both poverty and HIV. Indeed, the biases are pervasive enough to be felt even in those forums controlled by persons living with HIV/AIDS. Take, as an example, a recent article appearing in POZ, a magazine by and for people with AIDS. Entitled "A ranking of the nation's leading AIDS treatment centers," the analysis "draws on a groundbreaking mathematical model that combines three years' worth of U.S. News' reputational surveys, federal death-rate statistics, and nine categories of hard data" to determine the top 50 medical centers for the treatment of HIV/AIDS.[2] Such an approach to assessing the quality of AIDS care in this country highlights some of the deficiencies in the way we have responded to this epidemic. The ranking is based upon categories such as its "reputational score" among doctors surveyed; the ratio of residents, physicians, and nurses to beds; and "the number of high-tech services" offered by each hospital. The survey fails to ask how accessible these centers are to the poor, who constitute the majority of AIDS patients in this country; it makes no mention of how these services meet the complex needs of people facing poverty and HIV.

Research on agencies which deliver HIV-related services to poor women, however, has revealed that women use a different set of criteria when evaluating the quality of services they receive. The women surveyed in one study regarded comprehensive and accessible services provided by a sensitive, empathetic staff as the most important characteristics of an HIV agency.[3] Women surveyed reported that many service providers were unable to meet their full range of needs.

What barriers continue to prevent agencies from designing and implementing effective AIDS services for women? Why is there such an extreme difference in the ways that biomedicine, social services agencies, and HIV-positive women evaluate AIDS care?

This chapter is an effort to reexamine the challenges faced by community-based service organizations as they provide care and support for women confronted with both poverty and HIV. Our consideration of community-based organizations in this chapter attempts to meet two primary goals. First, it allows us to describe and discuss the complex issues and obstacles faced by poor women with HIV when trying to obtain services from organizations which fail—often in spite of their best intentions—to address their needs adequately. Second, it provides us with the background necessary to profile organizations which are sensitive to the needs of those living with poverty and able to incorporate a woman-focused approach in their HIV-related services. Descriptions of such organizations follow in Chapter 9, "Making Common Cause." We believe that the quality or benefits of these HIV services cannot be adequately determined through quantitative measures. Such experience-distant measures neglect to take into account the impact of poverty, racism, and sexism upon both the transmission of HIV and the experience of living with AIDS. In the pages that follow, therefore, we have not sought to systematically evaluate the quality of services offered to HIV-positive women, but rather to offer an overview of the various approaches to serving poor women with or at risk for HIV.

2. EVALUATING COMMUNITY-BASED ORGANIZATIONS

The agencies discussed in this and the following chapter were not chosen based on an exhaustive search, nor do they purport to be the best or most effective agencies of their kind. They represent a sample of domestic and international organizations which provide

HIV/AIDS services to poor women. Our selection of organizations to profile in these two chapters was also guided by our desire to reflect the geographical and structural diversity of agencies which serve HIV-positive poor women. Each organization confronts the epidemic of AIDS among women from a different perspective, based upon their own resources and the needs of the particular communities they serve. Despite this diversity of approaches, all of them face common challenges rooted in the many misconceptions and prejudices surrounding the myriad issues raised by women living with HIV. In fact, the concerns and experiences of these organizations are often strikingly similar, revealing new themes and trends as increasing numbers of women with AIDS seek social services. For example, many of these organizations reported that the challenges faced by HIV-positive mothers often hindered these women's ability to obtain care for themselves. Documenting the stories of these organizations and the women they serve creates an opportunity for us to learn from one another and to implement and improve programs to meet the needs of women living with HIV.

These two chapters are also intended to serve as a resource for those who recognize the effects of structural violence in the lives of poor women and are working with them to confront its effects. Solidarity comes in many forms, certainly, but here we address those concerned with such everyday problems as housing, transportation, and access to services. This is what we mean by the term "pragmatic solidarity." We hope that our book will promote the exchange of information and ideas between agencies, facilitate a deeper understanding of the obstacles which prevent organizations from serving poor women sensitively and effectively, and increase our collective commitment to eliminating these barriers. Only by continuing to press for sweeping changes in the current system of service delivery will we be able to offer pragmatic solidarity to women living with both poverty and AIDS.

The material for Part III of this book was gathered with the assistance of many individuals and sources.[4] Originally, these two chapters were envisioned as a single resource guide which would provide a more comprehensive list of exemplary domestic and international HIV/AIDS organizations which serve women, and a brief description of their services. We initially requested information from over one hundred domestic organizations which identified themselves in their literature (and in communication with us) as providing services for poor HIV-positive women. Many of them were included in national and local resource guides which listed woman-centered HIV programs; others appeared in articles or newsletters about women with HIV or were well known to us through personal contact or first-hand experience with their programs.

After receiving promotional material sent by scores of organizations, we realized that we had no way of objectively evaluating the content or quality of the services they provided. Thus, rather than profiling the services offered by a large number of providers, we decided to focus on several community-based organizations which attempt to offer comprehensive social services to women, have initiated progressive or innovative programs, or are the sole providers in an area with a high rate of HIV among women. From the group of 75 domestic organizations that responded to our inquiries, we chose 10 to profile, giving us the opportunity to explore their history, structure, and services in greater detail. With this more focused approach, we were able to request that their history include the story of a woman who had benefited from the organization's services, so that the profile would have a client's perspective. Our goal was to bring into relief the realities of organizing, funding, and developing services for HIV-positive women as well as to capture the issues faced each day by the recipients of care. These domestic organizations were then contacted, asked to participate in this project, and sent a list of questions to answer about themselves.

Over the next three months, this information was collected and compiled into short pieces detailing the history, demographics, funding sources, and challenges faced by each organization. When available, a case history of a client was included. While we have no means of determining the ultimate impact or effectiveness of these organizations, we believe that each organization has an approach to service delivery which is sensitive to women, and acknowledges the role of poverty and gender inequality in the transmission and treatment of HIV. These organizations have developed programs based on the basic premise that poverty and AIDS are inextricably connected. Each recognizes that profound institutional changes must accompany meaningful attempts to improve the lives and health of women confronting poverty and HIV. The inability of small community-based organizations to demand these changes does not cancel their chief contribution—to afford pragmatic solidarity to women living with HIV.

In examining the histories of the organizations presented in Chapter 9, it becomes apparent that many service providers began to realize early that AIDS affects poor women in a qualitatively different way than it affects men. We refer to more than the differences in the clinical manifestations of the illness, which are often minor when compared to the *social* differences between men and women. These organizations understood that women experienced additional pressures around issues of domestic violence, pregnancy, and homelessness. In the midst of their own trials, they remained the primary caregivers for children. Even prior to their ordeals with HIV, the vast majority of the women served were already marginalized within society through the forces of racism, sexism, and economic injustice.

The majority of the domestic organizations discussed in these two chapters were formed as the pandemic was rapidly expanding among poor women and as increased governmental funding became available in the late 1980s in response to the inadequacy of existing social services. Until recently, the models for AIDS prevention, care, and treatment have largely developed from the examples offered by organizations attempting to meet the needs of gay men, many of whom faced a different kind of stigma but were not living in poverty. The success of organizations such as Gay Men's Health Crisis served as an example of what could be done, but soon it became clear that making common cause with poor women living with HIV would pose even greater challenges. Service providers were unprepared for the rapid spread of HIV among women and unable to effectively confront the new and complex socioeconomic, legal, and medical issues faced by women.

Due to a long-standing dearth of services for poor women, there were few prototype models for woman-focused AIDS programs as late as a decade into the pandemic. Some of these model organizations began as grass-roots groups by initiating educational campaigns for at-risk or infected women and then developed additional services and programs as funding and resources became available over time. Several of the organizations profiled in Chapter 9 were formed through cooperative efforts between governmental or academic groups and community-based HIV service agencies. Others were established health and social service organizations which evolved into HIV-service providers as AIDS began to affect the women of their catchment areas. In the past few years, the number of organizations seeking to serve women with AIDS has increased dramatically.

Despite the resourcefulness and frequent ingenuity of these organizations, it is often impossible for any program to comprehensively meet all the needs of even a single woman living with HIV. These organizations are ultimately dependent upon an overburdened and fragmented health care system to ensure the health and well-being of their clients. Their stories of pragmatic solidarity are detailed in depth in the next chapter of this book.

3. JUMPING THROUGH THE HOOPS: MARIA'S EXPERIENCE

> As the prevalence of HIV among women in the United States rises, increasing numbers of women who are themselves infected by the virus are also caregivers for persons with AIDS who are their children, partners, and siblings. Yet in health services research about the utilization and financing of health services by people with AIDS, women kin vanish from sight as does their daily, onerous labor."
>
> Nina Glick Schiller, "The Invisible Women: Caregiving and the Construction of AIDS Health Services"[5]

As noted, the number of "AIDS agencies" has increased dramatically in recent years. But the relatively small number of agencies profiled in Chapter 9 reflects the fact that woman-focused AIDS programs which make common cause with the *poor* are few and far between. Even well-intentioned organizations are often hindered by internal and external pressures which prevent them from adequately serving women facing HIV and poverty. This has resulted in a fragmentation of services. The majority of HIV-positive women in the United States continue to depend upon a variety of disconnected service providers for their care.

To better understand the extent and complexity of the challenges most poor HIV-positive women face when seeking to obtain services for themselves and their children, we explore one woman's experience in a city that offers numerous resources to persons with HIV. Maria's story reveals the flaws and inadequacies of a service delivery system so decentralized that it ultimately fails those who most need it.[6]

Maria is a 28-year-old woman, originally from Puerto Rico, who lives in a working-class neighborhood in Boston. Diagnosed with HIV when she was 24, she is unable to use her left arm due to a neurological impairment resulting from toxoplasmosis. She lives with an abusive husband, who also has AIDS, and has three children, ages six, seven, and nine.

After Maria began to be covered by Medicaid due to her physical disability, she was instructed to choose a health maintenance organization (HMO). She picked Neighborhood Health Plan (NHP) so she could keep her doctor. When this new HMO began to "manage" her care, she was being seen by a psychiatric nurse for major depression and receiving four hours daily of household assistance from a home health aid who assisted Maria in preparing meals and caring for her children; these services were provided by the Boston Visiting Nurses Association (VNA). After Maria joined NHP, the administrators of the organization decided that she was no longer eligible for the home health aid. The HMO also stopped covering visits from her psychiatric nurse. Maria is only able to receive assistance when her husband is out of the house because of his abuse when they are together. He has also prevented her from attending an HIV support group for Latina women and from seeing her hospital social worker to receive supportive therapy for both HIV and domestic violence.

Further complicating Maria's ability to receive care is the fact that she, her husband, and her children all have different health plans and insurance providers. Her children are uninfected and are ineligible to receive certain services they desperately need. For example, when Maria's youngest daughter was five, her social worker tried to obtain child care for her since Maria's paralysis made it difficult to cook and look after her. The Children's AIDS Project, however, provides child care for infected children only. Maria's children were able to obtain four hours a week of "respite care" through Boston's Children's Services until her husband discontinued this arrangement. The social worker has also arranged for Maria's children to receive mental health treatment, but transportation is difficult, and their father believes they do not need psychological counseling. After her neighbors harassed her children for having parents with AIDS, Maria began working with the Latino Health Institute to obtain new housing for her family where her children might be safer. Maria has also been involved with the Dimock Community Health Center in Roxbury, which has reimbursed her niece for providing child care for Maria's children.

As Maria's disease progresses, her involvement with service providers becomes ever more complicated, as more organizations are necessary to meet her needs and those of her family. She recently became a client of the AIDS Action Committee, which has provided her with a lawyer to address issues of guardianship following the deaths of both parents and to help prepare wills. Yet her case manager from the Latino Health Institute has resigned and a replacement has not yet been hired, leaving Maria unable to obtain AIDS-specific housing for herself and her family. Maria has been assigned another case worker through MetroBoston, a subcontractor of NHP, who is working to put Maria's children into an after-school program. This case worker is considering filing a report with the Massachusetts Department of Social Services because she believes the children are suffering from physical and emotional neglect.

Maria's engagements with this dizzying number of providers will multiply further. Like many young people with terminal diseases,

Maria and her husband have had great difficulty acknowledging the severity of their illnesses. When they are prepared to address the issue of what will happen to their children after their deaths, they will be referred to Living Legacy II, an agency which deals with the legal and psychosocial issues surrounding HIV and future custody arrangements for orphaned children.

As will be seen, the experience of poor women in poor countries—where none of these services are available—is even worse. But Maria's experiences with AIDS service providers has been unnecessarily fragmented. She has received services from seven separate organizations and has had at least one case manager with each of them. While each of her case managers handled a particular aspect of Maria's care, none of them were responsible for coordinating services among the various agencies. Her case managers were often unable to follow up on the services Maria received, due to their own overwhelming caseloads. There is little communication among her case managers. When communication does occur, it is bureaucratic, creating unnecessary red tape and wasting scarce financial and human resources. Further complicating this situation is the lack of communication between the people coordinating her clinical care and the people managing the care of her husband and children.

Many of the administrators, social workers, and clients we contacted during the development of these two chapters agreed that the prevailing decentralized model of AIDS care for women is fundamentally problematic. They consistently stressed how the bureaucracy and rigidity of many health care systems prevent poor women from obtaining the type of services they need most. Several individuals felt that the HIV epidemic has simply highlighted some of the basic structural flaws of the current health care system. For example, Julie Marston, Director of Community Research Initiative of New England believes that the city of Boston "suffers in all its health care systems from a decentralized case management approach since there is no fiscal incentive for health providers to coordinate their services." Consequently, "there is little or no affiliation between some of the best research and teaching institutions in the country and the communities surrounding them."[7]

The crisis in HIV case management is indicative of the widespread fragmentation which plagues so many aspects of the health care industry. While the bureaucracy and structural flaws of the health care system are often burdens to all people with AIDS, they can have a particularly devastating effect upon the ability of poor women and their families to receive HIV-related services. For example, while many drug-treatment centers insist on separating a woman from her children during the course of the program, professionals who work with HIV-positive female addicts feel that these women would be better served by allowing them to stay with their families. It is commonly felt that programs for HIV-positive poor women should be designed to allow these women as much control over their lives as possible and must reinforce structures of support for those who are marginalized from the dominant institutions of society. Such goals could be facilitated by helping HIV-positive women find safe housing for themselves and their families and by providing opportunities for education and employment. Yet the lack of coordination between agencies and case managers often prevents women from accessing these programs. Marston further observes that "health care institutions are created and expanded with the needs and capabilities of the providers in mind. They are rarely developed with the people they serve in mind."[8]

Many of those working in solidarity with these women also believed that, by failing to offer centralized and comprehensive services, the established system of HIV care for women often obscures the importance of psychological and social factors which promote health and well-being. This approach ignores the life circumstances generally faced by many poor women with AIDS. Women facing the forces of both HIV and poverty are affected by AIDS in a multiplicity of ways, as infected persons, intimate partners, and mothers. Ellen Miller-Mack, a nurse practitioner with a large case load of poor HIV-positive women in Springfield, Massachusetts notes that "many of these women tend to have family responsibilities not shared by the men in their lives. In addition, we know in general that men with HIV are likely to be taken care of by women. In contrast, many women with HIV do not have caretakers."[9] Many HIV-positive women view their own needs as secondary to the needs of the people for whom they are caring.

The current health care system for HIV is not designed for people who face the additional pressures of being caretakers for their families. While health bureaucracies are intimidating to many people, they appear to be especially so to poor, marginalized women facing the responsibilities of being HIV-positive parents and partners. Marston explains that "the complexities of navigating systems of care at institutions often perceived to be impersonal and uncaring can be more difficult for women who may not only be ill but primary care givers as well."[10] The inherent intricacies of this system make it difficult for many women to fully utilize ostensibly available resources, a difficulty further compounded by the decentralized and overburdened system of HIV case management. What health care providers often view as "non-compliance" among poor HIV-positive women is often the result of their limited access to an already incomprehensible and inconvenient system of care.

The internal deficiencies of these institutions are yet another example of the structural violence faced by HIV-positive poor women seeking social services and treatment for AIDS. Without a system of centralized case management, women are forced to coordinate the care of their entire families, often ignoring their own pressing needs. As Kim Atkins, HIV Program Director for New York's Community Family Planning Council notes: "For these women, the next meal for them and their children, where they and their children are going to sleep that night, and how they are going to get clothes appropriate to the season—these are their concerns. If they can step beyond this, then getting substance abuse treatment, regular work, child care, regular housing, etc. are the main concerns. Only after this can attention be turned to appropriate medical care and ongoing treatment for HIV and mental health issues."[11] A centralized system of case management will help women to care for their families while receiving an optimum level of services for themselves.

The experiences of the medical providers, clients, and administrators who we interviewed have been substantiated and supported by research which has evaluated the quality of services for

HIV-positive women and the challenges faced by providers. A study conducted by researchers at Hunter College found that most HIV-service providers were unable to fully meet the complexity of women's needs.[12] The researchers surveyed 34 agencies in New York State which receive specific funding for AIDS-related services for women. They found that the client recruitment strategies most highly regarded by program administrators were the least widely used. Fewer than half the agencies offered child care services or transportation to their clients, despite the fact that a majority of staff members believed that these services would make the care they offered more accessible and appealing to infected women. Less than a third provided their clients with access to maternal-child health facilities and less than 40 percent had links with drug treatment centers, mental health centers, and housing agencies.

The study suggests that the inaccessibility of comprehensive care leads many women to prioritize the needs of their children and partners over their own needs, supporting the observations of many of the health professionals interviewed for this chapter. While many agencies are aware of ways to improve the quality and convenience of their AIDS-related services for women, limited funding, patchy insurance coverage, and poorly trained staff prevent them from offering comprehensive and accessible services for their clients. Thus it is not ignorance on the part of providers or clients, but rather the bureaucratic weaknesses of many HIV-service delivery systems, that restrict the capacity of providers to effectively serve women burdened by the combined pressures of poverty and HIV.

Despite these obstacles, however, our profiles of woman-centered HIV-service providers in the United States and abroad illustrate how organizations can design and implement programs which attempt to confront the particular forms of structural violence which plague their communities. The next section of this chapter addresses the specific challenges faced by international agencies which provide services for HIV-positive women. While domestic and international HIV-service organizations face many of the same issues regarding women and AIDS, there are several particular conditions which have facilitated the spread of AIDS among poor women outside of the United States.

4. NON-U.S. BASED ORGANIZATIONS

Gender, poverty, and their relation to HIV highlight both 'large scale' and 'local' social forces that seem to put women at risk of exposure to HIV early in their sexual experience. Such social forces are by no means only found in the poorest of countries; they cross the boundaries of societies of North and South, rich and poor."

Paul Farmer, Shirley Lindenbaum,
Mary-Jo Delvecchio Good,
Culture, Medicine and Psychiatry[13]

The general response of international organizations to the crisis of AIDS among women has been very similar to that of many agencies in the United States. Their HIV programs can be broadly characterized as focusing on the importance of changing individual behaviors. They do not lend themselves to analyzing and working to transform the structures which often force people into practices which increase their risk of infection. While organizations with this perspective on HIV prevention often recognize the connection between oppressive social conditions and AIDS, they fail to take this relationship into account in their intervention programs for HIV-positive women, who are in large part, poor.

A recent publication of the World Health Organization (WHO), *Facing the challenges of HIV/AIDS/STDs: a gender-based response,* typifies this approach.[14] It provides a large amount of quantitative data and numerous personal stories to illustrate how power and economic imbalances—rather than, say, women's ignorance - jeopardize the health of poor women in many countries. Despite the impressive presentation of this material, however, an awareness of the relative powerlessness of poor women is conspicuously absent from its proposed methods of intervention. The intervention programs described in WHO's material primarily involve educational tools designed to teach individuals how to avoid exposure to HIV. These programs thus fail to acknowledge the many layers of power that frequently exist between men and women, especially when negotiating safer sex or sharing injection drugs. Such programs in essence ignore the inconvenient fact that increased HIV risks are not distributed along cognitive lines. More importantly, their interventions assume that the poor will be able to protect themselves from HIV despite the many forces that conspire to increase their risk of infection.

While international organizations such as the WHO do not intentionally act against the best interests of the poor, their interventions do not square with their data. Their programs are often short-term solutions which obscure the roots of health problems rather than directly address them. This is significant, given the influence of these institutions. Consequently, many community-based HIV-related organizations for women which are funded by multilateral health agencies tend to be guided by this short-sighted agenda. There are, of course, organizations which have taken the initiative to develop programs which address the causes of structural violence as they battle its effects. In our profiles of international organizations serving HIV-positive women in the following chapter, we have highlighted a few programs which work in solidarity with the poor to fight the economic and political forces perpetuating powerlessness and increased AIDS risks. These organizations attempt to create programs which address structural change and community development in addition to focusing on issues of education and personal responsibility.

Due to the vast numbers of AIDS service providers outside of the United States, the international agencies profiled in Chapter 9 were contacted through colleagues who have been either directly involved with them or are familiar with their innovative approaches to serving poor women. These individuals were contacted, informed of our project, and asked to provide the requested information about each organization. The profiles were developed with assistance from people who work in close contact with these organizations.

We learned that both domestic and international organizations face common challenges. Like their counterparts in America, women-focused HIV-service providers outside of the United States are chronically under-funded and frequently unable to provide necessary medical and social services. Many face resistance from the dominant political, economic, and legal structures, which receive funding from multilateral lending organizations more interested in "restructuring" economies along neoliberal lines than in the elimination of poverty. Competing large-scale interests and institutions have often hindered the ability of non-governmental and community-based organizations to implement programs rooted in social and economic justice. Some have argued that the emergence of global economic markets and the "new world order" has had a devastating effect on the ability of HIV-services to protect the poor women who are already most vulnerable to infection by the virus.

AIDS is a political issue in all countries. The politicization of the pandemic has led some countries to create HIV organizations which merely respond to the needs of those who are most vocal and articulate within the language of the social elite. For example, in Abidjan, the capital of the Ivory Coast (which has the highest prevalence of HIV in West Africa), the government formed an organization to undertake prevention and care activities in response to the urgent protests of three well-educated young people with HIV who spoke out at a government-sponsored forum on AIDS. This organization receives support from the state and large non-governmental organizations, and its members have become highly visible representatives of people with AIDS. Having been incorporated into the bureaucracy of the Ministry of Health, however, this organization has come to reflect the inadequacy of the government's response to AIDS among the poor. One example of the problem is evident in the way the organization allocates its resources: it concentrates its efforts among urban, educated men and women, who, not surprisingly, make up the leadership of the group. The dynamic of the region's epidemic, however, seems to put a very different group at increased risk of infection.

The bureaucratic structure of the Ivoirien organization has unintentionally ensured that the needs of HIV-positive women remain largely unrecognized. Even when women are in leadership positions, as they often are through membership in the organization, they report that their lack of formal education and political power prevents their ideas from being heard within the larger group. Women with creative ideas for the care of poor women and the initiative to implement these ideas into programs are frequently silenced. This process of systematically muting women's voices closely mirrors the gender and class dynamics within the political arena of the Ivory Coast.[15]

The situation encountered by women in this organization is a common occurrence in well-meaning agencies around the world, and constitutes another factor which prevents poor women from obtaining HIV services. This makes them more vulnerable to infection. Other factors help render women in poor countries more vulnerable to HIV infection in ways less often encountered by women in the United States. For example, as Chapter 2 discusses, countries such as Thailand rely heavily upon revenue from sex tourism. In many instances, governments of these nations implicitly condone practices which put poor women at increased risk for HIV. For example, the Tourism Authority of Thailand has published pamphlets which praise the "night-life" of major sex centers such as Patpong and feature prominent advertisements for "escort services." While the government has no official links to the sex industry, it is a beneficiary of the money it brings into the region. One Thai official reinforces this idea: "Let's be frank: if there was no sex there wouldn't be much tourism, though no government wants to emphasize this."[16] Though the thriving industry of sex tourism has facilitated the explosive spread of HIV in Thailand, its importance to the national economy has hindered attempts to prevent HIV transmission in the region.

Child slavery and forced prostitution in many poor countries have also led to increased transmission of HIV. In some areas, women are pushed by their parents into sex work to provide poor families with additional financial support. Others are kidnapped or abducted into the sex industry. Widespread poverty and a lack of economic opportunities underpin these practices and contribute to the rapid spread of HIV among the most vulnerable inhabitants of many poor nations. The growing demand for younger sex workers also reflects the commonly held belief that children and teens are less likely to be infected with HIV. This idea, however, is clearly belied by estimates that as many as 50 percent of child prostitutes in Thailand are HIV-positive.[17]

The spread of HIV in some areas of the world has also been facilitated by the impact of a globalizing economy upon certain cul-

tural systems and practices. For example, there are in India an estimated 500,000 *hijras*, a group of transsexual men who constitute an
institutionalized third gender. The *hijras* have traditionally occupied
a religious role within Indian society. As devotees of the goddess
Bahuchara Mata, the *hijras* bless new-born male infants, praying for
health, fertility, and prosperity.[18] The declining practice of such ritu-
als, as economic change and urbanization impacts religious life, has
forced many of them to support themselves through sex work, catering to a clientele of both gay and bisexual men. The spread of AIDS
among *hijras* seems to be directly linked to their growing poverty. It
is estimated that a third of New Delhi's ten thousand *hijras* are HIV-
positive, though there is little reliable seroprevalence data on this
population.[19]

The weakening of rural and local economies has led to the
migration of many villagers to urban areas. These migrants nonetheless, remain tightly linked to their home villages. In Thailand, such
ties help to illuminate research showing higher incidence rates of
HIV among rural villagers than among the Thai population as a
whole.[20] Patricia Symonds, an anthropologist who works with the
Hmong of the northern Chiang Rai Province, notes that the rise of
AIDS among women in rural areas is directly related to their economic dependence upon the urban market: "As more Hmong men
are traveling to the lowlands in search of wage labor and the
exchange of goods and produce, they have had more opportunity and
inclination (as they absorb the cultural values of the global culture)
to visit Thai prostitutes. As economic problems continue to worsen,
hill tribe Hmong women go to the cities in search of work as well,
and many become prostitutes."[21] This combination of urban travel
and economic dependency puts rural women at increased risk for
HIV infection, further threatening the health of an already vulnerable population.

The challenges posed by AIDS prevention in such a setting are
emblematic of those posed elsewhere. To put it starkly: if the chief
forces promoting the transmission of HIV are fundamentally *economic*—in the Thai case, the dissolution of rural economies followed
by migration and its attendant effects on stable sexual union—how
can *educational* interventions hope to alter rates of transmission?

The challenges posed by AIDS prevention are by no means exclusively economic ones. AIDS is a stigmatized illness in settings throughout the world. Many countries have instituted policies which do not ensure the anonymity of those who receive HIV-related services or testing. Even if poor women have access to health care providers, they may choose not to obtain services, in order to avoid the public stigma of HIV infection. The effects of non-anonymous services are evident even in industrialized nations such as Canada. Vinh-Kim Nguyen, a physician at McGill University in Montreal, reports that many HIV-positive women do not seek AIDS-related services because they fear losing their jobs, their legal status as citizens in the country, or child custody battles.[22] The absence of anonymous HIV-related services forces people either to sacrifice their health in order to avoid discrimination or access services and run the risk of being further marginalized from society.

Issues such as sex tourism, forced prostitution, urban migration, and the influence of a globalizing economy upon cultural systems illustrate some of the specific challenges facing HIV-service providers in poor communities. We believe that the organizations profiled in the next chapter have established intervention programs which attempt to address these problems and seek to overcome the inequalities spawned by these structures. Even when facing overwhelming odds, these organizations confront AIDS in the spirit of pragmatic solidarity, working at the local level to protect the already precarious lives of poor women infected with, or at risk for, HIV.

5. CONCLUSION

In order to have the continued opportunity to express their 'generosity,' the oppressors must perpetuate injustice as well. An unjust social order is the permanent fount of this 'generosity,' which is nourished by death, despair, and poverty."

Paulo Freire,
Pedagogy of the Oppressed [23]

Community-based organizations which provide services to poor HIV-positive women are at the forefront of the battle against social injustice. They must constantly assist the most vulnerable members of society in confronting both the effects of the disease and the social conditions which both foster HIV transmission and aggravate the suffering of those already infected. At the same time, these organizations are usually inescapably bound to some of the institutions and structures which perpetuate the inequalities preventing many poor women from obtaining adequate HIV-care for themselves and their families. Most of the groups profiled in the following chapter are dependent upon these same sources of funding for the continued support of their programs. These funding organizations—which include federal governments, multilateral agencies, large philanthropic foundations, and corporations—determine who and what will receive financial support. These institutions have to a large extent shaped our responses to the crisis of HIV among women. Many people involved in community-based organizations report that their lack of financial independence inhibits their capacity to develop innovative interventions which address the root causes of HIV among poor women. This was a recurring theme in interviews with the community-based providers profiled in the next chapter. Dependence upon governmental and corporate funds often leads them to design and implement programs which provide a "band-aid" response to an epidemic spiraling out of control. The institutions providing funding for services for HIV-positive women thus inadvertently perpetuate another form of structural violence upon already beleaguered groups.

Many of the community-based organizations profiled in Chapter 9 have challenged this agenda by implementing programs which attempt to address the underlying social conditions facilitating the transmission of HIV. The groups we look at strive for a comprehensive approach to service delivery which helps HIV-positive and at-risk women escape the burdens of poverty. These organizations work in pragmatic solidarity with poor women, providing care and support to meet the complex needs of the HIV-positive woman as a caretaker for herself and her family. The experiences of these organizations provide valuable insights into ways that community-based service providers can positively impact the health of the poor.

CHAPTER NINE

Making Common Cause

Greg Rubin, editor

with Kim Atkins, Irma Azize, Ellen Bay, Wendy Blank, Mark Bonacci, Marie-Flore Chipps, Sarthak Das, Paul Farmer, Mary Inzana, Julie Marston, Ellen Miller-Mack, Vinh-Kim Nguyen, Chris Norwood, Juanita Ruano, Marge Samson, Brooke Schoepf, Debbie Scott-Young, Stacy Shoemaker, and Pat Symonds

1. U.S.-BASED ORGANIZATIONS

The Community Family Planning Council

Office for HIV Programs
92-94 Ludlow Street
New York, NY 10002
Phone: (212) 979-9014   Fax: (212) 477-8957
Contact: Kim Atkins

The Community Family Planning Council (CFPC) is a network of community health centers which provides health and social services to the homeless, substance abusers, and poor pregnant women in New York City. The CFPC aims to serve historically marginalized groups which are most in need: "We go after the hard to reach, the vulnerable, the sickest. We seek to make the whole city a better place to live for all its citizens," notes the network's coordinator.[1] Their eight clinics and two mobile health centers serve a client population which is over 85 percent African-American or Hispanic, 30 percent under the age of 20, and living in some of New York's most impoverished neighborhoods. To make their services financially accessible to all, they accept Medicaid, sliding fee payments, and private insurance; they use state and local funds to support services for adolescents, the uninsured, and others with low incomes. Since 1990, HIV-related services provided by CFPC have grown from four percent to 40 percent of their annual budget. The organization is currently participating in a range of HIV prevention and service activities in conjunction with New York City and New York State Health Departments. According to Executive Director Ana O. Dumois, CFPC is "defining a model of medical care for HIV-positive individuals based in the communities of need, delivered in the languages of the people we serve."[2]

The organization provides numerous HIV/AIDS services for women living in poverty, including case management, financial advocacy, transportation, counseling, childcare, and assistance with daily living tasks. With support from the New York State AIDS Institute and the State Department of Health, CFPC runs HIV education and outreach programs for high-risk women, providing condom distribution, group presentations, and individual counseling. Their HIV counseling, testing, and education services are funded by the New York State Bureau of Reproductive Health, allowing them to provide HIV testing for over 6,500 people each year. This funding has also enabled them to initiate a special program to provide testing and counseling to any woman or adolescent who comes to the clinic for a pregnancy test. This program is designed to educate women about perinatal transmission of HIV and the importance of knowing one's HIV status when pregnant.

CFPC provides the majority of its medical services for HIV-positive women through the H. Keith Williams Primary Care Program, which is located in four clinic sites and one mobile health center. This program was funded by the Bureau of Health Care Delivery and Assistance in order to "provide a model program for early intervention HIV care for women and to provide leadership in bringing other family-planning and community-based organizations into the fight against HIV."[3] It provides a full range of medical services for HIV-positive women, including gynecological, nutritional, and prenatal care; it aims to help them live longer with a higher quality of life. The mobile health center provides a broad array of HIV medical services and outreach programs to areas where HIV-positive or substance-abusing women gather or live.

This program has served over 800 HIV-positive clients since it began in 1991. It currently serves over 500 people, 55 percent of them women. CFPC is currently working in conjunction with the New York University Medical Center and Brooklyn Hospital to provide pediatric care within their clinics to better serve the needs of women and families. This partnership integrates services for HIV-positive mothers and children; services which have traditionally been provided in locations that have been more difficult for their clients to reach.

The effectiveness of this HIV primary care program for women is enhanced by CFPC's case management services, which are available at all CFPC sites throughout the city. Over 250 HIV-positive individuals currently receive assistance with entitlements and benefits, referrals, short-term crisis intervention, coordination of services with other providers, and transportation to appointments. With support from the United Way of New York City and the New York State AIDS Institute, CFPC has initiated a special case management program for women and families in East New York, Brooklyn, and Jamaica, Queens. This program provides the services listed above, as well as emergency financial aid, child-care, household assistance, legal counseling for guardianship and permanency planning, and family counseling. Since March of 1995, CFPC has also provided outpatient mental health services at all clinic sites.

CFPC is also one of a handful of community-based health agencies in the country to offer their HIV-positive patients access to clinical trials. They participate in the Clinical Directors Network (CDN) in federal Region II in order to "provide access to HIV/AIDS therapies for medically underserved populations and to provide access through community-based practitioners working in community health care centers."[4] CFPC is also involved in clinical trials involving alternative therapies, such as acupuncture and vitamins, which are of special interest to many of their clients.

CFPC reports that poor HIV-positive women face many obstacles and structurally-determined barriers when seeking services and treatment for their illness. Kim Atkins, Director of HIV Services, writes that "those who have a history of substance abuse, have been in prison, are sex workers, and are gay or bisexual often have been alienated from their families for years. At this point in their life, they may have a special need for family support, but find that it is unavailable to them."[5] Without these support networks many women are unable to find temporary care for their children as they address their own HIV-related issues. Furthermore, HIV is not always the most pressing concern for many HIV-positive poor women. They will often attend to issues such as food and housing for their children before seeking HIV-related services for themselves.

CFPC reports that care and treatment for HIV-positive poor women is exceptionally complicated, since women may depend on the services of several agencies for comprehensive care. This often makes it unclear which agencies should be paid or reimbursed for specific services and to which agency a client "belongs" It is therefore necessary for service coordination between agencies to be clearly defined and managed, to avoid duplication of services, to focus treatment and care in essential areas, and to prevent waste of precious financial and human resources.

Grants from the Centers for Disease Control (CDC), New York City Department of Health, The New York State AIDS Institute, and the Ryan White Act have been used to fund most of CFPC's programs and project initiatives. These funds have helped the organization to develop and implement peer-outreach programs, reach uninsured women for HIV testing and counseling, operate a mobile health center for high-risk adolescents, and provide same-site care for HIV-positive mothers and children. Despite their relative success in creating a comprehensive program for HIV-positive women, Kim Atkins notes, "the targeted funding is limited and doesn't encourage other providers to meet the needs of women. There is not enough incentive for programs to assume the responsibilities of meeting women's needs. Even in a program like CFPC's, which is geared toward women, there are many men who are provided with full services. On the other hand, there are not many programs that are established for men or for the general population where women can and do receive anywhere near the type of services they require."[6]

Community Research Initiative of New England

320 Washington Street, 3rd Floor
Brookline, MA 02146
Phone: (617) 566-4004
Fax: (617) 566-8226
Contact: Julie Marston

The Community Research Initiative (CRI) of New England was established in 1986 to study AIDS-related treatments which promise to improve the lives of people with HIV. The organization is specifically committed to making clinical trials more accessible to those who have been systematically excluded from participating in experimental AIDS treatment protocols, including the poor, people of color, and women.

Since its inception, CRI has initiated a number of community-based programs and research models aimed at increasing the accessibility of clinical trials for women struggling both with poverty and HIV. Central to this effort has been the implementation of fifteen research trials involving over 1,250 participants. These studies have included several which test the effectiveness of new treatments for HIV-related symptoms which are specific to women, including one to detect cervical disease and another to prevent yeast infections. CRI also develops educational programs for study participants, which address long-standing issues of mistrust between marginalized communities and the medical establishment. These programs provide information on individualized medical care, research protocols, and the history of clinical trials in the United States. In addition, CRI has implemented the HIV Drug Assistance Plan, which has offered over 3,000 people financial assistance for purchasing expensive AIDS-related medications.

In order to make these trials more convenient for poor HIV-positive women, the administration of many of CRI's clinical trials has been decentralized. This has allowed people with HIV to access experimental treatments through the primary care physicians in their own communities, rather than through research teams at a central location. By integrating clinical trials into the delivery of primary health care, CRI has sought to make accessibility to clinical trials not only a realistic option, but a priority for poor women with HIV.

According to Executive Director Julie Marston, CRI faces many obstacles in its attempts to increase services to HIV-positive women. Most clinical trials are conducted at large medical centers which are often inaccessible to poor women, due to difficulties in obtaining childcare, transportation or information about the study. These difficulties have led to some women being viewed as "non-compliant," further reducing the number of women who are asked to join clinical trials at centralized medical facilities. The community-based approach of CRI has been effective in placing more women in these studies and making the studies more "user-friendly" for women who are caretakers for their children or partners. Many of the women participating in trials through CRI have a history of not prioritizing their own health care needs, leading to fewer medical visits and an increased susceptibility to opportunistic infections. Marston notes: "A smaller, more personalized and friendly environment enables women to feel more in control and allows them to become more invested in their health care."[7] By designing its program to be more accessible to poor women and sensitive to their needs, CRI has been able to help its clients better utilize available options for care.

An interview with a CRI client reveals how involvement in clinical trials benefits poor, HIV-positive women in the Boston area. Ann is 21-year-old African-American woman who tested positive for HIV when she was 16. She has been participating in a protease inhibitor clinical trial for six months and reports that the treatment has contributed to an increase in her T-cells and improved overall health. CRI pays for her transportation to the clinical trial site and for the services of the medical professionals who monitor her progress. Ann reports: "A lot of my friends don't understand about the trial. They think research is bad for you and that everyone is using me, but they just don't get it. This is helping me and maybe it can help someone else someday."[8]

CRI receives funding from the Massachusetts AIDS Fund, the American Foundation for AIDS Research, and the Boston Department of Health and Hospitals. The organization is also supported by funds from pharmaceutical manufacturers and private donations. Spokespersons for CRI report that they have had great difficulty in generating additional funding to bring more women into clinical trials, since "private industry has not prioritized the inclusion of women into the research system, nor is it particularly responsive to the efforts required to incorporate the needs of women, poor people, and others into the design and application of clinical trials."[9] CRI faces additional challenges, since clinical trials have historically received a relatively small portion of the public funding available for HIV care and services.

The Empowerment Program: Women's AIDS Project

1245 East Colfax Avenue
Room 404
Denver, CO 80218
Phone: (303) 863-7817
Fax: (303) 863-0341
Contact: Debbie Scott-Young

The Empowerment Program was founded in the fall of 1984 to create alternatives to incarceration for female offenders. It began serving women directly in January 1986, and has provided comprehensive services to over 6,000 women since then. In 1989, with funding from the Robert Wood Johnson Foundation, the Empowerment Program developed the Women's AIDS Project, a "fully functioning program for women at risk for contracting or transmitting HIV disease, targeting those working in the sex industry or in prostitution-related activities."[10] Additional financial assistance for the formation of the Women's AIDS Project (WAP) was obtained through the Conference of Mayors and the Colorado Department of Health in 1990. This funding was used for HIV education, prevention activities, and case management for adolescent and adult women with HIV/AIDS. These services were expanded greatly in 1994, after the Empowerment Program received grants from the Piton Foundation, HOPWA, and the Ryan White Act to assist women living with HIV/AIDS. The organization is also funded by the CDC and various local churches. Though the Empowerment Program continues to serve women in prison and young women at risk for incarceration, the Women and AIDS Project has evolved as its primary program.

The Women and AIDS Project currently offers its HIV-positive clients counseling services and assistance in obtaining food, clothing and subsidized or low-cost housing. In addition, it provides transportation to HIV-related appointments and services. The Project offers outreach programs at sites which have a disproportionately high number of poor women at risk for HIV infection, such as drug and alcohol treatment centers, halfway houses, county jails, and community corrections facilities. Permanent housing is available for women living with HIV/AIDS through the group's Women in Transition House. WAP also offers financial assistance to their clients, including those women whose T-cell counts are too high for SSI or SSDI but who are not healthy enough to be employed. The average age of program participants is 32, and 80 percent are the sole caretaker for their young children. Forty percent of participants are African-American, 25 percent are Latina, and five percent are Native American. Sixty percent have not finished high school and 95 percent have a history of drug or alcohol abuse. About one-third of the participants are lesbian identified.

Penny, a client of the Empowerment Program, has been involved with WAP for three years. The Program has assisted her in finding and financing housing for herself and her three children, allowing her to distance herself from her violent and abusive partner. She receives case-management services and attends weekly social events through WAP. Penny is unable to work due to her health, and depends on WAP for food and financial assistance so she can remain in a safe apartment with her children. WAP has helped her obtain stability and safety in her personal life. She can now make her health care a priority.

WAP reports that it needs additional funding to provide clients with affordable housing, an adequate amount of healthy food, mental health counseling, and treatment for substance abuse. The problems caused by insufficient funding in these areas are exacerbated by the lack of HIV education in the community, the easy accessibility of street drugs and alcohol, and the growing conservatism among political leaders and the public.

Health Force: Women Against AIDS

Bronx Community College
295 St. Ann's Avenue
Bronx, NY 10454
Phone: (718) 585-8585
Fax: (718) 585-5041
Contact: Chris Norwood

Health Force, a project of Bronx Community College, was formed in 1990 to confront the growing impact of HIV on women. The group currently provides a variety of services to over 3,000 individuals annually in the poorest congressional district in the nation, which also has the highest pediatric and female AIDS rates in New York City. During its first year, Health Force initiated an intensive 40-day peer education program based upon the belief that "the best educators would be from communities most affected by AIDS—women who had personally experienced the devastation of the epidemic to their families and neighborhoods and therefore knew best where help was needed."[11] The twelve members of the first graduating class spoke about women and AIDS at clinics, churches and conferences throughout New York City. In honor of their efforts, Health Force won the first annual Recognition Award from the New York AIDS Coalition.

In 1991, Health Force trained a group of Latina women, "Las Mujeres Unidas," to ensure that Spanish-speaking women had equal access to woman-focused AIDS education. Their efforts have recently been expanded to include specific peer education programs for men, women with a history of crack abuse, and members of the Islamic community. These changes have enriched the range of services offered by Health Force, helping them become more responsive to the changing demographics of the epidemic in the Bronx.

In 1992, Health Force initiated a unique relapse-prevention program for HIV-positive women in recovery. The program aimed to reduce relapse and increase the quality of life for women living with HIV while providing outreach and support to substance-abusing women who are particularly isolated by homelessness, lack of services, and the social stigma of drug use. The program was designed to benefit both the peer facilitators and the women whom the program targets through outreach and education. During a recent two year period, 35 low-income candidates, 95 percent of whom were in recovery and half of whom were HIV-positive, entered a 14-week training program to become peer facilitators. Eighteen of the graduates established four ongoing support groups reaching 2,500 people in homeless shelters and welfare hotels. These groups were the sole source of social support and AIDS information and referrals for the majority of people participating in them. Furthermore, only 30 percent of the graduate peer facilitators relapsed into drug use within the first year; and half of those who relapsed recovered within six months.

In addition to its peer education and relapse prevention programs, Health Force coordinates ten HIV/AIDS support groups. These support groups, with a total enrollment of over 350, attempt to meet the needs of families, the homeless, those in recovery, and Spanish speakers with AIDS. They also offer courses on women's health and HIV prevention for women in drug recovery and classes on AIDS care for people with AIDS and their caretakers. Through their Family Services program, Health Force provides counseling for

HIV-positive parents and a mentoring program for their children. Health Force "incorporates the input of the community in the design and implementation of its services" in order to create an atmosphere which is attractive and non-threatening to HIV- affected individuals and families.[12]

The majority of Health Force's funding comes from the Ryan White Act and the New York City and New York State Departments of Health. Representatives of this organization report that they have difficulty accessing the flexible kinds of funding which would allow their services to be maintained consistently over each financial year and bridge the time between the start of a program and the actual receipt of funds. This type of financial support is necessary, they note, to "test out exciting and dynamic, yet unproven, models of service delivery, and to meet the needs of individuals who have not yet been identified or targeted by funders."[13]

Iris House

2271 Second Avenue
New York, NY 10035
Phone: (212) 423-9049
Fax: (212) 423-9193
Contact: Irma Azize

Iris House works to promote independent living for HIV-positive women and their families, educate public officials and health and service providers about the issues faced by these women, and advocates for policies and programs which are more responsive to their needs. According to the group's representatives, this "family-centered approach to service delivery has resulted in programs which are more realistic and comprehensive, have a higher level of service coordination, and minimize access barriers affecting the ability of women with HIV/AIDS to receive appropriate levels of quality service."[14]

The organization's case management programs offer a wide range of on-site and affiliated services. Case managers act as advisors and advocates, helping their clients understand and fully benefit from a variety of care options. On-site services include psychological counseling, legal and nutritional assistance, home and hospital visits, and child-care. Iris House also provides assistance for women seeking housing, financial benefits, mental health assessment, or placement in drug and alcohol abuse programs. The organization is currently developing recovery groups and individualized counseling for clients with substance abuse issues.

The scope and integration of its services allows Iris House to provide high quality services to HIV-positive poor women and their families. Gina, a 31-year-old African American woman, enrolled herself in the Iris House program in September 1994, three years after she was diagnosed with HIV. She is the mother of three children and the primary caretaker of two of them. Her personal history has been marked by domestic violence and an addiction to crack cocaine. Gina has a limited network of familial support and lives in fear of further abuse from the father of her children. She depends on her mother to care for her children during her hospitalizations, but has not revealed her HIV status to her.

After entering Iris House, Gina obtained the following services: family counseling, nutritional evaluation and counseling, financial assistance for food and furniture, help in securing benefits, eight hours of homemaking assistance a day, and home visits from a nurse twice a week. Iris House has also taken measures to help her plan for her children's future, despite Gina's reluctance to fully contemplate their separation. Through these services, Gina has increased her awareness of the care options available to her as an HIV-positive woman and mother and stabilized her living situation, giving her greater control over her life with HIV.

Iris House was established following a two-year planning process by the Women and AIDS Working Group, a coalition of 650 women affected by or infected with HIV, convened under the auspices of the Office of the Manhattan Borough President. The diverse experiences and perspectives of these women helped them to identify the inadequacies of existing programs for HIV-infected women and their families, and led them to design a more comprehensive model to improve the delivery of services to this population. In September 1993, Iris House began its first year of operation at a site in East Harlem, with funding provided by a grant from the Council of Fashion Designers of America-Vogue Initiative/New York City AIDS Fund of the New York Community Trust. The building included a childcare area, fully equipped kitchen, large meeting space, and resource library. During its first year of operation, Iris House obtained additional financial support from the United Way, the Aaron Diamond Foundation, and the Office of the Manhattan Borough President. Iris House is currently governed by a Board of Directors whose membership includes community representatives, HIV-positive women, and women with expertise in finance, fundraising, and public policy. The organization continues to receive funding through a variety of public and private sources including Seagrams, J.P. Morgan, American Express, Merrill Lynch, and the Liz Clairborne Foundation.

Life Force: Women Fighting AIDS, Inc.

165 Cadman Plaza East
Room 201
Brooklyn, NY 11201-1402
Phone: (718) 797-0937
Fax: (718) 797-4011
Contact: Juanita Ruano

Life Force, founded in 1989 by 19 women who were infected with or affected by HIV, was established as a community-based peer education project to reduce the incidence of HIV among local women and their families. In 1991, Life Force was incorporated as a non-profit, community-based organization "designed to give purpose to women with HIV and AIDS and give knowledge to those who are in high-risk populations or are already infected with HIV/AIDS."[15] Their organization is located in Brooklyn, where AIDS prevalence rates are among the highest in the United States, and women account for 30 percent of new AIDS cases. Of these women, 85 percent are African-American or Latina, reflecting the disproportionate impact of AIDS upon women of color in these communities.

Due to the growing numbers of HIV-positive poor women in Brooklyn and an absence of appropriate programs for this population, Life Force recruits women from local communities and prepares them to become peer educators through an intensive, three month training program. During this training program, the women address issues of family planning, STDs, tuberculosis, street and family violence, substance abuse, teen pregnancy, and case management. The peer educators are themselves from communities which have been devastated by AIDS. Many are HIV-positive or in recovery from substance abuse. Their personal involvements and connections with the communities they serve facilitate prevention education and outreach.

Peer educators are paid $3.00 an hour during training and $5.00 for their community outreach work. They receive compensation for travel and childcare expenses and participate in all aspects of organizational planning, development, and management. There are currently 43 active Life Force peer educators including 25 African-Americans, 13 Latinas, four Caucasian women, and one Caribbean-American woman of African descent. In serving as peer educators, Life Force believes that its "members use their own stories of personal transformation as a tool for effecting positive change in the lives of other women living with or at risk of HIV/AIDS."[16]

The staff at Life Force provides educational and outreach services to women at area hospitals and health clinics; to homeless and substance abusing women; to prisoners and women in work release programs; and to illegal aliens. These services include support groups, distribution of condoms and prevention and transmission information, individual counseling in person or by telephone, and referrals to other HIV service providers. They also provide clients with child care, transportation, and home attendants. Peer educators run weekly programs on prevention education and provide individual counseling services for women prisoners at Bayview Correctional Facility. With funding from the United Way of New York, Life Force is expanding its prison services to establish a support group for HIV-positive women on work release living in Brooklyn. The New York City Department of Health has provided Life Force with financial support for its home program, which is designed to facilitate open discussion about safer sex and risk reduction in a "non-threatening environment." Through these activities, they target women who may not be using organized health and social services for their HIV care.

LifeTies, Inc.

Rainbow House
2205 Pennington Road
Trenton, NJ 08638
Phone: (609) 771-1600
Fax: (609) 530-1648
Contact: Mary Inzana

Rainbow House is a group home for HIV-positive pregnant adolescents and teen mothers with children. Rainbow House is currently the only agency in the country which provides "residential support services to adolescents who have been rendered homeless because of their HIV infection or diagnosis with AIDS."[17] It was established in 1991 by LifeTies Inc., a non-profit organization dedicated to helping adolescents in crisis. With the financial support of the State Department of Health and Division of Youth and Family Services, Rainbow House is able to provide long-term medical care and support services for up to ten female adolescents and their children at a time. The services offered by Rainbow House are available to HIV-positive residents of New Jersey, aged 12-21, and their children. Many of their clients are homeless, victims of sexual or domestic violence, have histories of drug or alcohol abuse, and come from families who are either unable or unwilling to care for them.

Each resident of Rainbow House receives an individualized treatment plan designed to provide comprehensive medical, psychological, and educational services. Rainbow House is affiliated with a number of area hospitals, clinics, and individual health providers who work together to ensure that all the needs of its residents and their children are met. Primary and preventive medical care, including prenatal and gynecological treatments, prophylaxis for opportunistic infection, and monitoring of disease progression are available through the Robert Wood Johnson Medical Center. Emergency medical care, dental care, psychological counseling, and drug or alcohol treatment are provided by local agencies in the Trenton area. Visiting nurses see residents at least once a week to monitor the health of newborn children and teach parenting skills. Through the financial support of the New Jersey State Department of Education, residents receive HIV education and are tutored in basic academic skills, vocational skills, and job skills. Residents of the program are also prepared for their GED or helped to gain admission into the public school system or a community college.

Lisa, a 19- year-old resident with a fifteen month old son was diagnosed as being HIV-positive three years ago. Before coming to Rainbow House in April 1994, she was receiving services from a hospital in northern New Jersey. Although pleased with the services she was receiving, she came to Rainbow House for the "safe and stable" living environment it provided for her and her son. Since entering the program, Lisa reports that her health has stabilized, due to regular medical care, improved nutrition, and a decreased amount of stress. She has been able to save money, hold a part-time job, and earn her GED; she is currently taking classes at a community college. Lisa also reports that the staff and residents at Rainbow house have provided her with much-needed emotional and parenting support. She believes that her experiences at Rainbow House have given her with the skills to be self-sufficient and live independently after she leaves the program.

The major obstacles faced by Rainbow House have been the lack of neighborhood acceptance and difficulty with funding for its programs. Representatives of the organization report, "When Rainbow House first started, we had difficulty finding a neighborhood. Even though we have been open for four years, our acceptance in the neighborhood is tenuous. Neighbors do not want to see our program expand. The house was recently the brunt of vandalism, windows were broken and garbage was strewn on our front lawn. Neighborhood resistance to our program is due to a lack of education, which breeds fear."[18] Rainbow House also faces difficulty paying for older residents, since the Division of Youth and Family Services will not fund services for clients older than eighteen. Many of these clients are not prepared to live independently but have not yet been diagnosed with AIDS and are thus unable to obtain entitlements or benefits. The staff at Rainbow House seeks to provide ongoing support for HIV-positive young adults who are not yet eligible for many forms of governmental assistance.

Prototypes
4410 Sepulveda Blvd.
Culver City, CA 90230
Phone: (310) 313-5139
Fax: (310) 313-5137
Contact: Wendy Blank

Prototypes is a non-profit community-based agency founded in 1986 to develop programs which serve women and their families. Based in the Los Angeles area, this organization serves an economically disadvantaged client population, 80 percent of whom are women of color and 46 percent of whom are homeless when they first receive services. Since its inception, Prototypes has provided services for HIV-positive or at-risk women in four areas: HIV/AIDS Prevention and Education, Community Health and HIV Services, Substance Abuse Treatment, and Training/Consultation/Technical Assistance. Based upon this strategy for service delivery, the organization has developed and implemented several programs designed to meet the unique needs of women living with or affected by HIV.

The group's Women's Center provides residential, outpatient, and day treatment for women addicted to drugs or alcohol. In contrast to many other such programs, children are allowed to live in this residence with their mothers as the mothers obtain rehabilitation services. The Women's Center serves over 100 women and their children at any one time.

Since 1989, Prototypes has coordinated AIDS outreach services to educate high-risk women about HIV transmission and prevention. These services are provided to over 500 women each month by a culturally sensitive and multilingual staff of 30 street outreach workers. In June 1994, WomensLink, a program which provides support services to women living with AIDS, was opened. WomensLink currently offers case management, housing assistance, family support services, psychological counseling, and a variety of support groups. All services are available in English, Spanish, and American Sign Language. In addition, WomensLink provides its clients with child care and personal hygiene necessities. This program currently provides assistance to over 120 women and their families.

According to Wendy Blank, the Program Director of WomensLink: "The majority of women served by WomensLink are women of color. Many are or have been substance misusers. A significant number of women served have been involved in sex work, are homeless or at risk of becoming homeless, have been incarcerated, or are recent immigrants."[19] The services offered by WomensLink were augmented in April 1995, when the WomensCare project opened at Queen of Angels Hospital in Hollywood. This program offers medical care and follow-up, case management, mental health and nutritional counseling, treatment advocacy, and transportation to and from appointments at WomansCare. These services are provided in cooperation with the AIDS Healthcare Foundation, Being Alive, and the L.A. Shanti Project. Services are available in both English and Spanish.

The WomansLink and WomensCare programs were "designed to fill some of the critical gaps that we see in services addressing the needs of HIV infected women," including the limited number of medical providers who are knowledgeable about HIV in women, the lack of services which treat HIV-positive, pregnant women, and the widespread insensitivity to cultural, class, and economic barriers women face when attempting to access treatment.[20] The organization is supported by federal, state, county, and city funding, and has received additional grants from Permanent Charities, Blue Cross, Kaiser Permanente, and the McCarthy Foundation. The WomensCare program is funded through the California State Office on AIDS and the Los Angeles County AIDS Program Office.

Jasmine, a 41-year-old, African-American woman who tested positive for HIV in 1993, claims that her participation in WomensLink has had a dramatic impact upon her ability to cope with her illness. "Before WomensLink, I saw only HIV, it was my whole life. Now I see other facets of life. For the first year and a half there was a wall, this distance. WomensLink has made an extreme change in my life."[21] Prior to entering WomensLink, Jasmine received outpatient HIV services from one of Los Angeles County's Hospitals. She reports feeling "isolated and depressed" during this time and had to place her youngest daughter, age 8, in the care of her eldest, age 19. She enrolled at WomansLink after meeting an HIV-positive woman who was involved with one their 12-Step programs. Since this time, she has received case management assistance, individual therapy, housing assistance, and childcare; she has entered support and recovery groups. She was also referred to a clinic where she is able to receive her HIV and gynecological care from female practitioners who are familiar with the special needs of poor women with HIV. According to Jasmine, WomansLink "provided a safe and supportive atmosphere at the right time," which has benefited her "mentally, spiritually, and financially."[22]

Simon House

16260 Dexter Avenue
Detroit, MI 48221
Phone: (313) 863-1400
Fax: (313) 863-0218
Contact: Marge Samson

Detroit's Simon House was founded in April 1990 in response to the urgent need for "emergency residential care and transitional housing for HIV-positive women and their infected and non-infected children."[23] Simon House provides food and clothing, counseling, child care, transportation services and legal assistance to residents and their children and refers clients to appropriate medical and drug treatment services. This non-profit organization is based in a five-bedroom house which is able to accommodate up to ten people at a time. It has served over 250 women and children infected with or affected by HIV since it was opened. During 1994, Simon House was home to 35 women and 19 children. An additional 32 women and 58 children who had recently moved from Simon House into permanent housing continued to receive food, clothing, and other support services through their Continuum of Care program.

All of the families served by Simon House are homeless upon admission into the program. Residents tend to stay at Simon House for an average of 90-120 days. During this time they are prepared to make the transition into permanent housing. Clients are provided with classes on nutrition, HIV education, and parenting skills. Tutoring is available for women who are illiterate. Simon House is designed to "support, rather than replace the existing family structure" and ensure that "mothers receive the help they need to remain the primary caregivers for their children."[24] Fifty percent of their clients with children remain the primary caregiver for their children one year after entering Simon House. Simon House assists all its clients in obtaining government entitlements and benefits within 90 days. Eighty percent of the women are drug users, and these women are enrolled in a treatment program within 72 hours of entry into Simon House. Of these women, 50 percent remain drug-free after leaving Simon House for long-term housing. Through the effectiveness of these services and programs, only eight percent of clients are homeless one year after being enrolled in Simon House.

Simon House reports that its client demographics have changed drastically since 1990: "In 1990 our residents were in fairly good health, between the ages of 22 and 31, with an average of two to three children. Now they are older, between 31 and 51, have more medical problems, and are unable to care for their children. Many are admitted to Simon House directly from the hospital. The women are requiring more care and cannot live alone."[25] Along with the changing demographics of their clientele, Simon House has also faced challenges rooted in the ignorance, sexism, and racism which surround the issue of women and HIV/AIDS. Director of Development Marge Samson attributes these obstacles "to ignorance and lack of understanding of the disease itself, and, of course, the prejudice towards people who are HIV-positive."[26]

Simon House is funded by money from HUD, the Ryan White Act, HOPWA, and private foundations and donations. In 1995 they were awarded a $607,250 grant from the City of Detroit as a part of a national effort by HUD to help the homeless. This money will be used to purchase and rehabilitate a multi-unit residence which will house as many as 40 women and children at a time. This expansion of services will allow Simon House to provide its services to a greater number of people and "transition individuals and families from the chaos of crisis to the relative security of an environment where people can help each other in mutually supportive ways."[27] With these new housing facilities, the organization will be able to focus on the long-term needs of clients and help them gain the skills and access the support services necessary for high-quality independent living.

Special Audiences

75 Ferry Street
Newark, NJ 07105
Phone: (201) 465-3999
Fax: (201) 465-4326
Contact: Ellen Bay

Newark's Special Audiences was formed in 1980 to promote the use of the arts in addressing social issues. This organization began working with HIV-positive people in 1988, in response to the rapid spread of HIV in Newark and the continued absence of honest discussion about issues of sexuality and drug use in the community. By 1991, 34 percent of new AIDS cases in Newark were registered in women, the highest percentage of any city in the country. Newark also has the highest percentage of HIV-positive people under 25 in the country, reflecting the increasing prevalence of HIV among the area's teen-age populations. In addition, nearly five percent of all live births in the city are HIV-positive. Due to the growing rates of HIV infection among women and young adults in Newark, Special Audiences has helped coordinate and provide a variety of services for poor women who have or are at risk for HIV/AIDS.

In 1988, Special Audiences produced the People with AIDS Theater Workshop, operated by a group of HIV-positive actors from New York City. The success of this production led to the formation of the Teen-to-Teen program, a theater group composed of African-American and Latino teenagers who are at increased risk for HIV infection. Teen to Teen has produced an AIDS-related play for each of the past seven years, performing for high school and young adult audiences across the state. Special Audiences reports that 99 percent of their clients come from low-income backgrounds. Currently, half of the students in the program are women. In a city where only 40 percent of high school freshman graduate, 90 percent of Teen-to-Teen participants have successfully pursued higher education.

Special Audiences also sponsors the Newark AIDS Group (NAG), a coalition of self-identified HIV-positive men and women who lobby state and local organizations to ensure that people with AIDS have appropriate access to services and are not discriminated against. Half of NAG's members and most of their leaders and orga-nizers are women. Since 1994, Special Audiences has coordinated Street Smarts, the largest HIV outreach program in the state, which brings AIDS education to areas where IV drug users live or congre-gate. Outreach workers hand out male and female condoms, bilin-gual literature on HIV prevention and refer people to drug treatment centers. Street Smarts is designed, administered, and staffed by HIV-positive people, the majority of whom are in recovery programs for drug or alcohol abuse, and half of whom are women.

A 1995 pilot study of eight female participants in the Street Smarts Program found that "HIV-positive female outreach workers feel strongly that their employment supports their recovery from sub-stance abuse. It is also clear that their active recovery gives them tools that are utilized on the job, particularly significant when one realizes they are working with substance abusers on an intimate daily basis."[28] One woman reported that her employment in the Street Smarts program "helps me in my recovery because I'm around a lot of recovering addicts. It's like having a meeting without having a meeting....It's a support group and it's a network within itself."[29] The racially mixed group ranged in age from 29 to 45. Six of the women were former injection drug users, five had been incarcerated, and all eight had been physically battered as adults. All the participants had engaged in commercial sex work to support themselves for varying lengths of time. During the course of the study, three women left the Street Smarts program, due to incarceration, illness, or placement in a shelter for battered women and children. The study notes that the remaining five participants had an unusually low rate of absenteeism, reflecting "a clear need for the women to present themselves as reliable employees who do not need to be treated differently due to their HIV-status."[30] In the words of one African-American woman, "it [Street Smarts] gave me a purpose once I got this disease; it gave me a whole new outlook on life."[31]

Special Audiences reports that many of the obstacles it faces arise from the lack of communication and persistent misconceptions about AIDS in Newark's political and public discourse. They claim that people in the city still perceive AIDS as a "male disease" which must be accepted as a "chronic, manageable illness" rather than urgently fought. Furthermore, they report that there are few women in local government who are in positions to advocate for HIV-positive or at-risk women. This has created an atmosphere which is especially insensitive and unresponsive to the spread of HIV among poor women of color. Specifically, the group's staff cite the lack of centralized social services and advocacy, a poor city-wide transportation system, and the lack of day care for HIV-positive mothers as factors which make life more difficult for their women clients. Special Audiences currently receives funding from state and city health agencies, including the State Division of Alcohol, Drug Abuse, and Addiction Services, and corporate funding from the Prudential Insurance Company.

2. NON-U.S. BASED ORGANIZATIONS

Danaya So

Immeuble Sosso
B.P. E 62
Bamako Mali
Phone: 011-223-22 -3186
Fax: 001-223-22-7635

Danaya So is an NGO project which provides peer-led education and prevention services for women living with HIV/AIDS. The organization operates under the aegis of ENDA Tiers-Monde, an organization doing AIDS work in several countries in West Africa. Located in Mali's capital, Danaya So aims to provide economic alternatives and social support for sex workers and women who are trying to leave the sex industry. It is estimated that twenty to seventy-two percent of Mali's sex workers were HIV-positive in 1994. The imprecision of this figure reflects how the widespread stigmatization of HIV-positive women in Mali makes it difficult to obtain an accurate measure of seroprevalance and to implement programs for this community.

Danaya So works in solidarity with poor women to help them obtain food, basic medical care, and a safe haven from violence. Sex workers are trained as peer educators and work in groups to disseminate information about HIV transmission in areas frequented by prostitutes and their clients. They distribute condoms, provide social support, and assist women in accessing necessary health services. Danaya So also helps women develop small businesses so they are not economically dependent upon the sex industry.

The project is administered by a former-sex worker who is familiar with the risks faced by many poor women in Bamako. When Danaya So first began, she coordinated a participatory needs assessment of sex workers to better understand how HIV has impacted this population. This survey found that sex workers in Bamako were frequently harassed by pimps and police officers and lived in constant fear of abuse. Danaya So has since obtained a lawyer to ensure that the basic human rights of sex workers are not violated and women are not punished for their HIV-positive status. The organization is continuing its work to increase the visibility of HIV-positive women in Mali, so that there is a network of services and support for people affected by AIDS.

Empower Thailand

Concrete House - 2nd Floor
57/60 Tivanond Road
Nontburi 11000
Bangkok, Thailand
Phone: 001-662-526-3294
Fax: 001-662-526-3294
Contact: Noi Apisuk

Empower Thailand is an NGO which has provided social services to Bangkok's sex workers since 1983. Since 1991, their work has increasingly focused on HIV/AIDS education. Twenty-five full and part-time employees maintain direct contact with thousands of sex workers, about 40 percent of whom are HIV-positive. Additional volunteers and technical assistance are provided by International Voluntary Services, a Washington, D.C. based organization which has been active in AIDS prevention efforts in southeast Asia. Noi Apisuk, the director of Empower Thailand estimates that the organization provided HIV-preventive services to approximately 100,000 people during 1994.

Empower Thailand holds safer sex training sessions, STD detection workshops, and alternative job skills training twice per day. Over eighty women attend classes at least once a week, learning such skills as sewing, cooking, and secretarial skills. They teach English and Thai to women from the tribal hill communities of Thailand in order to help them gain employment opportunities in the hotel and restaurant industries. Classes in Dutch and German are given to about 30 sex workers a day, in order to help them negotiate safer sex with European tourists. Language classes are offered at both the social services center and in brothels where women are literally locked in. Empower Thailand has also instituted a non-formal education program which allows women to obtain an official graduation certificate of Primary and Secondary School in about one and a half years. Over 50 sex workers have enrolled as students in this program over the past two years.

In addition to these programs, Empower Thailand runs a theater group which presents plays depicting the lives of prostitutes and addresses issues regarding the negotiation of safer sex. These performances are seen by over 400 people per week. The organization distributes a newsletter which discusses health, drug abuse, and educational and employment opportunities to 4,000 sex workers each month. Empower Thailand has also developed picture-based "comic book-like publications" aimed at educating non-literate women about HIV transmission and safer sex and teaching English to women who are unable to attend language classes offered by the organization.

In 1992, Empower Thailand opened a social services center for the sex worker and injection drug using population of Chiang Mai, a northern city with Thailand's second largest sex industry and the country's highest concentration of injection drug users. The center is staffed by three full time workers and five volunteers who educate sex workers and injection drug users on methods to reduce the risk of HIV transmission. They also provide HIV-testing and counseling services for residents of Chiang Mai. This program currently has over 300 registered clients and provides over 160 women with language and job skills classes once a week. The center in Chiang Mai has opened a handcrafts shop which sells their client's embroideries, allowing these women to support themselves outside of the sex industry. The proceeds from the shop are used to fund this cooperative of women supporting themselves outside of the sex industry. Former sex workers are currently being hired to administer the Chiang Mai center.

Many of Empower Thailand's efforts have focused on educating the public about the lives of sex workers and challenging the widespread cultural acceptance of men who visit prostitutes. The organization has also been working to dissuade poverty-stricken families in rural areas from selling their children into the urban sex industry.

Members of the organization report that the spread of HIV throughout Thailand has contributed to an increase in child slaves who are sold into prostitution. An increased demand for these child prostitutes is due to the perception that younger sex workers are more likely to be disease-free. As future program initiatives, Empower Thailand plans to open additional social service centers, train additional sex workers for educational campaigns, and establish support groups for HIV-positive people.

Saheli Project

c/o: Indian Health Organization
J.J. Hospital Compound
Bombay, India 400 008

The Saheli Project (*saheli* is the Hindi term for "friend") was initiated in 1991 by Dr. I.S. Gilada, head of the Indian Health Organization. The program trains sex workers from Bombay's two major red light districts (where HIV seroprevalence rates are estimated at 50-60 percent) to be peer educators. This program currently has over 200 peer educators, 60 of whom are paid honoraria for their services. It is estimated that these women regularly reach over 5,500 sex workers in the local area. Participants in this program learn the basics of HIV transmission and AIDS prevention and spend several hours a day visiting brothels, passing out condoms, and training their peers to become AIDS educators themselves.

During the project's first year, responses from the red light community were overwhelmingly negative. Vans used as mobile health clinics were repeatedly vandalized, as madams and pimps perceived the presence of project staff as detrimental to their business. As one sex worker remarked, "In the earlier days, AIDS seemed an imaginary creation of people who were out to dismantle Bombay's sex industry. It took some time for us to believe they actually wanted to protect us."[32]

As the program began to evolve during its second year, staff members realized that it was necessary to recruit madams as peer educators, since they hold the most authority in the brothel's power structure and have an economic interest in the continuing health of their workers. The madams educate the sex workers and their clients about HIV transmission and the importance of safer sex. The Saheli Project has also developed a newsletter for sex workers, in which women write about their daily lives in the red light district and provide information on preventing the spread of AIDS.

The Saheli Project currently distributes over 130,000 condoms per week, though studies have revealed that condom usage remains fairly low, since many men are willing to pay more for unprotected sex. Mira, a prostitute in Kamathipura, notes: "For every girl who refuses to have sex without a condom, I'm sure there are ten who will. There are simply too many hungry mouths."[33] Condom use is also negatively associated with family planning and population programs, and several prostitutes reported that men will assume that sex workers are diseased if they insist on using them. The Saheli Project is continuing to develop additional programs which address these issues, in an effort to hinder the spread of AIDS between sex workers and their clients.

Women's Union of Viet Nam
39 Hang Chuoi
Hanoi, Viet Nam
Phone: 001-84-4257225
Fax: 001-84-4253143
Contact: Dr. Nguyen Kim Cuc

The Women's Union of Viet Nam established its AIDS prevention program in 1992, in collaboration with International Voluntary Services. The Women's Union is the largest NGO in Viet Nam, with eleven million members. The AIDS program primarily targets sex workers, their clients, and injection drug users. It is based in Ho Chi Minh City, home to over half of the nation's HIV-infected individuals. Despite over 1,300 documented cases of HIV in the city (as of the summer of 1995), "there is no program or plan to offer case management for persons living with HIV/AIDS. What few services are available are not integrated or coordinated....often after testing, there is very little follow-up of HIV-positive persons."[34] Approximately 14 percent of HIV infections in Viet Nam have been diagnosed in women; at least half of these women were involved in sex work. With assistance from IVS, the Women's Union provides testing services, educational outreach, and opportunities for economic development for women infected with or at risk for HIV.

During the first half of 1995, the Women's Union tested over 2,500 women for STDs, most of whom were sex workers. These examinations took place at both a centralized health clinic and in local bars and brothels. The clinic is staffed by two doctors, two nurses, and two social workers, all of whom are Vietnamese citizens. Women with STDs were provided with treatment, and all women were provided with information on HIV and family planning. In addition, 27 former sex workers were employed as peer educators. These women were paid $35 dollars a month (approximately the wage of a high school teacher) to provide condoms and AIDS-related information to prostitutes and their clients in the red-light district. In the past year, this group reached over 4,000 sex workers and distributed 37,000 condoms.

The Women's Union has established a program to increase the amount of AIDS-related information in the popular media. Viet Nam has one of the highest literacy rates in the non-industrialized world, and has many widely-read news periodicals for the general population. The organization has hired an editor and four full-time writers to publish weekly articles on the epidemic in Viet Nam, concentrating on family issues surrounding HIV infection. The Women's Union also offers vocational training and a loan program for women who wish to leave the sex industry. The average loan is $50, and 85 percent are paid back in full. More than 180 women have received these services over the past year. There are plans to expand this program with the assistance of Trickle Up, a U.S.-based NGO which specializes in this type of small enterprise development.

Zanmi Lasante

Boîte Postale 2182
Port-au-Prince, Haiti
Contact: Marie-Flore Chipps

Zanmi Lasante, a community-based organization located in Haiti's lower Central Plateau, has been a provider of health care for HIV-positive women for well over a decade. The organization supports a large clinic, a free women's health project, and community health outreach programs serving over 30 villages. Zanmi Lasante's guiding philosophy and approach to service delivery have been shaped by liberation theology and the experience of serving a squatter community of peasants who were displaced by the building of a hydroelectric dam as part of a development project during the 1950s. The organization explicitly makes a "preferential option for the poor" and recognizes the damaging effects that "development" has had on the health of the people it serves. Zanmi Lasante employs over 200 individuals, all of them Haitian, and the majority natives of the Central Plateau.

Zanmi Lasante began its HIV prevention activities in the mid-eighties as AIDS began to appear in the rural areas of Haiti. In 1988, all medical services were made free of charge for anyone with HIV disease and for children of seropositive women. The organization's prevention program was expanded significantly in 1991, when Zanmi Lasante and Partners In Health of Cambridge, Massachusetts received funds from the World AIDS Foundation to jointly inaugurate "Une Chance à Prendre" (UCAP). This project introduced HIV training programs for Haitian health workers ranging from midwives to Vodou priests. A primary goal of UCAP was to improve clinical care for those already infected with HIV and to enhance providers' abilities to quickly and accurately diagnose opportunistic infections and other complications of HIV.

UCAP projects have also been women-centered. For example, UCAP supported the efforts of a group of women to design a series of AIDS-prevention tools for other women like themselves: poor, landless, and subject to discrimination on many levels. Since most rural

Haitians do not read or write, and UCAP had funds for a video recorder and a portable generator, the women's group settled on making a video based on the life story of Jocelyne, the first woman from the area to die of AIDS. This video was named *Chache Lavi, Detwi Lavi* (literally translated as "Looking for Life, Destroying Life), an expression which is used whenever someone dies in the course of honest efforts to make a living. The educational potential of this type of narrative is evident in the words of Marie, an HIV-positive woman who worked on this video and has since died of AIDS. "We're telling this story to show how the circumstances of our lives have forced us to enter into bad situations like Jocelyne's. As poor women, we are committed to sharing what we've learned from other women like ourselves, especially those who don't have the means to create a video like this one."[35] Zanmi Lasante continues to expand its prevention efforts, recently introducing literacy and job programs to help poor women survive the oppressive social conditions which put them at increased risk for HIV infection.

Endnotes

Rebecca Wolfe, editor

INTRODUCTION

1. Sampson and Neaton, 1994, p. 1100.
2. See Selik, Chu, and Buehler, 1993.
3. Centers for Disease Control, 1996.
4. See Chapter 2 for a review of these data.
5. Ward, 1993a, p. 414.
6. A videotaped version of this exchange is available from the IHSJ.
7. Schoepf, 1993b, p. 55.
8. Lurie, Hitzen, and Lowe, 1995, p. 544.
9. Feachem, Musgrave, and Elmendorf, 1995, p. 982.

CHAPTER ONE

1. Centers for Disease Control, 1981.
2. See Oppenheimer, 1988, for a review of the ways in which data gathering was structured in the early years of the epidemic.
3. Langone, 1985, p. 52. As Paula Treichler notes of this essay, "Though more vivid and apodictic (i.e., presented as unarguable), Langone's conclusion parallels the conclusion on many scientists." See Treichler, 1988, p. 250n72.
4. For a review of these and other data, see Slutsker, Brunet, Karon *et al.*, 1992, pp. 610-614. It should be noted, however, that changing AIDS incidence was patterned among gay men, with decreases registered among white, middle-class gay men. Among poorer gay men, and gays of color, no such declines were registered. See Lemp, Hirozawa, Givertz, *et al.*, 1994; Osmond, Page, Wiley, *et al.*, 1994.
5. Cited in Treichler, 1988, p. 193. The image was epidemiologically inaccurate as far as HIV was concerned— white, yuppie couples were not those falling ill with heterosexually acquired HIV infection—but probably accurate in its depiction of which "us" concerned the editors of the magazine.
6. Fumento, 1993, p. 32. The first edition was published in 1990. The 1993 paperback edition is prefaced with unrepentant claims that heterosexual AIDS remains a myth.
7. Slutsker, Brunet, Karon *et al.*, 1992, pp. 612, 613.
8. See Selik, Chu, and Buehler, 1993. In 1991, the Centers for Disease Control reported that, in 15 U.S. cities, AIDS has become the leading cause of death among women aged 25 to 44 years.
9. Treichler, 1988, p. 193.
10. A recent editorial in the *American Journal of Public Health* would seem to support these claims, as it notes that it was only in the 1994 HIV/AIDS conference in Yokohama that women's voices were at last heard. See Stein, 1994, pp. 1887-1888.
11. See Centers for Disease Control, 1995c; Gwinn, Pappaioanou, George, *et al.*, 1991; Wasser Gwinn, and Fleming, 1993. See Chapter 2 for a more thorough review.
12. These data are taken from reports from the U.S. Centers for Disease Control and from the overview by Mann, Tarantola, and Netter, 1992, passim.
13. Global AIDS Policy Coalition, 1995.

14. United Nations Development Programme, 1992, p. 2.

15. World Health Organization, 1995a.

16. For more detail, see Pivnick, 1993, and Pivnick, Jacobson, Eric, *et al.*, 1991. The sociography of AIDS in New York is compellingly detailed in the work of Mindy and Robert Fullilove, Michael Clatts, Alisse Waterston, Samuel Friedman, Don DesJarlais, Dooley Worth, and Rodrick Wallace, among others. Their works, some of which are reviewed in Chapter 5, are cited in the bibliography.

17. For more details on the nature of HIV transmission in Haiti, see Farmer 1990, 1992, and 1995a.

18. See the fine ethnographic study by Sarthak Das, 1995, who collected the material used here. For overviews of the AIDS situation in India, see Chapter 2, and also Naik, Sarkar, Singh, *et al.*, 1991; Mathai, Prasad, Jacob, *et al.*, 1990.

19. See Hunter, 1995, p. 37.

20. Mitchell *et al.*, cited in Schneider and Stoller, 1995, p. 4.

21. Centers for Disease Control, 1995c. For a review of these data, see Lewis, 1994, p. 57.

22. Preliminary data from HERS (Paula Shuman, personal communication) suggests that 60% were African American, 17.5% Latina, and 21.5% white. Papers from the HER Study are slated for 1996 publication.

23. Wallace, 1988. See also Singer, 1994.

24. See Fullilove, 1995, p. 96, and also Fullilove, Fullilove, Haynes *et al.*, 1990. The Fulliloves draw heavily on the work of Wallace (e.g., 1988 and 1990). See also the 1990 study by McCord and Freeman, which reports that, in some groups, age-specific mortality rates are higher in Harlem than in Bangladesh. For an excellent and responsible ethnographic account of injection drug users in New York, see the above-cited work of Anitra Pivnick. For an overview of AIDS in U.S. African-American communities and public health responses, see Wilson and Pounds, 1993.

25. For an overview of the study, see Farmer, 1995a. Other studies of AIDS in Haiti are referenced in the bibliography.

26. See the review by Das, 1995.

27. See the account by Shyamala Nataraj, 1990, and also the helpful review by Priscilla Alexander, 1995.

28. Denison, 1995, p. 205.

29. Ward, 1993b, p. 61.

30. For more on structural violence, see Farmer, 1996.

31. Schoepf, 1993b, p. 57.

32. Ellerbrock, Lieb, Harrington, *et al.*, 1992, p. 1707. Italics mine.

33. The women in the HER Study have even lower per capita incomes (Shuman, personal communication).

34. On the rural-urban distribution of AIDS, see Wasser, Gwinn, and Fleming, 1993. The HER Study also suggests that geography is a far less significant determinant of AIDS risk than are many other criteria. Although results from the study have not yet been published, the women enrolled, when compared with those studied in Florida, have similar "risk profiles" and AIDS outcomes, but are all from urban settings scattered across the United States (Paula Shuman, personal communication).

35. See, for example, Miller, 1993.

36. Zierler, in press, p. 4. Zierler later humanely adds that, "These strangling forces of disenfranchisement are likely to include partners of women as well, given class and racial/ethnic distribution of women most at risk for HIV and violence. People who are violent against women may have experienced assaults against their own humanity, through racial discrimination, economic impoverishment and the social alienation that accompanies it."

37. Treichler, 1988, p. 194.

38. Treichler, 1988, p. 207. Italics mine.

39. For more about this group and about their AIDS-prevention efforts, see the "Zanmi Lasante" entry in Chapter 9.

40. Many other assessments concur: "It is worth noting that despite the portrayal of prostitute-as-vector, as of January 1989, in the United States, '... there [had] been no documented cases

of men becoming infected through contact with a specific prostitute'" (Carovano, 1991, p. 136).

41.   Ward, 1993, p. 60.

42.   Wyatt, 1995.

43.   Grover, 1988, p.30.

44.   The effects on explorations of suffering of these (witting and unwitting) obfuscations are examined in a recent essay (Farmer, 1996). For an overview on the inattention to class in U.S. health data, see Krieger and Fee, 1994; Navarro, 1990. The subject is discussed throughout Part II of *Women, Poverty, and AIDS*.

45.   Schoepf, 1993b, p. 59. For a similarly critical rereading of the literature on drug addicts in the United States, see Alisse Waterston's (1993) *Street Addicts in the Political Economy*.

46.   Epidemiologist Nancy Krieger and co-workers conclude their magisterial review of this subject with a sharp reproach: "The minimal research that simultaneously studies the health effects of racism, sexism, and social class ultimately stands as a sharp indictment of the narrow vision limiting much of the epidemiological research conducted within the United States" (see Krieger, Rowley, Herman *et al.*, 1993, p. 99).

47.   Nyamathi, Bennett, Leake *et al.*, 1993, p. 68.

48.   Nyamathi, Bennett, Leake *et al.*, 1993, p. 70.

49.   Holmes and Aral, 1991, p. 337. It should be noted that these interventions do not really square with their excellent analysis of the nature of the problem.

50.   Denison, 1995, p. 205. This phenomenon is by no means unique to AIDS. Anthropologist Alisse Waterston (1993, p. 245) has powerfully argued that street addicts, too, "have, de facto, joined hands with the larger public in believing the ideology of deviance and the myth of the defiant dope fiend. As such, their roles in social reproduction are obscured, actual resistant is subverted, and other alternatives are suppressed." See also Connors, 1995a.

51.   A recent study conducted in the state of Nebraska revealed that a single woman with two children would have to have an annual income greater than $21,887 to make ends meet— about $9,000 dollars more than the 1994 federal poverty level. "These numbers are a conservative estimate of a decent but no-frills standard of living," noted the report's author."There's no room here for savings to buy a home, pay for college or build up a nest egg for retirement— all items which have typically defined a middle-class standard of living." See "Federal Poverty Level Not Realistic," *Omaha World Herald*, October 18, 1994, p. 9.

52.   Polakow, 1995b, p. 592. Her book, *Lives on the Edge*, was recently published by the University of Chicago (Polakow, 1995a).

53.   In a moving and lucid essay, William Ryan (1971) explores the theme of blaming the victim and its significance in twentieth century American thought. As regards the blaming the victim in the context of the AIDS pandemic, see Part IV of *AIDS and Accusation* (Farmer, 1992).

54.   This project is described more fully in *Life Studies/Death Studies*, forthcoming from Common Courage Press as the next volume in this series.

55.   See "Improved STD treatment: a message of hope," *AIDS Analysis Africa* 5(5), pp. 10-11.

56.   For an overview of these studies, which come from both Europe and North America, see the recent work of Don DesJarlais and co-workers, cited in the bibliography.

57.   For examples of AIDS-related repression against sex workers, and for insights concerning the importance of organization among prostitutes, see the papers by Priscilla Alexander (1988, 1995) and Gloria Lockett (1995). It is important to underline the enormous differences in the constraints faced by sex workers in different settings. As Alexander (1995, pp. 107-113) shows, prostitutes have had an easier time organizing in Europe, North America, and Australia; the lot of women in the sex industry in poor countries has been far bleaker. Within these countries, there is also immense variation in the nature of sex work.

58.   Alexander, 1995, p. 105. See her overview of the effects of providing poor care to sex workers.

59.   There are several investigations of the underrecognition of HIV infection among poor women living in the United States. See the recent study by Schoenbaum and Webber (1993), which showed that in one Bronx emergency room serving the poor, only 11% of women were assessed for HIV risks. Other studies continue to reveal significant variation in the knowledge of AIDS

management in the United States, with the expected attendant results. See Chapters 4 and 7 for an overview.

60. Centers for Disease Control, 1995c.
61. These are unpublished and preliminary data from the HER Study. They are available from the Centers for Disease Control, and will be published in 1996.
62. An important new study by Chaisson, Keruly, and Moore suggests that if first-rate HIV care is provided to a cohort of poor persons, then "access to medical care is a more important predictor of survival" than are sex, race, and income level" (1995, p. 755). This is a remarkable claim and, if true, heartening news for physicians and other providers. It is particularly important coming from one of the groups that in 1991 reported significant race-based differences in outcomes (Easterbrook *et al.*, 1991). Again, see Chapters 4 and 7 for an overview.
63. See Nina Glick Schiller's 1993 study of this phenomenon, abstracted in Chapter 5 of this volume.
64. Das, 1995, p. 8.
65. Hollibaugh, 1995, p. 225. The essay does not cite data showing that lesbians of color account for a large number of the U.S. women living with HIV, but her comments are helpful in their clarity and candor. Other writers do underscore divisions between white and black feminists. "When it came down to it," notes Veronica Chambers, an African-American feminist, "I could not trust most white women to have my back." See Chambers, 1995, p. 25. The name of her essay is "Betrayal Feminism."
66. JeeYeun Lee, 1995, p. 211. In a recent review Nancy Krieger and Sally Zierler note that, "although women, as a group, may share experiences of being biologically female, these experiences occur in diverse gendered societies, located within a global economy, and simultaneously split, internally, by social class, race/ethnicity, and other social divisions" (Krieger and Zierler, 1995, p. 251).
67. Schoepf, 1993b, p. 70.
68. Collins, 1990, p. 10.

Chapter Two

1. See, for example, Altman's *AIDS in the Mind of America*, 1987.
2. Statistical data not attributed to another source are drawn from the following reports published by The Global AIDS Policy Coalition and the Francois-Xavier Bagnoud Center for Health and Human Rights of the Harvard School of Public Health: *Status and Trends of the HIV/AIDS Pandemic as of January 1, 1996* and *Status and Trends of the HIV/AIDS Pandemic as of January 1, 1995*. We are grateful for the assistance of colleagues there.
3. For a more comprehensive overview of this concept, see Mann, Tarantola, and Netter, 1992.
4. Mann, Tarantola, and Netter, 1992, p. 1.
5. Ickovics and Rodin, 1992.
6. Centers for Disease Control, September, 1995b.
7. Reported in Wasserheit, 1995, p. 142.
8. For an overview, see the papers by Des Jarlais and co-workers. For a report on the efficacy of needle exchange as a means of diminishing new infections among injecting drug users, see Des Jarlais, Hagan, Friedman, *et al.* 1995.
9. Hu, Fleming, Mays, *et al.*, 1994.
10. See, for example, the studies by Burke, Brundage, Bernier, *et al.*, 1987; Burke, Brundage, Goldenbaum, *et al.*, 1990; Centers for Disease Control, 1988; Cowan, Brundage, Miller, *et al.*, 1989; St. Louis, Rauch, Peterson, *et al.* 1990. A helpful 1992 review is *Searching for Women: A Literature Review on Women, HIV and AIDS in the U.S.*, produced by the University of Massachusetts, Boston, and the Multicultural AIDS Coalition, Inc., also of Boston, MA.
11. Smith, 1992, p. 85, cited in Doyal, 1995, p. 81.
12. Centers for Disease Control, 1990; Ickovics and Rodin, 1992.
13. Centers for Disease Control, 1995c, p. 83.
14. Guinan and Leviton, 1995.

15. Weniger, Limpakarnjanarat, Ungschusak, *et al.*, 1991, p. S81.
16. De Cock, Ekpini, Gnaore, *et al.*, 1994
17. Bassett and Mhloyi, 1991; Gershy-Damet, Koffi, Soro, *et al.*, 1991.
18. Bizimungu, Ntilivamundo, Tahimana, *et al.*, 1989.
19. Carovano, 1991, p. 135.
20. Fuller, 1991, p. 5.
21. Boylan and Stein, 1991.
22. Dabis in de Bruyn, Jackson, Wijermars, *et al.*, 1995, p. 5.
23. See Levine and Stein, 1994, for a discussion of the needs of orphaned HIV-negative children in six major urban centers in the United States and Puerto Rico.
24. de Bruyn, Jackson, Wijermars, *et al.*, 1995, p. 5.
25. de Bruyn, Jackson, Wijermars, *et al.*, 1995, p. 5.
26. Centers for Disease Control, 1995c, p. 83.
27. See Robinson, 1993; *The New York Times*, November 25, 1995.
28. *The New York Times*, November 25, 1995. See also Raffaelli, Squerira, Payne-Merritt, *et al.*, 1995 and Ramiro and Ramos, 1993.
29. UNICEF, 1995, p. 22.
30. Balzar, "In Africa, Families Orphaned by AIDS," *The Boston Globe*, November 23, 1995.
31. Wallace, 1988. Singer (1994) also discusses the concentrated presence of disease and difficulty in the lives of poor women and refers to HIV infection among these women as a "syndemic."
32. See Glick Schiller's (1993) excellent discussion of this underexamined topic.
33. Global AIDS Coalition, 1996.
34. World Bank, 1995, p. 160.
35. Padian, Shiboski and Jewell, 1991; European Study Group on Heterosexual Transmission of HIV, 1992; de Vincenzi, 1994; Nicolosi, Leite, Musicco *et al.*, 1994.
36. Bassett and Mhloyi, 1991, p. 146.
37. Obbo, 1989.
38. Abdool Karim, Quarraisha, Abdool Karim, *et al.*, 1995; Michal-Johnson, 1994; Schwartz, 1991.
39. For an overview of the local meanings associated with the use of condoms in the urban United States, see the papers by Pivnick (1993) and Sobo (1993); for Central Africa, see Schoepf, 1988; Schoepf, Rukarangira, Payanzo, *et al.*, 1988; and, Schoepf, 1992.
40. This was noted almost a decade ago by Dooley Worth, 1989.
41. Carovano, 1991, p. 136.
42. McBarnett, 1988, p. 55.
43. European Study Group on Heterosexual Transmission of HIV, 1992.
44. See the study by Padian, Shiboski, and Jewell (1991), which observed a 1 percent rate of transmission from females to males and a 20 percent rate of transmission from males to females in a study of 379 discordant couples in California.
45. de Bruyn, Jackson, Wijermars, *et al.*, 1995.
46. Sotoramirez, Renjifo, Mclane, *et al.*, 1996.
47. Duncan, Tibaux, Pelzer, *et al.*, 1990, discuss how first coitus before menarche can be a risk factor for acquiring sexually transmitted diseases. They note, as well, that menarche tends to occur later in females in Africa than in the West.
48. See Piot and Laga, 1989; Simonsen, Plummer, Ngugi, *et al.*, 1990; Moses, Manji, Bradley, *et al.*, 1992.
49. Laga, Manoka, Kivuvu, *et al.*, 1993.
50. Wasserheit, 1991.
51. Aral and Holmes, 1991, p. 67.
52. Fox, Williamson, Cates, *et al.*, 1995, p. 130.
53. Fox, 1995, p. 129
54. de Bruyn, Jackson, Wijermars, *et al.*, 1995.
55. Pickering and Wilkens, 1993.
56. For a discussion, see Dixon-Mueller and Wasserheit, 1991.
57. Heise and Elias, 1995, p. 933.

58.   For a more comprehensive review of women and violence, see Davies, 1994.
59.   de Bruyn, 1992, p. 250.
60.   Cited in de Bruyn, 1992, p. 255.
61.   Krieger and Margo, 1994b, p. 107.
62.   See Nicolosi, Leite, Musicco et al., 1994.
63.   Zierler, 1994b, p. 566.
64.   Carovano, 1991, p. 140.
65.   See Aral and Holmes, 1991. See also Fox, Williamson, and Cates, 1995, p. 129.
66.   United Nations Development Program, 1992, p. 4.
67.   United Nations, 1994.
68.   Zwi and Cabral, 1991, p. 1527. See also the excellent 1995 editorial by Anthony McMichael.
69.   Institute for Health and Social Justice, 1995.
70.   United Nations, 1994.
71.   United Nations, 1994.
72.   Jacobson, 1992, p. 3.
73.   Jacobson, 1991, cited in Jacobson, 1992, p. 4.
74.   Islam, 1991, cited in Jacobson, 1992, p. 5.
75.   Sabatier, 1988, pp. 15-16.
76.   Farmer, 1995a, p. 16.
77.   World Health Organization, 1995a.
78.   Anastos and Marte, 1989.
79.   Norwood, 1988, cited in Anastos and Marte, 1989, p. 7.
80.   Centers for Disease Control, 1981.
81.   Centers for Disease Control, 1981.
82.   Centers for Disease Control, 1983.
83.   Masur, cited in Oppenheimer, 1988, p. 279. See also Harris, Small, Klein, et al., 1983.
84.   Cited in Oppenheimer, 1988, p. 279; Centers for Disease Control, 1982.
85.   Boston Women's Health Book Collective, 1992, p. 327.
86.   Centers for Disease Control, 1986, pp. 757-760, 765-766.
87.   See Corea, 1992, for an account of activism around the subject of women and AIDS in the United States.
88.   Guinan and Hardy, 1987, p. 2041.
89.   Guinan and Hardy, 1987, p. 2041.
90.   Padian, Shiboski, and Jewell, 1991.
91.   Denenberg, 1990, Boston Women's Health Book Collective, 1992, p. 329.
92.   Centers for Disease Control, 1995.
93.   Wasserheit, 1995, p. 143.
94.   Guinan and Leviton, 1995.
95.   Centers for Disease Control, 1995.
96.   Kohn, Freeman, Mann, et al., eds., 1992, p. 160.
97.   Centers for Disease Control, 1995c.
98.   Amman, cited in Rogers, Mofenson and Moseley, 1995.
99.   Fuller, 1991, p. 5.
100. Rogers, Mofenson and Moseley, 1995.
101. Michaels and Levine, 1993, p. 11.
102. Levine and Stein, 1994, p. 1.
103. Levine and Stein, 1994, p. 1.
104. Schoepf, 1991a.
105. Sobo, 1995.
106. See Clumeck, Sonnet, Taelman, et al., 1984a and 1984b; Van de Perre, Rouvroy, Lepage, et al., 1984. For early work, see the articles collected by Koch-Weser and Vanderschmidt, as The Heterosexual Transmission of AIDS in Africa, 1988.
107. de Bruyn, Jackson, Wijermars, et al., 1995.
108. de Bruyn, Jackson, Wijermars, et al., 1995.

109. World Health Organization, 1995, p. 160.
110. de Zalduondo, Msamanga and Chen, 1989.
111. For an overview of "Lost Science in the Third World," see the 1995 essay by Gibbs.
112. Mann, Tarantola and Netter, 1992, p. 15.
113. Mann, Tarantola and Netter, 1992.
114. Schoepf, 1991a, 1991b.
115. Caldwell, Caldwell and Quiggin, 1989. See the discussion of this matter in Ahlberg, 1994.
116. Cited in Sabatier, 1988, p. 62.
117. For a review of these exotica and their pernicious effects, see Farmer, 1992, Schoepf, 1991a, 1991b; and Treichler, 1988.
118. Schoepf, 1992.
119. Hunt, 1989; Bassett and Mhloyi, 1994, p. 127.
120. de Zalduondo, Msamanga, and Chen, 1989; Schoepf, 1993b.
121. Wawer, (1992) notes that transportation and long distance trade play a role in HIV transmission in small towns and neighboring villages in the Rakai District, as HIV spreads from truck drivers to commercial sex workers to other local villagers.
122. de Zalduondo, Msamanga, and Chen, 1989, p. 425.
123. Nzila, Laga, Thiam, *et al.*, 1991.
124. Simonsen, Plummer, Ngugi, *et al.*, 1990.
125. Simonsen, Plummer, Ngugi, *et al.*, 1990, p. 143.
126. See, for example, D'Costa, Plummer, Bowmer, *et al.*, 1985; Simonsen, Plummer, Ngugi, *et al.*, 1990, p. 143.
127. Bwayo, Mutere, Omari *et al.*, 1991a and 1991b.
128. See also Carswell, Lloyd, and Howells, 1989; Bwayo, Mutere, Omari, *et al.*, 1991a and 1991b.
129. See Simonsen, Cameron, Gakinya, *et al.*, 1988.
130. Carovano, 1991, p. 136.
131. Simonsen, Plummer, Ngugi, *et al.*, 1990, p. 144.
132. Ngugi, Plummer, Simonsen, *et al.*, 1988.
133. N'Galy, Ryder, Kapita, *et al.*, 1988; Ryder, Nsa, Hassig, *et al.*, 1989.
134. Temmerman, Moses, Kiragu, *et al.*, 1990.
135. Temmerman, Ali, Ndinya-Achola, *et al.*, 1992.
136. Miotti, Dallabetta, Ndovi, *et al.*, 1990.
137. Rwanda Seroprevalence Study Group, 1989.
138. Bizimungu, Ntilivamunda, Thimana, *et al.*, 1989.
139. Lindan, Allen, Carael, *et al.*, 1991.
140. Allen, Lindan, Serufilira, *et al.*, 1991.
141. Bulterys, Musanganire, Chao, *et al.*, 1994.
142. Moran, 1994; O'Neil, 1995; African Rights, 1995.
143. de Bruyn, 1992, p. 253.
144. Moses, Manji, Bradley, *et al.*, 1992.
145. Lindan, Allen, Carael, *et al.*, 1991; Moses, Manji, Bradley, *et al.*, 1992.
146. Sen and Grown, 1985; Contributors to Gladwin, 1991.
147. Schoepf Rukarangira, Schoepf, *et al.*, 1988.; Schoepf and Walu, 1990; Schoepf, Walu, Russell, *et al.*, 1991.
148. World Bank, 1995.
149. Quinn, 1995, p. 93.
150. Farmer, 1995a.
151. Jochelson, Mothibeli, and Leger, 1994.
152. Jochelson, Mothibeli, and Leger, 1994, p. 141.
153. See Jochelson, Mothibeli, and Leger, 1994, p. 151
154. See Jochelson, Mothibeli, and Leger, 1994, p. 152.
155. Quinn, 1995, p. 82.
156. Quinn, 1995, p. 94.
157. Osborn, 1989, p. 126.

158. For a review of these data, see Farmer, 1990, 1992.
159. Kimball, González, and Zacarias, 1993, p. 179. The authors also state that "The male:female ratio (the most frequently used indicator of the relationship between male and female cases) for AIDS cases in the Region as a whole in 1991 is 7:1; from a low of 2:1 in the Caribbean to 13:1 in the Andean Area. A high male:female ratio is not necessarily stable, and, therefore, the number of cases in women may be expected to rise with respect to cases in men in many countries. In Peru, for example, the male:female ratio went from 7.9:1 in 1989 to 1.8:1 in 1990; the incidence rate jumped from 1.2 per million women in the prior year (13 cases reported) to 4.5 million (50 cases) in the latter. Incidence rates for males decreased slightly between 1989 and 1990, from 9.4 to 8.1, respectively."
160. In a key paper published in 1984, Guérin and coworkers from Haiti, North America, and Canada stated that "17 percent of our patients had sexual contact with [North] American tourists." See Guérin, Malebranche, Elie, et al., 1984, p. 256.
161. For reviews of this research, see Desvarieux and Pape, 1991; Farmer, 1990, 1992; Pape and Johnson, 1988.
162. Desvarieux and Pape, 1991, p. 275. For a more recent study of STDs in urban Haiti, see Behets, Desormeaux, Joseph, et al., 1995.
163. Farmer, 1995a.
164. Feilden, Allman, Montague et al., 1981, p. 4.
165. Locher, 1984, p. 329.
166. Neptune-Anglade, 1986, p. 209.
167. For an overview, see Mintz, 1964; Neptune-Anglade, 1986; Nicholls, 1985.
168. Neptune-Anglade, 1986, p. 155.
169. See, for example, the important work by Liautaud, Mellon, Denizé, et al., 1992, and Mellon, Liautaud, Pape, et al., 1995.
170. Lief, 1990, p. 36.
171. Goldstein, 1994. This author further notes that it may be especially difficult to warn women in Brazil about the growing numbers of HIV infection among women. She states: "From the perspective of a poor Brazilian woman in 1992, however, these numbers do not directly impinge upon her life. Statistically, and in her own subjective view of the world, she is more likely to die of hunger or of a poorly done abortion or other health complication before dying of AIDS. This makes the problem of education for this particular group even more difficult." (p. 219).
172. Goldstein, 1994.
173. Lurie, Hintzen, and Lowe, 1995.
174. Lurie, Hintzen, and Lowe, 1995, p. 543.
175. Lurie, Hintzen, and Lowe, 1995.
176. Global AIDS Policy Coalition, 1995.
177. Bonacci, 1992, p. 16.
178. Quinn, 1995, p. 89.
179. Vanichseni, Wongsuwan, Choopanya, et al., 1991; Choopanya, Banichseni, Des Jarlais, et al., 1991.
180. Quinn, 1995, p. 89.
181. Weniger, Limpakarnjanarat, Ungschusak, et al., 1991, p. 81.
182. Quinn, 1995, p. 90.
183. Weniger, Limpakarnjanarat, Ungschusak, et al., 1991, p. 80.
184. Weniger, Limpakarnjanarat, Ungschusak, et al., 1991, p. 81.
185. Kammerer and Symonds, 1992, p. 23; Kammerer, Hutheesing, Maneprasert, et al., 1995, p. 57.
186. Kammerer, Hutheesing, Maneeprasert et al., 1995, p. 59.
187. Bonacci, 1992, p. 17.
188. Jain, John, and Keusch, 1994a and 1994b.
189. Quinn, 1995, p. 92.
190. Jain, John, and Keusch, 1994.
191. Naik, Sarkar, Singh, et al., 1991.
192. Center for International Research, United States Bureau of the Census, cited in Quinn, 1995.

193. Mathai, Prasad, Jacob, *et al.*, 1990.
194. Quinn, 1995, p. 91.
195. Chakraborty, Jana, Das, *et al.*, 1994.
196. John, Bhushan, Babu, *et al.*, 1993.
197. See Jain, John, and Keusch, 1994b, p. S72-S73.
198. Shreedhar, 1995, pp. 2,11.
199. Xinhua, Janhua, and Qili, 1994.
200. Zheng, Tian, Choi, *et al.*, 1994.
201. Gil, 1991.
202. Xinhua, Junhua, and Qili, 1994.
203. Gil, 1994a and 1994b.
204. Tan and Dayrit, 1994.
205. Tan and Dayrit, 1994.
206. Tan and Dayrit, 1994.
207. Bonacci, 1992.
208. Bonacci, 1992, p. 93.
209. Tan and Dayrit, 1994.
210. Tan and Dayrit, 1994. The authors further stress that this "devolution" of health services combined with an increase in the number of cases of HIV seen in the Philippines could be a recipe for disaster in this country.
211. Kitamura, 1994. Miyazaki and Naemura (1994). Using the same data, Miyazaki and Naemura (1994) also note that "one of the epidemiological characteristics of HIV infection and AIDS in Japan is the rapid increase of cases of transmission through heterosexual contact since 1991" (pp. 276-277). The authors also underline the importance to the Japanese epidemic of people who emigrated to Japan from another country. Among women in Japan who are infected with HIV and less than nineteen years old, seven are Japanese and 60 are termed "foreign females." In the 20-29 year old age group, 36 of the HIV infected women are Japanese females while 365 of these women are "foreign born." The article also states that many of the foreigners are "young females from Southeast Asia, most of who were employed in the entertainment and amusement trade."
212. In fact, some researchers feel that the mistaken belief that AIDS would not spread to Asia may have led to complacency when dealing with the epidemic there. See Kaldor, Sittitrai, John, *et al.*, 1994.
213. Kaldor, Sittitrai, John, *et al.*, 1994, p. S2.
214. See Brown, Mulhall, and Sittitrai, 1994, p. S173. According to these authors, more attention needs to be paid to social factors which affect HIV transmission, particularly among women. They state that "Societal risk factors are those that affect a country's vulnerability as a whole to an HIV/AIDS epidemic and provide challenges to the implementation of prevention strategies. They include poverty, cultural and linguistic diversity, rates of economic expansion, the status of women, and rapid urbanization. These factors encourage or reinforce risk behaviors among populations and conditions that create or increase vulnerability to risk behavior. For example, poverty and the low status of women combine with the lack of educational and employment opportunities to pressure many young rural women into commercial sex."

CHAPTER THREE

1. Jacobs, 1989, p. 72.
2. Direct quotations used in this chapter come from the author's research between 1987 and 1992. These include two intervention-based ethnographic studies. The first was a two-year study of the social world of injection drug users and their adoption of AIDS prevention practices "on the street" and in a variety of drug treatment programs in Worcester, Massachusetts. The other project was a two-year, five-site National Institute on Drug Abuse ethnographic study of ethnic minority drug users and their sexual partners. Almost half of all the AIDS cases among these five ethnic groups (African Americans, Mexican Americans, Puerto Rican Americans, and Native

Americans of Arizona [Yaqui and Tohono O'odham] were linked to injection drug use when the study began in 1991.

3. Jaffe, Harold Dr. at the Centers for Disease Control, as quoted in *The Boston Globe*, January 31, 1995, p. 36.

4. *The Boston Globe*, January 26, 1994, p. 1.

5. With the feminization of AIDS, we will also see changes in access to care, the ethnic distribution of the disease, and length of survival. A recent national study of 2,500 people newly diagnosed with HIV found that nearly 60 percent did not get tested until they were already sick with an AIDS-related disease. Not surprisingly, almost half of these late diagnoses were among those infected through heterosexual sex. Given that 70 percent of those infected through unprotected sex are women, we can summize that a large percentage of delayed diagnoses are among women. Consequently, women whose lives could be improved and prolonged through early treatment are dying instead.

6. Centers for Disease Control, 1994.

7. See deGroot and Work, 1995. "Minorities are the Silent Multitude of AIDS victims in South Florida. The Cost of AIDS: No One is Immune." Sun Sentinel, Florida.

8. Centers for Disease Control, 1995a, p. 850 and 1995c, p. 82.

9. Centers for Disease Control, 1994. U.S. HIV and AIDS cases reported through June 1994. By 1994, 43 percent of Massachusetts adults diagnosed with AIDS reported injection drug use as compared to 35 percent who reported only male to male sex. (Trends in Massachusetts AIDS Cases By Risk Factor and Year of Diagnosis. Mass Dept. of Public Health 4/1/96).

10. See reference to the research of Dr. Anne deGroot in *The Boston Globe*, December 11, 1995, p. 32.

11. Centers for Disease Control, 1995c, p. 82.

12. Connors, 1992 (based on research conducted in 1987-1990); Brown, 1993.

13. In a national study conducted for the National Institute on Drug Abuse, we found that significantly more female than male IDUs (54% vs. 38% of a 225-person sample) had sexual partners who were also IDUs (Connors, Brown, Escolano, *et al.* 1992). See also Worth, 1989; Sotheran, Wenston, Des Jarlais *et al.* 1992.

14. See GAO, March 1993a. *Psychiatric News*, March 1994, p. 6; Saltus, *The Boston Globe* 1995, p. 16.

15. See the Washington D.C. pilot syringe exchange study in which 80 percent of the participants were male: (Vlahov and Brookmeyer, 1994). Boston's needle exchange participants are 76% male, according to its Public Health Dept. AIDS Bureau. One innovative program in New York City added "for women only" hours and found a dramatic increase (2% to 32% in three years) in women who reported syringe exchange as their most important source of sterile injection equipment (DesJarlais and Friedman 1990).

16. Brown, 1990; Wallace, 1976; Tucker, 1979; Sotheran, Wenston, Des Jarlais, *et al.*, 1992. See also Freeman and French, 1995 who conducted a 160-person interview series two weeks following the 12 fentanyl-related deaths from "bad dope." They found information networks for male and female IDUs in New Jersey to be distinctly different. These finding parallel Sotheran's observations. Women utilized personal networks as information sources, whereas men more often were informed through formal communication channels (TV, radio, newspapers) and through direct communication with the police.

17. Friedman, Neaigus, Jose, *et al.*, 1995.

18. Doherty, Gerfein, Monterossa, *et al.*, 1995.

19. AIDS Bureau, Massachusetts Dept. of Public Health, 1996.

20. Tortu, Beardsley, Deren, *et al.*, 1994; Wallace and Weiner, 1995; Ellerbrock, Bush, Chamberland, *et al.*, 1995; Forney, Incaidi, and Lockwood, 1992.

21. See Dr. Joyce Wallace as quoted by Goldsmith, *The New Yorker*, April 26, 1993, p. 65; Chirgwin, Dehovitz, Dillon *et al.*, 1991; Porter and Bonilla 1993; Mitchell-Lewis, Phelan, Kelly, *et al.*, 1994.

22. Connors, 1992.

23. In a number of states, women are also forced to submit to an HIV test when arrested for prostitution. Other legislation makes it a felony for sex workers to provide sexual services if they know

they are HIV-positive, even if the sexual practice is completely safe, for example manual stimulation (Leigh, 1988).

24. See Farmer and Kleinman, 1989, for a powerful discussion on AIDS and suffering.
25. Herbert, 1995, p. 116.
26. Worth, Drucker, Eric, et al., 1990
27. Goldsmith, *The New Yorker Magazine*, April 26, 1993, p. 65.
28. See Fullilove, Fullilove, Kennedy, et al., 1992.
29. National Institute of Justice and Centers for Disease Control and Prevention 1994 Update: HIV/AIDS and STDs in Correctional Facilities. See also deGroot as quoted in *The Boston Globe*, December 11, 1995, p. 32.
30. See Alegria, Vera, Freeman, et al., 1994, for details of a study finding high rates of depressive symptoms regardless of HIV status among drug-using sex workers interviewed in Puerto Rico. For further details see Fullilove, Lown, and Fullilove, 1992, and for how subcultural and community discrimination and subjugation by male drug users traumatize women, causing shame, grief, and depression.
31. There has been considerable controversy among social scientists as to whether needles are shared for the purposes of social bonding. Many have proposed that needle sharing is purely an economic necessity. Whereas others, including myself, find that while needle lending and borrowing occurs primarily as a result of limited supplies, the practice is more complex and serves multiple purposes, one of which is the need for social bonding.
32. See Brietbart, Chavkin, and Wise, 1994.
33. See Brietbart, Chavkin, and Wise, 1994.
34. General Accounting Office, HEHS 95-114 Services for Young Foster Children, 1995b.
35. General Accounting Office, HEHS 95-114 Services for Young Foster Children, 1995b.
36. Briethart, Chavkin, and Wise, 1994.
37. According to an editorial in *America* (October 28, 1995, p. 3), only after the class action litigation in 1993 did the government acknowledge that HIV-related illnesses brought on by a woman's weakened immune system —like bacterial pneumonia and cervical cancer—could qualify for disability benefits accorded Persons with AIDS.
38. See editorial, "Women, AIDS and Budget Cuts," in *America*, 1995.
39. See DesJarlais and Friedman, 1994.
40. According to Boston's director of the Center for Research Initiatives, women make up less than 10 percent of participants in AIDS clinical trials nationwide. A study by the Urban Institute on health care access and financing found that nearly one-third of non-elderly families living 100 percent below the poverty line have no health insurance coverage. Of those who do, Medicaid accounts for three-quarters of their coverage - leaving 40 percent of those living in dire poverty without any health care. In other words, there is a direct relationship between one's level of poverty and one's health care access (Winterbottom, Liska, and Obermaier, 1995). While this relationship is not surprising, it is further indication that the poorest in America receive little assistance in easing the burden of their poverty.
41. Salpingitis is an infection of the fallopian tubes.
42. Himmelstein and Woolhandler, 1994.
43. Trends in Massachusetts AIDS Cases by Risk Factor and Year of Diagnosis, Massachusetts Dept. of Public Health, 4/1/96; and "Mass AIDS rate triples that of '92: Cases outstrip projection." *The Boston Globe*, May 26, 1993.
44. Murphy, *The Boston Globe*, January 27, 1994, p. 21, and Fiscal Overview, Massachusetts Dept. of Public Health Bureau of Substance Abuse 1996.
45. Dalton goes on to say that public health officials have virtually ignored the perspective of poor and minority communities while they have taken account of other groups' needs with respect to the AIDS epidemic. It became apparent that to reach the gay community, public health officials had to view the epidemic from their perspective. He emphasizes, "today even the most control-minded health officials take care to involve the gay community in decision making, for white gay opposition to testing and for enhanced laws against discrimination." Dalton stresses that if

pressed, the public health establishment "can recognize that its targets are, in an important sense, its teachers" (1989, p. 207).

46. Even in cities where legal needle exchange programs operate, law enforcement frequently continue to arrest and charge drug users with possession of drug paraphernalia (Pelia, Singer, Himmelgreen, 1994). After nearly two years in operation, Boston's needle exchange program has claimed to refer 16 percent of eligible clients to treatment programs. Yet, only 60% actually received treatment according to the Massachusetts Dept. of Public Health AIDS Bureau.

47. See Shapiro and Greenstein, 1993.

48. GAO Testimony/T-HEHS-95-63, January 25, 1995a.

49. See Plotnick, 1993.

50. GAO Testimony/T-HEHS-95-63, January 25, 1995a.

51. See Tilly and Albelda in *Dollars and Sense* (Nov-Dec., 1994, pp. 8-11) for more on the topic of the toll of welfare reform on single mothers.

52. See Pavetti, 1993; GAO, August, 1993.

53. Recently, the governor of Massachusetts, William Weld, introduced cuts in welfare benefits available to mothers raising children out of wedlock by stating that, "children without fathers leads to violence in everyone's life" (October 12, 1995). Ironically, welfare provision remains profoundly anti-family. Laws in 29 states exclude two-parent families, no matter how poor, from receiving welfare payments or Medicaid (see Harrington, 1984).

    The walls of injustice are collapsing on women from both sides. Women neither get the support they need from public assistance nor from a stable family unit due to the increasing incarceration of men. See Tucker and Mitchell-Kerman, 1995, for further information on the trend of single parenting among African Americans in the last decade.

54. Federal Bureau of Prisons, December 1995. An important aside to the increasing size of the prison population is that as capitalism paves new roads in the privatization of the penal system, sheriffs are offered stock with profit based on full occupancy.

55. Recent statistics show that increasing numbers of inmates are, in fact three-strikers (National Institute on Justice, 1995). Three strikes can occur if the first two strikes are non-violent felonies and the third is a violent; or if the first two strikes are serious or violent and the third is a felony. What constitutes a serious felony or a violent crime is determined by state penal codes which often differ from FBI crime classification. In California, for example, a violent crime is classified as anything from murder to first degree burglary and a serious felony is anything from murder to prisoner assault on a non-inmate and robbery. The way the law is written, it is entirely possible to receive a 25 years to life sentence without commiting a violent crime. For example two robberies (considered a serious felony) and a car theft (a minor felony) would qualify as three strikes in California. One highly publicized incident in which the three strikes sentencing was imposed was the recent case of a Californian offender who stole a pizza and got life (see Greenwood, Rydell, Abrahamse, *et al.*, 1995). In 30 other states, bills similar to three strikes are under active consideration, including Massachusetts, which currently has a mandatory minimum sentencing law for drug-related crimes.

56. Many see these laws as institutional racism. The Supreme Court will soon review a racial bias claim in crack prosecution in which the last 24 prosecutions and convictions for crack possession in the state of California were all Black men (Nightline, November 18, 1995).

57. See Flint, *The Boston Globe*, October 19, 1995, p. 29.

58. Polakow, *The Nation*, May 1, 1995b, p. 592.

59. See Gifford, 1993, for discussion of public health risk discourse and its effect on human agency.

60. The victim-blaming ideology that attributes criminality to the poor is the norm, says William Ryan, author of *Blaming The Victim*. Ryan suggests that the ideology goes something like this: First that crime is prevalent among the poor. Second, the criminality of the poor is the result of social conditions that warp their character and behavior. Third, these lower class criminals make up a distinct subgroup in the population. And fourth, the purpose of police activity is to suppress and control the activities of this subgroup. Ryan goes on to say that "the real truth is that arrest, trial, and punishment of persons accused of breaking the law is very tenuously related to the enforcement of the law and the deterrence of crime, and has only a remote relationship with

any such abstract entity as justice" (1976, p. 197).

61. See Reed, 1988.
62. See Eleanor Holmes Norton, 1985. Regardless of data that show that the poor who receive government welfare are, in fact, working poor, this concept of a poor who leach strength from the nation as a whole casts the poor as both "untouchable" and certainly unreformable.
63. See Wacquant, 1993.
64. Beginning with the international modernization of poverty during the cold war, poverty became a social problem whose solution was framed in the context of "development," putting in place a whole new set of mechanisms for social control (see Escobar, 1995).
65. While there are new structures that determine the longevity of poverty in the United States, social polices have effectively maintained an underclass since slavery. In 1965, Assistant Labor Secretary Moynahan argued that "a tangle of pathology" had led to one-fourth of black marriages being dissolved, one-fourth of black babies being born illegitimate, and one-fourth of black families being headed by females. The result he called "a startling increase in welfare dependency."
66. Harrington, 1984, p. 36.
67. See The Center on Budget and Policy Priorities, 1995.
68. To make matters worse, AIDS is disproportionately affecting women at a time when Americans, we're told, are "burnt out on AIDS." For further reporting on this topic see deGroot and Work, 1995.
69. Among the exceptions is the work of Singer, Friedman and Des Jarlais, Farmer and Kim, Schoepf, Ward, Mason and Kane, and Pivnick, among others whose important contributions are reviewed in Chapter 5. Some of the best-known contributions of social science research include research methodologies such as: 1) social network analysis which has served in mapping drug users' social units as a way of identifying pivotal members of these units for targeting AIDS prevention messages; 2) promotion of the European harm reduction model, in which the welfare of injection drug users comes first, not last, in prevention planning; 3) the critique of the uses of such terms such as "subculture" and "risk groups" to describe drug users and gay men; and 4) the critique of psychological models such as the "health belief model" and the "theory of reasoned action," which are insufficient and even detrimental to preventing HIV.
70. Not included in any category of risk for HIV are transgenders who are both conscious of themselves as women and do, in fact, become women. Their socio-political vulnerabilities are very much like those of women in that they often engage in prostitution and are victims of drug abuse. One of the few HIV studies of this population found that 71 percent and 56 percent of transgender sex workers in two areas of Atlanta used crack cocaine (Elifson, Boles, and Posey, et al., 1993). A recent needs assessment for HIV prevention found that transgenders are at extremely high risk for HIV and many have already died in the Boston area (Mason, Connors, and Kammerer, 1995).
71. Singer, 1991.
72. Nyamathi, Lewis, Leake, et al, 1995 p. 171.
73. Nyamathi, Lewis, Leake, et al., 1995 p. 166.
74. Nyamathi, Lewis, Leake, et al., 1995 p. 170.
75. Nyamathi, Lewis, Leake, et al., 1995 p. 171.
76. Lewis and Watters, 1989.
77. Lewis and Watters, 1989, p. 1074.
78. Ward, Kleinman, Douglas et al., 1988.
79. Their argument goes something like this: reducing family size among the world's poor would result in fewer poor families because raising fewer children demands fewer resources. This logic is something that the poor do not seem to grasp; they continue to have children despite their poverty. Of course, this approach to alleviating poverty is myopic in at least two ways. First, the foremost problem of the world's poor is landlessness in a predominantly agrarian economy; redistribution of land to the poor will impact poverty more than restriction of family size. Second, it is only when the overwhelming distress of poverty is alleviated that choice about family size becomes a reality. From another perspective, the middle class in wealthy nations is able to perceive and act on the need to control their family size. Members of the middle class know that

the low rate of infant mortality will not threaten them with childlessness, and they actually have "experienced" cash surplus consistently enough to know that reducing family size will make a difference in their net income.

80. Lewis and Watters, 1989, p. 1075.

81. In cases where something like denial is suspected, it may be better depicted as ambivalence and ought to be seen as a normal response (rather than pathological), given the stigma surrounding AIDS and drug use (Miller and Rollnick, 1991). Ambivalence stems from uncertainty as to who should really own this disease, given the history of perceived plots to exterminate drug users and minorities. Understandably, AIDS is sometimes seen more as the property of medicine and government than as the personal problems of drug users. (see Miller and Rollnick, 1991; Connors, 1995a).

82. As anthropologist Sandra Gifford has commented, "the embodiment of risk has led to new ways of managing and disciplining the body"—other peoples' bodies, that is (1993, p. 4).

83. Connors, 1992.

84. See Farmer, 1995b.

85. Bayer, 1994.

86. Bayer, 1994, p. 895.

87. Bayer, 1989, p. 95.

88. Ankrah, Mhloyi, Manguyu, et al., 1994; Bayer, 1989; Dalton, 1989; Goldstein, 1987; Moore, Harrison and Doll, 1994 (although these authors acknowledge that denial is handled superficially and that disempowered women are most vulnerable, p. 261); Quimby, 1992; Sobo, 1993; Waterston, 1992; Worth and Rodriquez, 1987.

89. A.H. Maxwell (1988) points out that over the last few decades ethnographic inquiry with respect to the issue of poverty has explored how individuals and groups behave under externally-imposed conditions of poverty, but has failed to explain those external forces and their role in perpetuating poverty. This seems to be the case in social science research on AIDS as well. It has been three decades since social scientists Elliot Liebow (1967) and Hylan Lewis (1963) debunked the concept of culture as a useful construct for understanding class-based conditions and responses. Lewis, for example, suggests: "It is probably more fruitful to think of lower class families reacting in various ways to the fact of their position and to relative isolation, rather than to the imperatives of a lower class culture" (p. 43).

90. See Singer, 1994 for a discussion of the AIDS epidemic as a syndemic—the interrelationship of political and social factors on health. Individual behavior change becomes a less reliable measure of effective intervention when we consider the powerful forces of poverty, racism, and social isolation. In fact, there is growing evidence that decreased HIV risk-taking does not reduce one's overall risk of exposure to HIV (see Friedman, Stepherson, Woods et al., 1992, pp. 74-75). Reducing the number of sharing partners or incidents of unprotected sex may not significantly reduce infection rates if drug users' sharing circles are over 50% HIV-positive, a statistic not uncommon in low-income minority communities. Such high rates of infection are better explained and affected by addressing insufficient health care, job training, and income. Similarly, understanding the role that poverty plays in exposure to HIV can be crucial to understanding why black and Hispanic drug users continue to seroconvert at rates higher than whites, despite lower risk profiles vis-a-vis numbers of sexual partners and numbers in personal needle-sharing circles. If the effectiveness of HIV prevention continues to be measured by the amount of individual behavior change, women and minorities will continue to become disproportionately infected, despite reported positive behavior change, because the underlying determinants of risk and their causes have not been factored into prevention efforts.

91. See Connors, 1995a and Waitzkin, 1991.

92. Farmer, lecture transcript, May 1995, Department of Social Medicine, Harvard Medical School, and The Institute for Health and Social Justice, Health and Social Justice Seminar Series.

CHAPTER FOUR

1. Simon, Hu, Diaz, et al., 1995; Fife and Mode, 1992.

2. Centers for Disease Control, 1993a and 1993b; Chu and Diaz, 1993.

3. Fein, 1995; Krieger and Fee, 1994b; Navarro, 1990; Doyal, 1995.

4. Poverty as a risk factor for mortality and morbidity has been the subject of several books and articles. For reviews of this topic see *Daedalus*, volume 123, number 4, 1994, in which a series of experts review the very large literature treating this topic. For other reviews, see Hahn, Eaker, Barker, *et al.*, 1995; Kitagawa and Hauser, 1973; Krieger, Rowley, Herman, *et al.*, 1993; Najman, 1993; Pappas, 1993; Williams, 1990; Evans, Barer, and Marmor, 1994.

5. For example, Hogg, Strathdee, Craib, *et al.*, 1994, found that gay men in Vancouver who had low incomes had a 60% higher mortality rate than men with higher incomes. This difference could not be solely attributed to differential access to health care. Hoover, Rinaldo, He, *et al.*, 1995, found that higher economic status was related to longer disease-free survival after significant immunologic suppression was reached. Sha, Benson, Pottage, *et al.*, 1995, found no differential progression or survival among 82 women with HIV whom they observed. However, their sample size may have been too small to ascertain such an effect. A landmark study by Chaisson, Keruly, and Moore, 1995, also demonstrated no survival differences between people with high and people with lower incomes. However, these patients, unlike most inner-city, poor Americans, received first-class health care.

6. Weissman, Stern, and Fielding, 1991.

7. Horner, Bennett, Rodriguez, *et al.*, 1995.

8. Loue, Slymen, Morgenstern, *et al.*, 1995.

9. Sha, Benson, Pottage, *et al.*, 1995.

10. Rothenberg, Woelfel, Stoneburner, *et al.*, 1987; Freidland, Saltzman, Vileno, *et al.*, 1991; Lemp, Hirozawa, Cohen, *et al.*, 1992; Bastian, Bennett, Adams, *et al.*, 1993.

11. For reviews see Clancy and Massion, 1992; Krieger, Rowley, Hernan, *et al.*, 1993.

12. Coodley, Coodley, and Thompson, 1995.

13. Makadon and Silin, 1995.

14. Wortley, Chu, Diaz, *et al.*, 1995.

15. Allen, Serufilira, Bogaerts, *et al.*, 1992. See also Muller, Barugahare, Schwartlander, *et al.*, 1992, and Phanuphak, Muller, Sarangbin, *et al.*, 1994, for research on HIV testing programs in Uganda and Thailand, respectively. These articles discuss the impact of HIV testing on risk reduction and note that HIV testing is not widely available in either of these countries.

16. Barbacci, Repke, and Chaisson, 1991.

17. Ward, Kleinman, Douglas, *et al.*, 1988.

18. Porter and McAdam, 1994; Bloom and Murray, 1992; Leroy, Msellati, Lepage, *et al.*, 1995.

19. Her CD4 count was unusually high for an AIDS patient with diarrhea due to *Isospora belli*, although tuberculosis and pregnancy may have contributed to her net state of immunosuppression.

20. Turner, Markson, McKee, *et al.*, 1994; Moore, Hidalgo, Sugland, *et al.*, 1991; Stein, Leibman, Watchel, *et al.*, 1991.

21. Paula Schuman, personal communication.

22. Moore Hidalgo, Sugland, *et al.*, 1991; Moore, Stanton, Gopalan, *et al.*, 1994; Stein, Leibman, Watchel, *et al.*, 1991.

23. Easterbrook, Keruly, Creagh-Kirk, *et al.*, 1991; Moore, Stanto, Goplan, *et al.*, 1994.

24. Lemp, Hirozawa, Cohen, *et al.*, 1992.

25. Rothenberg, Woelfel, Stoneburner, *et al.*, 1987; Melnick, Sherer, Louis, *et al.*, 1994; Stein, Leibman, Wachtel, *et al.*, 1991.

26. Hellinger, 1993.

27. Hogan, Solomon, Bouknight, and Solomon, 1991.

28. Gloeb, Lai, Efantis, *et al.*, 1992.

29. Jaccard, Wilson, and Radecki, 1995; Coodley, Coodley, and Thompson, 1995. For an overview of this topic, see Sabatier, 1988.

30. Ryder, Batter, Nsuami, *et al.*, 1991.

31. Zierler, in press.

32. Kelly, St. Lawrence, Smith, *et al.*, 1987; Hunter and Ross, 1991.

33. For overviews of tuberculosis among the poor, see Bloom and Murray, 1992; Kearney, Warklyn, Teale, et al., 1993; and Spence, Hotchkiss, Williams, et al., 1993; for an overview of tuberculosis among minorities see Centers for Disease Control, 1993c; O'Farrell, Lau, Yognathan, et al., 1995; Rose, 1992; and Zolopa, Hahn, Gorter, et al., 1994; for an overview of human papilloma virus and women see Kharsany, Hoosen, Moodley, et al., 1993; McBarnett, 1988; Vermund and Melnick, 1995; Reeves, Rawls, and Brinton, 1989; Standaert and Meheus, 1985.
34. Hankins and Handley, 1992, p. 957.
35. For review on medical management of HIV in women, see Minkoff, DeHovitz, and Duerr, 1994, and Kelly, Holman, Rothenberg et al., 1995. Johnson and Johnstone, 1992.
36. Cotton, Finkelstein, He et al., 1993.
37. International Federation of Gynecology and Obstetrics, 1992.

CHAPTER FIVE

1. Welsh and Butorin, 1990, p. 808.
2. Boff and Boff, 1994, p. 4. Boff and Boff also note the dangers of endlessly "subdividing" poverty into different categories. When discussing the question "Who are the poor?", the Boffs note that academics "come up with so many definitions and subdivisions of poverty that any real meaning in the term is dissipated" (Boff and Boff, 1994, p. 46).
3. Schneider and Stoller, 1995b, p. 1. For another work on the perspectives of women living with AIDS, see Rudd and Taylor, 1992.
4. Esu-Williams, 1995, p. 30.
5. Esu-Williams, 1995, p. 29.
6. Hunter, 1995, pp. 32-33. Emphasis added.
7. In fact, the concept of "community" itself is difficult to define. For a review of concepts of community, see Laumann, 1995. For a discussion of the use of the term community with respect to HIV, see Clatts, 1994.
8. For reviews of HIV-risk reduction behaviors among gay men, see Lemp, Hirozawa, Givertz, et al., 1994; Ekstrand and Coates, 1990; Silvestre, Kingsley, Weham, et al., 1993.
9. See Pollak, 1988.
10. For discussions of sex as a survival strategy among the at-risk population of transgenders—particularly male-to-female transgendered people—see Mason, Connors, and Kammerer, 1995 and Elifson, Boles, Posey, et al., 1993.
11. Furthermore, legislation to protect the free speech of programs will not help if the programs themselves are underfunded or cut.
12. Ward, 1993b, p. 61.
13. This is, again, a general problem and closely related to culturally sanctioned tendencies to restrict the social field in analytic exercises. For another example of a well-intentioned book that reflects similar class biases, see Good Patients, Good Doctors: Partners in HIV Treatment, edited by Rabkin, Remien, and Wilson, 1994.
14. Mtshali, 1995, p. 167.
15. Mtshali, 1995, p. 169.
16. Bloom and Murray, 1992.
17. Mtshali, 1995, p. 166.
18. Schneider and Stoller, 1995b, p. 2.
19. Schneider and Stoller, 1995b, p. 3.
20. "I come from a poor-white-trash, working-class background, and I am a high-femme dyke passionately committed to butch and femme lives" (Hollibaugh, 1995, p. 220).
21. Hollibaugh, 1995, p. 230.
22. Hollibaugh, 1995, p. 229.
23. Fraser and Jones, 1995, p. 287.
24. Fraser and Jones, 1995, p. 290.
25. Fraser and Jones, 1995, p. 297. Paragraphing altered.
26. Rodriguez-Trias and Marte, 1995, p. 320.
27. Pies, 1995, p. 327.

28. Pies, 1995, pp. 330-331.
29. Bianco, 1995, p. 338.
30. Bianco, 1995, p. 337.
31. Denison, 1995, p. 195.
32. Denison, 1995, p. 196.
33. Denison, 1995, p. 200.
34. Denison, 1995, p. 197.
35. Denison, 1995, p. 205.
36. Denison, 1995, p. 201.
37. Denison, 1995, p. 206.
38. Alexander, 1995, p. 113.
39. Alexander, 1995, p. 99.
40. Alexander, 1995, p. 105.
41. Carovano, 1991, p. 136.
42. Alexander, 1995, p. 106.
43. Iliffe, 1987, p. 184.
44. Dirasse, cited in Iliffe, 1987, p. 185.
45. Alexander, 1995, p. 112.
46. Clearly, a gulf exists between the occasional wealthy woman who works as a prostitute (for example, the American prostitute who was the rich daughter of a rich doctor and who served a wealthy clientele in Hollywood) and poor women like Lata, was sold into sexual slavery so her family could survive. Alexander notes that in Thailand the highest HIV prevalence rates are among women in locally supported, low-income brothels. In the United States also, class differences in sex workers' HIV risk are significant. For a discussion of this topic in Brazil, see Lurie, Fernandes, Hughes, et al., 1995.
47. Lockett, 1995, p. 215.
48. See Luise White's ground breaking study of prostitution in Nairobi (1990).
49. Reback, 1995, p. 170.
50. Reback, 1995, p. 173.
51. Reback, 1995, p. 187.
52. Reback, 1995, p. 182.
53. Reback, 1995, p. 186.
54. Reback, 1995, p. 190.
55. Reback, 1995, p. 171.
56. Reback, 1995, p. 175.
57. Denison, 1995, p. 205.
58. Many of the ethnographic claims—"Like other minority youth, these women seldom discussed sex within their families" (p. 146)—are commonly heard, but are seldom bolstered by careful research. It seems unnecessarily splenetic for anthropologists to cry "foul" upon reading the author's claim that she had "immersed myself in their world for 14 weeks,"(p. 146) but it is worth saying that it is unwise to speak too much of "inability to discuss sex" and "inner fears" without experience in standard participant-observation. For most ethnographers, fieldwork is a full-time endeavor extended over many years.
59. Sosnowitz, 1995, p. 144.
60. Sosnowitz, 1995, p. 147. These exercises served, Sosnowitz further notes, to create "a place where questions about sexuality would be treated seriously." Some would draw the opposite conclusion.
61. Sosnowitz, 1995, p. 148.
62. Sosnowitz, 1995, p. 141.
63. Sosnowitz, 1995, pp. 142-143.
64. Sosnowitz, 1995, p. 149.
65. Sosnowitz, 1995, p. 153.
66. One of us (P.F.) was the lead editor of the special issue; we review its contents here with the hope of sharing the essays with a larger audience.
67. Gupta and Weiss, 1993b, p. 400.
68. Gupta and Weiss, 1993b, p. 400.

69. Gupta and Weiss, 1993b. See Table 2, p. 402.
70. Gupta and Weiss, 1993b.
71. Ward, 1993a, p. 418.
72. Ward, 1993a, p. 422.
73. Ward, 1993a, p. 424.
74. Pivnick, 1993, p. 447.
75. Pivnick, 1993, p. 442.
76. Sobo, 1993, p. 472.
77. Sobo, 1993, p. 472.
78. Farmer, Lindenbaum, and Delvecchio Good, 1993, p. 394.
79. Glick Schiller, 1993, p. 487.
80. Glick Schiller, 1993, p. 489.
81. Glick Schiller, 1993, pp. 506-507.
82. Farmer, Lindenbaum, and Delvecchio Good, 1993, p. 395.
83. Farmer, Lindenbaum, and Delvecchio Good, 1993, pp. 395-396.
84. Ward, 1993a, p. 422.
85. For a commentary on this subject as it relates to ethnographic research in general, see Asad, 1994. Asad notes that ethnographic research may ignore larger social, economic, and political forces that affect people's lives. These forces are often "conceptualized as being external to locally observable discourse and behavior or as being abstract and having little to do with the belief and conduct of people 'on the ground'" (Asad, 1994, p. 58).
86. Hollibaugh, 1995, p. 224.
87. The few international perspectives presented seem to be responses to a liberal American agenda instead of responses to the radical demands of the world's destitute.
88. In spite of the difficulties inherent in doing so, some scholars have attempted to create generic psychologies of gender and race. For example, see Jones, 1991, *Black Psychology*; Matlin, 1987, *The Psychology of Women*; Denmark and Paludi, 1993, *Psychology of Women: A Handbook of Issues and Theories*.
89. Coates, Temoshok, and Mandel, 1984, p. 1311.
90. For a review of the problems inherent in focusing only on individual agency outside of socioeconomic, political, and cultural contexts, see the 1995 Institute of Medicine report, *Assessing the Social and Behavioral Science Base for HIV/AIDS Prevention and Intervention*.
91. Batchelor, 1984, p. 1277.
92. Satcher, 1995, p. 4.
93. Institute of Medicine, 1995, p. 4.
94. "Epidemiology today, in developed countries, thus assigns a primary importance to studying interindividual variations in risk. By concentrating on these specific and presumed free-range individual behaviors, we thereby pay less attention to the underlying social-historical influences on behavioral choices, patterns, and population health" (McMichael, 1995, pp. 633-634).
95. Several researchers have pointed out some of the problems of a narrow scope of analysis in AIDS research. For example, see the Institute of Medicine report, 1995; Ewart, 1995; Fischoff, 1995; Heckathorne, 1995. Although the focus is not on AIDS research in particular, Asad, 1994, also points out the limitations of using a narrow scope of analysis in the social sciences.
96. See the Institute of Medicine report, 1995. Although not reviewed in this chapter, the volume by Laumann, Gagnon, Michael, *et al.*, 1994 entitled *The Social Organization of Sexuality: Sexual Practices in the United States* is another example of work which looks at structural conditions and HIV risk behaviors. For a bibliographic review of the literature on AIDS in anthropology, see Bolton, Lewis, and Orozco, 1991.
97. For particular problems inherent in the individualistic approach see Friedman and Wypijewska, 1995; Fullilove, 1995; Connors, 1995c.
98. Ross, 1990, p. 21.
99. See Chomsky's devastating review of Skinnerian behaviorism for a tour de force of critical, and still relevant, analysis: "The task of scientific analysis is not—as Skinner believes—to demonstrate that the conditions to which he restricts his attention fully determine human behavior, but

rather to discover whether in fact they do (or whether they are at all significant), a very different matter" (Chomsky, 1973, p. 322).

100. Hart, cited in Ross, 1990, p. 21.

101. Becker and Joseph, 1988, p. 394.

102. Becker and Joseph, 1988, p. 394.

103. Becker and Joseph, 1988, p. 394.

104. Becker and Joseph, 1988, p. 395.

105. This is problematic in that the term "community" is used and conceptualized in numerous ways. See Laumann, 1995, for a review of the various definitions and constructions of community.

106. See the Chapter 1 discussion of Ellerbrock and co-workers' study of HIV among women in "rural" Florida. Terms ranging from "inner city" to "tropical medicine" may also perform this obfuscatory function.

107. For a more thorough critique of KABP studies, see Farmer and Good, 1991.

108. Becker and Joseph, 1988, p. 403.

109. Becker and Joseph, 1988, p. 403.

110. For example, Becker and Joseph state: "The direction and magnitude of the relationship between substance use and unsafe sexuality, as well as their relationship to other potentially causal variables (such as personality predispositions), require further exploration." (p. 402; emphasis added)

111. Nyamathi, Bennett, Leake, et al., 1993.

112. Nyamathi, Bennett, Leake, et al., 1993, p.70.

113. Nyamathi, Bennett, Leake, et al., 1993, p.70.

114. For example, see Flaskerud and Thompson, 1991, which is reviewed in Chapter 7 of *Women, Poverty, and AIDS*.

115. Mak and Plum, 1991, p. 963.

116. Furthermore, the authors do not examine how or why these women became sex workers. Perhaps some of these women freely chose this career. But one has to wonder about the many women who have less than a secondary education and about the 28 percent who are foreign nationals, including the women from Africa.

117. Brown, Okako, and Brown, 1993, p. 993.

118. Wyatt, 1991, p. 37.

119. Wyatt, 1991, p. 39.

120. Wyatt, 1991, p.40.

121. Wyatt, 1991, p. 41.

122. Mays and Cochran, 1988, p. 949.

123. Mays and Cochran, 1988, p. 949.

124. Mays and Cochran, 1988, p. 950.

125. Mays and Cochran, 1988, p. 951.

126. Mays and Cochran, 1988, p. 951. And yet Cochran and Mays seem pulled back towards the "prefab" conclusions so commonly drawn in social-science research on AIDS: "The incidence of AIDS infection among Black and Latina women will continue if risk reduction education is not presented in its appropriate context—that of an interpersonal decision-making framework" (Mays and Cochran, 1988, p. 952). Similarly, the suggestion that "interventions need to be tailored to the cultural realities of the particular group in question" (Mays and Cochran, 1988, p. 952) also seems somewhat gratuitous, so long as cultural realities refer only to linguistic or stylistic matters.

127. Brown, Melchior, Reback, et al., 1994.

128. Brown, Melchior, Reback, et al., 1994, p. 87.

129. Amaro, 1995, p. 437.

130. Amaro, 1995, pp. 444-445.

131. See, for example, the Institute of Medicine report, 1995; Wallace, 1993; Fullilove, 1995; Friedman, Stepherson, Woods, et al., 1992; Ward, 1993a and 1993b.

132. Wallace and colleagues propose that actual and predicted transmission rates between "core groups" in major urban epicenters (New York, Washington, D.C., Los Angeles) and peripheral groups (particularly non-poor heterosexuals) are determined by a series of characteristically pat-

terned diffusion routes. These include *hierarchical diffusion* (spread from larger communities to subordinate or smaller places, generally through a network of transportation lines), *spatial contagion* (diffusion largely constrained to the outer limits of an already infected geographic epicenter); and *network diffusion* (spread occurring within personal and community networks which are generally of much smaller scale).

133. See also, for example, Wallace, 1988; Wallace, 1990; Wallace, 1991; Wallace, 1993; Fullilove, 1995.

134. Wallace, Fullilove, Fullilove, *et al.*, 1994, p. 1060.

135. Friedman, 1993, p. 30.

136. Friedman, Stepherson, Woods, *et al.*, 1992.

137. See also Friedman, de Jong, and Des Jarlais, 1988; Friedman, Sotheran, Abdul-Quader *et al.*, 1987; Friedman, Sufian, Curtis, *et al.*, 1992; Friedman, Sufian, and Des Jarlais, 1990.

138. Friedman, Stepherson, Woods, *et al.*, 1992, p. 84.

139. Friedman, Stepherson, Woods, *et al.*, 1992, p. 74.

140. Singer, 1994.

141. Other factors which put women at greater risk for HIV have to do with the gender inequality which exists in many relationships. For example, du Guerny and Sjöberg, 1993, discuss the role of gender relations in the spread of HIV and point out that a gender perspective could help design and implement better HIV-related policies and programs. The essay draws attention to the issue of poverty and discusses the plight of poor women in developing countries. Some examples of the difficulties encountered by poor women include: their economic dependence and subordination in the sexual division of labor. Although original data are not presented in their essay, du Guerny and Sjöberg remind us of the "triple jeopardy" facing women, who must assume, as mothers and workers, a disproportionate burden for caring with those with AIDS.

142. Worth, 1989, p. 305.

143. Des Jarlais, Friedman, and Ward, 1993.

144. The problem of underreporting among the urban poor is both classificatory, the result of inappropriate diagnostic criteria, and structural, the resulting of lack of access to medical care. The former problems have been to some extent remediated, as many of these conditions are now considered AIDS-defining. The latter problem—lack of access to medical care for the U.S. poor— is perhaps even worse at this writing.

145. For another perspective on HIV prevention among IDUs see Singer, Jia, Schensul, *et al.*, 1992.

146. Seidel, 1993, p. 176.

147. Seidel, 1993, pp. 176, 179, 180-183.

148. Seidel, 1993 p. 187. Seidel also links many barriers to HIV and AIDS prevention and care in sub-Saharan Africa to discourses on control and exclusion, including medical discourses which focus on "promiscuous people" and medico-moral discourses which view AIDS as "God's punishment."

149. Seidel, 1993, p. 187. Emphasis added.

150. For a review of this lacuna in the clinical and epidemiological literatures, see Chapters 6 and 7 of *Women, Poverty, and AIDS*.

151. Smeltzer, 1992, p. 154.

152. Ankrah, Mhloyi, Manguyu, *et al.*, 1994, p. 544.

153. Ankrah, Mhloyi, Manguyu, *et al.*, 1994, p. 543.

154. Ankrah, Mhloyi, Manguyu, *et al.*, 1994, p. 536.

155. Ankrah, Mhloyi, Manguyu, *et al.*, 1994, p. 536

156. Ankrah, Mhloyi, Manguyu, *et al.*, 1994, p. 537.

157. Ankrah, Mhloyi, Manguyu, *et al.*, 1994, p. 536.

158. Ankrah, Mhloyi, Manguyu, *et al.*, 1994, p. 541.

159. Ankrah, Mhloyi, Manguyu, *et al.*, 1994, p. 544.

160. de Bruyn, 1991.

161. The specific countries from which studies are cited includeZaïre, Senegal, Guatemala, Uganda, Belize, Brazil, Malawi, and Thailand. "From 1986 to 1991," notes de Bruyn (1991, p. 10), "the rich industrialized countries spent $850 million on AIDS programs in developing countries; the same amount was spent in the U.S. to build 90 miles of highway. The perception that too much

is being spent on AIDS in Africa, Asia, and Latin America to the detriment of our own welfare needs to be attacked with vigor."

162. de Bruyn, 1991, pp. 7-9.

163. de Bruyn, 1991, pp. 6-7.

164. "Experimental research," they continue, "was shown to be vulnerable to expectancy effects, setting effects, even paid subject effects, and as method effects proved to be so substantial that slight changes in research method produced major alterations in the patternings of one's findings" (Shweder and Fiske, 1986, pp. 4-5).

165. Clatts, 1995, p. 251.

166. Clatts, 1995, p. 247.

167. Sociologists have been less guilty of such decontextualization, which is why we have concentrated so much on our critique of anthropology and psychology. See, for example, the papers edited by Huber and Schneider in a collection titled *The Social Context of AIDS* (1992). The papers by Schneider and by Wermuth, Ham, and Robbins examine women and AIDS.

168. Ward, 1993b, p. 60.

169. Kleinman, 1986, p. 225. Although the costs, to clinical medicine, of desocialization are real, the benefits of the restricted gaze have been real, too: the individual patient, if he or she is fortunate, can claim the undivided attention of the provider.

170. Kleinman, 1986, pp. 236-237.

171. Mills, 1959, p. 5.

172. A preliminary view of the effects of these changes on popular cultures emerges from reading, for example, the recent essays by Taylor, 1991; Gitlin, 1995; Lipovetsky, 1993. See also Bernstein, 1978, and Rosaldo, 1989.

173. Clatts, 1995, p. 250.

174. Bolton, 1995, p. 292. For a more thorough critique of the Health Belief Model vis-á-vis AIDS research, see Farmer and Good, 1991.

175. Bolton, 1995, p. 293.

176. Gergen, 1986, pp. 136-137. He continues somewhat archly: "In psychoanalysis, for example, practitioners demonstrate an uncanny ability to apply a restricted descriptive vocabulary to an immense range of life patterns. Regardless of the vicissitudes of one's life, for analytic purposes, it can be characterized by a relatively narrow range of descriptors. If one turns to the psychological laboratory, one continues to find investigators capable of retaining a given theoretical account regardless of the range of data brought to bear."

177. See "New Studies Urged on Cultural Factors in Spread of AIDS," *The Chronicle of Higher Education*, June 14, 1989, p. A5.

178. Frankenberg, 1992, p. 8.

179. Brummelhuis and Herdt, 1995, p. ix.

180. Bolton, 1995, p. 293.

181. See, for example, the study by Waterston: "Cultural factors...and variation in the social context of drug taking...may be important in shaping diversity among a population ultimately compelled by larger forces toward actual or symbolic homogeneity. It is these larger forces, however, that have been largely ignored by those seeking to understand the nature of addict life on our city streets" (Waterston, 1993, p. 239).

182. Frankenberg, 1992, p. 8.

183. Clatts, 1995, p. 250.

184. Notes Carovano: "One popular anecdote is of a poor, black seropositive woman who upon being accused by her physician of making an irresponsible decision in choosing to bear a child responded: `Fifty percent is the best odds I've been given since I was diagnoses as carrying this virus'" (Cited in Carovano, 1991, p. 138). The exaggeration of agency is seen not only in writings about poor women, but in reference to many poor and otherwised marginalized persons. Writing of a teenage hustler with AIDS, Clatts (1995, p. 249) makes a similar observation: "Over and over again, Jake has been told by health care providers that in order to get help `he has to do his share'—a poignant phrase for the kind of supply-side economics that engenders poverty and homelessness. Poignant also for what it says about some of the fundamental assumptions that

underpin much of AIDS prevention practice. For clearly, and quite apart from what he might like to do, the share that Jake is able to do is quite limited."

185. Blaming the victim is an important component of the AIDS pandemic. One Republican lawmaker recently advanced the "Protection for Innocent Victims of AIDS Transmission Act," which recommends the death penalty for any individual who "knowingly transfers the human immunodeficiency virus" to another "or attempts to do so." As Horton wearily notes in *The Lancet*: "Such is the mood of the 104th Congress" (Horton, 1995, p. 531).

186. Carovano, 1991, p. 132.

187. Boff and Boff, 1994, pp. 4-5.

188. See Gregory, 1993, and Laumann, 1995, for more critical discussions of this subject. As regards critical feminism, see the collection of essays edited by Findlen, 1995.

189. See Chapters 4 and 7 for a consideration of these issues, which have been the subject of numerous studies. Note, however, that it is possible to exaggerate physicians' lack of interest in such topics. A recent editorial in *The Lancet* concluded as follows: "Creating partnerships with addicts, commercial sex workers, and the homeless; producing culturally relevant and sensitive educational materials; meeting unmet needs of food, clothing, and shelter; overcoming barriers to service provision such as lack of childcare and transportation are all part of the providers' role" (Horton, 1995, p. 532).

190. Rosaldo, 1989, p. 189.

191. Bolton, 1995, p. 299. See Farmer, 1991, and Farmer and Kim, 1991, for more extended discussions of accountability in AIDS research. See also the entry under "behavioral sciences" in the 1968 Encyclopedia of the Social Sciences, which suggests that the term itself was the result of a major disbursement of Ford Foundation funds (Berelson, 1969; see also Miller, 1955).

CHAPTER SIX

1. For a review of the epidemiology of AIDS in women, see Centers for Disease Control, 1983; Centers for Disease Control, 1990; Centers for Disease Control, 1991; Centers for Disease Control, 1995c; Chu and Wortley, 1995; Guinan and Hardy, 1987; Hankins and Handley, 1992; Ellerbrock, Bush, Chamberland, *et al.*, 1991; Willoughby, 1989; Donohue, Danello, and Kirschstein, 1989; Allen, Lee, Schulz, *et al.*, 1990; Pappaioanou, George, Hannon, *et al.*, 1990. For a discussion of the methodological problems encountered in acquiring reliable epidemiologic data on HIV and women, see Shapiro, Schultz, Dondero, 1989; Spence, 1994; Buehler, Hanson, and Chu, 1992. For a more clinical discussion of problems of case definition in women, see Schoenbaum and Weber, 1993.

2. For a discussion of the way this thinking may have shaped the current understanding of the AIDS pandemic, see Oppenheimer, 1992.

3. For studies of HIV risk behaviors in women who exchange sex for drugs, money, or both, see: Astemborski, Vlahov, Warren, *et al.*, 1994; Mak and Plum, 1991; Worth, 1989; Roper, Peterson, and Curran, 1993; Fullilove, Lown, and Fullilove, 1992; Kreiss, Koech, Plummer, *et al.*, 1986.

4. Tortu, Beardsley, Deren, *et al.*, 1994, p. 1248.

5. See, for example, Elias and Heise, 1994.

6. For a discussion of the importance of gender relations in HIV prevention, see Wingood and DiClemente, 1995; du Guerny and Sjoberg, 1993; Worth, 1989; Pivnick, 1993; Sobo, 1993; Zierler, 1994b.

7. See Choi, Catania, and Dolcini, 1994, regarding the low levels of condom use in extramarital sex; see also Leigh, Temple, and Trocki, 1993; Roper, Peterson, and Curran, 1993. Valdiserri, Arena, Proctor, *et al.*, 1989, discuss the relationship between women's attitudes toward condom use and actual condom use. Feldblum and Fortney, 1988, review the literature on condoms, spermicides and HIV transmission.

8. For example, see Worth, 1989, for one perspective on the economic and other reasons that condom promotion among "vulnerable women" may likely fail. Pivnick, 1993, and Sobo, 1993, also discuss this topic. These studies are reviewed in Chapter 5 of *Women, Poverty, and AIDS*.

9.   See Zierler 1994b; Brown, Melchior, Reback, *et al.*, 1994; Ryder, Batter, Nsuami, *et al.*, 1991; Coodley, Coodley, and Thompson, 1995; North and Rothenberg, 1993; Zierler, in press.

10. Zierler, 1994b, p. 565.

11. One study of seroprevalence and risk behaviors in a group of lesbian and bisexual women was conducted by Lemp, Jones, Kellogg, *et al.*, 1995. See also Chu, Buehler, Fleming, *et al.*, 1990, who report AIDS cases in lesbians and Hollibaugh's 1995 discussion of HIV and lesbian women.

12. See, for example, Reinisch, Sander, and Ziemba-Davis, 1987; Drotman and Mays, 1988; Leonard, 1990 as cited in Young, Weissman, and Cohen, 1992.

13. Young, Weissman, and Cohen, 1992, p. 176.

14. Young, Weissman, and Cohen, 1992, p. 180.

15. Young, Weissman, and Cohen, 1992, p. 175.

16. Soto-Ramirez, Renjifo, McLane, *et al.*, 1996, p. 1291.

17. Soto-Ramirez, Renjifo, McLane, *et al.*, 1996, p. 1291.

18. Soto-Ramirez, Renjifo, McLane, *et al.*, 1996, p. 1293.

19. Soto-Ramirez, Renjifo, McLane, *et al.*, 1996, p. 1293.

20. Soto-Ramirez, Renjifo, McLane, *et al.*, 1996, p. 1293.

21. See Novick, 1991a; Onorato, Jones, and Forrester, 1990. See also the special issue of *Public Health Reports*, volume 105 number 2, 1990, on seroprevalence surveys.

22. See Tabet, Palmer, Wiese, *et al.*, 1992; Modan, Goldschmidt, Rubinstein, *et al.*, 1992; Elifson, Boles, Posey, *et al.*, 1993; Onorato, Klaskala, Morgan, *et al.*, 1995; Rosenberg and Weiner, 1988. See also the special issue of the *American Journal of Public Health*, 78(4), 1988.

23. See Wilson, Marelich, Lemp, *et al.*, 1993.

24. See Williams, David, 1990; McCusker, Koblin, Lewis, *et al.*, 1990; Lewis, Watters, Case, 1990; Mascola, Lieb, Iwakoshi, *et al.*, 1989; Chaisson, Moss, Onishi, *et al.*, 1987; Jones, Allen, Onorato, *et al.*, 1990; Allen, Onorato, Green, *et al.*, 1992; Hartgers, van den Hoek, Krihnen, *et al.*, 1992; Watters, 1994; Rebagliato, Aviñó, Hernández-Aguado, *et al.*, 1995; Davies, Dominy, Peters, *et al.*, 1995; Lange, Snyder, Lozovsky, *et al.*, 1988. Seroconversion studies in injection drug users have also been conducted; for example, see the work of Vlahov, Muñoz, Celentano, *et al.*, 1991, and Nicolosi, Musicco, Saracco, *et al.*, 1990.

25. See Hoxie, Vergeront, Frisby, *et al.*, 1990; Andrus, Fleming, Knox, *et al.*, 1989; Glass, Hausler, Loeffelholz, *et al.*, 1988; Hankins, Gendron, Handley, *et al.*, 1994; Patel, Hutchinson, and Sienko, 1990. See Smith, Mikl, Truman, *et al.*, 1991, and Gellert, Maxwell, Higgins, *et al.*, 1993, who obtained seroprevalence estimates specifically for female prisoners. See Kebede, Pickering, McDonald, *et al.*, 1991, for seroprevalence in one prison in Ethiopia. See also Glass, Hausler, and Loeffelholz, 1988.

26. See Susser, Valencia, and Conover, 1993.

27. See Stricof, Kennedy, Nattel, *et al.*, 1991.

28. See Metler, Conway, and Stehr-Green, 1991.

29. See Garland, Gorham, Cunnion, *et al.*, 1992. Because of routine testing, specimens are readily available to document seroconversion rates in military personnel; see Renzullo, McNeil, Wann, *et al.*, 1995.

30. See Capell, Vugia, Mordaunt, *et al.*, 1992; Hoxie, Vergeront, Pfister, *et al.*, 1992; Matuszak, Panny, Patel, *et al.*, 1990.

31. See Stricof, Nattell, Novick, *et al.*, 1991; Darney, Myhra, Atkinson, *et al.*, 1989. Fehrs, Hill, Kerndt, *et al.*, 1991, obtained seroprevalence estimates for a clinic population of mostly Hispanic women.

32. See Allen, Lee, Schulz, *et al.*, 1990; Mahomed, Kasule, Makuyana, *et al.*, 1991.

33. See Pappaioanou, George, Hannon, *et al.*, 1990.

34. See Novick, Glebatis, Stricof, *et al.*, 1991.

35. See McCray, Onorato, Miller, *et al.*, 1990.

36. See Hiatt, Capell, and Ascher, 1992.

37. See Petersen and White, 1990.

38. See Petersen, Dodd, and Dondero, 1990; Eisenstaedt and Getzen, 1988.

39. See Brunswick, Aidala, Dobkin, *et al.*, 1993.

40. See Guerena-Burgueno, Benenson, and Sepulveda-Amor, 1991.

41. St. Louis, Olivo, Critchley, *et al.*, 1990. See Henry and Campbell, 1992, for a discussion of the potential efficiency of routine testing for HIV infection in hospitalized patients. See also Schwartlander, Janssen, Satten, *et al.*, 1994, for the Centers for Disease Control guidelines for designing hospital seroprevalence surveys.

42. Novick, 1991b. A study by Petersen, Calonge, Chamberland, *et al.*, 1990, used primary-care outpatients as a sentinel population.

43. Guinan and Hardy, 1987, p. 2039.

44. Kreiss, Koech, Plummer, *et al.*, 1986, p. 417.

45. Kreiss, Koech, Plummer, *et al.*, 1986, p. 415, table 1.

46. For a discussion of socioeconomic and gender barriers for commercial sex workers in reducing their HIV risk, see Karim, Karim, Soldan, *et al.*, 1995; Kammerer and Symonds, 1992; Kammerer, Hutheesing, Maneprasert, *et al.*, 1995; Jochelson, Mothibeli, and Leger, 1994. Mak and Plum, 1991, found that among a group of commercial sex workers in Belgium, a majority of the women surveyed reported that male customers often asked to pay less for sex with a condom or threatened to look elsewhere for sex if condom use was demanded by the sex worker.

47. Tortu, Beardsley, Deren, *et al.*, 1994, p. 1249.

48. Quinn, Mann, Curran, *et al.*, 1986, p. 962.

49. Quinn, Mann, Curran, *et al.*, 1986, p. 962.

50. Figueroa, Brathwaite, Morris, *et al.*, 1994, also examined trends in the HIV pandemic outside of the United States. They worked in Jamaica and found a rise in HIV seroprevalence among men and women in this country. These authors—like many others who study HIV seroprevalence—stress prevention through education and do not address societal forces that may also be contributing to the spread of HIV. Their primary call is for "targeted intervention aimed at female prostitutes and their customers, control of syphilis and other STDs, the promotion of avoiding bruising during sex, and education of sexually active persons to reduce their number of partners and to use condoms" (p. 316).

51. Treichler, 1992b, pp. 400-401.

52. Chu, Peterman, Doll, *et al.*, 1992; Ekstrand, Coates, Guydish, *et al.*, 1994; Wood, Krueger, Pearlman, *et al.*, 1993.

53. Ellerbrock, Bush, Chamberland, *et al.*, 1991, p. 2975.

54. Ellerbrock, Bush, Chamberland, *et al.*, 1991, p. 2975.

55. Centers for Disease Control, 1990.

56. Centers for Disease Control, 1990, p. 845.

57. Centers for Disease Control, 1995c, p. 83.

58. Later in 1995, the Centers for Disease Control reported on the first 500,000 AIDS cases in the United States noting that "the disproportionate impact of the epidemic among racial/ethnic minorities is reflected by rates of reported AIDS cases that are six and three times higher for blacks and Hispanics, respectively, than for whites." (1995a, p. 852). Once again, data on socioeconomic status are not included in the report.

59. For a more recent study on the distribution of HIV in urban centers in the United States, see Holmberg, 1996.

60. See, for example, Butz, Hutton, and Larson, 1991; Goedert and Cote, 1994; *Public Health Reports*, 1994, volume 109, number 5, p. 718; Chorba, Holman, and Evatt, 1993; Boylan and Stein, 1991. Vertical transmission is one way for a mother to pass HIV to her child. There is also the possibility of infection during breastfeeding. The dilemma regarding breastfeeding and subsequent risk to the child is discussed in Heymann, 1990. See also Nagelkerke, Moses, Embree, *et al.*, 1995; Hu, Heyward, Byers, *et al.*, 1992; Datta, Embree, Kreiss, *et al.*, 1994; Palasanthiran, Ziegler, Stewart, *et al.*, 1993; Del Fante, Jenniskens, Lush, *et al.*, 1993; Cutting, 1994; WHO/UNICEF, 1992, as reported in the *Weekly Epidemiological Record*, volume 67, number 24, pp. 177-179.

61. Halsey, Boulos, Holt, *et al.*, 1990, p. 2088.

62. See also Boulos, Halsey, Holt, *et al.*, 1990. Butz, Hutton, and Larson, 1991, described the impact of maternal seropositivity on the growth and immune state of the child; De Cock, Fernande,

Adjorlolo, *et al.*, 1994, described the impact of maternal infection on child survival in Côte d'Ivoire; and Morse, Lessner, Medvesky, *et al.*, 1991, described an association between HIV infection in the newborn and low birthweight, maternal drug use, lower maternal education, and race/ethnicity. See also Kuhn, Stein, Thomas, *et al.*, 1994, and Dunn, Newell, Mayaux, *et al.*, 1994. See Boylan and Stein, 1991, who review the epidemiology of vertical transmission of HIV. Mayaux, Blanche, Rouzioux, *et al.*, 1995, recently published a seven-year follow-up study of vertical transmission of HIV.

63. In a later study (1992), Halsey, Coberly, Holt, *et al.*, focus on the risk factor of smoking in an article called "Sexual Behavior, Smoking, and HIV-1 Infection in Haitian Women."

64. See Chapter 2 of *Women, Poverty, and AIDS* for a discussion of this   phenomenon.

65. Chin, 1990, p. 222.

66. Krieger and Fee, 1994a, p. 275; Krieger and Fee, 1994b; Krieger, Rowley, Herman, *et al.*, 1993; Navarro, 1990.

67. For studies which review the data on differential survival, see Rothenberg, Woelfel, Stoneburner, *et al.*, 1987; Bastian, Bennett, Adams, *et al.*, 1993; Easterbrook, Keruly, Creagh-Kirk, *et al.*, 1991; Chaisson, Keruly, and Moore, 1995; Moore, Stanton, Gopalan, *et al.*, 1994; Curtis and Patrick, 1993.

68. See also Wasser, Gwinn, and Fleming, 1993. For a compelling memoir treating this subject, see Verghese, 1994.

69. See Rumley and Esinhart, 1993, pp. 517, 519, 520.

70. See Johnstone, Hamilton, and Gore, 1992, who described apparently premorbid low socioeconomic characteristics of pregnant women infected with HIV.

71. Chitwood, Griffin, Comerford, *et al.*, 1995; Booth, Watters, and Chitwood, 1993; Siegal, Carlson, Falck, *et al.*, 1995 examined risk factors among IDUs in Ohio; McElrath, Chitwood, Griffin, *et al.*, 1994 looked at consistency in self-reported behaviors of injection drug users; Diaz, Chu, Byers, *et al.*, 1994 examined the types of drugs that were used; Schilling, el-Bassel, Ivanoff, *et al.*, 1994, focused on incarcerated female injection drug users.

72. Elifson, Boles, and Sweat, 1993; Mak and Plum, 1991; Modan, Goldschmidt, Rubinstein, *et al.*, 1992; Jana, Chakraborty, Das, *et al.*, 1995; Kreiss, Koech, Plummer, *et al.*, 1986; Nzila, Laga, Thiam, *et al.*, 1991; Rosenberg and Weiner, 1988; Simonsen, Plummer, Ngugi, *et al.*, 1990; Greaves, 1989.

73. Penkower , Dew, Kingsley, *et al.*, 1991; Kelly, St. Lawrence, Brasfield, *et al.*, 1990; McCusker, Stoddard, Mayer, *et al.*, 1988 looked at risk behaviors among gay men in Boston; Darrow, Echenberg, Jaffe *et al.*, 1987; Rotheram-Borus, Reid, and Rosario, 1994 focused on factors mediating change in behavioral risk factors among gay and bisexual adolescents; Ekstrand and Coates, 1990, examined the maintenance of safer sex behavior in men having sex with men.

74. Walter, Vaughan, Gladis, *et al.*, 1992; Hingson, Strunin, Grady, *et al.*, 1991; Holtzman, Anderson, Kann, *et al.*, 1991; Smith, McGraw, Crawford, *et al.*, 1993; Main, Iverson, and McGloin, 1994; Astone, 1996.

75. Slonim-Nevo, 1992.

76. Rotheram-Borus and Koopman, 1991.

77. Lebow, O'Connell, Oddleifson, *et al.*, 1995.

78. Sikkema, Koob, Cargill, *et al.*, 1995; Nyamathi, Lewis, and Leake, 1995.

79. el-Bassel and Schilling, 1991.

80. Catania, Binson, Dolcini, *et al.*, 1995, focused on changes in risk factors among heterosexual adults in U.S. 1990-1992; Melnick, Jeffery, Burke, *et al.*, 1993; Mayer and Anderson, 1995; Aral, 1993.

81. McMichael, 1995, p. 633.

82. See also the more recent study by Nyamathi, Lewis, Leake *et al.*, 1995, which is discussed in Chapter 3.

83. See Mason and Kane, 1992 and Mason, Connors, and Kammerer, 1995 for the argument that risk group categories need to be dismantled if we are to reach all those at risk for HIV infection and transmission.

84. Kleyn, Simpson, and Wood, 1990., p. 174.

85. Waldorf, 1973

86. Waldorf, 1973.

87. Kleyn, Simpson, and Wood, 1990, p. 174.

88. Rumley and Esinhart, 1993; Connors, 1992; Pivnick, Jacobson, Eric, *et al.* 1991. See Fullilove, Lown and Fullilove, 1992 for an account of the stigmatization and marginalization experienced by female crack users. See Chapter 3 of *Women, Poverty, and AIDS* for documentation of women's exclusion from drug treatment.

89. That an individual's agency to share or not share needles is constrained by economic conditions is supported by the work of Mandell, Vlahov, Latkin, *et al.*, 1994. See also another discussion of barriers poor women face to needle cleaning as well as to condom use in Nyamathi, Lewis, Leake, *et al.*, 1995.

90. Kaplan, Knoshnood, Heimer, 1994, p.1993.

91. A GAO evaluation of the New Haven forecasting model, based on expert consultant review, found the model to be technically sound. The GAO also reviewed published data of nine projects nationwide and found that their existence did not increase drug use or injection frequency. Seven of these programs reported success in reaching out to IDUs and referring them to treatment. At the time of the report, there were 32 needle-exchange programs in operation in the United States of which 15 were legally sanctioned by state or city government. No federal money may be used to fund needle-exchange programs (GAO, 1993a, p.60.)

92. Centers for Disease Control, 1995c.

93. Brown and Primm, 1986, p. 654.

94. Brown and Primm, 1986, p. 654.

95. Brown and Primm, 1986, p. 655.

96. Shayne and Kaplan, 1991, p. 33.

97. Shayne and Kaplan, 1991, p. 27.

98. Similarly, Kelly, Murphy, Washington, *et al.*, 1994, conclude that it is possible to achieve "behavior change" in poor women by targeted interventions in primary health clinics serving "low income and high risk" patients. Other studies focus on education and behavior change in this group of women as well. See, for example, Flaskerud and Thompson, 1991; Nyamathi, Bennett, Leake, *et al.*, 1993; Nyamathi, Bennett, Leake, *et al.*, 1995.

99. Shayne and Kaplan, 1991, p. 33.

100. White, 1990.

101. Becker and Joseph, 1988; van Haastrecht, van den Hoek, Bardoux, *et al.*, 1991; Calsyn, Meinecke, Saxon, *et al.*, 1992; McCusker, Stoddard, Zapka, *et al.*, 1992; Wenger, Linn, Epstein, *et al.*, 1991; Celentano, Vlahov, Cohn, *et al.*, 1991; van den Hoek, van Haastrecht, and Coutinho, 1989; Des Jarlais, Friedman, and Ward, 1993; Des Jarlais, Choopanya, Vanichseni, *et al.*, 1994; van Ameijden, van den Hoek, and Coutinho, 1994; McCusker, Stoddard, Zapka, *et al.*, 1993; Dengelegi, Weber, and Torqato, 1990; Magura, Grossman, Lipton, *et al.*, 1989. See Schilling, el-Bassel, Schinke, *et al.*, 1991, for a discussion of a behavior-change intervention targeted particularly at female IDU attending a methadone clinic.

102. For a review of the effectiveness of high school-based prevention programs, see Kirby, Short, Collins, *et al.*, 1994. See also the study by Jemmott, Jemmott, and Fong, 1992, which focused on black male adolescents.

103. See Flaskerud and Nyamathi, 1990, for an example of one education program that targeted poor women.

104. See the study by Marin, 1989, for one attempt at elaborating this type of culture-based solution. See also Wyatt, 1991; Reback, 1995; Sosnowitz, 1995.

105. There are a few public health studies that have attempted to examine the social dynamics of HIV transmission. For example, a seroprevalence study by Wasser, Gwinn, and Fleming (1993) has shown that 88 percent of HIV-positive women giving birth in the United States come from only eight states. Des Jarlais, Padian, and Winkelstein (1994) show that, in the states of New Jersey and Philadelphia, zip code and census track data reveal that AIDS cases are clustered in neighborhoods with high levels of poverty and poor access to medical care.

106. Susser and Susser, 1996a, p. 668.

107. See Chirgwin, DeHovitz, Dillon, *et al.*, 1991, who identified an independent correlation between HIV infection and crack use, as well as between HIV infection and genital ulcer disease.
108. Fullilove, Lown, and Fullilove, 1992, p. 278.
109. See Zierler, Feingold, Laufer, *et al.*, 1991, who found that childhood sexual abuse is associated with increased prevalence of HIV infection. See also Rosenfeld and Lewis, 1993.
110. See also Potts, 1994; Gollub and Stein, 1993; Cates, Steward, and Trussell, 1992; Rosenberg and Gollub, 1992; Farr, Gabelnick, Sturgen, *et al.*, 1994; Stein and Saez, 1995.
111. Elias and Heise, 1994, p. 2.
112. Elias and Heise, 1994, p. 4.
113. See also Rothenberg and Paskey, 1995; Brown, Melchior, Reback, *et al.*, 1994; North and Rothenberg, 1993, for discussions of the issue of the risk for women of domestic violence subsequent to partner notification.
114. Eversley, Newstetter, Avins, *et al.* 1993, p. 95.
115. This subject is more fully explored in the final two chapters of this book.
116. Holtgrave, Qualls, Curran, *et al.*, 1995, p.137.
117. Holtgrave, Qualls, Curran, *et al.*, 1995, p. 135.
118. Krieger, Rowley, Herman, *et al.*, 1993; Krieger and Fee, 1994a.
119. For a commentaries on this subject, see Susser and Susser, 1996a and 1996b; Pearce, 1996; McMichael, 1995; Krieger, 1994c; Oppenheimer, 1992.
120. Halsey, Coberly, Holt, *et al.*, 1992, p. 2065.
121. Similar causal links were made about smoking and HPV infection but were not supported by research. See, for example, Cannistra and Niloff, 1996; Zazove, Reed, Gregoire, *et al.*, 1993; Winkelstein, 1990.
122. McMichael, 1995, p. 633-634. Pearce (1996) also adds to the possible reasons why social factors may be ignored in epidemiology by noting that: "In most countries, the main sources of funding [for research] are government or voluntary agencies that have little interest in, or sympathy for, studies of socioeconomic factors and health." (p. 679).
123. Kreiss, Koech, Plummer, *et al.*, 1986, p. 417.
124. Susser and Susser, 1996a and 1996b; Pearce, 1996; McMichael, 1995; Krieger, 1994c.
125. Pearce, 1996, p. 679.
126. Pearce, 1996, p. 679.
127. Pearce, 1996, p. 679.
128. McMichael, 1995, p. 634.

CHAPTER SEVEN

1. Krieger and Fee, 1994a, p. 275.
2. Minkoff and DeHovitz, 1991.
3. Hankins and Handley, 1992.
4. Spence, 1994.
5. Korn and Landers, 1995.
6. Maiman, Fruchter, Serur, *et al.*, 1990.
7. Wright, Ellerbrock, Chaisson, *et al.*, 1994.
8. Brabin, 1985.
9. Berrebi, Kobuch, Puel, *et al.*, 1990.
10. Alger, Farley, Robinson, *et al.*, 1993.
11. Lindan, Allen, Serufilira, *et al.*, 1992.
12. Lindan, Allen, Serufilira, *et al.*, 1992.
13. Fahey, Taylor, Detels, *et al.*, 1990.
14. Saksela, Stevens, Rubenstein, *et al.*, 1995.
15. Rothenberg, Woelfel, Stoneburner, *et al.*, 1987.
16. Friedland, Saltzman, Vileno, *et al.*, 1991.
17. Lemp, Hirozawa, Cohen, *et al.*, 1992.

18. Lemp, Hirozawa, Cohen, *et al.*, 1992, p. 74.
19. Turner, Markson, McKee, *et al.*, 1994.
20. Bastian, Bennett, Adams, *et al.*, 1993.
21. Easterbrook, Keruly, Creagh-Kirk, *et al.*, 1991, p. 2718.
22. Easterbrook, Keruly, Creagh-Kirk, *et al.*, 1991.
23. Moore, Hidalgo, Sugland, *et al.*, 1991, p. 1416.
24. Melnick, Sherer, Louis, *et al.*, 1994.
25. Hogg, Strathdee, Craib, *et al.*, 1994.
26. Chaisson, Keruly, and Moore, 1995.
27. Chaisson, Keruly, and Moore, 1995, p. 754.
28. Schneider, Hoepelman, Eeftinck Schattenkerk, *et al.*, 1992.
29. Sperling and Stratton, 1992.
30. Sperling and Stratton, 1992.
31. Nightingale, Cameron, Gordon, *et al.*, 1993.
32. Pape, Jean, Ho, *et al.*, 1993.
33. Gallant, Moore, and Chaisson, 1994.
34. Bartlett, 1994.
35. Fischl, Richman, Grieco, *et al.*, 1987.
36. Volberding, Lagakos, Koch, *et al.*, 1990.
37. Lenderking, Gelber, Cotton, *et al.*, 1994.
38. Volberding, Lagakos, Grimes, *et al.*, 1995.
39. Kinloch de Loes, Hirscel, Hoen, *et al.*, 1995.
40. Hamilton, Hartigan, Simberkoff, *et al.*, 1992, p. 442.
41. Lagakos, Fischl, Stein, *et al.*, 1991.
42. Cotton, Finkelstein, He, *et al.*, 1993.
43. Stein, Piette, Mor, *et al.*, 1991.
44. See Chaisson, Keruly, and Moore, 1995.
45. Connor, Sperling, Gelber, *et al.*, 1994.
46. Kreiss, Ngugi, Holmes, *et al.*, 1992.
47. Ickovics, Morrill, Beren, *et al.*, 1994.
48. Ickovics, Morrill, Beren, *et al.*, 1994, p. 448.
49. Flaskerud and Thompson, 1991.
50. Ferguson, Stapleton, and Helms, 1991.
51. Schoenbaum and Weber, 1993.
52. Minkoff, DeHovitz, and Duerr, 1995.
53. Chu and Wortley, 1995, p. 9.
54. Minkoff, DeHovitz, and Duerr, 1995, p. ix.
55. Minkoff, DeHovitz, and Duerr, 1995.
56. Novello, 1995, p xii.
57. Kelly, 1995, p. 279.
58. Sherr, 1995, p. 107.

CHAPTER EIGHT

1. Ward, 1993b, p. 61.
2. *U.S. News and World Report*, July 18, 1994, cited in *POZ*, 1994/95, p. 80.
3. Maslanka, Lee, and Freudenberg, 1995, pp. 121-126.
4. I'd like to thank Paul Farmer, Margaret Connors, Janie Simmons, Joyce Millen, Susan Larrabee, Sarthak Das, Julie Marston, Ellen Miller-Mack, Shelia Davis, Brooke Schoepf, Mark Bonacci, Vinh-Kim Nguyen, Stacey Shoemaker, Patricia Symonds, Elizabeth Joglar, and all others who have provided me with the guidance, information, and inspiration to make this chapter possible.
5. Glick-Schiller, 1993, pp. 488-489.
6. I'm especially indebted to Susan Larrabee for sharing Maria's story with me. "Maria" is a pseudonym from Larrabee, personal interview, October 9, 1995.

7.   Julie Marston, personal interview, January 10, 1996.
8.   Julie Marston, personal interview, January 10, 1996.
9.   Ellen Miller-Mack, personal communication, December 7, 1995.
10.   Julie Marston, personal communication, December 7, 1995.
11.   Kim Atkins, personal communication, September 11, 1995.
12.   Maslanka, Lee, and Freudenberg, 1995, pp. 121-126.
13.   Farmer, Lindenbaum, and DelVecchio Good, 1993, p. 388.
14.   *Facing the Challenges of HIV/AIDS/STDs: A Gender-Based Response*, World Health Organization, 1995b.
15.   Vinh-Kim Nguyen, personal communication, January 27, 1996.
16.   Bonacci, 1992, p. 71.
17.   Robinson, 1993, p. 494.
18.   Nanda, 1986, pp. 35-54.
19.   Shreedhar, 1995, p. 11.
20.   Vinh-Kim Nguyen and Stacey Shoemaker, personal communication, January 18, 1996.
21.   Patricia Symonds, personal communication, February 16, 1996. For more on this subject see Kammerer and Symonds, 1992.
22.   Patricia Symonds, personal communication, February 16, 1996.
23.   Freire, 1970, p. 29.

Chapter Nine

1.   *Community Family Planning Council Special Annual Report 1992-1993*, "Not Just Birth Control."
2.   *Community Family Planning Council Special Annual Report 1992-1993*, "Not Just Birth Control."
3.   *Community Family Planning Council Special Annual Report 1992-1993*, "Not Just Birth Control."
4.   Kim Atkins, personal communication, September 6, 1995.
5 .   Kim Atkins, personal communication, September 6, 1995.
6.   Kim Atkins, personal communication, September 6, 1995.
7.   Julie Marston, personal communication, December 7, 1995.
8.   Julie Marston, personal communication, December 7, 1995.
9.   Julie Marston, personal communication, December 7, 1995.
10.   Debbie Scott-Young, personal communication, August 30, 1995.
11.   Colleen Gillespie, personal communication, August 9, 1995.
12.   Colleen Gillespie, personal communication, August 9, 1995.
13.   Colleen Gillespie, personal communication, August 9, 1995.
14.   Irma Azize, personal communication, May 3, 1995.
15.   Juanita Ruano, personal communication, July 28, 1995.
16.   Juanita Ruano, personal communication, July 28, 1995.
17.   Mary Inzana, personal communication, August 28, 1995.
18.   Mary Inzana, personal communication, August 28, 1995.
19.   Wendy Blank, personal communication, September 7, 1995.
20.   Wendy Blank, personal communication, September 7, 1995.
21.   Wendy Blank, personal communication, September 7, 1995.
22.   Wendy Blank, personal communication, September 7, 1995.
23.   Marge Samson, personal communication, August 17, 1995.
24.   Marge Samson, personal communication, August 17, 1995.
25.   Marge Samson, personal communication, August 17, 1995.
26.   Marge Samson, personal communication, August 17, 1995.
27.   Marge Samson, personal communication, August 17, 1995.
28.   Ellen Bay, personal communication, August 30, 1995.
29.   Ellen Bay, personal communication, August 30, 1995.
30.   Ellen Bay, personal communication, August 30, 1995.
31.   Ellen Bay, personal communication, August 30, 1995.
32.   Sarthak Das, personal communication, October 3, 1995.

33.   Sarthak Das, personal communication, October 3, 1995.
34.   *Summer, 1995 Viet Nam Field Visit Report*, International Voluntary Services.
35.   Paul Farmer, personal communication, January 26, 1996.

Glossary

acid-fast bacilli	bacteria that retain a special dye when washed with powerful solvents; the most important of these bacilli is *Mycobaterium tuberculosis*, the agent that causes tuberculosis
acute retroviral syndrome	a mononucleosis-like illness (characterized by fever, sweats, muscle aches, sore throat, rash, headache, and swollen lymph nodes) may occur between one and six weeks after infection with HIV
aerosolized pentamidine	inhaled medication to prevent the development of *Pneumocystis carinii* pneumonia
afebrile	without a fever
agency	the capacity, condition, or state of acting or exerting power; the ability to make choices
AIDS	acquired immunodeficiency syndrome: HIV infection with a case-defining illness (such as Kaposi's sarcoma, or PCP) or a CD4 count of less than $200/\text{mm}^3$
amenorrhea	absence of menstruation for at least six months; can occur with weight loss or a chronic illness
anergic	diminished reactivity of the immune system to specific antigens as determined by a skin test

antiretroviral therapy	medications that inhibit the proliferation of HIV, e.g., AZT (zidovudine), ddI, ddC
apex	uppermost part, as in the apex of the lung
ARC	AIDS-related complex: a term previously used to describe HIV-related symptoms such as recurrent fevers, weight loss, or swollen lymph nodes
aspiration	accidental passage of mouth secretions into the lungs rather than into the stomach; can cause pneumonia
AZT	also called zidovudine or ZDV; first antiretroviral used to treat HIV; inhibits viral reverse transcriptase, an enzyme that permits HIV to replicate itself
bacillus	a rod-shaped bacterium; plural, bacilli
bacteremia	the presence of bacteria in the blood; usually a sign of severe infection
bacterium	microscopic organisms that can cause infection in humans
BAL	see bronchoalveolar lavage
boarder babies	infants abandoned at birth by mother or parents and cared for by hospital staff; increasingly, such children are HIV-infected
bronchoalveolar lavage (BAL)	a procedure in which a segment of the lung is washed with fluid, which is then collected and examined; usually done to diagnose suspected infections such as PCP
bronchodilators	medications which relax the muscles lining the airways; used in asthma and other conditions characterized by airway constriction
bronchoscopy	a procedure in which a small, flexible tube containing a light and a fiberoptic camera is advanced into the lungs; performed to collect specimens for diagnosing infections or malignancies

candidiasis	infection by the yeast *Candida*, most commonly found in the mouth; may herald an immunocompromised state
case-control study	an epidemiological study in which persons diagnosed as having a disease (cases) are compared with persons who do not (controls) in order to determine if a particular exposure is associated with the disease
cavitary lesions	hollow, abnormal areas in the lung which, when seen on chest radiographs (X-rays), may suggest infection with tuberculosis
CDC	Centers for Disease Control: an agency of the U.S. federal government that offers guidelines on public health issues, including HIV. The CDC is the nation's prevention agency
CD4 count	the count of CD4 lymphocytes in a person's blood, used as a marker for following HIV progression
CD4 lymphocytes	white blood cells critical in the body's defense against infections; HIV infects and destroys these lymphocytes and gradually depleting their numbers and resulting in a weakened immune system
cervical dysplasia	cellular abnormalities on the cervix, typically screened for by a Pap smear; more common among women with HIV
chancroid	a sexually transmitted disease that results in painful genital ulcers
CIN	cervical intraepithelial neoplasia: abnormalities in cervical cells, detected by Pap smears, that are early stages of cervical cancer
cohort study	an epidemiological study in which a group of individuals with a certain exposure and a group without that exposure are monitored for the development of a specific outcome or disease
co-infection	the presence of two or more infections at one time
cross-sectional study	a study where exposure and disease status are assessed simultaneously among persons in a well-defined population

cytomegaloviral pneumonia	lung infection with cytomegalovirus
cytomegalovirus	also known as CMV; a virus that may cause a mononucleosis-like syndrome in healthy people; in people with AIDS, CMV may cause severe, often fatal, infection of the eye, colon, or lung
ddC	a medication like AZT used to treat HIV; blocks viral reverse transcriptase, an enzyme that permits HIV to replicate itself
ddI	a medication like AZT used to treat HIV; blocks viral reverse transcriptase, an enzyme that permits HIV to replicate itself
discordant couples	partners in a sexual relationship, one of whom is seropositive and the other seronegative
dysplastic	premalignant cellular changes
dyspnea	labored or difficult breathing
endotracheal intubation	the insertion of a tube into the trachea ("windpipe") in order to assist in breathing; usually performed to mechanically ventilate a person in respiratory distress.
epidemic	the occurrence of disease, illness, or injury in a community or region clearly in excess of normal expectations
granuloma	the body's immune response to certain chronic infections, such as tuberculosis. Also seen in certain diseases characterized by inflammation
hematocrit	the percentage of blood that consists of red blood cells, usually 35-45% in healthy people. A low hematocrit signals anemia
hemoptysis	expectoration of bloody lung secretions, often associated with pulmonary tuberculosis or lung cancer
herpes zoster	see shingles
hilum	the part of the lung where the main bronchus or airway begins

HIV RNA	the RNA found in HIV; used as a marker of HIV disease progression; see RNA
human papilloma virus	a sexually transmitted virus that causes certain genital warts; can lead to cervical cancer when it infects the cervix
hypoxia	low oxygen levels in body tissues and blood
immune system	the body's complex array of defenses against infection and certain malignancies
immunocompromised	having a severely weakened immune system, possibly due to HIV infection, congenital defects in the immune system, or other diseases such as leukemia; can also be caused by malnutrition and by certain medical treatments
incidence	the number of new cases of a disease in a population over a period of time
index case	the first person identified with a specific disease
induced sputum	secretions from deep in the lungs that are expressed (induced) by coughing while a therapist taps on the chest; usually such sputum is stained and examined under a microscope or cultured to look for infection
infiltrates	abnormal areas seen on chest radiographs that often signal lung infection (pneumonia)
informal sector	that sector of the economy that is outside the purview of official planning and management; many poor people, including street vendors and other petty merchants, are employed only in the informal sector
intubation	see endotracheal intubation
isoniazid	antibiotic medication for treating or preventing tuberculosis
Isospora belli	protozoan parasite that causes diarrhea; typically found in tropical and subtropical climates; often prolonged in AIDS

IDU	injection drug user: a person who injects illicit drugs such as heroin or cocaine; at high risk for HIV or viral hepatitis if the person shares injection needles with other IDUs; previously called IVDU or intravenous drug users
Kaposi's sarcoma	the most common tumor associated with HIV in the United States; typically produces skin lesions, and sometimes visceral lesions
Karnofsky score	subjective score from 0 to 100 that a physician can assign to describe a patient's mental and physical condition
lymphadenopathy	swollen lymph nodes
lymphocytes	see CD4 lymphocytes
MAC	*Mycobacterium avium* complex; the most common systemic infection in AIDS patients with very low CD4 counts. The M. *avium* complex consists of the non-tuberculous mycobacteria M. *avium*, M. *intracellulare*, and some other, as yet unclassified, strains of atypical mycobacterium
MAI	see MAC
mebendazole	a medication used to treat intestinal parasites
miliary	characterized by numerous small lesions, as in diffuse infection with tuberculosis
morbidity	suffering and disability caused by disease
mortality	death
mucosa	a moist membrane lining a body cavity
multivariate logistic regression analysis	a type of statistical analysis in which multiple factors thought to influence the outcome of interest are taken into account so that the effect of a single variable can be measured. For instance, a study that tries to measure the effect of coffee consumption on heart attacks would have to factor into its analysis all the known variables which contribute to heart disease—such as smoking, high blood pressure, and elevated cholesterol—so that the

	independent effect of coffee consumption on heart attacks may be measured
mycobacteria	microscopic organisms that can cause infection; usually slower-growing and harder to eradicate than other bacterial infections; see MAC, tuberculosis
myelosuppression	inhibition of the bone marrow's production of infection-fighting white blood cells, red blood cells, and platelets; often caused by HIV-related medications or by HIV infection itself
NIDA	U.S. federal agency responsible for conducting research and formulating policy on addiction
non-diagnostic	not helpful in ascertaining a diagnosis or cause of a person's illness
odds ratio	in a case-control study, a measure of how much influence a specific exposure has on causing a disease; approximates relative risk
opportunistic infection	infections that occur in people with AIDS and other immunocompromised states but which do not usually occur in people with normal immune systems. Examples would include PCP and MAC
oral hairy leukoplakia	raised, white lesions on mouth and tongue; associated with HIV infection
oropharynx	the upper part of the throat
pandemic	the worldwide distribution of disease, illness, or injury. Poverty and AIDS are pandemic
paratracheal	next to the trachea (windpipe)
parturient	ready to give birth; in labor
PCP	*Pneumocystis carinii* pneumonia: a disease occurring only in immunocompromised patients; caused by the organism *P. carinii*, which infects the lungs; one of the most common AIDS-related opportunistic infections

perinatal
  transmission   transmission of an infectious agent from mother to
                          fetus, as in the passage of HIV from a mother to her
                          infant around the time of birth

pneumococcal
  pneumonia   lung infection caused by *Streptococcus pneumoniae*,
                          the most common community-acquired bacterial
                          pathogen to infect the lung

pneumothorax   fully or partially collapsed lung, which can cause
                          chest pain or shortness of breath

prednisone   a steroid used as an anti-inflammatory medicine in
                          a variety of diseases

PPD   purified protein derivative: substance extracted
                          from the tubercle bacillus; used in a skin test to
                          screen for exposure to tuberculosis

prevalence   the number of people in a population who have a
                          certain disease at a given point in time

progressive
  multifocal leuko-   opportunistic infection of the nervous system seen
  encephalopathy   in advanced AIDS; caused by a virus that damages
                          the brain; results in death usually within three
                          months

prophylaxis   measures taken to prevent infection or disease
                          before they occur

prophylactic
  medications   medications that prevent new infection or reacti-
                          vation of previous infection; for example, people
                          with AIDS are given TMP/SMX to prevent PCP

reactivation   see tuberculosis, shingles

relative risk   the likelihood that someone with a specific expo-
                          sure will develop a certain disease divided by the
                          likelihood that someone without the exposure will
                          develop the disease. For example, a relative risk of
                          2 means that an exposed person is twice as likely to
                          develop the disease as compared to a person who
                          was not exposed

retrospective study	a study which collects data about an outcome that has already occurred
rhonchi	coarse breathing sounds emanating from the lungs, heard through a stethoscope
rifabutin	an antibiotic medication used for preventing or treating MAC in advanced AIDS
RNA	ribonucleic acid: a molecule which carries the genetic information of many viruses, including HIV
septic shock	a rapid, life-threatening drop in blood pressure due to severe infection
serosurveys	when blood of a particular population or subpopulation is tested for the presence of infection
shingles	a skin rash along a nerve distribution, caused by the reactiviation of varicella zoster virus; occurs in patients with a past history of chickenpox; often seen in immunocompromised patients
structural adjustment	a series of economic policies mandated by international financial agencies, such as the World Bank
structural violence	a series of large-scale forces— ranging from gender inequality and racism to poverty— which structure unequal access to goods and services
subepidemic	local variant of a large epidemic or pandemic
surveillance data	data collected to monitor the occurrence and spread of a disease
tachypneic	of or pertaining to rapid breathing
thrush	oral candidiasis; sometimes associated with HIV infection
TMP/SMX	trimethoprim/sulfamethoxazole: a medication for treating or preventing PCP and a host of other common infections
trichomoniasis	a sexually-transmitted infection caused by a protozoan parasite that often results in inflammation of the vagina (vaginitis)

tuberculosis	a disease caused by infection with the bacterium M. *tuberculosis*; begins in the lungs, but may spread to other organs. Many people, most of whom are poor, in countries throughout the world become exposed to this organism during childhood, develop a mild infection, and recover completely, although the mycobacterium lies dormant. If they develop other debilitating disease (e.g. AIDS) later in life, their tuberculosis may reactivate and cause a life-threatening infection
vector	an agent that carries and transmits a disease, e.g. certain mosquitoes are the vectors of malaria
vesicular	characterized by vesicles, which are small, raised, fluid-filled skin lesions
zidovudine	see AZT

Bibliography

Rebecca Wolfe, editor

1988a "Condoms for Prevention of Sexually Transmitted Diseases." *Public Health Reviews* 16(1-2): 13-20.
1988b "New Technique Reveals Extent of Viral Variations." *New Scientist* 118(1618): 37.
1988c "Report of the Second Public Health Service AIDS Prevention and Control Conference. Report of the Workgroup on Epidemiology and Surveillance." *Public Health Reports* 103(S1): 10-18.
1988d "Understanding AIDS: An Information Brochure Being Mailed to all U.S. Households." *Public Health Reviews* 16(1-2): 21-33.
1990 "The Sentinel HIV Seroprevalence Surveys." *Public Health Reports* 105(2): 113-171.
1992 "Global Programme on AIDS. Consensus Statement from the WHO/UNICEF Consultation on HIV Transmission and Breast-Feeding." *Weekly Epidemiological Record* 67(24): 177-179.
1993 "Human Immunodeficiency Virus Infections: ACOG Technical Bulletin Number 169—June 1992." Paper presented at the International Journal of Gynecological Obstetrics.
1994 "A New Strategy: The AIDS Pandemic." *Women's Health Journal* (2/3): 103-106.
1995a "Acting Against Anthrax. U.S. Military Veterinarian Helps Haitians and their Animals." *Journal of the American Veterinarian Association* 207(12): 1533.
1995b"Bangladeshi Women Suffer Health Risks Despite Good Record on Family Planning." *AIDS Analysis* 1(5): 1.
1995c "UNFPA Maintains Pressure to Achieve Cairo Goals." *AIDS Analysis* 5(1): 3.
1995d "Women, AIDS and Budget Cuts (Editorial)." *America* 173(13): 3.

AABY, PETER, BADARA SAMB, FRANÇOIS SIMONDON, ET AL.
1995 "Non-Specific Beneficial Effect of Measles Immunisation: Analysis of Mortality Studies from Developing Countries. " *British Medical Journal* 311(7003): 481-485.

ABBOTT, R., A. N'DOUR-SARR, A. DIOUF, ET AL.
1994 "Risk Factors for HIV-1 and HIV-2 Infection in Pregnant Women in Dakar, Senegal." *Journal of Acquired Immune Deficiency Syndromes* 7(7): 711-717.

ABDOOL KARIM, QUARRAISHA, SALIM S. ABDOOL KARIM, KATE SULDAN, ET AL.
1995 "Reducing the Risk of HIV Infection among South African Sex Workers: Socioeconomic and Gender Barriers." *American Journal of Public Health* 85(11): 1521-1525.

ABIMIKU, ALASH'LE G. AND ROBERT C. GALLO
1995 "HIV: Basic Virology and Pathophysiology." In *HIV Infection in Women.* Howard Minkoff, Jack A. DeHovitz, and Ann Duerr, eds. New York: Raven Press. Pp. 13-32.

AFRICAN RIGHTS
1995 *Rwanda: Death, Despair, and Defiance.* 11 Marshalsea Road, London, England, SEI1EP.

AHLBERG, BETH MAINA
1994 "Is there a Distinct African Sexuality?" *Africa* 64(2): 220-242.

ALBELDA, RANDY
1993 "Making Work Pay: The Unfinished Agenda." *Dollars and Sense* (November/December): 42-43.

ALBERS, PATRICIA
1989 "Anthropological Scholarship on Gender in the English-Speaking Caribbean. In *Gender and Anthropology.* Sandra Morgen, ed. Washington, D.C.: American Anthropological Association. Pp. 132-170.

ALEGRIA, MARGARETA, MILDRED VERA, DANIEL H. FREEMAN, ET AL.
1994 "HIV Infection, Risk Behaviors, and Depressive Symptoms among Puerto Rican Sex Workers." *American Journal of Public Health* 84(12): 2000-2003.

ALEXANDER, PRISCILLA
1988 *Prostitutes Prevent AIDS: A Manual for Health Educators.* San Francisco: CAL-PEP.
1995 "Sex Workers Fight against AIDS: An International Perspective." In *Women Resisting AIDS: Feminist Strategies of Empowerment.* Beth E. Schneider and Nancy Stoller, eds. Philadelphia: Temple University Press. Pp. 99-123.

ALGER, LINDSAY S., JOHN S. FARLEY, BARBARA A. ROBINSON, ET AL.
1993 "Interactions of Human Immunodeficiency Virus Infection and Pregnancy." *Obstetrics and Gynecology* 82(5): 787-796.

ALLARD, R.
1990 "A Family of Mathematical Models to Describe the Risk of Infection by a Sexually Transmitted Agent." *Epidemiology* 1(1): 30-33.

ALLARD, R. AND J. BOIVIN
1993a "Measures of Effect Based on the Sufficient Causes Model 1. Risks and Rates of Disease Associated with a Single Causative Agent." *Epidemiology* 4(1): 37-42.
1993b "Measures of Effect Based on the Sufficient Causes Model 2. Risks and Rates of Disease Associated with a Single Preventive Agent." *Epidemiology* 4(6): 517-523.

ALLEN, D., N. LEE, S. SCHULZ, ET AL.
1990 "Determining HIV Seroprevalence among Women in Women's Health Clinics." *Public Health Reports* 105(2): 130-134.

ALLEN, D., I. ONORATO, AND T. GREEN
1992 "HIV Infection in Intravenous Drug Users Entering Drug Treatment, United States, 1988 to 1989. The Field Services Branch of the Centers for Disease Control." *American Journal of Public Health* 82(4): 541-546.

ALLEN, JAMES R. AND VALERIE P. SETLOW
1991 "Heterosexual Transmission of HIV: A View of the Future." *Journal of the American Medical Association* 266(12): 265-276.

ALLEN, S., A. SERUFILIRA, J. BOGAERTS, ET AL.
1992 "Confidential HIV Testing and Condom Promotion in Africa. Impact of HIV and Gonorrhea Rates." *Journal of the American Medical Association* 268(23): 3338-3343.

ALLEN, S., A. SERUFILIRA, V. GRUBER, ET AL.
1993 "Pregnancy and Contraception Use among Urban Rwanda Women after HIV Testing and Counseling." *American Journal of Public Health* 83(5): 705-710.

ALLEN, SUSAN, JEAN BATUNWANAYO, KARLA KERLIKOWSKE, ET AL.
    1992 "Two-Year Incidence of Tuberculosis in Cohorts of HIV-Infected and Uninfected
        Urban Rwandan Women." *American Review of Respiratory Diseases* 146(6): 1439-
        1444.

ALLEN, SUSAN, CHRISTINA LINDAN, ANTOINE SERUFILIRA, ET AL.
    1991 "Human Immunodeficiency Virus Infection in Urban Rwanda: Demographic and
        Behavioral Correlates in a Representative Sample of Childbearing Women." *Jour-
        nal of the American Medical Association* 266(12): 1657-1663.

ALMOND, BRENDA AND CAROLE ULANOWSKY
    1990 "HIV and Pregnancy." *Hastings Center Report* 20(2): 16-21.

ALTMAN, DENNIS
    1987 *AIDS in the Mind of America.* Garden City, NY: Anchor Press.

ALTVATER, ELMAR, KURT HÜBNER, JOCHEN LORENTZEN, ET AL., EDS.
    1991 *The Poverty of Nations: A Guide to the Debt Crisis—from Argentina to Zaire.* London:
        Zed Books Ltd.

AMARO, HORTENSIA
    1995 "Love, Sex and Power." *American Psychologist* 50(6): 437-447.

AMMANN, ARTHUR
    1995 "Unrestricted Routine Prenatal HIV Testing: The Standard Care." *Journal of the
        American Medical Women's Association* 50(3/4): 83-84.

ANASTOS, KATHRYN AND CAROLA MARTE
    1989 "Women—The Missing Persons in the AIDS Epidemic." *Health/PAC Bulletin*
        19(4): 6-18.

ANDRUS, J., D. FLEMING, C. KNOX, ET AL.
    1989 "HIV Testing in Prisoners: Is Mandatory Testing Mandatory?" *American Journal of
        Public Health* 79(7): 840-842.

ANKRAH, E. MAXINE
    1991 "AIDS and the Social Side of Health." *Social Science and Medicine* 32(9): 967-980.

ANKRAH, E. MAXINE, MARVELLOUS M. MHLOYI, FLORENCE MANGUYU, ET AL.
    1994 "Women, Children and AIDS." In *AIDS in Africa.* Max Essex, Souleymane Mboup,
        Phyllis Kanki, *et al.,* eds. New York: Raven Press. Pp. 533-546.

ANTHONY, JAMES C., DAVID VLAHOV, DAVID D. CELENTANO, ET AL.
    1991 "Self-Report Interview Data for a Study of HIV-1 Infection among Intravenous
        Drug Users: Description of Methods and Preliminary Evidence on Validity." *The
        Journal of Drug Issues* 21(4): 739-757

APTER, DAVID E.
    1987 *Rethinking Development: Modernization, Dependency and Post-Modern Politics.* New-
        bury Park, CA: Sage.

ARAL, SEVGI
    1993 "Heterosexual Transmission of HIV: The Role of Other STDs and Behavior in its
        Epidemiology, Prevention, and Control." *Annual Reviews in Public Health* 14: 451-
        467.

ARAL, SEVGI AND KING HOLMES
    1991 "Sexually Transmitted Diseases in the AIDS Era." *Scientific American* 264(2): 64-69.

ARMSTRONG, SUE
    1993 "Women Hit Hardest by HIV in Divided South Africa." *New Scientist* 139(1880):
        10.

ARUFFO, JOHN F., JOHN COVERDALE, VALORY PAVLIK, ET AL.
    1993 "AIDS Knowledge in Minorities: Significance of Locus of Control." *American Jour-
        nal of Preventive Medicine* 9(1): 15-20.

ARUFFO, J. F., J. COVERDALE, C. VALBONA, ET AL.
    1991 "AIDS Knowledge in Low-Income and Minority Populations." *Public Health Reports*
        106(2): 115-119.

ASAD, TALAL
    1994 "Ethnographic Representation, Statistics, and Modern Power." *Social Research*
        61(1): 55-88.

ASHERY, R., R. CARLSON, R. FALCK, ET AL.
    1995 "Female Condom Use among Injection Drug- and Crack Cocaine-Using Women."
        American Journal of Public Health 85(5): 736-737.

ASTEMBORSKI, J., D. VLAHOV, D. WARREN, ET AL.
    1994 "The Trading of Sex for Drugs or Money and HIV Seropositivity among Female
        Intravenous Drug Users." *American Journal of Public Health* 84(3) 382-387.

ASTONE, JANETTA
    1996 "Having Sex and Using Condoms: Adolescents' Beliefs, Intentions, and Behavior."
        Current Issues in Public Health 2(1): 29-33.

BACCHETTI, PETER, DENNIS OSMOND, RICHARD E. CHAISSON, ET AL.
    1988 "Survival Patterns of the First 500 Patients with AIDS in San Francisco." *The Jour-
        nal of Infectious Diseases* 157(5): 1044-1047.

BACCHETTI, PETER, DENNIS OSMOND, RICHARD E. CHAISSON, ET AL.
    1988 "Survival with AIDS in New York." *The New England Journal of Medicine* 318(22):
        1464.

BACHRACH, LEONA L.
    1987 "Homeless Women: A Context for Health Planning." *The Milbank Quarterly* 65(3):
        371-396.

BARBACCI, MARGUERITE, JOHN T. REPKE, AND RICHARD E. CHAISSON
    1991 "Routine Prenatal Screening for HIV Infection." *The Lancet* 337(8743): 709-711.

BARNARD, MARINA A.
    1988 "Needle Sharing in Context: Patterns of Sharing among Men and Women Injectors
        and HIV Risks." *Addiction* 88: 805-812.

BARTLETT, J.G.
    1994 *The Johns Hopkins Hospital Guide to Medical Care of Patients with HIV Infection*. Bal-
        timore: Williams & Wilkins.

BASSETT, MARY AND MARVELLOUS MHLOYI
    1991 "Women and AIDS in Zimbabwe: The Making of an Epidemic." *International Jour-
        nal of Health Services* 21(1): 143-156.
    1994 "Women and AIDS in Zimbabwe: The Making of an Epidemic." In *AIDS: The Pol-
        itics of Survival*. Nancy Krieger and Glenn Margo, eds. Amityville, NY: Baywood
        Publishing Co. Pp. 125-140.

BASTIAN, LORI, CHARLES BENNETT, JOHN ADAMS, ET AL.
    1993 "Differences between Men and Women with HIV Related *Pneumocystis carinii*
        Pneumonia: Experience from 3,070 cases in New York City in 1987." *Journal of
        Acquired Immune Deficiency Syndromes* 6(6): 617-623.

BATALLA, JOAN, JOSEPH M. GATELL, JOAN A. CAYLÀ, ET AL.
    1989 "Predictors of the Survival of AIDS Cases in Barcelona, Spain." *AIDS* 3(6): 355-
        359.

BATCHELOR, WALTER F.
    1984 "AIDS: A Public Health and Psychological Emergency." *American Psychologist*
        39(11): 1279-1284.

BAYER, RONALD
    1989 "AIDS, Privacy and Responsibility." *Daedalus* 118(3): 79-99.

1994 "AIDS Prevention and Cultural Sensitivity: Are they Compatible?" *American Journal of Public Health* 84(6): 895-897.

1995 "Women's Rights, Babies Interests: Ethics, Politics and Science in the Debate of Newborn HIV Screening." In *HIV Infection in Women*. Howard Minkoff, Jack A. DeHovitz, and Ann Duerr, eds. New York: Raven Press. Pp. 293-308.

BECKER, MARSHALL H.
1988 "AIDS and Behavior Change." *Public Health Reviews* 16(1-2): 1-11

BECKER, MARSHALL H. AND JILL G. JOSEPH
1988 "AIDS and Behavioral Change to Reduce Risk: A Review." *American Journal of Public Health* 78(4): 394-410.

BEEVOR, A.S. AND J. CATALAN
1993 "Women's Experience of HIV Testing: The Views of HIV Positive and HIV Negative Women." *AIDS Care* 5(2): 177-186.

BEHETS, F.M., J. DESMORMEAUX, D. JOSEPH, ET AL.
1994 "High Prevalence of Reproductive Tract Infections (RTI) among Pregnant Women of Low Socioeconomic Status (SES) in Haiti." *International Conference on AIDS* 10(2): 289. Abstract Number PC0540.

1995 "Control of Sexually Transmitted Diseases in Haiti: Results and Implications of a Baseline Study among Pregnant Women Living in Cité Soleil Shantytowns." *Journal of Infectious Diseases* 172(3): 764-771.

BEHRENDT, CAROLYN, NEWTON KENDIG, CLAUDE DAMBITA, ET AL.
1994 "Voluntary Testing for Human Immunodeficiency Virus (HIV) in a Prison Population with a High Prevalence of HIV." *American Journal of Epidemiology* 139(9): 918-926.

BELEC, L., T. BROGAN, F. KEOU, ET AL.
1994 "Surveillance of Acquired Immune Deficiency Syndrome in Africa. An Analysis of Evaluations of the World Health Organization and Other Clinical Definitions." *Epidemiological Reviews* 16(2): 403-417.

BELLAH, ROBERT
1985 *Habits of the Heart: Individualism and Commitment in American Life*. Los Angeles: University of California Press.

BENENSON, A., ED.
1970 *Control of Communicable Diseases in Man*. Eleventh Edition. New York: American Public Health Association.

BERLESON, BERNARD
1969 "Behavioral Sciences." In *International Encyclopedia of the Social Sciences*. David Sills, ed. New York: The Free Press. Pp 41-45.

BERER, MARGE
1993 *Women and AIDS*. London: Pandora Press.

BERMAN, S., M. LINDSAY, AND A. HADGU
1993 "Reaching Minority Women at Risk for HIV: The Potential for Pregestational Access by Churches and Inner-City Hospitals." *International Conference on AIDS* 9(2): 842. Abstract number PO-D13-3746.

BERNIER, M. AND P. ASCENSIO
1995 "Enfants de la Rue et SIDA en Haiti." *Santé* 5(2): 125-130.

BERNSTEIN, R.
1978 *The Restructuring of Social and Political Theory*. Philadelphia: University of Pennsylvania Press.

BERREBI, ALAIN, WILHEIM E. KOBUCH, JACQUELINE PUEL, ET AL.
    1990 "Influence of Pregnancy on Human Immunodeficiency Disease." *European Journal of Obstetrics, Gynecology and Reproductive Biology* 37: 211-217.

BERRY, DAVID E.
    1993 "The Emerging Epidemiology of Rural AIDS." *The Journal of Rural Health* 9(4): 293-304.

BERTRAND, J., B. MAKANI, B. HASSIG, ET AL.
    1991 "AIDS-Related Knowledge, Sexual Behavior, and Condom Use among Men and Women in Kinshasa, Zaïre." *American Journal of Public Health* 81(1): 53-58.

BIANCO, MABEL
    1995 "How AIDS Changes Development Priorities." In *Women Resisting AIDS: Feminist Strategies of Empowerment.* Beth E. Schneider and Nancy E. Stoller, eds. Philadelphia: Temple University Press. Pp. 335-339.

BIANCO, M., C. GONZALEZ, AND M.I. RE
    1994 "Heterosexual Behavior and Risk Perception for HIV/AIDS in Argentinian Women." *International Conference on AIDS* 10(2): 381. Abstract Number PD0705.

BIGGAR, R. AND M. MELBYE
    1992 "Response to Anonymous Questionnaires Concerning Sexual Behavior: A Method to Eliminate Potential Biases." *American Journal of Public Health* 82(11): 1506-1512.

BIGGARE, R. AND P. ROSENBERG
    1993 "HIV Infection/AIDS in the United States During the 1990s." *Clinical Infectious Diseases* 17(S1): S19-S23.

BIRN, ANNE-EMANUELLE, JOHN SANTELLI AND LAWANDA G. BURWELL
    1994 "Pediatric AIDS in the United States: Epidemiological Reality Versus Government Policy." In *AIDS: The Politics of Survival.* Nancy Krieger and Glenn Margo, eds. Amityville, NY: Baywood Publishing Company. Pp. 89-106.

BIZIMUNGU, C., A. NTILIVAMUNDA, M. TAHIMANA, ET AL.
    1989 "Nationwide Community-Based Serological Survey of HIV-1 and Other Human Retrovirus Infections." *The Lancet* 335(8644): 941-943.

BLOOM, B.R., AND C.J. MURRAY
    1992 "Tuberculosis: Commentary on a Reemergent Killer." *Science* 257(5073): 1055-1064.

BLOWER, S., G. VAN GRIENSVEN, AND E. KAPLAN
    1995 "An Analysis of the Process of Human Immunodeficiency Virus Sexual Risk Behavior Change." *Epidemiology* 6(3): 238-242.

BLUMENTHAL, DAVID S., JOANNE E. LUKOMNIK AND DANIEL R. HAWKINS, JR.
    1993 "A Proposal to Provide Care to the Uninsured through a Network of Community Health Centers." *Journal of Health Care for the Poor and Underserved* 4(3): 272-286.

BOEKELOO, B., L. SCHIAVO, D. RABIN, ET AL.
    1994 "Self-Reports of HIV Risk Factors by Patients at a Sexually Transmitted Disease Clinic: Audio vs. Written Questionnaires." *American Journal of Public Health* 84(5):754-760.

BOFF, LEONARDO AND CLODOVIS BOFF
    1994 *Introducing Liberation Theology.* Maryknoll, NY: Orbis Books.

BOLTON, RALPH
    1995"Rethinking Anthropology: The Study of AIDS." In *Culture and Sexual Risk: Anthropological Perspectives.* Han ten Brummelhuis and Gilbert Herdt, eds. New York: Gordon and Breach. Pp. 285-314.

BOLTON, R., M. LEWIS, AND G. OROZCO
1991 "AIDS Literature for Anthropologists: A Working Bibliography." *Journal of Sex Research* 28(2): 307-346.

BONACCI, MARK A.
1992 *Senseless Casualties: The AIDS Crisis in Asia.* Washington, D.C.: International Voluntary Services and Asia Resource Center.

BOOTH, R.
1995 "Gender Differences in High-Risk Sex Behaviors among Heterosexual Drug Injectors and Crack Smokers." *American Journal of Drug and Alcohol Abuse* 21(4): 419-432.

BOOTH, R., J. WATTERS, AND D. CHITWOOD
1993 "HIV Risk-Related Sex Behaviors among Injection Drug Users, Crack Smokers, and Injection Drug Users Who Smoke Crack." *American Journal of Public Health* 83(8): 1144-1148.

BOSTON WOMEN'S HEALTH BOOK COLLECTIVE
1992 *The New Our Bodies, Ourselves.* New York: Simon and Schuster, Inc.

BOULOS, R., N. HALSEY, E. HOLT, ET AL.
1990 "HIV-1 in Haitian Women 1982-1988. The Cité Soleil/JHU AIDS Project Team." *Journal of Acquired Immune Deficiency Syndromes* 3(7): 721-728.

BOWLER, SUZANNE, AMY R. SHEON, LAWRENCE J. D'ANGELO, ET AL.
1992 "HIV and AIDS among Adolescents in the United States: Increasing Risk in the 1990s." *Journal of Adolescence* 15(4): 345-371.

BOXER, A., J. COOK, M. COHEN, ET AL.
1990 "AIDS Education for Minority, Low-Income Women: A Public Hospital and Jail Based Prevention Program in Chicago. *International Conference on AIDS* 6(3): 265. Abstract Number S.C. 707.

BOYLAN, LAURA AND ZENA A. STEIN
1991 "The Epidemiology of HIV Infection in Children and Their Mothers—Vertical Transmission." *Epidemiologic Reviews* 13: 143-177.

BRABIN, B.J.
1985 "Epidemiology of Infection in Pregnancy." *Reviews in Infectious Disease* 7: 579-603.

BREITBART, VICKI, WENDY CHAVKIN AND PAUL H. WISE
1994 "The Accessibility of Drug Treatment for Pregnant Women: A Survey of Programs in Five Cities." *American Journal of Public Health* 84(10): 1658-1661.

BRETTLE, R.P.
1992 "Pregnancy and its Effect on HIV/AIDS." *Balliere's Clinical Obstetrics and Gynecology* 6(1): 125-136.

BRITTON, CAROLYN BARLEY
1995 "An Argument for Universal HIV Counseling and Voluntary Testing of Women." *Journal of the American Medical Women's Association* 50(3/4): 85-86.

BROWN, B.S.
1990 "Editorial, NIDA Network." C# 271-88-8231. Bethesda, Maryland: Nova Research Company.

BROWN, JUDITH E., BIBI AYOWA OKAKO AND RICHARD C. BROWN
1993 "Dry and Tight: Sexual Practices and Potential Risk in Zaire." *Social Science and Medicine* 37(8): 989-994.

BROWN, KATE H.
1993 "Descriptive and Normative Ethics: Class, Context and Confidentiality for Mothers with HIV." *Social Science and Medicine* 36(3): 195-202.

BROWN, LAWRENCE, JR. AND BENY J. PRIMM
    1986 "Sexual Contacts of Intravenous Drug Abusers: Implications for the Next Spread of the AIDS Epidemic." *Journal of the National Medical Association* 80(6): 651-656.

BROWN, RICHARD, JUDITH BROWN AND OKAKO BIBI AYOWA
    1992 "The Use and Physical Effects of Intravaginal Substances in Zairian Women." *Sexually Transmitted Diseases* 20(2): 96-99.

BROWN, TIM, BRIAN MULHAL, AND WERASIT SITTIRAI
    1994 "Risk Factors for HIV Transmission in Asia and the Pacific." *AIDS* 8(S2): S173-S182.

BROWN, VIVIAN B., LISA A. MELCHIOR, CATHY J. REBACK, ET AL.
    1994 "Mandatory Partner Notification of HIV Test Results: Psychological and Social Issues for Women." *AIDS & Public Policy Journal* 9(2): 86-92.

BRUMMELHUIS, HAN TEN
    1994 "Between Action and Understanding." Paper presented at the Workshop in Sociocultural Dimensions of HIV/AIDS Control and Care in Thailand, Chiang Mai, Thailand (January).

BRUMMELHUIS, HAN TEN AND GILBERT HERDT
    1995 "Anthropology in the Context of AIDS." In *Culture and Sexual Risk: Anthropological Perspectives*. Han ten Brummelhuis and Gilbert Herdt, eds. New York: Gordon and Breach. Pp. ix-xxiv.

BRUNSWICK, A., A. AIDALA, J. DOBKIN, ET AL.
    1993 "HIV-1 Seroprevalence and Risk Behaviors in an Urban African-American Community Cohort." *American Journal of Public Health* 83(10): 1390-1394.

BUEHLER, JAMES W., DEBRA L. HANSON AND SUSAN Y. CHU
    1992 "The Reporting of HIV/AIDS Deaths in Women." *American Journal of Public Health* 82(11): 1500-1505.

BUEHLER, J., L. PETERSEN, J. WARD, ET AL.
    1994 "Defending HIV Seroprevalence Surveys." *American Journal of Public Health* 84(2): 319-320.

BULLOUGH, BONNIE
    1972 "Poverty, Ethnic Identity and Preventive Health Care." *Journal of Health and Social Behavior* 13: 347-359.

BULTERYS, M., F. MUSANGANIRE, A. CHAO, ET AL.
    1994 "Traditional Mourning Customs and the Spread of HIV-1 in Rural Rwanda: A Target for AIDS Prevention?" *AIDS* 8(6): 858-859.

BURKE, D., J. BRUNDAGE, W. BERNIER, ET AL.
    1987 "Demography of HIV Infections among Civilian Applications for Military Service in Four Counties in New York City" *New York State Journal of Medicine* 87(5): 262-264.

BURKE, D.S., J.F. BRUNDAGE, M. GOLDENBAUM, ET AL.
    1990 "Human Immunodeficiency Virus Infections in Teenagers. Seroprevalence among Applicants for U.S. Military Service. The Walter Reed Retrovirus Research Group." *Journal of the American Medical Association* 263(15): 2074-2077.

BUTZ, A., N. HUTTON, AND M. JOYNER
    1993 "HIV-Infected Women and Infants. Social and Health Factors Impeding Utilization of Health Care." *Journal of Nurse-Midwifery* 38(2): 103-109.

BUTZ, A., N. HUTTON, AND E. LARSON
    1991 "Immunoglobulins and Growth Parameters at Birth of Infants Born to HIV Seropositive and Seronegavtive Women." *American Journal of Public Health* 81(10): 1323-1326.

BWAYO, J.J., A.N. MUTERE, M.A. OMARI, ET AL.
    1991a "Long Distance Truck-Drivers: Prevalence of Sexually Transmitted Diseases." *East African Medical Journal* 68(6): 425-429.
    1991b "Long Distance Truck Drivers 2: Knowledge and Attitudes Concerning Sexually Transmitted Diseases and Sexual Behavior." *East African Medical Journal* 68(9): 714-719.

CALDWELL, JOHN C. AND PAT CALDWELL
    1994a "The Nature and Limits of the Sub-Saharan African AIDS Epidemic: Evidence from Geographic and Other Patterns." In *Sexual Networking and AIDS in Sub-Saharan Africa: Behavioral Research and the Social Context.* I.O. Orubuloye, John C. Caldwell, Pat Caldwell, *et al.*, eds. Canberra, Australia: The Australian National University. Pp. 195-216.
    1994b "African Families and AIDS Context, Reactions, and Potential Interventions." In *Sexual Networking and AIDS in Sub-Saharan Africa: Behavioral Research and the Social Context.* I.O. Orubuloye, John C. Caldwell, Pat Caldwell, *et al.*, eds. Canberra, Australia: The Australian National University. Pp. 235-248.

CALDWELL, JOHN C., PAT CALDWELL AND PAT QUIGGIN
    1989 "The Social Context of AIDS in Sub-Saharan Africa." *Population and Development Review* 15(2): 185-234.
    1994 "The Social Context of AIDS in Sub-Saharan Africa." In *Sexual Networking and AIDS in Sub-Saharan Africa: Behavioral Research and the Social Context.* I.O. Orubuloye, John C. Caldwell, Pat Caldwell, *et al.*, eds. Canberra, Australia: The Australian National University. Pp. 129-162.

CALDWELL, JOHN C., I.O. ORUBULOYE AND PAT CALDWELL
    1994a "Underreaction to AIDS in Sub-Saharan Africa." In *Sexual Networking and AIDS in Sub-Saharan Africa: Behavioral Research and the Social Context.* I.O. Orubuloye, John C. Caldwell, Pat Caldwell, *et al.*, eds. Canberra, Australia: The Australian National University. Pp. 217-234.
    1994b "The Destabilization of the Traditional Yoruba Sexual System." In *Sexual Networking and AIDS in Sub-Saharan Africa: Behavioral Research and the Social Context.* I.O. Orubuloye, John C. Caldwell, Pat Caldwell, *et al.*, eds. Canberra, Australia: The Australian National University. Pp. 45-68.

CALSYN, D., C. MEINECKE, A. SAXON, ET AL.
    1992 "Risk Reduction in Sexual Behavior: A Condom Giveaway Program in a Drug Abuse Treatment Clinic." *American Journal of Public Health* 82(11): 1536-1538.

CALSYN, D., A. SAXON, G. FREEMAN, JR. ET AL.
    1992 "Ineffectiveness of AIDS Education and HIV Antibody Testing in Reducing High-Risk Behaviors among Injection Drug Users." *American Journal of Public Health* 82(4): 573-575.

CAMPBELL, CAROLE A.
    1990 "Women and AIDS." *Social Science and Medicine* 30(4): 407-415.
    1991 "Prostitution, AIDS, and Preventive Health Behavior." *Social Science and Medicine* 32(12): 1367-1378.

CAMPBELL, DONALD
    1986 "Science's Social System of Validity-Enhancing Collective Belief Change and Problems of the Social Sciences." In *Metatheory in Social Science: Pluralisms and Subjectives.* D. Fiske and R. Shweder, eds. Chicago: University of Chicago Press. Pp 108-135.

CAMPBELL, T. AND M. KELLY
    1995 "Women and AIDS in Zimbabwe: A Review of the Psychosocial Factors Implicated in the Transmission of HIV." *AIDS Care* 7(3): 365-373.

CAMPOSTRINI, S. AND D. MCQUEEN
    1993 "Sexual Behavior and Exposure to HIV Infection: Estimates from a General-Population Risk Index." *American Journal of Public Health* 83(8): 1139-1143.

CANNISTRA, S. AND J. NILOFF
    1996 "Cancer of the Uterine Cervix." *New England Journal of Medicine* 334(16): 1030-1038.

CAPELL, F., D. VUGIA, V. MORDAUNT, ET AL.
    1992 "Distribution of HIV Type 1 Infection in Childbearing Women in California." *American Journal of Public Health* 82(2): 254-256.

CARAËL, MICHEL
    1991 "Women, Sexually Transmitted Diseases and AIDS in Sub-Saharan Africa." *Vena* 5(1): 15-21.

CARLIN, E.M. AND F.C. BOAG
    1995 "Women, Contraception and STDs Including HIV." *International Journal of STDs and AIDS* 6(6): 373-386.

CARLSON, ROBERT G., HARVEY A. SIEGEL AND RUSSEL S. FLACK
    1994 "Ethnography, Epidemiology, and Public Policy: Injecting Drug Users in the Midwest." In *Global AIDS Policy*. Douglas Feldman, ed. Westport, Connecticut: Bergin and Garvey.

CARMEL, S.
    1990 "The Health Belief Model in the Research of AIDS-Related Preventive Behavior." *Public Health Reviews* 18(1): 73-85.

CAROVANO, K.
    1991 "More than Mothers and Whores: Redefining the AIDS Prevention Needs of Women." *International Journal of Health Services* 21(1): 131-142.

CARPENETER, C., K. MAYER, A. DESAI ET AL.
    1989 "Natural History of Acquired Immunodeficiency Syndrome in Women in Rhode Island." *American Journal of Medicine* 86(6; Part 2): 771-775.

CARPENTER, CHARLES C. J., KENNETH H. MAYER, MICHAEL D. STEIN, ET AL.
    1991 "Human Immunodeficiency Virus Infection in North American Women: Experience with 200 Cases and a Review of the Literature." *Medicine (Baltimore)* 70(5): 307-325.

CARRIER, JOSEPH, BANG NGUYEN AND SAMMY SU
    1992 "Vietnamese American Sexual Behaviors and HIV Infection." *The Journal of Sex Research* 29(4): 547-560.

CARROLL, NINA
    1994 "Gynecological Terms and Definitions for Women with HIV." *Wellspring* (Summer): 12, 19.

CARSWELL, J. WILSON, GRAHAM LLOYD, AND JULIAN HOWELLS
    1989 "Short Communication: Prevalence of HIV-1 in East African Lorry Drivers." *AIDS* 3(11): 759-761.

CATANIA, J., D. BINSON, M. DOLCINI, ET AL.
    1995 "Risk Factors for HIV and Other Sexually Transmitted Diseases and Prevention Practices among U.S. Heterosexual Adults: Changes from 1990 to 1992." *American Journal of Public Health* 85(11): 1492-1499.

CATES, W., JR., AND G. BOWEN
    1989 "Education for AIDS Prevention: Not Our Only Voluntary Weapon." *American Journal of Public Health* 79(7): 871-873.

CATES, W. JR., F. STEWART, AND J. TRUSSELL
1992 "Commentary: The Quest for Women's Prophylactic Methods—Hopes vs. Science." *American Journal of Public Health* 82(11): 1479-1482.

CAUSSY, DEORAJ, STANLEY H. WEISS, WILLIAM A. BLATTNER, ET AL.
1990 "Exposure Factors for HIV-1 Infection among Heterosexual Drug Abusers in New Jersey Treatment Programs." *AIDS Research and Human Retroviruses* 6(12): 1459-1467.

CELENTANO, DAVID D., DAVID VLAHOV, S. COHN, ET AL.
1991 "HIV Knowledge and Attitudes among Intravenous Drug Users: Comparisons to the U.S. Population and by Drug Use Behaviors." *The Journal of Drug Issues* 21(3): 635-649.

CENTER ON BUDGET AND POLICY PRIORITIES
1995 *The Final Republican Welfare Bill*. Washington, D.C.: Center on Budget and Policy Priorities.

CENTERS FOR DISEASE CONTROL
1981 "Pneumocytis Pneumonia—Los Angeles." *Morbidity and Mortality Weekly Report* 30(21): 250-252.
1982 "Update on Kaposi's Sarcoma and Opportunistic Infections in Previously Healthy Persons—United States." *Morbidity and Mortality Weekly Report* 31(22): 294-301.
1983 "Immunodeficiency among Female Sexual Partners of Males with Acquired Immunodeficiency Syndrome (AIDS)—New York." *Morbidity and Mortality Weekly Report* 31: 697-698.
1986 "Update: Acquired Immunodeficiency Syndrome—United States." *Morbidity and Mortality Weekly Report* 35(49): 757-760; 765-766.
1988 "Prevalence of Human Immunodeficiency Virus Antibodies in U.S. Active-Duty Military Personnel." *Morbidity and Mortality Weekly Report* 37(30): 461-463.
1989a "Guidelines for Prophylaxis against *Pneumocystis carinii* Pneumonia for Persons Infected with Human Immunodeficiency Virus." *Morbidity and Mortality Weekly Report* 38(S5): 1-9.
1989b "Tuberculosis and HIV Infection: Recommendations of the Advisory Committee for the Elimination of Tuberculosis." *Morbidity and Mortality Weekly Report* 38(14): 236-238, 243-250.
1990 "AIDS in Women—United States." *Morbidity and Mortality Weekly Report* 39(47): 845-846.
1991 "Characteristics of, and HIV Infection among Women Served by Publicly Funded HIV Counseling and Testing Services—United States, 1989-1990." *Morbidity and Mortality Weekly Report* 40(12): 195-204.
1993a "Update: Mortality Attributable to HIV Infection/AIDS among Persons Aged 25-44 Years—United States, 1990 and 1991." *Morbidity and Mortality Weekly Report* 42(25): 481-486.
1993b "Update: Acquired Immune Deficiency Syndrome—United States, 1992." *Morbidity and Mortality Weekly Report* 42(28): 547-551; 557.
1993c "Tuberculosis among Pregnant Women–New York City, 1985-1992." *Morbidity and Mortality Weekly Report* 42(31): 605-611.
1994a "AIDS among Racial/Ethnic Minorities—United States, 1993." *Morbidity and Mortality Weekly Report* 43(35): 644-647; 653-655.
1994b "Dengue Fever among U.S. Military Personnel—Haiti, September-November, 1994." *Morbidity and Mortality Weekly Report* 43(46): 845-848.
1994c *HIV/AIDS Surveillance Report*. Atlanta: Centers for Disease Control. 6: 1-39.
1994d "Recommendations of the U.S. Public Health Service Task Force on the Use of Zidovudine to Reduce Prenatal Transmission of Human Immunodeficiency Virus." *Morbidity and Mortality Weekly Report* 43(RR-11): 1-20.

1995a "First 500,000 AIDS Cases—United States, 1995." *Morbidity and Mortality Weekly Report* 44(46): 849-852.

1995b *HIV/AIDS Surveillance Report.* Atlanta: Centers for Disease Control 7(1): 3-4; 30-34.

1995c "Update: AIDS among Women—United States, 1994." *Morbidity and Mortality Weekly Report* 44(5): 81-85.

1996 "Update: Mortality Attributable to HIV Infection among Persons Aged 25-44 Years—United States, 1994." Morbidity and Mortality Weekly Report 45(6): 121-124.

CHAISSON, R., J. KERULY AND R. MOORE

1995 "Race, Sex, Drug Use and Progression of Human Immunodeficiency Virus Disease." *The New England Journal of Medicine* 333(12): 751-756.

CHAISSON, R., A. MOSS, R. ONISHI, ET AL.

1987 "Human Immunodeficiency Virus Infection in Heterosexual Intravenous Drug Users in San Francisco." *American Journal of Public Health* 77(2): 169-172.

CHAKRABORTY, A.K., S. JANA, A. DAS, ET AL.

1994 "Community Based Survey of STD/HIV Infection among Commercial Sex Workers in Calcutta (India). Part I: Some Social Features of Commercial Sex Workers." *Journal of Communicable Diseases* 26(3): 161-167.

CHAMBERS, VERONICA

1995 "Betrayed Feminism." In *Listen Up: Voices from the Next Feminist Generation.* Barbara Findlen, ed. Seattle, WA: Seal Press. Pp. 21-28.

CHAO, A., M. BULTERYS, F. MUSANGANIRE, ET AL.

1991 "Risk Factors for HIV-1 Seropositivity among Pregnant Women in Rwanda." *International Conference on AIDS* 7(1): 322. Abstract Number M.C. 3097.

CHAVKIN, WENDY

1990 "Preventing AIDS, Targeting Women." *Health/PAC Bulletin* 20(1): 19-23.

1995 "Editorial." *Journal of the American Medical Women's Association* 50(3/4): 72.

CHICAGO WOMEN'S AIDS PROJECT

1992 "The Finer Points on Safer Sex." *Well-Woman Journal* 3(1): 3.

CHIN, J.

1990 "Current and Future Dimensions of the HIV/AIDS Pandemic in Women and Children." *The Lancet* 336(8709): 221-224.

CHIRGWIN, KEITH, JACK DEHOVITZ, STEPHEN DILLON, ET AL.

1991 "HIV Infection, Genital Ulcer Disease, and Crack Cocaine Use among Patients Attending a Clinic for Sexually Transmitted Diseases." *American Journal of Public Health* 81(12): 1576-1579.

CHIRMUUTA, R.C., AND R.J. CHIRIMUUTA

1987 *AIDS, Africa and Racism.* Privately Published in U.K.

CHITWOOD, D.

1994 "HIV Risk and Injection Drug Users—Evidence for Behavioral Change." *American Journal of Public Health* 84(3): 350.

CHITWOOD, D., D. GRIFFIN, M. COMERFORD ET AL.

1995 "Risk Factors for HIV Seroconversion among Injection Drug Users: A Case-Control Study." *American Journal of Public Health* 85(11): 1538-1542.

CHOI, K., J CATANIA, AND M. DOLCINI

1994 "Extramarital Sex and HIV Risk Behavior among U.S. Adults: Results from the National AIDS Behavioral Survey." *American Journal of Public Health* 84(12): 2003-2007.

CHOMSKY, NOAM
1973 *For Reasons of State*. New York. Vintage Books.

CHOOPANYA, K., S. VANICHSENI, D. DES JARLAIS, ET AL.
1991 "Risk Factors and HIV Seropositivity among Injecting Drug Users in Bangkok." *AIDS* 5(12): 1509-1513.

CHORBA, T., R. HOLMAN, AND B. EVATT
1993 "Heterosexual and Mother-to-Child Transmission of AIDS in the Hemophilia Community." *Public Health Reports* 108(1): 99-105.

CHOWDHURY, N.N.
1992 "Problems of AIDS in India especially in Women." *Early Human Development* 29(1-3): 225-229.

CHU, SUSAN Y., JAMES W. BUEHLER AND RUTH L. BERKELMAN
1990 "Impact of the Human Immunodeficiency Virus Epidemic on Mortality in Women of Reproductive Age, United States." *Journal of the American Medical Association* 264(2): 225-229.

CHU, S.Y., J.W. BUEHLER, P. FLEMING, ET AL.
1990 "Epidemiology of Reported Cases of AIDS in Lesbians, United States, 1980-89." *American Journal of Public Health* 80(11): 1380-1381.

CHU, S. Y., J.W. BUEHLER, L. LIEB, ET AL.
1993 "Causes of Death among Persons Reported with AIDS." *American Journal of Public Health* 83(10): 1429-1432.

CHU, S. Y., J.W. BUEHLER AND M. ROGERS
1991 "Characteristics of Infant Deaths Due to HIV/AIDS." *American Journal of Public Health* 81(8): 1076-1077.

CHU, S. AND T. DIAZ
1993 "Living Situation of Women with AIDS." *Journal of Acquired Immune Deficiency Syndromes* 6(4): 431-432.

CHU, S., T. PETERMAN, L. DOLL, ET AL.
1992 "AIDS in Bisexual Men in the United States: Epidemiology and Transmission to Women." *American Journal of Public Health* 82(2): 220-224.

CHU, SUSAN AND PASCALE M. WORTLEY
1995 "Epidemiology of HIV/AIDS in Women." In *HIV Infection in Women*. Howard Minkoff, Jack A. DeHovitz, and Ann Duerr, eds. New York: Raven Press. Pp. 1-12.

CHUANG, C.Y., P.Y. CHANG, AND K.C. LIN
1993 "AIDS in the Republic of China, 1992." *Clinical Infectious Diseases* 17(S2): 337-340.

CICOUREL, AARON
1986 "Social Measurement as the Creation of Expert Systems." In *Metatheory in Social Science: Pluralisms and Subjectives*. Fiske, D. and R. Shweder, eds. Chicago: University of Chicago Press. Pp 246-270.

CLANCY, CAROLYN M. AND CHARLES T. MASSION
1992 "American Women's Health Care: A Patchwork Quilt with Gaps." *Journal of the American Medical Association* 268(14): 1918-1920.

CLATTS, MICHAEL C.
1994 "All the King's Horses and All the King's Men: Some Personal Reflections on Ten Years of AIDS Ethnography." *Human Organization* 53(1): 93-95.
1995 "Disembodied Acts: On the Perverse Use of Sexual Categories in the Study of High-Risk Behaviour." In *Culture and Sexual Risk: Anthropological Perspectives*. Han ten Brummelhuis and Gilbert Herdt, eds. New York: Gordon and Breach. Pp. 241-256.

CLATTS, MICHAEL C., W.R. DAVIS, SHERRY DEREN, ET AL.
   1994 "AIDS Risk Behavior among Drug Injectors in New York City: Critical Gaps in Pre-
      vention Policy." In *Global AIDS Policy*. Douglas Feldman, ed. Westport, Con-
      necticut: Bergin and Garvey. Pp. 215-235.
CLEARY, P., N. VAN DEVANTER, T. ROGERS, ET AL.
   1991 "Behavior Change after Notification of HIV Infection." *American Journal of Public
      Health* 81(12): 1586-1590.
CLEMENTS, MARY LOU
   1995 "HIV Vaccines." In *HIV Infection in Women*. Howard Minkoff, Jack A. DeHovitz,
      and Ann Duerr, eds. New York: Raven Press. Pp. 33-56.
CLUMECK, N. J. SONNET, H. TAELMAN, ET AL.
   1984a "Acquired Immune Deficiency Syndrome in Belgium and its Relation to Central
      Africa." *Annals of the New York Academy of Sciences* 437: 264-269.
   1984b "Acquired Immune Deficiency Syndrome in African Patients." *New England Jour-
      nal of Medicine* 310(8): 492-497.
COATES, THOMAS J., LYDIA TEMOSHOK AND JEFFREY MANDEL
   1984 "Psychosocial Research is Essential to Understanding and Treating AIDS." *Ameri-
      can Psychologist* 39(11): 1309-1314.
COHEN, D.
   1994 "The Efficacy of Counseling in Limiting HIV Transmission." *American Journal of
      Public Health* 84(2): 321.
COHEN, E., H. NAVALINE, AND D. METZGER
   1994 "High-Risk Behaviors for HIV: A Comparison between Crack-Abusing and Opoid-
      Abusing African American Women." *Journal of Psychoactive Drugs* 26(3): 233-241.
COLE, REBECCA AND SALLY COOPER
   1990-1991 "Lesbian Exclusion from HIV/AIDS Education: Ten Years of Low-Risk Iden-
      tity and High-Risk Behavior." *Siecus Report* 19(2): 18-23.
COLLINS, PATRICIA HILL
   1990 *Black Feminist Thought: Knowledge, Consciousness, and the Politics of Empowerment*.
      New York: Routledge.
COMMUNITY FAMILY PLANNING COUNCIL
   1993 *Not Just Birth Control*. New York: Community Family Planning Council.
CONCORDE COORDINATING COMMITTEE
   1994 "MRC/ANRS Randomized Double-Blind Controlled Trial of Immediate and
      Deferred Zidovudine in Symptom-Free HIV Infection." *The Lancet* 343(8902):
      871-881.
CONNOR, EDWARD M., RHODA S. SPERLING, RICHARD GELBER, ET AL.
   1994 "Reduction of Maternal-Infant Transmission of Human Immunodeficiency Virus
      Type 1 with Zidovudine Treatment: Pediatric AIDS Clinical Trials Group Proto-
      col 076 Study Group." *The New England Journal of Medicine* 331(18): 1173-1180.
CONNORS, M., S. BROWN, AND I. ESCOLANO
   1992 The National Institute on Drug Abuse MAIDEP Final Report. NIDA Contract
      Number 271-90-8400.
CONNORS, MARGARET M.
   1992 "Risk Perception, Risk Taking and Risk Management among Intravenous Drug
      Users: Implications for AIDS Prevention." *Social Science and Medicine* 34(6): 591-
      601.
   1994 "Stories of Pain and the Problem of AIDS Prevention: Injection Drug Withdrawal
      and its Effect on Risk Behavior." *Medical Anthropology Quarterly* 8(1): 47-68.

1995a "The Politics of Marginalization: The Appropriation of AIDS Prevention Messages among Injection Drug Users." *Culture, Medicine and Psychiatry* 19(4): 1-28.

1995b "Women, Poverty and HIV Risk." *HIV Infection in Women: Setting a New Agenda.* Washington, D.C. (February 22-24) Pp. S46. Abstract Number TF-162.

1995c "Response to Social Science Models for Reducing HIV Transmission." In *Assessing the Social and Behavioral Science Base for HIV/AIDS Prevention and Intervention Workshop Summary.* Washington, D.C.: National Academy Press. Pp. 45-53.

CONTI, LISA, SPENCER LIEB, TRACY SPRADLING, ET AL.
1993 "AIDS Epidemic among Florida Women." *Journal of Florida Medical Association* 80(4): 246-249.

CONVERSE, PHILIP
1986 "Generalization and the Social Psychology of 'Other Worlds'. In *Metatheory in Social Science: Pluralisms and Subjectives.* D. Fiske and R. Shweder, eds. Chicago: University of Chicago Press. Pp 42-60.

COODLEY, GREG O., MARCIA K. COODLEY, ANDREA F. THOMPSON, ET AL.
1995 "Clinical Aspects of HIV Infection in Women." *Journal of General Internal Medicine* 10(2): 99-110.

COOK, JUDITH A., ANDREW M. BOXER, MARGE H. COHEN, ET AL.
1991 "The Elusive Concept of AIDS Risk Factor: Reports by Women Attending an Inner City Public Hospital HIV Clinic." *Sociological Practical Review* 2(2): 921-928.

COREA, GENA
1992 *The Invisible Epidemic: The Story of Women and AIDS.* New York: Harper Collins.

COTTON, DEBORAH, DIANE FINKELSTEIN, WEILI HE, ET AL.
1993 "Determinants of Accrual of Women to a Large Multicenter Clinical Trials Program of Human Immunodeficiency Virus Infection." *Journal of Acquired Immune Deficiency* 6(12): 1322-1328.

COTTON, D. AND D. WATTS, EDS.
in press *The Medical Management of AIDS in Women.* New York: Wiley-Liss, Inc.

COUTSOUDIS, A., R. BOBAT, H. COOVADIA, ET AL.
1995 "The Effects of Vitamin A Supplementation on the Morbidity of Children Born to HIV-Infected Women." *American Journal of Public Health* 85(8; Part 1): 1076-1081.

COWAN, D.N., J. BRUNDAGE, R. MILLER, ET AL.
1989 "Prevalence of HIV Infection among U.S. Army Reserve Component Personnel." *International Conference on AIDS* 5: 78.

COWAN, D.N., J.F. BRUNDAGE, AND R.S. POMERANTZ
1994 "HIV Infection among Women in the Army Reserve Components." *Journal of Acquired Immune Deficiency Syndrome* 7(2): 171-176.

COWAN, D.N., J.F. BRUNDAGE, R.S. POMERANTZ, ET AL.
1991 "HIV Infection among Members of the Army Reserve Components Residing in New York City." *New York State Journal of Medicine* 91(11): 479-482.

1994 "HIV Infection among Members of the U.S. Army Reserve Components with Medical and Health Occupations." *Journal of the American Medical Association* 265(21): 2826-2830.

CRAVEN, DONALD E., KATHLEEN A. STEGER AND CECELIA JAREK
1994 "Human Immunodeficiency Virus Infection in Pregnancy: Epidemiology and Prevention of Vertical Transmission." *Infection Control and Hospital Epidemiology* 15(1): 36-47.

CRIMP, D., ED.
1987 *AIDS: Cultural Analysis: Cultural Activism.* Cambridge, MA: MIT Press.

CRONBACH, LEE
1986 "Social Inquiry by and for Earthlings." In *Metatheory in Social Science: Pluralisms and Subjectives*. D. Fiske and R. Shweder, eds. Chicago: University of Chicago Press. Pp. 83-107.

CRUMBLE, D., T. HECKMAN, K. SIKKEMA, ET AL.
1995 "Inner-City, Older Adult Women's Risk of HIV Infection." *HIV Infection in Women: Setting a New Agenda*. Washington, D.C. (February 22-24) Pp. S45. Abstract Number TE-157.

CURRIER, JUDITH S.
1995 "Medical Management of HIV Disease in Women." In *HIV Infection in Women*. Howard Minkoff, Jack A. DeHovitz, and Ann Duerr. New York: Raven Press. Pp. 125-156.

CURTIS, J. AND D. PATRICK
1993 "Race and Survival Time with AIDS: A Synthesis of the Literature." *American Journal of Public Health* 83(10): 1425-1428.

CUTTING, W.
1994 "Breast-Feeding and HIV—A Balance of Risks." *Journal of Tropical Pediatrics* 40(1) 6-11.

CWIKEL, J.
1994 "After Epidemiological Research: What Next? Community Action for Health Promotion." *Public Health Reviews* 22(3-4): 375-394.

D'ANDRADE, ROY
1986 "Three Scientific World Views and the Covering Law Model." In *Metatheory in Social Science: Pluralisms and Subjectives*. D. Fiske and R. Shweder, eds. Chicago: University of Chicago Press. Pp. 19-41.

D'AQUILA, RICHARD, ANN B. WILLIAMS, HERBERT D. KLEBER, ET AL.
1986 "Prevalence of HTLV-III Infection among New Haven, Connecticut, Parenteral Drug Abusers in 1982-1983." *The New England Journal of Medicine* 314(2): 117.

D'COSTA, L.J., F.A. PLUMMER, ET AL.
1985 "Prostitutes are a Major Reservoir of Sexually Transmitted Diseases in Nairobi, Kenya." *Sexually Transmitted Diseases* 12(2): 64-67.

D'ERCOLE, ANN AND ELMER STRUENING
1990 "Victimization among Homeless Women: Implications for Service Delivery." *Journal of Community Psychology* 18(2): 141-152.

DADA, ABINBOLA J., FEMI OYEWOLE, RONKE ONOFOWOKAN, ET AL.
1993 "Demographic Characteristics of Retroviral Infections (HIV-1, HIV-2, and HTLV-1) among Female Professional Sex Workers in Lagos, Nigeria." *Journal of Acquired Immune Deficiency Syndromes* 6(12): 1358-1363.

DALEY, DANIEL
1994 "Reproductive Health and AIDS-Related Services for Women: How Well are They Integrated?" *Family Planning Perspectives* 26(6): 264-269.

DALLABETTA, G., P. MIOTTI, J. CHIPANGWI, ET AL.
1993 "High Socioeconomic Status as a Risk Factor for Human Immunodeficiency Virus Type-1 (HIV-1) Infection but not for Sexually Transmitted Diseases in Women in Malawi: Implications for HIV-1 Control." *Journal of Infectious Diseases* 167(1): 36-42.

DALTON, HARLON
1989 "AIDS in Blackface." *Daedalus* 118(3): 205-227.

DANIEL, HERBERT
1994 "We are All People Living with AIDS: Myths and Realities of AIDS in Brazil." In *AIDS: The Politics of Survival.* Nancy Krieger and Glenn Margo, eds. Amityville, NY: Baywood Publishing Co. Pp. 197-212.

DANZIGER, SHELDON H., GARY D. SANDEUR AND DANIEL H. WEINBURG
1994 *Confronting Poverty: Prescriptions for Change.* New York: Russell Sage Foundation.

DARROW, W., D. ECHENBERG, H. JAFFE, ET AL.
1987 "Risk Factors for Human Immunodeficiency Virus (HIV) Infections in Homosexual Men." *American Journal of Public Health* 77(4): 479-483.

DARNEY, P., W. MYHRA, E. ATKINSON, ET AL.
1989 "Serosurvey of Human Immunodeficiency Virus Infection in Women at a Family Planning Clinic: Absence of Infection in an Indigent Population in San Francisco." *American Journal of Public Health* 79(7): 883-885.

DAS, A., S. JANA, A.K. CHAKRABORTY, ET AL.
1994 "Community Based Survey of STD/HIV Infection among Commercial Sex-Workers in Calcutta (India). Part III: Clinical Findings of Sexually Transmitted Diseases." *Journal of Communicable Diseases* 26(4): 192-196.

DAS, SARTHAK
1995 *AIDS in India: An Ethnography of HIV/AIDS amongst Bombay's Commercial Sex Workers.* Cambridge, MA: Departments of Anthropology and Sanskrit and Indian Studies, Harvard University.

DATTA, P., J. EMBREE, J. KREISS, ET AL.
1994 "Mother-to-Child Transmission of Human Immunodeficiency Virus Type I: Report from Nairobi Study." *Journal of Infectious Diseases* 170(5): 1134-1140.

DAVIES, ANTHONY, NICOLA DOMINY, ANDREW PETERS, ET AL.
1995 "HIV in Injecting Drug Users in Edinburgh: Prevalence and Correlates." *Journal of Acquired Immune Deficiency Syndromes* 8(4): 399-405.

DAVIES, MIRANDA, ED.
1994 *Women and Violence: Realities and Responses Worldwide.* London: Zed Books.

DE BRUYN, M., H. JACKSON, M. WIJERMARS, ET AL.
1995 *Facing the Challenges of HIV, AIDS, STDs: A Gender-Based Response.* Geneva, Switzerland: World Health Organization.

DE BRUYN, MARIA
1991 "Gender-Related Problems of Self-Protection against HIV Infection." *Vena* 5(1): 6-11.
1992 "Women and AIDS in Developing Countries." *Social Science and Medicine* 34(3): 249-262.

DE COCK, KEVIN M., EHOUNOU EKPINI, EMANUEL GNAORE, ET AL.
1994 "The Public Health Implications of AIDS Research in Africa." *Journal of the American Medical Association* 272(6): 481-486.

DE COCK, KEVIN M., ZADI FERNANDE, GEORETTE ADJORLOLO, ET AL.
1994 "Retrospective Study of Maternal HIV-1 and HIV-2 Infections and Child Survival in Abidjan, Côte d'Ivoire." *British Medical Journal* 308(6925): 441-443.

DE LA CANCELA, VICTOR
1989 "Minority AIDS Prevention: Moving Beyond Cultural Perspectives Towards Sociopolitical Empowerment." *AIDS Education and Prevention* 1(2): 141-153.

DE VINCENZI, ISABELLE
1994 "A Longitudinal Study of Human Immunodeficiency Virus Transmission by Heterosexual Partners." *The New England Journal of Medicine* 331(6): 341-346.

DE WAAL, A. AND R. OMAAR
    1995 "Famine in Somalia." *The Lancet* 341(8858): 1479.

DE ZALDUONDO, BARBARA, GERARD MSAMANGA, AND LINCOLN CHEN
    1989 "AIDS in Africa: Diversity in the Global Pandemic." *Daedalus* 118(3): 165-204.

DECOSAS, J., F. KANE, J.K. ANARFI, ET AL.
    1995 "Migration and AIDS." *The Lancet* 346(8978): 826-828.

DEHOVITZ, JACK A.
    1995 "Natural History of HIV Infection in Women." In *HIV Infection in Women*. Howard
        Minkoff, Jack A. DeHovitz, and Ann Duerr, eds. New York: Raven Press. Pp. 57-
        72.

DELACOSTE, FREDERIQUE AND PRISCILLA ALEXANDER, EDS.
    1987 *Sex Work: Writings by Women in the Sex Industry*. San Francisco: Cleis Press.

DEL FANTE, P., F. JENNISKENS, L. LUSH, ET AL.
    1993 "HIV, Breast-Feeding, and Under-5 Mortality: Modeling the Impact of Policy Deci-
        sions For or Against Breast-Feeding." *Journal of Tropical Medicine and Hygiene*
        96(4): 203-211.

DEL RIO-ZOLEZZI, A., A. LIGUORI, C. MAGIS-RODRIGUEZ, ET AL.
    1995 "La Epidemia de VIH/SIDA y la Mujer en Mexico." Salud Publica de Mexico 37(6):
        581-591.

DENENBERG, RISA
    1990 "What the Numbers Mean," In *Women, AIDS and Activism*. The ACT Up/ New
        York and AIDS Book Group, eds. Boston: South End Press. Pp. 159-164.

DENENBERG, RISA
    1992 "Invisible Women: Lesbians and Health Care." *Health/PAC Bulletin* 22(1): 14-21.

DENGELEGI, L., J. WEBER, AND S. TORQUATO
    1990 "Drug Users' AIDS-Related Knowledge, Attributes, and Behaviors Before and After
        AIDS Education Sessions." *Public Health Reports* 105(5): 504-510.

DENIAUD, F.
    1994 "Premature Removal of Condoms by Young Men in Abidjan, Côte d'Ivoire: An
        Example of an AIDS Prevention Dilemma." *AIDS* 8(1): 140.

DENISON, REBECCA
    1995 "Call Us Survivors! Women Organized to Respond to Life-Threatening Diseases
        (WORLD)," In *Women Resisting AIDS: Feminist Strategies of Empowerment*. Beth
        E. Schneider and Nancy E. Stoller, eds. Philadelphia: Temple University Press. Pp.
        195-207.

DENMARK, F. AND M. PALUDI, EDS.
    1993 *Psychology of Women: A Handbook of Issues and Theories*. Westport, Connecticut:
        Greenwood Press.

DESCHAMPS, M.M., J. PAPE, P. WILLIAMS-RUSSO, ET AL.
    1993 "A Prospective Study of HIV-Seropositive Asymptomatic Women of Childbearing
        Age in a Developing Country. *Journal of Acquired Immune Deficiency Syndromes*
        6(5): 446-451.

DES JARLAIS, D., K. CHOOPANYA, S. VANCHSENI, ET AL.
    1994 "AIDS Risk Reduction and Reduced HIV Seroconversion among Injection Drug
        Users in Bangkok." *American Journal of Public Health* 84(3): 452-455.

DES JARLAIS, D., S. FRIEDMAN, AND C. CASREIL.
    1990 "Target Groups for Preventing AIDS Among Intravenous Drug Users: 2. The Hard
        Data Studies." *Journal of Counseling and Clinical Psychology* 58(1): 50-56.

DES JARLAIS, D., J. WESTON, S. FREIDMAN, ET AL.
1992 "Implications of the Revised Surveillance Definition: AIDS among New York City Drug Users." *American Journal of Public Health* 82(11): 1531-1533.

DES JARLAIS, DON C. AND SAMUEL R. FRIEDMAN
1988 "Needle Sharing among IVDUs at Risk for AIDS." *American Journal of Public Health* 78(11): 1498-1499.
1994 "AIDS and the Use of Injected Drugs." *Scientific American* 270(2): 82-87.

DES JARLAIS, DON C., SAMUEL R. FRIEDMAN AND JO L. SOTHERAN
1992 "The First City: HIV among Intravenous Drug Users in New York City," In *AIDS: The Making of a Chronic Disease*. Elizabeth Fee and Daniel M. Fox, eds. Berkeley: University of California Press. Pp. 279-298.

DES JARLAIS, DON C., SAMUEL R. FRIEDMAN AND THOMAS WARD
1993 "Harm Reduction: A Public Health Response to the AIDS Epidemic among Injecting Drug Users." *Annual Review of Public Health* 14: 413-450.

DES JARLAIS, DON C., HOLLY HAGAN, SAMUEL R. FRIEDMAN, ET AL.
1995 "Maintaining Low HIV Prevalence in Populations of Injecting Drug Users." *Journal of the American Medical Association* 274(15): 1226-1231.

DES JARLAIS, DON C., NANCY S. PADIAN AND WARREN WINKLESTEIN, JR.
1994 "Targeted HIV-Prevention Programs." *The New England Journal of Medicine* 331(21): 1451-1453.

DESVARIEUX, M. AND J.W. PAPE
1991 "HIV and AIDS in Haiti: Recent Developments." *AIDS Care* 3(3): 271-279.

DIAZ, T., J. BUEHLER, K. CASTRO, ET AL.
1993 "AIDS Trends among Hispanics in the United States." *American Journal of Public Health* 83(4): 504-509.

DIAZ, THERESA, SUSAN Y. CHU, JAMES W. BUEHLER, ET AL.
1994 "Socioeconomic Differences among People with AIDS: Results from a Multistate Surveillance Project." *American Journal of Preventive Medicine* 10(4): 217-222.

DIAZ, THERESA, SUSAN Y. CHU, R. BYERS, ET AL.
1994 "The Types of Drugs Used by HIV-Infected Injection Drug Users in a Multistate Surveillance Project: Implications for Intervention." *American Journal of Public Health* 84(12): 1971-1975.

DIAZ, THERESA, SUSAN Y. CHU, LISA CONTI, ET AL.
1994 "Risk Behaviors of Persons with Heterosexually Acquired HIV Infection in the United States: Results of a Multistate Surveillance Project." *Journal of Acquired Immune Deficiency Syndromes* 7(9): 958-963.

DICKER, B.
1989 "Risk of AIDS among Lesbians." *American Journal of Public Health* 79(11): 1569.

DICLEMENTE, RALPH J. AND GINA WINGOOD
1995 "A Randomized Controlled Trial of an HIV Sexual Risk-Reduction Intervention for Young African-American Women." *Journal of the American Medical Association* 274(16): 1271-1276.

DIETRICH, U., J.K. MANIAR, AND H. RUBSAMEN-WAIGMANN
1995 "The Epidemiology of HIV in India." *Trends in Microbiology* 3(1): 17-21.

DIFERDINANDO, GEORGE
1993 "Tuberculosis: An Epidemic Reemerges. I: The New Face of an Old Disease." *Emergency Medicine* 25(2): 141-158.

DINGELSTAD, A., E. DE VROOME, M. PAALMAN, ET AL.
1994 "Trends in Condom Use among Nonmonogamous Heterosexual Men in The Netherlands." *American Journal of Public Health* 84(7): 1184.

DIXON-MUELLER, R. AND J. WASSERHEIT
    1991 *The Culture of Silence: Reproductive Tract Infections among Women in the Third World.*
        New York: International Women's Health Coalition.

DOS SANTOS, J., M. LOPES, E. DELIEGE-VASCONCELOS, ET AL.
    1995 "Seroprevalence of HIV, HTLV-I/II, and Other Perinatally-Transmitted Pathogens
        in Salvador, Bahia." *Revista do Instituto de Medicina Tropical de Sao Paulo* 37(4):
        343-348.

DOHERTY, M.C., R.S. GARFEIN, E.R. MONTERROSO, ET AL.
    1995 "Circumstances of Women Initiating Injection Drug Use." *HIV Infection in Women:
        Setting a New Agenda.* Washington, D.C. (February 22-24) Pp. S53. Abstract
        Number FEI-188.

DONDERO, T., JR. AND J. CURRAN
    1991 "Serosurveillance of Human Immunodeficiency Virus Infection." *American Journal
        of Public Health* 81(5): 561-562.

DONDERO, T., JR., M. PAPPAIOANOU, AND J. CURRAN
    1988 "Monitoring Levels and Trends of HIV Infection: The Public Health Service's HIV
        Surveillance Program." *Public Health Reports* 103(3): 213-220.

DONOHUE, AGNES H., MARY ANN DANELLO AND RUTH L. KIRSCHSTEIN
    1989 "HIV Infection in Women: An Inventory of Public Health Service Initiatives."
        AIDS & Public Policy Journal 4(2): 120-124.

DOWDLE, W.
    1983 "The Epidemiology of AIDS." *Public Health Reports* 98(4): 308-312.

DOWNING, MOHER
    1995 "Some Comments on the Beginnings of AIDS Outreach to Women Drug Users in
        San Francisco." In *Women Resisting AIDS: Feminist Strategies of Empowerment.*
        Beth E. Schneider and Nancy E. Stoller, eds. Philadelphia: Temple University
        Press. Pp. 231-245.

DOYAL, L.
    1995 *What Makes Women Sick: Gender and the Political Economy of Health.* New
        Brunswick, New Jersey: Rutgers University Press.

DROTMAN, P. AND M. MAYS
    1988 "AIDS and Lesbians: IV Drug Use is the Risk." Paper Presented at the Fourth Inter-
        national Conference on AIDS, Stockholm.

DRUCKER, ERNEST
    1994 "Epidemic in the War Zone: AIDS and Community Survival in New York City." In
        AIDS: The Politics of Survival. Nancy Krieger and Glenn Margo, eds. Amityville,
        NY: Baywood Publishing Company. Pp. 73-88.

DUARTE, G., S.M. QUINTANA, E. GIR, ET AL.
    1994 "Poor Pregnant Women and HIV-1 Infection: Maternal Prognosis in a Brazilian
        Community." *International Conference on AIDS* 10(1): 253. Abstract Number
        PB0440 .

DUERR, ANN AND GENE E. HOWE
    1995 "Contraception." In *HIV Infection in Women.* Howard Minkoff, Jack A. DeHovitz,
        and Ann Duerr, eds. New York: Raven Press. Pp. 157-172.

DU GUERNY, JACQUES AND ELISABETH SJÖBERG
    1993 "Inter-Relationship Between Gender Relations and the HIV/AIDS Epidemic: Some
        Possible Considerations for Policies and Programmes." *AIDS* 7(8): 1027-1034.

DUNCAN, ELIZABETH, GERAUD TIBAUX, ANDRÉE PELZER, ET AL.
    1990 "First Coitus before Menarche and Risk of Sexually Transmitted Disease." *The
        Lancet* 335(8685): 338-340.

DUNN, D., M. NEWELL, M. MAYAUX, ET AL.
　　1994 "Mode of Delivery and Vertical Transmission of HIV-1: A Review of Prospective Studies." *Journal of Acquired Immune Deficiency Syndromes* 7(10): 1064-1066.

DUNN, FREDERICK L. AND CRAIG R. JANES
　　1986 "Introduction: Medical Anthropology and Epidemiology." In *Anthropology and Epidemiology*. Craig R. Janes, Ron Stall and Sandra Gifford, eds. Boston: D. Reidel Publishing Company. Pp. 3-34.

DUPRAT, C., Z. MOHAMMED, P. DATTA, ET AL.
　　1994 "Human Immunodeficiency Virus Type 1 IgA in Breast Milk and Serum." *Pediatric Infectious Disease Journal* 13(7): 603-608.

DYCHES, HAYNE AND BETH RUSHING
　　1993 "The Health Status of Women in the World-System." *International Journal of Health Services* 23(2): 359-371.

EASTERBROOK, PHILIPPA J., JEANE C. KERULY, TERI CREAGH-KIRK, ET AL.
　　1991 "Racial and Ethnic Differences in Outcome in Zidovudine Treated Patients with Advanced HIV Disease." *Journal of the American Medical Association* 266(19): 2713-2718.

EDLIN, BRIAN R., KATHLEEN L. IRWIN, SAIRUS FARUQUE, ET AL.
　　1994 "Intersecting Epidemics: Crack Cocaine Use and HIV-Infection in Inner-City Young Adults. Multicenter Crack Cocaine and HIV Infection Study Team." *New England Journal of Medicine* 331(21): 1422-1427.

EISENSTAEDT, RICHARD AND THOMAS GETZEN
　　1988 "Screening Blood Donors for Human Immunodeficiency Virus Antibody: Cost-Benefit Analysis." *American Journal of Public Health* 78(4): 450-454.

EKSTRAND, M. AND T. COATES
　　1990 "Maintenance of Safer Sexual Behaviors and Predictors of Risky Sex: The San Francisco Men's Health Study." *American Journal of Public Health* 80(8): 973-977.

EKSTRAND, M., T. COATES, J. GUYDISH, ET AL.
　　1994 "Are Bisexually Identified Men in San Francisco a Common Vector for Spreading HIV Infection to Women?" *American Journal of Public Health* 84(6): 915-919.

EL-BASSEL, N. AND R. SCHILLING
　　1991 "Drug Use and Sexual Behavior of Indigent African-American Men." *Public Health Reports* 106(5): 586-590.

EL-BASSEL, N. AND R. SCHILLING
　　1992 "15-Month Followup of Women Methadone Patients Taught Skills to Reduce Heterosexual HIV Transmission." *Public Health Reports* 107(5): 500-504.

EL SALVADOR INFORMATION PROJECT
　　1995 *Salvador Free Trade Zones and Women*. El Salvador Information Project (February 11).

ELDERS, M. JOYCELYN
　　1993 "Portrait of Inequality." *Journal of Health Care for the Poor and Underserved* 4(3): 153-162.

ELFORD, JONATHAN
　　1987 "Moral and Social Aspects of AIDS: A Medical Students' Project." *Social Science and Medicine* 24(6): 543-549.

ELIAS, CHRISTOPHER J. AND LORI L. HEISE
　　1994 "Challenges for the Development of Female-Controlled Vaginal Microbicides." *AIDS* 8(1): 1-9.

ELIFSON, K., J. BOLES, E. POSEY, ET AL.
    1993 "Male Transvestite Prostitutes and HIV Risk." *American Journal of Public Health*
        83(2): 260-262.
ELIFSON, K., J. BOLES, AND M. SWEAT
    1993 "Risk Factors Associated with HIV Infection in Male Prostitutes." *American Journal
        of Public Health* 83(1): 79-83.
ELLERBROCK, T.V., S. LIEB, P.E. HARRINGTON, ET AL.
    1992 "Heterosexually Transmitted Human Immunodeficiency Virus Infection among
        Pregnant Women in a Rural Florida Community." *The New England Journal of
        Medicine* 327(24): 1704-1709.
ELLERBROCK, TEDD V., TIMOTHY J. BUSH, MARY E. CHAMBERLAND, ET AL.
    1991 "Epidemiology of Women with AIDS in the United States, 1981 through 1990: A
        Comparison with Heterosexual Men with AIDS." In *Journal of the American Med-
        ical Association* 265(22): 2971-2975.
ELMENDORF, A. EDWARD AND WENDY ROSEBERRY
    1993 "Structural Adjustment: What Effect on Health? On Vulnerability to HIV?" Paper
        presented at the Tenth International Conference on AIDS, Berlin, (June 10).
ENVIRONMENT ET DÉVELOPPEMENT DU TIERS MONDE
    1991 "Sex Workers, Health, and Human Rights in Africa." *Vena* 5(1): 26.
EPIDEMIOLOGICAL BULLETIN
    1988a "AIDS Situation in the Americas 1988." *Epidemiological Bulletin* 9(4): 1-11.
    1988b "AIDS Surveillance in the Americas. Cumulative Number of Cases and Deaths."
        Epidemiological Bulletin 9(3): 16.
    1989a "AIDS Surveillance in the Americas. Cumulative Number of Cases and Deaths as
        of December, 1989." *Epidemiological Bulletin* 10(3): 16.
    1989b "AIDS Surveillance in the Americas. Cases Reported by Year and Cumulative
        Number of Cases and Deaths by Country and Subregion. 1986 to 1989." *Epidemi-
        ological Bulletin* 10(2): 10.
    1990 "AIDS Surveillance in the Americas." *Epidemiological Bulletin* 11(4): 12.
    1991 "AIDS Surveillance in the Americas." *Epidemiological Bulletin* 12(3): 15.
    1992a "AIDS in Latin America and the Caribbean: Current Situation." *Epidemiological
        Bulletin* 13(1): 1-8.
    1992b "AIDS Surveillance in the Americas." *Epidemiological Bulletin* 13(3): 15.
    1993a "AIDS Surveillance in the Americas." *Epidemiological Bulletin* 14(2): 13.
    1993b "HIV and AIDS Research in Latin America and the Caribbean: 1983-1991." *Epi-
        demiological Bulletin* 14(1): 10-12.
    1995a "AIDS Surveillance in the Americas." *Epidemiological Bulletin* 15(3): 16.
    1995b "AIDS Surveillance in the Americas." *Epidemiological Bulletin* 16(2): 15.
ESSEX, MAX, SOULEYMANE MBOUP, PHYLLIS KANKI, ET AL., EDS.
    1994 *AIDS in Africa*. New York: Raven Press.
ESCOBAR, ARTURO
    1995 *Encountering Development: The Making and Unmaking of the Third World*. Princeton,
        NJ: Princeton University Press.
ESU-WILLIAMS, EKA
    1993 "Needs for a Female-Controlled Method of HIV Transmission: A Woman's Per-
        spective." *Society for Women & AIDS in Africa* (November).
    1995 "AIDS in the 1990s: Individual and Collective Responsibility." In *Women Resist-
        ing AIDS: Feminist Strategies of Empowerment*. Beth E. Schneider and Nancy
        Stoller, eds. Philadelphia: Temple University Press. Pp. 23-31.

EUROPEAN STUDY GROUP ON HETEROSEXUAL TRANSMISSION OF HIV
    1992 "Comparison of Female to Male and Male to Female Transmission of HIV." *British Medical Journal* 304(6830): 809-813.

EVANS, R., M. BARER, AND T. MARMOR
    1994 *Why are Some People Healthy and Others Not? The Determinants of the Health of Populations*. New York: Aldine.

EVERSLEY, RANI B., AMANDA NEWSTETTER, ANDREW AVINS, ET AL.
    1993 "Sexual Risk and Perception of Risk for HIV Infection among Multiethnic Family-Planning Clinics." *American Journal of Preventive Medicine* 9(2): 92-95.

EWART, CRAIG
    1995 "HIV/AIDS Prevention: Models of Individual Behavior in Social and Cultural Contexts." In *Assessing the Social and Behavioral Science Base for HIV/AIDS Prevention and Intervention Workshop Summary*. Washington, D.C.: National Academy Press. Pp. 1-30.

FADEN, RUTH R., ANDREA C. GIELEN, NANCY KASS, ET AL.
    1994 "Prenatal HIV-Antibody Testing and the Meaning of Consent." *AIDS & Public Policy Journal* 9(3): 151-159.

FAHEY, JOHN L., JEREMY M.G. TAYLOR, ROGER DETELS, ET AL.
    1990 "The Prognostic Value of Cellular and Serologic Markers in Infection with Human Immunodeficiency Virus Type I." *The New England Journal of Medicine* 322(3): 166-172.

FAIRCHILD, AMY AND EILEEN TYNAN
    1994 "Policies of Containment: Immigration in the Era of AIDS." *American Journal of Public Health* 84(12): 2011-2022.

FARMER, PAUL
    1990 "Sending Sickness: Sorcery, Politics, and Changing Concepts of AIDS in Rural Haiti." *Medical Anthropology Quarterly* 4(1): 6-27.
    1991 "New Disorder, Old Dilemmas: AIDS and Anthropology in Haiti." In *Social Analysis in the Time of AIDS*. G. Herdt and S. Lindenbaum, eds. Beverly Hills: Sage Publications.
    1992 *AIDS and Accusation: Haiti and the Geography of Blame*. Berkeley: University of California Press.
    1994 *Uses of Haiti*. Monroe, ME: Common Courage Press.
    1995a "Culture, Poverty, and the Dynamics of HIV Transmission in Rural Haiti." In *Culture and Sexual Risk: Anthropological Perspectives on AIDS*. Han ten Brummelhuis and Gilbert Herdt, eds. New York: Gordon and Breach. Pp. 3-28.
    1995b "Medicine and Social Justice." *America* 173(2): 13-17.
    1996 "On Suffering and Structural Violence: A View from Below." *Daedalus* 125(1): 261-283.

FARMER, PAUL AND BYRON GOOD
    1991 "Illness Representations in Medical Anthropology: A Critical Review and a Case Study of the Representation of AIDS in Haiti." In *The Mental Representation of Health and Illness*. J. Skelton and R. Croyle, eds. New York: Springer-Verlag. Pp. 131-167.

FARMER, PAUL AND JIM KIM
    1991 "Anthropology, Accountability, and the Prevention of AIDS." *Journal of Sex Research* 28(2): 203-221.

FARMER, PAUL AND ARTHUR KLEINMAN
    1989 "AIDS as Human Suffering." *Daedalus* 118(2): 135-162.

FARMER, PAUL, SHIRLEY LINDENBAUM AND MARY-JO DELVECCHIO GOOD
    1993 "Women, Poverty and AIDS: An Introduction." *Culture, Medicine and Psychiatry*
    17(4): 387-397.

FARMER, PAUL, SALLY ZIERLER, AND WILLIAM RODRIQUEZ
    1995 "Women, Poverty and AIDS: On Scholarship and Social Justice." *HIV Infection in
    Women: Setting a New Agenda.* Washington, D.C. (February 22-24) Pp. S46.
    Abstract Number TF-163.

FARR, G., H. GABELNICK, K. STURGEN, ET AL.
    1994 "Contraceptive Efficacy and Acceptability of the Female Condom." *American Jour-
    nal of Public Health* 84(12): 1960-1964.

FEACHEM, R., P. MUSGROVE, AND A. ELMENDORF
    1995 "Comment from the World Bank." *AIDS* 9(8): 982-984.

FEE, ELIZABETH AND DANIEL M. FOX, EDS.
    1992 *AIDS: The Making of a Chronic Disease.* Berkeley: University of California Press.

FEE, ELIZABETH AND NANCY KRIEGER
    1993 "Understanding AIDS: Historical Interpretations and the Limits of Biomedical
    Individualism." *American Journal of Public Health* 83(10): 1477-1486.
    1994 "Thinking and Rethinking AIDS: Implications for Health Policy." In *AIDS: The
    Politics of Survival.* Nancy Krieger and Glenn Margo, eds. Amityville, NY: Baywood
    Publishing Co. Pp. 227-254.

FEHRS, L., D. HILL, P. KERNDT, ET AL.
    1991 "Targeted HIV Screening at a Los Angeles Prenatal/Family Planning Health Cen-
    ter." *American Journal of Public Health* 81(5): 619-622.

FEILDEN, RACHEL, JAMES ALLMAN, JOEL MONTAGUE, ET AL.
    1981 *Health, Population and Nutrition in Haiti: A Report Prepared for the World Bank.*
    Boston: Management Sciences for Health.

FEIN, OLIVER
    1995 "The Influence of Social Class on Health Status: American and British Research on
    Health Inequalities." *Journal of General Internal Medicine* 10(10): 577-586.

FELDBLUM, P. AND J. FORTNEY
    1988 "Condoms, Spermicides, and the Transmission of Human Immunodeficiency Virus:
    A Review of the Literature." *American Journal of Public Health* 78(1): 52-54.

FELDMAN, DOUGLAS A.
    1994a "Conclusion." In *Global AIDS Policy.* Douglas Feldman, ed. Westport, Connecti-
    cut: Bergin and Garvey. Pp. 236-240.
    1994b "Introduction." In *Global AIDS Policy.* Douglas Feldman, ed. Westport, Connecti-
    cut: Bergin and Garvey. Pp. 1-6.

FELDMAN, DOUGLAS A., ED.
    1990 *Culture and AIDS.* New York: Praeger.
    1994 *Global AIDS Policy.* Westport, Connecticut: Bergin and Garvey.

FENTON, THOMAS P. AND MARY J. HEFFRON, EDS.
    1987 *Women in the Third World: A Directory of Resources.* Maryknoll, NY: Orbis Books.

FERENCIC, NINA
    1991 "Women and HIV/AIDS: Situation and Action." *Vena* 5(1): 12-14.

FERGUSON, KRISTI J., JACK T. STAPLETON AND CHARLES M. HELMS
    1991 "Physician's Effectiveness in Assessing Risk for Human Immunodeficiency Virus
    Infection." *Archives of Internal Medicine* 151(4): 561-564.

FERRARA, ANTHONY J.
    1984 "My Personal Experience with AIDS." *American Psychologist* 39(11): 1285-1287.

FERREIRA, A. AND S. MALLOL
1994 "Training Health Agents for Prevention in Urban Low Socioeconomic Status Women." *International Conference on AIDS* 10(1): 382. Abstract Number PD0135.

FERRY, BENÔIT
1994 "Measuring Sexual Behavior in the General Population in Developing Countries–Lessons from Recent Studies." *Sociétés d'Afrique & SIDA* 4: 3-4.

FIFE, DANIEL AND CHARLES MODE
1992 "AIDS Incidence and Income." *Journal of Acquired Immune Deficiency Syndromes* 5(11): 1105-1110.

FIGUEROA, J.P., A. BRATHWAITE, J. MORRIS, ET AL.
1994 "Rising HIV-1 Prevalence among Sexually Transmitted Disease Clinic Attenders in Jamaica: Traumatic Sex and Genital Ulcers as Risk Factors." *Journal of Acquired Immune Deficiency Syndromes* 7(3): 310-316.

FINDLEN, BARBARA, ED.
Listen Up: Voices from the Next Feminist Generation. Seattle, WA: Seal Press.

FISCHL, MARGARET, DOUGLAS D. RICHMAN, MICHAEL H. GRIECO, ET AL.
1987 "The Efficacy of Azidothymidine (AZT) in the Treatment of Patients with AIDS and AIDS-Related Complex." *The New England Journal of Medicine* 317(4): 185-191.

FISCHHOFF, BARUCH
1995 "Response: What do People Need to Know About AIDS?" In *Assessing the Social and Behavioral Science Base for HIV/AIDS Prevention and Intervention Workshop Summary.* Washington, D.C.: National Academy Press. Pp. 31-44.

FISHER, BARBARA, MEL HOVELL, C. RICHARD HOFSTETTER, ET AL.
1995 "Risks Associated with Long-Term Homelessness among Women: Battery, Rape, and HIV Infection." *International Journal of Health Services* 25(2): 351-369.

FISKE, DONALD AND RICHARD SHWEDER, EDS.
1986a *Metatheory in Social Science: Pluralisms and Subjectives.* Chicago: University of Chicago Press.
1986b "Pluralisms and Subjectives." In *Metatheory in Social Science: Pluralisms and Subjectives.* D. Fiske and R. Shweder, eds. Chicago: University of Chicago Press. Pp. 362-370.

FLASKERUD, J.H. AND E. CAVILLO
1991 "Beliefs about AIDS, Health, and Illness among Low-Income Latina Women." *Research in Nursing and Health* 14(6): 431-438.

FLASKERUD, JACQUELYN H. AND ADELINE NYAMATHI
1990 "Effects of an AIDS Education Program on the Knowledge, Attitudes and Practices of Low Income Black and Latina Women." *Journal of Community Health* 15(6): 343-355.

FLASKERUD, JACQUELYN H. AND JOYCE THOMPSON
1991 "Beliefs About AIDS, Health, and Illness in Low-Income White Women." *Nursing Research* 40(5): 266-271.

FLEISHMAN, J.A., D.C. HSIA, AND F.J. HELLINGER
1994 "Correlates of Medical Service Utilization among People with HIV Infection." *Health Services Research* 29(5): 527-548.

FLEMING, P.L., C.A. CIESIESKI AND R.L. BERKELMAN
1991 "Sex-Specific Differences in the Prevalence of AIDS-Indicative Diagnoses, United States 1988-1989." Paper presented at the Seventh International Conference on AIDS, Florence, Italy.

FLORA, JUNE, EDWARD MAIBACH, AND DAVID HOLTGRAVE
　　1995 "Communication Campaigns for HIV Prevention: Using Mass Media in the Next Decade." In *Assessing the Social and Behavioral Science Base for HIV/AIDS Prevention and Intervention Workshop Summary*. Washington, D.C.: National Academy Press. Pp. 129-154.

FORD, K. AND A. NORRIS
　　1995 "Substance Use and Risk Taking Behaviors among Urban, Low Income, African American and Hispanic Young Women." *HIV Infection in Women: Setting a New Agenda*. Washington, D.C. (February 22-24) Pp. P118. Abstract Number TP-506.

FORLAND, F. AND K. ERIKSEN
　　1994 "HIV-Prevalens I Mutoko, Zimbabwe. En Studie Blant Gravide og Pasienter med Kjonnssykdommer." *Tidsskr Nor Laegeforen* 114(9): 1050-1052.

FORNEY, MARY ANN, JAMES A. INCIARDI AND DOROTHY LOCKWOOD
　　1992 "Exchanging Sex for Crack-Cocaine: A Comparison of Women from Rural and Urban Communities." *Community Health* 17(2): 73-86.

FOX, LAURIE, NANCY E. WILLIAMSON, WILLIARD CATES, ET AL.
　　1995 "Improving Reproductive Health: Integrating STD and Contraceptive Services." *Journal of the American Medical Women's Association* 50(3/4): 129-138.

FRANKEL, BARBARA
　　1986 "Two Extremes on the Social Science Commitment Continuum." In *Metatheory in Social Science: Pluralisms and Subjectives*. Fiske, D. and R. Shweder, eds. Chicago: University of Chicago Press. Pp 353-361.

FRANKENBERG, RONALD
　　1992 "What Identity's at Risk? Anthropologists and AIDS." *Anthropology in Action* 12: 6-9.

FRASER, MARCY AND DIANE JONES
　　1995 "The Role of Nurses in the HIV Epidemic." In *Women Resisting AIDS: Feminist Strategies of Empowerment*. Beth E. Schneider and Nancy E. Stoller, eds. Philadelphia: Temple University Press. Pp. 286-298.

FREEMAN, ROBERT C. AND JOHN F. FRENCH
　　1995 "What's the Addict's Grapevine When There's 'Bad Dope'?" *Public Health Reports* 110(September/October): 621-624.

FREIRE, PAULO
　　1970 *Pedagogy of the Oppressed*. New York: Continuum.

FREUDENBERG, NICHOLAS
　　1994 "AIDS Prevention in the United States: Lessons from the First Decade." In *AIDS: The Politics of Survival*. Nancy Krieger and Glenn Margo, eds. Amityville, NY: Baywood Publishing Company. Pp. 61-72.

FREUDENBERG, NICHOLAS AND URAYOANA TRINIDAD
　　1992 "The Role of Community Organizations in AIDS Prevention in Two Latino Communities in New York City." *Health Education Quarterly* 19(1): 219-232.

FRIEDLAND, GERALD H., BRIAN SALTZMAN, JOAN VILENO, ET AL.
　　1991 "Survival Differences in Patients with AIDS." *Journal of Acquired Immune Deficiency Syndromes* 4(2): 144-53.

FRIEDMAN, LAWRENCE, LEE STRUNIN AND RALPH HINGSON
　　1993 "A Survey of Attitudes, Knowledge, and Behavior Related to HIV Testing of Adolescents and Young Adults Enrolled in Alcohol and Drug Treatment." *Journal of Adolescent Health* 14(6): 442-445.

FRIEDMAN, S., A. NEAIGUS, B. JOSE, ET AL.
    1995 "Gender Differences in HIV Seroprevalence among New Drug Injectors Vary by
        City and by Social Network." *HIV Infection in Women: Setting a New Agenda*.
        Washington, D.C. (February 22-24) Pp. P82. Abstract Number WP-365.

FRIEDMAN, S., J. SOTHERAN, A. ABDUL-QUADER, ET AL.
    1987 "The AIDS Epidemic among Blacks and Hispanics." *The Milbank Quarterly* 65(S2):
        455-499.

FRIEDMAN, S., L. STRUNIN, AND R. HINGSON
    1993 "A Survey of Attitudes, Knowledge, and Behavior Related to HIV Testing of Ado-
        lescent and Young Adults Enrolled in Alcohol and Drug Treatment." *Journal of
        Adolescent Health* 14(6): 442-445.

FRIEDMAN, S., M. SUFIAN, R. CURTIS, ET AL.
    1992 "Organizing Drug Users Against AIDS." In *The Social Context of AIDS*. J. Huber
        and B. Schneider, eds. Newbury Park, California: Sage. Pp. 115-130.

FRIEDMAN, S., M. SUFIAN, AND D. DES JARLAIS
    1990 "The AIDS Epidemic among Latino Intravenous Drug Users." In *Drug Use in His-
        panic Communities*. R. Glick and J. Moore, eds. New Brunswick, New Jersey: Rut-
        gers University Press. Pp. 45-54.

FRIEDMAN, SAMUEL
    1993 "AIDS as a Sociohistorical Phenomenon." *Advances in Medical Sociology* 3: 19-36.

FRIEDMAN, SAMUEL, W. DE JONG, AND DON DES JARLAIS
    1988 "Problems and Dynamics of Organizing Intravenous Drug Users for AIDS Preven-
        tion." *Health Education Research* 3: 49-57.

FRIEDMAN, SAMUEL R., BRUCE STEPHERSON, JOYCE WOODS, ET AL.
    1992 "Society, Drug Injectors and AIDS." *Journal of Health Care for the Poor and Under-
        served* 3(1): 73-92.

FRIEDMAN, SAMUEL AND CHRISTINA WYPIJEWSKA
    1995 "Social Science Intervention Models for Reducing HIV Transmission." In *Assessing
        the Social and Behavioral Science Base for HIV/AIDS Prevention and Intervention
        Workshop Summary*. Washington, D.C.: National Academy Press. Pp. 53-74.

FUJIMURA, JOAN AND DANNY CHOU
    1994 "Dissent in Science: Styles of Scientific Practice and the Controversy over the
        Cause of AIDS." *Social Science and Medicine* 38(8): 1017-1036.

FULLER, J.
    1991 *AIDS and the Church: A Stimulus to Our Theologizing*. Cambridge, MA: Weston
        School of Theology.

FULLILOVE, M., A. LOWN, AND R.E. FULLILOVE, III
    1992 "Crack 'Hos and Skeezers: Traumatic Experiences of Women Crack Users." *Journal
        of Sex Research* 29(2): 275-287.

FULLILOVE, MINDY THOMPSON, ROBERT E. FULLILOVE, III, KATHERINE HAYNES, ET AL.
    1990 "Black Women and AIDS Prevention: A View Towards Understanding the Gender
        Rules." *Journal of Sex Research* 27(1): 47-64.

FULLILOVE, MINDY THOMPSON, ROBERT E. FULLILOVE, III, GAIL KENNEDY, ET AL.
    1992 "Trauma, Crack and HIV Risk." Presented at the Eighth International Conference
        on AIDS, Amsterdam (July 19-24).

FULLILOVE, ROBERT E., III
    1995 "Community Disintegration and Public Health: A Case Study of New York City."
        In *Assessing the Social and Behavioral Science Base for HIV/AIDS Prevention and
        Intervention Workshop Summary*. Washington, D.C.: National Academy Press. Pp.
        93-116.

FUMENTO, MICHAEL
    1993 *The Myth of Heterosexual AIDS*. Washington, D.C.: Regnery Gateway.

GAIL, MITCHELL, PHILIP ROSENBERG AND JAMES GOEDERT
    1990 "Therapy May Explain Recent Deficits in AIDS Incidence." *Journal of Acquired Immune Deficiency Syndromes* 3(4): 296-306.

GALAVOTTI, C. AND C. BEEKER
    1993 "Changing HIV Risk Behaviors: The Case Against Pessimism." *American Journal of Public Health* 83(12): 1791-1792.

GALLANT, JOEL E., RICHARD D. MOORE AND RICHARD E. CHAISSON
    1994 "Prophylaxis for Opportunistic Infections in Patients with HIV Infection." *Annals of Internal Medicine* 120(11): 932-944.

GAMURORWA, A., D. LUKENGE, J. NAHAMYA, ET AL.
    1993 "Young Women and HIV: Risk Taking in Uganda." *International Conference on AIDS* 9(2): 929. Abstract Number PO-D30-4266.

GARLAND, MIRIAM, BAKER N. MAGGWA, JAPETH K. MATI, ET AL.
    1993 "Knowledge of AIDS and Other Sexually Transmitted Diseases among Women Attending a Family Planning Clinic in Nairobi, Kenya." *American Journal of Preventive Medicine* 9(1): 1-5.

GARLAND, F., E. GORHAM, S. CUNNION, ET AL.
    1992 "Decline in Human Immunodeficiency Virus Seropositivity and Seroconversion in U.S. Navy Enlisted Personnel: 1986 to 1989." *American Journal of Public Health* 82(4): 581-584.

GATTER, PHILIP
    1995 "Anthropology, HIV and Contingent Identities." *Social Science and Medicine* 41(11): 1523-1533.

GAY, CARYL L., F. DANIEL ARMSTRONG, DONNA COHEN, ET AL.
    1995 "The Effects of HIV on Cognitive and Motor Development in Children Born to HIV-Seropositive Women with No Reported Drug Use: Birth to 24 Months." *Pediatrics* 96(6): 1078-1082.

GELLERT, G., R. MAXWELL, K. HIGGINS, ET AL.
    1993 "HIV Infection in the Women's Jail, Orange County, California, 1985 through 1991." *American Journal of Public Health* 83(10): 1454-1456.

GENERAL ACCOUNTING OFFICE (GAO)
    1993a *Needle Exchange—Research Suggest Promise as an AIDS Prevention Strategy*. Washington, D.C.: United States General Accounting Office.
    1993b *Self-Sufficiency: Opportunities and Disincentives on the Road to Economic Independence*. Washington, D.C.: United States General Accounting Office, HRD-93-23.
    1995a *Low Income Families: Comparison of Incomes of AFDC and Working Poor Families*. Washington, D.C.: United States General Accounting Office, 95-63, (January 25).
    1995b *Services for Young Foster Children*. Washington, D.C.: United States General Accounting Office, HEHS 95-114.

GERGEN, KENNETH
    1986 "Correspondence versus Autonomy in the Language of Understanding Human Action." In *Metatheory in Social Science: Pluralisms and Subjectives*. D. Fiske and R. Shweder, eds. Chicago: University of Chicago Press. Pp. 136-162.

GERSHY-DAMET, G., K. KOFFI, B. SORO, ET AL.
    1991 "Seroepidemiological Survey of HIV-1 and HIV-2 Infections in the Five Regions of Ivory Coast." *AIDS* 5(4): 462-463.

GESHEKTER, CHARLES L.
    1995 "Outbreak? AIDS, Africa and the Medicalization of Poverty: Is Africa Facing a Lethal Pandemic?" *Transition* 67: 4-14.

GIBBS, WAYT
    1995 "Lost Science in the Third World." *Scientific American* 273(2): 92-99.

GIFFORD, S.
    1993 "Broken Promises or Missed Understandings? Rationalities of Risk in Public Health." Paper presented at the 89th Annual Meeting of the American Anthropological Association, Washington, D.C. (November 17-21).

GIL, VINCENT E.
    1991 "An Ethnography of HIV/AIDS and Sexuality in The People's Republic of China." *Journal of Sex Research* 28(4): 521-537.
    1994a "Behind the Wall of China: AIDS Profile, AIDS Policy." In *Global AIDS Policy*. Douglas Feldman, ed. Westport, Connecticut: Bergin and Garvey. Pp. 7-27.
    1994b "Sinic Conundrum: A History of HIV/AIDS in the People's Republic of China." *Journal of Sex Research* 31(3): 211-217.

GINZBURG, HAROLD M.
    1984 "Intravenous Drug Users and the Acquired Immune Deficiency Syndrome." *Public Health Reports* 92(2): 206-212.

GINZBURG, HAROLD M., STANLEY H. WEISS, MHAIRI G. MACDONALD, ET AL.
    1985 "HTLV-III Exposure among Drug Users." *Cancer Research* 45(Supplement): 4605s-4608s.

GIRI, T.K., J.P. WALI, H.S. MEENA, ET AL.
    1995 "Sociodemographic Characteristics of HIV Infection in Northern India." *Scandinavian Journal of Infectious Diseases* 27(2): 105-108.

GITLIN, T.
    1995 *The Twilight of Common Dreams: Why American is Wracked by Cultural Wars*. New York: Metropolitan Books.

GIVEN, MICHAEL J., M. ANEES KHAN AND LEE B. REICHMAN
    1994 "Tuberculosis among Patients with AIDS and a Control Group in an Inner-City Community." *Archives of Internal Medicine* 154: 640-645.

GLADWIN, CHRISTINA H.
    1991 *Structural Adjustment and African Women Farmers*. Gainsville, FL: University of Florida Press.

GLASCH, HELEN D., MICHAEL POULSON, ROBERT E. FULLILOVE III, ET AL.
    1991 "Shaping AIDS Education and Prevention Programs for African Americans amidst Community Decline." *Journal of Negro Education* 60(1): 85-96.

GLASS, G., W. HAUSLER, P. LOEFFELHOLZ, ET AL.
    1988 "Seroprevalence of HIV Antibody among Individuals Entering the Iowa Prison System." *American Journal of Public Health* 78(4): 447-449

GLOBAL AIDS POLICY COALITION
    1995 *Status and Trends of the HIV/AIDS Pandemic as of January 1, 1995*. Cambridge, MA: Harvard School of Public Health/François-Xavier Bagnoud Center for Health and Human Rights.
    1996 *Status and Trends of the HIV/AIDS Pandemic as of January 1, 1996*. Cambridge, MA: Harvard School of Public Health/François-Xavier Bagnoud Center for Health and Human Rights.

GLOEB, D.J., S. LAI, J. EFANTIS, ET AL.
    1992 "Survival and Disease Progression in Human Immunodeficiency-Infected Women after an Index Delivery." *American Journal of Obstetrics and Gynecology* 167(1): 152-157.

GOEDERT, J. AND T. COTE
    1994 "Public Health Interventions to Reduce Pediatric AIDS." *American Journal of Public Health* 84(7): 1065-1066.

GOEMAN, J., A. MEHÉUS, AND P. PIOT
    1991 "L'Epidémiologie des Maladies Sexuellement Transmissibles dans les Pays en Développement à l'Ere du SIDA. *Annales de la Société Belge de Médicine Tropicale* 71(2): 81-113.

GOICOECHEA-BALBONA, ANAMARIA
    1994 "Why We Are Losing the AIDS Battle in Rural Migrant Communities?" *AIDS & Public Policy Journal* 9(1): 36-48.

GOLDBERG, D. AND F. JOHNSTONE
    1992 "HIV Testing Programs in Pregnancy." *Balliere's Clinical Obstetrics and Gynecology* 6(1): 33-51.

GOLDSTEIN, DONNA M.
    1994 "AIDS and Women in Brazil: The Emerging Problem." *Social Science and Medicine* 39(7): 919-929.

GOLLUB, E., AND Z. STEIN
    1993 "Commentary: The New Female Condom—Item 1 on Women's AIDS Prevention Agenda." *American Journal of Public Health* 83(4): 498-500.

GÓMEZ, ELSA GÓMEZ
    1993 *Gender, Women, and Health in the Americas.* Washington, D.C.: Pan American Health Organization.

GONZALEZ, C. AND M. BIANCO
    1994 "Young Women's Vulnerability to HIV/AIDS in Argentina." *International Conference on AIDS* 10(1): 377. Abstract Number PD0114.

GOOD, MARY-JO DELVECCHIO, LINDA HUNT, TSUNETSUGU MUNAKATA, ET AL.
    1993 "A Comparative Analysis of the Culture of Biomedicine: Disclosure and Consequences for Treatment in the Practice of Oncology." In *Health and Health Care in Developing Countries.* Peter Conrad and Eugene Gallagher, eds. Philadelphia: Temple University Press. Pp. 205-209.

GOODMAN, E.
    1994 "Knowledge, Preference, or Both? It's Hard to Tell without the Data." *American Journal of Public Health* 84(5): 867-868.

GOODMAN, ELIZABETH AND ALWYN T. COHALL
    1989 "Acquired Immunodeficiency Syndrome and Adolescents: Knowledge, Attitudes, Beliefs and Behaviors in a New York City Adolescent Minority Population." *Pediatrics* 84(1): 36-42.

GORMAN, M.
    1986 "The AIDS Epidemic in San Francisco: Epidemiological and Anthropological Perspectives. In *Anthropology and Epidemiology.* Craig Janes, Ron Stall, and Sandra Gifford, eds. Pp. 157-174.

GRABARD, STEPHEN, PHYLLIS BENDELL, AND AMY TAYLOR, EDS.
    1994 "Health and Wealth." *Daedalus* 123(4).

GREAVES, WAYNE
    1989 "HIV Infection among Prostitutes." In *AIDS and Intravenous Drug Abuse among Minorities.* NIDA 90-1637. Pp. 84-87.

GREEN, EDWARD CROCKER
    1994 *AIDS and STDs in Africa: Bridging the Gap between Traditional Healing and Modern Medicine*. Boulder: Westview Press.

GREENBERG, W.
    1987 "On HIV Transmission in Homosexual/Bisexual Men." *American Journal of Public Health* 77(12): 1552-1553.

GREENBLAT, CATHY
    1995 "Women in Families with Hemophilia and HIV: Improving Communication about Sensitive Issues." In *Women Resisting AIDS: Feminist Strategies of Empowerment*. Beth E. Schneider and Nancy E. Stoller, eds. Philadelphia: Temple University Press. Pp. 124-138.

GREENWOOD, PETER W., C. PETER RYDELL, AND ALLAN F. ABRAHAMSE
    1995 *Estimated Benefits and Costs of California's New Mandatory Sentencing Law*. Santa Monica, CA: Rand.

GREGORY, STEPHEN
    1993 "Race, Rubbish, and Resistance: Empowering Difference in Community Politics." *Cultural Anthropology* 8(1): 24-48.

GROSS, MICHAEL
    1994 "Hospitals: Inhospitable to AIDS Outreach Demonstration Projects for High-Risk Women." *AIDS & Public Policy Journal* 8(2): 73-78.

GROSSMAN, CHARLES J.
    1991 *The Effect of Oral Contraceptives on Immune Function in HIV Positive Women*. Cincinnati: Department of Veterans Affairs Medicine Center (November 3).

GROVER, JAN ZITA
    1988 "AIDS: Keywords." In *AIDS: Cultural Analysis/ Cultural Activism*. Douglas Crimp, ed. Cambridge, MA: MIT Press. Pp. 17-31.

GRUND, J., C. KAPLAN, AND N. ADRIAANS
    1991 "Needle Sharing in the Netherlands: An Ethnographic Analysis." *American Journal of Public Health* 81(12): 1602-1607.

GUERENA-BURGUENO, F., A. BENESON AND J. SEPULVEDA-AMOR
    1991 "HIV-1 Prevalence in Selected Tiajuana Sub-Populations." *American Journal of Public Health* 81(5): 623-625.

GUÉRIN, J., R. MALEBRANCHE, R. ELIE, ET AL.
    1984 "Acquired Immune Deficiency Syndrome: Specific Aspects of the Disease in Haiti." *Annals of the New York Academy of Sciences* 437: 254-261.

GUINAN, MARY E. AND ANN HARDY
    1987 "Epidemiology of AIDS in Women in the United States, 1981 through 1986." *Journal of the American Medical Association* 257(16): 2039-2042.

GUINAN, MARY E. AND LAURA LEVITON
    1995 "Prevention of HIV Infection in Women: Overcoming Barriers." *Journal of the American Medical Women's Association* 50(3/4): 74-77.

GUNBY, PHIL
    1995 "UN's Ins, Outs Affect U.S. Military Medicine." *Journal of the American Medical Association* 273(13): 980.

GUPTA, GEETA RAO AND ELLEN WEISS
    1993a *Women and AIDS: Developing a New Health Strategy*. Washington, D.C.: International Center for Research on Women (October).
    1993b "Women's Lives and Sex: Implications for AIDS Prevention." *Culture, Medicine and Psychiatry* 17(4): 399-412.

GUTTMACHER, SALLY, LISA LIEBERMAN, WAI HOI-CHANG, ET AL.
    1995 "Gender Differences in Attitudes and Use of Condom Availability Programs among
        Sexually Active Students in New York City Public High Schools." *Journal of the
        American Medical Women's Association* 50(3/4): 99-102.

GWINN, MARTA, MARGUERITE PAPPAIOANOU, J. RICHARD GEORGE, ET AL.
    1991 "Prevalence of HIV Infection in Childbearing Women in the United States: Sur-
        veillance Using Newborn Blood Samples." *Journal of the American Medical Associ-
        ation* 265(13): 1704-1708.

HAHN, R.A., E. EAKER, N.D. BARKER, ET AL.
    1995 "Poverty and Death in the United States—1973 and 1991." *Epidemiology* 6(5): 490-
        497.

HALL, R., D. WILDER, P. BODENROEDER, ET AL.
    1990 "Assessment of AIDS Knowledge, Attitudes, Behaviors, and Risk Level of North-
        western American Indians." *American Journal of Public Health* 80(7): 875-877.

HALSEY, NEAL A., REGINALD BOULOS AND ELIZABETH HOLT
    1990 "Transmission of HIV-1 Infections from Mothers to Infants in Haiti: Impact on
        Childhood Mortality and Malnutrition." *Journal of the American Medical Associa-
        tion* 264(16): 2088-2092.

HALSEY, NEAL A., JACQUELINE S. COBERLY AND ELIZABETH HOLT
    1992 "Sexual Behavior, Smoking and HIV-1 Infection in Haitian Women." *Journal of the
        American Medical Association* 267(15): 2062-2066.

HAMBLIN, JULIE AND ELIZABETH REID
    1991 "Women, the HIV Epidemic and Human Rights: A Tragic Imperative." Interna-
        tional Workshop on 'AIDS: A Question of Rights and Humanity,' International
        Court of Justice. The Hague: United Nations Development Programme (May).

HAMILTON, JOHN D., PAMELA M. HARTIGAN, MICHAEL S. SIMBERKOFF, ET AL.
    1992 "A Controlled Trial of Early Versus Late Treatment with Zidovudine in Sympto-
        matic Human Immunodeficiency Virus Infection." *The New England Journal of
        Medicine* 326(7): 437-443.

HANDLEY, P.
    1990 "Dangerous Liaisons." *Far Eastern Economic Review* (June): 25-28.

HANKINS, C., S. GENDRON, M. HANDLEY, ET AL.
    1994 "HIV Infection among Women in Prison: An Assessment of Risk Factors Using a
        Nonnominal Methodology." *American Journal of Public Health* 84(10): 1637-1640.

HANKINS, C., C. LABERGE, N. LAPOINTE, ET AL.
    1990 "HIV Infection among Quebec Women Giving Birth to Live Infants." *Canadian
        Medical Association Journal* 143(9): 885-893.

HANKINS, CATHERINE A.
    1990 "Issues Involving Women, Children, and AIDS Primarily in the Developed World."
        Journal of Acquired Immune Deficiency Syndromes 3(4): 443-448.

HANKINS, CATHERINE A. AND MARGARET A. HANDLEY
    1992 "HIV Disease and AIDS in Women: Current Knowledge and a Research Agenda."
        Journal of Acquired Immune Deficiency Syndromes 5(10): 957-971.

HARDY, A. AND D. DAWSON
    1990 "HIV Antibody Testing among Adult in the United States: Data from 1988 NHIS."
        American Journal of Public Health 80(5): 586-589.

HARRINGTON, MICHAEL
    1984 *The New American Poverty.* New York: Penguin Books.

HARRIS, C., C. BUTKUS SMALL, G. FRIEDLAND, ET AL.
    1983 "Immunodeficiency among Female Sexual Partners of Males with Acquired
        Immune Deficiency Syndrome (AIDS)—New York." *Morbidity and Mortality
        Weekly Report* 31(52): 697-698.

HARRIS, CAROL, CATHERINE BUTKUS SMALL, ROBERT S. KLEIN, ET AL.
    1983 "Immunodeficiency in Female Sexual Partners of Men with the Acquired Immun-
        odeficiency Syndrome." *The New England Journal of Medicine* 308(20): 1181-1184.

HARTGERS, C., A. VAN DE HOEK, P. KRIJNEN, ET AL.
    1992 "HIV Prevalence and Risk Behavior among Injecting Drug Users Who Participate
        in 'Low-Threshold Methadone Programs' in Amsterdam." *American Journal of
        Public Health* 82(4): 547-551.

HARTIGAN, PAMELA
    1994 "The Response of Nongovernmental Organizations in Latin America to HIV Infec-
        tion and AIDS: A Vehicle for Grasping the Contribution NGOs Make to Health
        and Development." In *Global AIDS Policy*. Douglas Feldman, ed. Westport, Con-
        necticut: Bergin and Garvey. Pp. 47-60.

HARTMANN, BETSY
    1995 *Reproductive Rights and Wrongs: The Global Politics of Population Control*. Boston:
        South End Press.

HAVERKOS, H.W. AND R.J. BATTJES
    1992 "Female-to-Male Transmission of HIV." *Journal of the American Medical Association*
        268(14): 1855-1857.

HAVERKOS, H., AND E. STEEL
    1991 "Crack Cocaine, Fellatio, and the Transmission of HIV." *American Journal of Public
        Health* 81(8): 1078-1079.

HEAGARTY, MARGARET C. AND ELAINE J. ABRAMS
    1992 "Caring for HIV-Infected Women and Children." *The New England Journal of Med-
        icine* 326(13): 887-888.

HECKATHORN, DOUGLAS
    1995 "Response: Cognitive Psychology, Social Networks, and AIDS." In *Assessing the
        Social and Behavioral Science Base for HIV/AIDS Prevention and Intervention Work-
        shop Summary*. Washington, D.C.: National Academy Press. Pp. 45-52.

HEGGENHOUGEN, H.K.
    1984 "Traditional Medicine and the Treatment of Drug Addicts: Three Examples from
        Southeast Asia." *Medical Anthropology Quarterly* 16(1): 3-6.
    1986 "Cultural Components of Behavioral Epidemiology: Implications for Primary
        Health Care." *Social Science and Medicine* 22(11): 1235-1245.

HEISE, L.L. AND C. ELIAS
    1995 "Transforming AIDS Prevention to Meet Women's Needs: A Focus on Developing
        Countries." *Social Science and Medicine* 40(7): 931-943.

HEISE, L.L., ET AL.
    1994 *Violence against Women: The Hidden Health Burden*. World Bank Discussion Paper,
        No. 255. Washington, D.C.: World Bank.

HEISE, LORI
    1993 "Violence against Women: The Missing Agenda." In *The Health of Women: A Glob-
        al Perspective*. Marge Koblinsky, Judith Timyan and Jill Gay, eds. Boulder, CO:
        Westview Press. Pp. 171-196.
    1995 "Violence, Sexuality and Women's Lives." In *Concerning Sexuality: Approaches to Sex
        Research in a Post-Modern World*. Richard Parker, ed. Pp. 109-143.

HELLINGER, FRED J.
1993 "The Use of Health Services by Women with HIV Infection." *Health Services Research* 28(5): 543-561.

HENRION, R. AND L. MANDELBROT
1990 "Conséquences Socio-Economiques de l'Infection à VIH Chez la Femme et l'Enfant." *Bulletin de l'Academie Nationale de Médecine* 174(8): 1151-1159.

HENRY, K AND S. CAMPBELL
1992 "The Potential Efficacy of Routine HIV Testing of Hospitalized Patients—Data from a CDC Sentinel Hospital." *Public Health Reports* 107(2): 138-141.

HENRY, K., M. OSTERHOLM, AND K. MACDONALD
1988 "Reduction of HIV Transmission by Use of Condoms." *American Journal of Public Health* 78(9): 1244.

HERB, ALICE
1995 "Standby Guardianship: A Viable Legal Option for the Future Care of Children." *Journal of the American Medical Women's Association* 50(3/4): 95-98.

HERBERT, B.
1995 "Women Battering and HIV Infection." *HIV Infection in Women: Setting a New Agenda.* Washington, D.C. (February 22-24) Pp. P116. Abstract Number TP-500.

HERDT, GILBERT AND SHIRLEY LINDENBAUM, EDS.
1992 *The Time of AIDS: Social Analysis, Theory and Method.* Newbury Park, CA: Sage Publications.

HEYMANN, SALLY JODY
1990 "Modeling the Impact of Breast-Feeding by HIV-Infected Women on Child Survival." *American Journal of Public Health* 80(11): 1305-1309.

HIATT, R., F. CAPELL, AND M. ASCHER
1992 "Seroprevalence of HIV-Type I in a Northern California Health Plan Populations: An Unlinked Survey." *American Journal of Public Health* 82(4): 564-567.

HIMMELSTEIN, DAVID V. AND STEFFIE WOOLHANDLER
1994 *The National Health Program Book: A Source Guide for Advocates.* Monroe, ME: Common Courage Press.

HINGSON, R. AND L. STRUNIN
1993 "Validity, Reliability, and Generalizability in Studies of AIDS Knowledge, Attitudes, and Behavioral Risks Based on Subject Self-Report. *American Journal of Preventive Medicine* 9(1): 62-64.

HINGSON, R., L. STRUNIN, M. GRADY, ET AL.
1991 "Knowledge About HIV and Behavioral Risks of Foreign-Born Boston Public School Students." *American Journal of Public Health* 81(12): 1638-1641.

HIRSCHHORN, LISA R.
1995 "HIV Infection in Women: Is It Different?" *The AIDS Reader* (May/June): 99-105.

HOCH, D.E. AND K.R. WILCOX
1991 "Transmission of Multidrug-Resistant Tuberculosis from an HIV-Positive Client in a Residential Substance-Abuse Treatment Facility—Michigan." *Morbidity and Mortality Weekly Report* 40(8): 129-131.

HOFF, RODNEY, VICTOR P. BERARDI, BARBARA J. WEIBLEN, ET AL.
1988 "Seroprevalence of Human Immunodeficiency Virus among Childbearing Women: Estimation by Testing Samples of Blood from Newborns." *The New England Journal of Medicine* 318(9): 525-530.

HOGAN, A.J., D.J. SOLOMON, R.R. BOUKNIGHT, ET AL.
1991 "Under-Utilization of Medical Care Services by HIV-Infected Women? Some Preliminary Results from the Michigan Medicaid Program." *AIDS* 5(3): 338-339.

HOGG, ROBERT S., STEPHANIE A. STRATHDEE, KEVIN J.P. CRAIB, ET AL.
 1994 "Lower Socioeconomic Status and Shorter Survival Following HIV Infection." *The Lancet* 344(8930): 1120-1124.

HOLLISTER, ROBINSON G. AND JENNIFER HILL
 1995 "Problems in the Evaluation of Community-Wide Initiatives." Working Paper No. 70. New York: Russell Sage Foundation.

HOLLIBAUGH, AMBER
 1995 "Lesbian Denial and Lesbian Leadership in the AIDS Epidemic: Bravery and Fear in the Construction of a Lesbian Geography of Risk." In *Women Resisting AIDS: Feminist Strategies of Empowerment.* Beth E. Schneider and Nancy E. Stoller, eds. Pp. 219-230.

HOLLOWAY, MARGUERITE
 1994 "Trends in Women's Health: A Global View." *Scientific American* 271(2): 76-83.

HOLMAN, SUSAN AND BARBARA L. MCTAGUE
 1995 "Providing HIV Counseling and Testing Services to Women." In *HIV Infection in Women.* Howard Minkoff, Jack A. DeHovitz, and Ann Duerr, eds. New York: Raven Press. Pp. 263-292.

HOLMBERG, S.
 1996 "The Estimated Prevalence and Incidence of HIV in 96 Large U.S. Metropolitan Areas." *American Journal of Public Health* 86(5): 642-654.

HOLMES, K., J. KARON, AND J. KREISS
 1990 "The Increasing Frequency of Heterosexually Acquired AIDS in the United States, 1983-88." *American Journal of Public Health* 80(7): 858-863.

HOLMES, KING AND SEVGI ARAL
 1991 "Behavioral Interventions in Developing Countries." In *Research Issues in Human Behavior and Sexually Transmitted Diseases in the AIDS Era.* Judith Wasserheit, Sevgi Aral and King Holmes, eds. Washington, D.C.: American Society for Microbiology. Pp. 318-344.

HOLTGRAVE, DAVID, NOREEN L. QUALLS, JAMES W. CURRAN, ET AL.
 1995 "Overview of HIV Intervention Prevention Programs." *Public Health Reports* 110(2): 134-146.

HOLTZMAN, D., J. ANDERSON, L. KANN, ET AL.
 1991 "HIV Instruction, HIV Knowledge, and Drug Injection among High School Students in the United States." *American Journal of Public Health* 81(12): 1596-1601.

HOLZMAN, PHILIP
 1986 "Similarity and Collaboration within the Sciences." In *Metatheory in Social Science: Pluralisms and Subjectives.* D. Fiske and R. Shweder, eds. Chicago: University of Chicago Press. Pp. 347-352.

HOOK, EDWARD W., III
 1995 "HIV/Sexually Transmitted Disease Interactions in Women." In *HIV Infection in Women.* Howard Minkoff, Jack A. DeHovitz, and Ann Duerr, eds. New York: Raven Press. Pp. 229-240.

HOOVER, D.R., C. RINALDO, Y. HE, ET AL.
 1995 "Long-Term Survival without Clinical AIDS after CD4+ Cell Counts Fall Below 200 x 10(6)/l." *AIDS* 9(2): 145-152.

HORNER, P.J., M. MCBRIDE, R.J. COKER, ET AL.
 1993 "Outpatient Follow-Up in Women with HIV Infection in Parkside Health Authority." *Genitourinary Medicine* 69(5): 370-372.

HORNER, RONNIE D., CHARLES L. BENNETT, DAN RODRIGUEZ, ET AL.
 1995 "Relationship between Procedures and Health Insurance for Critically Ill Patients with *Pneumocystis carinii* Pneumonia." *American Journal of Respiratory and Critical Care Medicine* 152: 1435-1442.

HORTON, RICHARD
 1995 "Women as Women with HIV." *The Lancet* 345(8949): 531-532.

HOXIE, N., J. VERGERONT, H. FRISBY, ET AL.
 1990 "HIV Seroprevalence and the Acceptance of Voluntary HIV Testing among Newly Incarcerated Male Prison Inmates in Wisconsin." *American Journal of Public Health* 80(9): 1129-1131.

HOXIE, N., J. VERGERONT, J. PFISTER, ET AL.
 1992 "Improving Estimates of HIV-1 Seroprevalence among Childbearing Women: Use of Smaller Blood Spots." *American Journal of Public Health* 82(10): 1370-1373.

HU, D., W. HEYWARD, R. BYERS, ET AL.
 1992 "HIV Infection and Breast-Feeding: Policy Implications Through a Decision-Analysis Model." *AIDS* 6(12): 1505-1513.

HU, DALE J., PATRICIA L. FLEMING, MITZI A. MAYS, ET AL.
 1994 "The Expanding Regional Diversity of the Acquired Immunodeficiency Syndrome Epidemic in the United States." *Archives of Internal Medicine* 154(6): 654-659.

HUBER, JOAN AND BETH SCHNEIDER, EDS.
 1992 *The Social Context of AIDS.* Newbury Park, Ca: Sage.

HUNT, CHARLES W.
 1989 "Migrant Labor and Sexually Transmitted Disease: AIDS in Africa." *Journal of Health and Social Behavior* 30(4): 353-373.

HUNTER, CHRISTINE E. AND MICHAEL W. ROSS
 1991 "Determinants of Health-Care Workers' Attitudes toward People with AIDS." *Journal of Applied Social Psychology* 21(11): 947-956.

HUNTER, GILLIAN, MARTIN C. DONOGHOE, GERRY STIMSON, ET AL.
 1995 "Changes in the Injecting Risk Behavior of Injecting Drug Users in London, 1990-1993." *AIDS:* 9(5): 493-501.

HUNTER, NAN D.
 1995 "Complications of Gender: Women, AIDS, and the Law," In *Women Resisting AIDS: Feminist Strategies of Empowerment.* Beth E. Schneider and Nancy E. Stoller, eds. Philadelphia: Temple University Press. Pp. 32-56.

HYPPOLITE, P.R. AND J.W. PAPE
 1995 "Infección por VIH y Tuberculosis en Haiti." *Bol Oficina Sanit Panam* 118(2): 161-169.

ICKOVICS, JEANNETTE R., ALLISON C. MORRILL, SUSAN E. BEREN, ET AL.
 1994 "Limited Effects of HIV Counseling and Testing for Women: A Prospective Study of Behavioral and Psychological Consequences." *Journal of the American Medical Association* 272(6): 443-448.

ICKOVICS, JEANNETTE R. AND JUDITH RODIN
 1992 "Women and AIDS in the United States: Epidemiology, Natural History, and Mediating Mechanisms." *Health Psychology* 11(1): 1-16.

IDE, MARY, WENDY SANFORD AND AMY ALPERN
 1992 *AIDS, HIV Infection and Women.* NY: Simon & Schuster.

ILIFFE, JOHN
 1987 *The African Poor: A History.* Cambridge: Cambridge University Press.

IMAM, NAIYER, CHARLES C. J. CARPENTER, KENNETH H. MAYER, ET AL.
    1990 "Hierarchical Pattern of Mucosal Candida Infections in HIV Seropositive Women."
        American Journal of Medicine 89(2): 142-146.

INGSTAD, BENEDICTE
    1990 "The Cultural Construction of AIDS and Its Consequences for Prevention in
        Botswana." Medical Anthropology Quarterly 4(1): 28-40.

INSTITUTE FOR HEALTH AND SOCIAL JUSTICE
    1995 "The New World Order and the Health of the Poor." Critical Essay. Cambridge,
        MA: Partners In Health.

INSTITUTE OF MEDICINE
    1995 Assessing the Social and Behavioral Science Base for HIV/AIDS Prevention. Washington,
        D.C.: National Academy Press.

INTERNATIONAL BANK FOR RECONSTRUCTION AND DEVELOPMENT/THE WORLD BANK
    1995 Workers in an Integrating World. New York: Oxford University Press.

INTERNATIONAL FEDERATION OF GYNECOLOGY AND OBSTETRICS (FIGO)
    1992 "AIDS and Women." International Journal of Gynecology and Obstetrics 37(4): 323.

INTERNATIONAL VOLUNTARY SERVICES
    1995 Viet Nam Field Visit Report. Washington, D.C.: International Voluntary Services
        (Summer).

JACCARD, JAMES J., TRACEY E. WILSON AND CARMEN M. RADECKI
    1995 "Psychological Issues in the Treatment of HIV-Infected Women." In HIV Infection
        in Women. Howard Minkoff, Jack A. DeHovitz, and Ann Duerr, eds. New York:
        Raven Press. Pp. 87-106.

JACOBS, SALLY
    1989 "Dying and Living With AIDS." Boston Globe Magazine: 72.

JACOBSON, JODI L.
    1992 "Women's Health: The Price of Poverty." In The Health of Women: A Global Per-
        spective. Marge Koblinsky, Judith Timyan and Jill Gay, eds. Boulder, CO: West-
        view Press. Pp. 1-24.

JAIN, M.K., T.J. JOHN, AND G.T. KEUSCH
    1994a "Epidemiology of HIV and AIDS in India." AIDS 8(S2): 61-75.
    1994b "A Review of Human Immunodeficiency Virus Infection in India." Journal of
        Acquired Immune Deficiency Syndromes 7(11): 1185-1194.

JAMETON, ANDREW
    1994 "Casuist or Cassandra." Cambridge Quarterly of Health Care Ethics 3: 449-466.
    1995 "Sustainable Justice and Resources in Support of the Disabled." Mount Sinai Journal
        of Medicine 62(2): 1-4.

JAMISON, DEAN T. AND W. HENRY MOSLEY
    1991 "Disease Control Priorities in Developing Countries: Health Policy Responses to
        Epidemiologic Change." American Journal of Public Health 81(1): 15-22.

JANA, S., A.K. CHAKRABORTY, A. DAS, ET AL.
    1995 "Community Based Survey of STD/HIV Infection among Commercial Sex-Work-
        ers in Calcutta (India). Part II: Sexual Behavior, Knowledge and Attitude towards
        STD." Journal of Communicable Diseases 26(3): 168-171.

JEMMOTT, J., III, L. JEMMOTT, AND G. FONG
    1992 "Reductions in HIV Risk-Associated Sexual Behaviors among Black Male Adoles-
        cents: Effects of an AIDS Prevention Intervention." American Journal of Public
        Health 82(3): 372-377.

JENNY, CAROLE, THOMAS HOOTEN, ANN BOWERS, ET AL.
    1990 "Sexually Transmitted Diseases in Victims of Rape." *The New England Journal of Medicine* 322(11): 713-716.

JOCHELSON, KAREN, MONYAOLA MOTHIBELI, AND JEAN PATRICK LEGER
    1994 "Human Immunodeficiency Virus and Migrant Labor." In *AIDS: The Politics of Survival.* Nancy Krieger and Glenn Margo, eds. Amityville, NY: Baywood Publishing Co. Pp. 141-160.

JOHN, T.J., N. BHUSHAN, P.G. BABU, ET AL.
    1993 "Prevalence of HIV Infection in Pregnant Women in Vellore Region." *Indian Journal of Medical Research* 97: 227-230.

JOHNSON, A.
    1992 "Epidemiology of HIV Infection in Women." *Balliere's Clinical Obstetrics and Gynecology* 6(1): 13-31.

JOHNSON, ALICE K. AND LARRY W. KRUEGER
    1989 "Toward a Better Understanding of Homeless Women." *Social Work* 34(6): 537-540.

JOHNSON, ANNE M.
    1994 "Condoms and HIV Transmission." *The New England Journal of Medicine* 331(6): 391-392.

JOHNSON, MARGRET A. AND FRANK D. JOHNSTONE, EDS.
    1992 *HIV Infection in Women.* New York: Churchill Livingstone.

JOHNSTONE, F., B. HAMILTON, AND S. GORE
    1992 "Socio-Economic Factors Associated with HIV Infection in Pregnant Women." *Health Bulletin* 50(2): 156-162.

JONES. R.
    1991 *Black Psychology.* Berkeley, California: Cobb and Henry Publishers.

JONES, T., D. ALLEN, I. ONORATO, ET AL.
    1990 "HIV Seroprevalence in Drug Treatment Centers." *Public Health Reports* 105(2): 125-130.

JOSEPH, JILL G., CAROL-ANN EMMONS, RONALD C. KESSLER, ET AL.
    1984 "Coping with the Threat of AIDS: An Approach to Psychosocial Assessment." *American Psychologist* 39(11): 1297-1302.

KALEEBA, NOERINE
    1990 "From a Uganda Casebook." *World Health* (November-December): 20-21.

KALDOR, JOHN M., PAUL EFFLER, RABIN SARDA, ET AL.
    1994 "HIV and AIDS in Asia and the Pacific: An Epidemiological Overview." *AIDS* 8(S1): 165-172.

KALDOR, JOHN, WERASIT SITTITRAI, T. JACOB JOHN, ET AL.
    1994 "The Emerging Epidemic of HIV Infection and AIDS in Asia and the Pacific." *AIDS* 8(S2): S1-S2.

KALICHMAN, SETH C., JEFFREY A. KELLY, TRICIA L. HUNTER, ET AL.
    1993 "Culturally Tailored HIV/AIDS Risk-Reduction Messages Targeted to African-American Urban Women: Impact on Risk Sensitization and Risk Reduction." *Journal of Consulting and Clinical Psychology* 61(2): 291-295.

KAMBON, A.
    1993 "Cultural and Socio/Economic Factors as an Impediment to HIV Prevention among Rural Women in Trinidad and Tobago." *International Conference on AIDS* 9(1): 107. Abstract Number WS-D04-2.

KAMENGA, MUNKOLENKOLE C., KEVIN M. DE COCK, MICHAEL E. ST. LOUIS, ET AL.
> 1995 "The Impact of Human Immunodeficiency Virus Infection on Pelvic Inflammatory Disease: A Case-Control Study in Abidjan, Ivory Coast." *American Journal of Obstetrics and Gynecology* 172(3): 919-925.

KAMMERER, CORNELIA ANN
> Unpublished "AIDS Among Akha Highlanders in Thailand: A Pandemic Analysis." Paper presented at the University of Chicago Anthropology Alumni Conference, 1993.

KAMMERER, CORNELIA ANN, OTOME HUTHEESING, RALANA MANEEPRASERT, ET AL.
> 1995 "Vulnerability to HIV Infection among Three Hill Tribes in Northern Thailand." In *Culture and Sexual Risk: Anthropological Perspectives.* Han ten Brummelhuis and Gilbert Herdt, eds. New York: Gordon and Breach. Pp. 53-78.

KAMMERER, CORNELIA ANN AND PATRICIA SYMONDS
> 1992 "AIDS in Asia: Hill Tribes Endangered at Thailand's Periphery." *Cultural Survival Quarterly* 16(3): 23-26.

KAPLAN, EDWARD H., KAVEH KHOSHNOOD AND ROBERT HEIMER
> 1994 "A Decline in HIV-Infected Needles Returned to New Haven's Needle Exchange Program." *American Journal of Public Health* 84(12): 1991-1993.

KARIM, QUARRAISHA ABDOOL, SALIM S. ABDOOL KARIM, KATE SOLDAN, ET AL.
> 1995 "Reducing the Risk of HIV Infection among South African Sex Workers: Socioeconomic and Gender Barriers." *American Journal of Public Health* 85(11): 1521-1525.

KASS, NANCY E., RUTH R. FADEN, PATRICIA O'CAMPO, ET AL.
> 1992 "Policy Options for Prenatal Screening Programs for HIV: The Preferences of Inner-City Pregnant Women." *AIDS & Public Policy Journal* 7(4): 225-233.

KATSIVO, M. AND L. MUTHAMI
> 1991 "Social Characteristics and Sexual Behavior of Women at High Risk of HIV Infection in a Town in Central Province of Kenya." *East African Medical Journal* 68(1): 34-38.

KATZ, IRWIN, GLEN HASS, AND NINA PARISI
> 1987 "Lay People's and Health Care Personnel's Perceptions of Cancer, AIDS, Cardiac, and Diabetic Patients." *Psychological Reports* 60(2): 615-629.

KAVUMA, L.
> 1994 "Factors that Influence Counseling of Women Infected with HIV." *International Conference on AIDS* 10(2): 394. Abstract Number PD0757.

KEARNEY, M.T., P.D. WARKLYN, C. TEALE, ET AL.
> 1993 "Tuberculosis and Poverty." *British Medical Journal* 307(6912): 1143.

KEBEDE, Y., J. PICKERING, J. MCDONAD, ET AL.
> 1991 "HIV Infection in an Ethiopian Prison." *American Journal of Public Health* 81(5): 625-627.

KELLER, PAULA ANNE
> 1995 "Enhancing Family-Centered Care through the Ryan White Title IV Program." *Journal of the American Medical Women's Association* 50(3/4): 94.

KELLY, J., S. CHU, AND J. BUEHLER
> 1993 " AIDS Deaths Shift From Hospital to Home: AIDS Mortality Project Group." *American Journal of Public Health* 83(10): 1433-1437.

KELLY, J., T. HECKMAN, S. HELFRICH, ET AL.
> 1995 "HIV Risk Factors and Behaviors among Men in a Milwaukee Homeless Shelter." *American Journal of Public Health* 85(11): 1585.

KELLY, J., D. MURPHY, C. WASHINGTON, ET AL.
    1994 "The Effects of HIV/AIDS Intervention Groups for High-Risk Women in Urban Clinics." *American Journal of Public Health* 84(12): 1918-1922.

KELLY, J., J. ST. LAWRENCE, T. BRASFIELD, ET AL.
    1990 "AIDS Risk Behavior Patterns among Gay Men in Small Southern Cities." *American Journal of Public Health* 80(4): 416-418.

KELLY, JEFFREY, JANET ST. LAWRENCE, STEVE SMITH, ET AL.
    1987 "Stigmatization of AIDS Patients by Physicians." *American Journal of Public Health* 77(7): 789-791.

KELLY, PATRICIA
    1995 "Starting a Clinic for Women with HIV Disease." In *HIV Infection in Women*. Howard Minkoff, Jack A. DeHovitz, and Ann Duerr, eds. New York: Raven Press. Pp. 279-292.

KELLY, PATRICIA, SUSAN HOLMAN, ROSALIE ROTHENBERG, ET AL.
    1995 *Primary Care of Women and Children with HIV Infection: A Multidisciplinary Approach*. London: Jones and Bartlett Publishers.

KEMPEN, PAUL MARTIN
    1988 "Equipment Modifications to Reduce Needlesticks." *The New England Journal of Medicine* 319(5): 308.

KENNEDY, MEGHAN B., MARGARET I. SCARLETT, ANN C. DUERR, ET AL.
    1995 "Assessing HIV Risk among Women Who Have Sex with Women: Scientific and Communication Issues." *Journal of the American Medical Women's Association* 50(3/4): 103-107.

KENT, MARY BETH
    1994 "Pregnancy and Zidovudine Study: Update." *Ruah—Breath of Life* (June): 5.

KEOGH, P., S. ALLEN, C. ALMEDAL, ET AL.
    1994 "The Social Impact of HIV Infection on Women in Kigali, Rwanda: A Prospective Study." *Social Science and Medicine* 38(8): 1047-1053.

KHARSANY, A.B., A.A. HOOSEN, J. MOODLEY, ET AL.
    1993 "The Association between Sexually Transmitted Pathogens and Cervical Intra-Epithelial Neoplasia in a Developing Community." *Genitourinary Medicine* 69(5): 357-360.

KIMBALL, ANN MARIE, ROXANNE SALVATIERRA GONZÁLEZ AND FERNADO ZACARÍAS
    1993 "Women and the AIDS Epidemic: An Impeding Crisis for the Americas. In *Gender, Women and Health in the Americas*. E. Gómez, ed. Washington, D.C.: Pan American Health Organization. Pp. 178-183.

KING, DONNA
    1990 "'Prostitutes as Pariah in the Age of AIDS: A Content Analysis of Coverage of Women Prostitutes in *The New York Times* and *The Washington Post* September 1985-April 1988." *Women and Health* 16(3/4): 155-176.

KINGMAN, SHARON AND STEVE CONNOR
    1988 "The Answer is Still a Condom." *New Scientist* 118(1618): 33-36.

KINLOCH DE LOES, S., B.J. HIRSCEL, B. HOEN, ET AL.
    1995 "A Controlled Trial of Zidovudine in Primary Human Immunodeficiency Virus Infection." *The New England Journal of Medicine* 333(7): 408-413.

KIRBY, D., L. SHORT, J. COLLINS, ET AL.
    1994 "School-Based Programs to Reduce Sexual Risk Behaviors: A Review of Effectiveness." *Public Health Reports* 109(3): 339-360.

KIRUHI, M., E. NGUGI, P. KAMAU, ET AL.
  1994 "The Impact of Social Economic and Sexual Empowerment: Commercial Sex Workers." *International Conference on AIDS* 10(2): 39. Abstract Number 447D.

KISEKKA, MERE N.
  1990 "AIDS in Uganda as a Gender Issue." *Women and Therapy* 10(3): 35-53.

KITAGAWA, EVELYN AND PHILIP HAUSER
  1973 *Differential Mortality in the United States: A Study in Socioeconomic Epidemiology.* Harvard University Press. Cambridge, Massachusetts.

KITAMURA, TAKASHI
  1994 "Summary of the Epidemiology of HIV/AIDS in Japan." *AIDS* 8(S2): 595-597.

KLEINMAN, ARTHUR
  1986 "Some Uses and Misuses of the Social Sciences in Medicine." In *Metatheory in Social Science: Pluralisms and Subjectives.* D. Fiske and R. Shweder, eds. Chicago: University of Chicago Press. Pp 222-245.

KLEYN, JEANNE, EDITH E. SIMPSON AND ROBERT WOOD
  1990 "Intravenous Drug Users' Sexual Partners: Gender and Drug Injection Practices." *AIDS & Public Policy Journal* 6(4): 173-174.

KLINE, ANNA, EMILY KLINE AND EMILY OKEN
  1992 "Minority Women and Sexual Choice in the Age of AIDS." *Social Science and Medicine* 34(4): 447-457.

KLINE, ANNA, JENNIFER STRICKLER AND JUDITH KEMPF
  1995 "Factors Associated with Pregnancy and Pregnancy Resolution in HIV Seropositive Women." *Social Science and Medicine* 40(11): 1539-1547.

KOCH-WESER, DIETER AND HANNELORE VANDERSCHMIDT, EDS.
  1988 *The Heterosexual Transmission of AIDS in Africa.* Cambridge, MA: Abt Books.

KOHN, NANCY, PHYLLIS FREEMAN, MARIE-PAULE MANN, ET AL., EDS.
  1992 *Searching for Women: A Literature Review on Women, HIV, and AIDS in the United States.* Boston: Law Center, College of Public and Community Service, University of Massachusetts and the Multicultural AIDS Coalition.

KONOTEY-AHULU, FELIX I.D.
  1987 "Clinical Epidemiology, Not Seroepidemiology, is the Answer to Africa's AIDS Problem." *British Medical Journal* 294(6587): 1593-1594.

KOOPMAN, C., M. ROSARIO, AND M. ROTHERAM-BORUS
  1994 "Alcohol and Drug Use and Sexual Behaviors Placing Runaways at Risk for HIV Infection." *Addictive Behaviors* 19(1): 95-103.

KOOPMAN, C., M. ROTHERAM-BORUS, L. DOBBS, ET AL.
  1992 "Beliefs and Behavioral Intentions Regarding Human Immunodeficiency Virus Testing Among New York City Runaways." *Journal of Adolescent Health* 13(7): 576-581.

KORN, ABNER P., AND DANIEL V. LANDERS
  1995 "Gynecologic Disease in Women Infected with Human Immunodeficiency Virus Type I." *Journal of Acquired Immune Deficiency Syndromes* 9(4): 361-370.

KREISS, JOAN, ELIZABETH NGUGI, KING HOLMES, ET AL.
  1992 "Efficacy of Nonoxynol-9 Contraceptive Sponge Use in Preventing Heterosexual Acquisition of HIV in Nairobi Prostitutes." *Journal of the American Medical Association* 268(4): 477-482.

KREISS, JOHN K., DAVY KOECH, FRANCIS A. PLUMMER, ET AL.
  1986 "AIDS Virus Infection in Nairobi Prostitutes: Spread of the Epidemic to East Africa." *The New England Journal of Medicine* 314(7): 414-418.

KRIEGER, N., D. ROWLEY, A. HERMAN, ET AL.
　　1993 "Racism, Sexism and Social Class: Implications for Studies of Health, Disease, and Well-Being." *American Journal of Preventive Medicine* 9(Supplement): 82-122.

KRIEGER, NANCY
　　1994a "The Histories of AIDS—Introduction." In *AIDS: The Politics of Survival*. Nancy Krieger and Glenn Margo, eds. Amityville, NY: Baywood Publishing Co. Pp. 223-226.
　　1994b "Solidarity and AIDS—Introduction." In *AIDS: The Politics of Survival*. Nancy Krieger and Glenn Margo, eds. Amityville, NY: Baywood Publishing Co. Pp. 161-166.
　　1994c "Epidemiology and the Web of Causation: Has Anyone Seen the Spider?" *Social Science and Medicine* 39(7): 887-903.

KRIEGER, NANCY AND ROSE APPLEMAN
　　1994 "The Politics of AIDS." In *AIDS: The Politics of Survival*. Nancy Krieger and Glenn Margo, eds. Amityville, NY: Baywood Publishing Co. Pp. 3-54.

KRIEGER, NANCY AND ELIZABETH FEE
　　1994a "Man-Made Medicine and Women's Health: The Biopolitics of Sex/Gender and Race/Ethnicity." *International Journal of Health Services* 24(2): 265-283.
　　1994b "Social Class: The Missing Link in the U.S. Health Data." *International Journal of Health Services* 24(1): 25-44.

KRIEGER, NANCY AND GLENN MARGO
　　1994a "AIDS: Community Survival in the United States—Introduction." In *AIDS: The Politics of Survival*. Nancy Krieger and Glenn Margo, eds. Amityville, NY: Baywood Publishing Co. Pp. 55-60.
　　1994b "Women and AIDS—Introduction." In *AIDS: The Politics of Survival*. Nancy Krieger and Glenn Margo, eds. Amityville, NY: Baywood Publishing Co. Pp. 107-110.

KRIEGER, NANCY AND GLENN MARGO, EDS.
　　1994 *AIDS: The Politics of Survival*. Amityville, NY: Baywood Publishing Co.

KRIEGER, NANCY AND SALLY ZIERLER
　　1995 "Accounting for Health of Women." *Current Issues in Public Health* 1: 251-256.

KRISTAL, A.
　　1988 "Sexual Behavior and Risks of HIV Infection." *American Journal of Public Health* 78(1): 91-92.

KRZYNOWEK, K.A.
　　1995 "Haitian Centers Council, Inc. v. Sale: Rejecting the Indefinite Detention of HIV-Infected Aliens." *Journal of Contemporary Health Law Policy* 11(2): 541-562.

KU, L., F. SONENSTEIN, AND J. PLECK
　　1993 "Young Men's Risk Behaviors for HIV Infection and Sexually Transmitted Diseases, 1988 through 1991." *American Journal of Public Health* 83(11): 1609-1615.

KUHN, LOUISE, ZENA A. STEIN, PAULINE A. THOMAS, ET AL.
　　1994 "Maternal-Infant HIV Transmission and Circumstances of Delivery." *American Journal of Public Health* 84(7): 1110-1115.

KUMAR, R.M., S.A. UDUMAN, AND A.K. KHURRANNA
　　1995 "Impact of Maternal HIV-1 Infection on Perinatal Outcome." *International Journal of Gynecology and Obstetrics* 49(2): 137-143.

LAGA, MARIE, ABIB MANOKA, MAYIMONA KIVUVU, ET AL.
　　1993 "Non-Ulcerative Sexually Transmitted Diseases as Risk Factors for HIV-1 Transmission in Women: Results from a Cohort Study." *AIDS* 7(1): 95-102.

LAGAKOS, STEPHEN, MARGARET A. FISCHL, DANIEL S. STEIN, ET AL.
    1991 "Effects of Zidovudine Therapy in Minority and Other Subpopulations with Early
        HIV Infection." *Journal of the American Medical Association* 266(19): 2709-2712.

LAL, S.
    1994 "Current Status of AIDS and HIV Infection in India." *Journal of the Indian Medical
        Association* 92(1): 3-4.

LANG, NORRIS G.
    1994 "HIV, Immigration Policy and Latinos/as: Public Health Safety versus Hidden
        Agendas." In *Global AIDS Policy*. Douglas Feldman, ed. Westport, Connecticut:
        Bergin and Garvey. Pp. 61-69.

LANGE, W. ROBERT, FREDRICK SNYDER, DAVID LOZOVSKY, ET AL.
    1988 "Geographic Distribution of Human Immunodeficiency Virus Markers in Parenter-
        al Drug Abusers." *American Journal of Public Health* 78(4): 443-446.

LANGONE, JOHN
    1985 "AIDS: The Latest Scientific Facts." *Discover* (December): 40-56.

LARRABEE, K.D. M. MONGA, N.L. ERIKSEN, ET AL.
    1995 "Quality of Life Assessment in Indigent HIV Positive Pregnant Women." *HIV Infec-
        tion in Women: Setting a New Agenda*. Washington, D.C. (February 22-24) Pp. P77.
        Abstract Number WP-347.

LAUMANN, EDWARD
    1995 "On the Concept of Community." In *Assessing the Social and Behavioral Science Base
        for HIV/AIDS Prevention and Intervention Workshop Summary*. Washington, D.C.:
        National Academy Press. Pp. 81-92.

LAUMANN, EDWARD, JOHN GAGNON, ROBERT MICHAEL, ET AL.
    1994 *The Social Organization of Sexuality: Sexual Practices in the United States*. Chicago:
        University of Chicago Press.

LAWYERS COMMITTEE FOR HUMAN RIGHTS
    1995 *Haiti: Learning the Hard Way*. Washington, D.C.: Lawyers Committee for Human
        Rights.

LEBOW, JOAN, JAMES O'CONNELL, STEPHANIE ODDLEIFSON, ET AL.
    1995 "AIDS among the Homeless of Boston: A Cohort Study." *Journal of Acquired
        Immune Deficiency Syndromes* 8(3): 292-296.

LEE, JEEYEUN
    1995 "Sisterhood may be Global, but Who is in that Sisterhood?" In *Listen Up: Voices from
        the Next Feminist Generation*. Barbara Findlen, ed. Pp. 205-211.

LEIBMAN, B., N. IMAM, S. DANFORTH, ET AL.
    1990 "Clinical and Immunologic Features in HIV Positive Women from 3 Distinctive
        Behavioral Risk Groups: A Prospective Study." *International Conference on AIDS*
        6(3): 266. Abstract Number S.C. 710.

LEIGH, C., M. TEMPLE, AND K. TROCKI
    1993 "The Sexual Behavior of U.S. Adults: Results from a National Survey." *American
        Journal of Public Health* 83(10): 1400-1408.

LEIGH, CAROL
    1988 "Further Violations of Our Rights." In *AIDS Cultural Analysis, Cultural Division*.
        David Crimp, ed. Cambridge, MA: MIT Press. Pp. 177-181.

LEMP, G.F., A.M. HIROZAWA, D. GIVERTZ, ET AL.
    1994 "Seroprevalence of HIV and Risk Behaviors among Young Homosexual and Bisex-
        ual Men: The San Francisco/Berkeley Young Men's Survey." *Journal of the Ameri-
        can Medical Association* 272(6): 449-454.

LEMP, G., M. JONES, T. KELLOGG ET AL.
    1995 "HIV Seroprevalence and Risk Behaviors among Lesbians and Bisexual Women in San Francisco and Berkeley, California." *American Journal of Public Health* 85(11): 1549-1552.

LEMP, GEORGE, ANNE HIROZAWA, JUDITH COHEN, ET AL.
    1992 "Survival for Women and Men with AIDS." *Journal of Infectious Diseases* 166(1): 74-79.

LENDERKING, WILLIAM R., RICHARD D. GELBER, DEBORAH J. COTTON, ET AL.
    1994 "Evaluation of the Quality of Life Associated with Zidovudine Treatment in Asymptomatic Human Immunodeficiency Virus Infection." *The New England Journal of Medicine* 330(11): 738-743.

LEONARD, TERRI L.
    1990 "Male Clients of Female Street Prostitutes: Unseen Partners in Sexual Disease Transmission." *Medical Anthropology Quarterly* 4(1): 41-55.

LEONARD, Z.
    1990 "Lesbians in the AIDS Crisis." In *Women, AIDS, and Activism*. C. Chris and M. Pearl, eds. Boston: South End Press.

LERNER, SHARON
    1995 "An Evaluation of Community-Based HIV Services for Women in New York State." *Journal of the American Medical Women's Association* 50(3/4): 127-128.

LEROY, VALERIANE, PHILLIPPE MSELLATI, PHILLIPPE LEPAGE, ET AL.
    1995 "Four Years of Natural History of HIV-1 Infection in African Women: A Prospective Cohort in Kigali (Rwanda), 1988-1993." *Journal of Acquired Immune Deficiency Syndromes* 9(4): 415-421.

LESSNER, L.
    1991 "Projection of AIDS Incidence in Women in New York State." *American Journal of Public Health* 81(Supplement): 30-34.

LESTER, P., J. PARTRIDGE, AND M. CHESNEY
    1993 "Consequences of Perinatal HIV Testing for Women." *International Conference on AIDS* 9(2): 910. Abstract Number PO-D25-4152.

LEVINE, C. AND G.L. STEIN
    1994 *Orphans of the HIV Epidemic: Unmet Needs in Six U.S. Cities*. New York: The Orphan Project.

LEVINE, CAROL AND NANCY NEVELOFF DUBLER
    1990 "HIV and Childbearing: Uncertain Risks and Bitter Realities: The Reproductive Choices of HIV-Infected Women." *The Milbank Quarterly* 68(3): 321-351.

LEVINE, DONALD
    1986 "The Forms and Functions of Social Behavior." In *Metatheory in Social Science: Pluralisms and Subjectives*. D. Fiske and R. Shweder, eds. Chicago: University of Chicago Press. Pp 271-283.

LEWIS, DIANE K.
    1995 "African-American Women at Risk: Notes on the Sociocultural Context of HIV Infection." In *Women Resisting AIDS: Feminist Strategies of Empowerment*. Beth E. Schneider and Nancy E. Stoller, eds. Philadelphia: Temple University Press. Pp. 57-73.

LEWIS, DIANE K. AND JOHN K. WATTERS
    1989 "Human Immunodeficiency Virus Seroprevalence in Female Intravenous Drug Users: The Puzzle of Black Women's Risk." *Social Science and Medicine* 29(9): 1071-1076.

LEWIS, DIANE K., JOHN K. WATTERS AND PATRICIA CASE
1990 "The Prevalence of High-Risk Sexual Behavior in Male Intravenous Drug Users with Steady Female Partners." *American Journal of Public Health* 80(4): 465-466.

LEWIS, HYLAN
1963 "Culture, Class and the Behavior of Low Income Families." Paper presented at the National Conference on Social Welfare, New York City (June 27-29).

LI, V.C., B.L. COLE, S.Z. ZHANG, ET AL.
1993 "HIV-Related Knowledge and Attitudes among Medical Students in China." *AIDS Care* 5(3): 305-312.

LIAUTAUD, B., B. MELLON, J. DENIZÉ ET AL.
1992 "Preliminary Data on STDs in Haiti." Presented at the Eighth International Conference on AIDS, Amsterdam. Abstract Number C4302. (July 19-24).

LIEBOW, ELLIOT
1967 *Tally's Corner: A Study of Negro Streetcorner Men.* Boston: Little, Brown and Company.

LIEF, LOUISE
1990 "Where Democracy isn't about to Break Out." *U.S. News and World Report* (February 12): 34-36.

LIFSON, ALAN R., SUSAN ALLEN, WILLIAM WOLF, ET AL.
1995 "Classification of HIV Infection and Disease in Women from Rwanda: Evaluation of the World Health Organization HIV Staging System and Recommended Modifications." *Annals of Internal Medicine* 122(4): 262-270.

LILLIE-BLANTON, MARSHA, JAMES C. ANTHONY AND CHARLES R. SCHUSTER
1993 "Probing the Meaning of Racial/Ethnic Group Comparisons in Crack Cocaine Smoking." *Journal of the American Medical Association* 269(8): 993-997.

LINDAN, CHRISTINA, SUSAN ALLEN, MICHAEL CARAEL, ET AL.
1991 "Knowledge, Attitudes, and Perceived Risk of AIDS among Urban Rwandan Women: Relationship to HIV Infection and Behavior Change." *AIDS* 5(8): 993-1002.

LINDAN, CHRISTINA P., SUSAN ALLEN, ANTOINE SERUFILIRA, ET AL.
1992 "Predictors of Mortality among HIV-Infected Women in Kigali, Rwanda." *Annals of Internal Medicine* 116(4): 320-328.

LIPOVETSKY, G.
1993 *L'ère du Vide: Essais sur l'Individualisme Contemporain.* Second Edition. Paris: Gallimard

LOCHER, ULI
1984 "Migration in Haiti." In *Haiti—Today and Tomorrow: An Interdisciplinary Study.* C. Foster and A. Valdman, eds. Lanham, MD: University Press of America. Pp. 325-336.

LOCKETT, GLORIA
1995 "CAL-PEP: The Struggle to Survive." In *Women Resisting AIDS: Feminist Strategies of Empowerment.* Beth E. Schneider and Nancy E. Stoller, eds. Philadelphia: Temple University Press. Pp. 208-218.

LONGWE, SARA AND ROY CLARKE
1991 "The Need for NGOs to Address Gender Issues in AIDS Prevention and Control." *Vena* 5(1): 33-38.

LOUE, SANA, DONALD J. SLYMEN, HAL MORGENSTERN, ET AL.
1995 "Health Insurance and Utilization in *Pneumocystis carinii* Pneumonia." *Journal of General of Internal Medicine* 10(8): 461-463.

LOWENTHAL, IRA
    1984 "Labor, Sexuality and the Conjugal Contract in Rural Haiti." In *Haiti—Today and Tomorrow: An Interdisciplinary Study*. C. Foster and A. Valdman, eds. Lanham, MD: University Press of America. Pp. 15-33.

LOWNDES, C.M., A. DOMINGUES, N. BASSO, ET AL.
    1994 "*Chlamydia Trachomatis* Infection in Women in Rio de Janerio, Brazil." *International Conference on AIDS* 10(1): 316. Abstract Number PC0193.

LUGALLA, JOE L.P.
    1994 *Structural Adjustment Policies and Health Policy in Tanzania: Their Impact on Women's and Children's Health*. Dar-Es-Salaam, Tanzania: University of Dar-Es-Salaam.

LUO, C.C., C. TIAN, AND D.J. HU
    1995 "HIV-1 Subtype C in China." *The Lancet* 345(8956): 1051-1052.

LURIE, PETER, EUGENIA FERNANDES, VERONICA HUGHES, ET AL.
    1995 "Socioeconomic Status and Risk of HIV-1, Syphilis, and Hepatitis B Infection among Sex Workers in São Paulo State, Brazil." *AIDS* 9(S1): S31-S37.

LURIE, PETER, PERCY HINTZEN AND ROBERT A. LOWE
    1995 "Socioeconomic Obstacles to HIV Prevention and Treatment in Developing Countries: The Roles of the International Monetary Fund and the World Bank." *AIDS* 9(6): 539-546.

LYE, M.S., C. ARCHIBALD, A.A. GHAZALI, ET AL.
    1994 "Patterns of Risk Behavior for Patients with Sexually Transmitted Diseases and Surveillance for Human Immunodeficiency Virus in Kuala Lumpur, Malaysia." *International Journal of STD & AIDS* 5(2): 124-129.

LYKETSOS, C. AND E. FEDERMAN
    1995 "Psychiatric Disorders and HIV Infection: An Impact on One Another." *Epidemiological Reviews* 17(1): 152-164.

MACILWAIN, C.
    1995 "Forensic Team Digs up Haiti's Deadly Past." *Nature* 377(6547): 278.

MAGGWA, BAKER N., DAVID J. HUNTER, SUSAN MBUGUA, ET AL.
    1993 "The Relationship between HIV Infection and Cervical Intraepithelial Neoplasia among Women Attending Two Family Planning Clinics in Nairobi, Kenya." *AIDS* 7(4): 733-738.

MAGID, DAVID
    1990 "AIDS Education in the Emergency Department." *Annals of Emergency Medicine* 19(7): 57-62.

MAGURA, S., J. GROSSMAN, D. LIPTON, ET AL.
    1989 "Correlates of Participation in AIDS Education and HIV Antibody Testing of Methadone Patients." *Public Health Reports* 104(3): 231-240.

MAHOMED, K., J. KASULE, D. MAKUYANA, ET AL.
    1991 "Seroprevalence of HIV Infection amongst Antenatal Women in Greater Harare, Zimbabwe." *Central African Journal of Medicine* 37(10): 322-325.

MAIMAN, MITCHELL, RACHEL G. FRUCHTER, ELI SERUR, ET AL.
    1990 "Human Immunodeficiency Virus Infection and Cervical Neoplasia." *Gynecologic Oncology* 38(3): 377-382.

MAIMAN, MITCHELL, NICHOLAS TARRICONE, JEFFREY VIEIRA, ET AL.
    1991 "Colposcopic Evaluation of Human Immunodeficiency Virus-Seropositive Women." *Obstetrics and Gynecology* 78(1): 84-88.

MAIN, D., D. IVERSON, AND J. McGLOIN
    1994 "Comparison of HIV-Risk Behaviors and Demographics of Adolescents Tested and not Tested for HIV Infection." *Public Health Reports* 109(5): 699-702.

MAK, RUDOLPH P. AND JEAN R. PLUM
1991 "Do Prostitutes Need More Health Education Regarding Sexually Transmitted Diseases and the HIV Infection? Experience in a Belgian City." *Social Science and Medicine* 33(8): 963-966.

MAKADON, HARVEY J. AND JONATHAN G. SILIN
1995 "Prevention of HIV Infection in Primary Care: Current Practices, Future Possibilities." *Annals of Internal Medicine* 123(9): 715-719.

MALDONADO, M.
1994 "Socio-Cultural Factors Impacting HIV Prevention among Latina Women in New York City." *International Conference on AIDS* 10(2). Abstract Number PD0657.

MALES, MICHAEL
1996 *The Scapegoat Generation: America's War on Adolescents.* Monroe, ME: Common Courage Press.

MANDELL, W., D. VLAHOV, C. LATKIN, ET AL.
1994 "Correlates of Needle Sharing among Injection Drug Users." *American Journal of Public Health* 84(6): 920923.

MANJI, F., S. MOSES, J.E. BRADLEY, ET AL.
1992 "Impact of User Fees on Attendance for Sexually Transmitted Diseases." *International Conference on AIDS* 8(2): Abstract number D843.

MANN, JONATHAN
1991 "Global AIDS: Critical Issues for Prevention in the 1990s." *International Journal of Health Services* 21(3): 553-559.

MANN, JONATHAN, DANIEL TARANTOLA AND THOMAS NETTER, EDS.
1992 *AIDS in the World.* Cambridge, MA: Harvard University Press.

MARASCA, GIUSEPPE AND MARIAN McEVOY
1986 "Length of Survival of Patients with Acquired Immune Deficiency Syndrome in the United Kingdom." *British Medical Journal* 292(6537): 1727-1729.

MARAZZI, M.C., L. PALOMBI, S. MANCINELLI, ET AL.
1994 "Care Requirements of People with ARC/AIDS in Rome: Non-Hospital Services." *AIDS Care* 6(1): 95-104.

MARIN, B., C. GOMEZ, AND J. TSCHANN
1993 "Condom Use among Hispanic Men with Secondary Female Sexual Partners." *Public Health Reports* 108(6): 742-750.

MARIN, G.
1989 "AIDS Prevention among Hispanics: Needs, Risk Behaviors, and Cultural Values." *Public Health Reports* 104(5): 411-415.

MARINS, H. AND M. LIMA
1994 "Social and Cultural Aspects of Women with AIDS in Rio de Janeiro." *International Conference on AIDS* 10(1): 379. Abstract Number PD0125

MARSHALL, ELIOT
1995 "International Experts Help Probe Haiti's Bloody Past." *Science* 269(5232): 1812.

MARSHALL, PATRICIA A. AND LINDA A. BENNETT
1990 "Anthropological Contributions to AIDS Research." *Medical Anthropology Quarterly* 4(1): 3-5.

MARSTON, J.K., E. MILLER-MACK, AND V. ANDRADAS
1995 "Women, Poverty, AIDS and the Role of Community Based HIV/AIDS Research." *HIV Infection in Women: Setting a New Agenda.* Washington, D.C. (February 22-24) Pp. S46. Abstract Number TF-160.

MARTE, CAROLA AND KATHRYN ANASTOS
    1990 "Women—The Missing Persons in the AIDS Epidemic, Part II." *Health/PAC Bulletin* 20(1): 11-23.

MARTIN, JOHN L. AND CAROLE S. VANCE
    1984 "Behavioral and Psychosocial Factors in AIDS: Methodological and Substantive Issues." *American Psychologist* 39(11): 1303-1308.

MARTORELL, R. AND U. RAMAKRISHNAN
    1995 "Vitamin A Supplementation and Morbidity in Children Born to HIV-Infected Women." *American Journal of Public Health* 85 (8;Part 1): 1049-1051.

MASCOLA, L., L. LIEB, K. IWAKOSHI, ET AL.
    1989 "HIV Seroprevalence in Intravenous Drug Users: Los Angeles, California, 1986." *American Journal of Public Health* 79(1): 81-82.

MASLANKA, HALINA, JACALYN LEE AND NICHOLAS FREUDENBERG
    1995 "An Evaluation of Community-Based HIV-Services for Women in New York State." *Journal of the American Women's Association* 5(3/4): 121-126.

MASON, T. AND S. KANE
    1992 "'IV Drug Users and 'Sex Partners': The Limits of Epidemiological categories and the Ethnography of Risk." In *The Time of AIDS: Social Analysis, Theory, and Method*. G. Herdt and S. Lindenbaum, eds. Newbury Park, CA: Sage Publications.

MASON, T.H., MARGARET M. CONNORS AND CORNELIA A. KAMMERER
    1995 *Transgenders and HIV Risks: Needs Assessment*. Massachusetts Department of Public Health: HIV/AIDS Bureau, Massachusetts (August).

MASSAGLI, M., J. WEISSMAN, G. SEAGE, III, ET AL.
    1994 "Correlates of Employment after AIDS Diagnosis in the Boston Health Study." *American Journal of Public Health* 84(12): 1976-1981.

MASUR, HENRY, MARY ANN MICHELIS, GARY P. WORMSER, ET AL.
    1982 "Opportunistic Infection in Previously Healthy Women: Initial Manifestations of a Community-Acquired Cellular Immunodeficiency." *Annals of Internal Medicine* 97(4): 533-539.

MATHAI, R., P.V. PRASAD, M. JACOB, ET AL.
    1990 "HIV Seropositivity among Patients with Sexually Transmitted Diseases in Vellore." *Indian Journal of Medical Research* 91: 239-241.

MATLIN, M.
    1987 *The Psychology of Women*. New York: Holt, Rinehart, and Winston.

MATUSZAK, D., S. PANNY, J. PATEL, ET AL.
    1990 "HIV Antibody Seroprevalence among Childbearing Women Surveyed in Maryland." *Public Health Reports* 105(6): 562-566.

MAXWELL, A.H.
    1988 "The Anthropology of Poverty in Black Communities: A Critique and Systems Alternative." *Urban Poverty* 17(2-3): 171-191.

MAYAUX, M., S. BLANCHE, C. ROUZIOUX, ET AL.
    1995 "Maternal Factors Associated with Perinatal HIV-1 Transmission: The French Cohort Study: 7 Years of Follow-Up Observation." *Journal of Acquired Immune Deficiency Syndromes* 8(2): 188-194.

MAYER, KENNETH H. AND DEBORAH J. ANDERSON
    1995 "Heterosexual Transmission of HIV." In *HIV Infection in Women*. Howard Minkoff, Jack A. DeHovitz, and Ann Duerr, eds. New York: Raven Press. Pp. 73-86.

MAYES, S., V. ELSESSER, J. SCHAEFER, ET AL.
    1992 "Sexual Practices and AIDS Knowledge among Women Partners of HIV Infected Hemophiliacs." *Public Health Reports* 107(5): 504-514.

MAYS, VICKIE M. AND SUSAN D. COCHRAN
    1988 "Issues in the Perception of AIDS Risk and Risk Reduction Activities by Black and
        Hispanic/Latina Women." *American Psychologist* 43(11): 949-956.

MCBARNETT, LORNA M.
    1988 "Women and Poverty: The Effects on Reproductive Status." In *Too Little, Too Late:
        Dealing with the Needs of Women in Poverty.* Cesar Perlas and Lauren S. Young, eds.
        New York: Haworth. Pp. 55-81.
    1993 "National Health Insurance: Is This the Answer for the Poor and Underserved?"
        Journal of Health Care for the Poor and Underserved 4(3): 163-169.

MCCOMBIE, SUSAN
    1989 "Dealing with AIDS: Lessons from Hepatitis B." *Medical Anthropology* 10(2-3): 151-
        157.

MCCORD, COLIN AND HAROLD P. FREEMAN
    1990 "Excess Mortality in Harlem." *The New England Journal of Medicine* 322(3): 173-177.

MCCRAY, E., I. ONORATO, B. MILLER, ET AL.
    1990 "Estimating HIV Levels and Trends among Patients of Tuberculosis Clinics." *Public
        Health Reports* 105(2): 135-140.

MCCURDY, SHERYL
    1992 "Colonialist Concepts of AIDS." *Links* (Fall): 20-25.

MCCUSKER, J., A. STODDARD, J. ZAPKA, ET AL.
    1992 "AIDS Education for Drug Abusers: Evaluation of Short-Term Effectiveness." *Amer-
        ican Journal of Public Health* 82(4): 533-540.

MCCUSKER, J., B. KOBLIN, B. LEWIS, ET AL.
    1990 "Demographic Characteristics, Risk Behaviors, and HIV Seroprevalence among
        Intravenous Drug Users by Site of Contact: Results from a Community-Wide HIV
        Surveillance Project." *American Journal of Public Health* 80(9): 1062-1067.

MCCUSKER, J., A. STODDARD, K. MAYER, ET AL.
    1988 "Behavioral Risk Factors for HIV Infection among Homosexual Men at a Boston
        Community Health Center." *American Journal of Public Health* 78(1): 68-71.

MCCUSKER, J., A. STODDARD, J. ZAPKA, ET AL.
    1993 "Behavioral Outcomes of AIDS Educational Interventions for Drug Users in Short-
        Term Treatment." *American Journal of Public Health* 83(10): 1463-1466.

MCDONALD, M., L. KLEPPEL, AND D. JENSEN
    1990 "Developing AIDS Education for Women in County WIC Clinics." *American Jour-
        nal of Public Health* 80(11): 1391-1392.

MCELRATH, K. D. CHITWOOD, D. GRIFFIN, ET AL.
    1994 "The Consistency of Self-Reported HIV Risk among Injection Drug Users." *Amer-
        ican Journal of Public Health* 84(12): 1965-1970.

MCGRATH, JANET, CHARLES RWABUKWALI, DEBRA SCHUMANN, ET AL.
    1993 "Anthropology and AIDS: The Cultural Context of Sexual Risk Behavior among
        Urban Baganda Women in Kampala, Uganda." *Social Science and Medicine* 36(4):
        429-439.

MCKENNA, M., J. BUEHLER, J. QUALTERS, ET AL.
    1993 "HIV and Trends in Cervical Cancer Death Rates among Young Women." *Ameri-
        can Journal of Public Health* 83(12): 1792-1793.

MCKENZIE, ROBIN, WILLIAM D. TRAVIS, STEPHEN A. DOLAN, ET AL.
    1991 "The Causes of Death in Patients with Human Immunodeficiency Virus Infection:
        A Clinical and Pathologic Study with Emphasis on the Role of Pulmonary Dis-
        ease." *Medicine (Baltimore)* 70(5): 326-343.

MCKUSICK., L., W. HORSTMAN, AND T. COATES
    1985 "AIDS and Sexual Behavior Reported by Gay Men in San Francisco." *American Journal of Public Health* 75(5): 493-496.

MCKUSIK, L., J. WILEY, T. COATES, ET AL.
    1985 "Reported Changes in the Sexual Behavior of Men at Risk for AIDS, San Francisco, 1982-1984—The AIDS Behavioral Research Project." *Public Health Reports* 100(6): 622-629.

MCMICHAEL, ANTHONY J.
    1995 "The Health of Persons, Populations, and Planets: Epidemiology Comes Full Circle." *Epidemiology* 6(6): 633-636.

MCNAMARA, R.
    1993 *Female Genital Health and the Risk of HIV Transmission.* New York: HIV and Development Programme, UNDP, Issues Paper No. 3.

MCQUILLAN, G., T. EZZATI-RICE, A. SILLER, ET AL.
    1994 "Risk Behavior and Correlates of Risk for HIV Infection in the Dallas County Household HIV Survey." *American Journal of Public Health* 84(5): 747-753.

MEEHL, PAUL
    1986 "What Social Scientists Don't Understand." In *Metatheory in Social Science: Pluralisms and Subjectives.* D. Fiske and R. Sweder, eds. Chiacgo: University of Chicago Press. Pp 315-338

MELLON, R., B. LIAUTAUD, J. PAPE, ET AL.
    1995 "Association of HIV and STDs in Haiti: Implications for the Blood Banks and HIV Vaccine Trials." *Journal of Acquired Immune Deficiency Syndromes* 8(2): 214.

MELNICK, SANDRA L., GREGORY L.BURKE, L. PERKINS, ET AL.
    1993 "Sexually Transmitted Diseases among Young Heterosexual Urban Adults." *Public Health Reports.* 108(6): 673-679.

MELNICK, SANDRA L., ROBERT W. JEFFREY, GREGORY L. BURKE, ET AL.
    1993 "Changes in Sexual Behavior by Young Urban Heterosexual Adults in Response to the AIDS Epidemic." *Public Health Reports* 108(5): 582-588.

MELNICK, SANDRA L., RENSLOW SHERER, THOMAS A. LOUIS, ET AL.
    1994 "Survival and Disease Progression According to Gender of Patients with HIV Infection. The Terry Beirn Community Programs for Clinical Research on AIDS." *Journal of the American Medical Association* 272(24): 1915-1921.

MELNICK, SANDRA L., WENDY J. WERTHEIMER, AND VIVIAN W. PINN
    1995 "Women and HIV/AIDS Research in the United States." *Journal of the American Medical Women's Association* 50(3/4): 137-138.

MELODY, M.E.
    1994 "Acting Up Academically: AIDS and the Politics of Disempowerment." In *Global AIDS Policy.* Douglas Feldman, ed. Westport, Connecticut: Bergin and Garvey. Pp. 160-184.

MENENDEX, B., S. VERMUND, E. DRUCKER, ET AL.
    1989 "Race/Ethnic-Specific AIDS Risk in New York City, 1981-1987." *American Journal of Public Health* 79(12): 1679-1680.

MERKATZ, RUTH B., ELYSE I. SUMMERS, AND THERESA TOIGO
    1995 "FDA: Making a Difference for Women and HIV/AIDS." *Journal of the American Medical Women's Association* 50(3/4): 108.

MEREDITH, ANN
    1992 "Until That Last Breath: Women with AIDS," In *AIDS: The Making of a Chronic Disease.* Elizabeth Fee and Daniel M. Fox, eds. Berkeley: University of California Press. Pp. 229-244.

METLER, R., G. CONWAY, AND J. STEHR-GREEN
1991 "AIDS Surveillance among American Indians and Alaska Natives." *American Journal of Public Health* 81(11): 1469-1471.

MEYER-BAHLBURG, H., A. EHRHARDT, T. EXNER, ET AL.
1988 "Sexual Risk Behavior Assessment Schedule-Adult, Baseline Interview for Female Drug Users (SERBAS-A-DF-1). Available from H. Meyer-Bahlburg, HIV Center for Clinical and Behavioral Studies, Columbia University, Unit 10, 722 West 168 Street, New York, NY 10032.

MICHAELS, DAVID AND CAROL LEVINE
1992 "Estimates of the Number of Motherless Youth Orphaned by AIDS in the United States." *Journal of the American Medical Association* 268(24): 3456-3461.
1993 "The Youngest Survivors: Estimates of the Number of Motherless Youth Orphaned by AIDS in New York City." In *A Death in the Family*. Carol Levine, ed. New York: United Hospital Fund. Pp. 1-12.

MICHAL-JOHNSON, PAULA
1994 "The Dark Side: Barriers to Changing High-Risk Behaviors." *AIDS & Public Policy Journal* 9(1): 18-19.

MICROBICIDE RESEARCH ADVOCACY PROJECT
1994 *Questions and Answers about the Need for a Woman-Controlled Method of HIV and STD Prevention*. Washington, D.C.: Center for Women and Policy Studies and Reproductive Technologies Project.

MIGUEZ-BURBANO, M., M. BAUM, B. PAGE, ET AL.
1993 "Risk of HIV Infection in Runaway Children in Colombia." *The Lancet* 342(8869): 98.

MILLER, J.
1993 "'Your Life is on the Line Every Night You're on the Streets': Victimization and the Resistance among Street Prostitutes." *Humanity and Society* 17: 422-446.

MILLER, JAMES
1955 "Toward a General Theory for the Behavioral Sciences." *American Psychologist* 10: 513-531.

MILLER, WILLIAM R. AND STEPHEN ROLLNICK
1991 *Motivational Interviewing: Preparing People for Changing Addictive Behavior*. New York: Guilford Press.

MILLS, C.
1959 *The Sociological Imagination*. New York: Oxford University Press.

MILLSTEIN, RICHARD A.
1992 "The National Impact of Alcohol and Drug Problems and HIV Infection and AIDS among the Poor and Underserved." *Journal of Health Care for the Poor and Underserved* 3(1): 21-29.

MINKOFF, HOWARD L.
1987 "Care of Pregnant Women Infected with Human Immunodeficiency Virus." *Journal of the American Medical Association* 258(19): 2714-2717.
1995 "Pregnancy and HIV Infection" In *HIV Infection in Women*. Howard Minkoff, Jack A. DeHovitz, and Ann Duerr, eds. New York: Raven Press. Pp. 173-188.

MINKOFF, HOWARD L. AND JACK A. DEHOVITZ
1991a "Care of Women with the Human Immunodeficiency Virus." *Journal of the American Medical Association* 266(16): 2253-2258.
1991b "HIV Infection in Women." *AIDS Clinical Care* 3(5): 33-35.

MINKOFF, HOWARD, JACK A. DEHOVITZ, AND ANN DUERR, EDS.
1994 *HIV Infection in Women*. New York: Raven Press.

MINKOFF, HOWARD, JACK A. DEHOVITZ AND ANN DUERR
    1995 "Preface." In *HIV Infection in Women*. Howard Minkoff, Jack A. DeHovitz, and Ann Duerr, eds. New York: Raven Press. Pp. ix.

MINKOFF, HOWARD L. AND LEONARD FEINKIND
    1989 "Management of Pregnancies of HIV-Infected Women." *Clinical Obstetrics and Gynecology* 32(3): 467-476.

MINKOFF, HOWARD L. AND J.D. MORENO
    1990 "Drug Prophylaxis for HIV-Infected Pregnant Women: Ethical Considerations." *American Journal of Obstetrics and Gynecology* 163(4): 1111-1114.

MINTZ, S.
    1964 "The Employment of Capital by Market Women in Haiti." In *Capital, Saving, and Credit in Peasant Societies*. R. Firth and B. Yamey, eds. Chicago: Aldine.

MIOTTI, P.G., G. DALLABETTA, E. NDOVI, ET AL.
    1990 "HIV-1 and Pregnant Women: Associated Factors, Prevalence, Estimate of Incidence and Role in Fetal Wastage in Central Africa." *AIDS* 4(8): 733-736.

MITCHELL, JANET, JOHN TUCKER, PATRICIA LOFTMAN, ET AL.
    1992 "HIV and Women: Current Controversies and Clinical Relevance." *Journal of Women's Health* 1(1): 35-39.

MITCHELL-LEWIS, DENNIS, JOAN PHELAM, RODRICK KELLY, ET AL.
    1994 "Identifying Oral Lesions Associated with Crack Cocaine Use." *Journal of the American Dental Association* 125(8): 1104-1108.

MIYAZAKI, M. AND M. NAEMURA
    1994 "Epidemiological Characteristics on Human Immunodeficiency Virus Infection and Acquired Immunodeficiency Syndrome in Japan." *International Journal of STDs & AIDS* 5(4): 273-278.

MMARI, E.
    1993 "Women in Developing Countries: The Case Study of Economic Factors as a Function of HIV Sexual and Behavioral Risks among African Women." *International Conference on AIDS* 9(1): 107. Abstract Number WS-D04-1.

MODAN, B.
    1993 "Combating AIDS—High Hopes and Doomed Realities." *Public Health Reviews* 21(3-4): 295-296.

MODAN, B., R. GOLDSCHMIDT, E. RUBINSTEIN, ET AL.
    1992 "Prevalence of HIV Antibodies in Transsexual and Female Prostitutes." *American Journal of Public Health* 82(4): 590-592.

MONGELLA, G.
    1995 "Global Approaches to the Promotion of Women's Health." *Science* 269(5225): 789-790.

MOORE, JANET S., JANET S. HARRISON AND LYDIA DOLL
    1994 "Interventions for Sexually Active, Heterosexual Women in the United States." In *Preventing AIDS: Theories and Methods of Behavioral Interventions*. Ralph DiCelemente and John L. Peterson, eds. New York: Plenum Press. Pp. 243-266

MOORE, RICHARD, JULIA HIDALGO, BARBARA SUGLAND, ET AL.
    1991 "Zidovudine and the Natural History of the Acquired Immunodefiency Syndrome." *The New England Journal of Medicine* 324(20): 1412-1416.

MOORE, RICHARD, DAVID STANTON, RAMANA GOPALAN, ET AL.
    1994 "Racial Differences in the Use of Drug Therapy for HIV Disease in an Urban Community." *The New England Journal of Medicine* 330(11): 763-768.

MOR, VINCENT, JOHN A. FLEISHMAN, MARGUERITE DRESSER, ET AL.
    1992 "Variation in Health Service Use among HIV-Infected Patients." *Medical Care* 30(1): 17-29.

MORAGA, CHERRÍE AND GLORIA ANZALDÚA, EDS.
    1981 *The Bridge Called My Back: Writings by Radical Women of Color.* New York: Kitchen Table: Women of Color Press.

MORAN, J., S. ARAL, W. JENKINS, ET AL.
    1989 "The Impact of Sexually Transmitted Diseases on Minority Populations." *Public Health Reports* 104(6): 560-565.

MORAN, MARY
    1994 *Populations at Risk: Fleeing Terror in Rwanda.* Report for the Women's Commission of the International Rescue Committee, New York.

MORENO, SANTIAGO, JOSU BARAIA-ETXABURU, EMILIO BOUZA, ET AL.
    1993 "Risk for Developing Tuberculosis among Anergic Patients Infected with HIV." *Annals of Internal Medicine* 119(3): 194-198.

MORIN, STEPHEN F.
    1984 "AIDS in One City: An Interview with Mervyn Silverman, Director of Health." *American Psychologist* 39(11): 1294-1296.

MORIN, STEPHEN F., KENNETH A. CHARLES AND ALAN K. MAYLON
    1984 "The Psychological Impact of AIDS on Gay Men." *American Psychologist* 39(11): 1288-1293.

MORLAT, P., P. PARNEIX, D. DOUARD, ET AL.
    1992 "Women and HIV Infection: A Cohort Study of 483 HIV-Infected Women in Bordeaux, France, 1985-1991." *AIDS* 6(10): 1187-1193.

MORSE, D., L. LESSNER, M. MEDVESKY, ET AL.
    1991 "Geographic Distribution of Newborn HIV Seroprevalence in Relation to Four Sociodemographic Variables." *American Journal of Public Health* 81(Supplement): 25-29.

MORRIS, L., C. WARREN, AND S. ARAL
    1993 "Measuring Adolescent Sexual Behaviors and Related Health Outcomes." *Public Health Reports* 108(S1): 31-36.

MOSHER, WILLIAM D. AND WILLIAM F. PRATT
    1993 "AIDS-Related Behavior among Women 15-44 Years of Age: United States, 1988 and 1990." *Advance Data* 239: 1-15.

MOSES, S., F. MANJI, J.E. BRADLEY, ET AL.
    1992 "Impact of User Fees on Attendance at a Referral Centre for Sexually Transmitted Diseases in Kenya." *The Lancet* 340(8817): 463-466.

MOSS, ANDREW R., GERALD MCCALLUM, PAUL A. VOLBERDING, ET AL.
    1984 "Mortality Associated with Mode of Presentation in the Acquired Immune Deficiency Syndrome." *Journal of the National Cancer Institute* 73(6): 1281-1284.

MOULTON, LAWRENCE H., ELIZABETH A. HOLT, JAYAKRAN S. JOB, ET AL.
    1995 "Percentile Regression Analysis of Correlated Antibody Responses." *Statistics in Medicine* 14(8): 777-787.

MOYNIHAN, DANIEL P.
    1965 *The Negro Family: The Case for National Action.* Washington, D.C.: United States Department of Labor.

MTSHALI, NTOMBIFUTHI AGNES
    1995 "Transferability of American AIDS Prevention Models to South African Youth." In *Women Resisting AIDS: Feminist Strategies of Empowerment.* Beth E. Schneider and Nancy E. Stoller, eds. Philadelphia: Temple University Press. Pp. 162-169.

MUIR, D. AND M. BELSEY
    1980 "Pelvic Inflammatory Disease and its Consequences in the Developing World."
         American Journal of Obstetrics and Gynecology 138(7; Part 2): 913-928.

MULCAHY, F., G. KELLY AND M. TYNAN
    1994 "The Natural History of HIV Infection in Women Attending a Sexually Transmit-
         ted Disease Clinic in Dublin." *Genitourinary Medicine* 70(2): 81-83.

MULDER, DAAN W., ANDREW J. NUNN, ANATOLI KAMALI, ET AL.
    1994 "Two-Year HIV-1-Associated Mortality in a Ugandan Rural Population." *The Lancet*
         343(8904): 1021-1023.

MULEMWA, JANE N.
    1990 "Women and AIDS: Theoretical Overview and Strategic Initiatives." Paper pre-
         sented at the Sixth International Women and Health Meeting, Quezon City,
         Philippines (November 3-9).

MULLEN, GEORGE E., ARTHUR L. SHEPPELL AND JOSEPH R. MASCI
    1988 "Survival with AIDS in New York." *The New England Journal of Medicine* 318(22):
         1465.

MULLER, O., L. BARUGAHARE, B. SCHWARTLANDER, ET AL.
    1992 "HIV Prevalence, Attitudes and Behaviour in Clients of a Confidential HIV Test-
         ing and Counselling Centre in Uganda." *AIDS* 6(8): 674-689.

MUREKEZI, C. AND J. KEMIGABO
    1993 "Why Women Carry Out Prostitution in Uganda: Aren't They at Risk of STD/HIV
         Infection?" *International Conference on AIDS* 9(2): 826. Abstract Number PO-
         D09-3649.

MURPHY, TIMOTHY F.
    1994 *Ethics in an Epidemic: AIDS, Morality, and Culture.* Berkeley: University of Califor-
         nia Press.

N'GALY, BOSENGE, ROBERT W. RYDER, BILA KAPITA, ET AL.
    1988 "Human Immunodeficiency Virus Infection among Employees at an African Hos-
         pital." *The New England Journal of Medicine* 319(17): 1123-1127.

NAGELKERKE, N., S. MOSES, J. EMBREE, ET AL.
    1995 "The Duration of Breast-Feeding by HIV-1 Infected Mothers in Developing Coun-
         tries: Balancing Benefits and Risks." *Journal of Acquired Immune Deficiency Syn-
         dromes* 8(2): 176-181.

NAIK, T.N., S. SARKAR, H.L. SINGH, ET AL.
    1991 "Intravenous Drug Users—A New High-Risk Group for HIV Infection in India."
         AIDS 5(1): 117-118.

NAJMAN, J.M.
    1993 "Health and Poverty: Past, Present, and Prospects for the Future." *Social Science and
         Medicine* 36(2): 157-166.

NANDA, DEEPAK AND HOWARD MINKOFF
    1992 "Pregnancy and Women at Risk for HIV Infection." *Primary Care: Clinics in Office
         Practice* 19(1): 157-169.

NANDA, SERENA
    1986 "The Hijras of India: Cultural and Individual Dimensions of an Institutionalized
         Third Gender Role." In *The Many Faces of Homosexuality: Anthropological
         Approaches to Homosexual Behavior.* Evelyn Blackwood, ed. New York: Harrington
         Park Press. Pp. 36-54.

NARAIN, J.P., A. JHA, S. LA, ET AL.
    1994 "Risk Factors for HIV Transmission in India." *AIDS* 8(S2): S77-S82.

NASH, JUNE
    1989 "Gender Studies in Latin America." In *Gender and Anthropology*. Sandra Morgen, ed. Washington, D.C.: American Anthropological Association. Pp. 228-245.

NATARAJ, SHYAMALA
    1990 "Indian Prostitutes Highlight AIDS Dilemmas." *Development Forum* (November-December): 1,16.

NATIONAL INSTITUTE ON DRUG ABUSE
    1992 *MAIDEP Final Report*. National Institute on Drug Abuse, 271-90-8400.

NATIONS, MARILYN K.
    1986 "Epidemiological Research on Infectious Disease: Quantitative Rigor or Rigormortis? Insights from Ethnomedicine." In *Anthropology and Epidemiology*. Craig Janes, Ron Stall and Sandra Gifford, eds. Boston: D. Reidel Publishing Company. Pp. 97-123.

NAVARRO, VICENTE
    1990 "Race or Class versus Race and Class: Mortality Differentials in the United States." *The Lancet* 336(8725): 1238-1240.

NEGRA, MARINELLA DELLA, WLADIMIR QUEIROZ AND YU CHING LIAN
    1991 "Women and AIDS in Brazil." *Vena* 5(1): 27-28.

NELSON, EDWARD
    1991 "Sexual Self-Defense Versus the Liaison Dangereuse: A Strategy for AIDS Prevention in the '90s." *American Journal of Preventive Medicine* 7(3): 146-149.

NEPTUNE-ANGLADE, MIREILLE
    1986 *L'Autre Moité du Dévelopment: À Propos du Travial des Femmes en Haïti*. Petion-Ville, Haïti: Editions des Alizes.

NEWMEYER, JOHN, HARVEY FELDMAN, PATRICK BIERNACKI, ET AL.
    1989 "Preventing AIDS Contagion among Intravenous Drug Users." *Medical Anthropology* 10(2-3): 167-175.

NGUGI, E., F. PLUMMER, J. SIMMONSEN, ET AL.
    1988 "Prevention of HIV Transmission in Africa: The Effectiveness of Condom Promotion and Health Education among High-Risk Prostitutes." *The Lancet* 2(8615): 887-890.

NICHOLLS, DAVID
    1985 *Haiti in Caribbean Context: Ethnicity, Economy and Revolt*. New York: St. Martin's Press.

NICOLL, ANGUS, MARIE-LOUISE NEWELL, ERIC VAM PRAAG, ET AL.
    1995 "Infant Feeding Policy and Practice in the Presence of HIV-1 Infection." *AIDS* 9(2): 107-119.

NICOLOSI, ALFREDO, MARIA LÉA CORREA LEITE, MASSIMO MUSICCO, ET AL.
    1994 "The Efficiency of Male-to-Female and Female-to-Male Sexual Transmission of the Human Immunodeficiency Virus: A Study of 730 Stable Couples. Italian Study Group on HIV Heterosexual Transmission." *Epidemiology* 5(6): 570-575.

NICOLOSI, ALFREDO, MASSIMO MUSICCO, A. SARACCO, ET AL.
    1990 "Incidence and Risk Factors of HIV Infection: A Prospective Study of Seronegative Drug Users from Milan and Northern Italy, 1987-1989." *Epidemiology* 1(6): 453-459.

NIGHTINGALE, STEPHEN D., D. WILLIAM CAMERON, FRED M. GORDON, ET AL.
    1993 "Two Controlled Trials of Rifabutin Prophylaxis Mycobacterium Avium Complex Infection in AIDS." *The New England Journal of Medicine* 329(12): 828-833.

NORTH, RICHARD L. AND KAREN H. ROTHENBERG
1993 "Partner Notification and the Threat of Domestic Violence against Women with HIV Infection." *The New England Journal of Medicine* 329(16): 1194-1196.

NORTON, ELEANOR HOLMES
1985 "Restoring the Traditional Black Family." *New York Times Magazine*. (June 2).

NORWOOD, C. AND R. CORDOVA
1992 "Health Force: Three Years Successful Experience Empowering Women Affected by AIDS as Educators, Advocates, and Leaders in a Poor Urban Area." *International Conference on AIDS* 8(2): D461. Abstract Number POD 5447.

NOSTLINGER, C., B. WIMMER-PUCHINGER, M. BARTH, ET AL.
1992 "Promoting Safe Sex and Sexual Health to Socially Disadvantaged Young Women and Girls." *International Conference on AIDS* 8(2): D461. Abstract Number POD 5446.

NOVELLO, ANTONIA COELLO
1995 "Introduction." In *HIV Infection in Women*. Howard Minkoff, Jack A. DeHovitz, and Ann Duerr, eds. New York: Raven Press. Pp. xi-xiv.

NOVICK, L.
1991a "HIV Seroprevalence Surveys: Impetus for Preventive Activities." *American Journal of Public Health* 81(Supplement): 61-63.
1991b "New York State HIV Seroprevalence Project: Goals, Windows, and Policy Consideration." *American Journal of Public Health* 81(Supplement): 11-14.

NOVICK, L., D. GLEBATIS, R. STRICOF, ET AL.
1991 "Newborn Seroprevalence Study: Methods and Results." *American Journal of Public Health* 81(Supplement): 15-21.

NWANYANWU, O., L. CONTI, C. CIESIELSKI, ET AL.
1993 "Increasing Frequency of Heterosexually Transmitted AIDS in Southern Florida: Artifact or Reality?" *American Journal of Public Health* 83(4): 571-573.

NYAMATHI, ADELINE M.
1992 "Relationship of Resources to Emotional Distress, Somatic Complaints, and High-Risk Behaviors in Drug Recovery and Homeless Minority Women." *Journal of Health Care for the Poor and Underserved* 3(1): 93-106.

NYAMATHI, ADELINE, CRYSTAL BENNETT, JACQUELYN FLASKERUD, ET AL.
1994 "Evaluation of Two AIDS Education Programs for Impoverished Latina Women." *AIDS Education and Prevention* 6(4): 296-309.

NYAMATHI, ADELINE, CRYSTAL BENNETT, AND BARBARA LEAKE
1995 "Predictors of Maintained High-Risk Behaviors among Impoverished Women." *Public Health Reports* 110(5): 600-606.

NYAMATHI, ADELINE, CRYSTAL BENNETT, BARBARA LEAKE, ET AL.
1993 "AIDS Related Knowledge, Perceptions, and Behaviors among Impoverished Minority Women." *American Journal of Public Health* 83(1): 65-71.

NYAMATHI, ADELINE, BARBARA LEAKE, JACQUELYN FLASKERUD, ET AL.
1993 "Outcomes of Specialized and Traditional AIDS Counseling Programs for Impoverished Women of Color." *Research in Nursing and Health* 16(1): 11-21

NYAMATHI, ADELINE M., CHARLES LEWIS, BARBARA LEAKE, ET AL.
1995 "Barriers to Condom Use and Needle Cleaning among Impoverished Minority Female Injection Drug Users and Partners of Injection Drug Users." *Public Health Reports* 110(2): 166-172.

NZILA, NZILAMBI, MARIE LAGA, MANOKA ABIB THIAM, ET AL.
1991 "HIV and Other Sexually Transmitted Diseases among Female Prostitutes in Kinshasa." *AIDS* 5(6): 715-722.

NZILA, NZILAMBI, KEVIN M. DE COCK, DONALD FORTHAL, ET AL.
  1988 "The Prevalence of Infection with Human Immunodeficiency Virus over a 10-Year Period in Rural Zaire." *The New England Journal of Medicine* 318(5): 276-279.

O'FARRELL, N., R. LAU, K. YOGANATHAN, ET AL.
  1995 "AIDS in Africans Living in London." *Genitourinary Medicine* 71(6): 358-362.

O'NEIL CATHERINE
  1995 *Rwanda: Recovering from Genocide*. Report for the Women's Commission of International Rescue Committee. (January).

OBBO, CHRISTINE
  1989 "Women, Children and AIDS in Rakai District, Uganda." Presentation at African Studies Association, Atlanta.
  1992 "Gender, Age and Class: Discourses on HIV Transmission and Control in Uganda." Paper presented at the Workshop on Culture, Sexual Behavior, and AIDS, University of Amsterdam.
  1993a "HIV Transmission: Men are the Solution." *Population and Environment* 14(3): 211-243.
  1993b "HIV Transmission through Social and Geographical Networks in Uganda." *Social Science and Medicine* 36(7): 949-955.

OLLE, GOIG J.E.
  1995 "Carta Urgente Desde Haiti." *Medicina Clinica* 105(8): 302-303.

ONOGE, O.
  1975 "Capitalism and Public Health: A Neglected Theme in the Medical Anthropology of Africa." In *Topias and Utopias in Health*. S. Ingman and A. Thomas, eds. The Hague: Mouton. Pp. 219-232.

ONORATO, I, M. GWINN, AND T. DONDERO, JR.
  1994 "Applications of Data from the CDC Family of Surveys." *Public Health Reports* 109(2): 204-211.

ONORATO, I, T. JONES, AND W. FORRESTER
  1990 "Using Seroprevalence Data in Managing Public Health Programs." *Public Health Reports* 105(2): 163-166.

ONORATO, I., W. KLASKALA, M. MORGAN, ET AL.
  1995 "Prevalence, Incidence, and Risk for HIV-1 Infection in Female Sex Workers in Miami, Florida." *Journal of Acquired Immune Deficiency Syndromes* 9(4): 395-400.

ONORATO, I, E. MCCRAY, M. PAPPAIOANOU, ET AL.
  1990 "HIV Seroprevalence Surveys in Sexually Transmitted Disease Clinics." *Public Health Reports* 105(2): 119-124.

ONORATO, I. T. O'BRIEN, C. SCHABLE, ET AL.
  1993 "Sentinel Surveillance for HIV-2 Infection in High-Risk U.S. Populations." *American Journal of Public Health* 83(4): 515-519.

OPPENHIEMER, GERALD
  1988 "In the Eye of the Storm: The Epidemiological Construction of AIDS," In *AIDS: The Burdens of History*. Elizabeth Fee and Daniel Fox, eds. Berkeley, CA: University of California. Pp. 267-300.
  1992 "Causes, Cases, and Cohorts: The Role of Epidemiology in the Historical Construction of AIDS." In In *AIDS: The Making of a Chronic Disease*. Elizabeth Fee and Daniel Fox, eds. Los Angeles: University of California Press. Pp. 49-83.

OPPONG, CHRISTINE
  1991 "Sexual Coercion in the Workplace: The Need for Protection." *Vena* 5(1): 39-42.

ORR, S., D. CELENTANO, J. SANTELLI, ET AL.
    1994 "Depressive Symptoms and Risk Factors for HIV Acquisition among Black Women
        Attending Urban Health Centers in Baltimore." *AIDS Education and Prevention*
        6(3): 230-236.

ORUBULOYE, I.O., JOHN C. CALDWELL AND PAT CALDWELL
    1994a "African Women's Control over their Sexuality in an Era of AIDS: A Study of the
        Yoruba of Nigeria." In *Sexual Networking and AIDS in Sub-Saharan Africa: Behav-
        ioral Research and the Social Context*. I.O. Orubuloye, John C. Caldwell, Pat Cald-
        well, *et al.*, eds. Canberra, Australia: The Australian National University. Pp. 69-
        88.
    1994b "Commercial Sex Workers in Nigeria in the Shadow of AIDS." In *Sexual Net-
        working and AIDS in Sub-Saharan Africa: Behavioral Research and the Social Context*.
        I.O. Orubuloye, John C. Caldwell, Pat Caldwell, *et al.*, eds. Canberra, Australia:
        The Australian National University. Pp. 101-116.
    1994c "The Role of High-Risk Occupations in the Spread of AIDS: Truck Drivers and
        Itinerant Market Women in Nigeria." In *Sexual Networking and AIDS in Sub-Saha-
        ran Africa: Behavioral Research and the Social Context*. I.O. Orubuloye, John C.
        Caldwell, Pat Caldwell, *et al.*, eds. Canberra, Australia: The Australian National
        University. Pp. 89-100.

ORUBULOYE, I.O., JOHN C. CALDWELL, PAT CALDWELL, ET AL., EDS.
    1994 *Sexual Networking and AIDS in Sub-Saharan Africa: Behavioral Research and the Social
        Context*. Canberra, Australia: The Australian National University.

OSMOND, D.H., K. PAGE, J. WILEY, ET AL.
    1994 "HIV Infection in Homosexual and Bisexual Men 18 to 29 Years of Age: The San
        Francisco Young Men's Health Study." *American Journal of Public Health* 84(12):
        1933-1937.

OSBORN, JUNE
    1989 "Public Health and the Politics of AIDS Prevention." *Daedalus* 118(3): 123-144.
    1990 "Policy Implications of the AIDS Deficit." *Journal of Acquired Immune Deficiency
        Syndromes* 3(4): 293-295.

OSTROW, D. AND J. LANGE
    1994 "Heterosexual Human Immunodeficiency Virus Risk and Cocaine Use." *Epidemiol-
        ogy* 5(4): 389-390

OSTROW, DAVID
    1990 *Behavioral Aspects of AIDS*. New York: Plenum Press.

O'SULLIVAN, M.J., AND J. SAJOUS, M.R. BLEUS, ET AL.
    1995 "HIV Counseling and Testing of Multi-Ethnic Indigent Women." *HIV Infection in
        Women: Setting a New Agenda*. Washington, D.C. (February 22-24) Pp. P78.
        Abstract Number WP-349.

OTTEN, M., JR., A. ZAIDI, J. WROTEN, ET AL.
    1993 "Changes in Sexually Transmitted Disease Rates after HIV Testing and Posttest
        Counseling, Miami, 1988 to 1989." *American Journal of Public Health* 83(4): 529-
        533.

OVER, M. AND P. PIOT
    1993 "HIV Infection and Sexually Transmitted Diseases." In *Disease Control Priorities in
        Developing Countries*. D.T. Jamison, ed. Oxford: Oxford University Press. Pp. 455-
        527.

PAAUW, DOUGLAS S., MARGOIRE D. WENRICH, J. RANDALL CURTIS, ET AL.
    1995 "Ability of Primary Care Physicians to Recognize Physical Findings Associated with
        HIV Infection." *Journal of the American Medical Association* 274(17): 1380-1382.

PACKARD, RANDALL
    1989 *White Plague, Black Labor: Tuberculosis and the Political Economy of Health and Disease in South Africa*. Berkeley: University of California Press.

PACKARD, RANDALL AND PAUL EPSTEIN
    1991 "Epidemiologists, Social Scientists, and the Structure of Medical Research on AIDS in Africa." *Social Science and Medicine* 33(7): 771-783, 793-794.

PADIAN, NANCY S.
    1987 "Heterosexual Transmission of Acquired Immunodeficiency Syndrome: International Perspectives and National Projections." *Reviews of Infectious Diseases* 9(5): 947-960.

PADIAN, NANCY S.
    1990 "Sexual Histories of Heterosexual Couples with One HIV Infected Partner." *American Journal of Public Health* 80(8): 990-991.

PADIAN, NANCY S., STEPHEN C. SHIBOSKI AND NICHOLAS P. JEWELL
    1991 "Female-to-Male Transmission of the Human Immunodeficiency Virus." *Journal of the American Medical Association* 266(12): 1664-1667.

PAGE, J. BRYAN, DALE D. CHITWOOD, PRINCE C. SMITH, ET AL.
    1990 "Intravenous Drug Use and HIV Infection in Miami." *Medical Anthropology Quarterly* 4(1): 56-71.

PAL, N.K., M.S. CHAKRABORTY, A. DAS, ET AL.
    1994 "Community Based Survey of STD/HIV Infection among Commercial Sex Workers in Calcutta (India). Part IV: Sexually Transmitted Diseases and Related Risk Factors." *Journal of Communicable Diseases* 26(4): 197-202.

PALASANTHIRAN, P., J. ZIEGLER, G. STEWART, ET AL.
    1993 "Breast Feeding during Primary Maternal Human Immunodeficiency Virus Infection and Risk of Transmission from Mother to Infant." *Journal of Infectious Diseases* 167(2): 441-444.

PALCA, JOSEPH
    1990 "African AIDS: Whose Research Rules?" *Science* 250(4978): 199-200.

PALTROW, LYNNE M.
    1992 *Criminal Prosecutions against Pregnant Women: National Update and Overview*. New York: American Civil Liberties Union.

PAN AMERICAN HEALTH ORGANIZATION (PAHO)
    1995 "Humanitarian Assistance in Haiti." *Bulletin of the Pan American Health Organization* 29(2): 171-175.

PANOS INSTITUTE
    1990 "Who Cares, Who Pays?," In *Triple Jeopardy: Women and AIDS*. Washington: Budapest. Pp. 60-72.
    1992 *The Hidden Cost of AIDS: The Challenge of HIV to Development*. London: The Panos Institute.

PAONE, DENISE, STEPHANIE CALOIR, QUIHU SHI, ET AL.
    1995 "Sex, Drugs, and Syringe Exchange in New York City: Women's Experiences." *Journal of the American Medical Women's Association* 50(3/4): 109-114.

PAPE, J.W., S.S. JEAN, J.L. HO, ET AL.
    1993 "Effect of Isoniazid Prophylaxis on Incidence of Active Tuberculosis and Progression of HIV Infection." *The Lancet* 342(8866): 268-272.

PAPE, JEAN AND WARREN JOHNSON
    1988 "Epidemiology of AIDS in the Caribbean." *Ballière's Clinical Tropical Diseases* 3(1): 31-42.

PAPPAIOANOU, M., T. DONDERO, L. PETERSEN, ET AL.
    1990 "The Family of HIV Seroprevalence Surveys: Objectives, Methods, and Uses of Sentinel Surveys for HIV in the United States." *Public Health Reports* 105(2): 113-119.

PAPPAIOANOU, MARGUERTIE, J. RICHARD GEORGE, W. HARRY HANNON, ET AL.
    1990 "HIV Seroprevalence Surveys of Child-Bearing Women—Objectives, Methods, and Uses of the Data." *Public Health Reports* 105(2): 147-152.

PAPPAS, P.G.
    1993 "Syphilis 100 Years Ago: Parallels with the AIDS Pandemic." *International Journal of Dermatology* 32(10): 708-709.

PARDO, J.A.
    1995 "Excluding Immigrants on the Basis of Health: The Haitian Centers Council Decision Criticized." *Journal of Contemporary Health Law Policy* 11(2): 523-540.

PARKER, RICHARD G.
    1987 "Acquired Immune Deficiency Syndrome in Urban Brazil." *Medical Anthropology Quarterly* 1(2): 155-175.
    1994 "Public Policy, Political Activism and AIDS in Brazil." In *Global AIDS Policy*. Douglas Feldman, ed. Westport, Connecticut: Bergin and Garvey. Pp. 28-46.

PARTNERS IN HEALTH
    1991 "Women, Poverty and AIDS: A Project in Haiti." *Vena* 5(1): 29.

PATEL, K., C. HUTCHINSON, AND D. SIENKO
    1990 "Sentinel Surveillance of HIV Infection among New Inmates and Implications for Policies of Corrections Facilities." *Public Health Reports* 105(5): 510-514.

PATTERSON, JAMES T.
    1986 *America's Struggle Against Poverty*. Cambridge, MA: Harvard University Press.

PATTON, CINDY
    1994 *Last Served?: Gendering the HIV Pandemic*. Bristol, PA: Taylor & Francis.

PAVETTI, LADONNA A.
    1993 *The Dynamics of Welfare and Work: Exploring the Process by which Women Work their Way Off Welfare*. Cambridge, MA: Harvard University Press.

PAVIA, A., M. BENYO, L. NILER, ET AL.
    1993 "Partner Notification for Control of HIV: Results after Two Years of a Statewide Program in Utah." *American Journal of Public Health* 83(10): 1418-1424.

PAXTON, S.
    1994 "Prioritizing Women's Ability to be Self-Sufficient." *International Conference on AIDS* 10(1): 378. Abstract Number PD0119.

PEARCE, N.
    1992 "Time-Related Confounders and Intermediate Variables." *Epidemiology* 3(4): 279-281.
    1996 "Traditional Epidemiology, Modern Epidemiology, and Public Health." *American Journal of Public Health* 86(5): 678-683.

PEGUES, D., M. ENGELGAU, AND C. WOERNLE
    1994 "Prevalence of Illicit Drugs Detected in the Urine of Women of Childbearing Age in Alabama Public Health Clinics." *Public Health Reports* 109(4): 530-538.

PELIA, P., M. SINGER AND D. HIMMELGREEN
    1994 "Police, Community, Services and Client Response toward a Needle Exchange Program." Abstracts of the 93rd Annual Meetings of the Anthropological Association. Atlanta, GA.

PENKOWER, L., M. DEW, L. KINGSLEY, ET AL.
    1991 "Behavioral, Health, and Psychosocial Factors and Risk for HIV Infection among Sexually Active Homosexual Men: The Multicenter AIDS Cohort Study." *American Journal of Public Health* 81(2): 194-196.

PEQUEGNAT, W., J. KELLY, G. WYATT, ET AL.
    1995 "Challenging Assumptions about Women in Order to Design More Effective HIV Prevention Programs." *HIV Infection in Women: Setting a New Agenda.* Washington, D.C. (February 22-24) Pp. P122. Abstract Number TP-524.

PEREIRA, CILENE AND MALU OLIVEIRA
    1994 "Mulher e AIDS: Eu Passo AIDS." *Istoé* 1314: 40-5.

PEREIRA, T.M., V. SANTOS, AND C.M. FONSECA
    1994 "Women and AIDS: Steady Partners, Are They Safe?" *International Conference on AIDS* 10(1): 381. Abstract Number PD0130.

PEREZ, V., D. SCOTT, AND G. SANTIAGO
    1993 "Postive Women: Organizing for Community and Family in a Poor Urban Area." *International Conference on AIDS* 9(2): 881.

PERGALLO, N.
    1995 "Risk Behaviors for HIV Infection among Latino Women." *HIV Infection in Women: Setting a New Agenda.* Washington, D.C. (February 22-24) Pp P124. Abstract Number TP-531.

PESCE, L., C. SOSA, AND M. PEREIRA
    1994 "We, Women, Facing HIV/AIDS; What Can We do about It?" *International Conference on AIDS* 10(1): 382. Abstract Number PD0134.

PETERMAN, T., D. DROTMAN, AND J. CURRAN
    1985 "Epidemiology of the Acquired Immune Deficiency Syndrome (AIDS)." *Epidemiologic Reviews* 7: 1-21.

PETERMAN, T. AND L. PETERSEN
    1990 "Stalking the Epidemic: Which Tracks to Follow and How Far?" *American Journal of Public Health* 80(4): 401-402.

PETERSEN, LYLE, NED CALONGE, MARY CHAMBERLAND, ET AL.
    1990 "Methods of Surveillance for HIV Infection in Primary Care Outpatients in the United States." *Public Health Reports* 105(2): 158-162.

PETERSEN, LYLE, ROGER DODD, AND TIMOTHY DONDERO, JR.
    1990 "Methodological Approaches to Surveillance of HIV Infection among Blood Donors." *Public Health Reports* 105(2): 153-157.

PETERSEN, L. AND C. WHITE
    1990 "Premarital Screening for Antibodies to Human Immunodeficiency Virus Type 1 in the United States: The Premarital Screening Study Group." *American Journal of Public Health* 80(9): 1087-1090.

PETERSON, JOHN L., JOSEPH A. CATANIA, M. MARGARET DOLCINI, ET AL.
    1993 "Multiple Sexual Partners among Blacks in High-Risk Cities." *Family Planning Perspectives* 25(6): 263-267.

PETERSON, JOHN L., T. COATES, JOSEPH A. CATANIA, ET AL.
    1992 "High-Risk Sexual Behavior and Condom Use among Gay and Bisexual African-American Men." *American Journal of Public Health* 82(11): 1490-1494.

PHANUPHAK, P., O. MULLER, S. SARANGBIN, ET AL.
    1994 "Knowledge, Attitudes and Behaviour among HIV-Positive and HIV-Negative Clients of a Confidential HIV Counselling and Testing Centre in Thailand." *AIDS* 8(9): 1315-1319.

PICKERING, HELEN AND H. ANDREW WILKENS
1993 "Do Unmarried Women in African Towns Have to Sell Sex or Is it a Matter of Choice." In *Sexual Networking and HIV/AIDS in West Africa—Supplement to Health Transition Review 3*. Canberra: The Australian National University. Pp. 17-27.

PIES, CHERI
1995 "AIDS, Ethics, Reproductive Rights: No Easy Answers." In *Women Resisting AIDS: Feminist Strategies of Empowerment*. Beth E. Schneider and Nancy E. Stoller, eds. Philadelphia: Temple University Press. Pp. 322-334.

PIETTE, JOHN D., ORNA INTRATOR, SALLY ZIERLER, ET AL.
1992 "An Exploratory Analysis of Survival Time with AIDS Using a Nonparametric Tree-Structure Approach." *Epidemiology* 3(4): 310-318.

PIOT, P. AND LAGA, M.
1989 "Genital Ulcers, Other Sexually Transmitted Diseases and Sexual Transmission of HIV." *British Medical Journal* 298(6674): 623-624.

PIVNICK, ANITRA
1993 "HIV Infection and the Meaning of Condoms." *Culture, Medicine and Psychiatry* 17(4): 431-453.

PIVNICK, ANITRA, AUDREY JACOBSON, KATHLEEN ERIC, ET AL.
1991 "Reproductive Decisions among HIV-Infected, Drug-Using Women: The Importance of Mother-Child Coresidence." *Medical Anthropology Quarterly* 5(2): 153-69.
1994 "AIDS, HIV Infection, and Illicit Drug Use within Inner-City Families and Social Networks." *American Journal of Public Health* 84(2): 271-274.

PIZZI, M.
1992 "Women, HIV Infection, and AIDS: Tapestries of Life, Death, and Empowerment." *American Journal of Occupational Therapy* 46(11): 1021-1027.

PLOTNICK, ROBERT D.
1993 "Changes in Poverty, Income, Inequality, and the Standard of Living in the U.S. during the Reagan Years." *International Journal of Health Services* 23(2): 347-358.

PLOURDE, PIERRE J., FRANCIS A. PLUMMER, JACQUES PEPIN, ET AL.
1992 "Human Immunodeficiency Virus Type I Infection in Women Attending a Sexually Transmitted Diseases Clinic in Kenya." *Journal of Infectious Diseases* 166(1): 86-92.

PLUMMER, FRANCIS A., NEIL J. SIMONSEN, DAVID W. CAMERON, ET AL.
1991 "Cofactors in Male-Female Sexual Transmission of HIV-I." *Journal of Infectious Diseases* 163(2): 233-239.

POINDEXTER, ALFRED N., MARGARET L. FRANK, GABRIELA VILLARREAL, ET AL.
1992 "Risk Factors for Infection with Human Immunodeficiency Virus among Low-Income Women Undergoing Voluntary Sterilization." *Texas Medicine* 88(10): 70-74.

POLAKOW, VALERIE
1995a *Lives on the Edge*. Chicago: University of Chicago.
1995b "Lives of Welfare Mothers: On a Tightrope Without a Net." *The Nation* (May 1): 590-592.

POLLAK, MICHAEL
1988 *Les Homosexuels et le SIDA: Sociologie d'une Epidémie*. Paris: A.M. Matailie.

POMERANTZ, ROGER J., SUZANNE DE LA MONTE, S. PATRICK DONEGAN, ET AL.
1988 "Human Immunodeficiency Virus (HIV) Infection of the Uterine Cervix." *Annals of Internal Medicine* 108(3): 321-327.

PORTER, J.D. AND K.P. MCADAM
1994 "The Re-Emergence of Tuberculosis." *Annual Review of Public Health* 15: 303-323.

PORTER, JUDITH AND LOUIS BONILLA
    1993 "Cracked Lips: An Additional HIV Risk Factor." *American Journal of Public Health*
        83(10): 1409-1410.

PORTER, ROBERT W.
    1994 "AIDS in Ghana: Priorities and Policies." In *Global AIDS Policy*. Douglas Feldman,
        ed. Westport, Connecticut: Bergin and Garvey. Pp. 90-106.

PORTER, S.B.
    1993 "Public Knowledge and Attitudes about AIDS among Adults in Calcutta, India."
        AIDS Care 5(2): 169-176.

POSHYACHINDA, V.
    1993a "Drugs and AIDS in Southeast-Asia." *Forensic Science International* 62(1-2): 15-18.
    1993b "Drug Injecting and HIV Infection Among the Population of Drug Abusers in
        Asia." *Bulletin on Narcotics* 45(1): 77-90.

POTTS, M.
    1994 "The Urgent Need for a Vaginal Microbicide in the Prevention of HIV Transmis-
        sion." *American Journal of Public Health* 84(6): 890-891.

PRIOLO, L. AND H. MINKOFF
    1992 "HIV Infection in Women." *Balliere's Clinical Obstetrics and Gynecology* 6(3): 617-
        628.

QUAM, MICHAEL D.
    1994 "AIDS Policy and the United States Political Economy." In *Global AIDS Policy*.
        Douglas Feldman, ed. Westport, Connecticut: Bergin and Garvey. Pp. 142-159.

QUIMBY, ERNEST
    1992 "Anthropological Witnessing for African Americans: Power, Responsibility, and
        Choice in the Age of AIDS." In *The Time of AIDS*. Gilbert Herdt and Shirley Lin-
        denbaum, eds. Newbury Park, CA: Sage. Pp. 159-184.

QUINN, THOMAS C.
    1995 "Population Migration and the Spread of Types 1 and 2 Human Immunodeficiency
        Viruses." In *Infectious Diseases in an Age of Change*. Bernard Roizman, ed. Wash-
        ington, D.C.: National Academy of Sciences, Pp. 77-97.

QUINN, THOMAS C., JONATHAN MANN, JAMES CURRAN, ET AL.
    1986 "AIDS in Africa: An Epidemiologic Paradigm." *Science* 234(4779): 955-963.

QUIRK, MARK E., MICHAEL A. GODKIN AND ELIZABETH SCHWENZFEIER
    1993 "Evaluation of Two AIDS Prevention Interventions for Inner-City Adolescent and
        Young Adult Women." *American Journal of Preventative Medicine* 9(1): 21-26.

RABKIN, JUDITH, ROBERT REMIEN, AND CHRISTOPHER WILSON
    1994 *Good Doctors, Good Patients: Partners in HIV Treatment*. New York: NCM Publish-
        ers.

RAFFAELLI, M., R. CAMPOS, A. PAYNE-MERRITT, ET AL.
    1993 "Sexual Practices and Attitudes of Street Youth in Belo Horizonte, Brazil. The
        Street Youth Group Study." *Social Science and Medicine* 37(5): 661-670.

RAFFAELLI, M., E. SIQUEIRA, A. PAYNE-MERRITT ET AL.
    1995 "HIV-Related Knowledge and Risk Behaviors of Street Youth in Belo Horizonte,
        Brazil. The Street Youth Group Study." *AIDS Education and Prevention* 7(4): 287-
        297.

RAGNI, M., P. GUPTA, C. RINALDO, ET AL.
    1988 "HIV Transmission to Female Sex Partners of HIV Anti-Body Positive Hemophili-
        acs." *Public Health Reports* 103(1): 54-58.

RAMIRO, L.S. AND M.T. RAMOS
    1993 "Risk-Taking Behavior in Relation to AIDS among Child Sex Workers." *International Conference on AIDS* 9(2): 906.

RAMPERSAD, SHEILA
    1994 "Caribbean-Population: Women Feel the Heavy Hand of Poverty." *International Press Service Third World News Agency* (December 22): 1-3.

RAPHAEL, DANA
    1994 "The Politics of International Health: Breastfeeding and HIV." In *Global AIDS Policy*. Douglas Feldman, ed. Westport, Connecticut: Bergin and Garvey. Pp. 129-141.

RAYMOND, CHRIS ANNE
    1988 "Pilot Project: Preventing Further AIDS Spread among Women, General Heterosexual Population." *Journal of American Medical Association* 259(22): 3224-3225.

REBACK, CATHY J.
    1995 "Constructing the Outreach Movement: Street Interventions to Women at Risk." In *Women Resisting AIDS: Feminist Strategies of Empowerment*. Beth E. Schneider and Nancy E. Stoller, eds. Philadelphia: Temple University Press. Pp. 170-192.

REBAGLIATO, M., M. JOSÉ AVIÑÓ, I. HERNÁNDEZ-AGUADO, ET AL.
    1995 "Trends in Incidence and Prevalence of HIV-1 Infection in Intravenous Drug Users in Valencia, Spain." *Journal of Acquired Immune Deficiency Syndromes* 8(3): 297-301.

REED, ADOLPH, JR.
    1988 "The Liberal Technocrat." *The Nation* (February): 167-170.
    1991 "The 'Underclass' as Myth and Symbol: The Poverty of Discourse about Poverty." *Radical America* (Summer).

REEVES, W.C., W.E. RAWLS, L.A. BRINTON, ET AL.
    1989 "Epidemiology of Genital Papillomaviruses and Cervical Cancer." *Review of Infectious Diseases* 11(3): 426-439.

REID, ELIZABETH
    1990a "Placing Women at the Centre of the Analysis." Paper presented at the Women and AIDS: Strategies for the Future Conference, Quebec, Canada, (December 6).
    1990b "Two Voices." *World Health* (November-December): 10-12.
    1993 *The HIV Epidemic and Development: The Unfolding of the Epidemic*. New York: United Nations Development Programme (November).

REID, ELIZABETH AND MIKE BAILEY
    1989 "Young Women: Silence, Susceptibility and the HIV Epidemic." In *AIDS and Society*. Mary Merki, ed. Mission Hills, CA: Glencoe Publishing Co.
    1993 *Young Women: Silence, Susceptibility and the HIV Epidemic*. New York: HIV and Development Programme, UNDP, Issues Paper No. 12.

REINISCH, J., S. SANDER, AND M. ZIEMBA-DAVIS
    1987 "Self-Labeled Sexual Orientation, Sexual Behavior, and Knowledge about AIDS: Implications for Biomedical Research and Education Programs." In *Women and AIDS: Promoting Health Behaviors:* papers from a Workshop Sponsored by NIMH and NIDA. (September 27-29).

REMINGTON, P., M. SMITH, D. WILLIAMSON, ET AL.
    1988 "Design, Characteristics, and Usefulness of State-Based Behavioral Risk Factor Surveillance." *Public Health Reports* 103(4): 366-375.

REMIS, ROBERT S., ERICA L. EASON, ROBERT W. PALMER, ET AL.
    1995 "HIV Infection among Women Undergoing Abortion in Montreal." *Canadian Medical Association Journal* 153(9): 1271-1279.

RENZULLO, P., J. MCNEIL, Z. WANN, ET AL.
    1995 "Human Immunodeficiency Virus Type 1 Seroconversion Trends among Young
        Adults Serving in the United States Army, 1985-1993." *Journal of Acquired
        Immune Deficiency Syndromes* 10(2): 177-185.

RICHTER, FRANK
    1986 "Non-Linear Behavior." In *Metatheory in Social Science: Pluralisms and Subjectives*. D.
        Fiske and R. Shweder, eds. Chiacgo: University of Chicago Press. Pp. 163-196.

RIVER, M., C. NORWOOD, B. ADDRESSEE, ET AL.
    1994 "Stages of Women's Condom Use." *International Conference on AIDS* 10(2): 369.
        Abstract Number PD0655.

ROBES, R., H. COLON, A, GONZALEZ, ET AL.
    1990 "Social Relations and Empowerment of Sexual Partners of IV Drug Users." *Puerto
        Rico Health Science Journal* 9(1): 99-104.

ROBES, R., C. MERRIER, H. COLON, ET AL.
    1992 "Comparison of Risk Behaviors and HIV Infection among Drug Injector Women:
        Puerto Ricans in Puerto Rico; Puerto Ricans and Non-Hispanic Whites in the
        U.S." *International Conference on AIDS* 8(2): D469. Abstract Number POD 5495.

ROBINSON, LILLIAN S.
    1993 "Touring Thailand's Sex Industry." *The Nation* 257(14): 492-496.

RODRIGUEZ, J.J., SM.. MEHENDALE, M.E. SHEPARD, ET AL.
    1995 "Risk Factors for HIV Infection in People Attending Clinics for Sexually Transmit-
        ted Diseases in India." *British Medical Journal* 311(7000): 283-286.

RODRIGUEZ, L.
    1995 "Obstacles to Treatment for HIV Positive Women of Color in Primary Setting."
        HIV Infection in Women: Setting a New Agenda. Washington, D.C.(February 22-
        24) Pp. P108. Abstract Number TP-466.

RODRIGUEZ, WILLIAM, PAUL FARMER, AND SALLY ZIERLER
    1995 "Socioeconomic Factors Influencing Access to Care and Survival in Women with
        HIV." *HIV Infection in Women: Setting a New Agenda*. Washington, D.C. (Febru-
        ary 22-24) Pp. S46. Abstract Number TF-161.

RODRIGUEZ-TRIAS, HELEN
    1995 "Promoting Women's Rights to Promote Women's Health Care." *Journal of the
        American Medical Women's Association* 60(3/4): 73.

RODRIGUEZ-TRIAS, HELEN AND CAROLA MARTE
    1995 "Challenges and Possibilities: Women, HIV, and the Health Care System in the
        1990s." In *Women Resisting AIDS: Feminist Strategies of Empowerment*. Beth E.
        Schneider and Nancy E. Stoller, eds. Philadelphia: Temple University Press. Pp.
        301-321.

ROGERS, MARTHA F., LYNNE M. MOFENSON, AND ROBIN R. MOSELY
    1995 "Reducing the Risk of Perinatal HIV Transmission through Zidovudine Therapy:
        Treatment Recommendations and Implications for Perinatal HIV Counseling and
        Testing." *Journal of the American Medical Women's Association* 50(3/4): 78-82.

ROMER, D., M. BLACK, I. RICARDO, ET AL.
    1994 "Social Influences on the Sexual Behavior of Youth at Risk for HIV Exposure."
        American Journal of Public Health 84(6): 977-985.

ROMERO-DAZA, NANCY
    1994 "Multiple Sexual Partners, Migrant Labor, and the Makings of an Epidemic: Knowl-
        edge and Beliefs about AIDS among Women in Highland Lesotho." *Human Orga-
        nization* 53(2): 192-205

ROPER, W.

1991a "A Comprehensive HIV Prevention Program." *Public Health Reports* 106(6): 601-603.

1991b "Current Approaches to Prevention of HIV Infections." *Public Health Reports* 106(2): 111-115.

ROPER, W., H. PETERSON, AND J. CURRAN

1993 "Commentary: Condoms and HIV/STD Prevention—Clarifying the Message." *American Journal of Public Health* 83(4): 501-503.

ROSALDO, RENATO

1989 *Culture and Truth: The Remaking of Social Analysis.* Boston, Massachusetts: Beacon.

ROSE, D.N.

1992 "The Epidemiology of HIV Infection and AIDS in East and Central Harlem, NY." *Mount Sinai Journal of Medicine* 59(6): 493-497.

ROSENBERG, ALEXANDER

1986 "Philosophy of Science and Potentials for Knowledge in the Social Sciences." In *Metatheory in Social Science: Pluralisms and Subjectives.* D. Fiske and R. Shweder, eds. Chiacgo: University of Chicago Press. Pp 339-346.

ROSENBERG, E., M. BAYONA, C. BROWN, ET AL.

1994 "Epidemiologic Factors Correlated with Multiple Sexual Partners among Women Receiving Prenatal Care." *Annals of Epidemiology* 4(6): 472-479.

ROSENBERG, M. AND E. GOLLUB

1992 "Commentary: Methods Women Can Use that May Prevent Sexually Transmitted Disease, Including HIV." *American Journal of Public Health* 82(11): 1473-1478.

ROSENBERG, M.J. AND J.M. WEINER

1988 "Prostitutes and AIDS: A Health Department Priority?" *American Journal of Public Health* 78(4): 418-423.

ROSENBERG, PHILIP S.

1995 "Scope of the AIDS Epidemic in the United States." *Science* 270(5240): 1372-1375.

ROSENBERG, PHILIP S., ROBERT J. BIGGAR AND JAMES L. GOEDERT

1994 "Declining Age of HIV Infection in the United States." *The New England Journal of Medicine* 330(11): 789.

ROSENBERG, PHILIP S., MARTIN E. LEVY, JOHN F. BRUNDAGHE, ET AL.

1992 "Population-Based Monitoring of an Urban HIV/AIDS Epidemic: Magnitude and Trends in the District of Columbia." *Journal of the American Medical Association* 268(4): 495-503.

ROSENFELD, SHOSHANA AND DEBORAH LEWIS

1993 "The Hidden Effect of Childhood Sexual Abuse on Adolescent and Young Adult HIV Prevention: Rethinking AIDS Education, Program Development and Policy." In *AIDS and Public Policy Journal* 8(4): 181-185.

ROSS, MICHAEL W.

1990 "Psychovenereology: Psychological Aspects of AIDS and Other Sexually Transmitted Diseases." In *Behavioral Aspects of AIDS.* David Ostrow, ed. New York: Plenum Publishing. Pp. 19-40.

ROTHENBERG, KAREN H. AND STEPHEN J. PASKEY

1995 "The Risk of Domestic Violence and Women with HIV Infection: Implications for Partner Notification, Public Policy and the Law." *American Journal of Public Health* 85(11): 1569-1576.

ROTHENBERG, KAREN H., STEPHEN J. PASKEY, MELISSA M. REULAND, ET AL.
1995 "Domestic Violence and Partner Notification: Implications for Treatment and Counseling of Women with HIV." *Journal of the American Medical Women's Association* 50(3/4): 87-93.

ROTHENBERG, RICHARD, RAND STONEBURNER, MARY WOELFEL, ET AL.
1988 "Survival with AIDS in New York: Authors' Reply." *The New England Journal of Medicine* 318(22): 1465.

ROTHENBERG, RICHARD, MARY WOELFEL, RAND STONEBURNER, ET AL.
1987 "Survival with the Acquired Immunodeficiency Syndrome: Experience with 5833 Cases in New York City." *The New England Journal of Medicine* 317(21): 1297-1302.

ROTHERAM-BORUS, M. AND C. KOOPMAN
1991 "Sexual Risk Behaviors, AIDS Knowledge, and Beliefs about AIDS among Runaways." *American Journal of Public Health* 81(2): 208-210.

ROTHERAM-BORUS, M., H. MEYER-BAHLBURG, M. ROSARIO, ET AL.
1992 "Lifetime Sexual Behaviors among Predominantly Minority Male Runaways and Gay/Bisexual Adolescents in New York City." *AIDS Education and Prevention* (Supplement): 34-42.

ROTHERAM-BORUS, M., H. REID, AND M. ROSARIO
1994 "Factors Mediating Changes in Sexual HIV Risk Behaviors among Gay and Bisexual Male Adolescents." *American Journal of Public Health* 84(12): 1938-1946.

ROTHMAN, KENNETH J. AND KARIN B. MICHELS
1994 "Sounding Board: The Continuing Unethical Use of Placebo Controls." *The New England Journal of Medicine* 331(6): 394-398.

RUDD, ANDREA AND DARIEN TAYLOR, EDS.
1992 *Positive Women: Voices of Women Living with AIDS*. Toronto: Second Story Press.

RUGG, D., R. MACGOWAN, K. STARK, ET AL.
1991 "Evaluating the CDC Program for HIV Counseling and Testing." *Public Health Reports* 106(6): 708-713.

RUMLEY, RICHARD L. AND JAMES D. ESINHART
1993 "AIDS in Rural North Carolina." *North Carolina Medical Journal* 54(10): 517-522.

RWABUKWALI, CHARLES B., DEBRA A. SCHUMANN, AND JANET W. MCGRATH
1994 "Culture, Sexual Behavior, and Attitudes toward Condom Use among Baganda Women." In *Global AIDS Policy*. Douglas Feldman, ed. Westport, Connecticut: Bergin and Garvey. Pp. 70-79.

RYAN, C., M. LEVY, J. JACKSON, ET AL.
1992 "HIV Prevention in U.S. Correctional System, 1991." *Journal of the American Medical Association* 268(1): 23-24.

RYAN, MARY KAY AND ARTHUR D. SHATTUCK
1994 *Treating AIDS with Chinese Medicine*. Berkeley: Pacific View Press.

RYAN, WILLIAM
1971 *Blaming the Victim*. New York: Vintage Books.

RYDER, R.W., W. NSA, S.E. HASSIG, ET AL.
1989 "Perinatal Transmission of the Human Immunodeficiency Virus Type 1 to Infants of Seropositive Women in Zaire." *The New England Journal of Medicine* 320(25): 1637-1642.

RYDER, ROBERT W., VÉRONIQUE L. BATTER, MALANDA NSUAMI, ET AL.
1991 "Fertility Rates in 238 HIV-1-Seropositive Women in Zaire Followed for 3 Years Post-Partum." *AIDS* 5(12): 1521-1527.

ST. LOUIS, M., G. CONWAY, C. HAYMAN, ET AL.
　　1991 "Human Immunodeficiency Virus in Disadvantaged Adolescents." *Journal of the Amercian Medical Association* 266(17): 2387-2391.

ST. LOUIS, M., N. OLIVO, S. CRITCHLEY, ET AL.
　　1990 "Methods of Surveillance for HIV Infection at U.S. Sentinel Hospitals." *Public Health Reports* 105(2): 140-146.

ST. LOUIS, M., K RAUCH, L. PETERSEN, ET AL.
　　1990 "Seroprevalence Rates of Human Immunodeficiency Virus Infection at Sentinel Hospitals in the United States." *New England Journal of Medicine* 323(4): 213-218.

SABATIER, RENÉE
　　1988 *Blaming Others: Prejudice, Race and Worldwide AIDS.* Philadelphia: New Society Publishers.

SABO, C. AND V. CARWEIN
　　1994 "Women and HIV/AIDS." *Journal of the Association of Nurses in AIDS Care* 5(3): 15-21.

SACKOFF, J., K. LAWTON, L. TORIAN, ET AL.
　　1995 "Characteristics of Women with TB and AIDS in New York City." *HIV Infection in Women: Setting a New Agenda.* Washington, D.C. (February 22-24) Pp P91. Abstract Number WP-400.

SAKSELA, KALLE, CLADD STEVENS, PABLO RUBINSTEIN, ET AL.
　　1995 "HIV-1 Messenger RNA in Peripheral Blood Mononuclear Cells as an Early Marker of Risk for Progression to AIDS." *Annals of Internal Medicine* 123(9): 641-648.

SALTZMAN, S., A. STODDARD, J. MCCUSKER, ET AL.
　　1987 "Reliability of Self-Reported Sexual Behavior Risk Factors for HIV Infection in Homosexual Men." *Public Health Reports* 102(6): 692-697.

SAMPSON, JAMES H. AND JAMES NEATON
　　1994 "On Being Poor with HIV." *The Lancet* 344(8930): 1100-1101.

SAMUALS, JACK F., DAVID VLAHOV, JAMES C. ANTHONY, ET AL.
　　1992 "Measurement of HIV Risk Behaviors among Intravenous Drug Users." *British Journal of Addiction* 87(3): 417-428.

SANCHEZ, S., D. WOOLCOTT, A. MEJIA, ET AL.
　　1994 "STD/HIV Prevention Program for Women of Low Socioeconomic Status in Lima, Peru." *International Conference on AIDS* 10(2): 68. Abstract Number 548D.

SANTANA, SARAH, LILY FAAS AND KAREN WALD
　　1994 "Human Immunodeficiency Virus in Cuba: The Public Health Response of a Third World Country." In *AIDS: The Politics of Survival.* Nancy Krieger and Glenn Margo, eds. Amityville, NY: Baywood Publishing Company. Pp. 167-196.

SATCHER, DAVID
　　1990 "Crime, Sin, or Disease: Drug Abuse and AIDS in the African-American Community." *Journal of Health Care for the Poor and Underserved* 1(2): 212-218.
　　1995 "Emerging Infections: Getting Ahead of the Curve." *Emerging Infectious Diseases* 1(1): 1-6.

SCHERR, LORRAINE
　　1995 "Psychosocial Aspects of Providing Care for Women with HIV Infection." In *HIV Infection in Women.* Howard Minkoff, Jack A. DeHovitz, and Ann Duerr, eds. New York: Raven Press. Pp. 107-124.

SCHEPER-HUGHES, NANCY AND MARGARET M. LOCK
　　1987 "The Mindful Body: A Prolegomenon to Future Work in Medical Anthropology." *Medical Anthropology Quarterly* 1(1): 6-42.

SCHILLER, NINA GLICK
  1992 "What's Wrong with this Picture? The Hegemonic Construction of Culture in AIDS Research in the United States." *Medical Anthropology Quarterly* 6(3): 237-254.
  1993 "The Invisible Women: Caregiving and the Construction of AIDS Health Services." *Culture, Medicine and Psychiatry* 17(4): 487-512.

SCHILLING, ROBERT, NABILA EL-BASSEL, ANDRE IVANOFF, ET AL.
  1994 "Sexual Risk Behavior of Incarcerated, Drug-Using Women, 1992." *Public Health Reports* 109(4): 539-547.

SCHILLING, ROBERT, NABILA EL-BASSEL, S. SCHINKE, ET AL.
  1991 "Building Skills of Recovering Women Drug Users to Reduce Heterosexual AIDS Transmission." *Public Health Reports* 106(3): 297-304.

SCHNEIDER, BETH E.
  1992 "AIDS and Class, Gender, and Race Relations." In *The Social Context of AIDS*. Joan Huber and Beth Schneider, eds. Newbury Park, CA: Sage. Pp. 19-43.

SCHNEIDER, BETH E. AND VALERIE JENNESS
  1995 "Social Control, Civil Liberties, and Women's Sexuality." In *Women Resisting AIDS: Feminist Strategies of Empowerment*. Beth E. Schneider and Nancy E. Stoller, eds. Philadelphia: Temple University Press. Pp. 74-96.

SCHNEIDER, BETH E. AND NANCY E. STOLLER, EDS.
  1995a *Women Resisting AIDS: Feminist Strategies of Empowerment*. Philadelphia: Temple University Press.
  1995b "Introduction: Feminist Strategies of Empowerment." In *Women Resisting AIDS: Feminist Strategies of Empowerment*. Beth E.Schneider and Nancy E. Stoller, eds. Philadelphia: Temple University Press. Pp. 1-20.

SCHNEIDER, MARGARET M.E., ANDY I. HOEPELMAN, JAN KAREL M. EEFTINCK SCHATTENKERK, ET AL.
  1992 "A Controlled Trial of Aerosolized Pentamidine or Trimethoprim-Sulfamethoxazole as Primary Prophylaxis against *Pneumocystis carinii* Pneumonia in Patients with Human Immunodeficiency Virus Infection." *The New England Journal of Medicine* 327(26): 1836-1841.

SCHOENBAUM, E.E., K. DAVENNY AND K. HOLBROOK
  1992 "The Management of HIV Disease in Pregnancy." *Balliere's Clinical Obstetrics and Gynecology* 6(1): 101-124.

SCHOENBAUM, ELLIE E. AND MAYRIS P. WEBBER
  1993 "The Underrecognition of HIV Infection in Women in an Inner-City Emergency Room." *American Journal of Public Health* 83(3): 363-368.

SCHOEPF, BROOKE GRUNDFEST
  1986 "CONNAISSIDA: AIDS Control Research and Interventions in Zaïre." Proposal Submitted to the Rockefeller Foundation (November 12).
  1988 "Women, AIDS, and Economic Crisis in Zaïre." *Canadian Journal of African Studies* 22(3): 625-644.
  1991a "Ethical Methodological and Political Issues of AIDS Research in Central Africa." *Social Science and Medicine* 33(7): 749-763.
  1991b "Représentations du SIDA et Pratiques Populaires à Kinshasa." *Anthropological Société* 15: 149-166.
  1992a "AIDS, Sex and Condoms: African Healers and the Reinvention of Tradition in Zaïre." *Medical Anthropology* 14(2-4): 225-242.
  1992b "Gender Relations and Development: Political Economy and Culture," In *Twenty-First Century Africa: Toward a New Vision of Self-Sustainable Development*. Ann Seidman and Frederick Anang, eds. Trenton, NJ: Africa World Press. Pp. 203-241.

1992c "Women at Risk: Case Studies from Zaïre." In *Social Analysis in the Time of AIDS*. Gilbert Herdt and Shirley Lindenbaum, eds. Newbury Park: Sage. Pp. 259-286.

1993a "AIDS Action-Research with Women in Kinshasa, Zaïre." *Social Science and Medicine* 37(11): 1401-1413.

1993b "Gender, Development, and AIDS: A Political Economy and Culture Framework." In *Women and International Development Annual*. Rita Gallin, Anne Ferguson and Janice Harper, eds. Boulder, CO: Westview. Pp. 53-85.

1995a "Action-Research and Empowerment in Africa." In *Women Resisting AIDS: Feminist Strategies of Empowerment*. Beth E. Schneider and Nancy E. Stoller, eds. Philadelphia: Temple University Press. Pp. 246-269.

1995b "Culture, Sex Research and AIDS Prevention in Africa." In *Culture and Sexual Risk: Anthropological Perspectives on AIDS*. Han ten Brummelhuis and Gilbert Herdt, eds. New York: Gordon and Breach. Pp. 29-51.

1995c "Genocide and Gendered Violence in Rwanda." Paper Presented at the 94th Annual Meeting of the American Anthropological Association, Invited Session on "Surviving Gendered Violence" (November 15): Submitted to *Medical Anthropology Quarterly*.

SCHOEPF, BROOKE GRUNDFEST AND ENGUNDU WALU

1990 "Women's Trade and Contributions to Household Budgets in Kinshasa." In *The Second Economy in Zaïre*. J. MacGaffey, ed. London: James Currey.

SCHOEPF, BROOKE GRUNDFEST, ENGUNDU WALU, WA NKERA RUKANGIRA, ET AL.

1988 "Community-Based Risk-Reduction Support." In *AIDS Prevention Through Health Promotion*. R. Bervens, ed. Geneva: World Health Organization.

1991 "Gender, Power and Risk of AIDS in Central Africa." In *Women and Health in Africa*. M. Turshen, ed. Trenton, NJ: Africa World Press. Pp. 187-203.

SCHOEPF, BROOKE GRUNDFEST, ENGUNDU WALU, DIANE RUSSELL, ET AL.

1991 "Women and Structural Adjustment in Zaïre. In *Structural Adjustment and African Women Farmers*. C. Gladwin, eds. Gainesville: University of Florida Press. Pp. 151-168.

SCHOEPF, BROOKE GRUNDFEST, WA NKERA RUKARANGIRA AND MAHOYA M. MATUMOMA

1986 "Étude des Réactions à une Nouvelle Maladie Transmissible (SIDA) et des Possibilités de Démarrage d'un Programme d'Éducation Populaire." Paper presented at the Research proposals submitted to Zaïre, Conseil Executif and USAID, Kinshasa, Zaïre.

SCHOEPF, BROOKE GRUNDFEST, WA NKERA RUKARANGIRA, NTSOMO PAYANZO, ET AL.

1988 "AIDS, Women, and Society in Central Africa." In *AIDS 1988: AAAS Symposia Papers*. Ruth Kulstad, ed. Washington, D.C.: The American Association for the Advancement of Science. Pp. 175-181.

1989 "SIDA, Sexologie et Culture en Afrique Centrale." *International Conference on AIDS* 5: 860.

SCHOEPF, BROOKE GRUNDFEST, WA NKERA RUKARANGIRA, CLAUDE SCHOEPF, ET AL.

1988 "AIDS and Society in Central Africa: A View from Zaïre." In *The Heterosexual Transmission of AIDS in Africa*. Dieter Koch-Weser and Hannelore Vanderschmidt, eds. Cambridge, MA: Abt Books. Pp. 265-282.

SCHRAGER, LEWIS K., GERALD H. FRIEDLAND, AND C. FEINER

1991 "Demographic Characteristics, Drug Use, and Sexual Behavior of IV Drug Users with AIDS in Bronx, New York." *Public Health Reports* 106(1): 78-84.

SCHRAGER, LEWIS K., GERALD H. FRIEDLAND, DIANA MAUDE, ET AL.

1989 "Cervical and Vaginal Squamous Cell Abnormalities in Women Infected with Human Immunodeficiency Virus." *Journal of Acquired Immune Deficiency Syndromes* 2(6): 570-575.

SCHUMAN, P., A. EYLER, AND S. NEWELL
1995 "An Association between Tubal Sterilization and HIV Seropositivity among Low-Income Urban Women." *HIV Infection in Women: Setting a New Agenda.* Washington, D.C. (February 22-24). Pp. S38. Abstract Number TE2-131.

SCHUSTER, C.
1988 "Intravenous Drug Use and AIDS Prevention." *Public Health Reports* 103(3): 261-266.

SCHWARTLANDER, B., R. JANSSEN, G. SATTEN, *ET AL.*
1994 "Guidelines for Designing Rapid Assessment Surveys of HIV Seroprevalence among Hospitalized Patients. Centers for Disease Control and Prevention." *Public Health Reports* 109(1): 53-59.

SCHWARTZ, IVY L.
1991 "Sexual Violence against Women: Prevalence, Consequences, Societal Factors, and Prevention." *American Journal of Preventive Medicine* 7(6): 363-373.

SCHWARTZ, R. AND E. MAYNARD
1990 "Hospital Policy, Practice Regarding HIV Testing for Pregnant Women and Newborns." *American Journal of Public Health* 80(10): 1276.

SECK, A.M. COLL AND M. MONNET
1991 "African Women and AIDS: The Case of Senegal." *Vena* 5(1): 22-25.

SECORD, PAUL
1986 "Explanation in the Social Sciences and in Life Situations." In *Metatheory in Social Science: Pluralisms and Subjectives.* D. Fiske and R. Sweder, eds. Chiacgo: University of Chicago Press. Pp 197-221.

SEELEY, JANET, SAM MALAMBA, ANDREW NUNN, *ET AL.*
1994 "Socioeconomic Status, Gender, and Risk of HIV-1 Infection in a Rural Community in South West Uganda." *Medical Anthropology Quarterly* 8(1): 78-89.

SEIDEL, GILL
1993 "The Competing Discourses of HIV/AIDS in Sub-Saharan Africa: Discourses of Rights and Empowerment vs. Discourses of Control and Exclusion." *Social Science and Medicine* 36(3): 175-194.

SEIDMAN, S., C. STERK-ELIFSON, AND S. ARAL
1994 "High Risk Sexual Behavior among Drug-Using Men." *Sexually Transmitted Diseases* 21(3): 173-180.

SEIDMAN, STUART N., WILLIAM D. MOSHER AND SEVGI O. ARAL
1992 "Women with Multiple Sexual Partners: United States, 1988." *American Journal of Public Health* 82(10): 1388-1393.

SEKAR, B., M. JAYASHEELA, D. CHATTOPADHYA, *ET AL.*
1994 "Prevalence of HIV Infection and High-Risk Characteristics among Leprosy Patients of South India: A Case-Control Study." *International Journal of Leprosy and Other Mycobacterial Diseases* 62(4): 527-531.

SELIK, R.M., K. CASTRO, AND M. PAPPAIOANOU
1988 "Racial/Ethnic Differences in the Risk of AIDS in the United States." *American Journal of Public Health* 78(12): 1539-1545.

SELIK, R.M., K. CASTRO, M. PAPPAIOANOU, *ET AL.*
1989 "Birthplace and the Risk of AIDS among Hispanics in the United States." *American Journal of Public Health* 79(7): 836-839

SELIK, R.M., S.Y. CHU,, AND J.W. BUEHLER
1993 "HIV Infection as Leading Cause of Death among Young Adults in U.S. Cities and States." *Journal of the American Medical Association* 296(23): 2991-2994

SELWYN, PETER A., PATRICK G. O'CONNOR, AND RICHARD S. SCHOTTENFELD
    1995 "Female Drug Users with HIV Infection: Issues for Medical Care and Substance Abuse Treatment." In *HIV Infection in Women.* Howard Minkoff, Jack A. DeHovitz, and Ann Duerr, eds. New York: Raven Press. Pp. 241-262.

SEN, GITA AND KAREN GROWN
    1985 *Development Crises and Alternative Visions: Third World Women's Perspectives.* New York: Monthly Review Press.

SERWADDA, D., N.K. SEWANKAMBO, A.C. BAYLEY, ET AL.
    1985 "Slim Disease: A New Disease in Uganda and its Association with HTLV-III Infection." *The Lancet* 335(8693): 849-852.

SHA, BEVERLY E., CONSTANCE A. BENSON, JOHN C. POTTAGE JR., ET AL.
    1995 "HIV Infection in Women: An Observational Study of Clinical Characteristics, Disease Progression, and Survival for a Cohort of Women in Chicago." *Journal of Acquired Immune Deficiency Syndromes* 8(5): 486-495.

SHAH, P. N., J.R. SMITH, C. WELLS, ET AL.
    1994 "Menstrual Symptoms in Women Infected by the Human Immunodeficiency Virus." *Obstetrics and Gynecology* 83(3): 397-400.

SHAPIRO, CRAIG N., SUSAN LLOYD SCHULTZ AND TIMOTHY J. DONDERO
    1989 "Review of Human Immunodeficiency Virus Infection in Women in the United States." *Obstetrics and Gynecology* 74(5): 800-808.

SHAPIRO, ISSAC AND ROBERT GREENSTEIN
    1993 *Making Work Pay: The Unfinished Agenda.* Center on Budget and Policy Priorities.

SHAYNE, VIVIAN T. AND BARBARA J. KAPLAN
    1991 "Double Victims: Poor Women with AIDS." *Women and Health* 17(1): 21-37.

SHERR, LORRAINE
    1995 "Psychosocial Aspects of Providing Care for Women with HIV Infection." In *HIV Infection in Women.* Howard Minkoff, Jack A. DeHovitz, and Ann Duerr, eds. New York: Raven Press. Pp. 107-124.

SHIBOSKI, C., J. HILTON, D. GREENSPAN, ET AL.
    1994 "HIV-Related Oral Manifestations in Two Cohorts of Women in San Francisco." *Journal of Acquired Immune Deficiency Syndromes* 7(9): 964-971.

SHREEDHAR, J.
    1995a "HIV Thrives in Ancient Traditions." *Harvard AIDS Review.* Cambridge, MA: The Harvard AIDS Institute (Fall).
    1995b "Passage through India: HIV Maps a Deadly Course." *Harvard AIDS Review.* Cambridge, MA: The Harvard AIDS Institute (Fall).

SHTARKSHALL, R.
    1993 "Some Difficulties in Basing HIV/AIDS Prevention Policies in Israel on Previously Proposed Modes of Analysis and the Available Data. *Public Health Reviews* 21(3-4): 297-307.

SHUMAN, P., A. EYLER, S. NEWELL, ET AL.
    1995 "An Association between Tubal Sterilization and HIV Seropositivity among Low-Income Urban Women." *HIV Infection in Women: Setting a New Agenda* Washington, D.C. (February 22-24) Pp. S38. Abstract Number TE2-130.

SHWEDER, RICHARD
    1986 "Divergent Rationalities." In *Metatheory in Social Science: Pluralisms and Subjectives.* D. Fiske and R. Shweder, eds. Chiacgo: University of Chicago Press. Pp 163-196.

SHWEDER, RICHARD AND DONALD FISKE
    1986 "Introduction: Uneasy Social Science." In *Metatheory in Social Science: Pluralisms and Subjectives*. D. Fiske and R. Shweder, eds. Chiacgo: University of Chicago Press. Pp 1-18.

SIBTHORPE, BEVERLY
    1992 "The Social Construction of Sexual Relationships as a Determinant of HIV Risk Perception and Condom Use among Injection Drug Users." *Medical Anthropology Quarterly* 6(3): 255-270.

SIEGAL, H., R. CARLSON, R. FALK, ET AL.
    1991 "HIV Infection and Risk Behaviors among Intravenous Drug Users in Low Seroprevalence Areas in the Midwest." *American Journal of Public Health* 81(12): 1642-1644.
    1995 "Drug Abuse Treatment Experience and HIV Risk Behaviors among Active Drug Injectors in Ohio." *American Journal of Public Health* 85(1): 105-108.

SIKKEMA, K., J. KOOB, V. CARGILL, ET AL.
    1995 "Levels and Predictors of HIV Risk Behavior among Women in Low-Income Public Housing Developments." *Public Health Reports* 110(6): 707-713.

SILVESTRE, A., L. KINGSLEY, P. WEHMAN, ET AL.
    1993 "Change in HIV Rates and Sexual Behavior among Homosexual Men, 1984 to 1988/92." *American Journal of Public Health* 83(4): 578-80.

SIMON, PAUL A., DALE J. HU, THERESA DIAZ, ET AL.
    1995 "Income and AIDS Rates in Los Angeles County." *AIDS* 9(3): 281-284.

SIMONON, A., P. LEPAGE, E. KARITA, ET AL.
    1994 "An Assessment of the Timing of Mother-to-Child Transmission of Human Immunodeficiency Virus Type 1 by Means of the Polymerase Chain Reaction." *Journal of Acquired Immune Deficiency Syndromes* 7(9): 952-957.

SIMONSEN, J.N., D.W. CAMERON, M.N. GAKINYA, ET AL.
    1988 "Human Immunodeficiency Virus Infection among Men with Sexually Transmitted Diseases: Experience from a Center in Africa." *The New England Journal of Medicine* 319(5): 274-278.

SIMONSEN, J., F. PLUMMER, E. NGUGI, ET AL.
    1990 "HIV Infection Among Lower Socio-Economic Strata Prostitutes in Nairobi." *AIDS* 4(2): 139-144.

SINGER, MERRILL
    1991 "Confronting the AIDS Epidemic among IV Drug Users: Does Ethnic Culture Matter?" *AIDS Education and Prevention* 3(3): 258-283.
    1992 "AIDS and U.S. Ethnic Minorities: The Crisis and Alternative Anthropological Responses." *Human Organization* 51(1): 89-95.
    1994 "AIDS and the Health Crisis of the U.S. Urban Poor: The Perspective of Critical Medical Anthropology." *Social Science and Medicine* 39(7): 931-948.

SINGER, MERRILL, CANDIDA FLORES, LANI DAVIDSON, ET AL.
    1990 "SIDA: The Economic, Social and Cultural Context of AIDS among Latinos." *Medical Anthropology Quarterly* 4(1): 72-114.
    1991 "Puerto Rican Community Mobilizing in Response to the AIDS Crisis." *Human Organization* 50(1): 73-81.

SINGER, MERRILL, ZHONGKE JIA AND JEAN J. SCHENSUL
    1992 "AIDS and the IV Drug User: The Local Context in Prevention Efforts." *Medical Anthropology Quarterly* 14(3): 285-306.

SINGH, Y.N. AND A.N. MALVIYA
    1994a "Experience of HIV Prevention Interventions among Female Sex Workers in Delhi, India." *International Journal of STD & AIDS* 5(1): 56-57.

1994b "Long Distance Truck Drivers in India: HIV Infection and their Possible Role in Disseminating HIV into Rural Areas." *International Journal of STD & AIDS* 5(2): 137-138.

SINGH, Y.N., K. SINGH, R. JOSHI, ET AL.
1993 "HIV Infection among Long-Distance Truck Drivers in Delhi, India." *Journal of Acquired Immune Deficiency Syndromes* 6(3): 323.

SISCOVICK, D., L. COBB, M. COPASS, ET AL.
1992 "HIV Seroprevalence among Adults Treated for Cardiac Arrest Before Reaching a Medical Facility." *Journal of the American Medical Association* 268(1): 24.

SKOLNICK, ANDREW A.
1995a "Forensic Scientists Helping Haiti Heal." *Journal of the American Medical Association* 274(15): 1181-1182.
1995b "Military Physicians Lend Healing Hands to Haiti." *Journal of the American Medical Association* 274(21): 1664-1666.

SLATER, P.
1993 "Sutton's Law and AIDS Prevention in Israel." *Public Health Reviews* 21(3-4): 285-291.

SLATER, P. AND C. COSTIN
1989 "Trends in Human Immunodeficiency Disease in Israel." *Public Health Reviews* 17(4): 269-277.

SLONIM-NEVO, V.
1992 "AIDS Related Knowledge, Attitudes, and Behaviors among Juvenile Delinquents in Israel." *Public Health Reviews* 20(3-4): 241-250.

SLONIM-NEVO, V., W. AUSLANDER, J. MUNRO, ET AL.
1994 "Knowledge and Attitudes Related to AIDS among African-American Women." *Ethnicity and Disease* 4(1): 68-76.

SLUTSKER, LAURENCE, JEAN-BAPTISTE BRUNET, JOHN KARON, ET AL.
1992 "Trends in the United States and Europe." In *AIDS in the World*. Jonathan Mann, Daniel Tarantola and Thomas Netter, eds. Cambridge, MA: Harvard University Press. Pp. 605-616.

SMELTZER, SUZANNE C.
1992 "Women and AIDS: Sociopolitical Issues." *Nursing Outlook* 40(4): 152-157.

SMITH, BRENDA V. AND CYNTHIA DAILARD
1994 "Female Prisoners and AIDS: On the Margins of Public Health and Social Justice." *AIDS & Public Policy Journal* 9(2): 78-85.

SMITH, D.
1990 "Thailand: AIDS Crisis Looms." *The Lancet* 335(8692): 781-782.

SMITH, K., S. MCGRAW, S. CRAWFORD, ET AL.
1993 "HIV Risk among Latino Adolescents in Two New England Cities." *American Journal of Public Health* 83(10): 1395-1399.

SMITH, P., J. MIKL, S. HYDE, ET AL.
1991 "The AIDS Epidemic in New York State." *American Journal of Public Health* 81(Supplement): 54-60.

SMITH, P., J. MIKL, B. TRUMAN, ET AL.
1991 "HIV Infection among Women Entering the New York State Correctional System." *American Journal of Public Health* 81(Supplement): 35-40.

SOBO, E.J.
1993 "Inner-City Women and AIDS: Psychosocial Benefits of Unsafe Sex." *Culture, Medicine and Psychiatry* 17(4): 454-485.

1995 "Human Immunodeficiency Virus Seropositivity Self-Disclosure to Sexual Partners: A Qualitative Study." *Holistic Nursing Practice* 10(1): 18-28.

SOLOMON, D.J., A.J. HOGAN, R.R. BOUKNIGHT, ET AL.
1989 "Analysis of Michigan Medicaid Costs to Treat HIV Infection." *Public Health Reports* 104(5): 416-424.

SOLOMON, E.
1995 "The Synthesis of Research Priorities and Community Interventions Related to Women, Poverty and HIV." *HIV Infection in Women: Setting a New Agenda.* Washington, D.C. (February 22-24) Pp. S47. Abstract Number TF3-164.

SORKIN, J., P. BOLTON, J. GREENBLATT, ET AL.
1995 "Age, Gender, and Other Predictors of the Wasting Syndrome among HIV-1 Infected Injecting Drug Users." *Epidemiology* 6(2): 172-177.

SOSNOWITZ, BARBARA G.
1995 "AIDS Prevention, Minority Women, and Gender Assertiveness." In *Women Resisting AIDS: Feminist Strategies of Empowerment.* Beth E. Schneider and Nancy E. Stoller, eds. Philadelphia: Temple University Press. Pp. 139-161.

SOTHERAN, JO L., JOHN A. WENSTON, DON C. DES JARLAIS, ET AL.
1992 "Injecting Drug Users: Why Women Share Syringes More Often Than Men?" Abstracts of the American Public Health Association. Washington, D.C.: National Development and Research Institutes Beth Israel Medical Center (November 8-12).

SOTO-RAMIREZ, L.E., B. RENJIFO, M.F. MCLANE, ET AL.
1996 "HIV-1 Langerhans' Cell Tropism Associated with Heterosexual Transmission of HIV." *Science* 271(5253): 1291-1293.

SPENCE, D.P., J. HOTCHKISS, C.S. WILLIAMS, ET AL.
1993 "Tuberculosis and Poverty." *British Medical Journal* 307(6907): 759-761.

SPENCE, MICHAEL R.
1994 "HIV Infections in Women." *Current Opinion in Obstetrics and Gynecology* 6(4): 383-388.

SPENCE, MICHAEL R. AND ANNETTE C. REBOLI
1991 "Human Immunodeficiency Virus Infection in Women." *Annals of Internal Medicine* 115(10): 827-829.

SPERLING, R AND P. STRATTON
1992 "Treatment Options for Human Immunodeficiency Virus-Infected Pregnant Women. Obstetric-Gynecologic Working Group of the AIDS Clinical Trials Group of the National Institute of Allergy and Infectious Diseases." *Obstetrics and Gynecology* 79(3): 443-448.

STALL, RON, SUZANNE HEURIN-ROBERTS, LEON MCKUSICK, ET AL.
1990 "Sexual Risk for HIV Transmission among Singles-Bar Patrons in San Francisco." *Medical Anthropology Quarterly* 4(1): 115-128.

STANDAERT, B. AND A. MEHÉUS
1985 Le Cancer du Col Utérin en Afrique. *Médecine en l'Afrique Noire* 32: 406-415.

STEIN, MICHAEL, JOHN PIETTE, VINCENT MOR, ET AL.
1991 "Differences in Access to Zidovudine (AZT) among Symptomatic HIV-Infected Persons." *Journal of General Internal Medicine* 6(1): 35-40.

STEIN, MICHAEL D., BRIAN LEIBMAN, TOM J. WACHTEL, ET AL.
1991 "HIV-Positive Women: Reasons They are Tested for HIV and their Clinical Characteristics on Entry into the Health Care System." *Journal of General Internal Medicine* 6(4): 286-289.

STEIN, Z. AND H. SAEZ
1995 "The HIV Vaginal Virucide." *Current Issues in Public Health* 1(3): 110-113.

STEIN, ZENA
1990 "HIV Prevention: The Need for Methods Women Can Use." *American Journal of Public Health* 80(4): 460-462.
1992 "The Double Bind in Science Policy and the Protection of Women from HIV Infection." *American Journal of Public Health* 82(11): 1471-1472.
1993 "HIV Prevention: An Update on the Status of Methods Women Can Use." *American Journal of Public Health* 83(10): 1379-1382.
1994 "What's was New at Yokohama—Women's Voices at the 1994 International HIV/AIDS Conference." *American Journal of Public Health* 84(12): 1887-1888.
1995 "More on Women and the Prevention of HIV Infection." *American Journal of Public Health* 85(11): 1485-1488.

STERK-ELIFSON, C.
1993 "Outreach among Drug Users: Combining the Role of Ethnographic Field Assistant and Health Educator." *Human Organization* 52(2): 162-168.

STEVENS, A., C. VICTOR, L. SHERR, ET AL.
1989 "HIV Testing in Antenatal Clinics: The Impact on Women." *AIDS Care* 1(2): 165-171

STIPP, HORST AND DENNIS KERR
1989 "Determinants of Public Opinion about AIDS." *Public Opinion Quarterly* 53: 98-106.

STOLLER, NANCY
1995 "Lesbian Involvement in the AIDS Epidemic: Changing Roles and Generational Differences." In *Women Resisting AIDS: Feminist Strategies of Empowerment.* Beth E. Schneider and Nancy E. Stoller, eds. Philadelphia: Temple University Press. Pp. 227-285.

STONE, V.E., M.Y. MAUCH, K. STEGER, ET AL.
1995 "Provider Attitudes Regarding the Participation of Women and Persons of Color in AIDS Clinical Trials." *Journal of General Internal Medicine* (Abstracts) 10: 126.

STRATTON, PAMELA, LYNNE MOFENSON AND ANNE WILLOUGHBY
1992 "Human Immunodeficiency Virus Infection in Pregnant Women under Care at AIDS Clinical Trials Centers in the United States." *Obstetrics and Gynecology* 79(3): 364-368.

STRICOF, R., J. KENNEDY, T. NATTELL, ET AL.
1991 "HIV Seroprevalence in a Facility for Runaway and Homeless Adolescents." *American Journal of Public Health* 81(Supplement): 50-53.

STRICOF, R., T. NATTELL, AND L. NOVICK
1991 "HIV Seroprevalence in the Clients of Sentinel Family Planning Clinics." *American Journal of Public Health* 81(Supplement): 41-45.

STRUNIN, L. AND R. HINGSON
1992 "Alcohol, Drugs, and Adolescent Sexual Behavior." *International Journal of the Addictions* 27(2): 129-146.

STUNTZNER-GIBSON, DENISE
1991 "Women and HIV Disease: An Emerging Social Crisis." *Social Work* 36(1): 22-28.

SUSSER, M. AND E. SUSSER
1996a "Choosing a Future for Epidemiology: I. Eras and Paradigms." *American Journal of Public Health* 86(5): 668-673.
1996b "Choosing a Future for Epidemiology: II. From Black Box to Chinese Boxes and Eco-Epidemiology" *American Journal of Public Health* 86(5): 674-677.

SUSSER, E., E. VALENCIA, AND S. CONOVER
   1993 "Prevalence of HIV Infection among Psychiatric Patients in a New York City Men's Shelter." *American Journal of Public Health* 83(4): 568-570.

SUWANAGOOL, S., P. CHAIYAKUL, W. RATANASUWAN, ET AL.
   1995 "HIV-1 Infection among Low Income Women Attending a Siriraj Sexually Transmitted Disease Clinic: Sociodemographic Differentials." *Journal of the Medical Association of Thailand* 78(7): 355-361.

SWAA (SOCIETY FOR WOMEN AND AIDS IN AFRICA)
   1989 Report of the 1st International Workshop on Women and AIDS in Africa. Harare, Zimbabwe (May 10-12).

TABET, S., D. PALMER, W, WIESE, ET AL.
   1992 "Seroprevalence of HIV-1 and Hepatitis B and C in Prostitutes in Albuquerque, New Mexico." *American Journal of Public Health* 82(8): 1151-1154.

TAN, M.L.
   1993 "Socio-Economic Impact of HIV/AIDS in the Philippines." *AIDS Care* 5(3): 283-288.

TAN, MICHAEL L. AND MANUEL M. DAYRIT
   1994 "HIV/AIDS in the Philippines." *AIDS* 8(S2): S125-S130.

TAYLOR, C.
   1991 *Ethics of Authenticity.* Cambridge: Harvard University Press.

TAUER, CAROL
   1989 "AIDS: Human Rights and Public Health." *Medical Anthropology* 10(2-3): 177-192.

TEMMERMAN, M., F.M. ALI, J. NDINYA-ACHOLA, ET AL.
   1992 "Rapid Increase of Both HIV-1 Infection and Syphilis among Pregnant Women in Nairobi, Kenya." *AIDS* 6(10): 1181-1185.

TEMMERMAN, M., E. CHOMBA, J. NDINYA-ACHOLA, ET AL.
   1994 "Maternal Human Immunodeficiency Virus-1 Infection and Pregnancy Outcome." *Obstetrics and Gynecology* 83(4): 495-501.

TEMMERMAN, M., S. MOSES, D. KIRAGU, ET AL.
   1990 "Impact of Single Session Post-Partum Counselling of HIV Infected Women on their Subsequent Reproductive Behaviour." *AIDS Care* 2(3): 247-252.

TEMMERMAN, M., A. NYONG'O, J. BWAYO, ET AL.
   1995 "Risk Factors for Mother-to-Child Transmission of Human Immunodeficiency Virus-1 Infection." *American Journal of Obstetrics and Gynecology* 172(2; Part 1): 700-705.

TEZLAK, E.E., M.A. CHAISSON, P.J. BEVIER, ET AL.
   1993 HIV-1 Seroconversion in Patients with and without Genital Ulcer Disease: A Prospective Study." *Annals of Internal Medicine* 119(12): 1181-1186.

THOMAS, STEPHEN B. AND SANDRA CROUSE QUINN
   1991 "The Tuskegee Syphilis Study, 1932 to 1972: Implications for HIV Reduction and AIDS Risk Education Programs in the Black Community." *American Journal of Public Health* 81(11): 1498-1505.

THOMAS, STEPHEN B. AND SANDRA CROUSE QUINN
   1993 "The Burdens of Race and History on Black Americans' Attitudes Toward Needle Exchange Policy to Prevent HIV Disease." *Journal of Public Health Policy* 14(3): 320-347.

TILLY, CHRIS AND RANDY ALBELDA
   1994 "It's Not Working—Why Many Single Mothers Can't Work their Way Out of Poverty." *Dollars and Sense* 196: 8-11.

TORIAN, LUCIA V., ISSAC B. WEISFUSE, HADI A. MAKKI, ET AL.
    1995 "Increasing HIV-1 Seroprevalence Associated with Genital Ulcer Disease, New York City, 1990-1992." *AIDS* 9(2): 177-181.

TORTU, STEPHANIE, MARK BEARDSLEY, SHERRY DEREN, ET AL.
    1994 "The Risk of HIV Infection in a National Sample of Women with Injection Drug-Using Partners." *American Journal of Public Health* 84(8): 1243-1249.

TRAISUPA, AMNUAY, CHAINARONG WONGBA AND DAVID TAYLOR
    1987 "AIDS and Prevalence of Antibody to Human Immunodeficiency Virus (HIV) in High Risk Groups in Thailand." *Genitourinary Medicine* 63(2): 106-108.

TREICHLER, PAULA A.
    1987 "AIDS, Homophobia and Biomedical Discourse. An Epidemic of Signification." In *AIDS: Cultural Analysis, Cultural Activism,* D. Crimp, ed. Cambridge, MA: The MIT Press.
    1988 "AIDS, Gender, and Biomedical Discourse: Current Contests for Meaning." In *AIDS: The Burdens of History.* Elizabeth Fee and Daniel M. Fox, eds. Berkeley: University of California Press. Pp. 190-266.
    1990 "Uncertainties and Excesses." *Science* 248(4952): 232-233.
    1992a "Beyond Cosmo: AIDS, Identity and Inscriptions of Gender." *Camera Obscura* 28: 21-76.
    1992b "AIDS and HIV Infection in the Third World: A First World Chronicle." In *AIDS: The Making of a Chronic Disease.* Elizabeth Fee and Daniel Fox, eds. Los Angeles: University of California Press. Pp 377-412.

TROSTLE, JAMES
    1986 "Early Work in Anthropology and Epidemiology: From Social Medicine to the Germ Theory, 1840 to 1920." In *Anthropology and Epidemiology* Craig R. Janes, Ron Stall and Sandra Gifford, eds. Boston: D. Reidel Publishing Company. Pp. 35-57.

TU, XIN MING, XIAO-LI MENG AND MARCELLO PAGANO
    1993 "Survival Differences and Trends in Patients with AIDS in the United States." *Journal of Acquired Immune Deficiency Syndromes* 6(10): 1150-1156.

TUCKER, BELINDA
    1979 "A Descriptive and Comparative Analysis of the Social Support Structure of Heroin-Addicted Women." In *Addicted Women: Family Dynamics, Self Perceptions, and Support Systems.* Rockville, Maryland: U.S. Department of Health, Education, and Welfare. Pp. 37-76.

TUCKER, BELINDA AND CLAUDIA MITCHELL-KERMAN, EDS.
    1995 *Decline in Marriage Among African Americans.* New York: Russell Sage Foundation.

TURNER, BARBARA J., LEONA E. MARKSON, LINDA J. MCKEE, ET AL.
    1994 "Health Care Delivery, Zidovudine Use and Survival of Women and Men with AIDS." *Journal of Acquired Immune Deficiency Syndromes* 7(12): 1250-1262.

TURSHEN, M. AND D. HILL
    Unpublished "Sex Tourism, the Military and the Spread of AIDS in Asia." Edward J. Bloustein School of Planning and Public Policy, Rutgers University, New Brunswick, New Jersey.

TURSHEN, MEREDETH
    1984 *The Political Ecology of Disease in Tanzania.* New Brunswick, New Jersey: Rutgers University Press.
    1995 "Response: Societal Instability in International Perspective: Relevance to HIV/AIDS Prevention." In *Assessing the Social and Behavioral Science Base for HIV/AIDS Prevention and Intervention. Workshop Summary.* Washington, D.C.: National Academy Press. Pp. 117-128.

ULIN, PRISCILLA R.
1992 "African Women and AIDS: Negotiating Behavioral Change." *Social Science and Medicine.* 34(1): 63-73.

UNITED NATIONS
1994 *World Social Situation in the 1990's.* New York: United Nations Publications.

UNITED NATIONS CHILDREN'S FUND (UNICEF)
1995 *State of the World's Children.* Oxford: Oxford University Press.

UNITED NATIONS DEVELOPMENT PROGRAMME (UNDP)
1992 *Young Women: Silence, Susceptibility and the HIV Epidemic.* New York: UNDP.
1995 *Human Development Report.* Published for the United Nations Development Program. New York: Oxford University Press.

VALDISERRI, R., V. ARENA, D. PROCTOR, ET AL.
1989 "The Relationship between Women's Attitudes about Condoms and their Use: Implications for Condom Promotion Programs." *American Journal of Public Health* 79(4): 499-501.

VALDISERRI, R., W. BRANDON, AND D. LYTER
1984 "AIDS Surveillance and Health Education: Use of Previously Described Risk Factors to Identify High-Risk Homosexuals." *American Journal of Public Health* 74(3): 259-260.

VALLEROY, L., D. MACKELLAR, C. HAYMAN, ET AL.
1995 "HIV Seroprevalence among Disadvantaged Out-of-School Young Women." *HIV Infection in Women: Setting a New Agenda.* Washington, D.C. (February 22-24) Pp. S54. Abstract Number FE1-189.

VAN AMEIJDEN, E., A. VAN DE HOEK, AND R. COUTINHO
1994 "Injecting Risk Behavior among Drug Users in Amsterdam, 1986 to 1992, and its Relationship to AIDS Prevention Programs." *American Journal of Public Health* 84(2): 275-281.

VAN DE PERRE, P.D. ROUVROY, P. LEPAGE, ET AL.
1984 "Acquired Immunodeficiency in Rwanda." *The Lancet* 2(8394): 62-65.

VAN DE VILET, VIRGINA
1994 "Apartheid and the Politics of AIDS." In *Global AIDS Policy.* Douglas Feldman, ed. Westport, Connecticut: Bergin and Garvey. Pp. 107-128.

VAN DOORNUM, G.J.J., J.A.R. VAN DEN HOEK, E.J.C. VAN AMEIJDEN, ET AL.
1993 "Cervical HPV Infection among HIV-Infected Prostitutes Addicted to Hard Drugs." *Journal of Medical Virology* 41(3): 185-190.

VAN HAASTRECHT, H., J. VAN DEN HOEK, C. BARDOUX, ET AL.
1991 "The Course of the HIV Epidemic among Intravenous Drug Users in Amsterdam, The Netherlands." *American Journal of Public Health* 81(1): 59-62.

VAN DEN HOEK, J., H. VAN HAASTRECHT, AND R. COUTINHO
1989 "Risk Reduction among Intravenous Drug Users in Amsterdam under the Influence of AIDS." *American Journal of Public Health* 79(10): 1355-1357.

VANICHSENI, S., B. WONGSUWAN, K. CHOOPANYA, ET AL.
1991 "A Controlled Trial of Methadone Maintenance in a Population of Intravenous Drug Users in Bangkok: Implications for the Prevention of HIV." *International Journal of Addictions* 26(12): 1313-1320.

VEENOFF, ANN
1993 "Women and AIDS." *Vena* 5(1): 1-72.

VERGHESE, ABRAHAM
1994 *My Own Country: A Doctor's Story.* New York: Vintage Books.

VERGHESE, I., D. ONG, Y. LEO, ET AL.
   1994 "Women with HIV Infection in Singapore." *International Conference on AIDS* 10(1): 380. Abstract Number PD0129.

VERMUND, STEN H.
   1995 "Casual Sex and HIV Transmission." *American Journal of Public Health* 85(11): 1488-1489.

VERMUND, STEN H. AND SANDRA L. MELNICK
   1995 "Human Papillomavirus Infection." In *HIV Infection in Women*. Howard Minkoff, Jack A. DeHovitz, and Ann Duerr, eds. New York: Raven Press. Pp. 189-228.

VIADRO, CLAIRE AND JO ANNE EARP
   1991 "AIDS Education and Incarcerated Women: A Neglected Opportunity." *Women and Health* 17(2): 105-117.

VIEUX, SERGE
   1989 *Le Plaçage: Droit Coutumier et Famille en Haiti*. Paris: Editions Publisud.

VLAHOV, DAVID, JAMES C. ANTHONY, ALVARO MUÑOZ, ET AL.
   1991 "The Alive Study: A Longitudinal Study of HIV-1 Infection in Intravenous Drug Users: Description of Methods." *The Journal of Drug Issues* 21(4): 759-776.

VLAHOV, DAVID AND RONALD S. BROOKMEYER
   1994 "Editorial: The Evaluation of Needle Exchange Programs." *American Journal of Public Health* 84(12): 1889.

VLAHOV, DAVID, ALVARO MUÑOZ, D. CELENTANO ET AL.
   1991 "HIV Seroconversion and Disinfection of Injection Equipment among Intravenous Drug Users, Baltimore, Maryland." *Epidemiology* 2(6): 444-446.

VLAHOV, DAVID, CAITLIN RYAN, LIZA SOLOMON, ET AL.
   1994 "A Pilot Syringe Exchange Program in Washington, D.C." *American Journal of Public Health* 84(2): 303-304.

VOELLER, BRUCE
   1991 "AIDS and Heterosexual Anal Intercourse." *Archives of Sexual Behavior* 20(3): 233-276.

VOELLER, BRUCE, JUNE MACHOVER REINISCH, AND MICHAEL GOTTLIEB
   1990 *An Integrated Biomedical and Biobehavioral Approach*. New York: Oxford University Press.

VOLBERDING, PAUL A., STEPHEN W. LAGAKOS, JANET M. GRIMES, ET AL.
   1995 "A Comparison of Immediate with Deferred Zidovudine Therapy for Asymptomatic HIV-Infected Adults with CD4 Cell Counts of 500 or More per Cubic Millimeter." *The New England Journal of Medicine* 333(7): 401-407.

VOLBERDING, PAUL A., STEPHEN W. LAGAKOS, MATTHEW A. KOCH, ET AL.
   1990 "Zidovudine in Asymptomatic Human Immunodeficiency Virus Infection: A Controlled Trial in Persons with Fewer than 500 CD4-Positive Cells per Cubic Millimeter." *The New England Journal of Medicine* 322(14): 941-949.

WACQUANT, LOÏC J.D.
   1993 "Urban Outcasts: Stigma and Division in the Black American Ghetto and the French Urban Periphery." *International Journal of Urban and Regional Research* 17(3): 366-383.

WAHMAN, A., S. MELNICK, F. RHAME, ET AL.
   1991 "The Epidemiology of Classic, African, and Immunosuppressed Kaposi's Sarcoma." *Epidemiologic Reviews* 13: 178-199.

WAITZKIN, HOWARD
   1986 "The Micro-Politics of Medicine: Theoretical Issues." *Medical Anthropology Quarterly* 17(5): 134-135.

WALDORF, D.
　　1973 *Careers in Dope.* Englewood Cliffs, NJ:Prentice Hall Press.
　　1991 *The Politics of Medical Encounters.* New Haven: Yale University Press.

WALLACE, J. AND A.P. WEINER
　　1995 "Intravenous Drug Use, Inconsistent Condom Use and Fellatio in Relationship to Crack Smoking Streetwalkers." *HIV Infection in Women: Setting a New Agenda.* Washington, D.C. (February 22-24) Pp. S62. Abstract Number FE2-218.

WALLACE, N.
　　1976 "Support Networks among Drug Addicted Men and Women. W.O.M.A.N. Evaluation Project." Report to National Institute on Drug Abuse (August).

WALLACE, RODERICK
　　1988 "A Synergism of Plagues: 'Planned Shrinkage,' Contagious Housing Destruction and AIDS in the Bronx." *Environmental Research* 47: 1-33.
　　1990 "Urban Desertification, Public Health and Public Order: 'Planned Shrinkage,' Violent Death, Substance Abuse and AIDS in the Bronx." *Social Science and Medicine* 31(7): 801-813.
　　1991 "Social Disintegration and the Spread of AIDS: Thresholds for Propagation along 'Sociogeographic' Networks." *Social Science and Medicine* 33(10): 1155-1162.
　　1993 "Social Disintegration and the Spread of AIDS-II: Meltdown of Sociogeographic Structure in Urban Minority Neighborhoods." *Social Science and Medicine* 37(7): 887-896.

WALLACE, RODERICK, MINDY FULLILOVE, ROBERT FULLILOVE, III, *ET AL.*
　　1994 "Will AIDS be Contained within U.S. Minority Urban Populations?" *Social Science and Medicine* 39(8): 1051-1062.

WALLERSTEIN, IMMANUEL
　　1987 "World-Systems Analysis." In *Social Theory Today.* A. Giddens and J. Turner, eds. Stanford: Stanford University Press. Pp. 309-324.

WALTER, H., R. VAUGHAN, M. GLADIS, *ET AL.*
　　1992 "Factors Associated with AIDS Risk Behaviors among High School Students in an AIDS Epicenter." *American Journal of Public Health* 82(4): 528-532.

WARD, J.W., S.H. KLEINMAN, D.K. DOUGLAS, *ET AL.*
　　1988 "Epidemiologic Characteristics of Blood Donors with Antibody to Human Immunodeficiency Virus." *Transfusion* 28(4): 298-301.

WARD, MARTHA C.
　　1993a "A Different Disease: HIV/AIDS and Health Care for Women in Poverty." *Culture, Medicine and Psychiatry* 17(4): 413-430.
　　1993b "Poor and Positive: Two Contrasting Views from Inside the HIV/AIDS Epidemic." *Practicing Anthropology* 15(4): 59-61.

WASHINGTON, C., J. KELLY, D. MURPHY, *ET AL.*
　　1993 "Effects of Group Behavior Change Intervention for High-Risk Women Seen in Urban Primary Health Care Clinics." *International Conference on AIDS* 9(2): 741. Abstract Number PO-C22-3143.

WASSER, S.C., M. GWINN, AND P. FLEMING
　　1993 "Urban-Nonurban Distribution of HIV Infection in Childbearing Women in the United States." *Journal of the Acquired Immune Deficiency Syndrome* 6(9): 1035-1042.

WASSERHEIT, JUDITH
　　1991 "Epidemiological Synergy: Interrelationships between HIV Infection and Other STDs" In *AIDS and Women's Reproductive Health: Science for Policy and Action.* J. Sepulveda and S. Segal, eds. New York: Plenum Press.

1995 "Effect of Human Ecology and Behavior on Sexually Transmitted Diseases, Including HIV Infection." In *Infectious Diseases in an Age of Change*. Bernard Roizman, ed. Washington, D.C.: National Academy of Sciences. Pp. 141-156.

WATERSTON, ALISSE
1993 *Street Addicts in the Political Economy*. Philadelphia: Temple University Press.

WATTERS, JOHN
1994 "Trends in Risk Behavior and HIV Seroprevalence in Heterosexual Injection Drug Users in San Francisco, 1986-1992." *Journal of Acquired Immune Deficiency Syndromes* 7(12): 1276-1281.

WATTERS, JOHN K., MICHELLE J. ESTILO, GEORGE L. CLARK, ET AL.
1994 "Syringe and Needle Exchange as HIV/AIDS Prevention for Injection Drug Users." *Journal of the American Medical Association* 271(2): 115-120.

WAWER, MARIA
1992 "HIV Risk Factors in Three Geographic Strata of Rural Raki District, Uganda." *AIDS* 6(9): 983-989.

WEINER, M., C. MARTINEZ, T. PRIHODA, ET AL.
1989 "AIDS Knowledge, Language Use, and Response to Spanish and English Radio Messages of Low-Income, Mexican-American Women in South Texas." *International Conference on AIDS* 5: 836. Abstract Number M.E.P. 13.

WEISS, E., G. GUPTA, AND D. WHELAN
1995 "Findings from the Women and AIDS Research Program." *HIV Infection in Women: Setting a New Agenda*. Washington, D.C. (February 22-24) Pp. P115. Abstract Number TP-493.

WEISSMAN, GLORIA, LISA MELCHIOR, GEORGE HUBA, ET AL.
1995 "Women Living with Substance Abuse and HIV Disease: Medical Care Access Issues." *Journal of the American Medical Women's Association* 50(3/4): 115-120.

WEISSMAN, JOEL S., ROBERT STERN, STEPHEN L. FIELDING, ET AL.
1991 "Delayed Access to Health Care: Risk Factors, Reason, and Consequences." *Annals of Internal Medicine* 114(4): 325-331.

WELLS, ELIZABETH A., PEGGY L. PETERSON, RANDY R. GAINEY, ET AL.
1994 "Outpatient Treatment for Cocaine Abuse: A Controlled Comparison of Relapse Prevention and Twelve-Step Approaches." *American Journal of Drug and Alcohol Abuse* 20(1): 1-17.

WELSH, BRIAN AND PAVEL BUTORIN, EDS.
1990 *Dictionary of Development: Third World Economy, Environment, Science*. New York: Garland Publishers.

WENGER, N., F. KUSSELING, AND M. SHAPIRO
1995 "Misunderstanding of 'Safer Sex' by Heterosexually Active Adults." *Public Health Reports* 110(5): 618-621.

WENGER, N., L. LINN, M. EPSTEIN, ET AL.
1991 "Reduction of High-Risk Sexual Behavior among Heterosexuals Undergoing HIV Antibody Testing: A Randomized Clinical Trial." *American Journal of Public Health* 81(12): 1580-1585.

WENIGER, B., K. LIMPAKARNJANARAT, K. UNGSCHUSAK, ET AL.
1991 "The Epidemiology of HIV Infection and AIDS in Thailand." *AIDS* 5(S2): S71-S85.

WERMUTH, L.
1995 "HIV Risk Behaviors in Rural Northern California Women Respondents." *HIV Infection in Women: Setting a New Agenda*. Washington, D.C. (February 22-24) Pp. P73. Abstract Number WP-329.

WERMUTH, LAURIE, JENNIFER HAM, AND REBECCA ROBBINS
  1992 "Women Don't Wear Condoms: AIDS Risk among Sexual Partners of IV Drug
        Users." In *The Social Context of AIDS*. Joan Huber and Beth Schneider, eds. New-
        bury Park, CA: Sage. Pp. 72-94.

WERNER, DAVID
  1994 "The Economic Crisis, Structural Adjustment and Health Care in Africa." *Third
        World Resurgence* (42/43): 15-22.

WHELAN, V., D. McBRIDE, AND R. COLBY
  1993 "Public Health Department Tracking of High-Risk Drug Users." *Public Health
        Reports* 108(5): 643-645.

WHITE, LUISE
  1990 *The Comforts of Home: Prostitution in Colonial Nairobi*. Chicago: University of
        Chicago Press.

WHYTE, BRUCE M., CHERYL E. SWANSON AND DAVID A. COOPER
  1989 "Survival of Patients with the Acquired Immunodefiency Syndrome in Australia."
        The Medical Journal of Australia 150: 358-362.

WILLIAMS, DAVID R.
  1990 "Socioeconomic Differentials in Health: A Review and Redirection." *Social Psy-
        chology Quarterly* 53(2): 81-99.

WILLIAMS, M.
  1990 "HIV Seroprevalence among Male IVDUs in Houston, Texas." *American Journal of
        Public Health* 80(12): 1507-1509.

WILLOUGHBY, ANNE
  1989 "AIDS in Women: Epidemiology." *Clinical Obstetrics and Gynecology* 32(3): 429-
        436.

WILSON, JANE
  1993 "Women as Carers, Scotland." In *Women and HIV/AIDS*. Marge Berer and Sunan-
        dra Ray, eds. London: Pandita. Pp. 287-288.

WILSON, M., W. MARELICH, G. LEMP, ET AL.
  1993 "HIV-1 Seroprevalence among Women Attending Sexually Transmitted Disease
        Clinics in California. California Family of Surveys and Sentine Surveillance Con-
        sortia." *Western Journal of Medicine* 158(1): 40-43.

WILSON, RUT AND MOSES POUNDS
  1993 "AIDS in African-American Communities and the Public Health Response: An
        Overview." *Transforming Anthropology* 4: 9-16.

WILSON, SCOTT AND BRENDA LEIN
  1992 "HIV Disease in Women." *The Gay Men's Health Crisis Newsletter of Experimental
        AIDS Therapies* (Summer/Fall): 1-6.

WIMSATT, WILLIAM
  1986 "Heuristics and the Study of Human Behavior." In *Metatheory in Social Science: Plu-
        ralisms and Subjectives*. D. Fiske and R. Shweder, eds. Chiacgo: University of
        Chicago Press. Pp 293-314.

WINGOOD, G. AND R. DICLEMENTE
  1995 "The Role of Gender Relations in HIV Prevention Research for Women." *Ameri-
        can Journal of Public Health* 85(4): 592.

WINKELSTEIN, W., JR.
  1990 "Smoking and Cervical Cancer—Current Status: A Review." *American Journal of
        Epidemiology* 131(6): 945-957.
  1996 "Editorial: Eras, Paradigms, and the Future of Epidemiology." *American Journal of
        Public Health* 86(5): 621.

WINKELSTEIN, W., JR., S. PADIAN, J. WILEY, ET AL.
 1987 "The San Francisco Men's Health Study: III. Reduction in Human Immunodeficiency Virus Transmission among Homosexual/Bisexual Men, 1982-1986." *American Journal of Public Health* 77(6): 685-689.

WINTERBOTTOM, C., D.W. LISKA AND K.M. OBERMAIER
 1995 *State-Level Databook on Health Care Access and Financing*. Princeton, NJ: Robert Wood Johnson Publication.

WLERINGA, NICOLEIN
 1994 "An Integrated Approach is Needed." *Women's Health Journal* (February/March): 19.

WOOD, R., L. KRUEGER, T. PEARLMAN, ET AL.
 1993 "HIV Transmission: Women's Risk from Bisexual Men." *American Journal of Public Health* 83(12): 1757-1759

WORLD BANK
 1994 *Social Indicators of Development*. Baltimore: The Johns Hopkins University Press.
 1995 *Social Indicators of Development*. Baltimore: The Johns Hopkins University

WORLD HEALTH ORGANIZATION
 1995a *Bridging the Gaps: The World Health Report*. Geneva: World Health Organization.
 1995b *Facing the Challenge of HIV/AIDS/STDs: A Gender Based Response*. Geneva: World Health Organization.

WORLD HEALTH ORGANIZATION AND INTERNATIONAL FEDERATION OF GYNECOLOGY AND OBSTETRICS
 1992 "AIDS and Women." *International Journal of Gynecological Obstetrics* 37: 323.

WORLD HEALTH ORGANIZATION AND UNITED NATIONS CHILDREN'S FUND (UNICEF)
 1992 "Global Programme on AIDS. Consensus Statement from the WHO/UNICEF Consultation on HIV Transmission and Breast-Feeding." *Weekly Epidemiological Record* 67(24): 177-179.

WORTH, DOOLEY
 1989 "Sexual Decision-Making and AIDS: Why Condom Promotion among Vulnerable Women is Likely to Fail." *Studies in Family Planning* 20(6; Part 1): 297-307.
 1990 "Minority Women and AIDS: Culture, Race and Gender." In *Culture and AIDS*. Douglas Feldman, ed. New York: Praeger. Pp. 111-136.

WORTH, D., E. DRUCKER, E. ERIC, ET AL.
 1990 "Sexual and Physical Abuse as Factors in Continued Risk Behavior of Women IV Drug Users in a South Bronx Methadone Clinic." *Sixth International Conference on AIDS* 6(1): 322.

WORTH, DOOLEY AND RUTH RODRIGUEZ
 1987 "Latina Women and AIDS." *Radical America* 20(6): 63-67.

WORTLEY, P.
 1993 "Use of AZT and Primary Prophylaxis for PCP among Pregnant HIV-Infected Women." Paper presented at the Ninth International Conference on AIDS, Berlin (June 6-11).

WORTLEY, PASCALE M., SUSAN Y. CHU, THERESA DIAZ
 1995 "HIV Testing Patterns: Where, Why and When were Persons with AIDS Tested for HIV?" *AIDS* 9(5): 487-492.

WRIGHT, THOMAS C. JR., TEDD V. ELLERBROCK, MARY ANN H. CHAISSON, ET AL.
 1994 "Cervical Intraepithelial Neoplasia in Women Infected with Human Immunodeficiency Virus: Prevalence, Risk Factors, and Validity of Papanicolaou Smears." *Obstetrics and Gynecology* 84(4): 591-597.

WU, Z., Z. LIU, AND R. DETELS
1995 "HIV-1 Infection in Commercial Plasma Donors in China." *The Lancet* 346(8966): 61-62.

WYATT, GAIL ELIZABETH
1991 "Examining Ethnicity versus Race in AIDS Related Sex Research." *Social Science and Medicine* 33(1): 37-45.
1995 "Transaction Sex and HIV Risks: A Women's Choice?" *HIV Infection in Women: Setting a New Agenda*. Washington, D.C. (February 22-24) Pp. S2. Abstract Number WA1-1.

XIA, M., J.K. KREISS, AND K.K. HOLMES
1994 "Risk Factors for HIV Infection among Drug Users in Yunnan Province, China: Association with Intravenous Drug Use and Protective Effect of Boiling Reusable Needles and Syringes." *AIDS* 8(12): 1701-1706.

XINHUA, SUN, NAN JUNHUA AND GUO QILI
1994 "AIDS and HIV Infection in China." *AIDS* 8(S2): S55-S59.

YANKAUER, ALFRED
1989 "The Deadliest Plague." *American Journal of Public Health* 79(7): 821-822.

YARBER, WILLIAM L. AND MOHAMMAD R. TORABI
1991 "HIV Prevention Knowledge Test for Teenagers." *Siecus Report* 19(2): 28-32.

YEAGER, GERTRUDE M., ED.
1994 *Confronting Change, Challenging Tradition: Women in Latin American History*. Wilmington, DE: Scholarly Resources, Inc.

YELIBI, S., P. VALENTI, C. VOLPE, ET AL.
1993 "Sociocultural Aspects of AIDS in an Urban Peripheral Area of Abidjan (Côte d'Ivoire)." *AIDS Care* 5(2): 187-197.

YELLIN, E., R. GREENBLATT, H. HOLLANDER, ET AL.
1991 "The Impact of HIV-Related Illness on Employment." *American Journal of Public Health* 81(1): 79-84.

YOUNG, MARY A. AND P. PIERCE
1990 "Natural History of HIV in an Urban Cohort of Women." Paper presented at the International Conference on AIDS, San Francisco.

YOUNG, REBECCA M., GLORIA WEISSMAN AND JUDITH B. COHEN
1992 "Assessing Risk in the Absence of Information: HIV Risk Among Women Injection-Drug Users Who Have Sex with Women." *AIDS & Public Policy Journal* 7(3): 175-183.

YOUNGE, RICHARD
1989 "Report from the Frontlines." *Health/PAC Bulletin* 19(4): 16-18.

ZAZOVE, P., B. REED, L. GREGOIRE, ET AL.
1993 "Presence of Human Papillomavirus Infection of Uterine Cervix as Determined by Different Detection Methods in a Low-Risk Community-Based Population." *Archives of Family Medicine* 2(12): 1250-1258.

ZEKENG, LEOPOLD, PAUL FELDBLUM, REGINA M. OLIVER, ET AL.
1993 "Barrier Contraceptive Use and HIV Infection among High-Risk Women in Cameroon." *AIDS* 7(5): 725-731.

ZHENG, X., C. TIAN, K.H. CHOI, ET AL.
1994 "Injecting Drug Use and HIV Infection in Southwest China." *AIDS* 8(8): 1141-1147.

ZHENG, X.W., J.P. ZHANG, C.Q. TIAN, ET AL.
1993 "Cohort Study of HIV Infection among Drug Users in Ruili, Longchuan and Luxi of Yunnan Province, China." *Biomedical and Environmental Sciences* 6(4): 348-351.

ZIERLER, S., L. FEINGOLD, D. LAUFER, ET AL.

    1991 "Adult Survivors of Childhood Sexual Abuse and Subsequent Risk of HIV Infection." *American Journal of Public Health* 81(5): 572-575.

ZIERLER, SALLY

    1994a Anthropology Seminar. Cambridge, MA: Institute for Health and Social Justice (August 12).

    1994b "Women, Sex and HIV." *Epidemiology* 5(6): 565-567.

    in press "Hitting Hard: HIV and Violence." In *Gender Politics of HIV.* N. Goldstein and J. Manlowe, eds. New York: New York University Press.

ZOLOPA, A.R., J.A. HAHN, R. GORTER, ET AL.

    1994 "HIV and Tuberculosis Infection in San Francisco's Homeless Adults. Prevalence and Risk Factors in a Representative Sample." *Journal of the American Medical Association* 272(6): 455-461.

ZWI, A.B. AND A.J. CABRAL

    1991 "Identifying 'High Risk Situations' for Preventing AIDS." *British Medical Journal* 303(6816): 1527-1529.

Index

Q

R

T

About the Editors

Paul Farmer, author of *AIDS and Accusation* (1992) and *The Uses of Haiti* (1994), is assistant professor at the Harvard Medical School, an attending physician at Boston's Brigham and Women's Hospital, and the director of the Institute for Health and Social Justice. He conducts his research and medical practice in rural Haiti, where he has lived and worked for 14 years specializing in community-based efforts to improve the health of the poor.

Margaret Connors, a medical anthropologist, is currently Associate Director of the Institute for Health and Social Justice and a fellow in the Department of Social Medicine at the Harvard Medical School. During the past eight years her work has focused on the prevention of HIV infection among drug users. She has conducted street-based ethnographic research in Massachusetts and more recently worked on developing comprehensive HIV prevention strategies, as well as analyzing the "war on drugs" as it affects options for recovery within poor communities.

Janie Simmons is a critical ethnographer who has worked to bridge academic and community interests in AIDS research and prevention since 1989. She is a fellow in the Division of Aging in the Department of Social Medicine at the Harvard Medical School. Before serving as a Fellow at the Institute for Health and Social Justice, she worked with poor adolescents in Boston and caregivers of elders with Alzheimer's disease in Massachusetts, as well as on the education of the deaf.